The Other Within

The Other Within

The Marranos

Split Identity and Emerging Modernity

Yirmiyahu Yovel

PRINCETON UNIVERSITY PRESS   PRINCETON AND OXFORD

Published by Princeton University Press, 41 William Street, Princeton, New Jersey 08540

In the United Kingdom: Princeton University Press, 6 Oxford Street,
Woodstock, Oxfordshire OX20 1TW

ISBN: 978-0-691-13571-7

British Library Cataloging-in-Publication Data is available

Library of Congress Cataloging-in-Publication Data

Yovel, Yirmiyahu.
The other within : the Marranos : split identity and emerging modernity / Yirmiyahu Yovel.
p.   cm.
Includes bibliographical references and index.
ISBN 978-0-691-13571-7 (hardcover : alk. paper) 1. Jews—Spain—History.
2. Marranos—Spain—History. 3. Jews—Spain—Identity. 4. Spain—Ethnic relations.
I. Title. II. Title: Marranos : split identity and emerging modernity.
DS135.S7Y68 2009
305.892′4046—dc22
2008026794

This book has been composed in Minion

Printed on acid-free paper. ∞

press.princeton.edu

Printed in the United States of America

1 3 5 7 9 10 8 6 4 2

For Daniella, Maya, and Tamara,
who will soon be able to read

Contents

Preface

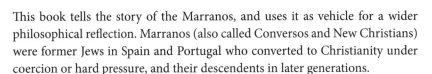

This book tells the story of the Marranos, and uses it as vehicle for a wider philosophical reflection. Marranos (also called Conversos and New Christians) were former Jews in Spain and Portugal who converted to Christianity under coercion or hard pressure, and their descendents in later generations.

My first adult encounter with the Marrano theme occurred in the early 1970s. A visiting junior professor at Princeton, I was invited to some event in Miami Beach. My host lent me a car, which I parked near the beach and went for a swim with my wife. On our return we found that the car had been broken into and all our things stolen, including an expensive watch I had received as present. Nearby I saw a band of local youngsters, the kind that hangs around places of tourist leisure. Suspecting them, I approached the guy who looked like their leader and asked in somewhat provocative irony if "by any chance" he had an idea who had broken into my car. (Nature endowed me with a strong body and a silly manly pride.) I got what I deserved: the young man denied in a challenging tone and looked me fiercely in the eye, while the others closed in around us. A dangerous confrontation resulted, on the brink of violence. Then, suddenly, my eyes fell on a kind of a gilded medallion on his neck, shaped in the form of a Star of David with a Cross inlaid in its middle. I was surprised and got curious, and within a second I turned from a young macho into an anthropologist. "Excuse me, what is this thing?" I asked in a new, matter-of-fact, almost friendly tone, which surprised and softened the young man. The tension evaporated. He explained that it was something quite exceptional—his family had come from the Caribbean, and there are Christians there who are also Jews, it's hard to explain but it is a fact, and it goes back to very old times in which such and such had happened—I got a confused, instant history of the Marranos. We parted as friends. I never found the actual thieves. (The Miami Beach mafia still owes me a watch.)

Perhaps the most poignant anecdote, which highlights the ironies in the Marrano dualities—a recurring theme in this book—was told to me by my friend and colleague, Professor Eddy Zemach. In his student days Eddy was staying in New York with another philosophy student, Bill, who earned his rent by showing tourists around town. One day Bill took a group of Spanish visitors to the Cathedral of St. John the Divine and noticed that on entering the church, an elegant young Spaniard was murmuring something strange while making the sign of the Cross. When the visit was over Bill dared to ask the man what that was about. "Oh, it's an ancient custom in our family," the visitor said. "We are devout Catholics, and on entering a church we say this special benediction as sign of extra piety."—"And what are you saying, if I may ask?"—"I don't really understand it, it's rather opaque, a mystical formula; but I can write it down for you." He scribbled a string of letters that read: SAKESTESAKSENU. The puzzled Bill showed it to Eddy, who turned it around in his head until he finally had a flash: it was the Hebrew Biblical phrase *shakets teshaktsenu* [שקץ תשקצנו]—"Thou should loathe it"—a commandment in the Torah (Deuteronomy 7:26) in which Moses bids the Israelites to abominate idolatry and destroy the idols. The devout Spanish Catholic, as a sign of extra piety, was repeating an ancient formula by which his Marrano ancestors used to curse and anathemize the church they were entering as a place of idolatry![1]

Since then I have come across many other testimonies and traces of the Marrano experience that keep popping up here and there. A Colombian painter, for example, told me that while staying overnight in a village in the Andes he saw a torn Hebrew parchment on the mantelpiece; his host, a Catholic villager, explained that it was a family talisman passed down through many generations. Such stories abound. A distinguished colleague, Nathan Wachtel, has found many Marrano traces even in the deep Amazonian forest (as did Anita Novinsky in Brazil's urban culture). In Spain and Portugal it has recently become fashionable to discover (and, sometimes, to invent) Marrano ancestors, after centuries in which this had been repressed as a social shame (and a great risk). And then there is the actual, living Marrano community in Belmonte, northern Portugal, which cordially hosted my wife and me in 1986 (see the epilogue).

In childhood, like my contemporaries in Israel, I too had been exposed to exciting stories and novels about the Marranos. I too believed that Marranos had all been leading a covert Jewish religious life under the nose of the Inquisition, engaging in clandestine fraternities and often dying as martyrs for their forbidden faith; and that their Christianity was merely a superficial mask, while in their minds and hearts, they were purely and untaintedly Jewish. Popular writers and serious historians alike contributed to this romantic picture. Perhaps they wished to heighten the sense of Jewish national loyalty and Zionist pride.

Upon critical reflection, I found it untenable that the Marranos, even those who observed certain Jewish rites in secret, were completely and faithfully Jewish in their inmost hearts and acted as Christians only externally, in pure make-believe. As if a person's identity, especially religious identity, is a pure golden coin, free of dross, that can be hidden in the safe of the heart and interior life; and as if a person's life can be so divided in two distinct parts that the outer life neither affects the inner nor is affected by it. This naive view is more conso-

nant with romantic aspirations than with the philosophical and psychological
dynamics of human identity.

Spanish Marranism burst into existence in two waves of mass conversions (1391–
1414 and 1492). Despite economic success and some political emancipation,
the Marranos suffered social stigma and were persecuted by the Inquisition.
They were "The Other Within"—both belonging and not belonging, rejected
by most Jews as renegades and by most veteran Christians as Jews, and stigmatized as having impure blood. As a result of their partial social exclusion—and,
especially, of their mixing Jewish and Christian notions and life-forms—many
Marranos manifested a split identity, restlessness, and social and religious dissent, which became their most interesting and distinctive characteristic.

My serious interest in the Marranos began when I worked on the philosophy
of Baruch/Benedictus Spinoza. No modern thinker was as radical as Spinoza
in shedding the mental worlds of both Christianity and Judaism, and in transcending all historical religion. I wondered how this young Jewish man was
able to perform such a huge feat. What enabled him to tear himself so drastically from the theistic tradition that defined the Western medieval world and
replace it with a radical "philosophy of immanence" (as I called it), which influenced and became present in decisive turns of modern thought?

I found a promising clue in Carl Gebhardt, a major Spinoza editor and
scholar, which led me to look attentively at the Marrano features in Spinoza's
background and early life. Using textual and historical materials, I worked out
Spinoza's "Marrano connection"—the recurring Marrano patterns that his life
and mind manifested and transformed. The result allowed me (in volume 1 of
my *Spinoza and Other Heretics*) to call Spinoza a "Marrano of reason."[2]

But why stop with Spinoza? It did not take long to discover that the fascinating Marrano saga has important intellectual ramifications in itself, beyond
any particular person or case. So over the years I plunged into the Marrano
topic for its own sake. Fortunately, a great deal of research has been done in
this field since World War II (see the appendix), mostly in specialized studies,
and many primary documents are now available in print. Having intermittently
devoted long periods to this exciting subject, I felt that my contribution might
consist of a critical integrative study, intended for a broad intellectual audience
and organized in view of the philosophical themes that the story suggests and
brings forth.

The result is a historico-philosophical essay rather than a standard study in
either of these fields. I chose this mode of writing (already present in my *Spinoza
and Other Heretics*, and variously practiced by authors such as Ernst Bloch, Hans
Blumenberg, Hannah Arendt, Michel Foucault, Charles Taylor, Julia Kristeva,

and others) because I am among those who believe that philosophical issues cannot be detached from the historical and existential context in which they arise and ripen for reflection. I cannot share the Platonic belief, held by many philosophers of the analytic tendency, that ideas exist in a pure logical space of their own and can be fruitfully treated by logical and linguistic analysis alone, with no regard to the impurities and dialectic of time, history, and desire.

In this book, therefore, the philosophical reflection rides on an empirical-historical narrative as its vehicle, and is expressed mainly through it. Focusing on the Judeo-Marranos, the base narration refers to the evolution of historical events in time; at the same time (and on another plane), the historical account seeks to explicate the Marranos' peculiar phenomenological traits—in which, I suggest, more universal features and possibilities of the human mind can be traced—and to articulate the relevance of those traits for the rise of modern forms of life.

An underlying theme is the Marrano duality, or split identity, which the narrative works out in its diverse, and sometimes opposing, shapes and forms. Thereby the book throws into relief the nonintegral character of human identities as a basic structure of the human condition, which the Marrano phenomenon brings to light in anticipation of the late-modern situation. In earlier times, split identities were considered illicit and illegal, a grave social and metaphysical sin punished by the Inquisition (and later, by nationalism and similar "integralist" movements). Yet, far from being a marginal anomaly, such identities are, I suggest, a genuine and necessary form of human existence, which deserves recognition as a basic form of freedom, indeed a human right. In contrast, the romantic notion of an *integral person* (and even *authenticity* in some of its senses) is doubtful as an ideal and potentially harmful. Under certain interpretations it will breed existential self-deception, and, when politicized, can lead to intolerance and persecution.

Beyond this issue, the book's philosophical dimension revolves around several families of notions and ideas.

(1) *Identity and Otherness.* This category includes:
- *New forms of otherness:* for example, the Jew as traditional Other replaced by the Marrano as the "Other Within."
- *Split or multiple identities:* this is manifest in almost all types of Marranos.
- *Passions of identity:* these play an important role in explaining (1) the conflicts between Old and New Christian burghers; (2) the action of the Inquisition; (3) the policies of *pure blood*; (4) a variety of Converso characters, from the devout Judaizer (and even martyr) to the ardently anti-Jewish convert, to the Converso reformer of Christianity.

- *The illusion of homogeneous identity:* this is manifest in the reigning Spanish ideology from the fifteenth through the nineteenth centuries.

(2) *Subjectivity and Self.* This category includes:
  - *Discovering the inner domain* and its vast peculiar potential.
  - *The sense of subjectivity* as the center of one's existence.
  - *The rise of individual conscience* and dissent from established traditions.
  - *Placing the source of worth in individual achievement* rather than in innate status or *blood*; the emerging domain of privacy; and the drive for selfhood as a new ideal.

(3) *Early Secularization.* This, in several degrees, is manifest in phenomena such as
  - *Indifference to Judaism and Christianity alike,* transcending historical religion altogether.
  - *Stressing this-worldliness* as the person's main horizon; doubting or negating the afterlife.
  - *Turning to deism or to a "universal" religiosity;* adopting a tacit metaphysics of immanence.

(4) *Basic Features of the Rise of Modernity.* These are prefigured in most of the other categories listed here, and in other patterns the Marrano experience displays (see list in chapter 19).

In addition, as an enabling medium for the processes just listed, we should mention *the need for ironic discourse* and for underground communication patterns based on allusion and dual language.

These issues are not treated in the abstract. For the most part they are presented through their actual manifestation in historical experience. Consequently, the book's reflective dimension is interlaced into the way the narrative is told and the historical picture is drawn. Yet some philosophical issues are also extracted from the narrative and spelled out separately (as in chapters 19–20, on Western modernity and on Jewish modernity, and partly in chapters 5 and 14).

Mode of Writing

A cross-disciplinary work like this, which addresses itself to a wide range of intellectuals, is best served by an essay-style mode of writing. It cannot be composed as an academic historical treatise, with intensive discussions each step of the way, explaining the author's every choice (of facts, materials, positions, and so on) and debating with other scholars while describing their controversies and the history of each question. (I do, however, describe the major trends and scholars in the field in the appendix.) I opted for a bird's eye view that highlights main outlines in the complex Marrano story and fleshes them out with illustrative detail—pertinent events, figures, conflicts, trials, analysis of literary texts, and so forth—allowing readers to appreciate the *several* faces of this peculiar phenomenon, and its broader implications.

I drew all materials from the voluminous historical research done by Converso scholars (see the appendix), to whom I owe an immense debt. I did not discover any new information: my work consisted in a critical reinterpretation of the existing materials, and in their partial synthesis. I thus worked as a philosophical reader of history (and literature). I absorbed the historians' work, reread original documents they published, reflected on their goals and conclusions, and tried to understand their conceptual schemes. I also used a few of my own specific studies, the essence of which is distilled in chapters 6, 7, 15, 16, and 18. The result, the book's actual account, does not present the whole process of study and deliberation, but already uses its conclusions in telling the story.

Georg Wilhelm Friedrich Hegel, the philosopher of modernity par excellence, placed the gist of the modern era in the rise of the principle of subjectivity (the subjective mind discovering and asserting itself as the source of value, justification, rights, and actuality itself) rather than depending on a compact, thinglike, nonreflective tradition (understood as mere "substance"), or on God's external revelation.[3] And he saw this shift prefigured in religion—specifically, in the Lutheran Reformation, which had been, he believed, the first to recognize the value of the interior, subjective mind. I think we can identify an earlier and more distinctive source in the Marranos—first those who Judaized and, following them, those converts of Jewish descent who created a "religion of the interior" within Catholic Christianity (see chapters 14–15). Hegel, however, understood the modern subject not only as torn and fractured, but also as potentially harmonious, capable of being reconciled to itself and achieving a higher unified identity; whereas the Marrano subject arose from the start as fissured in its very identity and incapable of fully repairing it. Thus an unsatisfied, split, yet creative modern Self was constituted, which is closer to the unsettled realities of our late-modern experience than to Hegel's reconciliatory expectations (and illusions) of modernity.

Three Vital Dimensions

Although no account of the Marranos can be comprehensive—their saga lasted four centuries and spilled into three continents—it must, I believe, cover all *three* dimensions in which the Marrano experience unfolded—the Jewish, the

Hispano-Christian, and the cosmopolitan. To leave any of these dimensions out, or to reduce it to the others, is a common flaw which, because of ideological reasons, even the best historians sometimes commit. Historians who see their work as constructive of the national identity (as did many Jewish and Spanish scholars in the twentieth century) tend to appropriate the Marranos exclusively to their own nation and culture. Thereby they flatten and even mutilate a peculiar human phenomenon whose distinguishing and most interesting feature is that it defies national and religious boundaries.

Yitzhak Fritz Baer, a founding historian of the Jews in Christian Spain, declared that the Marranos were an integral part of the Jewish people, and that most of them were "consciously linked to the living Jewish tradition." This implausible statement has no factual support. Yet Baer did not write this as a descriptive statement: the distinguished historian assumed here the posture of a secular rabbi, who rules on a normative question. Baer's dictum gave a scholarly cachet to the romantic popular legend mentioned earlier, that Iberia was full of secret Jews whose hearts were purely Jewish, while Christianity was merely a disposable mask with no hold in their minds.

Some of Baer's disciples in the "Jerusalem school," such as Haim Beinart, have unearthed large and invaluable material (especially from inquisitorial records) in apparent support of Baer's thesis; yet much of this testimony is better construed as demonstrating the *dualities* of most Judaizers rather than their integral Jewish position. The irony of this school is that it shares the same conceptual attitude, and fallacy, as the Inquisition. Both tend to see a Jew in anyone whose mixed or dual mind manifests a few remaining Jewish habits and/or beliefs.

Among Spanish scholars, the concern with Spanish identity and what is genuinely Spanish is often as vivid as the concern with Jewish identity among Jewish scholars. The fresh and novel voice in the Spanish debate was that of Américo Castro, who started a new trend in Spain's self-understanding by breaking away from the sacrosanct conservative myth of a true Spanish essence that is exclusively Christian and homogeneous (see the appendix). Castro and his disciples highlighted the roles of the Jewish and Arab/Muslim elements in constituting Spain's history and what is genuinely Spanish. And because their interest lies with the Spanish national and cultural identity, they tend to appropriate the Marranos to their vision of Spanishness, and to submerge them in it. Especially, in assessing the outstanding impact of Conversos on Spanish culture in the sixteenth century—a truly remarkable phenomenon—they see it as proof that those Conversos were integrated members of the Hispano-Catholic social body. This is another mode of national/identitarian appropriation which, like Baer's, does not do justice to the unique phenomenon at hand.

To me, what gives the Marrano story its significance and interest is that it *breaks integral identities and transcends any single culture*. To interpret the Judeo-Conversos as integral members of any nation is to impose upon them a modern nationalist outlook, and to miss their complexity and inherent interest as people caught between two religions, two identities (or more), who became the Other of both, and often lived in dual exile. No integral position was available to the Marranos. No unified "Marrano subject" can be reconstructed from their diverse dualities—and it is as such that the Marranos deserve a phenomenological study and reinterpretation.

Note on Terminology

I am using the three terms—*Marranos, Conversos,* and *New Christians*—interchangeably, as referring to the largest group of Judeo-converts and their descendents. Some scholars restrict *Marranos* to Judaizers whose intent was to remain Jews. But how are we to clearly determine and recognize them? This is a theoretical question rather than a simple lexical matter. Restricting the term *Marrano* to such indeterminate cases will often create more confusion than it resolves. So, following Révah, Netanyahu, Yerushalmi, C. Roth, N. Wachtel, and the French school, I chose to use the three terms synonymously and, where necessary, to add a further specification or adjective (such as: "a Judaizing Marrano," or "an assimilating New Christian," or "dissident Conversos," and so forth).

Even so, as the Greek sage Cratilus knew, no synonyms are fully equivalent. They differ at least in ring and connotation. So, in choosing which of the three synonyms to use in a given context, I often follow its current ring as guideline. The basic semantics does not change, though the music, perhaps, does.

No doubt, *Marrano* had initially been a bad word, a kind of expletive. (Some believe it meant a pig.) But so were also *Confeso* and *Converso*: appellations draw their emotive charge from public usage, not the dictionary. Otherwise, euphemisms would work, which after a while they usually do not. Today, of course, the originally prejudiced word *Marrano* is used as a neutral scholarly term.

Acknowledgments

My great debt to available scholarship is reflected in the notes and the list of works cited. I learned no less from scholars whose interpretations I could not share than from those I agree with. Baer, Révah, Netanyahu, Beinart, Domínguez Ortiz, Caro Baroja, Roth, Sicroff, Carrete Parrondo, Kamen, and Elliott have all been valuable sources, as well as many others. With Américo Castro (and his more restrained disciples, such as Márquez Villanueva), and with Marcel Bataillon, Yosef Yerushalmi, Stephen Gilman, Angela Selke, and Nathan Wachtel, I found many intellectual affinities (not always without differences). With Maurice Kriegel I have entertained a long and rewarding exchange over the years

Because, intermittently, this book has been in the making over a long period, I am also indebted to former students and assistants (several of whom have meanwhile become scholars and teachers): Moshe Meller, Marta Topel, Diego Ulstein, Tal Aviran, Pini Ifergan, Nimrod Ben Cnaan, Dror Yinon, Avner Inbar, Noa Limone, and Gal Katz in Israel, and Monica Vilhauer, Beatrice Preciado, Maria Alexandra Tortorelli, and especially Daniel Jove at the New School for Social Research, New York. Avner Inbar was also my "assistant surgeon" in cutting a much-too-long original manuscript to its present size, a delicate and painful operation.

Some of the materials in this book were previously published in articles. An early outline of the book appeared in Hebrew as: "The Jews in History: Marranos in Early Modernity," in *Zionism and the Return to History: A Reevaluation* (Heb.), ed. S. N. Eisenstadt and M. Lissak (Jerusalem: Yad Ben-Zvi, 1989), 211–248. An analysis of Marrano dualities in literature appeared in "Converso Dualities in the First Generation: The *Cancioneros*," *Jewish Social Studies* 4, no. 3 (1998): 1–28. And an early version of chapter 5 (an axial chapter in the book) was delivered in invited guest lectures in several countries: (1) the Swig Program for Judaic Studies of the University of San Francisco; (2) the Centre Alberto Benveniste pour les études et la culture sépharades at the Sorbonne (École Pratique des Hautes Études); and (3) the Herman-Cohen-Akademie in Germany. The texts, in English and French, were published as: Yirmiyahu Yovel, *The New Otherness: Marrano Dualities in the First Generation. The 1999 Swig Lecture, September 13, 1999* (San Francisco: Swig Judaic Studies Program, University of San Francisco, 1999); and *La nouvelle altérité: Dualités marranes des premières générations* (Paris: Centre Alberto Benveniste, 2002). I thank these institutions and their directors—Professors Andrew Heinze (University of San Francisco), Esther Benbassa (École Pratique), and Evelyn Goodman-Tau (Herman-Cohen-Akademie) for these esteemed invitations.

For moral and intellectual support I am deeply indebted to the novelist Shoshana Yovel, to whom I am fortunate to be married; to my beloved son, Jonathan Yovel, a keen intellectual and poet; and to Yitzhak Torchin of Paris and Barbizon, recently departed, whose generosity equaled the breadth of his learning. Eva Shorr, the associate editor of the *Jerusalem Philosophical Quarterly IYYUN* and a devoted collaborator and friend, was always there for judicial counsel.

It is not customary to thank agents, but I feel Georges Borchardt of New York has taken an interest in this topic beyond the call of professionalism, as did Michelle Lapautre in Paris. I thank Jean-Louis Schlegel, my Paris editor at Éditions du Seuil, for his patience, and Ian Malcolm, my Princeton University Press editor, for his wise handling of the project. The readers for Princeton University Press deserve thanks for both their praise and helpful criticism, and Madeleine B. Adams for her contribution to copyediting the manuscript. The pains of cutting the longer version of the manuscript were made more bearable by the Rockefeller Foundation, whose fellowship allowed me to spend a month at their exquisite Villa Serbelloni in Bellagio, Italy, and by a case of superb Barolo '97 found in the village.

PART ONE

A Millennium of Jewish Spain

1

Sefarad, the Spanish Jerusalem

When the Jews, crushed and subdued, were driven out of Spain in 1492, they had been living there for over a millennium, the greatest, most affluent and most civilized Jewish community in the world, and certainly the proudest. The Spanish Expulsion was their direst national calamity in fourteen centuries, comparable in popular memory only to the destruction of the Temple of Jerusalem. It was the summer of 1492, the same year Columbus landed in what today we call America; his vessels were actually preparing to leave for the westbound voyage to India as the last ships carrying Jewish exiles were sailing out of the same port, to no less unknown destinations. The modern era in Western history began with a massive, state-organized destruction of Jewish life on a scale unknown to the "dark" Middle Ages.

Famous dates, such as 1492, are signposts for more complex events. Their dry numerals are loaded with passionate human quality, and almost always conceal a longer story. In sailing out to sea, the exiles' memories were often heavier than their baggage: images of families split, homes abandoned, property hastily sold for almost no price at all, projects, designs, personal dreams destroyed in the ebb, ongoing life abruptly shattered. Beyond these recent personal memories, a veil of more distant, perhaps partly mythical reminiscences compounded the agony. What these exiles were leaving was not a foreign country but literally their fatherland, the land where their fathers' fathers were born and—so they felt and remembered— had lived since time immemorial. Many Jews had come to see Sefarad—Hebrew for Spain—as their other Zion, a temporary new Jerusalem where God granted them relative repose in waiting for the Messiah. Now, instead of the Messiah, the grand inquisitor Torquemada was shattering their identity, and the Spanish crown was celebrating the end of the Reconquista (the Christian recapture of Spain) by forcing the Jews to renounce either their religion or their country.

Early Jewish Settlement in Iberia

Like most beginnings, the dawn of Jewish Spain is shredded in legend. In the Middle Ages, when Spain became the leading center of the Jewish Diaspora, it endowed itself with a mythological ancestry going back to the biblical Adoni-ram, King Solomon's tax-controller and emissary to the west, whose tomb was still shown in Spain. Still later, Jewish converts to Christianity used a similar story to disclaim responsibility for Jesus's death, because, they argued, their ancestors were already living in Spain when Jesus was crucified.

Legend apart, Jews could have lived in Spain since the early Christian era and possibly earlier. In the first millennium B.C., the Phoenician ships going to Spain from Carthage and Lebanon may have included Jews as well;[1] and the remote *Tarshish*, which fired traders' imagination in biblical times, is some-times identified as the city of Tartessus in southwestern Spain, on the edge of the then-known world.[2] Later, a large Jewish Diaspora stretched around the Mediterranean in Roman times, from Mesopotamia through Asia Minor to Greece, Sicily, Italy, Egypt, and North Africa, brushing the southern shores of France and plausibly also Spain; and, following the two devastations of Judea by the Romans (A.D. 70 and 135), new waves of Jewish exiles were heading west-ward, sometimes as far as they could reach.

Solid records, however, exist (for now) only from around A.D. 300. A little before that date, the infant Annia Salomonula died at the age of one year, four months, and one day—too young to know she was Jewish, and unaware that her tombstone would make her the first recorded Jew in Spain.[3] In symbolic anticipation of the future, the first paper document mentioning Jews in Spain is an anti-Jewish decree passed in A.D. 308 by a council of bishops. Among other things, it prohibited all Christians from dining with Jews or marrying them. Especially, a rabbi should never be invited to celebrate the first harvest (origi-nally a Jewish holiday) because his presence might usurp the Catholic priest's power of benediction. Clearly, the young Catholic Church in Spain was still fighting against the shadows of its Jewish beginnings and, in order to stress its separate identity, had taken an offensive stance against the Jews.

The Catholic missionaries knew of course—if only dimly, with self-repressive unease—that the message they were transmitting to the pagans was originally drawn from Judaism. But that made them even more uneasy and often more furious. Now that the Jews' election and divine mission were superseded by Christ's church, how could the Jews persist in claiming they alone were God's chosen people? That made Jews worse than pagans. Pagans were frequently crude and rough; yet spiritually, toward the Cross, they were remarkably passive, even submissive. Jews were politically docile, but spiritually a provocation.

Anything inexplicable, when strong passions are at stake, is likely to be vili-fied as diabolical by its opponents, especially if secretly, unconsciously, it aspires to greatness. Most Christians could not fathom the Jews' stubborn stand, which they found to be wildly incomprehensible; and since they did not admit any spirituality or divine grace in the Jews' persistence, they tended to associate it with the Devil.

The Jews, on their part, experienced their persistence as a sign of valor. To them, the unbounded fidelity they showed to God's original message bore witness that God had willed their sacrifice and maintained his covenant with them despite their sins and suffering.

To prove the Jews wrong, the church had two alternatives. It could debunk the Jews' testimony by the sword and forced conversions; or it could try reversing the *meaning* of their testimony, by permitting the Jews to maintain their identity in a humiliated form. The Jews' debasement would make their persistence look like a curse, and testify that God had forsaken them because they had rejected his Son.

A famous advocate of forced conversion was Bishop Severus of Minorca. In A.D. 418, he organized a debate between Christians and Jews, which drove the mob to burn down the Jewish synagogue, and 540 Jews were terrorized into accepting Christianity. Triumphantly, Severus propagated his exploits in a letter to all Christendom, exhorting Christians everywhere to force the Jews to convert.[4] Severus's tract made it into the corpus of church fathers, though not into church doctrine. Jews, the church eventually decided, must be persuaded rather than coerced to see the Christian light. Meanwhile, they should be both debased and tolerated.

With noticeable exceptions, the latter approach was to become the official church doctrine. But that took several centuries of strife and irresolution. In the early years of European Catholicism, the doctrine concerning Jews was still equivocal and unsettled. Time and again Jews were compelled to accept Christianity by legal decrees or brute force, not only in Spain but also in Burgundy, Paris, Languedoc, and other places in today's France. Yet France was later to change track,[5] whereas in Spain forced conversions recurred over large spans of time and nearly became a hallmark of Spanish history.

The Visigoth Pendulum

Temporary relief came to Iberian Jews—if eight decades can count as "temporary"—from those who later became their worst enemies.

In 416 Spain fell to the Visigoths, a Germanic warrior people who adopted the Arian form of Christianity. Arians (from Arius of Alexandria, their founding theologian) opposed the Catholic doctrine of the Trinity and Rome fiercely denounced them as heretics. The Visigoths used to keep to themselves in the lands they have invaded. In Spain they had for three generations kept their separate

German laws, dress, and customs. To balance off the indigenous Catholic population, the Visigoth invaders protected the legal status of the Jews.

In King Alaric II's legal code of 506, the Jews, although restricted, were treated with "astonishing liberality," says a historian of Visigoth Spain.[6]

Matters were radically reversed in 589, when King Reccared abolished Arianism and launched Visigoth Spain on the road that made it a militant Catholic state, seeking unity through religious uniformity.

The conversion to Catholicism signaled the end of the Visigoths' peregrinations, which had taken them from Scandinavia to Iberia, fighting and looting their way through many countries. Spain was journey's end, the edge not only of Europe, but of the world, from which there was nowhere else to go but inward.

In 589, when, after a century, this recognition finally matured in the Visigoths' mind, they were ready to assimilate into the local Roman culture and religion. Along with the Arian religion they abolished the dual legal system for Goths and Romans, and eventually abandoned their Gothic dress, linguistic habits, burial customs, artistic forms, and tastes, down to the typical insignia on their belts.

If that was a major self-sacrifice for the Goths, then its pains may explain the fire with which they started persecuting the Jews. Demanding the same permutation and sacrifice from all others, including the Jews, they turned Visigoth Spain into a militant Catholic state based on a bizarre mixture of politics and religion that the Christian West had hardly ever seen. The council of bishops and the provincial synods became a state institution working to create a single nation under the Catholic faith. Political unity, the Visigoth rulers now felt, was to be attained through Catholic conformity and imposed by a central state organ.

The Jews were ready victims of the Visigoths' fresh Catholic energies. Reccared, Sisebut, Sisenant, Chintila, Recceswinth, Wamba, Egica, and Roderic—all are names of Visigoth kings who, successively, declared war on the Jews' existence in their land. Details are as dismal as they are monotonous to repeat; they are recorded in successive decrees, canons, preambles, and resolutions passed against the Jews for over a century (589–694).[7] Official royal documents now referred to Jews as *plague* and *leprosy*. Some measures against them were harsher than others, and all were even more severe on paper than in real life. As usual, bribes, inefficient government, and complex commercial interests of their persecutors were the Jews' natural allies in the Middle Ages. Occasionally the pendulum swung back and there was a short reprieve when a more secular-minded ruler took office, such as Swinthila in the 620s, or Chindaswinth in the 640s. But the general trend was ominous.

The First Conversos

One set of rules put the Jews' economic existence in jeopardy by barring them from owning Christian slaves, or hiring Christian labor. If, to maintain his labor force, a Jewish master persuaded his slave to become Jewish and even be circumcised, the master would be put to death and his property confiscated. But should the dead Jew's son accept Catholicism (and thus, we may add, nullify his father's sacrifice), he could retrieve part of his inheritance and slaves. A crude decree, joining the stick to a bitter carrot—and still producing meager results from the king's standpoint. So in 613, hoping to solve the Jewish problem in a single stroke, Sisebut ordered all Jews to become Catholics or leave his realm.

King Sisebut was unaware of the historical precedent he was setting. Nor did he have sufficient means to enforce his sweeping decree. So, rather than putting an end to the problem, Sisebut started a new one. With him, Jewish *Conversos* (forced converts) make their first collective entry onto the Spanish stage.

Sisebut's decree was revoked twenty years later. But now a new group was living alongside the overt Jews—Christians who went to Mass but kept Jewish rites at home, read the Talmud, and abstained from pork and other foods prohibited to the Jews.

How were they to be treated? It took some time and several bishopric councils before a doctrine could take shape. In essence, it drew a rigid distinction between ordinary Jews and baptized Jews. Ordinary Jews, though Christ's opponents, owed him no allegiance; they could practice their rites in private while keeping a low profile. Yet baptized Jews were full-fledged Christians; by practicing Judaism in secret they became rebels and renegades, desecrating the sacrament of baptism and cheating not only the king, but Christ himself.

That was a tragic pit, a one-way street with no U-turn allowed. At its background, rigorously interpreted, was the Catholic view that sacraments are objective metaphysical powers, independent of the individual's feeling and intention. Hence, baptism is binding and irreversible even when performed against a person's will.

In a pathetic manifesto to King Recceswinth, the baptized Jews confessed that for a long time they were unable to believe in Christ and the Trinity; but henceforth, they promised, they would accept the Savior with a pure and sincere heart. They vowed to sever all ties with the "abominable sect of unbaptized Jews," to scrupulously observe the Catholic holidays and never again keep the Jewish Sabbath or Passover. They also vowed to eat nonkosher food, but begged for the king's understanding if, "because of natural revulsion," there was one single item they could not eat—pork. To prove their sincerity, they humbly promised to eat everything else cooked in the same pot as pork.

This remarkable document, a study in forced self-humiliation, highlights the double hypocrisy that was imposed upon the Jewish converts. The paradoxes and disguise in this letter make it sound like a political ritual, a game of gestures. How can one sincerely promise to change one's inner belief? (And how "natural" is a revulsion from which no Christian suffers but all Jews do?) It seems the converts' vows were seemingly not meant to be taken too seriously, except perhaps as a statement of political submission.[8]

Ethnic and Religious Jews

By speaking of "Jews whether baptized or unbaptized," Recceswinth's legislation made a significant distinction—between the converts' religion and their ethnic definition. The converts themselves used that distinction in referring to their group. Thus, in promising to keep away from "the sect of unbaptized Jews," they imply there is also a sect of *baptized* Jews—their own. And in their vehement manifesto of Christian devotion, they call themselves "Hebrew citizens of Toledo."

So Visigoth Spain upheld the notion of a Jewish or Hebrew people—an ethnic group distinct from the Jewish religion. These terms should not be understood in quite the same way they are used today because of their different ideological context. The Visigoth view had Pauline origins; in addition, it mixed, so it seems, the idea of a natural *tribe* with that of a supernatural *people of God*. Though the Jews were believed to have been deserted by God, their former divine election still clung to them in a negative mode, the mode of *not anymore*, of *having been superseded*—a metaphysical cadaver and dead religious shell which, as such, retained a supernatural significance, now turned partly diabolical.

Jews have long seen themselves and been seen by others as a people, a separate ethnic group. The religion they had been given (or gave themselves) through Moses was so revolutionary that it took many centuries of inner strife before they were able to fully accept it themselves. When finally they did, they injected their sense of religious mission, of Covenant and Election, into that which made them a separate people, so that the nation and its religion became intertwined.

That bond was reinforced in the Diaspora, when the Jewish state no longer existed and Jews had to contend with the Christian challenge. Pauline Christianity contested that bond, however. After Jesus had failed to reform the Jewish religion from within, Paul carried his message outside the Jewish people. He created a universal (catholic) religion open to all the nations, and called upon his fellow Hebrews to join it. Most of the Jews declined; indeed, it was in confrontation with the Pauline challenge—and in defense of their exclusive Election—that Diaspora Jews fused religion and people into one.

Spain's Visigoth rulers considered St. Paul's call still effective; and by putting coercive force behind it, they made many Jews succumb to the Cross. Did these converts cease thereby to be Jews, or Hebrews? Certainly not, was the Visigoth answer; saying otherwise would admit the Jewish rabbis' standpoint. Jews can relinquish their religious error, yet remain ethnically what they had been before[9]—Hebrews, or Jews.

The Persecution Heightens

In the last decades of Visigoth reign (about 681–711) both baptized and non-baptized Jews went through their most ferocious period. In 681 a new king, Erwig, outlawed Jewish rites for both groups. Observing a Jewish holiday was to be punished by flogging, yanking the culprit's hair, confiscation of property, and exile. In a crude, physical eye-for-an-eye, a woman's nose was to be cut off if she circumcised her son. Then Egica, the next king, prohibited all commerce between Jews and Christians, thus breaking the Jews' international trade. By then Muslim power was building up in North Africa, and the king suspected that Jews were favoring the buildup. Claiming he had conclusive proof of Jewish treason, Egica proposed to the council of bishops that the Jews be either freed "from their paternal error" or "cut off by the scythe of justice," a formula smacking of massacre.[10] The council resisted the latter extravagance, but made all Jews slaves of the Crown. They were absolutely to stop practicing Judaism. All Jewish children were to be taken away from their parents at the age of seven and given to Christian families to raise—a decree, on paper, of pharaonic magnitude.

Egica's ruling is the first major occasion proclaiming the principle of *servitus iudaeorum*—that Jews were the king's slaves. Egica had meant it literally; the Jews were to be actual slaves, suffering affliction and calamity. Yet, ironically, when this principle later became fundamental in Christian Europe, it produced benign consequences for the Jews. As the king's property they were under his protection. No one else could enslave or possess the Jews. Nor were they to be killed or plundered by hostile barons or city councils. On the other hand, unlike real serfs, Jews enjoyed the freedom to move, resettle, engage in trade, and acquire various privileges. The actual meaning of their "serfdom" was economic: the crown reserved for itself the right to bleed the Jews financially. As a result, the Jews' nominal serfdom became one of their assets, a status definition under which their existence was made possible in later Christian Europe.

The Muslims Are Coming

In late April 711, Arab and Berber warriors led by Tarik Bin Ziad crossed the narrow straits separating Africa from Europe and landed on the cliff now called Gibraltar (Jabl a Tarik, or Tarik's mountain). That was a crucial moment in western history: Islam's first major assault against Europe, ushering in more than seven centuries of Muslim dominion in Spain.[11]

Tarik defeated and killed Roderic, the last Visigoth king, and started heading for Toledo, the glittering prize of his invasion. But his blitzkrieg was too daring to succeed without local help. With an army of only twelve thousand, Tarik needed allies to cover his rear and hold the captured cities for him. These allies he found among a disgruntled Visigoth faction, local Ibero-Roman peasants resenting their Gothic overlords, and the Jews.

Almost everywhere, Jews welcomed Tarik as liberator. In Cordova, Malaga, and later in Toledo, Jews organized in a local militia to guard the captured cities for him, thus freeing Tarik's warriors to resume active combat. While Arab chroniclers praised the Jews' role in the invasion, Christian sources, of course, condemned it. The Jews themselves chose to define their friends and foes according to how they treated them. How could they feel allegiance to a Christian kingdom that had for a whole century tried to eradicate them? But the tale of "Jewish treason" established itself in Christian memory and, eight centuries later, when the Christians had reconquered Spain, it was revived as an excuse for harassing not so much the Jews, but, especially, the Marranos.

For the next two decades the Muslims continued their thrust into Europe. Periodically they crossed the Pyrenees, marched up the Rhône valley, and, finally, launched the deep incursion into southeastern France, which Carl Martel, the great Hammer, broke at the gates of Poitiers in 732. Thereby Martel reversed a tide of conquests that had begun in the Arabian desert a century earlier, and went down in European memory as the savior of Christendom.

Thus the Jews, with no global design, were assisting the Muslims during their greatest challenge to Europe. At the same time, again unknowingly, the Jews started their own, slow ascent to one of the high points in their social and cultural history.

Migrations followed the sword into Spain. First from North Africa, then from almost everywhere in the Muslim empire came Arabs, Berbers, Syrians, Yemenites, Slavs, and also Jews. Spain was a new world to them, luring with promises—of loot and adventure for some, of new beginnings for others. For men from the Sahara and the Atlas ridges, Spain had the legendary attraction that urban civilizations exercise on more nomadic people. Poor Muslims from other regions were eager to join the privileged ruling caste. And, like immigrants everywhere, many were trying to leave behind them adversaries, debtors, tyrannical fathers, painful memories, or sheer bad luck.

Jews were swept along with these tides. Now that the Muslim empire was stretching from western India to the Atlantic Ocean, most of the Jews in the world were living for the first time under a single Muslim empire and dominant culture. (Ashkenazi Jews, or their forebears, barely existed).[12] Jewish Spain, freed of Visigoth harassment, was part of the alluring western land; and now, through the empire's system of commerce, communication, and law, Spain was linked to the Jewish communities in the east, including the great scholarly center in Babylon (Mesopotamia, today's Iraq). As a result, not only was Jewish Spain revived demographically but, for several centuries, it became a preferred destination for Jews on the verge of moving, as Jews often are.

These demographic changes assumed their true dimension under the Ummayad dynasty which ruled Spain for two and a half centuries, almost until the end of the first millennium. During all that time the Jews suffered no official persecution, a rare phenomenon in the history of the Jewish Diaspora. Social harassment, which did exist, was counterbalanced by the central government's favors. The Ummayad rulers used to rely on non-Arabs as their closest aids. The Arabs were in frequent revolt against the prince and in rivalry with each other, whereas Christians and, especially, Jews were too weak to be ambitious; relying on their service as councillors, financial directors, and the like was part of a wider policy that led Abd-a-Rahman I, the founder of the dynasty, to fill his army with Berbers, import Slav warriors from the Balkans, and use black Africans as his bodyguard.

No less significant was the shifting Jewish image in Ummayad mythology. In one of the dynasty's founding legends, a clairvoyant Jew saves the life of the young Abd-a-Rahman I by foretelling the rise of the dynasty and providing a ground for its legitimacy: quite a change from the Jews' diabolical image under the late Visigoths!

Still, all was not roses for the Jews. The Ummayad also consolidated the inferior legal status of Jews and Christians in Muslim society, as laid down by the Prophet Muhammad and later modified by his Sunni descendents. Though Muhammad included some abusive language against the Jews in the Qur'an (because the Jewish tribes in Arabia refused to admit him as *rasul-Allah*, God's messenger), he recognized Moses and Jesus as true prophets and set the ground for the doctrine of the *dhimmi*. According to that patronizing-tolerant doctrine, Christians and Jews, though infidels, are "peoples of the book" who deserve Muslim protection, as long as they are politically submissive and prove it by paying a poll tax.

The "infidel tax" made toleration profitable to the Muslim establishment at a time when its missionary ardor was receding before the practical needs of government. The state needed money, and the advocates of toleration praised their policy as being both theologically correct and financially advantageous, a kind of self-rewarding virtue. Others, the more purist or bigoted crusaders, pressed for the Islamization of all the conquered peoples, but they were a minority. The Muslim government needed infidels. "One believer more was one poll-payer less."[13] The official doctrine, in any case, was against forced conversions: the sword had to be used to expand Muslim government, but belief in Allah and Muhammad must be voluntary.[14]

The result was a mixed one. In the following centuries, driven by fear, greed, social pressure, economic anxiety, and also by the desire to conform, to join the ruling caste, or simply to avoid the infidel tax, mass Islamization of the Iberian population actually took place. At first moving in low gear, the process seems to have attained a swirling acceleration by the end of the millennium.[15] At the height of Ummayad rule the New Muslim population was estimated at over five million,[16] mostly former Catholics, and also a certain number of Jews.

A word of caution is needed here. *Islamization* has two senses in our story, a religious sense and a broader cultural one. Many Christians and Jews who resisted Islam as a religion nevertheless accepted the culture, language, and tastes of the Muslim elite. Another ambivalent term, *Arabization*, must also be taken in a wide cultural sense rather than in a purely ethnic one. Ethnic Arabs remained a minority in Spain.[17] Yet most other groups assimilated into the manners, language, dress, food, fashion, craftsmanship, artistic design, and even body language of the ruling Arab civilization, as imported from Baghdad, Damascus, and North Africa. The educated class, including Christians and Jews, was versed in Arab poetry and literary associations.

The Arabization of Christians and Jews was facilitated by the many secular aspects of Arab culture. Although Islam links religion to the state, it can leave a wide range of cultural concerns relatively free of religion, as it did during the Arab golden age. Art, poetry, science, linguistics, music, manners, and craftsmanship were high concerns of the Arab educated class in which Jews or Catholics could participate without compromising their own religious affiliation. This relative secularization of wide areas of life, so obnoxious to Islamic fundamentalists today, existed in Islam's golden age and must have been partly responsible for it.

Arabization among the Christians produced a phenomenon known as *Mozarabs*, meaning *Arabizers*; and the spectacle arose in Spain of Arabic-speaking Christians, dressed and moving like Arabs, going to church to confess or listen to a Christmas Mass; then, in the marketplace, in private homes and gardens, or in a secular party, negotiating like the rest of the population, reciting poems and songs in Arabic or debating a point of Arabic grammar. A similar phenomenon existed among the Jews, although there was no special term to denote it. In the end, Spanish Jews had become so widely Arabized in the cultural sense that Arab historians today have a point when they list Abu Imran Musa, better known as Maimonides, the celebrated Jewish philosopher and rabbi, among the figures of the Arab golden age in Spain.

The Cordova Caliphate

The tenth century saw the pinnacle of Muslim power and civilization in Spain. Under Abd-a-Rahman III, the Ummayad state became a powerful caliphate, challenging the supremacy of eastern Islam and the power of both Christian empires, the Latin and the Byzantine. Abd-a-Rahman III was a sophisticated, strong-willed autocrat, tolerant in religious matters and dexterous in balancing off friends, foes, and especially minorities. From his sparkling capital city of Cordova,[18] where visitors today can still admire the forest of arches in the Grand Mosque, he ruled for a remarkable half-century (912–961) and gave *al-Andalus* (Muslim Spain) political stability, effective administration, economic prosperity, international prestige, military might, and cultural glamour.

"Never before was Cordova so prosperous, al-Andalus so rich, and the state so triumphant," raves a modern Arab historian.[19] He also extols Cordova as "the most cultured city in Europe"[20]—not an unlikely praise since Christian Europe at that time was lagging behind the Muslim world in culture and urbanism. The Ummayads were avid patrons of arts and learning. They attracted poets, philologists, musicians, architects, calligraphers, and men of learning; and encouraged the ruling elite and social aspirants to follow their example. They founded a university and dozens of schools, commissioned the writing of books, and built a splendid royal library.

Language, in particular, was an overriding passion in al-Andalus—language in all its modes and forms. Poetry was part of the ruling elite's daily life. Ranging from the crude to the exquisite, from inflated images to subtle combinations of word and sensibility, Arab (and soon after, Hebrew) poets were writing about everything under and above the sun—friendship, ambition, love, the tribulations of personal fate, and the delights of sex and the table no less than metaphysics and the exalted states of religious faith. Poetry—or at least, rhyming—was also a means of daily communication, used for writing letters, transmitting hidden messages, praising, aggrandizing, suggesting, equivocating, and sometimes conspiring and spreading libel. It was an instrument of life and death. Poetry was life, and life itself was lived through images, metaphor, meter, and rhyme.

Not surprisingly, the tenth century was a high point for Spanish Jews, as well. Arabized Jews and Mozarab Christians were not only tolerated, but given high roles in running the state. The Caliphs, tolerant by temper and education, mistrusted the powerful Arab factions and preferred relying on members of the politically powerless *dhimmi*. If ever the myth of "Spain of the three religions" came close to reality, it was not under the Cross, but under the Ummayad Crescent (and its heirs in the twelfth century). The Jews, subdued and heavily taxed, but protected by the caliph's policy of treating minorities, were free to exercise their religion and obey their autonomous law. They could own land, work in most professions, mingle with non-Jews and emigrate at will—though very few had that will: Rather, Jews in great numbers were streaming into al-Andalus throughout the tenth century. The few who left went mostly to the Christian north—León, Old Castile, and Navarre—where Jews, now grudgingly tolerated, followed the Mozarab merchants to set up their own trading bases and thereby set the groundwork for the future Jewish communities in Christian Spain. As the numbers and prosperity of Andalusian Jews were growing, their self-assurance and cultural identity became more pronounced, both in relation to non-Jews and to the older Jewish centers abroad.

Like most Muslim lands, al-Andalus was a highly urbanized society. At a time when major Frankish cities like Aix-la-Chapelle, Charlemagne's capital, had only a few thousand inhabitants, Muslim cities such as Baghdad, Samarkand, and Damascus counted several hundred thousand, and Cordova could have neared half a million. Smaller urban centers included Seville, Granada, Malaga, Saragossa, and Toledo. The immense size of the Muslim world (*dar al Islam*)— from India to Spain and from Samarkand to Mozambique—provided a quasi-uniform system of language, law, and monetary exchange. This facilitated international trade. The golden *dinar* was accepted everywhere, and money orders (called *suftadja*) were also sometimes trusted.[21] Protected by the caliph's power, the Muslims built a merchant marine that crisscrossed the Mediterranean (mostly along the coasts, since even the caliph could not shield them from storms). The Muslims used Jews and Mozarabs to trade with the Christian countries and relied on venture merchants—in many cases, Jews again—to trade with India, China, central Asia, and the faraway regions of dar al Islam. Traders usually preferred the smoother sea routes to cumbersome caravans— and Jews preferred them even more because ships, unlike camels, were not obliged to stop for the Sabbath.

A steady flow of money streamed into the caliph's vaults as a result of the economic prosperity: the annual royal income, mostly from duties and customs

on trade, averaged one hundred thousand gold bars. The figure was given by
Hisdai ibn Shaprut, the caliph's Jewish doctor and political favorite who was in
a position to know, because he was also the royal commissioner of customs, and
a chief adviser and diplomat for the caliph.

The Jewish "Caliph"

The senior Jew in the caliphate, Hisdai ibn Shaprut, climbed to power on the
only effective, yet always fragile, ladder available in a system of personal government—the caliph's favor and trust. The brilliant and ambitious young doctor had
become a polished courtier and politician who looked after his master's two most
precious assets—his body and his treasury. Abd-a-Rahman III was too prudent
to officially appoint a Jew as his minister of finance, and too clever not to use
Hisdai's services in that capacity as a matter of fact, so he made him commissioner of customs—the main source of royal income[21]—and appointed no one
above him. Hisdai was also involved in delicate foreign missions. He had to be
on his guard incessantly, catering to his master's every wish and whim (though
Abd-a-Rahman III, on the whole, was not a whimsical ruler), and warding off
the envy and intrigue of rival dignitaries who often used Hisdai's Judaism as
their target. "The prophet by whose virtue alone you are respected," a resentful
theologian once shot at the caliph in public, "is called a liar by this Jew."[23]

Hisdai's Jewish profile was indeed high. The caliph made him preside over all
the Jewish communities in al-Andalus. The Jews called him *nassi* (chief, prince),
though in some respects he was a semblance of "caliph" to them, providing the
Jews with protection, access to power, deals, and appointments, and accepting
their ceaseless respect and flattery, some of it, of course, in verse. Just as the
Ummayad caliphate challenged the supremacy of Baghdad, so Hisdai strove to
free Jewish al-Andalus from the preponderance of Jewish Mesopotamia (Babylon). He was an Ummayad courtier to the bone, deeply versed in Arabic ways
and, following the example of his caliph, he too was trying to attract poets,
linguists, and scientists to Cordova—to work as Jews and extensively use the
Hebrew language, which had to be resuscitated and fitted for secular use. His
own elegant home served as meeting place for intellectuals and scientists in
fields such as astronomy, mathematics, and medicine, whose work he commissioned and helped publish. And his emissaries went everywhere in the Jewish
Diaspora to collect books and persuade literary and rabbinical figures to come
to Cordova.

Until that time, Jewish culture was doubly limited in Spain: it was restricted to
legal-religious matters, and it lacked full authority even in them. All important

questions had to be referred to Babylon, where the main version of the Talmud had been created[24] and where subsequent rabbinical masters, called *geonim*, continued to exercise worldwide authority for several centuries. Jewish Spain did not have such prominent Talmudists; but perhaps the real reason for its dependency was lack of status and recognition rather than of scholarship. That was what Hisdai set forth to change. He knew that Babylon was already in decline, while the younger, vibrant Jewish Spain was rapidly growing in wealth and prestige.

Like any new institution of power—or declaration of independence—this one had its founding myth. One day, we are told,[25] Rabbi Moshe ben Hanoch, an eminent Italian Talmudist, was sailing with his wife and son when Andalusian ships attacked their ship. Rabbi Moshe's wife drowned herself to avoid being raped and he and the boy were taken prisoner and brought to Cordova, where the local Jews ransomed them. At first Rabbi Moshe lived anonymously until one day he heard the local chief rabbi, Nathan, stumbling before a problem in Jewish law. Modestly, Moshe produced the answer, and Nathan instantly recognized the stranger as his superior. Rabbi Moshe was appointed (presumably by Hisdai) chief Talmudic judge and teacher for al-Andalus—to the great satisfaction of the caliph, who was delighted "that the Jews of his domain no longer had need of the people of Babylonia."[26] The quotation sounds authentic, but the rest of the story has the fancy ring of a minimessianic legend: the redeemer's sudden emergence, his suffering and early loneliness, then his disclosure and immediate recognition. It is more likely (and prosaic) to suppose that the eminent Rabbi Moshe came to Cordova of his own will (perhaps he was en route when the incident occurred), knowing that Talmudic studies were already quite developed in Spain and its Jewish community was on the rise.[27] But that makes a weaker founding myth: a miraculous deus ex machina captivates the imagination far more than the banality of organic growth.

Thus two processes were taking place under Hisdai: Jewish Spain was being recognized as an independent Talmudic power, and it was linking into the secular (Arab and Arabized Greek) culture of the age. Jewish culture expanded beyond rabbinical studies to embrace poetry, art, and science—and it did so creatively, not by simple imitation but often by Hebraizing that culture, that is, investing it with different linguistic sensibilities and cultural associations.

Without relinquishing their covenant with their fathers' transcendent God, Spanish Jews discovered the earthbound joys he made available to men and women who take interest in his creation and are open to the pleasures of the intellect, language, the imagination, and not least (though within reason), the senses. Here was a permanent feature of the Spanish-Jewish "golden age" which started under the Ummayads and outlived them by far. Adding the fact that Jews outside the cities lived on the land and closer to its products, we get a life experience of Sephardi Jews which is significantly different from that of most of the Ashkenazim, and is quite unlike the common image of the Diaspora Jew whose material life revolves mostly on commerce and finance and whose spirit is almost exclusively invested in religious practice and rabbinical studies.

Fragility and Dreams of Power

Hisdai's fragile but steady position in court, and his fulfilling life, anticipated and symbolized the Sephardi golden age in general, which was similarly long and, on balance, a fortunate existence, at times even glorious, yet precarious at bottom, built on moving waters rather than stable ground, but, nevertheless, rolling fairly smoothly with the waves.

Hisdai keenly felt the deficiencies of Jewish power in the Diaspora. No other Jew in the middle ages was as influential as Hisdai—that is, as prominent in a major world power—yet no other knew better than he how contingent and precarious it all was. The Mozarabs could look to the strong Christian states around them; Jews had only other Jews to rely upon, all equally outside the pale of real power. Hisdai intervened on behalf of oppressed Jewish communities abroad, corresponded, made inquiries, and kept abreast of the Jewish situation in many lands. But what really flared his imagination were reports about a remote Jewish kingdom beyond the Ararat and the Caucasus—the Khazars, a Turkish warrior tribe whose elite had accepted some diluted form of Judaism and maintained it until the tenth century.

In an engaging Hebrew letter he sent through various intermediaries to Joseph, the Khazar king, Hisdai described the glory of the Cordova caliphate, its economy, its politics, and his own high position, and made innumerable inquiries about the legendary Jewish kingdom: How does its government work? Who are its tributaries? Do the Khazars fight on the Sabbath? And do they possess a calculation of the end of days, when the Messiah will come? Hisdai assured the king—sincerely? rhetorically?—that he was ready to "renounce my honor and give up my greatness" and cross half the world in order to watch an independent Jewish monarch and observe the refuge he can provide "for the survivors of Israel." Such words could only be written by a Jew who knew his greatness to be borrowed and who felt that however much the Jews are integrated in the host society—himself being a prime example—they remain uneasy guests whose yearning tells them they lack something essential both in their country and beyond its horizons.

If Hisdai ever received an answer, it was lost. The so-called reply that has been circulating for the last millennium is probably a fake.[28] But even if King

Joseph had invited Hisdai to come, there was not much time left for the dream: in 965, shortly before Hisdai's death, the Khazar kingdom was overrun and destroyed by the Russians.[29] And, as human affairs are volatile, the Caliphate of Cordova itself did not survive beyond the year 1009 and two more caliphs. The new millennium saw its irreversible collapse.

Splinter and Flourish: The "Petty Kingdoms"

The last two caliphs were as different as can be. Hakkam II was, like his father, a mature politician educated to rule, and a true scholar and bibliophile. His death in 976 left the most powerful kingdom in Europe to Hisham II, a boy of 12 who grew to become merely a shadow ruler. Real power was held by his first minister, the famous al-Mansur, remembered by Christians as the fearful Almanzor, who periodically plundered the Christian kingdoms and carried away their church bells as tokens of their humiliation. Al-Mansur used to collect dust from his numerous military campaigns, and willed that it be buried in his grave. When his wish was fulfilled in 1002, he could not know that the caliphate was also buried with him.

Seven years later, al-Mansur's son and successor perished in obscure circumstances which led to a long period of chaos and civil wars. The caliphate, it turned out, was not a stable institution commanding universal allegiance, but a mosaic of self-centered groups and ethnic elites, held together by the ruler's personal power and skill. Now Arabs, Berbers, and "Slavs" (European Muslims) were in deadly conflict over the spoils of a kingdom they were jointly destroying. Within twenty-two years, nine different caliphs, three of whom held the office more than once, were successively crowned and dethroned. Meanwhile Cordova was sacked, the countryside depleted, people lost their livelihood and security, and atrocities were committed everywhere: a doleful story reminding us that politics, and political history, are often more important in determining other dimensions of human life than today's historiography is ready to admit.

In 1031 the long-defunct caliphate was officially pronounced dead. Al-Andalus was splintered into petty kingdoms dominated by warring ethnic factions (Arab-Andalusians in Seville, Berbers in Granada, Slavs in Valencia and Almería, and so on). The divided Muslim states lost their strategic hegemony on the peninsula and now had to pay tribute to some Christian kingdom—a reversal of roles that started the Reconquista, the slow rolling back of Christian power southward that was to last for another two centuries.

The breakdown of the caliphate was also a consolidation—of a new status quo. A new peninsular order emerged which enabled the still-vigorous Andalusian civilization to express its creative energies in accordance with the new conditions. As in fifteenth-century Italy, political fragmentation and a measure of habitual violence, contingent but contained, proved to be compatible with economic recovery and cultural stir and flourish.

The title of caliph connotes the Prophet's vicar, and the old caliphate had a religious significance underneath its worldly culture. Not so the splinter rulers, who had no other mission than their own gain and glory. Most of them were this-worldly oriented, "not deeply attached to the Islamic religion, but . . . chiefly interested in poetry, belles letters and the arts generally."[30] The breakdown of central power allowed art and learning to proliferate as many petty rulers tried to imitate the Ummayad splendor in their own courts, and Jewish magnates followed their example.

A Mitigated Peak

The eleventh century is often seen as the first peak of the Jewish golden age, but this is true only in regard to culture. The economic picture was more uneven. Many Jews had their land depleted or their trade disrupted by the wars, and for the first time there was a significant Jewish emigration to the Christian north.[31] On the other hand, the petty rulers were more comfortable than the Ummayads had been about non-Muslims serving in high places. If, seventy years before, Hisdai ibn Shaprut could not be officially appointed finance minister in Cordova, now the Jew, Ismail ibn Nagrila—known to Jews as Shmuel HaNagid (the Governor, or Chieftain)[32]—was officially chief minister in Granada, and other Jews were serving in high places elsewhere. As at no other time before late modernity, people in Spain were judged by their utility, sometimes even their merit, rather than by their race or religion. Tolerance, though not a moral command, was a utilitarian precept and inbred mentality, which may be the reason it worked (more or less).

The petty kingdoms proved beneficial to Arabic culture and even more so to Jewish culture. Hebrew became the dominant language in Jewish poetry; Talmudic studies rose to prominence; and, as if to counterbalance them, philosophy made a serious start in Jewish Spain. Poems in Hebrew were being written everywhere, and countless new phrases, idioms, declensions and inflections were invented in the process, some ingenious, others rather wooden (because they imitated Arabic forms much too mechanically). An unlikely topic provoking strong feelings was, of all things, Hebrew grammar. This seemingly dry subject was given a systematic basis (by Joseph Hayuj and, especially, by Jonah ibn Jinah); and, together with progress in Hebrew semantics, this enabled scholars to take a fresh look at biblical texts and debate no less an issue than the true meaning of God's word. The study of language thus became as crucial and sensitive among the Jews as it was among the Arabs, and in some respects prefigured the work of European humanists of the sixteenth century. When Ibn Jinah published his monumental works on grammar (using Hayuj, but also severely criticizing him), the polemics were such that Ibn Nagrila/HaNagid himself, the most prominent Jew of the century, was prompted to personally write a rebuttal. At stake were such matters as irregular three-letter radicals, not so exciting in themselves but relevant to reading the Bible—and to the future of scholarly reputations.

Ibn Nagrila/HaNagid, held the highest office that any Spanish Jew ever attained; in addition he was an important scholar in his time, and a major name in Hebrew poetry of any time. Officially, as first wazir of Granada, his position was higher than Hisdai ibn Shaprut's, yet his overall power was far more provincial and restricted since he served solely in the small state of Granada, enmeshed in local politics and intrigue. A man of amazing capabilities, Ibn Nagrila's most important talent consisted in knowing how to use his other talents politically; that is, how to translate them into instruments of power.

The list of countless plots, machinations, and wars in which Ibn Nagrila/HaNagid was involved is too long to recount. No less extensive was his literary production: three books of poems, many of which still make captivating reading today, a dictionary of biblical terms, and essays on Hebrew grammar and Talmudic issues (he was also chief rabbi of Granada and a former disciple of Rabbi Hanoch). His most daring work was a polemical analysis of the contradictions in the Qur'an, to which the Muslim scholar Ibn Hazm responded by exposing the contradictions in the Bible. Both scholars were basically right, and jointly, if inadvertently, produced a foundation for canonical criticism (biblical and Qur'anic). The striking thing about their polemic was its very existence. A Jew running a Muslim state was quite enough; that he should be allowed to openly criticize its religion was inordinately tolerant even for that period. (Think of the fierce Islamist reactions today to any slight criticism of the Qur'an.) The Islamic backlash that was soon to occur had some real grievances with which to fuel its zeal.

Jewish historians, dazzled by HaNagid's fascinating personage, saw him as embodying the Jewish golden age in Spain. Yet his political eminence was, in the end, an episode based on personalities, and it ended in disaster. Upon his death his son Yehoseph was made wazir and rabbi but, lacking his father's skills, he finally succumbed to his enemies. Disgraced, he escaped the palace disguised as a black African but was exposed and butchered instantly. After his death, a pogrom and massacre raged in Granada's Jewish neighborhoods, fueled by resentment against both Ibn Nagrilas. This final catastrophe is no less telling than the Nagid's earlier glory. It is only by insisting on *both* its ends—and its essentially personal nature—that the Ibn Nagrila/HaNagid saga can be significant of the Jewish situation in that inconstant age, golden as it may have been.

Ibn Gabirol or Avicebron?

Towering above all other writers was Shlomo ibn Gabirol, a melancholic, sometimes bitter poetical prodigy who was equally at home in earthly affairs and muddles and in the lofty spheres of divine emanations. No one in Spain could write Hebrew poetry more smoothly, and everyone, including Ibn Gabirol himself, knew it. His sense of metaphysical nullity and poetic superiority—of being insignificant in the universe, yet deserving preeminence among men—produced a fascinating contrast. An orphaned child, lonely, sickly, unattractive to women, and practically without family, he was often as arrogant as only a self-conscious genius can be in the company of social superiors he considers to be his intellectual inferiors. His talent was overflowing. In a lifespan shorter than Mozart's, he produced every kind of work, from custom flattery and birthday verses written for money, to deeply lyrical poems, personal revelations, metaphysical poetry, songs, prayers, riddles, moral admonitions, poems depicting natural landscapes and complex human moods and desires, or remonstrating against the "vacuity of the world" (this-worldly affairs). His masterpiece was *Keter Malkhut* (Kingdom's Crown),[33] a poetic-philosophical penetration into God's mysteries and the act of creation. The rabbis found this work so essentially Jewish that they incorporated parts of it into the prayer book; yet Ibn Gabirol's purely philosophical treatise on comparable topics—his Neoplatonic treatise, *Source of Life* (known as *fons vitae* to centuries of Latin readers), written in Arabic, was so devoid of Jewish content that until the nineteenth century it had been attributed to an obscure Muslim author named Avicebron.[34] This duality between Ibn Gabirol's philosophical and Jewish identity recurs in other Hispano-Jewish intellectuals (for example, Maimonides); and, in different ways, we shall meet it again among Converso intellectuals of the sixteenth and seventeenth centuries (and still differently, among modern Jews today).

The Crescent Darkens

The regime of the petty states came to an end in the last decade of the eleventh century, prey to its endemic weakness and two crusading movements. On both sides of the Christian-Muslim divide, holy war was in the air. An army of Christian crusaders was soon to march into the Holy Land and capture Jerusalem from the Muslims, and in Iberia, fifteen years earlier, the Christian north led by Alfonso VI of Castile had already mounted an offensive. Clearly, the Christians were the vital force in Spain now, fresher, rougher, more determined, and less affected by doubt or spoiled by self-indulgence than their Muslim adversaries.

When Toledo, the ancient Iberian capital, fell to Alfonso in 1085, a high point was reached in the Reconquest. The victorious Christians felt they had come half way to their Jerusalem. The Muslim rulers faced a harsh dilemma: either succumb to the Christian onslaught, or summon help from the sturdier, more fanatical Berber warriors of the Moroccan desert, who might save Andalusia but spell the doom of its way of life. Either way, as al-Mu'tamid, the poet-prince of Seville, knew when he made his fateful decision to call in the Berber armies, life would no longer be the same.

He was right. The Berber armies were animated by a crusade of their own— the spirit of *Jihad* (holy war), whose target (like that of Muslim Jihadists today) was not only the infidel but lax Islam as well. They succeeded in stopping the Castilian onslaught, but also abolished the petty Muslim states (al-Mu'tamid was sent in chains to Morocco), and imposed a stern Islamic rule upon the country, shrinking tolerance to a receding minimum.

These Berbers belonged to the religious ascetics (*Murabitun*, Spanish Almoravides), a military brotherhood whose religion was more puritanical than learned; today they would pass as fundamentalists in the sense which combines zeal with the lack of religious sophistication. Through them, Muslim Spain is said to have become acutely conscious of its religious vocation;[35] yet in the six decades in which they ruled cultivated Andalusia, the Murabits submitted to a pattern known in other reformers: they had learned to appreciate some of the virtues and amenities—from poetry to wine shops—of the culture they had wished to subdue.

This provoked the wrath of a still more fanatical Berber movement, the Unitarians (*Al-Muwahiddun*, Almohades), who expelled the Murabits in 1149 and established a second, and harsher, Islamic regime. Their religion was more intellectual (also more dogmatic) than the Murabits'; among other things they fought against anthropomorphism, the contamination of God's abstract unity by human-like images. That made them fiercely opposed not only to Christianity, the religion of the man-God, but to most forms of popular religion, including those existing in Judaism and Islam itself. No wonder they became detached from the people, repressive and domineering—as fanatical establishments often do.

With them, the Spanish Crescent darkened for a whole century. Not that they did not build a magnificent mosque in Seville, their capital since 1170: its tower, the splendid Giralda, still stands today. But prior to that they destroyed the city's synagogues and killed, exiled, or forcibly converted thousands of Jews and Christians, from Cordova and Almería to the island of Majorca (and also in North Africa).

"A cataclysm, alas, descended on Sefarad,"[36] lamented the Jewish poet and scholar Abraham ibn Ezra. Cordova lies in shambles, Granada's Jews have been expelled, in Malaga and Majorca people are starving, and in Jaén and Almería "not a single Jew is left." The Talmud is "lonely" for lack of learners, synagogues are turned into "places of idolatry" (mosques), and Jewish children are "given to a foreign religion."

Poetic Peregrinations: Yehuda Halevi, the Ibn Ezras

The Jews' situation in those turbulent days is well reflected in the peregrinations—geographic and mental—of a few major intellectuals.

Yehuda Halevi (*Abu l'Hassan*) is the most renowned poet of Jewish Spain. His life is reflected as a puzzle from his numerous (over 700) poems. Born around 1075, he was ten years old when the Castilians took Toledo and sixteen when the Murabits annexed Muslim Spain. His later life, several decades of it, was spent wandering between many cities, Muslim and Christian—not as a refugee but in ease and comfort, as becoming the well-off physician, writer, and part-merchant he was; which indicates that the drive for Yehuda Halevi's wanderings came from within himself. Spain, he felt, was a fatherland to the Jews, though nowhere in it was he quite at home. He likewise wandered between poetry and philosophy, frivolity and personal depth, mundanity and messianism, the love of women and young boys and the love of God.

A half millennium before Pascal, Halevi argued against "the God of the philosopher" (Aristotle) and for "the God of Abraham," who is not viewed just as a cosmic principle known to the intellect, but as Yahweh, the God of history and of Israel, whom the Jews know from the direct, even sensuous experience of Mount Sinai. Thus Halevi's theology, unlike Ibn Gabirol's, was distinctly Jewish.

One of Halevi's major stations was Christian-held Toledo, where a prosperous Jewish community existed, still Arabized but starting to adapt to Christian rule. Such reacculturation was now common in the peninsula as Jews and Mozarabs were emigrating to the north in order to share in its rising fortunes or escape Murabit pressure; meanwhile they acted as cultural agents who transmitted Muslim idioms, techniques, and lifestyles to the cruder Christian elite. Yet Abu l'Hassan/Halevi was too deeply Arabized to sustain this role. He felt doubly exiled in Castile: his cultural self remained in the Muslim south and his religious heart was beating in the east (Jerusalem)—so he returned to wander between Muslim cities.

Then came a crisis. "Will you chase frivolity past your fiftieth year / when your days are counted and ready to disappear?" Thus Halevi admonished himself as he went through an inward-oriented conversion. In his fifties, then an old age, he set out for his farthest and loneliest journey—to Jerusalem, then held by the Christian crusaders. Jerusalem was the object of great messianic yearning in Halevi's poems ("My heart is in the East while I am at the far end of the West"; "O Zion, ask how those imprisoned by you are doing!"), and in taking the road to Jerusalem Halevi seems to have performed a counter-crusade of his own, challenging both the Christians and the Muslims. Romantic legend has him killed incognito at the foot of the Wailing Wall, but legend is often more generous than life. Halevi, it seems, never made it past the Jewish community of Egypt, where he died.

The spirit of countercrusade is also embodied in the setting of the *Kuzari*, Halevi's chief theoretical work, in which the king of the Khazars organizes a debate between a Jew, a Muslim, a Christian, and a rationalist philosopher in order to know which religion to adopt. That the Jew wins—not only a debate, but a kingdom—was not merely a theological point for Halevi: it alluded, perhaps as wish-fulfillment, to the more violent "debate" then raging between Muslim and Christian crusaders. The Jews were too powerless to even count as contenders in this debate—they only paid its price in suffering—yet they alone, the *Kuzari* argues, are the true bearers of God's revelation; so all they can do is dream of power, either in the symbolic form of a return to Zion, or in the more worldly form of the Khazar kingdom, which still fired Halevi's imagination as once it had Hisdai's.

The Ibn Ezras

Another poetic wanderer symbolizing the age was Moshe ibn Ezra, Halevi's elder friend, whose life was also divided in two, although in a different manner. Born to wealth and learning in flourishing Granada, he was singing of springtime gardens and the joys of wine and bisexual love ("caressing a beauty's breasts nightly" and "sucking the lips of a young deer" [boy-lover]), and also of wisdom and life's brevity, when the Murabit invasion shattered Jewish Granada and sent him wandering for the rest of his life in Christian Spain—bitter, resentful, unable (for some obscure reason) to return to Granada and refusing to acculturate in the north, where he felt "like a man in the company of savages / a lion among monkeys and parrots."[37] In Jewish life he signifies the pain of

Spain's Muslim parts retreating before the Christian north—a kind of Jewish replica of the Reconquista.

Even more nomadic was his younger relative Abraham ibn Ezra, the most multifaceted Jew of his time—poet, mathematician, astronomer, penetrating biblical exegete and critic (the most audacious before Spinoza), and eternal pauper—who practically lived on the road. In 1140, the year Yehuda Halevi sailed to Egypt and seven years before the Al-Muwahiddun calamity, Ibn Ezra left Spain for good—in the other direction. He went to Rome, Pisa, Mantova, Narbonne, Bordeaux, Angers, Rouen, London, and other cities in Christian Europe—writing essays and poems, propagating Sephardi culture to local Jews, chasing his luck and rarely finding it. Yet he was hardly ever bitter, but maintained a splendid self-irony and comforted himself with the thought that he needed no external honors—no "place" in either the literal or the social sense—because "*I am the place and the place is with me.*" With a confidence untainted by arrogance, he assures himself that "My honor lies in the place I choose, however low it be."[38] No one prior to the late European Renaissance had better expressed the sense of self of the person of excellence, replacing the outer insignia of honor with individual worth and merit.[39]

It is quite remarkable to observe the creative height that, through such wandering intellectuals, the Arabized Jews of Spain attained in the period of their great political and demographic decline. Muslim culture (especially poetry) was already past its prime in the twelfth century, becoming routinized and repetitive;[40] but the Judeo-Arabic culture went through a period of fruition and propagation—a burst of flourishing on the brink of the precipice.

Islam's Forced Converts

The times were bleak indeed. Together with the shattering of the Jews' political status by the Berber dynasties, their numbers were dropping through massive emigration to the Christian north and periodical conversions to Islam. Already the Murabits had tried to convert Jews; their relative success is recorded in Yehuda Halevi's sad lines about the "dove" (the Jewish people) whom "foreigners entice with other gods" while she "weeps in secret for the husband of her youth."[41] There is also a story about the Murabit conqueror of Spain who, in 1005, told the rabbis that the Prophet Muhammad had allowed their ancestors to wait for the Messiah for another five hundred years, after which the Jews had to accept Islam. As Muslim years are shorter than Jewish years (by seven months every nineteen years), the sultan proclaimed that Muhammad's extension was about to expire in two years![42] That the Jews, in the end, ransomed themselves with money was a classic, if temporary, solution which proved far less effective under the later Al-Muwahiddun.

Historians debate whether the Al-Muwahiddun oppression of the Jews was planned or sporadic, permanent or intermittent;[43] but no one denies that under their rule, Spain humiliated its Jews and Mozarabs as never before. Brutal force was periodically used to convert Jews and Christians to Islam, sometimes en masse. Thus, under the darkened Crescent, Jewish forced converts (*anussim*) reappear on the Spanish scene for the first time since the Visigoth period. They were not the exclusive creation of Christian Spain, but were produced by Muslim Spain as well, and thereby became a recurrent phenomenon in Spanish history.[44]

Many conversions were superficial. A convert's duty was to accept and regularly recite the Muslim credo ("There is no God but Allah and Muhammad is his messenger"), together with a few rudimentary prayers. Many converts used to mentally annul what their lips were uttering. Some were practicing Jewish rites in private, an offense that was severely punished—sometimes by death—when detected, though the law was loosely enforced. Still, caution was imperative: in Tunisia until the twentieth century there were Jewish families who refused to admit guests on holidays—contrary to Jewish tradition, but conforming to the rules of prudence eight centuries ago, in Tunisia as well as in Andalusia.

Some conversions were voluntary. A moving apology of such a convert is made in a poem by Yizhak ibn Ezra, Abraham's son. Yes, he says half-defiantly, I have sinned, but didn't all our great men sin too? Didn't Moses break God's tables? Didn't Judah fornicate with his daughter-in-law Tamar, Samson with Delilah, King David with Bath-Sheba? Myself, I have always refrained from eating nonkosher meat whilst I was a Muslim, and when my lips declared that the "lunatic" (Muhammad) was God's prophet, my heart always responded: "thou art lying!" At last I returned to the true God and now expect His pardon![45]

Ben Maimon and the Forced Converts

Again a wandering intellectual encapsulates the times. Moshe ben Maimon (Maimonides, also known as Musa Ibn Maimun and Abu Imran Musa) was a young prodigy approaching his bar mitzvah in Cordova when the Al-Muwahiddun calamity sent him wandering in Andalusia with his rabbi-father and brother. Despite their itinerant life he continued with his superb education, covering the whole Bible and Talmud, much of rabbinical literature, and everything available in Greco-Arabic philosophy and science (including medicine, his later profession), together with philology and some poetry.[46] It was a typically Spanish combination of sacred and secular studies; but for Maimonides, at least in maturity, the secular itself acquired a sacred dimension: philosophy and natural science, he maintained, are not outside the religious domain; they have a profound religious significance in themselves, a significance so fundamental that the other elements of religion—prophecy, revelation, popular fables and myths, and the system of Jewish commands (mitzvoth)—are ultimately grounded in these rational-philosophical foundations.

Around 1160 the Maimon family crossed the sea to Morocco—right into the lion's den, the center of the persecuting empire. Why they did so has not been explained. Either the capital city was more lenient than the province, or by then the Maimons themselves had nominally converted to Islam for appearance's sake (the evidence for that is strong but inconclusive).[47] In any case, sometime later Maimonides wrote a manifesto on conversion in which he violently denounced a rabbi who had indiscriminately damned all converts, whatever their motives and circumstances. Applying his logical mind to this burning (and perhaps personal) question, Maimonides discerned several modalities and degrees of conversion, and ruled that a forced convert must "abandon everything he possesses and walk day and night until he finds a place where he can reconstitute his [Jewish] religion";[48] meanwhile, he should keep a maximum of Jewish laws in secret.

The writer took his own advice. In 1165 the Maimon family crossed Al-Muwahiddun lines into Egypt and settled in Fustat (ancient Cairo). Moshe practiced medicine in the court of Salah-a-Din ("Saladin") and eventually rose to chief rabbi and *nagid* (leader) of all Jewish communities in Egypt. Though his free time in Egypt was scarce,[49] his outstanding concentration and lightening-quick grasp, supported by a phenomenal memory, enabled him, despite other duties, to compose two very different works which, independent of each other, made him the greatest rabbi and legal authority ever to arise in the Diaspora, and the most significant Jewish philosopher before Spinoza.

It was of him that the epigram was made: "From Moses [the prophet] to Moses [Ben Maimon] there was no one like Moses." In his *Mishne Torah* (literally: "Repetition of the Torah," 1180) Ben Maimon offered, in fourteen tracts, the clearest, most comprehensive, topically organized systematization of all the rulings in Jewish law. The book was intended to put an end to the Talmudic spirit of perpetual exegesis and ratiocination about the law, and return the law to what it essentially was—a directive for action. This, in turn, was supposed to liberate the Jews' intellectual energies and redirect them to where they ought to be invested: the study of God and his creations—namely, rational metaphysics and natural science—which the prophets themselves, Maimonides claimed, have studied and allegorized in the bible's secret linguistic layer. This Maimonidean revolution is announced and performed, half-covertly, in his philosophical opus, *The Guide of the Perplexed* (1190), which deliberately perplexed as many people as it has guided, because it is addressed to an enlightened minority and often uses equivocation and intentional contradictions to conceal its meaning from those whom Maimonides calls the "rabbinical multitude."

Maimonides' project was as daring as only an Arabized Hispano-Jewish elitist could conceive. But historically, it failed. The rabbinical multitude had the upper hand. For although the *Mishne Torah* had been accepted and eventually hailed as a major authority in Judaism, the *Guide*, its inseparable complement, was mistrusted from the start. It was even banned and burned at the heat of the conflict—and was shoved into that alcove of Jewish religious life where philosophy and rationalism have been struggling for their legitimate existence in face of the unflinching supremacy of legal Talmudic studies and periodic surges of mysticism. In the end, not only did the Talmud remain dominant in Jewish learning, but—supreme irony—the *Mishne Torah* itself has become the object of Talmud-like ratiocination and interminable exegesis.

Thus the connection closest to Maimonides' heart—between his rabbinical and philosophical work—was broken. Beside being his personal setback, this was another failed attempt of Andalusian Jews to impress the rest of the Jewish world with the distinct combination of the secular and the sacred, however configured, which characterized their unique and multifarious culture.

However, within the peninsula this was still a valid and working combination; and now it was making its way toward the north, where Christian Spaniards were preparing for the decisive phase of the Reconquest, and where the hub of Jewish life was now shifting. The Jewish Star was parting way with the darkened Crescent and moving back toward the Cross.

2

Reconquest and Revival: The Cross Is Back

———————— ⬨ ————————

A full cycle had turned since Visigoth oppression pushed the Jews into Tarik's camp. Now, after more than a century of Berber intolerance, Spanish Jews were moving back into the Christian camp, not only politically, but geographically too, by immigrating en masse into the Christian kingdoms. The Christian rulers welcomed the Jews as needed allies in building a new Hispano-Christian empire—for that, nothing less, had become the goal and vision of the leaders of the Reconquest.

Muslim power in Spain was irreversibly broken in the battle of Las Navas de Tolosa in 1212; and, with the fall of Seville in 1248, the work of the Reconquista was practically done. Only Granada with its coastal region was left to the Muslims, their last bastion in Iberia, which curiously survived until 1492, the same year that Jewish life was also eradicated in Spain.

The centuries-long Reconquest had left its mark on the spirit of religious crusade which persisted in Spain even after it became an empire, and in the cult of birth and *hidalgo* values, which prized noble birth, personal venture, and prowess, and disdained the world of work, production, and commerce—though not its fruits, which a Spanish hidalgo was considered entitled to pluck as a matter of natural right.

The latter attitude was to assign the Jews further tasks in Christian Spain, both as producers of wealth and as those who, through the tax administration, helped the ruling class reap its fruits. But first they had a colonizing role.

One of the handicaps of the Reconquest was the widening gap between its geography and its demography. As more territories were captured, a stream of Muslim refugees was heading southward, leaving their areas half-depopulated and in economic decay. The result was a "desperate shortage" of civilian manpower to hold and develop the new territories.[1] The Muslim exodus left considerable property behind, which the new rulers distributed among petty knights, soldiers, and veteran free peasants—and also among Jews, who bore the promise of economic recovery.

Jews indeed (especially immigrants) were in great demand in the frontier's shifting zones.[2] Most Jews were now opposed to the Al-Muwahiddun, and therefore considered loyal; their knowledge of Arabic language and custom was important in dealing with the Muslims; and they possessed the trades and crafts necessary to make the abandoned areas economically viable. In all, the Reconquest treated the Jews well—indeed, so favorably that, despite the inevitable pains of adaptation, the Jews knew a kind of second golden age, or at least many occasions to flourish.

The Reconquest gave rise to a tremendous effort toward urbanization in Christian Spain, one of the most impressive in the Middle Ages. Dozens of cities, old and new, big and small, were eventually active in Castile alone,[3] founded by royal charters that gave them many freedoms. The cities were jealous of their autonomy and always considered it insufficient.

The Jews and the Economic Engine

What made the Jews in such demand was not only their knowledge of trade and finance, but also their age-old expertise in the crafts that make a city work—producing clothes, footwear, furniture, tools, weapons, and the like. In all these areas the Jews had an advantage over the upcoming Christian burghers who, coming from the ranks of the military, had little urban experience and needed much training. Jews also served the kings—they supplied the army, helped collect the king's taxes, leased and ran royal monopolies (such as salt mines), and lent money to nobles, gentry, and the incipient burghers. It is therefore fair to say that Jews helped start the economic engine of Christian Spain in the critical generations after the Reconquest, and gave it shape and impetus. However, in the fourteenth century the Christian burghers started taking over many of the urban functions that Jews had dominated (excepting the royal finances); and this produced a long and harsh rivalry between them and their former Jewish mentors.

Jewish Self-Rule and the Cities

The Jews' status in Christian Spain was anchored in legal grounds. Living and often flourishing in separate neighborhoods, called *juderías*, the Jews were treated as an inferior variety of burghers. This made their existence in Christian Spain less arbitrary, though no less fragile, in times of crisis. The Jews formed a self-ruling corporate body called *Aljama* (Arabic for "community"). The members of the *Aljama* were authorized—indeed, required—to live by Jewish laws and obey the rabbinical courts in most matters. Although barred from a whole range of honors and opportunities, the Jews' service to the royal court gave them advantages, which the local burghers resented. The burghers constantly complained that the Jews were more loyal to the Crown than to the city. The complaint, though partisan, was not groundless. Their link to the Crown allowed the Jews to enjoy a dual autonomy—as an urban corporation vis-à-vis the nobility, and as a semi-independent community within the city, directly subject to the king. This duality was a permanent cause of grievance and conflict between the cities and their Jewish citizens. The history of the fourteenth century is overcast by this bitter struggle, which eventually tore a lethal wound in the body of Jewish existence in Spain.[4]

Cultural Dualities and Interdependence

Apart from their economic role, the Jews for many generations continued to transmit Arab knowledge and civilization to Christian Spain, while themselves maintaining a mixed cultural identity. It is striking how long the Jews in Christian Spain have preserved their Arabic names, language, and many tastes. In 1305, almost all the Jewish oligarchs in Tudela, a town in the far north, had Arabic names (Abassi, Falkira, Sha'ib, Da'oud, and so on).[5] Visitors to Toledo today can still admire the intricate Muslim-like beauty of El Tránsito, a private synagogue built in 1360, a full century after the heyday of the Reconquest, by Shemuel Halevi Abulafia, a Jewish courtier bearing an Arabic name and serving a Catholic king, who decorated this shrine with Hebrew and Arabic inscriptions.

In their own scholarly writing, however, the use of Arabic was declining among the Jews. Now Hebrew and sometimes Aramaic were used to write the treatises, sermons, and moral admonitions of which the Jews' prose in Christian Spain mainly consisted. Poetry emigrated with the Jews to Christian Spain but its days of glory were behind it. The Jews' original creation in Christian Spain was the mystical and messianic movement known as Kabbalah, which took shape as a semi-underground movement and gave itself a canonical work (the *Zohar*). Rather than plunge into legal Talmudic studies, the Kabbalists indulged in elaborate mystical allegories and image-rich combinations of words and numbers, by which they sought to decipher the secrets of creation and the covert meaning of the Torah hidden under the plain text. Their doctrine of salvation involved a mystical practice by which the Kabbalist was said to affect the divine sphere itself and mend the state of the whole universe, albeit in a small, cumulative way.

Philosophy, meanwhile, was fighting for its life. A fierce struggle had developed over Maimonides' *Guide*. At stake was the role of rational philosophy, which many rabbis saw as a menace to the habitual directness of popular faith—and to the nascent Jewish mysticism. Eventually philosophy was considerably delegitimized and ejected from current Jewish life into the possession of a small elite minority, which was thereby marginalized.

The Kings and "Their" Jews

The backbone of Jewish existence in Christian Spain was the assiduous protection of the Crown. Elsewhere in Western Europe Jews were being expelled (from England in 1290 and from France in 1306) yet in Spain, except for a few local pogroms, every king protected the Jews, and Aragon even admitted Jewish exiles from France. The pogroms occurred when the king was either dead, a minor, or challenged by rebellion. When, in 1355, Pedro I was dubbed "king of the Jews" by his insurgent brother Enrique, this was a hostile exaggeration of an image that, in a milder form, had been latent in most of Pedro's predecessors.

This royal constancy owed much to high-ranking Jews who served the kings as administrators and as tax farmers (those who "lease" the right to collect taxes, for which they pay a fee to the Crown) and tax collectors. Taxes, from the Crown's standpoint, were too important to consign to a Christian peer, who might use them to build an independent power base rivaling the monarch. And the Jewish communities paid a higher share of taxes than the rest of the population, most of which went directly to the royal treasury.

No less important, all Spanish monarchs were anxious to build a loyal central administration that could restrain the divisive barons and rationalize the government's work in the intricate maze of medieval conditions then in effect. The Jews possessed the required skills and lacked any perspective of independent power. With all their proud airs and grandee postures, the Jewish dignitaries were actually the king's political eunuchs; as such, they responded, in a medieval way, to the need for loyalty and centralized "impartiality" in the royal administration.[6]

Consequently, the history of Christian Spain is studded with Jewish courtiers and administrators, each coupled with his respective king. On the long list of names—Yuçaf de Écija, Shlomo Bonafos, Yoseph Revalia, Don Çac de la Maleha (Don Yizhak of the salt mines), and so forth—we might single out Don Yehuda ben Lavi de La Caballería, the founder of an illustrious Jewish dynasty (and later, a Marrano dynasty), whose members we shall meet in later chapters. The occasional downfall or even execution of a Jewish courtier, as happened to Don Çac, signified an integral part of the system rather than its breakdown: it highlights the inherent fragility of the relation. Unlike Muslim times, the monarch's dependence on his Jewish favorite was now structural, transcending the singular individual. The king could dispose of this or that particular Jew, but he needed the Jewish administrators as an informal *institution*.

When speaking of administration, the word must not be understood in the modern sense. Much of the government's business was carried out through leasing and contracting of state functions to private entities—a kind of medieval privatization. The top Jewish entrepreneurs often employed other Jews as secretaries or subcontractors (royal papers were sometimes signed in Hebrew, or carried Hebrew comments), which gave the Jews a high profile in positions of authority, too visible to avoid resentment.

Ironically, without knowing it, the successive Jewish administrators were engaged in a long and tortuous process of premodernization in Spain, which culminated around 1500 in the semicentralized, premodern state of Ferdinand and Isabella. When that stage was reached, the Jews were expelled from Spain. Ferdinand and Isabella could afford the Expulsion because by then they had Conversos at their disposal, former Jews who now were under threat of the Inquisition and thus, again, dependent on the Crown.

The Native Other

It was the Jews' status as both indigenous and *Other*—as the native Other—that helped them attain such high rank in Christian Spain. Their position was due to their stigmatized image no less than to material considerations. The Jews were more dependable than Spanish peers in doing the Crown's work because, as members of an irremediably stained group, they did not have sufficient political legitimacy to contend for real power.[7] Paradoxically, therefore, it was their basic illegitimacy that allowed the Jews to attain high office and thus survive and flourish in Spain. In this respect, the Jews' living both inside the city, and yet separately from it, reflected their broader situation.

In a word, the Jews' alienness played in their favor, much as it also played against them; and this tension defined the Jews' situation in Christian Spain. They were tolerated and resented, granted opportunities and envied for using them, and always seen as utter strangers. Their support came mainly from the crown and from a thin Christian elite, yet even their patrons felt the Jews to be disquieting aliens and Christianity's irreconcilable Other. King Alfonso the Sage, a learned ruler and poet who protected the Jews in his policies and legislation, depicted them in his poetry as the enemies of God's mother, and as associated with the "devil's disciples," the epitome of otherness; and he expressed a pious, if not realistic, longing for their voluntary conversion. The contradiction, if there was one, is symbolic of Christian Spain's attitude toward the Jews.

From another angle, the Jews were integrated into Spanish society in the special medieval sense that differentiated all layers of society. Alongside the Christians, the Muslims, the old Mozarabs, the new Mudejares (former Muslims newly converted to Christianity, who maintained Arabic art and culture), and others, the Jews participated in Spain's social mosaic not by transcending their unequalled otherness, but through it. The result was a certain stratified, medieval form of multiculturality. The reign of Ferdinand and Isabella, who expelled the Jews and started the Inquisition, signaled its end.

The Drive to Convert

Alongside the hostility of the burghers and of common folks, the Jews suffered from the ethos of conversion—an offshoot of the crusading spirit of the Reconquista, which now turned inward. Almost every monarch who protected the Jews also tried, at least outwardly, to persuade them to accept the Cross (although counting on not being fully successful). One king, Jaime I of Aragon, went in person to the synagogue to preach Christianity to the Jews. He also organized a public debate in Barcelona (1263) in which a famous rabbi, Nachmanides (*Ramban*), confronted the converted Jew Paulus Christiani in front of the entire court. Though the rabbi was not free to fully speak his mind, his performance was so prudent and effective that the king told him afterward he had "never heard anyone in the wrong argue so well."[8]

The enduring thrust to convert the Jews ran on two levels, deep and shallow, genuine and self-deceptive. The monarchs admitted the ideology of conversion, but only in their hearts, not in their deeds; so it became a pious hope for the future. Far more sincere in fighting Judaism were the monastic orders—Franciscan and, especially, Dominican friars, whose crusading spirit, now turned inward, injected a strong current of intolerance into a country that still allowed the three religions to coexist in a hierarchic, conflictual (yet workable) *convivencia*.

The Glory of Sheer Existence

To avoid a distorted perspective we should remember that finance was a relatively small part of the Jews' occupation in Spain. It gave their community political and economic muscle, but was rarely present in people's actual lives. The bulk of the Jewish society was made of small economic players—artisans, shopkeepers, some farmers and manual workers, transporters, petty clerics, and ordinary doctors and scholars—not all glamorous occupations or linked to a noble's court.

Thus, politically crucial as he was, the glamour of the Jewish courtier ought not to blind us. Rather, our historical imagination must clear the center stage for the ordinary Jewish men and women and visualize them working, studying, making a living (or failing to do so), celebrating religious occasions, looking for opportunities, defending their interests, admonishing each other, writing and reading poetry, competing, quarreling, uniting in common causes, raising children, trying to figure out what life is about and what lies in store for them in this world and the next: in other words, *living*, going on with the business of existing in a gentile environment that both accepts and denounces them.

Because the inglorious fourteenth century produced nothing outstanding in Jewish life—and since the documents about this time are not abundant—a major Jewish historian called it a "period of stagnation and decline."[9] However, sometimes we look too much in history for special events—major achievements or great suffering and downfall—to serve as signposts of meaning, and we fail to appreciate the power and worth of sheer *life* as it reengenders itself and its world. Even without big-letter signposts, there is a certain glory in sheer existence—in the nonmonumental, ongoing human experience in which men and women strive to create a life for themselves in the face of frequent adversity, engender progeny, fulfill dreams, produce or re-create cultural values, and look for some sense in their existence: and this was certainly part of the Jewish story in the fourteenth century.

The Jews Redemonized

Yet the fourteenth century also produced two new sources of anti-Jewish animosity: the Black Death and a civil war. This was the Calamitous Century in Europe,[10] when death was more rapid, fear more crippling, and suffering even more arbitrary than in most other periods. France was torn by foreign invasions and warfare known today as the Hundred Years War; Italy was at the mercy of brigands and *condottieri* (bands of mercenaries); and in Spain, too, private armies and highwaymen were intermittently ravaging the land.[11] The collapse of public order and security made life precarious and the future uncertain. Then, in midcentury, came the Black Death—a horrid plague that wiped out one-third of Europe's population and filled survivors with cold dread—of the unknown, the undeserved, the inexplicable. Such a cataclysm could not have been caused by either God or nature, so it had to be the work of occult, devilish powers. And who, besides the usual witches, was more occult, more devilish, more inexplicably alien, and more readily available for blame, than the Jews?[12]

Thus arose the demonic image of Jews as "contaminating wells," which generated pogroms across Europe. The pope and leading medical authorities were powerless to dispel the evil myth because the Black Death undermined people's respect for authority. It also shattered basic assurances and reshaped people's fears and prejudices. Hysterical self-flagellation and the demonizing of the Jews, were two new forms of expressing guilt and blame. Thus the Jews, who suffered from the plague like everyone else, also became its victims' victims.

As a result, the dormant, half-repressed, almost acquiesced image of the *Jew-as-demon* came back to life in a violent new form, like an old cancer in remission that suddenly turned malignant. Henceforth, this image affected the way Spanish Jews were viewed until the cataclysm which engulfed them at the end of the fourteenth century.

Halevi Abulafia and the "King of the Jews"

No sooner had the Black Death subsided than Castile became tormented by wars from without and within, which were also blamed on the Jews. In 1350 King Alfonso XI died of the plague and his two sons, the half-brothers Pedro and Enrique, disputed the throne for almost two decades. The legitimate heir was Pedro I, whom history dubbed *the Cruel*, although his brother was even more brutal. As his chief financier and, eventually, top adviser, King Pedro appointed Shemuel Halevi Abulafia (builder of the splendid Toledo synagogue mentioned previously), who set up a semi-Jewish administration and brought Jewish power in Castile to a short-lived apogee.

That provided Enrique with his battle cry. "Down with Pedro, king of the Jews!" his followers shouted everywhere. By cold-blooded design, Enrique sent his rebel troops to massacre Jews and invited the local populace to join the killing: he knew this would make him popular. He also wanted to compromise the populace in a mutinous act, thus forcing them into his camp.

The strategy worked. Pedro eventually sacked and executed Abulafia on charges of fraud, but this late move could not erase the king's image as one fighting a Jewish war. Meanwhile the Jews were being killed and heavily taxed by all sides. In the end, Pedro was killed by his brother's hand. A triumphant Enrique II ascended the throne—and started protecting the Jews in his turn. New Jewish financiers were appointed to help Enrique run his kingdom. The long-standing royal pattern proved stronger than any princely prejudice, if one ever truly existed.

In the following decades, Castilian Jews were healing their wounds and starting to thrive again, as did their brethren in Aragon. Yet this short-lived recovery was a mere shadow of the Jews' former position. The shattering effects of the century poisoned the psychosocial scene, and the anti-Jewish venom acquired a new malignant nature. The trends begun in the thirteenth century—the pressure to convert, and the hostility of the Christian burghers—not only accelerated, but were now operating within the new cast of mind of the Calamitous Century. These trends generated a new anti-Judaism whose fervor expressed a sui generis aversion aimed at the *radical other* as such, and which cannot be reduced to mere economic reasons or to ordinary religious differences.

Actually, the economic struggle between Christian burghers and the Jews had all along been shaped and defined in terms of the Jews' otherness. The Jews were singled out as the opponents not merely because they were tradesmen, but because they were otherwise different, bearing a Jewish stigma. This is what made their rivalry unbearable and united the other burghers against them as a group, rather than competing individually with each other. To feel indignation and cry out against the Jews' position, the Christian burghers must already have experienced an aversion against the Jew as such—not as an economic player but, more fundamentally, as the bearer of a radically foreign and undeserving identity. The Jews were unworthy of economic privileges (thought the burghers), or of practicing authority over Christian tax payers (thought the populace), or even of enjoying the law's protection as money lenders (thought their debtors) because they were illegitimate aliens, marked by social anathema and theological guilt. Thus identity passions, expressed as social bigotry, were decisive in defining the socioeconomic frontline and framing its arguments.

The same identity passions, heightened by the post–Black Death demonization of the Jews, were also crucial in generating the pogrom of the late fourteenth century, which tore a lethal wound in the body of Jewish existence in Spain, and started the problem of the Marranos.[13]

A Storm Gathers

The new anti-Judaism lacked legitimization by the Spanish elite. Neither the church nor the secular government condoned it overtly. But, beneath the shell of restored order, it was suffusing and agitating in the Spanish social underground—a potential for dangerous aggression, ready to explode when circumstances are ripe.

For this to happen, several further conditions had to be fulfilled. A crisis in royal power had to occur, tempting the populace to break the reigns of established order. Additionally, the assault on the Jews had to receive ecclesiastical legitimization, or its appearance; and an able and determined leader was needed in order to drive the mob to action.

These conditions were fatally united in the early 1390s. Enrique II's heir died prematurely, leaving a power void in government. A similar vacuum was created in the Andalusian church. The man of the hour was now one Ferrán Martínez, archdeacon of Écija, a small town in the diocese of Seville.

Who was Ferrán Martínez?[14] He seemingly had low origins, which barred his promotion in the church but made him popular among simple people. Martínez had absorbed the new, embittered anti-Jewish mood of the fourteenth century and strove to give it ecclesiastical *legitimization*. A religious radical and popular demagogue, he transformed his abundant hatred into effective and persistent action. Martínez felt bitterly betrayed by Enrique II, who had massacred the Jews as long as he was fighting for the Crown and reverted to protecting them after he won his royal prize. To Martínez, this perfidy exposed the whole royal institution as a nest of petty utilitarian interests, which a true Christian believer should despise, and place his own authority above it. Thus Martínez seized an authority he did not possess and issued orders for the Jews to be expelled from several cities in Andalusia, boldly threatening to excommunicate city elders who failed to obey his command. Enrique II, encouraged by his Jewish adviser, Don Yoseph Pichón, told the cities to disregard Martínez's void instruction, and the matter was aborted. But a seed had been sown.

Some time later Enrique II died prematurely and was succeeded by Juan I. Martínez tested the new king's will and was rebuffed in strong language.[15] Yet his influence and prestige in popular circles were growing, mostly because of the bold challenge he presented to the system, and because the multitude perceived the anti-Jewish campaign as a hazy promise for anarchic liberation—from authority, debt, taxes, and the presence of the Devil himself.

Meanwhile the Jews' political standing had been shattered. Both Jewish high courtiers died, and King Juan I became increasingly dependent on city delegates, who were hostile to the Jews. In 1380 the Cortes (the medieval Castilian assembly) abolished Jewish autonomous jurisdiction in criminal matters, and five years later it barred Jews from living in Christian neighborhoods and holding posts in the royal court. The king was forced to appoint one-third of his council from among the city delegates.

The fatal consequences of this political downfall of the Jews cannot be exaggerated. Suddenly, Martínez's demands started to look less outlandish and slightly more realistic. The unbending cleric now came out with a new battle cry: all Jewish synagogues built after the Reconquista must be destroyed! The permits to build them—even those granted by the pope—were motivated by material interests and thus were void. Jewish leaders appealed to the higher church authorities and found an obdurate supporter in Martínez's superior, Archbishop Pedro Baroso of Seville. The archbishop viewed Martínez as a wild anarchist and a presumptuous radical who endangered church hierarchy and the established tradition.

In the summer of 1389, an internal investigation organized by Baroso declared Martínez "a rebel suspect of heresy" (because of his attacks on the pope), and announced he would stand trial; meanwhile, he was suspended of all his clerical functions and forbidden to preach in public.

This was the lowest point in Martínez's career. Twelve years of an anti-Jewish crusade strung with personal risks and sacrifice had led nowhere. But Martínez refused to give up, and within less than a year his fortunes changed completely.

At this point—we stand at the brink of the most momentous pogrom in the history of Spanish Jews—the story of the Marranos is about to begin.

But first, an anticipating reflection.

Who did not cross the Spanish space, and who did not leave their mark on its mix of cultures and races? Roman Spain had already been a mix of Celts, Greeks, Italians, and Phoenicians. Then, Germanic conquerors came from Scandinavia, Arabs emigrated from the Middle East, Berbers invaded from North Africa, and Slavs drifted in from southern Europe. In religion, Spain had hosted pagans, Jews, Arians, Catholics, and Muslims of several sects, and, most notably, had known waves of religious conversions in all directions. During the centuries-long Reconquista, Jews and Muslims wandered between the different worlds of the Spanish south and north. The cultural transfers that marked the peninsula have no parallel elsewhere in Europe. They left their marks not only on such typically mixed Spanish groups as the Mozarabs and Mudejares, Marranos and Moriscos, but on the general population in all parts of the still diverse peninsula—Andalusia and New Castile, Catalonia and the Basque country, proud Galicia and even hilly Navarre.

How ironic—though psychologically understandable—that this most heterogeneous of European countries developed an ardent mystique of *pure blood*, and a crushing policy of alleged homogeneity, which it imposed on its populace. The history of Spain since the fifteenth century is dominated by a delusion of purity, an impossible ideal that arose from the reality of its many mixtures. But rather than recognizing the blessings of its human and cultural variety, official Spain has tried for centuries to repress this diversity and pursue an illusory ideal of uniformity (religious, ethnic, and blood purity) for which it has paid in excessive human suffering and, so it seems, in its eventual decline.

The year 1391, in which the Marrano problem was born, also marks the beginning of Spain's flight from itself and into an imagined ideal essence it ascribed to itself in reaction to its actual history, as its invented opposite and antidote.

3

Pogroms and Mass Conversions

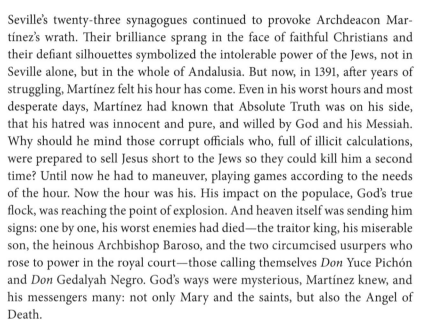

Seville's twenty-three synagogues continued to provoke Archdeacon Martínez's wrath. Their brilliance sprang in the face of faithful Christians and their defiant silhouettes symbolized the intolerable power of the Jews, not in Seville alone, but in the whole of Andalusia. But now, in 1391, after years of struggling, Martínez felt his hour has come. Even in his worst hours and most desperate days, Martínez had known that Absolute Truth was on his side, that his hatred was innocent and pure, and willed by God and his Messiah. Why should he mind those corrupt officials who, full of illicit calculations, were prepared to sell Jesus short to the Jews so they could kill him a second time? Until now he had to maneuver, playing games according to the needs of the hour. Now the hour was his. His impact on the populace, God's true flock, was reaching the point of explosion. And heaven itself was sending him signs: one by one, his worst enemies had died—the traitor king, his miserable son, the heinous Archbishop Baroso, and the two circumcised usurpers who rose to power in the royal court—those calling themselves *Don* Yuce Pichón and *Don* Gedalyah Negro. God's ways were mysterious, Martínez knew, and his messengers many: not only Mary and the saints, but also the Angel of Death.

What Martínez did not know was that Spanish Jewry no longer possessed the inner strength that its proud synagogues symbolized, and that his own action was about to prove this. Nor was Martínez aware that he himself, who had fought zealously to purify Christendom and isolate the Jews, was about to launch a major problem of ethnic and religious mixture that would cast a shadow on Iberian life for several centuries and send ripples to the rest of Europe—the problem of the Marranos.[1] It is usually impossible to determine the precise beginning of historical processes but sometimes a catalyst or occasional cause can be identified. And that single-minded hater, Ferrán Martínez, happened to play the ironic, though not uncommon, role of triggering a process that led finally to exactly the opposite of what he had wished and expected—although, in his day, it seemed to Martínez that God himself was guiding his moves.

The Clouds Darken

When, relying on his massive popular support, Martínez defied the order to step down from his office, he usurped the authority of the church and appointed himself its spokesman. A mood of anarchy spread in Seville, and the grim prospect of riot hovered over the Jewish neighborhoods. The simmering atmosphere produced local incidents and provocations. Threatened by the agitated populace, the urban nobles called upon the king's representative to intervene. The chief of the royal police, Alvar Pérez de Guzmán, arrested the leading agitators and flogged them in public, but that only intensified the rioters' fury. Storming the jail, they freed the prisoners and locked up Guzmán in their place. "To death!" "To be stoned!" the rioters shouted, eager to avenge themselves of the nobles. But their leaders restrained the uprising before it got out of hand. Martínez did not want to raise the nobles en bloc against him. His strategy was to divide them.

Meanwhile the crisis assumed nationwide proportions. All Spanish cities kept a vigilant eye on Seville. An emergency meeting of Jewish leaders in Madrid made a passionate appeal to the Council of Regents (there was no reigning king in Castile), but received sympathy instead of action. In order to control the situation, the regents had to send troops down to Seville, but they were badly divided and needed the army in their vicinity, so they ordered the cities to maintain public order by their own means. In an appeasing gesture, the regents dismissed the tough Sevillian commander, Pérez de Guzmán, and replaced him with a rival noble, who advocated a conciliatory line. The sacrifice of Guzmán proved unwise because it divided the nobility without reinforcing public authority.

The Storm

Now there was no power in Andalusia capable of restraining the mob. The local nobles were divided and royal troops camped far away. Clamoring for action, the populace denounced its leaders' hesitation, and Martínez renewed his incitement from the pulpit. Soon words became deeds. On June 4, 1391, the Sevillian rabble burst into the *Judería* (Jewish quarter) and spread havoc and death. A succinct letter in Hebrew, from Rabbi Hasdai Crescas, a philosopher and public leader, summarizes the event. The mob went berserk in Seville's large Judería, swept into a frenzy of murder and looting.[2] The Jews' only escape was to the churches to be baptized, but this was not always offered in the storm of events. About four thousand Jews perished anyway. Women and children were sold in slavery. A few Jews chose to "sanctify the name of God" (to die as martyrs rather than convert), yet, in Crescas's laconic and sad words, "many violated the Holy Covenant" between God and the Jews and, in fact, "the majority converted."

From Seville the riots spread to most of the Spanish provinces. Seized with social anger and religious righteousness, the populace broke the yoke of the ruling classes and assaulted the Jewish quarters in Cordova, Toledo, Madrid, Ciudad Real, Carmona, Soria, Burgos, Valencia, Barcelona, Gerona, Majorca, and several dozen other cities and localities. The fall of the Jewish quarter in one city gave the signal to assault another. The mob's craving for freedom soon transformed into a thirst for blood—and spoils. They broke into homes and shops, killing, looting, and dragging Jews to the baptismal font. Everywhere the outcry resounded: "Death or the Cross!"—the Jews must perish or convert to Christianity! Ideological justification for the riot was supplied by members of the lower clergy, most of them faithful to Martínez. Typically, the rioters also demanded the annulment of debts, and often, as in Barcelona, broke into the municipal court to burn the registrations of Jewish property and the records of debts owed by Christians to Jews.[3]

Wherever possible, the Jews took refuge in the local citadel (Alcázar, "the Tower") which belonged to the king. But the city authorities were unable or unwilling to provide adequate protection and sometimes handed the Jews over to their marauders. In several cities, the burghers, in order to satisfy their own anti-Jewish grudge or to ward off the oncoming riots, demanded that the Jews convert even before the populace arose. Meanwhile the Jews' money was dissipating in a stream of bribes and ransoms. Astruc Rimoch, a physician in the city of Fraga, appealed in a fervent letter to the Jews of Monzon for help: "You know what we have gone through in this place of torment.... And now that we ran out of money and cannot give any more ransom, we entreat your grace...: Do not allow our whole congregation, young and old, to be driven into Temptation [= conversion]."[4]

But only a few communities were able to assist others financially. Meanwhile the mob continued to clamor and demand its due. Theological arguments proving that Christ does not want forced conversions were of little use, and so were threats of the sword and the whip. The populace caught the political establishment in a failing moment and was eager to humiliate it. Like other pogroms in history, this anti-Jewish riot expressed a wider popular insurrection against the established order and the oppressing authority of the nobles and the royal agents. And contrary to the Jews' expulsion from Spain a century later, which was organized from the top, the riots of 1391 arose from below, from a popular radical anger that endangered the foundations of social order and existing authority.

Unable to repress the insurrection by force, the Spanish establishment tried to defuse it by a mixture of concessions and post-factum punishments; and the main concession they made to the rioters consisted in the possibility (if not tacit permission) of crushing the Jews.

Thus began the problem of the Marranos in post-Muslim Spain.

Seen from an all-European view, the riots that triggered Spanish Marranism were part of a chain of popular insurrections that took place at the end of the fourteenth century (1378–1383) from Italy and France to England and Hungary.[5] The growing bitterness accumulated in the lower classes during the Calamitous Century occasionally erupted into a revolt against the established order, and against order in general. In the eyes of many commoners, *order* signified oppression—a degrading constant pressure of poverty, hard labor, onerous debt, capricious lords, domineering priests, covetous tax collectors (often, though neither always nor even mostly, Jews) and servile obedience to various other authorities. It has been said of the revolts in Europe that they were always sudden, obscure in their origins and goals, and left behind them a dark memory of human anger, cruelty, and senselessness. The description fits Spain with one exception: The goal was not obscure. There were Jews everywhere in Spain, and Martínez's party succeeded in directing the social anger toward them. Spanish Jews were part of the established order of power—the least legitimate, and the easiest to hurt. As the king's "slaves," they enjoyed privileges that were denied the lower classes; and as royal agents and tax collectors, they held a position of authority that was doubly resented, both in itself and because its holders were the Savior's enemies. Also, Jews were more easily assailable; they seldom carried arms (a sign of honor they were denied) and depended on others for their protection; and their vulnerability tempted the mob. Martínez's faction exploited these factors in making the Jews the Satanic embodiment of all the wrongs of the ruling classes, and a prime target of the mob's assault. In so doing, Martínez, despite himself, did a service to the power system he hated.

Members of other social groups jumped on the rabble's murderous wagon. The records tell of whole families, complete with their slaves, and of entire suburban villages flowing into the city to participate in the violent orgy. The pogroms were further fueled by news about the violence. People rushed to the streets when they heard a riot was on, and news of a pogrom in one city often triggered a pogrom in another.[6]

In most cases, the Jews who had sought refuge in the citadel were rapidly overwhelmed. Hasdai Crescas gives a laconic account of the events in Barcelona, strung with personal grief: "Using bows and catapults, they fought against the Jews assembled in the Citadel, beating and smashing them in the Tower. Many sanctified the name of God [died for the Jewish religion], among them my own only son, an innocent bridal lamb.[7] . . . Some slew themselves, others jumped from the tower . . . and all the rest converted." He concludes with startling simplicity: "And because of our sins, today there is no one in Barcelona called an Israelite."[8]

In wave after wave, Jews flocked to the gates of churches in panic, either coerced by the sword or, confused and losing heart, following their neighbor's example. A few fresh converts crossed over to the enemy and helped drive their former coreligionists to the baptismal font. Some converts believed they had merely taken temporary shelter under the Cross, after which they would travel to a Muslim country and recant; but the realities of life were more compelling, so they remained in Spain as Christians. Others, accepting their lot, looked forward to a new beginning in their lives. As for the "sanctifiers of the Name," who preferred violent death to apostasy, they constituted a small minority. The number of converts is unknown but it was a massive phenomenon that led to a momentous mutilation of Jewish life in Spain in 1391, and to the creation of a large "New Christian" population. It seems that no Jewish community was spared. And, in Valencia, it was told that the Jews awaiting baptism were so numerous that only a miracle (which always intervenes in such cases) made it possible to complete the holy action.

In addition to the legends there are documents. They tell a story of divided families, estranged friends, and parents severed from their children. Baptism sometimes split the core family, with one spouse converting to Christianity while the other remained Jewish.[9] Problems of personal status arose—how to divide the family property, and how Jewish law (*halakha*) applies to such agonizing questions as unreleased widows (*yebamot*)[10] and the wives of missing husbands (*agunot*).[11] In one case, the queen of Aragon intervened on behalf of a Jewish widow, forcing her converted brother-in-law to perform a *Jewish* rite that would make the widow eligible to remarry.[12]

If, by the turn of the fifteenth century, Ferrán Martínez (wherever he was) could look back on the consequence of his action, he would have noted that Spanish Jewry did not, after all, possess the strength that its twenty-three Sevillian synagogues suggested. Why did Spanish Jews collapse so drastically? Baer, their foremost historian, blames the Jewish elite, saying it broke down in a moment of crisis and dragged the common people along with it. Baer writes of Jewish leaders who were so immersed in Christian lifestyle, or so involved in "Averroist" (Greek-inspired) ideas, that passing from one revealed religion to another did not look shocking to them. Baer's view agrees with his general folkish outlook on Jewish history, extolling common people's constancy and instinctive loyalty to their identity, and attributing the erosion of Jewish life to the study of philosophy and the adoption of European manners.[13] Yet common Jewish folk took to the Cross, just like their leaders. The major bulk of converts—tens of thousands—came from the popular ranks. If simple folks were as strongly devout to Judaism as Baer believes, why did they follow the alleged example of their elite? Terror and fear of death certainly played a role in both social strata, alongside confusion and demoralization. As for philosophy and secular studies, these are not necessarily opposed to Jewish life. In Muslim Spain, as chapter 1 has shown, philosophy, the sciences, linguistics, secular poetry, and aesthetics had coexisted among the Jews alongside a flourishing rabbinical culture.

The Jewish leaders' disarray was not caused by Averroist philosophy but, far more likely, by the overwhelming new situation they confronted: the collapse of Jewish influence in court; the tide of unchecked popular anarchy; the explosive violence running out of control; and—quite a rarity in Christian Europe—the semiofficial religious legitimacy, provided by Martínez, of converting the Jews by force. These were totally new conditions that the Jews did not know how to confront, except by using the old methods, which suddenly proved ineffective.

For many centuries, the Jews had followed established survival strategies. They learned how to manage the rulers under whose unstable protection they lived, how to bend during a storm, cut their losses, and go on. But now the ruling Spanish elite had lost control over the country, and quasi-revolutionary popular forces erupted from the underground. In face of these new forces, the Jews had no proven strategy of survival; they had no experience in coping with such a radical and widespread revolt which, legitimized by mutinous religious clerics, took almost unbridled control of the situation.

Jewish historians, sometimes in complaint, point out that martyrdom was rare among the Spanish Jews. Yet martyrdom is not an accepted Jewish norm. Maimonides, the chief codifier of Jewish law, viewed it as an exception that cannot be demanded of the multitude. When under threat of death, he said, the proper response is to convert in appearance, then emigrate and revert to Judaism in another country.[14] The rebuking question—"Why didn't they commit martyrdom?"—recalls, with due difference, the charge that Jews in Nazi Europe "went like sheep to the slaughter," and sounds equally facile. Under conditions reigning then, no other way was open to the wider public. Driven by terror and demoralization, some even converted when the actual assault had not yet occurred or was still uncertain. This is ordinary human conduct, unheroic and uninspiring, but quite natural. To condemn it from a latter-day historian's desk is to confuse realistic history with judgmental moralizing.

The Jewish Bishop and the Ascetic Monk

The forced conversions were followed by voluntary ones. The first signs appeared in Burgos, where Shlomo Halevi, the local rabbi, tried to persuade his congregates to accept Christianity even before the rioters arrived. The attempt failed. Only a handful of Jews followed their rabbi to the Cross. But what shocked the Jews throughout Spain was the discovery that Rabbi Shlomo Halevi had acted from inner conviction rather than fear. The imminent pogrom only made him carry out an intention he had already been cultivating for some time.

Halevi's wife refused to convert with him and paid a dear price. She was severed from her four children, whom the rabbi took with him to Christianity. Shlomo Halevi took the name Pablo de Santa María (alluding to his descent from Saint Mary's people), and went to study theology in Paris. Afterward he spent time—and made an impression—in the papal court in Avignon. Returning to Spain, he befriended the king of Aragon, rose in church hierarchy, and was made bishop of the city of Burgos, in which he had been rabbi.

Bishop Santa María/Shlomo Halevi was the most formidable apostate of his time. His threat to the Jews derived from his stunning personal example, no less than from the harsh polemic and anti-Jewish legislation he initiated. Shlomo Halevi had crossed over to Christianity from inside Judaism itself. Some Jews said he was motivated by ambition and glory, but that was a polemical simplification. Halevi/Santa María had been contemplating Christian texts long before he converted. He was tormented by the thought that, in rejecting Jesus, the Jews had committed a fatal error in terms of their own religion. This terrifying doubt led him to ponder the very foundations of the Mosaic religion, taking the risk of becoming a skeptic and heretic. Yet this wager, he said, had become his salvation. He discovered that Christianity is the necessary completion of Judaism, and is required from within Judaism itself. So Halevi went on to give a Christological meaning to Jewish texts. For example, a famous verse in the Psalms says, referring to the gate of the Jewish temple: "This is the Lord's Gate, through which the righteous will pass." Halevi/Santa María interprets: Judaism is the gate through which a righteous Jew (not traitors!) should pass—to Christianity, thus fulfilling God's promise to Abraham.

Halevi/Santa María was not merely showing off his tortuous gift for Hebrew exegesis. He believed his reading laid bare the secret meaning of the Jewish Bible and of Jewish history. And, if unable to make his move alone, Halevi/Santa María passionately wanted all Jews to acknowledge the same secret and follow his example—a passion that turned into vengeance, even hatred, when it was not fulfilled.

Opposing the Jewish bishop of Burgos was his childhood friend, Yehoshua Halorki. In a lengthy address, Halorki declared himself shocked and surprised by his friend's apostasy, and refuted his claim that the Messiah had already come. Are the sheep and the wolf living together? Is the Torah prevailing everywhere? Is Jerusalem rebuilt and the temple restored? And anyway, could Jesus be a true descendent of the house of David?[15] And yet, underneath Halorki's conventional polemic a disquiet already stirred. Halorki, who still loved and respected his friend, seemed to be sending a dual message. Could it be that Halevi had discovered some metaphysical truth hidden from the Jews? At times, Halorki's pro-Jewish polemic sounds as a hidden plea for help—to overcome Judaism.

Meanwhile, Don Pablo de Santa María made a brilliant career as Christian. His gifts were as outstanding as his ambitions. An acute intellectual and sophisticated politician, he impressed colleagues and patrons alike and had the knack for making friends in high places. His dark side was turned against his own past and former identity as embodied in the Jews. Don Pablo could not bear the fact that other Jews—even those in his own congregation—refused to follow his lead and personal example. Driven by pride, the need for justification, and possibly a sense of historical calling, he felt the irresistible drive to have all his former coreligionists share with him in the momentous step he had taken; and in order to make them comply, he used both intellectual and political weapons—polemic as well as legal pressure.

Halevi/Santa María's polemic against the Jews had the efficacy of an informant—in Jewish terms, a formidable *malshin*. Though he had confidence in his chosen way, Halevi/Santa María could have been resisting a sense of guilt or betrayal regarding the Jews that turned into anger and hatred; or perhaps in order to vindicate the rightness of his choice, he needed the Jews to reassure him by joining him. So he continued to address the Jews in the first person plural, as *we*.

Halevi/Santa María's line of thinking—that a Jew faithful to the deep legacy of his religion must fulfill his *Jewish* calling by converting to Christianity—was doubly unorthodox. The Jews saw it as self-betrayal, while orthodox Catholics resented the fact that it gave them, as Christians, an unwelcome parenthood in Judaism and established a continuous chain between the sacred and the anathema, between Christ's faithful and his alleged murderers. By this potentially provocative way of thinking, Santa María set himself aside from the mainstream Catholic establishment no less than from the Jews. He testified to a specific Marrano peculiarity—a special form of duality—that affected his mind and recurred, as we shall see, in the work of his son, Don Alonso de Cartagena (also bishop of Burgos), and in other Marrano theologians.

Complementing Halevi/Santa María's pressure on the Jews were two influential partners—a prophetic monk, Fray Vicente Ferrer, and a deposed pope, Benedict XIII.

The Maverick Saint

Fray Vicente Ferrer (1350–1419) combined in his charismatic person the profound and the theatrical, the real and the symbolic. His awe-inspiring presence and unwavering sense of divine mission startled the hearts and minds of simple folks. He quit a high post in the papal court of Avignon and descended to the common people, haunted by visions of the world's imminent end. He also was disgusted by the corruption in the Catholic Church—the lust for power and pleasures, the emphasis on external hierarchy, the hollowness of religious life. Ferrer was thus an early church reformer with populist and somewhat fundamentalist tendencies. At other times he could have been burned as a heretic; but in those days, when the church was split and three anointed popes were disputing Saint Peter's miter, Ferrer was able to gather considerable influence, owing to the multitudes that streamed to his sermons and public flagellations, and were driven to sobs and mass hysteria that he alone could control.

Ferrer demanded that his followers repent and flagellate themselves to the point of bleeding, as if to punish the flesh for its very existence. His band of monks would enter a city in procession, carrying torches, whipping themselves with leather lashes, and chanting the Savior's glory. The frightened people, who had been imbued with guilt feelings from childhood, were easily moved by those sights, which often provoked a kind of catharsis and thereby produced a measure of social restraint in the audience. Political thinkers like Machiavelli and Hobbes would see here an example of the stabilizing role of religion in the service of the state. Rather than letting the people's social discontent lead to anarchy, the feelings of guilt and repentance fanned by Ferrer worked to assuage the popular resentment and divert its power to other channels, away from protest and agitation. This was part of the reason for Ferrer's high political standing in both Castile and Aragon.

Another avenue for saving the world was a crusade to convert all Jews and Muslims to Christianity—not by coercion, but through persuasion and spiritual terror. Ferrer opposed the use of violent force in Martínez's style. Jews and Muslims must willingly ask to be baptized, but there was nothing wrong in helping them reach that decision. So Ferrer devised a two-way strategy: enacting laws that would make life outside the Catholic Church unbearable; and organizing an awesome campaign of persuasion that offered the Christian alternative amid sound and fury.

Traveling from city to city (from 1412 to 1414), Ferrer set out on a preaching crusade covering Castile and later Aragon. His appearances, not unlike the spectacles of a modern evangelist (though more stylized and frightening), were staged as divinely inspired theatrical events. Ferrer would break into a Jewish synagogue during service, holding a cross in one hand and a scroll of the Torah in the other and followed by a band of monks carrying torches and flagellating themselves. It is not hard to imagine the fright and dismay that seized the Jews. Many remembered the horrors of 1391 too well to gamble on the subtle theological difference between coerced baptism, which Ferrer rejected, and conversion by mental terror and concealed threat, which he practiced. Everywhere Jews succumbed to Ferrer's offensive. In some isolated places the Jewish community sometimes converted as a whole, and in big cities, such as Toledo, it was said that Ferrer, in a single day, won four thousand souls for Christ.

Ferrer's crusade caused numerous synagogues to be converted into churches. Among them was the splendid Toledo synagogue built by Shemuel Halevi Abulafia (see chapter 1) and later transformed into the church of El Tránsito, where visitors today still admire the superb Hebrew inscriptions and Mudejar stone lace. A contemporary Hebrew poet lamented its fate:

> [O] synagogue of lord Shemuel
> Halevi, chief of Israel,
> Cry, O cry, Ariel,
> Over the sacred glory of Israel.[16]

Ferrer used similar methods against Spanish Muslims in their mosques; to them, his assault signified the continuation of the Reconquista by other means. Without knowing or intending it, his action against the two religions fanned the Marrano and Morisco problems and helped prepare the new, intolerant and artificial conception of Spanish unity which took over at the end of the century.[17]

Driven by Ferrer and the "Jewish bishop" Santa María, the queen-regent of Castile, Catalina, signed in 1412 a series of draconian laws against Jews and Muslims,—the harshest ever passed in reconquered Spain. Known as the "infidel laws," they were meant to ostracize the non-Christians, break their livelihood and force them to convert. Among other humiliations, Jews and Muslims were required to carry a distinctive sign, wear inferior clothes, even refrain from trimming their beards. No work that involved contact with Christians was allowed—thus barring the Jews from most of their traditional occupations—in tax farming, banking, the royal administration, and even in commerce, artisanship, and medicine. Jews and Muslims were deprived of their communal autonomy and were placed under civil officers, who were instructed to take their religious laws into consideration. A Christian official was to pass judgment according to the Talmud and the Shariah!

Had these infidel laws been enforced to the letter, almost no Jews (and only a few Muslims) would have been left in Spain by 1420, when the laws were abrogated. But, fortunately for suppressed minorities in the Middle Ages, their real-life situation can hardly be inferred from the records of formal legislation. In an age lacking a strong central administration, when government was burdened with a cumbersome system of privileges and exemptions, and when laws made by the king were often ignored in the barons' domains, there was a built-in hiatus between the written legal word and the actual situation. So the harsh decrees were implemented only loosely and rather partially.

Even so, the infidel laws produced a shocking blow. Soon reenacted in Aragon, their brutality hit the Jews harder than the Muslims. Muslims lived in greater isolation and were much less involved in the Christian economy than the Jews. Yet the intention to shame, to humiliate, was the same for both communities.

A Show-Disputation in Tortosa

Meanwhile, a deposed Spanish pope crowned the proselytizing assault on Judaism by organizing a theatrical and well-publicized show-debate in the city of Tortosa.[18]

Benedict XIII (alias Pedro de Luna) was the last antipope in Avignon during the Great Schism in the Catholic Church. When Catholic unity was restored in 1407, he was deposed but refused to accept the verdict, and subsequently tried to build a power base for himself in his native Aragon. He organized the show-debate in Tortosa in order to break the spirit of the remaining Spanish Jews and drive them to baptism, if not by theological persuasion, then through demoralization and a sense of historical defeat.

Benedict set up the Disputation in concert with his physician, Master Gerónimo de Santa Fe (of the holy faith), whom the Jews called *Blasphemer* (*megadef*). This man was no other than Yehoshua Halorki, who two decades earlier had clamored against Shlomo Halevi's conversion. Instead of bringing his friend back to Judaism, he belatedly followed Halevi into Christianity. When he finally resolved to convert, a vibrant energy burst out in Halorki, as if to compensate for years of indecision. And, like Halevi, he wanted and needed other Jews to cross over the bridge with him.

The much publicized debate opened in great pomp on February 7, 1412, with cardinals, bishops, and high officials sitting in their colorful attire on gilded seats, and it dragged on for twenty-one months. Benedict set the rules of the game. The dogmas of Christianity were beyond argument and could not be debated. The goal was to make the Jews realize that the Christian truth is implied in their own texts. The Jews could voice doubts (so they could be answered) but must do so politely, without blaspheming or insulting Christianity.

Clearly, this was not a debate at all. It was a political show, translating the power relations between Judaism and Christianity. Halorki, now Santa Fe, was the star of the show. He presented the Christian theses, responded to his Jewish opponents, and interrogated them. Those two intense years were the climax of his previously irresolute life. He made threats when necessary, and did not shy from manipulating Jewish texts. On one theatrical occasion, Santa Fe misquoted the Talmud. Rabbi Astruc Halevi produced the original page and demanded that Santa Fe read it aloud. The latter hesitated, then collected himself and, pretending to read from the page, repeated the misquotation.[19]

Facing Gerónimo de Santa Fe were Jewish rabbis and dignitaries he had chosen himself. They were summoned by decree from around the country but lacked a recognized leader. Young Yosef Albo had not yet written the famous *Book of Principles* which was to make his name in Judaism. The ablest Jewish debater was Astruc Halevi, a fairly unknown rabbi from Halorki's town who had debated him in the past. At times it looked as though the two men, the rabbi and the apostate, were continuing their argument of old times amidst the grandiose décor of Tortosa. Another gifted Jewish speaker was Don Vidal de La Caballería, a Hebrew poet and a royal adviser, a scion of the distinguished Jewish-Aragonese family. Some of his relatives had converted to Christianity in 1391, and Don Vidal himself was to leave Tortosa a Catholic.

The sinister shadow of the infidel laws determined the atmosphere all along. Santa Fe drew confidence from them, while the Jewish leaders were struck with pessimism and felt they were treading on shifting sand. The pressures, the fears, and the awesome sense of responsibility produced acrimonious divisions among the Jewish spokesmen.

The core of the debate was the issue of the Messiah. Santa Fe quoted a (true) Talmudic saying, according to which the Messiah was born on the same day the Jewish Temple was destroyed. What better proof that the Messiah has already come—and replaced Judaism? Some rabbis hastened to answer that the saying was a mere allegory, meant to reassure the Jews that redemption was implicit in their very calamity. But other rabbis, furious at the concession, insisted on a literal reading of the Talmud: the Messiah has indeed been born, but has not yet come—he is still in waiting.

This required the rabbis to sharply define Judaism's difference from Christianity without offending the rival religion. So Rabbi Astruc Halevi offered a cutting demarcation. The Christian Messiah, he said, is God become man; his birth was supernatural; he gives a new Law, redeems original sin, and above all, saves souls from hell. By contrast, the Jewish Messiah is a man, his birth is natural, and he will save the Jewish body rather than the soul—namely, restore the Jews' political independence.[20] A Jew does not save his soul through the Messiah, but through the Torah—the law given to Moses.

Ordinary Jews rarely discuss salvation, or declare it is attained through the Law of Moses. But because of the audience, Halevi chose to use a Christian conceptual framework to state a fundamental Jewish creed. Inadvertently, he anticipated a formula that was to become the core belief of the *Judaizing Marranos* (converts who tried to remain Jewish in secret) for generations, indeed centuries, as their mark of identity and secret credo: Salvation is attained through the Law of Moses, not Christ.

As the debates dragged on, Jews staying in Tortosa were facing economic ruin because of endless expenses and the neglect of their businesses. Meanwhile Vicente Ferrer won several thousand more Jews for the Cross in Aragon, and a group of his fresh converts arrived in Tortosa declaring that their rabbis were wrong and Christianity wins. The depressing sight of Jews capitulating en masse to victorious Christianity produced a demoralizing snowball effect.

The first conversions started during the debate; the converts included several rich and learned Jews and a few rabbis. The most startling case was Don Vidal de La Caballería, the young Jewish diplomat and poet. He converted under stiff pressure from the king of Aragon, who wanted Don Vidal to remain in his service despite the new infidel laws. Three months later, Don Vidal had a new royal post and a new name (Gonzalo). A contemporary poet wrote that the sun went dark. But the sun was not alone—other lights went out, too, as further Jewish delegates converted with Don Vidal.

Don Vidal was relatively young, a courtier and man of letters looking into a rich future. As a Jew he had written Hebrew poems; as a Christian he translated Cicero into Spanish. Alongside him converted his elderly friend, the 70 year old poet Shlomo de la Piera, whose former poetry had lamented the 1391 disaster. A third poet, Shlomo Bonafed, remaining loyal to Judaism, complained of the betrayal of his two colleagues—"the kings of song"—and saw their act as primarily betraying the holy Hebrew *language*, which bemoans the lovers who forsook her.

Beside such leaders and intellectuals, a mass of simple people lost heart and also converted. The fatal combination of the infidel laws, Ferrer's crusade, and the Tortosa debacle, produced a second massive wave of converts whose act was often neither totally forced nor really voluntary. It was provoked by a break-down of morale and the desire to avoid persecution rather than by a direct threat to their lives. Numbers are hard to estimate, but tens of thousands (per-haps fifty thousand or more) were lost to Spanish Jewry in the years 1412–1415. Rabbi Astruc Halevi, in any case, returned to his town Alcañiz to find that no Jews were left in it. Halorki had defeated him in their common city.

Despite this debacle, the remaining Jews resumed their lives and returned to their synagogues. Realism led them to take a long breath, shorten the front line, and reorganize. The infidel laws were abrogated several years later (1420), and in the 1430s, Jews were again farming most of the indirect taxes in Castile. Religious incitement against them had become permanent, as had the slow ongoing individual conversions. Jewish Spain never regained its past great-ness. Yet the stem that had survived the two waves of mass conversion sent new roots into the Spanish soil and, until its uprooting in 1492, occasionally even flourished again.[21]

A dry juridical document concerning property summarizes the conversions and divisions of the Jewish elite—and the historical chapter we have traversed so far. It is the will of Doña Tolosana de La Caballería, widow of Benveniste de La Caballería and probably Don Vidal's mother. Doña Tolosana, who died laden with years and trials, remained loyal to Judaism to the end. In her will she divided part of her property between her four Christian sons and two Jewish daughters. The rest of her capital she endowed to the Jewish congregation of Saragossa with a special provision: should the congregation convert to Chris-tianity or otherwise cease to exist, the money should go to the second larg-est Jewish community in Aragon. The endowment was to be administered by Doña Tolosana's closest relative who remained Jewish and bore the name La Caballería. But if no such person existed, the realistic old lady added, then the heir should be a Jewish relative of hers, bearing any name.

PART TWO

Marrano Otherness and Dualities

4

Conversos: The Other Within

A new concept penetrated Christian Spanish society—the Conversos. Within a quarter century (1391–1415) the Jewish community had probably lost more than one hundred thousand people,[1] and a similar number of New Christians entered Christian society. In the span of a few generations these newcomers mixed into most social groups, except the agricultural poor. Some converts even penetrated into the top aristocratic families but the majority filled the ranks of the middle classes, promoting the creation of a new, productive, urban bourgeoisie, and fostering learning that prepared the way for the Spanish Renaissance. Equally, they introduced problems and paradoxes into Spanish society; and their own lives were marked by the social and existential complexities they engendered and embodied.

The Official Doctrine and Its Contradictions

If, in 1391 or later, there had been converts who believed they might take temporary refuge in the Cross and then return to Judaism, they soon discovered that their way of retreat was barred by the same government that had failed to protect them in the first place. According to Catholic canon law, the church did not want and could not accept coerced believers. But what does coercion mean exactly? Following a long and hard debate, it was determined by the end of the fourteenth century that a conversion was void—as if it had never occurred—if the victim was threatened with imminent death and kept protesting all the way.[2] In all other cases (the massive majority) baptism was valid and could not be annulled.[3] Baptism became an absolute barrier, a metaphysical crossroads dividing the destinies of individuals and whole families. Whoever persevered in Judaism was Jesus's foe and God's outcast; yet, except in rare cases, the church had no jurisdiction over these individuals, and the secular government had to tolerate and protect their person and property. Yet from the moment Jews crossed over to Catholicism, they had no way of returning. Transgressing Catholics remained Catholic. If they should revert to the religion of Moses, they would not be recognized as Jewish, but proclaimed as Christian heretics and criminals who must be severely punished to save their souls.

That was the official doctrine. Eighty years later it was to engender the Spanish Inquisition. But during the first generations of conversion this rule was not rigorously applied and did not generate a uniform policy. Christian society was facing a problem of unprecedented nature and proportions, and it was baffled. No one deluded themselves that mere baptism, whether forced or voluntary, could make people shed all the mental layers of their former world and become real Christians. And it was no secret that many converts continued to move in their old social circles, to eat *matzoth* alongside the Host, and observe some Jewish rites while also going to church. Who were these Conversos? Were they Christians, as canon law teaches? Were they Jews, as a suspicious inner voice insisted? Or perhaps they were hybrids, a composite entity in the middle? If they were full-fledged Christians, they ought to have been accepted into all social classes. If they were Jews, they should have been restricted as they had been in the past. And if they were both Jews and Christians, or neither the one nor the other, then everything, however contradictory, was possible.

Contradictory Patterns

For the most part, inner contradiction marked the Christian attitude toward the converts—and many converts' attitude toward themselves. The same missionary zeal that had engendered the Converso phenomenon—the will to melt all races and religions into the single pot of Catholic Spain—introduced an almost ineradicable otherness into Spanish society, an otherness that now lived in its midst. The Jewish Other, who formerly had confronted Christian society from without, had now become an inner component of that society without losing his otherness either in the eyes of the host society or, often, in his own self-perception. For several centuries, Iberian society proved unable to fully assimilate this internal Other or to evict it.

An important cause of that tie was, no doubt, the deep undercurrent that linked a steadfast minority of Conversos to their fathers' memory and religion. But whether they strove to remain Jewish or tried to assimilate into Christianity, the Conversos usually also manifested the identity marks of the group they were trying to shed. A distinct duality marked their situation, a duality that assumed diverse forms, some subtle and some more easily discernible, but that almost inevitably clung to all their identity efforts, whichever way they turned.

This was due to two sets of reasons. One set concerned the converts' mental world and symbolism and the general dynamics of cultural identity; the other depended on external forces, especially the tensions and contradictions at work in Spanish society. From a purely religious standpoint, the veteran Christian society had to welcome the mass Jewish conversion, and embrace the New Christians as brothers. Yet powerful identity passions, serving as carrier to economic and social rivalries, worked to reject the Conversos. Often these interests justified their purpose with arguments and emotions drawn from the same religious arsenal which, in theory, should have worked against such exclusion.

In the last quarter of the fifteenth century, the contradiction would be institutionalized in the Royal Inquisition—the first drastic instrument that Spanish society devised for dealing with the Converso problem. By burning thousands of New Christians on the stake or ruining their families' standing and property for several generations, the Inquisition succeeded in shrinking the size of the problem in one hand and intensifying it in the other. The climate of fear and persecution in which the Conversos lived, their being always held in suspicion and liable to sudden arrest, and the restrictions against citizens of "impure blood" that Spain later adopted, heightened many Conversos' awareness of their separate and alien identity. And since quite often they were victims of false accusations, even assimilated Conversos were driven against their will back into the group from which they had sought to escape. The Inquisition's campaign to purify the church had been at first basically religious, but with time it acquired the character of an ethnic, racial, and class conflict, and the problem was made more acute by the very attempt to resolve it.

For several generations after the first mass conversions, however, there was no effective Inquisition in Spain. Official policy toward Conversos was rather confused and inconsequent. Two years after the first riots, King Juan II of Aragon issued the first decrees for separating the Conversos from the Jews: "Henceforth no Converso, man or woman, shall live in the same house or the same room together with a Jew or a Jewess. . . . And it is prohibited to eat and drink with Jews, or to pray in their presence. . . . A Jew caught with a Christian woman in a place suggesting carnal copulation will be burnt without mercy."[4]

With all their harsh language, these laws were more rhetorical than practical, and barely enforced. In real life each locality treated the Conversos as it saw fit. In 1391, Conversos in the town of Morvedre were sentenced to a moderate fine for participating in a seder ceremony—an offense that a century later could send them to the flames. It was an open secret that many Conversos continued, in some degree, to practice their old religion. Tolerant Christians cited this fact to prove that forced conversions were ineffective. Crown Prince Alfonso of Aragon wrote to his father, King Ferdinand: "Experience proves that . . . recent converts continue to hold their perverse and perfidious beliefs even more ceremoniously than they did before." Intended to shield the Jews of

Daroca from imposed conversion, the prince's words were a realist's plea for relative tolerance. The same observation, in a different mode, is reiterated in Hebrew sources. In Shlomo (Solomon) ibn Verga's chronicle, *Shevet Yehuda*, a Christian scholar tells his king: "And what use is it to our king and Lord to pour holy waters on the Jews and call them by our names, Pedro or Pablo, when they preserve their religion like Akiba and Tarphon [famous rabbis who died as martyrs in Roman times]?"

The scholar summarizes the problem: "Know, our Lord, that the *anussim* [Hebrew for forced converts] pursue their old religion even more avidly after the forced conversion than before."[5]

This, however, was true only of a segment of the Converso population—those known as *Judaizers* (their appellation at the time, which modern scholarship adopted).[6] Others became faithful, even ardent, Christians. Fresh renegades penetrated into the Jewish neighborhoods in acts of provocation, or became self-appointed supervisors of the kosher Christian conduct of other converts. As told by Rabbi Yitzhak ben Sheshet: "Once they converted, even if at first it was by coercion, they later rebelled against Heaven and willingly followed the ways of the Pagans [meaning Gentiles]. Worse, they persecute the downcast Jews who live among them, and impute false accusations to them. As for the *Anussim* [forced converts] whose heart remains true to Heaven, those villains denounce them to the authorities."[7]

It is not surprising to see a group of people struggling to assimilate into a new identity that has been initially imposed on them by demonstrating hostility toward those who represent the old identity they are trying to shed. On the surface it may seem that nothing is more coherent and integral than such ardent submission. But on second look we see that what it projects is not real Christian self-confidence or integral identity, but inner duality and unrest that seeks to hide from itself (and thus involves self-deception in some measure). In persecuting the Jews and the other converts, these hard-line Conversos were fighting against their own image as reflected to them from their former coreligionists.

Between the two extreme groups—those observing Judaism in secret and those persecuting it in the open—a whole spectrum of intermediary attitudes arose: Conversos who willingly adopted Christianity, and even rose to high positions in the church—which they used to protect the Jews; those who accepted Christianity as socially useful, without a serious religious interest, and, because of nostalgia or pangs of conscience, would secretly donate money to a synagogue or send oil for its ceremonies; and others who, from habit or because of childhood memories, continued to practice certain Jewish rites and holidays although they had no intent of reverting to their old religion. Then there were Conversos who confused the two rival religions, and others who became equally indifferent to both.

Sorrow and remorse were common among converts. Many experienced a sense of sin, deprivation, and alienation. Yet, even without coercion, conversions continued throughout the fifteenth century. Some Conversos lived in split families or households, where one spouse was Jewish and the other Christian. A Jewish son living with his mother appealed to his converted father to convert him. The father refused: "Go away, son, for I am lost, I wish I had not converted! But you, you [still] have a good religion, stick with your mother!"[8]

Jewish Attitudes to the Conversos

How did the Jewish leaders in Spain and abroad view the Marranos? Focusing on practice rather than motivation, they saw the Judaizers as engaged in idolatry. While extremist rabbis called all the Marranos "complete Gentiles," some tried to distinguish between different generations of Marranos, and between those who could and those who couldn't emigrate to other countries; but these distinctions were impractical and hard to determine. The Marranos found Jewish advocates in the members of the Duran clan of rabbis—Rabbi Shimon ben Zemach Duran (the *Tashbez*), his son, and his grandson, together with Saadia ibn Dannan, the last rabbi of Granada. But these were minority voices.[9] Judaizing Marranos were doubly alienated: they were called Jews by the Inquisition and shunned as non-Jews by the people to whom they claimed to belong; so they were the Other of both sides. Marranos who chose the Cross were still rejected by "Christians of pure Christian origin," and those who kept the flame of their ancient religion were excluded from the essence they willed and imagined for themselves by those who embodied its seamless continuity—the Jews. As for Marranos who lacked any deep religious consciousness, they were sketching the profile of a new human type that was taking shape on the margins of Iberian society in the Renaissance—a type that lives beyond the spheres of conventional belief and mentality, and whose very constitution involves an ingredient of alienation, even to the self. Such people were to inject a measure of novelty, deracination, and skeptic freedom into the emerging European society.

The Conversos' Rapid Advancement

Many converts, especially among the well-to-do, continued practicing the old Jewish occupations—artisanship, commerce, medicine, and finance[10]—while others sought new fields and ventures for their energy. Common to most was their rapid advancement. From the moment they were freed of restrictions, the Conversos poured into Christian society, reaching into most of its crevices. Within one or two generations they could be found in the councils of Castile and Aragon, in royal advisory and administrative offices, in military and naval commands, and in every ecclesiastical rank—from parish priest to bishop and even cardinal. Those who wished to maintain a secret Jewish ingredient in their identity sometimes took refuge in Catholic monasteries. Conversos were priests and soldiers, politicians and professors, judges and theologians, writers, poets, and legal advisors—and of course, as before, physicians, accountants, and big-time traders. Some, through marriage, made their way into the most distinguished noble families in Spain. (Even the Catholic king Ferdinand, a founder of the Inquisition, was rumored to have had Jewish blood in his veins.)[11] Conversos obtained estates and titles—caballeros, counts, marquises—and established dynasties that were to overshadow some old noble families. Their social ascent and penetration was astonishing in its scope and rapidity.[12]

What made this initial success possible—and what backlash did it, inevitably, provoke?

The Conversos brought to Christian society not only Jewish occupations but many of the features of Jewish society as well. While age-old barriers were lifted away, the Conversos, as former Jews, were also free of many mental and normative inhibitions that impeded Christian Spain. The Spanish value system was dominated by ideals of chivalry, social prestige (honor), and the aspiration for *hidalguía*, the basic rank of nobility. These values stress a person's prestige, based on origin or "blood," and downgrade all forms of work, trade, and business. Learning was also not very highly regarded, for it was considered a form of service. In the fifteenth century, the Spanish elite were still rougher and less cultured than their counterparts in Renaissance Italy and France. This view of social value manifested itself in the amazingly large number of lower hidalgos, who played a passive and rather negative role in the Spanish economy. (They were satirized and attacked in much of the later picaresque literature, down to Cervantes; see chapter 16.) The Conversos now stepped into that partial economic void, bringing with them the positive Jewish outlook on work, personal effort, learning, and money. Their economic experience and legal acumen, sharpened by a long Talmudic tradition, now sought new avenues in which to assert itself; and their immense drive to advance and excel continued to rely on the Jewish tendency toward mutual help within the family and the community, a tradition that had often proven itself in hard times for the Jews and now, when external barriers were relaxed, played a role in the Conversos' leap forward.

Solidarity among the New Christians was a complex story, however, because they did not constitute a homogeneous group. They belonged to different social layers and political factions, and sharply diverged on the question of religious affiliation. As a result, Conversos of one kind sometimes tried to separate themselves from those of another kind. Yet their bonds, at least in the early generations, were usually sufficient to ensure mutual help even between Conversos whose attitudes to assimilation were quite different. And as the century progressed, and with it grew the reactive hostility of the Old Christian society and new obstacles put in the Conversos' way, a defensive solidarity imposed itself on most Converso factions.

But we are still in the early period, when the upper echelons of Christian society were relatively open to the Conversos. The great nobles, in particular, had not yet been swept by the intense anti-Jewish feelings that pervaded the common folk and were to mark Spain's overall attitude in the late fifteenth century. Marriages between converts and aristocratic Spanish families, which still went on, were due not only to the Conversos' wealth and education but, to some extent, also to their distinguished origin: a family such as the La Caballerías could claim to be descended from King David, and thereby related to Jesus himself—a distinction no pure Spanish noble could claim.

A contemporary New Christian, Fernán Díaz de Toledo, who was himself well networked in upper society, described the Converso penetration into the top Spanish families:

> In our time there was the reverend father Don Pablo, bishop of Burgos, of beloved memory, the king's chief chancellor and a member of his council. His grandchildren, great grandchildren, nephews and other descendants are to be found today in the lineages of Manriques, Mendozas, Rojas, Saravias, Pestines, Luxanes, Solis, Mirandas, Osorios, Salcedos, and other lineages and families. Indeed some of these descendants are great grandchildren of Juan Hurtado de Mendoza, the king's *mayordomo mayor*, and of the marshal, Diego Fernández de Córdoba, nephew of the greatest in the kingdom. Similarly there is the example of Juan Sánchez de Sevilla who was of this race and was the king's *contador mayor*. . . . I could fill the page with more examples.[13]

Actually, Fernán Díaz says that almost all aristocratic houses have kinship ties with former Jews. Undoubtedly he exaggerates; as his aim was to protect Conversos against excessive prying into their past, arguing this would hurt almost all the nobles of the land. But his testimony is so detailed and concrete that one can hardly ignore it. The writer himself was a royal secretary, a powerful post ("the most important" in the royal household, says MacKay) that several other Conversos also held, among them Juan Gonzales Pintado, Alvar Gómez,

Diego Romero, and a person we shall meet several times in this story—Diego Arias d'Avila, chief finance officer of Castile. We have already mentioned the La Caballería dynasty; no less successful was the Marmolejo clan, whose founder, a tax farmer who had converted prior to 1391, served as chief of finance to King Juan I, his descendants obtained the rank of caballero and held senior offices in many sectors of society. Other top Converso families who did the same were Benveniste, Abenamias, Abenxuxan, Abudaran, Levi, and Nasçi: their names appear both in official documents, and the *Libros de Rentas*, and sometimes also in the sharp satires of the age.

The chronicler Bernáldez gives further evidence (also exaggerated because of his hostility to the Conversos). Many of them, he says, not only did well but, within a short time, attained great fortunes and estates. They were able to accomplish this feat because they "had no moral scruples" in taking their usuries and "exercising their profiteering" methods, thus causing many evils.[14]

Alvaro de Luna and the Conversos

The Conversos' social advance was greatly assisted by the able and all-powerful chief minister of Castile, Alvaro de Luna, serving under King Juan II.[15] Juan had ascended the throne as a minor in 1412 (we came across his mother, Catalina, who enacted the "infidel laws" in his name), and had not completely matured politically even forty years later. During this king's lengthy rule, Alvaro de Luna was able to curb the power of the great nobles and to gain partial control over the cities, thereby endowing his sovereign—and the Castilian state—with a degree of central authority never attained before. Only the king's folly could undo his minister's achievement when, bowing to his wife, he sacrificed Luna to the nobles' vengeance. The execution of the powerful minister in 1453 set Castilian politics half-a-century backward.

The Making of an Exceptional Statesman

The illegitimate son of an Aragonese nobleman, young Luna had started as tutor and companion to Juan II while he was a minor. Both youths had grown up without parental love. The love and trust which the boy king had for Luna evolved into an almost obsessive dependency. In his early career Luna concealed his devotion to King Juan, and his personal ambition, under a mask of professionalism and indifference to politics. This mask was necessary in order to survive the series of purges and intrigues by which scheming relatives tried to isolate the young monarch from his loyal advisors and turn him into their puppet. Alvaro de Luna, though devoted to King Juan, pretended to be a mere opportunist, and thus avoided being purged. But when King Juan, with Luna's efficient help, took the reins of government, his secret adviser came out of the closet and was appointed chief minister (Constable of Castile), a status he continued to hold for a quarter century full of adventure, achievements, and intrigue.

Alvaro de Luna was driven by a strong desire to save "his" king from conspiring self-serving relatives, and to make him the real power in the land, in control of the nobles, the cities, and other semiautonomous powers. Of course, Don Alvaro understood that bolstering the king's authority would also reinforce his own. But alongside his personal ambition he was motivated by a broader political philosophy. Efficient government was a political good in itself to him—not simply a means for power. And since he was no longer a medieval man, he realized that the real basis of royal power was not just military, but primarily economic and administrative. But how can one set up an efficient and trustworthy royal administration when those aspiring to serve in it are precisely those it should restrain—the obdurate nobles, the domineering clerics, and city representatives who compete against the king's authority and jealously defend their privileges and special interests?

It was a trap. To evade it, Luna turned first to the Jews, and then to the Conversos. His choice to employ the Jews (which helped restore their standing in the kingdom) was based on a known political logic. Jews could not nurture a political ambition separate from the king on whom they totally depended, so they were the classic element he could trust. In addition, Jews possessed the required talents and an almost hereditary experience in finance and administration.

When Luna moved from the backstage into the office of first minister, he revised his strategy and preferred using Conversos. Conversos were as proficient in finance and administration as the Jews, and were unlikely to build a power center rivaling the king. On the contrary, with Luna's help, service and fidelity to the king became the chief avenue of mobility by which the Conversos could realize their new social aspirations, so they were determined to preserve it. And being Christians, Conversos were entitled to openly hold any government post, whether royal, municipal, or seigniorial—as clerics, judges, supervisors, treasurers, police constables, notaries, *regidores* (council members)—all the way to royal secretaries. The Jews were less essential to Luna now. They could continue to provide the king with "privatized" services such as tax farming, but the backbone of the royal administration had to be composed by men with an official post and title who were versed in Christian society and customs and were directly subject to the king and his minister—namely, by *Christians having all the advantages of Jews*. In this respect, the New Christians played the role of Jews for Luna, but Jews possessing the official status and education of Christians.

Luna's reliance on New Christians was so wide and conspicuous, and so mindless of the resentment it provoked, that his political fate became inexorably linked to theirs. And since the ambitious minister had penetrated into the realm's power centers in large measure through the Conversos' penetration into those centers, it was no accident that his time in office was parallel to the Conversos' social take off, and that his fall occurred shortly after 1449, the year that saw the first big offensive against the Conversos. The fact that Luna also conflicted with some powerful Conversos, such as the Santa Marías, only adds realism to the picture without changing its pattern.

In terms of deep historical currents, Alvaro de Luna was fateful to both Conversos and Jews. In boosting the Conversos' social rise and casting them in the role of his men, he encouraged the stream of envy and hatred that, in the second part of the century, led to anti-Converso riots and, eventually, the Inquisition. As for the Jews, although Luna started by restoring their standing and giving them, in Netanyahu's words, "a new lease on life," on a deeper level he unwittingly prepared the Jews' destruction by shifting the core of the royal service from Jews to Conversos, a trend which the Catholic monarchs, Ferdinand and Isabella, brought to its climax. Making the Jews look dispensable undermined the basis of their political standing in the land and, for the first time, made their expulsion from Christian Spain a conceivable option.

The Urban Bourgeoisie

Most of the New Christians were artisans and merchants of different levels—and also money changers, doctors, secretaries, scribes, and other professionals and service providers that filled the ranks of urban society. Herein lay their main importance for Spanish society: they helped create an energetic bourgeois class that promoted urban economic activity and gave it a vital boost in pre-Renaissance Spain.[16] Accordingly, Conversos in all social strata had higher incomes than Old Christians. Although they were not necessarily rich, their vibrant activity in the urban economy and culture provided a motor for creating the aggregate wealth of a country that looked down on productive activity as socially inferior, yet needed it badly.

A partial profile of the Converso occupations in 1497 (there are no data for the early part of the century) was drawn by Ladero Quesada from the records of the Inquisition.[17] Only a small number worked in agriculture; the greater majority were urban artisans.[18] Of these, between one-third and one-half worked in textiles:[19] weaving, dyeing, tailoring, sewing silk, and reworking old tissues. Second was the leather industry: makers of shoes, purses, bags, saddles, and so forth,[20] followed by the iron industry (smiths, metalworkers), and by goldsmiths and jewelers. The various branches of commerce, from big trading to shopkeeping and retail, occupied about 13–15 percent of urban Conversos,[21] while the financial sector, especially exchange and lending, was served by 5–6 percent[22] (here again the figures cover big financiers down to small money peddlers). The rate of tax farmers fell toward the end of the century. In addition, Conversos were active as physicians, pharmacists, barbers, lawyers, scribes, teachers, and educators. About 5–7 percent worked in the service of noble families and the upper clergy—as majordomos, accountants, and real estate and business managers: most of these jobs (excepting servants) were considered honorable and served as springboards for social promotion. Of those in public office,[23] a few held powerful posts, while most had middle-authority jobs: thus, among twenty-one Converso public officers in Baena and Sanluzar, eight were scribes and public notaries, as against three *regidores* (council members) and one *alguacil* (police commander).

These statistics calls for caution. In every society, the powerful are a small minority whose impact is far more visible in real life than in the numbers. The Conversos' actual economic weight and social impact are blurred in those average figures, which include both small and big time economic players. Also, the way the groups are cut and defined here does not express the distinct weight of those who initiate and move the wheels of the economy. So these figures shed more light on the social profile of the Conversos among themselves than on their influence and standing in the broader society. But with this reservation and a bit of imagination, we may trace in such figures the lines of a more vivid and lively portrait of the Converso community in its daily life.

A Conflict of Values: Productive Work versus Hidalguía

Contrary to common belief, Spain in the late medieval and early modern period was far from a rigid and frozen society. The ambition to climb the social ladder was driven in Spain in great measure by the lust for status and the marks of honor and prestige (*honra*). A widely coveted goal was *hidalguía*, the basic rank of nobility, and the title *caballero* (knight, chevalier), which carried a halo of social pride, in addition to the title *Don*, and tangible advantages such as exception from the king's taxes. Still, the passion for chivalry and *hidalguía* did not arise from monetary considerations primarily, but from the inherent value that was attributed to them, and also from the will (of those engaged in a lucrative economic activity) to wash off the negative stigma that many Spaniards attached to productive occupations. Not only manual labor, but any specialized work, small and big commerce, even medicine and banking, were looked on with disdain by the true hidalgo: lowly occupations that are better left to vulgar families—and also to Jews, Moors, Conversos, and foreigners. The Spanish noble needed and wanted the fruits of economic activity, but despised the process that generates them and looked down disdainfully on those engaged in it. Serving the cruder material needs, productive work was by nature dishonorable and unworthy of a Spanish noble, who should serve honor, faith, devotion, self-sacrifice, and the aspiration to great deeds.

The craving for *hidalguía* produced a complex genealogical art—the construction (or faking) of lineage. True and fabricated claims to hidalgo status piled up in government offices. In ironic contradiction to its very meaning, *hidalguía* even became an economic asset as the royal court started selling it for money, to the dismay of the older nobles. Yet neither abuse nor literary attacks (mostly by Converso writers) could overcome the power of *hidalguía*, or the dominance of the ideal of chivalry, as a system of values and aspirations. The thrust for honor and prestige drove many Spaniards to perform extraordinary deeds in which they could excel: the conquest of new lands, propagating God's word to the "savages," magnifying Spain's name in the world, and promoting its alleged civilizing mission. Even the hunt for gold could become at times a passion with some grandeur that transcended ordinary greed, and lead to daring adventures in which a person could demonstrate courage and character that would justify his claim to *honra*.

These values and drives contributed to Spain's Golden Age in the sixteenth century. They supplied energy and imagination at an appropriate moment. We can see them in action, spreading Spain's rule over two continents, helping to forge its self confidence and engendering deeds of greatness and heroism (also of cruelty and savage brutality) that built the power and glory of imperial Spain. But those same values and drives, when continuing into the seventeenth century, contributed to Spain's decline. Following the first great achievements, the time came for consolidation. And that meant (in terms of the period): adjust the economy of Spain and its colonies to the conditions of emerging mercantilism and early capitalism while giving priority to production, financing, and international trade. But the change that was now demanded seems to have lain beyond the cultural capability of imperial Spain—not beyond its economic potential, but beyond its system of values, the same that was also expressed in the Inquisition in the ideal of "blood purity," in the counter-Reformation in the sense of religious crusade, and in the unrealistic aspiration to Spanish homogeneity. Spain had an immense economic potential—its own production of wool; its large market and inner system of transport; its naval capacity; dominion over the Low Countries and parts of Italy, the two most civilized and economically sophisticated areas of Europe; and, of course, in the flow of precious metals from America. Spain missed this opportunity not only for purely economic, but also for cultural, reasons which always affect economics. Although the force of circumstance had swept it to the center of international economy as a major player, Spain fulfilled that role half-heartedly, still attached to the notions of honor, nobility, religious zeal, and the inherent worth of a Spanish hidalgo as such, regardless of what he has done or earned. And since the economic roles were fulfilled by many Conversos—who from the mid-fifteenth century onward were considered an internal Other, inferior to the "pure" Spaniard—the Converso stain reverted in a kind of feedback to the already bad reputation of the "coarse" economic occupations.

The Old Christians were partly trapped. They now started opposing the Conversos, as they had in the past fought the Jewish competition, but at the same time they failed to expand their own number and economically productive activity in the measure required by the time—that is, sufficient to translate Spain's great military and colonial power into economic and commercial strength. Thus Spain started to decline. Its primacy passed to England, Holland, and later, France, who were far more successful (and adjustable) in passing that early modern trial, which, in their case too, was cultural before being economic, related to social values and self-perceptions.

At the height of its power, Spain manifested greatness of ambition, vitality, and achievement. The fabled Spanish pride, though ostentatiously projected, was not without foundation in deed and character. In transporting the drive for Reconquest outside their borders and turning it into imperial domination, Spaniards had many opportunities for showing valor, perseverance, and nobility (alongside greed and cruelty)—and their sense of divine mission, together with their myth of purity and uniformity, did not produce an illusion only but, perhaps thereby, also bred the self-confidence necessary for extraordinary action.

Historically, however, Spain had already missed its great opportunity in the midst of its Golden Century, when a surge in economic demand arising form the demographic growth of metropolitan Spain and the needs of its American colonies was not exploited to achieve a parallel growth in Spanish productive capacity. Instead, the strong demand generated periodic inflationary waves that raged in Spain through the sixteenth century, intensified by the stream of precious metals—gold, and especially silver—from America. The precious metals served mostly for private and public consumption, or for enhancing the glamour and fortunes of the great families without contributing to Spain's productive capacity or aggregate national wealth. New wealth was not invested in dynamic means of production, but was mostly parked in landed property, precious objects and metals, and other stationary assets. Incidentally, the Spanish attachment to precious metals did not express only ordinary greed (although that too, of course). Symbolically, it represented the ideal of nonproductive nobility: here was a flow of easy wealth that was, or ought to be, available to the nobles without requiring them to worry about the processes that produce real goods and services, and enabled them to continue spurning those who were engaged in those lowly occupations.

The minority of nobles who did engage in commerce and finance kept this fact in low profile, preferring to boast about their lineage and aristocratic essence rather than their acquired wealth. (Inherited wealth was a different matter altogether, and considered dignified, a projection of blood-transmitted worth.) On the other hand, a good number of hidalgos, lacking family resources and being cut off the process of production, were wretchedly poor. A biting parody of hidalgo pride—and of their parasitic role in Spanish economy—is given in the picaresque novel *Lazarillo de Tormes*. The tramp Lazarillo finds a new master—a starving noble, whose only possession is the sword on his belt—and in a reversal of roles typical of the picaresque genre, the master has to live off the crumbs gathered by his thieving and parasitical servant. He would rather feed on garlic and squash than have to work, declares the proud, impoverished noble, who does not even possess garlic—and picks his teeth in public, to make believe he has just had a lavish meal (see chapter 16).

Muslims and Conversos: Filling the Void

By a common estimate, the hidalgos in golden age Spain reached the stunning rate of 13 percent of the population. No wonder they created a void in Spain's economics and deprived it of much of its potentially productive elite. That void was partly filled, first by the Muslims and later by the Judeo-Conversos. The Muslims provided the manual work force of Spanish society, especially in the south. They filled the ranks of agricultural laborers, workers in urban services, harbor hands (in Seville) and petty artisans. They also controlled the building industry, both as simple workers and as trained architects, masons, and decorators. To them Christian Spain—and visitors today—owe the magnificent, if somewhat overbearing Mudejar style, whose delicate plaster lace, bas-reliefs, and arabesques are widespread in the Iberian peninsula.

Part of the Muslims also converted to Christianity, either voluntarily or by force, and were known as *Moriscos*. Unlike the Judeo-Conversos, who strove to ascend socially and possessed the education to make it work, the Moriscos kept more to their old ways and places of residence. They refrained from mixing with the Old Christian society and retained their old communal structures and customs (including essential Islam) far more than the Judeo-Conversos. Often living in geographic vicinity to each other (in the Valencia region, Granada, the Alpujar mountains), the Moriscos were more cohesively organized; and when oppressed beyond their limit, they took to armed rebellion, which was mercilessly crushed. In 1609 all Moriscos—though they were Christians, and some rather devout—were brutally and cruelly expelled from Spain.

The Judeo-Conversos, on the other hand, were more dispersed and better assimilated than the Moriscos; they filled the productive urban classes and exploited the privileges granted to Christian sectors. Just as during the Reconquest the Jews had helped create the Spanish urban civilization, so now the Judeo-Conversos contributed to shaping a bourgeois class far greater and more energetic than had existed before their advent. This was made possible not only by their earth-bound drives and social values but also by the new economic conditions in Europe of the early Renaissance, and in the naval and commercial empire that Spain was to set up in the next century.

To a great extent, the Conversos' role in promoting the premodern bourgeois class in Spain defines (though neither uniquely nor exclusively) a socioeconomic function they would fulfill for many generations to come. It also explains the main contradictions in the attitude toward them. The Old Christian society both needed and despised the Conversos' economic and managerial roles. It wanted them to succeed in creating the national wealth whose fruits could be culled by the traditional elite, but often resented the Conversos' personal success, which rivaled the standing of the Old Christian burghers. This conflict was crucial for Spain's future. The Conversos embodied a drive to revolutionize the basic social values—to rehabilitate work and stress personal achievement rather than birth as the source of honor. This attempt failed on the broader, countrywide level, though it was incessantly stirring in the social undercurrents; its challenging, half-hushed voice, masked behind an ironic facade, came out in literary works—from *Lazarillo* to *Don Quijote*—which, as in an inverted mirror, critically reflect the official normative universe of Golden Age Spain (see chapter 16).

The Pursuit of City Offices

Alongside their craving for noble status, Spanish burghers manifested a strong desire for city offices: to serve in the city council and municipal administration or the local or royal police and judiciary, to supervise economic privileges, command the royal citadel, or represent the king in other capacities, high and low. A much-coveted office was that of city councilor, called *regidor* or "twenty-four man" (*veinticuatro*). The title referred to the fact that Spanish city councils were officially comprised of twenty-four members. However, by a special political arithmetic, many cities had up to ninety "twenty-four men" to serve in their councils. According to F. Márquez Villanueva, the first four decades of the fifteenth century saw a slow but persistent penetration of Conversos into city councils, and they were also heavily represented in other public offices.[24] Having, as Jews, been barred from the social honors of public office, the New Christians were now anxious to exploit their new opportunities, not only for economic advantage but as a symbolic way of realizing—and consummating—their new identity. (A similar psychosocial phenomenon was manifested in the early stage of modern Jewish emancipation in Western Europe.)

The Conversos' widespread presence in public office added fuel to an already burning fire. Compounded by the hatred toward Alvaro de Luna, the rising social resentment and anger started turning toward the Conversos. Some historians view this movement as a class struggle—between feudal nobles and the rising bourgeoisie; or between two strata of the city patriarchate; or between a centralist monarchy and the jealous defenders of city privileges. Yet these struggles did not constitute the defining pattern of the Marranos' social strife. The Marranos engaged in the struggles (when they did) with the flag of "former Jew" already flying over their heads, with all the identity passions and stereotypes attached to it. The Marranos inherited the Jews' alterity in a new mode, that of the *Other Within*; and their new otherness (which we shall study more closely) defined their social and existential situation from the outset, shaping also the pattern of the socioeconomic (and ideological) strife in which they engaged. Beyond, and through, the economic rivalry of the Old Christian bourgeoisie, a deeper complex of identity passions and interests was raging—the struggle of the similar against the stranger, of the self against the alien, and of claims for recognition against their persistent negation—than a narrow economic interpretation of history (be it Marxist or neocapitalist) is able to appreciate.

The Conversos' new form of otherness found expression in popular idiom, literary images, and, starting in the mid-fifteenth century, also in outbursts of violence and extraordinary acts of legislation. The term *New Christians*, which had been at first descriptive, gathered negative connotations; words like *Marrano*, *Converso*, and *Confeso* were used as invectives; and sharp satires started circulating in the popular literature depicting the Conversos as cheats and crooks, or as secret Jews who desecrate the name of the Crucified; and also, no less, as cynics and heretics lacking any religion except money. (This was a hostile way of referring especially to those Marranos who indeed lost interest in either Judaism or Christianity and adopted a this-worldly outlook.) Such propaganda resulted in several violent anti-Converso riots. A tendency emerged to perceive the Conversos as humanly inferior by birth, thus turning them into an outcast and degraded Christian caste defined by its vile and impure blood.

Purity of Blood—Act I

The "purity of blood" policies that were in effect in Spain (and later in Portugal) were of momentous importance in constituting the Marrano phenomenon. But the story of their genesis—how these laws were enacted and came into effect—is secondary to the issue itself and can be told briefly. I divide this drama in several "acts" and "scenes." Act I, scene 1 (1449) is told here; act I, scene 2 (1467) is told in chapter 8, and act II (the mid-1550s) is discussed in chapter 12. The purity of blood issue projected its shadow for centuries, and overlays most of the following chapters.

In the mid-fifteenth century it was clear that the old Spanish hope and ethos of converting the Jews had turned sour when its goal was partly achieved. A generation or two of relative toleration had not abolished the basic Old Christian hostility toward the newly baptized and their progeny, or the Jew's sense of alienness. Catholicism, to be sure, holds that baptism removes metaphysical barriers and all believers have an equal part in Jesus. Yet the Christian populace continued to see the foreign essence—Jewish and Moorish—within the convert's self; and when they could no longer rely on a religious distinction, they started looking for difference in other areas—above all, in blood. Thus the first racial theory of modern times was born in early Renaissance Spain.

We even have a specific birth certificate: Toledo, June 5, 1449. Two generations had passed since the Conversos first entered Spanish society. The relative openness initially shown to them by the ruling classes had invoked anger in the populace and concern among the burghers. The common people felt cheated: the Catholic religion, which had in the past served to justify mistreating the Jews, had become a shield that protected them following their conversion. One must be naive, the argument went, to believe that Jewish malice can be erased by holy water. And actually, the argument continued, many of these New Christians are not Christians at all, but falsely converted Jews who secretly observe all the abominable customs of their old religion—a fact that commoners could better ascertain than others. The commoners concurred with the Christian adviser's statement in *Shevet Yehuda* that "Judaism is one of the diseases to which there is no cure," and attributed this flaw to an immutable metaphysical Jewish essence. In other words, the flaw was Jewish blood, which flows irremediably in the converts' veins and which, as the commoners could assert with

Schadenfreude, had also penetrated into the Spanish nobility and infected it. And who is free of the infection? Only the common people, whom the converted Jews would never dream of marrying, and who would not accept them if they did. Purity of blood thus became a newly acquired advantage of the common folk—now they too had an inborn genetic distinction lifting them even above their rich and powerful oppressors. (Thus Sancho Panza, in *Don Quijote,* brags he is a pure "Old Christian," and therefore deserves to be a governor); while the urban merchants and craftsmen used the slogan of "pure blood" as compensation for the lack of hidalgo status and a sign of superiority over their New Christian rivals.

Blood purity thus became a principle in the popular struggle for identity and recognition, and a weapon in the urban class conflict. Yet purity of blood could not have played its role in socioeconomic conflicts unless it already had a deeper significance—a negative existential halo, rooted in identity passions, that made it possible to use a rival's problematic identity as a reason for discrimination on a socioeconomic level, too.

The crucial point is that now the opponent's radical otherness, or negative-demonic essence, was no longer defined in religious terms—such as lack of grace, baptism, faith, or the Eucharist, or the denial, murder, and desecration of the Savior—but in secular terms of blood and origin. In this way blood purity was integrated from the start into the traditional Spanish value system, which stressed a person's honorable status as the outcome of his or her origin and lineage; except that now *origin* was not tied to the identity of a noble ancestor, but determined by the measure of radically foreign blood that flowed in one's veins.

Soon writers and theologians emerged who gave ideological justification to this racial view. They did so as part of their own class interest and identity passion, since many clerics came from the lower social strata. Thereby, as in 1391—though from different motives—those clerics provided a seemingly ecclesiastical legitimation to the riots that ensued.

In January 1449 a new kind of pogrom erupted in Toledo. Its targets now were baptized Christians who no longer had the option of escaping through conversion. The fact that the riots were part of a broader rebellion against the royal government could not comfort the Conversos, but only remind them that their fate resembled that of Jews in other generations, including their ancestors in 1391. The direct trigger of the rebellion was a compulsory loan of one million maravedis that minister Alvaro de Luna imposed on Toledo. Luna had consigned the royal finance administration to Diego Arias d'Avila, a rich Converso of whom we shall hear more in this book, and his staff of other Conversos. The Converso Alonso de Cotta was charged with collecting Toledo's compulsory loan. In January the bells of the Toledo Cathedral tolled and tolled. The mob, whose ancestors had assaulted the Jewish quarter (the *Judería*) sixty years earlier, now stormed the *Magdalena*, a quarter of rich Conversos named after the Christian saint. The city leaders were headed by Pero Sarmiento, an ambitious noble whom the king had appointed his representative in Toledo, but who turned against his royal master. Sarmiento and the council closed the city gates in open rebellion. Unlike their Jewish ancestors, the Conversos took to arms. Many perished in the battle and their bodies were hanged upside down, in the manner that Jews used to be hanged.

But the main casualty that the Conversos suffered occurred in the judicial field five months later. On June 5, 1449, the city elders of Old Christian extraction gathered under Pero Sarmiento and signed the following statement:

> We the above mentioned, Pero Sarmiento . . . and the citizens and people of Toledo, declare that since the Conversos of Jewish origin are suspect of disbelief in Our Lord Jesus . . . and often return to their rot and Judaize, they will not be permitted to hold any posts or benefices, public and private, from which they could cause harm to Christians of pure origin. . . . [And this is done in accordance with] a privilege that this city had been granted by King Don Alfonso of glorious memory.[25]

This document, known as the *Sentencia Estatuto*, is the first document of blood purity in Spain (and in Europe). It was to be succeeded by many others. The authors justify the document's inordinate character by listing all the evils of the Conversos. They are corrupt people who steal public funds and impoverish the fatherland; they are traitors who give up Toledo to its enemies (meaning: the royal administration), just as their Jewish ancestors of seven centuries earlier had surrendered Toledo to the Muslims; they have been the enemies of the true faith from the day their ancestors caused the Savior's suffering on the cross, "and they continued doing so today"; they say that God's son was a man of their own stock who got himself hanged; and it is they who started the civil war by "gathering and collecting arms . . . with the intention to annihilate all the pure Christians, and me Pedro Sarmiento."

Actually, the Conversos took to arms in self-defense; but that was not the only falsehood in the document. King Alfonso of glorious memory, who supposedly had granted those privileges before, is unknown and probably never existed (a fact that did not prevent future Spanish generations from relying on his legendary precedent). But the most outstanding distortion was using canon law as the basis for racial discrimination. Catholic law forbids distinguishing between Christian believers on ethnic and racial grounds. The novel concept introduced by the Toledo statutes: "Christians of pure Christian origin," contradicts the universal (catholic) character of the church, which brought different peoples and races to reside under the Cross and made them all brothers in Jesus. From a strict judicial and theological standpoint, the Toledo ruling was scandalous.[26]

A major polemic broke out between Castilian statesmen, clerical leaders, and theologians. One of the first to denounce the aberration was Alonso de Cartagena, bishop of Burgos, a noted theologian and diplomat. If his arguments recall the views of Bishop Pablo de Santa María, the former rabbi of Burgos, this is no accident: Don Alonso was the Jewish-born son of Rabbi Shlomo Halevi. He was converted as child, along with his father, and followed his father in also becoming bishop of Burgos. Shlomo Halevi, we remember, argued that Christianity is the direct offshoot of Judaism and consummates its inner message; his son Alonso inferred from there that Christians of Jewish origin are fuller and more valuable Christians than those stemming from pagan peoples—that is, the Spanish Old Christians. A Jew who embraces the Cross does not adopt a foreign doctrine but culls the fruit of his own Old Testament, but a Gentile becoming Christian subordinates himself to a totally new faith. From a purely Christian standpoint, therefore, Jewish origin is a distinction rather than a drawback!

Perhaps the Jewish-born bishop did not notice that his proud words bore out his opponents' claim: the Jewish superior self-image, the sense of divine election, perseveres in the Jew's heart even after he embraces the Cross, and even when he becomes a bishop.

What is more, Don Alonso constructed a whole philosophy of history that assigned his Converso caste a special role in God's plan. All men descend from Adam: this is their unity of the flesh. God allowed them to split into many races, but elected one nation—the Jews—from which the "second Adam," Christ, was to issue, and he would unite all humans in the spirit, which is higher than the body. With Christ, all differences of the flesh (that is, of race) had been superseded and abolished by the believers' spiritual unity.

This is where Don Alonso's egalitarianism ends. In his thinking, Salvation in Jesus abolishes only differences of blood and race, but not the inborn *social* distinctions. The gap dividing nobles from commoners is basic to any human society and must be scrupulously observed. Ironically, Cartagena accepts what he was supposed to deny—that birth and origin do determine a person's worth. Moreover, he readily admits there are noble and ignoble *peoples*, but constructs a militant Converso ideology—or theology—that puts New Christians above Old Christians precisely because they are of Jewish stock.

Cartagena's variety of the Converso duality consisted in his seeking a higher, more privileged form of Christianity and finding it in his own Jewishness. While Judaizing (as religious practice) was repugnant, Jewishness (as origin) was a cause of pride to him. Bishop Alonso de Cartagena was most certainly a devout Christian, but in a distinct and uncommon way. His Christian devotion was informed by the Jewish ingredient in his identity, which he Christianized—but saw this very Christianization as fulfilling his ancient Jewish election. Thus, *Jewishness* and *Judaism* were two different concepts for Cartagena. The supreme combination was a Christian Jew, who negates Judaism as a religion but highlights his Jewish stock as a Christian advantage.[27]

In the short run, Cartagena could note with satisfaction that his goal was being served. The Toledo mutiny was crushed by Alvaro de Luna, and Pope Martin V published a bull denouncing the discrimination against New Christians. The bull was obtained with the help of senior Converso clerics, among them Cardinal Juan de Torquemada, one of the heads of the Castilian church who, like Cartagena, wrote an important essay defending the New Christians. Nevertheless, this was a temporary victory only. The deed done in Toledo could not be undone or erased from Spanish history, though its full consequences emerged only in the next century.

In retrospect, the *Sentencia Estatuto* proved to be a founding act that continued to simmer and reverberate in the Spanish background. Even after Sarmiento's mutiny was suppressed, strong social powers continued to press for the blood purity statutes. Henceforth these statues burst out periodically and retreated again, leaving their mark locally on specific segments of the society—until, under King Philip II, they raised their ugly head in triumph and retreated no more. (See "Purity of Blood: Act I, Scene 2" in chapter 8, and "Back to Spain: Blood Purity, Act II" in chapter 12.)

5

The New Otherness: Duality in Many Faces

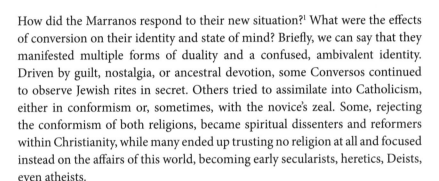

How did the Marranos respond to their new situation?[1] What were the effects of conversion on their identity and state of mind? Briefly, we can say that they manifested multiple forms of duality and a confused, ambivalent identity. Driven by guilt, nostalgia, or ancestral devotion, some Conversos continued to observe Jewish rites in secret. Others tried to assimilate into Catholicism, either in conformism or, sometimes, with the novice's zeal. Some, rejecting the conformism of both religions, became spiritual dissenters and reformers within Christianity, while many ended up trusting no religion at all and focused instead on the affairs of this world, becoming early secularists, heretics, Deists, even atheists.

Many of these responses were unsettled, and none of them provided the Conversos with a fully integrated identity and mode of life. Whether in the early generations the Conversos tried to preserve Judaism in secret, or assimilated into the host society, or mixed the two religions together, whether they became Christian reformers and dissenters or abandoned all religious traditions—they practically all ended in a state of incomplete identity—a mixed or divided self, in which the Other is preserved within the Self and partly constitutes it.

Two trends emerged in consequence, apparently excluding each other: constant assimilation on the one hand, and the ongoing attempt to preserve a modicum of Jewish identity on the other. Although opposing in theory, these two trends were often compatible in reality and sometimes existed within the same family, even within the same person. This produced some of the complex—and more fascinating—forms of duality that marked the lives of Conversos. Not only the wavering or ambivalent converts, but even those who had made a single-minded choice in favor of one option or the other (Catholicism or secret Judaism) often betrayed the rival option in their actual lives, in the way they reasoned and behaved, or in the very ardent choice they made against it. As we shall see, no pure unmitigated position was available to the Conversos. The secret Judaizer was not really a Jew, and the zealot Christian betrayed his Jewish background by his very zeal, or by the restlessness with which he embraced his new religion.

The New Otherness

What characterized the Conversos' existential situation was *a new way of being Other*. Formerly, in being Jewish, they had been the conspicuous Other of Spanish society, though a native Other. In a medieval culture dominated by religion, Judaism was an unambiguous mode of otherness, which sharply demarcated them from the rest of the social body. Now, through a shift of religion, they officially moved into the main body of Christian Spain—into its own Self, so to speak; yet even within that they remained Other, now in a variety of new modes, some overt and others more subtle and complex.

This otherness—this being the *Other Within*—initially took a religious form. It was expressed either as dissent *from* Christianity or as dissent *within* Christianity, and also as religious laxity or, on the contrary, as exaggerated zeal. In later years, when religion proved to be an insufficient cultural demarcation, the Conversos' otherness was also expressed in terms of race and blood, and thus was tacitly *secularized*. Conversos were marked as having "impure blood" and were barred from holding various positions and honors. Eventually, the task of so barring them was relegated to the Inquisition, which was trying to wrap a religious mantle over a racist, fundamentally un-Christian notion. Yet the Inquisition was able to do so only institutionally, by projecting and manipulating worldly power; and thereby the Inquisition itself was playing a secular role in disguise.

At the same time, the Conversos became estranged from the traditional Other of Spanish society from which they were issued—the Jews—and this compounded their overall otherness. Though Jews and Conversos sometimes socialized and associated on a practical level, their basic relation was severance and alienation: the Conversos, as the new Other, were also the traditional Other's Other, without thereby returning to the social Self; and this made the Conversos doubly estranged.

A major feeling affecting all Conversos was guilt. Many converts felt guilty of having betrayed their Jewish bonds, and Judaizers were often conscious of being false to their new religion. The unease, confusion, and mistrust that they came to feel toward both Christianity and Judaism led some of them to reject both religions alike. Thus, alongside the Judaizers and the assimilated converts, a third group was emerging: religious skeptics and sometimes outright (if secret) heretics who, instead of metaphysical salvation, were seeking personal fulfillment in the affairs of this world—in commerce, politics, love, family, or personal career. From their number arose some early rationalists and atheists, those who denied the existence of an afterlife, or a transcendent, supernatural world, or even a personal God.

Members of the openly Jewish community were often insensitive to Converso dualities. Ruy Martines "used to enter Jewish synagogues and recite Jewish prayers while gesturing like the other Jews," but they sent him away. So Ruy Martines protested, "Why do the Jews drive me away when all I want is to pray like them?"[2] More receptive to Conversos were some of their Jewish relatives: "On the night when Juan Rodrigues, the [Converso] *escribano*, died, . . . the witness saw two Jewish women coming out of his house. Later it was known in town that they had been going in and out throughout the whole night . . . and that many Jews and Jewesses were in Juan Rodrigues's house." This was surely a compressed Marrano version of the *Shiv'a*, the Jewish rite of consoling the mourner.

Their dual otherness pushed many Conversos to intermarry. "I embraced my wife a thousand times," one Converso exclaimed when all the couple's daughters were also married. "[It is good] to marry my daughter to someone of my own generation and stock, for if they call her a Jewess she could say 'Jew' to him, and if she cooks *Khamin* [a Jewish Sabbath dish] he will eat it with her." A particularly strong expression of the same kind is given by the Converso poet Antón de Montoro addressing his Conversa wife.[3]

Needless to say, each of the three main Converso groups we shall discuss had various subgroups and shades that sometimes overlapped. Especially, none was entirely *self-identical*, or fully capable of *accomplishing its own project and intention*. Yet with certain variations, the early patterns we traced have recurred in different periods of the Marrano experience and may be seen as the groundwork for its phenomenology.

It will be noticed that I did not assign a special category to the dualists who mixed both Judaism and Christianity. The reason is simply that almost everyone did so. Dualities, as mentioned before, were common to all Converso groups: membership in a group is here defined by a person's dominant posture and intent, not some pure or single-minded variety of it.[4]

The Judaizers

It is only among the first generation after conversion that genuinely struggling Jews could still be found in Spain—at least for a while, until their old Jewish self surrendered to assimilation, or to the more dualistic features of the so-called Judaizers. Resenting the violence perpetrated against them, or feeling guilt and shame for having broken their fathers' covenant, many converts indeed strove to sustain some form of Jewish identity in the privacy of their homes and through clandestine behavior. They used to observe certain Jewish rites in secret, abstained as best they could from eating foods forbidden to the Jews, practiced silent prayer, whispered old Jewish formulas and benedictions,[5] and initiated their children into the knowledge that they were to be saved by the Law of Moses rather than Christ; meanwhile, they considered themselves captives in "the land of idolatry," awaiting their own kind of Messiah.

The vicinity of a practicing Jewish community provided the early Judaizers with opportunities to receive Jewish instruction and occasionally participate in Jewish ceremonies. Only a small minority circumcised their sons—a dangerous practice that inscribed the parents' religious commitment, and society's anathema, onto their progeny's flesh. However, many feigned working on the Sabbath or eating pork, while doing neither. Some would rise in early morning for a Jewish-like prayer before starting their day as Catholics. A common practice was to greet the Jewish Sabbath by putting on new clothes on Friday night and lighting ritual candles, usually hidden in a closet or a fireplace. Some Marranos engaged in kosher slaughtering, and many still remembered—or learned again—how to drain away the blood and remove the forbidden sinew, in accordance with Jewish dietary law.

The more daring Judaizers celebrated Passover, Yom Kippur, and sometimes lesser Jewish holidays, either in solitude, or by paying an "innocent" visit to a Jewish neighbor in the *Judería*, or sometimes in clandestine company. Thus in Ciudad Real, secret assemblies by Judaizers were held in eighteen different houses between 1440 and 1480. The participants often covered themselves with a *talit* (prayer shawl), both as a Jewish symbol and also, it seems, in order to hide their faces from curious onlookers.[6]

All that time the Judaizers were regularly attending church, hearing Mass, taking Holy Bread, praying to the Virgin Mary, and appearing to adore her child. When confessing their sins to a priest, they sinned in that very confession because they concealed their most crucial secrets of Judaizing. A common practice was to mentally annul what the body was doing or the mouth was saying. Upon entering church, some Conversos used to whisper a damnation of the place as a shrine of idolatry; others turned their eyes away from Christ's effigy during religious ceremony, silently prayed to the God of Moses, or tried to evade taking the Host by pretending to be lost in prolonged orisons, or by getting busy with a rosary or a prayer book.

Particularly popular among Judaizers was the holiday of Purim, which commemorates the legendary deliverance of the Jews by Queen Esther of Persia, herself a clandestine Jew who, as the Bible tells, had saved her people from genocide by the evil vizier, Haman. In a striking example of religious duality, future Marrano generations anointed Queen Esther to be their patron saint (a Catholic concept absent in Judaism) and referred to her as "Queen *Santa* Esther."[7] This mixture of Jewish and Christian elements—the Jewish intent wrapped in a Catholic framework—is emblematic of the Judaizing Marrano experience throughout.

Jewish relics—a menorah, a goblet, prayer scrolls (*tefilin*), or bits of a *mezuzah*—were passed in Converso families from one generation to the next, and they were venerated as holy talismans, often Catholic talismans, long after the family had assimilated into Christianity and the object's original meaning had been forgotten. Such relics occasionally turn up in Latin America today, where they had emigrated with their former owners. In the early generations, possession of such objects could be mortally dangerous. During the anti-Converso riots in Ciudad Real in 1474, the cobbler Juan Alegre was spotted desperately trying to hide away a Hebrew amulet, while Juan Calvilio entreated his Old Christian neighbor, Juana Sánchez, to conceal his Jewish prayer book in her house.[8]

Some Marrano families started to Judaize a generation or two after they had been assimilated into Catholicism. Such reversions were often due to proselytizing efforts by other Conversos that worked on one's tacit sense of loss or regret. Marina Gonzales had been raised and was living in Ciudad Real as a Catholic in the 1480s when her two brothers-in-law persuaded her that she had been living in sin and could be saved (a Christian concept) only by the Law of Moses; so she started Judaizing and continued to do so for the next thirty-two years. In a similar vein, Beatrice Gonzales was "reconverted" by two of her Judaizing acquaintances, Juan Falcón and Alonso Díaz.[9] As often happens with proselytization, some of the inducements to convert were more ordinary and terrestrial than salvation. The Judaizer García Barbes, a clandestine kosher slaughterer and occasional proselytizer, promised Juan de Chinchila that his wife would return to him if he kept the Jewish law; he also gave Juan clothes and shoes in return for his promise to fast on Yom Kippur, and hugged and kissed the new "penitent" when he accepted.[10] (It was, presumably, a clandestine act of reconciling a deviant Judaizer back into the fold.)

There was almost no limit to the resourcefulness with which the Judaizers practiced their covert dissent. Dissimulation included the use of *verbal* masks—equivocation and doublespeak. Sending opposing messages in the same utterance was a life necessity that almost became a form of art. Some Judaizers found refuge in the lion's den by becoming monks and living in monasteries (see next chapter). A subtle way of Judaizing was to call God *Dio* (in the singular) rather than *Dios* (supposedly in the plural), as the Spanish language requires; the omission of the final *s* expressed dissent from the idea of the Trinity, which Jews find particularly absurd and which, logic aside, is the main doctrinal divide between Judaism and Christianity.[11] A similar omission was practiced by Inez López of

Ciudad Real, who used to stop after saying "in the name of the Father" (omitting "the Son, and the Holy Spirit"), and crossed herself only halfway, touching the forehead and the shoulder and then stopping.[12]

Women as "Quasi Rabbis"

Women played a considerable role in preserving and spreading Judaizing practices. Women were in charge of the home—the private domain par excellence—and had a more direct relationship with the children, so the tasks of initiating the new generation and instructing the family in Jewish-like practices fell, in many cases, to the women. This was so prevalent that Judaizing Marranism, though not outright matriarchal, became greatly feminized over time—a pattern which still exists today. Women controlled the inner space of the home, where secrets were kept; and they were responsible for the next generation's education, thus also for their crypto-Judaism. María Díaz, a Conversa who taught Jewish customs to Conversos in Ciudad Real and Palma in late fifteenth century, was considered a semirabbinical authority of such stature that she used to preside over clandestine Passover ceremonies.[13] Another Conversa, María Alonso, wife of Alonso, the notary and public writer, held Judaizing meetings in her home in Ciudad Real and determined the dates on which Jewish holidays were to be celebrated[14]—a major power reserved in ordinary Judaism for the rabbinical establishment. Nothing similar has been allowed women by orthodox Jews, then or today.[15]

It is noteworthy that Marrano women have retained this kind of authority for centuries, to this day.[16] In today's Belmonte (Portugal), where Marranos still exist (see the epilogue), women have been responsible for keeping and disseminating the prayers, and a wise elderly woman used to perform quasi-Jewish marriage ceremonies in private before a Catholic wedding was publicly celebrated. Moreover—and quite stunning for orthodox Jews—some Marranos had special prayers to be said by women, one of which runs: "The angels praise the Lord for having created me . . . and given me water to wash and a towel to clean myself, eyes to see, hands to touch, ears to hear, and for having made me a woman."[17] This is a flat rebuttal of the orthodox Jewish prayer thanking God daily "for not having made me a woman."[18]

Jewish Knowledge Drawn from the "Enemy"

In later generations, following the expulsion of the Jews from Spain, which removed Jewish books from the Marranos' reach, they had to look for other written—that is, stable—sources of Jewish knowledge. These they could find (if they knew Latin) in the Catholic literature that was accessible to them.[19] The Latin translation of the Bible (The Vulgate) could teach the Marranos about the great Jewish figures of antiquity and the main commands of the Law of Moses, which they claimed as their road to salvation. More ironically, anti-Jewish tracts, including the most ferocious ones, could be purged of their venomous intention and used to learn "what Jews do."

No less remarkably, inquisitors used to publish detailed lists of Jewish beliefs and customs intended for informers; and thus, inadvertently, the Inquisition became an elementary school of Judaism. And since some of the items on those lists were imprecise—or corresponded to dualistic Marrano customs rather than to authentic Jewish rites—the inquisitors were not only instructors, but even innovators in the matter of how to be Jewish, and became contributing founders of the "religion of the Marranos."[20]

Interiority and Hope

Not surprisingly, the experience of Judaizing produced a tendency to prefer the inner over the outer world—intentions over acts, silent mental prayer over verbal utterance. It encouraged its veterans to place true religious value in one's private world and accustomed people to view the inner will as the center of one's identity. In the next century this Marrano stress on inwardness would inject new forms of spirituality into Spanish Catholicism, including Spanish illuminism and Erasmianism.

Another characteristic state of mind in the Marrano experience was *hope*—that famous *esperanza*, which sustained and nourished the lives of the active, or more determined, Judaizers. As ostensible Jews, they shared the general Jewish hope for the coming of the Messiah; but they also lived in their *own* special exile, their Spanish "Egypt" or "Babylon," and yearned to be delivered from it first. The Old Christians—in poems, sermons, and daily barbs—mocked this Marrano *esperanza* as futile and grotesque; to them, the Jews failed to recognize that the Messiah had *already* come, and were therefore condemned to a life of futility and humiliation. To the Judaizing Marranos, however, as to the Jews, their messianic hope testified to the persistence of their faith and trust—faith in God's continued election and trust in His eventual recall.

In using their many stratagems of dissimulation (some sophisticated, others pathetically naive) the Conversos did not always express a positive Jewish impulse, but sometimes a denial, a refusal, or private protest against the violence through which a foreign identity had been imposed upon them. Their violated will retreated inward, where it reasserted itself in acts of arcane denial and dissension (see next chapter, on the "Judaizing" monks). Nevertheless, a good number maintained a strong *positive* interest in Judaism. Anxious to hold on to a Jewish experience they knew was vanishing from their actual lives, they clung to it with devotion, courage, and desperation. Still others, too weak to protest and not determined either way, drifted into their new Christian roles while still Judaizing in a passive, weak-willed manner, more habitual than insistent, and dictated by nostalgia rather than assertive hope.

Dialectical Paradoxes and Reversals

The ardent Judaizers frequently showed courage and devotion. But their situation was marred by several contradictions and paradoxes. They continued to feel like full-fledged Jews in captivity and took considerable risks for the sake of that which they considered, or *willed*, to be their real essence. Yet all Catholic theologians and most Jewish rabbis considered Judaizers to be Christians, not Jews; and one might wonder how Jewish a person can be when almost no one recognizes him or her as such. Theoretically, the Judaizers could dismiss the Catholic view as immaterial (even though an opponent's view is always relevant to one's identity) and respond to the rabbis by flaunting their private Judaism as superior to ordinary Jewish life since it was won through danger and sacrifice. Yet they knew only too well that underneath it all there was the "original sin" of conversion, which they had not tried to expunge by following Maimonides's precept and emigrating from Spain.[21] So all the Judaizers could claim was the higher worth of inward religion over external rites and works—a semi-*Protestant* view which, despite its origin in the ancient prophets, was not accepted as an official Jewish teaching until the nineteenth century.

Thus, the Judaizers were handicapped from the outset. They were estranged from their foes and those whom they considered their brethren alike. Neither religious establishment accepted their form of life as legitimate. Consequently they lived a triple exile: as purported Jews, they were exiled from Zion; as Conversos, they were cut off from the mainstream of Jewish life; and as Judaizers, they lived in exile from their host society.

Furthermore, dissimulation is not a mere facade, nor does it produce semblances only. A life of dissimulation has its own dialectic, which often breaks the simplistic line between what is considered *real* and what is taken to be *mere appearance*, and reverses their roles. Judaizers might have told themselves that their Catholicism was merely an appearance, yet in most cases it took up the lion's share of their actual lives, penetrated their thoughts, determined their social action and the targets of their ambition, and affected the way in which they applied their supposedly Jewish values to actual situations. Thereby, over time, that which had been considered *inessential* (Christianity) became the essential thing in their lives, whereas the supposedly *essential* aspect (being Jewish) receded into an abstract hope or illusion.

Nor is this the final stage. At a certain point, *duality as such*—the split identity, whose several faces mirror each other—becomes the actual substance of life, its very essence. At this stage, the former essential and the former inessential aspects *both become inessential*: both are inadequate characterizations of the Conversos' form of life because of their self-identity. Rather, Converso life consists of the inter-penetration and the back and forth shifts between these poles. The outer life affects the inner, and vice versa, and the Judaizer is *indeed*—not only in the view of rabbis and theologians—neither truly a Jew nor actually a Christian.

In one of many such dualities, Juana Rodrigues of Ciudad Real confessed to the Inquisition that she had chosen a Saturday as the day on which to baptize her two-year-old son into Catholicism because of her "affection" (*afición*) for the day Saturday and the opportunity this gave her to celebrate it as a legitimate holiday.[22] A more resentful duality was manifest in Inez López, who used to secretly rest on Saturdays but broke her habit and worked on one particular Saturday because it coincided with a Catholic holiday, the May Day of the Holy Cross, which she refused to celebrate![23]

Thus the Judaizers included several subgroups, some of which were in dynamic change: the disappearing genuine Jews; the determined Judaizers; the resenting protesters; and the enfeebled, nostalgic drifters, whose growing number made them overlap with the two other major groups: the assimilated Catholics on the one hand, and the religious skeptics and early rationalists on the other. Needless to say, further subgroups and individual varieties existed, some partly overlapping, so no classification should be taken too rigidly.

Exclusion or Syncretism?

We must not confuse the Judaizers' dualities with religious syncretism, as it is known especially in some Eastern (Asian) religions. In the East it is often legitimate to conjoin elements from different religions and cults; there is more than one single way to please the gods or reach metaphysical bliss. Yet the three Western monotheistic religions tend to be considered mutually exclusive, both by themselves and their rivals; therefore, mixing them together is illegitimate from the standpoint of each religion. This incompatibility was even more pronounced in late medieval Spain, when the forces of exclusion and particularism were gathering formidable momentum, and could not but affect their victims' minds as well. The semi-Christianized, Judaizing Marranos were split between two rival traditions and paths to salvation which they, too, considered incompatible. Thus they were not peacefully enjoying the syncretic benefits of different traditions, but living in an irresolvable ambivalence and tension—indeed, a contradiction—affecting both the single person and the group.[24]

One form of duality was the attempt to rationalize the religion to which one adhered by discovering the other religion hidden in it. Diego López, a simple Converso accepting his Catholicism, said: "To tell the truth, what is said in the Mass are the Psalms which the Jews say in their prayers, and the Epistles are prophesies of the Jews, and the Evangel is Genesis. So all is [actually] the Old Law, and all is good."[25] On the other side, a Judaizing Converso cited Jesus as his example: "The Law of Moses is a good law, which is why our Lord Jesus Christ wanted to be a Jew for thirty-three years, and to be circumcised."[26]

Is this a form of syncretism? Or a subjective compromise of elements that in themselves are irreconcilable? Syncretism implies a basic compatibility of foreign elements; yet Marrano dualities often involved an inner competition between the two paths to God and salvation, in which some particular ingredients were combined. Even so, subjectively, a person might wish to hold together two elements that in themselves deny the validity of such a conjunction. So, in terms of a person's state of mind, syncretism may seem possible even between incompatibles; but then it is no longer a reconciled, peaceful union, but inner tension, as described previously.

Moreover, syncretism is far from capturing the split identity of the New Christians, which was not purely theological but often involved ethnic, racial, familial, sociological, and even economic factors of identity. So the adequate terms for analyzing Marrano dualities must be taken from the broader issue of identity rather than the narrow theological context to which the concept of syncretism is confined.

A cynical form of incompatible duality was used by Juan de Talavera. Having broken a sworn promise, he explained that "he had two faiths, one good and one bad, and he had sworn in the name of the bad faith—the Jewish—keeping the good [Christian] faith to himself."[27] This cynic used a Judaizer's technique—the inner annulment of outer pronouncements—to justify ordinary treachery.

Discovering the Inner Self

With all their dualities, Judaizing Marranos shared a new pattern of experience. They learned to value religious truth as residing in the depth of the mind rather than in outer acts and behavior. Thus the inner domain rose in importance and worth, while opposing the outer world. One did not enter the inner world as something already given, however, but as a discovery, the revelation of something that has all along been unnoticed, disregarded, downgraded, or veiled by an excess of outer activity. Both Catholicism and Judaism are mostly outward-directed cultures, stressing works, acts, ritual; but now, with the Judaizing Marranos, the inner self became the most important dimension of the person's life, and the main source of meaning that justified what the Marrano is and does in opposition to society. To be vindicated in their opposition, the Marranos unwittingly sowed the seeds of a new principle—*inner conscience* (and the single self that bears it)—as a deeper and higher authority than convention, and as worthy of risk and sacrifice.

This process required stages. At first, the Marrano's dissent could rely on the support of an institutional religion—Judaism—which, although the Marrano was forbidden to practice, nevertheless existed in the Spanish space as a living tradition and institution. (The support was mental no less than practical, based on the belief that only traditions justify.) But after the Jews were expelled from Spain and the Inquisition went on to burn Judaizers, Judaism ceased to be a supporting reality for them and became a dream, an object of receding hope and fantasy. The Judaizers became increasingly lonely and secluded, depending more on the resources of their own solitary selves—on memory, hope, vision, and personal conviction. For them authentic religion had been *deinstitutionalized* and *privatized*—not merely in the sense that it was concealed inside the home, but also of depending on the inner heart as its almost sole support. There were, of course, supporting fragments of memory and custom, and the sense of a secret fraternity; but these could not offset the weight of the outer society without the rising force of personal truth and commitment (that is, of a personal religious conscience). In the end, and all along, the person had to face the most important religious truths—decisions about value, and about personal fate in this and the next world—within a private "inner forum." Thus emerges the Self—or human subjectivity—hesitantly and, again, in stages: first as the locus of true religious worth; then as the judge and bearer of value in general; and later, as the object of self-affirmation and of self-investigation and exploration. These are all hallmarks of modernity (see chapter 19), of which the

Marrano experience injected important rudiments into Renaissance Spain and early modern Europe.

The Assimilated

A similar and sometimes overlapping variety of Converso duality existed also among those who assimilated into Catholicism. A major goal of assimilation was social and economic integration. Former Jews hoped to reap the fruits of conversion by shedding their old restrictions and entering the dominant society as full members—even penetrating its higher echelons, which seemed to be possible at first. On a deeper level, these social and economic drives were linked to the person's self-image and existential prospect—to the realization of what this person was, or could become, as an individual in this world—which in many cases implied that the *present* world, and the person's individual standing within it, rose in importance relative to religious and communal concerns and the prospect of transcendent salvation.

This does not mean that assimilation to Catholicism was only instrumental or insincere. Many people seem to need a religion by which to structure and interpret their lives, to give them orientation and meaning. This was even more so in the fifteenth century. Various assimilated Conversos started looking to Catholicism to fulfill some of these roles for them. Even the more worldly Conversos often accepted Catholicism as the low-keyed ritual religion that now conformed to their new social or economic situation, while also infusing their ordinary lives with festive occasions and an arsenal of symbolic interpretations. Still, as human affairs are complex, this did not always keep them from also marginally indulging in residual Judaism as a personal inclination or weakness, lacking serious intent.

The Drifters and Accommodators

Indeed, the bulk of Conversos eventually assimilated to a significant (if not always to a full) degree. Among them, the majority seemed to have been the drifters and accommodators—those who wished to be absorbed into the dominant Christian society and culture in one way or another, though not necessarily in the submissive and mimetic manner demanded by the church. Alongside them there were the spiritual seekers (discussed later in this chapter), who wanted to assimilate to a less routine and conventional Catholicism.

The drifters did not manifest a strong determination either way, but accommodated themselves rather passively to their new sociocultural environment. They did so with little defiance and resolution and often without religious tension, letting the needs and circumstances of life be their guide. (As a popular saying had it: "More Jews have become Christians by pork and ham than by the Holy Faith.")[28]

Still, we must not think of this process as easy or simple in any way. As in any case of integrating a minority, there were hard obstacles to surmount, constraints to respect, social and emotional prices to pay, inner and outer difficulties to cope with, new friendships to cultivate, and opposing loyalties to balance. Thus, despite the overall passive nature in which their new Catholic identity was being assumed, accommodation often required activity and much exertion from those involved in it.

The forces of drifting and accommodating drew the assimilated Conversos toward a new center of gravity and a solidified Catholic routine. Accompanying this force, however, and constantly undermining its solidity, were *restlessness and confusion*. Having been first Jews and then Catholics, many assimilating Conversos tended—like the Judaizers—to mix the two religious cultures together (often in a natural, unintended way), and this kept them from finding rest in a stable new identity. Actually, religious disquiet and confusion were compatible with other diverse Converso features and often accompanied and underlay them.

For some Conversos, the blurring of the boundaries between the two religions made it easier to accept Catholicism, because it reduced the dissonance involved in conversion and the crisis it provoked. If Christianity was not that far from Judaism (or was its fruition, as some Converso theologians maintained), or if both religions were but popular beliefs that an enlightened rationalist should not take too seriously, or if people could be saved in whatever monotheistic religion into which they were born—then conversion signified a primarily social transformation rather than a deep personal and existential one. Yet even this stance was liable to produce an unclear identity and strengthen the sense of duality, leading to an even greater disharmony between the individual person and the whole religious culture.

Nostalgia versus Hope

Nostalgic Judaizing was a wide ranging phenomenon, especially among assimilated Marranos. Nostalgia is the reverse counterpart of hope; but there is also a major difference between the two. Nostalgia is essentially unreal longing, a relation to a memory whose object is known to have irrevocably passed away and is accepted as such. It is because of that fundamental acceptance that nostalgia draws its gloomy kind of pleasure from playing with the mere traces and vestiges of those disappeared objects, knowing the originals will never recur.[29] Nostalgia does not bear the seeds of change, it only indulges in the sadness arising from the knowledge its object can no longer be retrieved. Whereas hope (at least in one of its major varieties) looks forward to a different reality; it longs for a new real time, however distant, when the dream might be actualized. Both forms of longing are based on a leap of the imagination, a shortcut between a bypassed reality and some absent state in the past or the future; and nostalgia, furthermore, is often also based on an imagined memory; but of the two, hope alone has an outlet from the imagined to the possibly real. Therefore, while hope was a typical structure of the active Judaizers, nostalgic Judaizing characterized those Conversos who drifted and assimilated with neither the hope nor the wish to become Jewish again.

The Determined Neophytes

There were also those who, realizing there was no way back to actual Judaism, made the *voluntary* decision to accept their enforced situation and make the best of it, or rather, build a new identity around it. The phenomenon of neophytes who become more fervently attached to their new identity than its old guard is well known among immigrants, minorities, and ideological renegades. There is an urgent will to assert oneself through the new cultural medium: the anxiety to prove one's loyalty; the haste to leap over great cultural gaps unknown to the Old Christians; and the embarrassment and shame surrounding anything pertaining to one's old world, which sometimes evolves into outright hostility and hatred toward it.

The converts' Jewish background and Spain's intolerant atmosphere gave this phenomenon a special Marrano tinge. Precisely because, as former Jews, they were sensitive to the betrayal that conversion involved in Jewish terms, many Conversos were anxious to totally eradicate those Jewish terms and justify themselves by embracing their new religion with even greater ardor than was expected of them. It was as though by defying their old conscience (the product of a previous identity) they declared flagrantly, "Yes, this is what I will become!" Needless to say, this militant posture was far from expressing a natural integration into Catholicism. It was—like its opposite, active Judaizing—rather an act of the will, which is often severed from the person's actual life yet asserts itself as the superior principle. In this respect there was a self-induced Catholic identity in these Conversos, and their Catholic faithfulness, or at least their outward single-mindedness, was actually a form of duality (which quite often implies self-deception).

Over time, as one generation gave way to the next, this semiabstract, partly artificial acceptance of Catholicism started to breed more routine, perhaps more natural (though still not quite integral) forms of Catholic acculturation that, together with the phenomenon we called drifting, combined to produce the extensive movement of Converso assimilation that took place in the fifteenth century.[30]

Marrano Anti-Judaism

Actually, there were two kinds of eager Catholics among the Conversos, the dedicated and the resentful: those who found a positive meaning in their new religion and those who could find no rest and meaning in life except by negating and eventually persecuting their old way of life and the people who still embodied it. This form of *ressentiment* (as Nietzsche would call it) led some Conversos to become not only zealous Catholics but ferociously anti-Jewish. Shedding their Jewish identity meant to these Conversos that they must consider it a foe, an enemy that threatened both their old repressed conscience and their future existential prospects; so in order to suppress *their own* Jewish identity they had to repress it in *others*.

Thus a small but determined group of Conversos emerged, who strongly agitated against the Jews, denounced them in pamphlets and learned tracts, and lobbied for discriminatory policies against them. From their circles arose much of the fierce propaganda that led to the establishment of the Inquisition in the late 1470s and to the expulsion of the Jews from Spain by the end of the century. The irony was that the more these converts sought to disengage from the Jews by denouncing them, the more ammunition they provided their own enemies. For who were the Conversos in their foes' eyes if not Jews? With the introduction of the *blood purity* policies, the anti-Jewish polemic by Conversos boomeranged. The anti-Jewish tracts written by Conversos were still in circulation a century after no single Jew remained in Spain—and whom could they have targeted, if not the author's own Converso descendents and kinsmen?

The "Christianizers"

Of course, those who found positive meaning in Christianity were not passive drifters. They actively willed and intended to adopt their new religion. But this did not necessarily mean they fully understood what being Christian entailed. And many willing Christians, even in later generations, continued to manifest Jewish habits and modes of thinking and interpreting the world. Some even preferred to retain a few semi-Jewish residues (food, gesture, habit, or mental pattern) in their daily lives as Christians, without compromising their commitment to the Cross; and they expected their host society to accept, and their own Christian identity to sustain, this kind of variety. However, this presumed right was never openly admitted, and later in the century it was denied them with a bang by the Inquisition, which declared total war on variety and difference. The inquisitors classified these people as *Judaizers* regardless of their own will and intention. Yet, to be more discerning, we might rather call them *Christianizers*. By this concept I mean a certain duality of both religious cultures in which the will and intention to be Christian dominates. We can fairly assume that many of the victims of the Inquisition possessed this particular form of duality. They willed and intended to be Christians, but realized this choice in such a way that their dominant Catholicism was interlaced with Jewish ingredients or mentalities that lost their religious meaning and became forms of social tradition or folklore. This peculiar combination was maintained either as a conscious preference, or passively, even without full awareness.[31]

As defined above, the category of Christianizers could be used as an analytical tool for better comprehending (and classifying) the Converso phenomenon.[32]

The Spiritual Seekers

A special variety of Christian-oriented Marranos were the spiritual seekers, who proved to be of great historical consequence for Spanish culture (see chapter 15). These people, a minority group no doubt, refused to assimilate into Spanish Christianity as it was, and looked instead for a deeper, less conventional Christian experience with which they could identify. For these Conversos, the only way they could accept their new religion was by *changing* it—going beyond its routinized form toward a more complex, unorthodox, and spiritualized version of Christianity.

This was not always a conscious or well-defined demand. It was often vague, groping for something it did not quite articulate, and often needed external input and reinforcement from Christian humanists like Erasmus and other sources in order to take a more effective shape. But as a structural condition and drive, it was there from the start. People, who by personal inclination were more spiritually bent, or had deeper attitudes toward religion than the average person, felt it was improper, almost a sacrilege to simply exchange one religious routine for another. If they had to cast off their former religious identity, it had to be for the sake of a finer form of Christianity than the one practiced ordinarily. This trend became even more marked in subsequent generations, when the offspring of former Judaizers started to willingly assimilate into Christianity; it produced some interesting and exciting forms of duality, and in the sixteenth century it helped generate what is sometimes known as the Spanish *Pre-Reformation*.

A subgroup among the reform seekers looked for a Christian experience that incorporated elements of their Jewish past, and thereby recognized their legitimacy as Judeo-Christians. Why, they protested (usually to themselves), should being a faithful Christian require the complete eradication of all one's Jewish ingredients? Wouldn't the Christian experience be deepened and further spiritualized if it assimilated and sublimated some Jewish elements—as Christianity is said to have done in its origin? This was not a plea for Judaizing because it was made with a Christianizing intent. The aim was to make the new religion more congenial to those who could not accept its orthodox and/or exclusionist form.

The two objects of reform were not necessarily linked; but sometimes they coincided in the belief that a better, more spiritual Christianity must be more supple and receptive to its own Jewish origin. Psychologically, this allowed a subjective rapprochement of the two religious identities to take place under the sign of the Cross, now admitted as the higher and overall truth. (For more on the spiritual seekers see chapters 14 and 15.)

It is interesting that a similar (though not identical) pattern occurred among postemancipation Jews in the nineteenth century, who adhered to various ideological movements or utopias—liberalism, nationalism, socialism, and so on—in the (not always conscious) hope of rediscovering a rarefied form of the Jewish religion they were leaving in the shape of the modern world to which they were assimilating. However, those modern Jews were seeking a secular substitute to religion, whereas the Marrano spiritual seekers we are discussing had sought the answer within the traditional world of religion and, indeed within Christianity itself. The world outside the *aljama* (community) they were joining was not yet the modern world, but a universe still dominated by a medieval Christian culture.

The This-Worldly, the Skeptics, the Heretics

Alongside the Judaizers, the assimilated, and the spiritual seekers, we should consider a most important further category: those who, in one way or another, left both Judaism and Christianity and, in fact, transcended the boundaries of any historical revealed religion.

The Career Seekers: Early Individualism and Secularism

The fact that many Marranos had manifested a keen interest in their personal careers, and were eager to join mainstream Catholicism primarily for that reason, indicates a weakened religious interest among them. Less concerned with life before God and in the next world, they attached a major premium to one's *this-worldly* existence, individual person, achievements, and worth. This caused an early form of individualism—in some respects, even of protomodernity—to emerge on the Spanish and European scene along with the Marranos. Unlike the later Calvinists, whose disposition for this world was infused with religious significance and derived (on Weber's analysis) from a strong interest in salvation, here we can see the beginnings of a secularism that, on the contrary, was increasingly indifferent to religion and replaced transcendent salvation with a this-worldly *career* as a major drive in one's life.

A career is not just any kind of endeavor or achievement. One pursues a career on one's own—as an individual—and for the sake of personal (or familial) fulfillment in the present world. By contrast, people who are integrated in traditional societies, even when they seek success, are not quite following a *career* drive; the term applies more aptly to this-worldly interests and to a dominant personal perspective, quite detached from the person's communal roles and traditional social and religious allegiances. These features existed in many Conversos who no longer manifested the dominant medieval allegiance to a religious denomination. Torn from their traditional society, these particular Marranos were not really integrated into a new one, but were left by and large on their own, and many in the subgroup we are considering had worldly interests which overshadowed the transcendent perspectives of both Judaism and Catholicism.

In this way, the forced conversions that seemed to be a major victory for religion—even in its extremist and intolerant face—were actually, beneath the surface, seething with secular, this-worldly, individualistic rudiments that tacitly challenged the ruling Hispanic culture, even though they were still too weak to transform it.

In the opinion of Francisco Márquez Villanueva, a major historian of the Conversos, those who abandoned both religions and developed a heretical attitude "toward every supernatural perspective" (what I call an *immanentist* philosophy)[33] were much more numerous than the Judaizers and constituted a culturally more important group—so important, that Márquez Villanueva sees them as the key to "the widespread rationalist, restless, and irreverent spirit which sweeps the subterranean current" of Spanish culture in the next century.[34] While numbers are difficult to evaluate, there is no doubt that an important cultural and religious phenomenon was developing here, with far reaching effects in later generations.

The narrow-sighted records of the Inquisition, seeing Judaizing everywhere, tend to describe these earth-bound tendencies as crude Jewish materialism. Thus, in the city of Soria, Juan López was denounced to the Inquisition as having declared: "Say what you like, I don't believe there is any other god but money" (*FIRC*, 2, no. 325). And the Converso merchant Gonzalo del Rincón reportedly said: "You see? There is no other law in this world than acquisition; whoever possesses is respected, and he who has no possession is discarded" (*FIRC*, 2, no. 153). Another Converso flatly declared: "Acquiring is everything; there is no paradise but property" (*FIRC*, 2, no. 297). And in an even more pointed epigram, a Converso declared: "There is no more paradise but the market in Calatayud."[35] While these quotations would fit the hostile stereotype of the Jew as "worshiping only Mammon," here they echo the confused and dwindling religious mind of the Conversos who, caught between Judaism and Christianity, shift their concerns away from religion toward their secular, worldly, and, indeed, mainly economic interests. With the death of Transcendence, the immanent, actual world becomes the sole arena in which mortals can project their existence and realize their lives "between birth and death"; and with the decline of inherited authority, one's worldly will arises as a crucial factor. Conversos wavering between religious truths had to rely on their own will, and on the world in which it was exercised, as a substitute to salvation. Thus the combination of will plus world replaced religion as the center of existence.

The Proto-Universalists

Parallel and, in a way, contrary to the negation of all revealed faiths, an *affirmation* of all three monotheistic religions also arose from the ruptured Marrano experience. It reached articulation in the dictum that "every person can be saved by his own religion." This early universalist religious trend arose especially (though not exclusively) among former Judaizers and their descendants. Rather than abandoning the religious sphere altogether, they *broadened* it to make legitimate room—separate but equal—for both their new and older religious identities. This move made it possible for them to avoid the conflict of mutual exclusion between Christianity and Judaism, although it did not exempt the individual person from making a choice—or rather, from following the logic of a fundamental choice already made.

The point of this broad-minded approach was not so much to legitimize the practice of Judaism (after all, these people were officially Catholic, so they were supposed to be saved in this religion); the point was rather to defend a plural-ist view of the monotheistic experience, opposing the wave of intolerance then overtaking Spain. No wonder the Inquisition, the paragon of Spanish intoler-ance, set out to wipe away such heretical views with fire.

In an even stronger assertion of this outlook the Converso priest Juan Rodrigues declared that "God created three religions, and no one can tell which is the best" (*FIRC*, 2, no. 62). His words recall the famous fable of the three rings told by Boccaccio in the fourteenth century and retold by Lessing in the eigh-teenth. But in fifteenth-century Spain this motif assumed a Converso meaning and shape. It not only defied the closing of the Spanish mind but suggested a new kind of religious tolerance that went far beyond the old system of *conviven-cia* (the coexistence of the three monotheistic religions). In that celebrated sys-tem there was always one dominant religion (be it Islam or Christianity) which alone was true, while the other two religions, though tolerated and protected, were treated as false and inferior. By contrast, the Marrano dictum that no one can know which religion is the best could be construed as denying there is a *best* religion and putting all monotheistic creeds on equal footing. This view was infinitely more daring for its time than the (already discredited) support for *convivencia*.

Taking this bold idea a dangerous step further, one could attribute the equal-ity of the monotheistic religions to some essential features that are common to them all, and in which their true religious value resides. This protouniversalism planted the seeds (which took a long time to sprout) of a nonparticularistic *natural* religion open to everyone, that implicitly *negated* all historical religions as such.

In this way, the broad affirmation of the three religions touched base with the negation of all three. From claiming that all historical religions can lead to salva-tion, some people moved to the notion that no religion can save (precisely because of its excessive historical burden)—and even that the very project of salvation had to be abandoned, or redefined in terms of secular goals and achievements.

Early Secularism, Irreligiosity, and the Crisis of Transcendence

Secularism does not in itself mean agnosticism or atheism, though it can. Its basic or narrow sense indicates that religion has been removed from its central place, and that worldly affairs have gained the upper hand, not only in one's ordinary pursuits but also in one's perception of the source of authority, the meaning of life, worthwhile goals (such as happiness), and even salvation (or its worldly substitute).[36] In some Marranos this shift was linked to an even more radical move, which led them to religious skepticism and beyond. The mixture of Judaism and Christianity made some Conversos weary of both. Having first been *Jewish*, then *Christian*, then *both* Jewish and Christian, these Conversos ended up being *neither*. Transcending the very concept of a historical religion, they moved either to several forms of skepticism and utter irreligiosity, or toward a variety of deism—affirming God's existence on rational grounds, but denying his involvement in human affairs.

Consequently, religious ideas as basic as God's Revelation, Providence, the Incarnation, the next world, and divine law were either doubted or flatly rejected. Even the idea of a personal God was not totally immune to disbelief. But most negations aimed at the idea of transcendence—the existence and superior value of God's separate realm, the great beyond, in front of which our actual world is supposed to pale.

A heretical slogan made headway among these Conversos: *There is nothing but living and dying in this world; what allegedly lies beyond the world is empty speculation.* Another saying denying the world beyond was: *You won't see me suffer in this world or burn in the next.* This crude "philosophy of immanence" did not arise from the conscious meditation of a learned elite; more often it was a kind of lived philosophy, not clearly articulated. It was basically a practical attitude toward existence, based on sentiment and popular deliberation rather than on deep and thorough examination, and failing to attain systematic shape. Even so, it planted the seeds of a new rationalism in some Conversos, who hesitantly—and of course secretly—started relying on the powers of reason and this-worldly experience more than on revealed, transmitted tradition. (And, in the next step, they turned toward reliance on their own human and personal will.)

In Soria, Diego Mexía, a man of the church, was heard saying: "Don't let them put into your head, lady, that there is paradise and hell; for there is nothing but being born and dying, living in the company of a good female friend, and good food; there is but being born and dying" (*FIRC*, 2, no. 151).[37] Another witness saw and heard Pero Gómez el Chamorro "pouring abuse on time, the earth, and the air, saying there is nothing but to be born and to die." He also said, "I bet God that the soul doesn't exist" (*FIRC*, 2, no. 185). This is the same attitude we analyzed above, but tinged with defiant desperation, a sense of angry loss. A further step toward full atheism was taken by Alonso Carnicero who "was angry and said that *God does not exist* . . . heaven and earth were not created by God, and the sun moves in its own course" (*FIRC*, 2, no. 282, my emphasis). He too expresses metaphysical anger, a painful awakening or realization.

This evidence should modify a famous thesis by the French historian Lucien Febvre, denying that atheism was possible in the wake of the Middle Ages.[38] What was impossible or unheard of was not religious skepticism, or even atheism per se, but the attempt to legitimize and express them in public. Everything we hear about such attitudes was expressed in private, even in clandestine settings, as illicit thinking.[39]

The nascent atheism among the Conversos—in the sense, above all, of denying transcendence—had to be kept private with the same anxious concern with which Judaizers concealed their Law of Moses. As such, these Conversos became the precursors of a new type of Marranism that was to arise in future centuries, precursors of those I call the Marranos of Reason.[40]

In the Soria records a priest is reported to have asked of a New Christian, "why the Jews have converted, since they keep no religion, neither that of the Christians nor that of the Jews" (*FIRC*, 2, no. 231). And Juan de Salzedo, in prison on a life sentence, heard Pero Nuñes declare: "I disbelieve in both Jesus and Moses" (*FIRC*, 2, no. 129). This motif recurs in innumerable cases, satirical poems, and pamphlets, and in inquisitorial records.

A special dialectic was at work here, whereby the official repression of Judaism—especially in the second and third generations of Marranism—rekindled the memory of Judaism in certain assimilated Conversos, while in others, embarrassed and disgusted by that revival, it reinforced the denial of their Jewish past and the desire to discard it completely. The tension between those two trends favored the emergence of the third option—denying the exclusive way to salvation claimed by many, or even denying the very prospect of salvation, at least when understood as aiming at the next world and as mediated by a particular religious revelation and ritual.

Further indications of irreligiosity and heresy in the Soria records are described in the following pages.

Denial of Creation

Of course, like police reports, inquisitorial records tend to impoverish people's statements by framing their testimonies into preestablished formulas. Yet the saying "there is nothing but living and dying in this world" resounds in the files of the Inquisition in such diverse forms, times, and places, that it must have been drawn from actual usage. It served Conversos of a certain bent as a shortcut, a kind of code word for private confidences and communication. The existence of this worldview is indirectly attested by other materials in the files and by independent literary sources whose equivocal texts provide an abundance of covert information to anyone willing to read between the lines, as texts of this nature must be read.[41]

Here are a few more voices from Soria. Marín Pérez from Gormaz declared: "God does not have the power to do either good or bad" (FIRC, 2, no. 365). And Fernand de Guernica el Viejo went further: "After God had created the world, he left everyone to be on his own, for good or bad" (FIRC, 2, no. 373).[42] The first claim denies God's providence, the second adopts outright deism. And if these heresies were not enough, another Converso denied the Creation and even God's very existence: "He said there is no God, . . . and that the heavens and the earth had been there [always] and weren't created by God, and the sun too was turning in its course" (FIRC, 2, no. 282). When threatened with excommunication, this man answered in agitation: "Mind your [own] soul! For there is no God, no Santa María and no excommunication, all is sheer mockery [burla]."[43]

Some of these statements were made in anger. "I deny the son of a bitch Jewish God," one Converso blasted. By Jewish God he meant, of course, Jesus, but also the God of the Old Testament, thus packing a double blasphemy into a single outburst (FIRC, 2, no. 180). Calmer expressions of radical heresy were also reported. On several occasions, the blacksmith Pedro el Herrero "negated God or Saint Mary" (FIRC, 2, no. 50), and Pedro Texero avowed to a Franciscan that he "did not believe in God" (FIRC, 2, no. 105).

The speakers quoted above were simple people. But intellectuals too took part in this irreligious tendency to an even greater extent. An outstanding example is the Celestina, the classic Spanish play written at the end of the fifteenth century by the Converso Fernando de Rojas.[44] In addition to constantly alluding to the Converso predicament, it also contains a hidden irreligious metaphysics that depicts the universe as a metaphysical wasteland lacking any transcendent horizon, and thereby denies Christianity, Judaism, and revealed religion in general. The universe is but a disorderly play of forces, of which love—or rather, erotic passion—is the most powerful, yet is always in excess and never redeeming. As the action unfolds, the image of the desired woman ironically usurps the role of the Christian God as the true deity. She also becomes the aspired-to source of "salvation," which, however, turns sour in the play's unhappy end. The work culminates in a harsh secular metaphysics almost anticipating Nietzsche's: there is only this world, which is meaningless in itself, a "vale of tears" in which only personal achievement—planting trees, building ships, gathering wealth, rearing a beloved daughter—can adduce sense; and when this inner-worldly sense is lost, nothing is left and there is no redemption.[45]

Is it accidental that the author's father-in-law, Alvaro de Montalbán, was also heard declaring there is only life in this world? Alvaro was by then seventy years old. Many years earlier he had been the object of another accusation: presumably he had participated in a Passover celebration, and was caught breaking the fast of Lent by eating meat and drinking milk. Was he a Judaizer then? Only partly so, for he sinned against Judaism (by eating meat and dairy products together) just as he sinned against Christianity (by eating meat during Lent). Judging by Alvaro's later trial, he must by then already have been a religious skeptic and dualist who—like his famous son-in-law, but in a simpler and less sophisticated way—was a heretic to both religions and a believer, without much optimism, in this world alone.

Thus the negation of both religions had diverse shapes and results, including: (1) rationalism and religious skepticism; (2) spiritual reform of Christianity; (3) protouniversalism and deism; and (4) worldly secularism. In all these forms, the Marrano experience had later influenced important, if sometimes covert, cultural trends in Iberia and, even later, when Marranos started to emigrate from the Iberian Peninsula—in Western Europe as well.

It is noteworthy that with all the variations due to place and generation, the basic patterns recur in almost all periods. Secret Judaizing, uncertain assimilation, unorthodox Christianity, excessive Catholic zeal, a dissenting spiritual drive, a heightened sense of this-worldliness, as well as abandoning the religious orbit altogether and taking to skepticism, rationalism, and even semiatheism— all recur in later centuries, even as Conversos openly returned to Judaism in the seventeenth century,[46] or tried to cope with their ancestral memories and dualities in the New World, after having been manifest already in the first Marrano generations. What distinguished the fifteenth century is that the Conversos still lived alongside a large, tolerated Jewish community; and that until the middle of the century, Spanish society was still fairly receptive to the New Christians, and no Inquisition had yet existed to harass them.[47]

The categories of Marranos discussed in this chapter are still broad, and made for the sake of analysis. In real life several groups intersected and none is illustrated in its purity by one single individual. But as a recurring grid, present in most Marrano periods, they will facilitate a better understanding of the complexity of the Marrano phenomenon, which allowed no simple, *integral* Marrano self, but split the structures of identity (and allegiance) in several ways, all forbidden by the dominant Spanish culture, which had to resort to terror and violence in order to maintain its fantasy of a unique, integral Spanish identity. Powerful remnants of that illusion survived for five centuries. They started to disperse only in the last quarter of the twentieth century following the death of Generalissimo Franco. Today it has become almost fashionable for Spaniards and Portuguese to claim some Jewish-Marrano ancestry, or to speak with nostalgia of the "Spain of the three religions."[48] But even today, with its Basque and Catalan questions,

Spain still needs the broader framework of Europe in order to successfully deal with its unresolved problem of unified identity: it needs, that is, the late-modern view of plural identity and plural allegiance—the same ideas that the Judeo-Conversos have represented in their various dualities, and for which, consciously or not, they stood and struggled in the era of the Inquisition.

6

Marrano Mosaic I: Places, Persons, Poems

<hr>

The dualities of the Marrano situation—and mind—stand out from an abundance of materials—trial records, personal stories, prayers, customs, and popular poems. In the following cluster of illustrations we shall sketch the portraits of several different Marranos, visit a great Catholic monastery affected by Marranism, and listen to popular Marrano poets of the late fifteenth century, whose crude verses, often sad and ironical (and sometimes quite vulgar), depict, satirize, or lament their peculiar dualisms.[1] Such materials are priceless since the novels, poems, and even vulgar rhymes of another era can serve as cogent sources of historical understanding in a way that dry chronicles cannot.[2]

The Synagogue of Saint Jerome

In the popular fifteenth-century play written by the Converso Fernando de Rojas, an old procuress and archwhore, Celestina, promises a client: "I shall travel to monasteries where people 'are devoted to my worship' and order them to pray for the success of your [illicit sexual] designs." The surface irony refers to secret fornication by monks, yet on a more covert level it alludes to the fact that some Catholic convents in Spain were reputed to harbor Conversos who secretly practiced Jewish rites.[3]

Among these monasteries, none was more magnificent than Nuestra Señora de Guadalupe, the leading sanctuary of the order of St. Jerome. To this day it stands majestically on its hilltop, radiating its past splendor (and present enticement) over the green-and-brownish fertile landscape. Visitors flock to admire not only the imposing complex, an amalgam of church and military architecture, but also the mysterious effigy of the dark-faced Virgin. The Dark Lady is said to have been buried there by monks fleeing the Arab invasion in 714. After the Reconquest the Dark Lady made a miraculous apparition to a simple herdsman and revealed her place of burial. The house of prayer built on that venerated site evolved into a great Spanish place of worship, a longtime favorite of kings and popes.

In 1389, the order of Hieronymite monks turned the site into their main bastion. Amassing riches and political influence, the Guadalupe monastery in the next century developed an ethos that cherished spirituality but rejected asceticism. The same friars practiced solitary meditation *and* managed the monastery's vast assets in land, livestock, and cash. To critics who called Guadalupe "corrupt," a leading prior responded that his monastery's mission was not mendicancy, but the shaping of a different kind of religiosity. They sought a religious experience compatible with worldly work; they stressed celebration rather than asceticism; and they believed in *hospitality*—implying an early form of toleration—instead of the harsh religious intolerance practiced in Spain.[4]

These features made Guadalupe a magnet for Conversos. For nearly two generations, the monastery had been the site of covert Judaizing, which won it the sobriquet *the synagogue of Saint Jerome*. While Judaizing monks also lived in other Hieronymite convents (one near Toledo is also recorded),[5] Guadalupe was the most spectacular case. We know about it from an internal Hieronymite inquisition which, in 1485, put an abrupt end to this extraordinary phenomenon, the practice of Judaism—or what looked like Judaism—under the protection of a Catholic saint.[6]

The climate of suspicion blurred the inquisitors' eyes into branding all irregular conduct by Conversos as "Jewish," making them miss the complexity of the phenomenon before them. To assess their findings critically, we should make some crucial distinctions, as between:

(1) Dissent *from* Christianity, which is performed with an explicit Jewish intent and is expressed in actual Judaizing;
(2) Dissent *within* Christianity, which accepts the basic message of Jesus but looks for a more spiritual, enlightened, or less superstitious Christianity;
(3) The various shades of *residual Judaism* that can be traced in some converts, whether they are (a) sincere Catholics, or (b) marked by duality and existential confusion, or (c) skeptics who used these illicit residues to express dissent from any historical religion whatever.

Let us now imagine a contemporary visitor—a discerning spy—who spent time in the monastery and, having penetrated into some of its secrets, sends the following report to the Archbishop of M.[7]

Prayer, Sabbath, and pork:
I am sure Your Grace would have been as startled as I was when Fray Juan de Madrid told me in all candor that he "had become a monk for no other reason than for being able to better practice the law of the Jews."[8] This is not an isolated

case. The monks in Guadalupe spend hours of solitude in their cells, which gives them numerous opportunities to practice Jewish rites. As another active Judaizer, Brother Alonso de Toledo, explained to me, "among us no one could know what the others were praying" (ibid). Some acts are quite daring, perhaps because no strict measures are taken against them. For example, the master of novices, Fray Pedro de Madrid, lights Sabbath candles in his cell every Friday night. Several weeks ago he was surprised by a novice—and had the young man expelled from the monastery. This was by no means an isolated case. The unholy spectacle of Catholic monks greeting the Jewish Sabbath with candles in their cells has become so common in this monastery that Fray Diego de Paris, the prior, sternly warned a group of offenders against the practice. But lacking the necessary bite, I suspect that his warning will not eradicate this grave offense; it will only make it less conspicuous for a while.

At table, several monks show disgust for pork, the food Jews loath the most, and use various stratagems to avoid it. I saw Brothers Francisco de Burgos and Francisco de Toledo shove their pork plates to an Old Christian neighbor, claiming it was "bad for their stomach" (p. 98). Another monk goes regularly out of the refectory after eating pork and regurgitates his meal, while Fray Diego de Segovia simply skips all meals in which pork is served.

Sacrament or "torta":
Your Grace will be distressed to hear that New Christian monks in Guadalupe often show disrespect to Holy sacraments. Many evade communion, break fasts, make false confessions (inevitably so, because a true confession will expose their double game), and express doubt, even derision, concerning the fundaments of Christian dogma. A common target of theirs is the sacrament of the Eucharist, the cornerstone of our Holy Faith. Just as Jews and Moors have never been able to grasp how God could be embodied in a mortal man—nor how, by a mysterious ritual, ordinary bread and wine can transform into that man's body and blood—so, I discovered, there are monks in Guadalupe who carry the same disbelief to the point of sacrilege. When conducting holy Mass, some New Christian priests fail to consecrate the Host altogether; and during Elevation, one of them was seen raising the Host upside down. Converso recipients of the Eucharist sometimes say, "it is merely bread," and one of them called it a torta (cake)! (p. 102)

Strange and scandalous things occur during Mass. When in church, I noticed Brother Diego de Segovia mechanically turning the pages of a prayer book, which he was not reading (p. 100); later, he stared at the floor while the Host— our Lord's body—was raised to be adored. On several occasions I saw brother Diego de Marchena sitting stiff like stone during Mass. Other monks of Jewish origin tried to void the prayer of its Christian intention and redirect it to the Jewish God. This they did, for example, by saying a benediction or the Paternoster without adding the Ave Maria: in this way, by addressing God as simply "Our Father," they could intend *Yahve* in their hearts.

Indeed, the inner heart and the unspoken word are more important to some New Christian monks than performing the holy Catholic works and rites. The same Fray Diego claimed in my hearing that mental prayer is superior to oral prayer, because it is more spiritual. I suspect this tendency might catch up with Old Christians as well, misleading them into new paths and adventures that resemble the mood, though not the content, of the faith of these same Judaizers.[9]

Abraham's Mark:
As Your Grace is aware, some of these monks have entered our Holy Faith as children, others are Catholics of a second and sometimes even a third generation. Nevertheless, a few still carry the sign of Abraham in their flesh. One day, an Old Christian witness told me, when sitting near a river with a few friends, he had looked up into the raised skirts of Fray Juan de Segovia and was startled to discover a circumcised male organ. (The said friar, by the way, is the same one who tries to evade pork meals) (p. 95). To explain his own circumcision, another monk, Friar Diego de Segovia, could find no better excuse than saying that "he had been born that way" (p. 97). Your Grace will not believe the fantastic, and indeed pathetic, stories that some monks invent to deny the fact to which their flesh testifies. I can understand their anxiety, because admitting they are circumcised could imply that their parents had been unremitting Jews, or, worse, that the monk himself had remained so. For example, Fray Juan de Carranza (p. 97) claims that as a small boy he had been molested by other children who hurt his organ, so that now it looks "a little circumcised." Fray Pedro de Las Cuevas protests that what seems to be a circumcision was really a medical operation that a Jewish surgeon had performed on him years ago in order to cure him of some infant disease. And Fray Gonzalo de Guadalcanal, in a sensational story, says that a neighboring Conversa used to cuddle and play with him as a small child, keeping him naked in bed in her house: he insinuates that this unscrupulous woman, rather than his parents, either had him circumcised or, by her abuse, caused him a delicate physical harm in some other way.

Inner-Converso Solidarity:
New Christians in this Monastery are no exception to the well-known Jewish custom of helping each other in the face of Gentiles, even regardless of merit and the law. They all share a common blood which distances them from the rest

of our compatriots, and even when they do not profess the Law of Moses, they are held in suspicion by most other Christians, and keep together among themselves. This is quite clear in the monastery, too. New Christian monks are constantly favoring and protecting other converts, helping them reach positions of influence, and helping suspected and malefactor Conversos evade exposure and punishment (the most daring in this respect is Fray Diego de Marchena). The order of San Hieronymus is too lenient toward such behavior—so much so, that during the priorship of Diego de Paris a Jew had the impertinence of offering the monastery ten thousand maravedis if it harbored for one year a Converso who appeared to be a fugitive heretic.[10] The offer had no issue; yet the Jew who made it must have made prior inquiries about the monastery and taken seriously its unworthy reputation. It pains my heart to report to Your Grace that bad tongues have started calling this most holy shrine by the abusive and clownish name of the synagogue of San Jeronimo.

We should pause here to ask: are all the irregular phenomena we found in Guadalupe explicit Jewish signals? After all, avoiding pork, eluding sacraments, uttering Jewish benedictions, bearing a circumcision, deriding Christian dogmas and symbols, even lighting Sabbath candles, may have been simply nostalgic gestures, or residual habits and sensitivities which former Jews have been known to preserve over the centuries, even after becoming assimilated. (Remember the Visigoth Jews we met in chapter 1, or think of modern secular Jews who remain averse to pork). The probable answer is that both intentional and residual Judaizing existed in Guadalupe, as they did in Spain at large. Avoiding pork is the handiest, but not the only example of residual Judaizing: former Jews could also reject the Trinity or disdain certain Catholic rites without necessarily intending to return to Judaism. Their dissent sometimes expressed confusion and restlessness rather than a strong Jewish commitment; and in Guadalupe there were Conversos whose discontent with Catholicism pushed them toward a more spiritual Christianity (see Nogales and Augustine, below) and in some cases, outside the religious tradition altogether. Thus, the monastery was a microcosm of most varieties of Converso dissent.

Poetic Interlude I

The city of Cordova, in a move directed against Judaizing Conversos, seems to have ordered all butchers to sell pork only. The poet Antón de Montoro, born near Cordova to Jewish parents and converted into Catholicism as a child, responds thus:

To the Corregidor of Cordova Because the Butcher Shop Has Nothing But Pork

One of the true servants
Of our mighty Lord the King,
Has given the meat dealers
A reason to make me a perjurer.
Not finding, to my grief,
With what to kill my hunger,
They made me break the vow
I had made to my forefathers.[11]

This is a sad poem whichever way we read it. Who are the "forefathers" (*agüelos*) whose bond Antón was forced to betray? Are they the ancient Jewish prophets, in which case Montoro is an active Judaizer? Or are they his personal grandparents, who had remained Jewish amidst the waves of conversion and, painfully realizing that their grandson was about to convert, at least made him vow that, even as a Christian, he would not eat pork, the utmost abomination for Jews? I think the second is the appropriate reading. But even so, Montoro's overt moral reproach of the governor (*corregidor*) is remarkable. The poem is a poignant document which demonstrates that it was still legitimate for Conversos in the first Marrano generation to admit they did not eat pork. Later, when the Inquisition had been established, avoiding pork became a grave offense and a certified sign of heresy that could have disastrous results. Montoro had no Judaizing designs; he wanted to be a Christian and to be recognized as one; but in his poem to the corregidor he demands the moral right to have *some* free space for other loyalties, too: not to Judaism as such but, in this case, to the personal vow he had sworn to his grandparents; thus he claims the right to some dualism, to some plurality within his person.

Antón de Montoro was born in 1404 and converted to Christianity during the crisis provoked by Vicente Ferrer and the infidel laws of 1414. His Jewish name seems to have been Saul[12] and his nickname El Jabibe (Habib, Arabic for *dear*). In adult life he made a modest living in the clothing business. His first known poems date from the 1440s, when he was in his late thirties, so it took him a long time to develop the nerve and spirit required for writing the brash and provocative verses which made his name. But his personal state was declining even as his fame (or notoriety) grew. Conversos in that period started being barred from public office and honors because of the inherent defect attributed to them—their impure blood—and Montoro's writing bitterly echoed this novelty. Perhaps in a defying spirit, and no doubt with irony—that is, with a dual and contrary intent—Montoro flaunted and exaggerated his own lowly occupation and state in life.

Montoro was known as El Ropero, meaning roughly "the clothes peddler" (*shmate* vendor in today's colloquial Yiddish), and liked to refer to himself by that title as an ironic literary trademark. Perhaps the image of old clothes being sold, reused, and sold again, appealed to him as a figurative representation of his own inconstant and unsettled identity, a recurring theme in the text and subtext of his poems.

In the following poem Montoro addresses his Converso future wife with resigned realism:

More to His Wife

Since God had wanted us to be
Both unlucky [*desmazalados*, a Hebraism][13] you and I
And to have but little worth,
We had better both pervert
A single house only, not two.
For [wishing] to enjoy a good husband
Would be a waste of time for you,
And an offense to good reason;
So I, old, dirty, and meek,
Will caress a pretty woman. (Montoro, *Poesía completa*, 104)

In this bitter, ironic, "wooing poem," Montoro reimagines himself persuading his Converso wife to marry him. It is one of the many texts in which Montoro laments the Conversos' inability to fully shed their Jewish aspect and be accepted as Christians. Montoro alludes here specifically to the racial stigma attached to Conversos after midcentury, portraying them as base human beings unworthy of honors. If so, he says to the lady, why debase two households (by each of us marrying an Old Christian) when we can make do with one? Anyway, no marriage prospect outside the Converso fold is feasible for you nowadays, so come, pretty lady, into my old Converso arms, and let me draw some advantage from my inferior state!

Thus, through a classic ironical reversal, Montoro's bad luck as a Converso becomes the source of his good fortune.[14]

A Female Figure of Job: Donosa Ruyz

The records of the Inquisition in Teruel contain the story of Donosa Ruyz (Ruiz), the eighty-year-old widow of Juan Ruyz (the *Generalero*), who was tried as a Judaizer in the year 1484.[15] Born Jewish around 1404, young Donosa was nursed and educated by a Jewish woman who, the old lady says, "was like a mother to me."[16] At age nine or ten her family converted to Catholicism, probably following the onslaught of Vicente Ferrer and the 1414 anti-Jewish laws. Yet, in secret, the girl remained in close contact with her Jewish mentor who "taught me how to keep the laws of the Jews." This influence lasted well into Donosa's adult life. "When I grew up" she said, "because [this woman] had raised me as her daughter and given me two houses and seats in the [Jewish] synagogue . . . , I maintained close ties with her as long as she lived."[17] Among other things, her mentor instructed Donosa to fast on Yom Kippur and "to secretly avoid working on Saturdays, and to have my food sent to me" (from Jewish kosher butcher shops).

Donosa's baptized name had been Catalina, but she changed it later because, she explained, her household included a Moorish servant also called Catalina, "and when her name was called, it was unclear who was being meant." The inquisitors, with good reason, did not accept this explanation. Donosa's change of name was clearly not innocent. It symbolized her rejection of the very act of baptism and the new identity it had imposed upon her.[18]

The main house she received from her mentor was situated across the courtyard from the synagogue; so when unable to join the Jews in open ceremony (which was most of the time), Donosa used to go into her courtyard, pretending to take fresh air, and listen to the prayers emerging from the synagogue ("although I could not understand the words"). Standing there alone at a distance, taking passive part in a Jewish ceremony whose text she could not understand, can symbolize the situation of Judaizing Conversos generally.

Donosa was not lacking in ambivalence, however. "I did what she [her mentor] wanted me to do, but I also did the opposite," she tells with credible candor. This duality was amplified by her personal fate. Donosa had been an afflicted mother, a kind of female Job, who lost six sons and daughters to violence, war, and the more common grief of infant mortality. Once, after her first born had been killed, her other sons fell gravely ill. The anguished Donosa gave alms to both the synagogue and the church—to buy oil for Jewish services and to say Holy Mass for her children. Thus, the Judaizer's typical duality had a compelling extra reason in her case. Persuaded by the Jews that her eldest son had been killed because "everyone in my household was a good Christian and never . . . gave alms to the Jews," she sent charity to the Jewish poor and "fasted several times in secret on the same day as the Jews."

Finally, when her sons died, "I secluded myself at home and was weeping most of the time, and did not go out to Mass, only to the courtyard in front of my house" (that is, to her virtual synagogue). Thus, when this unhappy Marrana mother was agonizing in uncertainty she manifested her dualism; and when disastrous certainty set in, she returned to her dominant Judaizing tendency. It should be noted that Donosa's dualism entailed a split between conflicting allegiances. Her turning to the Cross in dire times, presumably on the argument that "it might do no harm," is very telling in this respect. A full-fledged Jew would see great harm in praying to Jesus, which in Jewish terms is an act of idolatry certain to evoke God's wrath. Precisely because the desperate Donosa was already facing high stakes, she could not afford taking this further risk unless she had some faith in Jesus, too, however uncertain and contradictory this faith might have been.[19]

Still, quasi Judaism was dominant in Donosa's unsettled religious life. Her portrait, as drawn by the prosecutor's one-sided pen, seems credible on several points. Not only did she light candles on Friday nights, she also celebrated "the Holiday of the Lamb" (Passover) and used to send wheat to Jewish bakers to make *matzot* for her. When buying meat she removed the nonkosher sinew and washed off the blood, according to Jewish law; and on Saturdays she used to eat *khamin*, the slow-cooking Jewish dish (containing "beans and spinach, or vegetables," according to a recipe inadvertently given by the prosecutor), prepared ahead of the Sabbath, which, the local Jews in Teruel used to send to Conversos. The aim was to help the Conversos avoid lighting fire on the Sabbath, yet many recipients, we may assume, accepted the Jewish dish as a nostalgic relic of their past while going on with their lives as partly assimilated Catholics.

Perhaps uncharacteristically, Donosa's Catholic mask was as defective as its religious content. She abstained from going to church, broke the fast of Lent, and failed to kneel when the church bells announced an important moment. Worse, upon examination, the more than eighty-year-old Donosa was found ignorant of the *credo*—the list of Catholic articles of faith—and unable to say the Paternoster and Ave Maria.

In the words of the prosecutor, Donosa had "hoped to be saved in the Law of Moses and [believed] that no one can be saved outside this law." We saw, however, that in times of crisis she also turned to Jesus, so the Law of Moses's monopoly on the way to salvation was not so clear in Donosa's split heart. "I recognize that I have erred and beg forgiveness of our Lord Jesus Christ," she declared to save her skin. But when ordered not to leave town, the old lady disappeared from sight. Her remaining son, a priest, returned empty-handed from a mission to find her. Donosa Ruyz was declared guilty in absentia, sentenced to be burned, and her property confiscated. Listing her many Judaizing offenses one by one, the verdict implicitly also recognized her dualities: "It is clear to us that she has no strong faith in Christian truth" they said (thereby attributing *some* faith to her); "and if she observed anything of the Evangelical doctrine, she observed it together with the Law of Moses."

Poetic Interlude II

In old age, Antón de Montoro, in a poem addressed to the young queen Isabella (Isabel in Spanish), who had just been crowned, took a sober look back at himself and the experience of the first Marrano generation. The first two stanzas draw a portrait of the artist as an old man, a disillusioned and entrapped Converso.

To the Queen Doña Isabel

O sad, bitter clothes-peddler
Who does not feel your sorrow![20]
Here you are, sixty years of age,
And have always said [to the Virgin]:
"You remained immaculate,"[21]
And have never sworn [directly] by the Creator.[22]
I recite the credo, I worship
Pots full of greasy pork,
I eat bacon half-cooked,
Listen to Mass, cross myself
While touching holy waters—
And never could I kill
These traces of the *confeso* [pejorative for Converso].

With my knees bent
And in great devotion
In days set for holiness
I pray, rosary in hand,
Reciting the beads of the Passion,[23]
Adoring the God-and-Man
As my highest Lord,
But because of the remnants of my guilt[24]
I cannot lose the name
Of an old Jewish son of a whore [*puto*]. (Montoro, *Poesía completa*, 35)

A moving and revealing poem. The last sentence alludes to the Converso's social image and standing, whereas the punch line of the first stanza ("never could I kill those traces of the *confeso*") alludes also to the Conversos' intellectual makeup and mind. Actually, Montoro betrays his Jewish traces in the very poem that laments their persistence, thus making his point twice, once overtly and a second time in the subtext. The phrase: "Here you are, sixty years of age, and have never . . . " (*sesenta años que nasciste . . . y nunca*) echoes a passage in the Passover Haggadah that every Jew, and every former Jewish boy, would recognize. Rabbi Eleazar ben Azarya declares in that passage that "here I am, seventy years of age," and have never seen the Exodus story being told at night.[25] Montoro situates his poetic self as an inverted Rabbi Eleazar and contemplates his own Converso-like *never*. He has never mocked or doubted Mary's virginity, as do the Jews. He has never addressed God directly, in the Jewish manner, but only through Mary or the saints. He has never sworn to God by calling him, vaguely, "the Creator," to avoid using the plural form *Dios* (as Judaizers do). Yet despite all this, he could never eradicate "those traces of the *confeso*" from his mind and identity.[26]

With pathetic irony the writer describes his ceaseless efforts to demarcate himself from the Jews. While Jews abhor pork, he has always "worship[ped] those greasy pots of pork" (the verb *adorar*, to worship, is a mock-religious pun), and whereas Jews are forbidden to eat rare meat, he consumed his bacon half cooked, thereby committing a dual sin against Judaism—yet still failed to prove his Catholic fidelity. In fact, a lifetime of prayers, devotions, and a strict (one is tempted to say *kosher*) Catholic observance did not make him look any better to the outward world than an "old Jewish son of a whore."[27]

There are two kinds of Converso traces that the poem finds impossible to erase: those inhering in the Converso's own mind and those residing in the minds of others. The latter includes the Converso's alleged baseness, satirized in the poem to his wife (quoted earlier), and also "the remnants of my guilt" (from the second poem): namely, the Jews' responsibility for the death of Jesus, which the Marranos were forced to inherit.

To resist this imputed guilt, which weighed quite heavily upon them, some Marranos claimed that their forefathers had already been living in Spain during Jesus's lifetime. They even invented the story that these ancient Hispanic Jews had sent a letter to the Jews in Judea protesting the crucifixion. The guilty shadow of the crucifixion recurs persistently in the *Cancioneros*, including in a poem by Montoro, written as a dialogue between himself and his horse. In the end, the horse declares:

> And now, Señor Antón,
> Because you have temporalized me,
> I grant you pardon
> For the one you have crucified.[28] (Montoro, *Poesía completa*, 116)

To understand this cryptic verse we should note that earlier in the poem the horse mentioned *Dios el temporal* (God the temporal), undoubtedly referring to Jesus. So *temporalization* alludes here to the Incarnation, God's entry into the world of time. Because Montoro has temporalized God, he gains pardon for having crucified Him. This means that because the converted poet has accepted the doctrine of the Incarnation, his share in the guilt of Jesus's crucifixion is annulled—or *ought* to be annulled. Montoro demands this annulment as his right, yet knows and decries that he can get the pardon only in theory, not real life, and not from the old Spanish society but only from his horse.[29]

Pedro de La Caballería

Bishop Pablo de Santa María, the former rabbi of Burgos, illustrates the renegade who turned fiercely against his former fellow Jews in a passionate attempt to obliterate his old identity. Yet not every Converso attacking his former religion did so out of zeal; expediency was also a motive. Pedro de La Caballería, of the famous family we met earlier, had converted to Christianity with his father Fernando and other members of the family following the Tortosa Disputation. Later in life he became a celebrated jurist loaded with titles and offices. He served in the city government of Saragossa and in the royal court, represented the queen in Cortes, was involved in national politics, and finally was killed (or murdered) during an uprising against King Juan II in 1461.

Pedro de La Caballería's paramount concern was his career, which dominated his life and, one might say, also his death. Although he was not an active Judaizer, he too lived a life of concealment because he invested great efforts and cunning in hiding his Jewish origin. At one point in 1447, he produced a notary attestation that stated, or looked as if it did, that Pedro de La Caballería had been born and educated a full-fledged Christian. The document, says Baer, is phrased in an elliptical way—a Marrano way, we might add—so as to avoid a direct lie yet make the desired false impression.[30]

Three years later, in a more drastic denial of his origin, Pedro de La Caballería published a tract entitled *Christ's Zeal against Jews, Saracens, and Infidels*, which became one of the sharpest anti-Jewish pamphlets circulating in mid-fifteenth-century Spain. To the eyes of a connoisseur (but there weren't many), this work could have revealed rather than concealed Pedro's Jewish credentials because it used Jewish sources with an ease that an Old Christian could rarely display. Why then did Pedro write it? Probably because he relied on the scarcity of such expert readers; meanwhile he was building for himself the desired reputation of a fervent Christian and Jew baiter.

However, that reputation was, in his case, only a mask. Unlike Pablo de Santa María, Pedro de La Caballería did not attack the Jews because of the Christian zeal he claimed to display, or because of aversion toward his Jewish past. The last thing that can be attributed to this new Spaniard is religious zeal of *any* kind. He disparaged Judaism in public in order to do the same to Christianity in private. What was really important to him was life itself, in its this-worldly course and achievement; he sought to become free by expanding his possibilities and shaping his career as richly as he could. By *career* I do not mean social advancement only, but the expansion of one's personality through the successful practice of a profession; the exploitation of knowledge and know-how; the assurance drawn from mastery of one's faculties and expertise; access to interesting people, places, and events; the enjoyment of the ups and downs of politics; and the intellectual and aesthetic pleasures attending a diverse and varied worldly life. Thus, behind the medieval facade of Christ's zeal, a secular Renaissance figure was hiding as a Marrano.

Alfonso de La Caballería

That such cultural patterns could pass on to further generations is illustrated in Pedro's son, Alfonso de La Caballería. He followed and surpassed his father in becoming the foremost jurist in Aragon (according the chronicler Palencia, his contemporary), while also acquiring a rich humanist education. In his youth he became associated with the young prince Ferdinand, the future Catholic king, and helped him negotiate his marriage arrangement with Isabella of Castile, leading to Spain's unification under their joint crowns. Later he was named the king's vice-chancellor for Aragon. A shrewd and pragmatic politician, he saw his way through the intricate web of privileges, powers, *fueros* (regional exemptions), corporative rights, and secular and religious authorities, which made the Spanish system—especially in his native Aragon—close to impossible to govern at the wane of the Middle Ages. Although Alfonso personally seems to have drawn intellectual pleasure from these intricate maneuverings, as a statesman he realized their harmful nature and, with King Ferdinand's support, set out to reform and simplify the obsolete politico-juridical system. Simplification meant greater centralization, so many particular interests felt threatened by the reform, and Alfonso de La Caballería won himself powerful enemies who were jealous of their traditional privileges. Yet his diplomatic talent, and the lesson of prudence he drew from his father's ill-fated end, made Alfonso a master of persuasion and negotiation. He used the leverage of royal power in moderation, sometimes only as a faint though very present hint, while offering creative juridical solutions to his negotiating partners. In the end he was instrumental not only in overcoming the proud Aragonian elite's opposition to the new political realities, but, ironically, also in helping to subject unwilling

Aragon to the new Inquisition, which was rightly perceived as an instrument of central royal power.

Interesting facts were revealed about Alfonso's dual life "in the closet." A Jewish notable, Don Jacob Hazan testified under interrogation that Don Alfonso had been "like a father"[31] to the Jews, secretly advising them on how to promote their interests, while giving them a cold shoulder in public. Jewish leaders who lacked skill incurred his wrath. Once he scolded Hazan for being incompetent as a politician, and said: "I pity you Jews. Your foolishness makes it impossible for me to help you." Then he added: "But I take comfort in knowing that while you undergo bodily suffering in this world, you have saved your soul in the next." Perhaps this was said in irritated irony, though Hazan did not think so; he claimed that Alfonso's words revealed a secret he had been keeping for thirty years. Yet on another occasion Alfonso was heard insisting "there is nothing but living and dying in this world,"[32] a statement which sounds truer to his character (even if it contradicts another statement, since contradictions were also in character for him).

In another testimony that calls for equal caution, Moshe Haninai Aderet, a Jewish merchant, testified that as a young man he had considered becoming a Christian against his father's opposition, but Don Alfonso, who was his father's friend, persuaded him to desist. Once when father and son came to warn Alfonso of a plot that was brewing against him Alfonso showed them a charm he was wearing, which an old Sicilian rabbi had given him and which, he said, protected him against his enemies.[33] Of course, neither of Aderet's stories bears out a charge of Judaism. Attachment to a magical device only indicates superstition, which is compatible with the lack of any religious faith; and showing greater loyalty to friends than to one's official religion can equally indicate a failing religious attachment. The facts reported by Aderet can be better explained by Alfonso's religious indifference than by his alleged adherence to Judaism.

That does not, of course, make his case or person a coherent one. Don Alfonso did not lack contradictions. Underlying them, his basic duality was that of a nonreligious Judeo-Christian seeking personal growth, perhaps even a substitute salvation, in the affairs of this world, while turning his former religion into a scholarly interest mixed with personal affection or nostalgia. The covert dimension of his life did not conceal an actual practice of Judaizing but its suspected image and, no less dangerous, a fundamental lassitude toward the official Christianity he was serving as the Catholic king's close adviser. That such a person, a modern man "in the closet," must have felt solitary and, therefore, had an acute sense of his individuality (which made him even more proto-modern) can, I think, be readily imagined.

Poetic Interlude III

Alfonso Alvarez Villasandino, perhaps a Marrano, attacks a Marrano enemy, Alfonso Ferrandes Semuel, by presenting his feigned "testament," which Semuel is said to have left when he died:

> Friends, who have so enjoyed
> Alfonso [Semuel] while he was alive,
> Now with his much lamented death . . .
> Perhaps you will laugh again
> When you read his will. . . .
> A testament and codicil
> He has ordered as [*commo*] a Christian . . .
> *In which his whole handicapped life* [*su vyda lasdrada*]
> *Is sketched in outline.*[34]

Read in a somewhat different light, Alvarez Villasandino's last claim may be very true indeed. There was something handicapped, fractured, or unfulfilled in this former Jew's life as an official Christian, as there was for many of his generation. The misspelled phrase *su vyda lasdrada* can be corrected either into *vida castrada* (castrated life) or into *vida lastrada* (handicapped, burdensome life).[35] In the first case, the writer would be alluding to Semuel's circumcision (and thereby, metaphorically, to his *Judaized self*), and also to the castrated mode of existence that Semuel was bound to lead as a duality-ridden Judeo-Christian, unable to bring his life and identity to fruition in either way.[36] The latter meaning is also compatible with reading *lasdrada* as signifying Semuel's handicapped or burdensome life as a Converso.

Now the content of the mock testament is spelled out:

> To the Trinity
> He wills a copper coin [*cornado*]
> Of the new ones.[37]
> To the Crusades
> He gives two eggs, in sign of [his] Christianity.
> And as a major charity
> He wills a hundred maravedis [a fairly nice sum]
> To Jews who won't work
> On the Sabbath.[38]
> He orders that a Cross
> Be laid—what madness—at his feet,

And the Koran, that false and stupid[39] scripture,
Be put on his chest,
And the Torah [*Atora*], his life and light,
He wants on his head. . . .

Semuel's various faces are a mix of sincerity and disguise. Even when facing death, no one, not even he, can decide or know for certain what he believes. He emerges as a Judaizer who looks down on the other Hispanic religions but also has some regard for them; and this, given the cultural climate, could mean that he lacked serious regard for any religion.

Further down his testament, fearing that his body might be dragged out of his grave as a heretic, Semuel orders his donkey and silk clothes to be converted into cash with which to bribe the authorities to avoid treating his remains cruelly. Although all three religions would consider Semuel a heretic, it is the Jewish element that, without fully determining his identity, dominates his memory and nostalgia; so

He leaves his white shirts [a hint of Judaizing]
To some *Samas* [Heb. שמש: synagogue attendant] in Salamanca
Because he prays from the *Homas* [Heb. חומש: Pentateuch]
And chants with a good voice
A hymn and a *pysmon* [Heb. פזמון: song, chant].

Finally, to accomplish all this Semuel appoints as his executor

A Jew of good standing,
By name of Jacob Çidario,
To whom he leaves his *sudario* [prayer shawl, i.e., his *talit*][40]
In sign of *çedaqua* [Heb. צדקה : charity]
So that he may say *tefyla* [Heb. תפילה : prayer]
Once he [Semuel] is buried in his *fonsario* [moat or grave].

For people of that period the testament was a shocking denunciation. To us, it offers some insight, distorted by the lens of satire, into the ambiguities of Judaizers and religious skeptics in the first Marrano generations, and reveals how they were presumed to cope with their existentially handicapped lives.[41]

Juan de Torquemada

Tomás de Torquemada is one of the most fear-inspiring names in Spanish history—the first grand inquisitor, who imprisoned, tortured, humiliated and burned thousands of Conversos. A few decades earlier, however, the name *Torquemada* was praised and blessed by Conversos everywhere. It belonged to Cardinal Juan de Torquemada, the future inquisitor's uncle and a highly respected church dignitary who became a staunch and militant defender of the Conversos. In all probability, he was partly of Jewish origin through his maternal grandmother.[42] (It is worth noting that his name appears in a list of Converso luminaries appended to a late manuscript copy of Pablo de Santa María's major book, *Scrutinium Scriptuarum*).

Cardinal Torquemada was particularly active in repulsing the protoracist attack against the Conversos launched in 1449 by the Toledo rebels. His counterattack appeared in a treatise entitled: *Against the Midianites and Ishmaelites— the Adversaries and Detractors of the Sons whose Origin is the People of Israel.* The title is revealing. The Conversos' foes are called "Ishmaelites" and thereby likened to the Muslims, who were still trying to destroy Christendom (the tract was written close to the fall of Constantinople, and while Granada was still in Muslim hands); whereas the Conversos are treated as "sons" in a triple sense. They are the sons of Israel, the nation of Jesus and Mary, and the original bearers of God's election. In the second sense, they are also now the sons of the Church, and thus brothers to all other Christians; and finally, they are "sons" in the sense of new arrivals in the family who deserve love and protection. That the Jews of all nations should accept Christianity—that they should become the sons of the Church while also being the sons of Israel—is an outstanding achievement that should be celebrated by all Christians; whoever stands against this happy combination is God's enemy.

"Thy enemies, O God . . . took malicious counsel against Thy people," Torquemada boldly quotes Psalms 83:3–5. "They said: Let us destroy them as a nation, so that Israel's name will be remembered no more." By referring to the Conversos as *God's people* Torquemada capitalizes on two elements of Christian doctrine. The Conversos belong to God's former people as Jews, and to God's present people as Christians.

Thus it is their *duality* that places the Marranos in a privileged position. In converting to Christianity they regained the divine election that their ancestors had lost and, in addition, they also retained a special value as the people of Jesus and Mary.

Thus far Torquemada joined Cartagena (see chapter 4); but he differed from him in sternly denying that moral and religious qualities are predetermined by ethnic origin. He denounced this view as profoundly un-Christian, "false, blasphemous, and erroneous." According to Cardinal Torquemada, Christianity has a universal message; its grace transcends ethnic differences and transforms every baptized person into a brother in Jesus. To deny this is to blaspheme against the sacrament of baptism; for what is baptism if not the purging of one's former sins, and the abolition of all carnal differences—of blood, origin, language, culture—allowing everyone to be reborn in Christ and to equally share his body, passion, and sacrifice?[43]

While this applied to Jews and Gentiles alike, the Jews enjoyed a special advantage that Torquemada, in order not to contradict himself, struggled to articulate in terms of their history and past greatness rather than blood. Seen from Torquemada's perspective, the fact that the people who had denied their own Messiah should turn back to him fifteen centuries later is a colossal historical event (the cardinal was thinking, of course, of *sacred* history, mainly the history of grace, revelation, and redemption) and a prize everyone should learn to cherish.

Cardinal Torquemada thus treated the Converso duality as preeminence, a sign of special distinction. No wonder his view, like Bishop Cartagena's, remained a minority position, a voice calling in the wilderness. The chasm between Cardinal Torquemada and most other Catholic theologians and publicists only grew wider with time.

Guadalupe Revisited: Portraits of Four Monks

Bearing in mind the distinctions we made above between dissent from Christianity and dissent within Christianity, we now return to Guadalupe to view the portraits of four ex-Jewish monks, each manifesting a different shape of Converso duality.

Marchena

Fray **Diego de Marchena** was an active and determined Judaizer. His case (and fate) "created a great sensation at the time."[44] During the adoration of Christ in church, this priest and monk used to sit frozen and self-distancing ("like a statue," say the records of the Inquisition), and he was heard reciting Jewish-sounding formulas and benedictions on more private occasions. As a priest, Marchena had to conduct services and consecrate the ritual bread (Host) but on several occasions he was observed abusing the holy sacrament. While performing at the altar he addressed the Host with irreverence and, presumably by accident, dropped it on the floor on five different occasions. And he used a Jewish doctor to claim that he was ill during Lent so he could break this Catholic fast.

Toward his own group, the Jewish-oriented Conversos, Marchena manifested remarkable solidarity. As father confessor he advised Conversos to marry exclusively among themselves. He traveled several times to Andalusia to provide help to prisoners of the Inquisition, and was heard on the road reciting *Jeremiah's Lamentations*, as Jews used to do on days of mourning. Yet Brother Diego de Marchena was not merely the lamenting type, but a man of courage and action. Constantly he was on the lookout for other Judaizers with whom he could establish clandestine relations. He raised money for the victims of the Inquisition, helped twenty prisoners escape trial, and protected Conversos who had given alms to synagogues. When two rabbis arrived in the adjacent city of Guadalupe to instruct and supervise the Judaizers, Marchena was aware of their visit but failed to inform the authorities.[45]

His views were no less daring. Father Marchena claimed that neither Jew nor Gentile would be condemned for lack of faith in Jesus, thereby challenging both the content and the dogmatic status of a crucial Christian belief. With the sober logic of Jews he dispelled Catholic mysteries. He agreed with another monk that, besides Jesus, Mary and Joseph must have had other children as well—implying that Mary was not a virgin, and Joseph was physically Jesus's father. In the end, this daring monk became a martyr. Put to trial, he was convicted of Judaism and burned at the stake.

Nogales

The monk with whom Marchena agreed about the Holy Family was Fray **Alonso de Nogales**, not a clear-cut Judaizer but a man of subtler dualities. There is little doubt he thought of himself as Catholic; yet his brand of Christianity was saturated with Jewish beliefs, gestures, attitudes—and doubts. Even his body language was Jewish. When praying at the altar he used to sway his body back and forth in the manner of Jews. When blessing someone, he put his hands on the person's head in what was called a "Jewish benediction." Like Marchena, Nogales opposed the prevailing Spanish intolerance and declared that Jews and Moors deserved to be loved by Christians. He too was ridden by typically Jewish doubts concerning Jesus's virgin birth. How, Nogales wondered, did the Holy Spirit enter Mary's body? Some have suggested it entered through the ear, when Mary heard the Annunciation; but Nogales resisted this solution. With irritated skepticism he repeated several times: "through the ear?!," and finally decided it was through "the normal place."

All these Jewish gestures and dispositions did not make Nogales a Jew. He was a different kind of Christian, a Jewish kind perhaps—heterodox, restless, and inquisitive. This was manifest in his rather Jewish demand that Catholicism, his new religion, should make more rational sense to him (and to others) than it actually does. Conversion did not involve passive assimilation for Nogales. He could not see why, as a new Christian, he should eradicate everything in his Jewish past. Thus he lived his own distinct form of ambiguity, a Judeo-Catholic wandering outside the pale of any orthodox tradition.[46]

Burgos el Mozo

A different kind of duality existed in Fray Diego de **Burgos** *el Mozo* (the younger), who declared he was glad to have "descended from the line of the Jews, as did our Lord Jesus Christ, rather than from the line of the Devil, as do the Gentiles." Statements in the same spirit were made by Bishop Alonso de Cartagena of Burgos (see chapter 4) and other high-ranking Conversos who flaunted their Jewish origin as a distinctly Christian advantage. But Fray Diego's claiming Jesus as an ethnic cousin was really a sign of ambivalence. The same Diego de Burgos *el Mozo* was known to be a devotee of the Old Testament—the *Jewish* Bible, which he used to read in Hebrew. And in the Bible, he took a particular liking to the story of the Jews' redemption from Egypt, a coded allusion to the Marranos' situation in Spain and to their *esperanza* (hope) for deliverance.

Augustín

Another monk, Fray **Augustín**, created a commotion in the monastery when he proclaimed in a sermon that Mary was not the only virgin who had given birth. A hot debate ensued over his meaning. Some understood him as implying that Mary had not been touched by divine grace, and that Jesus's birth was not miraculous. Augustín's defenders claimed he only meant that Mary could not have known that her child was divine because other virgins had also born children.[47]

We need not enter the details of this curious polemic; what matters is Augustín's obvious discontent with a central Christian dogma, which sounded so irrational to him that finally he declared it was not a mandatory dogma, but open to opinion. Less sensational, but even more serious, was the trouble he had with the Eucharist. This pillar of Christianity looked so crude and unspiritual to Augustín that he concluded Christ should not be adored in the body, and that the adoration need not necessarily take place in church (in other words, it should not be reduced to a ritual). Augustín clearly had a low view of both rituals and the church. On another occasion he was heard stating that moral virtue, probably the most essential thing to him, was better taught in synagogues and mosques than churches.

These were ominous views for the time. But it is significant that Augustín was never caught performing Jewish rites. He was not a Judaizer, but a latent Christian reformer who rejected a religion based on formalistic ritual and mandatory dogma. He was looking for a more enlightened Christian faith, free of irrational superstition, based on the inmost heart, stressing morality over ceremony (as did the Jewish prophets), and showing tolerance toward non-Christians. Unwittingly, Fray Augustín and Conversos like him were reaching toward some form of internal religiosity (or, as Sicroff suggests, of Erasmus's pre-Enlightenment),[48] thereby anticipating the Spanish spiritual movements of the sixteenth century (see chapter 15).

These four monks testify that Judaizing in Guadalupe, though sometimes active and determined, had other faces and shades as well. Dissent within Christianity was no less present among Guadalupe Conversos than dissent from Christianity. Ex-Jewish monks who felt unable to acquiesce in their new religion turned not only backward to the old Law of Moses, or forward to religious skepticism and even a kind of atheism, but also searched a more spiritual Christian experience to which they were yet unable to give a distinct shape.[49] This provoked an early reformist trend within medieval Spanish Catholicism. And when, in 1485, the ax fell on this remarkable exercise, a pattern had been created that, a few decades later, was to produce more distinct forms of Christian spirituality that will require our attention later.

A Judaizing Seer: The *Beata* of Herrera

The fifteenth century saw the appearance in Spain of the *beatas*, popular mystics and seers, who saw visions, rose to heaven, and foresaw apocalyptic events. Most of them were women, and quite a few were of Jewish origin. The *beatas* practiced a nonconformist form of Christianity, claiming to have direct access to the divinity as Christ's brides and lovers. At times a distinctly Marrano *beata* would also arise: such was the case of Inez of Herrera, the Judaizing *beata*, whose visions drove a group of partly assimilated Marranos to organize and secretly return to "Judaism"—more precisely, to a dualist form of crypto-Judaism heavily clothed in Catholic mentality.

On a business trip to the city of Herrera, Juan de Segovia, a maker of leather goods, heard of a wondrous event that had happened the night before. Inez, the daughter of Juan Esteban, had gone up to heaven where, guided by an angel, she saw those in pain and those in glory. Intrigued, Juan de Segovia asked to see the girl. He found her "a little embarrassed," but, encouraged by her father, the girl finally told him that her late mother had appeared to her in a vision and, taking her by the hand, told her not to fear but to follow an angel that had appeared to lead their way. Thus, in a Converso version of Dante's *Divine Comedy*, "they ascended to heaven and saw Purgatory with the souls suffering there [a distinct Christian image, absent in Judaism]. . . . They also saw the just, who reside in Glory, sitting in golden chairs [this is close to a Judaic image]." Then the girl heard a distant murmur and wondered what it might signify. The angel said: "Friend of God, what you are hearing are those who were burnt on earth [the Judaizing Marranos], and now they reside in Glory."

What we have is a Judaizer's martyrology fitted into the Christian model! The reversal of roles—the Judaizers burned on earth being the true saints in Heaven—shocked and impressed Juan. "I remained"—he testified at Inez's later trial—startled and puzzled, not knowing what was true and what I should believe."[50]

Juan de Segovia demanded a sign to prove the girl was genuine. The girl said she had asked herself for a sign, and the angel promised to deliver her a letter from God. Impressed even more, Juan de Segovia asked the girl's father to keep him informed—especially if the letter arrived. Then he left home for Toledo and his wife, "both not knowing . . . in what we ought to believe."

Sometime later, the glove-maker Luis, a business associate of Juan's, visited Toledo and brought the latest news from Herrera. The girl was now going to heaven once a week. People initiated into her secret were fasting, repenting, giving alms, and preparing for a great mysterious event. Did the girl bring the sign? Yes, Luis answered—she brought an olive, a large ear of corn, and a small letter. Her message was clear: no one would be saved in the life to come except those observing the Law of Moses.

The *beata* predicted a grand mystical event approaching—the redemption of the Conversos from captivity. God was preparing to lead them to the Promised Land. He had "erected a wondrous city in Heaven which would be transported to the Holy Land in one piece, and all the Conversos would live there in prosperity." Therefore, Luis urged, Juan had better join the movement, observe the Law of Moses, and start fasting—as everyone around Herrera was already doing in secret, even small children. "For no one cares for his business any more; and those who have [money] give it to those who have not, hoping to be taken to that Promised Land."

The mixture of Jewish and Christian symbolism is striking. The atmosphere of a secret sect in a high pitch of expectation recalls Jewish messianic outbursts at other times. Juan de Segovia and his wife took to fasting "in the manner of the Jews," and started observing the Jewish Sabbath, concealing their action from the servants. (To avoid suspicion, he pretended he was going out fishing on the Sabbath.) And they abstained from eating pork during that period in which, he later told the inquisitors, he had lived under this "blindness, false belief, and hope."

This is a telling testimony of the duality-ridden minds of simple folk, artisans, and shopkeepers undergoing a quasi-Jewish messianic fervor. There can hardly be a less Jewish story, yet its intent is Jewish. The narrator's conversion (or reconversion) to Judaism occurred in a very Christian way—based on a miracle, an angel, revelation, martyrdom, and a Dante-like visit to the Catholic heaven. The symbolic universe of this event is saturated with Christian motifs: The souls suffering in Purgatory (a concept absent in Judaism); a mystical city—the Heavenly Jerusalem (a Christian, basically anti-Jewish symbol) awaiting the Marranos as their worldly abode (a very Jewish hope); the prize of salvation—another mainly Christian concern being granted to those keeping the anti-Christian Law of Moses; and perhaps in the first place—Marrano martyrs burned on the stake, so powerfully recalling the early Christian martyrs whose doctrine they deny, are here given a privileged place in Paradise. This paradise is shaped in Christian fashion; yet all the Catholic motifs serve a Jewish intent. The Messiah is still to come—so he cannot be Jesus, but he must be the future Jewish Messiah, whom the prophet Elijah will precede, as the Jews believe;[51] and as in mainstream Judaism, redemption has a this-worldly, political character.[52] Above all, the intent here was to return to Judaism (however foggy its notion was), or rather, to that *Law of Moses* whose keeping was the true road to the (Christian) goal of salvation and worth the risk and the suffering.

This fascinating story shows in a spectacular fashion how Marranos from the second generation onward, even when they wanted to be Jews, were neither Jews nor Christians. They were marked by a duality whose Jewish-oriented content and intention were couched in a Christian framework and symbolic world.

On the other side of the same duality one could meet Fray Melchior, a male *beato* (a rare phenomenon), who also pronounced Jewish-like messianic prophesies. Melchior's apocalypse emerged from within the Catholic world and predicted its imminent destruction. Yet Melchior had no Jewish intent: the dead Catholic world, in his vision, was to be replaced by a new, superior Christianity that would be based not in Rome, but in Zion.[53]

7

The Arias d'Avilas:
Hidden Jews or Marrano Dualists?

———— ⇌ ————

The name of Diego Arias d'Avila has been mentioned several times in our story. As royal chief financier of Castile under Enrique, he was one of the most powerful, and most hated, figures in the land, a paragon of the Conversos' early success and later disdain and rejection.[1]

Born in the city of Avila as Ysaque (Isaac) Abenacar, Diego Arias was one of those Jewish children converted by their parents around 1412 to 1414—the generation of Donosa Ruyz and the poet Antón de Montoro. Little Ysaque was raised as a Jewish boy, learned to recite Hebrew chants and prayers, and sang so well that he must have been told that he should become a cantor.

Of his early life after the conversion little is known. The chronicler Palencia, who loathed him, says that Diego Arias had started as an itinerant spice peddler who cheated the villagers and barely escaped their wrath. Even harsher on Diego Arias were popular gossip and the salacious *Cancionero* poems that slighted his circumcision, mocked his assumed aristocratic manners, imputed to him greed, treachery, deicide, scheming, and every Jewish stereotype in the Christian book.[2] Yet during his and King Enrique's lifetimes no one dared challenge Diego Arias's Christian fidelity. The attack came decades later, when Diego Arias and Doña Elvira Goncález, his first wife, had long been dead and the newly created Inquisition was making its initial headway in Castile. The chief bearer of the Arias d'Avila name by then was their distinguished son Juan, the bishop of Segovia, whose high office and family prestige proved insufficient to bar the vengeful posthumous onslaught on his parents—and indirectly, on him.[3]

Officially, the trials of dead persons were motivated by Christian love—to save their souls from hell, or release them from purgatory. Yet the actual targets were the living: in this case, the bishop himself, his brother Pedro (Pedrarias), who controlled the family wealth, and their various relatives. Exposing their parents as Judaizers was to ruin the Arias dynasty, causing the loss of its fortune and standing, and the right to honors for its offspring.[4]

Ironically, it was Juan, as bishop, who invited the inquisitors to Segovia. Having concluded he could not stop them, he chose to project a false-confident image by inviting them himself. He knew he was a choice target for the Inquisition but he felt trapped; so after taking the first bold initiative, he started to procrastinate, obstructing the proceedings while appearing to support them. In the end he fled Spain and took his case to the pope's council in Rome. It was in this foreign city, pleading, soliciting, and disbursing the usual bribes, that he spent the last years of his life.

Although the bishop was not a Judaizer, his dualities leap to the eye. But first we must consider his father's posthumous trial.

Diego Arias—Worldly Power, Nostalgic Deprivation

A close review of the investigation against Diego Arias d'Avila and his first wife, Doña Elvira, is enlightening in several ways. It reveals the mere nostalgia, *social* religion, and/or basic secularism and this-worldliness that often are the reality behind charges of Judaizing; and it illustrates the pitfalls of an uncritical reading of the Inquisition's records.[5]

The bulk of evidence against Diego Arias and his wife was hearsay, often in the third degree (x told y that he heard from z), but the inquisitors admitted this information as evidence even when it all came from a single source (and thus was not corroborated). Witnesses were questioned under pressure, sometimes torture, and, always, paralyzing fear. This does not mean they all lied; but even when trying to tell the truth it was colored by their cognitive limitations—prejudice, lack of context, failed memory—or their wish to appease the inquisitors. More important, the inquisitors interpreted the data according to their own ideological and institutional bias—which is the foremost methodological problem in this kind of material, even greater (because it is more subtle) than the problem of fabricated evidence.

It took several years, and several rounds of cross-investigation, before the Inquisition was able to break posthumously into Diego Arias's inner circle and intimate behavior. What it found leaves little doubt of Diego Arias's unstable Christianity and outbursts of Jewish longing. The following facts seem to have been established:

(1) Diego Arias was observed on several different occasions chanting Jewish prayers. (This was mentioned in six primary testimonies and a stream of hearsay).
(2) Diego and his wife, Doña Elvira, often ate *khamin* on the Sabbath, a Jewish dish and custom. (Eight direct testimonies and much hearsay).
(3) Diego was seen treating a Christian saint with rage and disrespect, and was heard making occasional deprecating remarks about religion.

Following is a sample of the evidence.

On 20 January, 1486, Luis Mexía, *regidor* (city councilor) of Segovia, testified that Juan Cáceres had told him of a conversation he had had with Mosén Negro, a prominent Jew in Medellin. Negro remarked that Diego Arias used to have a very good voice. When Cáceres wondered how he knew this, Negro told him that once he had visited Diego Arias's house in Segovia, and seen him in the company of other Conversos "chanting psalms which the Jews say in their vespers, his head covered with a cloth."[6] Other hearsay testimonies refer to this story. (Two witnesses, quite ironically, call the cloth "a Jewish sanbenito.")[7]

Much later, Cáceres confirmed the story. On a visit to Medellín, Negro had told him that once in Segovia "he had seen Diego Arias with a *talit* (Taler, a prayer shawl) covering his head "like a rabbi," chanting a verse "which Jews say in the evening," and that his voice "sounded like an angel." With a sigh, Negro added cryptically: "Ah, what a black voice [probably meaning *melancholic*] he had!"[8]

Another first-hand testimony was given by the Jew Judá Caragoza, perhaps a distant relative of Diego Arias. One day when they both traveled to the town of Chinchón, Diego Arias reminisced about how, as a young child in synagogue, he used to say the Jewish *berakhot* (prayers) on the Sabbath while the rabbi was reading the Torah. Then, in an outburst of emotion, he exclaimed: "I want to say the *berakhot* now!" Upon which he "started chanting them aloud, like a Jew, in a voice full of grace."[9]

In addition, a Jewish rabbi testified that twenty-five years earlier he had heard it said in the house of Doña Zar (Sara) that Diego Arias used to retire to the kitchen with Don Yuce (Yosef) Mayor, "and they put on a sheet . . . and they said Jewish prayers, especially *nishmat kol hai*."[10]

Isn't this conclusive evidence that Diego Arias was a hidden Jew? The inquisitors wanted to draw this conclusion, and did. But we have no reason to follow their narrow interpretation. So far, these stories record a sense of personal loss, a nostalgia (expressed even in Diego's melancholic tone of voice) toward a broken childhood experience, and the attempt to retrieve a fragment of that experience for the sake of personal gratification. But they tell us little or nothing about Diego Arias's religious beliefs, his self-perception, or serious intent.

At long last—on May 19, 1489—Mosén Negro, the alleged source of so much hearsay about Diego Arias, appeared in the records in person. Negro quoted someone else ("Fernando Albarez's old uncle") who, twenty-eight years earlier, had told Negro that many people in Segovia "know the Bible" (meaning, read it in Hebrew), and that "Diego Arias, when he is in good spirits, covers his head and shoulders with a large cloth like a *talit* (*Taler*) and sings the Hebrew chant which the Jewish cleric says when taking out the Torah, and that he sings very well!"[11]

Perhaps Negro did not tell everything he knew. Even so, the side remarks of his testimony are significant. When this important source speaks, we learn that Diego Arias performed his Judaizing acts "when in good spirits"—that is, as a matter of mood, and mainly for personal fulfillment or pleasure. No religious intent or devotion is indicated, nor an attempt to be Jewish again.

The same conclusion emerges from the more colorful story told by Jacob Castellano, an official of the Jewish *aljama* (congregation), who recalled an episode that had taken place twenty-six years earlier. Castellano was then twelve years old.[12] It was, writes the trial clerk,

> a day in which the Jews do not work, a Sabbath or Passover and the said Diego Arias rose and told all the Christians to leave the room. . . . Upon seeing the witness, who had come in the company of his master Mayr, and making sure the boy was Jewish, he asked the other Jews whether the boy had brains, and when they said he had, he ordered: "let him stay." At that moment a servant entered and asked if they wanted to dine, and Diego Arias sent him away and locked the door. There was a dining table covered with a cloth, so he put some tablecloths on his head, the way a Jewish priest does with the large *talit* [*Taler Mayor*],[13] and stood on a stool, and started singing a lamentation which the Jews say on the Sabbath or any other Jewish holiday, in the graceful manner of the Jews and even more gracefully. And he recited the lamentation in Hebrew, the one beginning *nishmad colhai* [*nishmat kol hai*,—נשמת כל חי] until the *cadis* [*Kaddish*: a prayer for the deceased].
>
> Thus he said in Hebrew for a quarter of an hour. Then he got off the stool, sighed and said: "O Jews, Jews, when the Sabbath comes in, on a Friday night, and you are saying *vay hod lo asamay* [distortion of *vayehulu hashama'yim* (and the heavens were done), which is the actual Friday night prayer celebrating the end of the Creation], you have the whole world in your possession: [why] can't you appreciate it?!"

The recurrent mention of the prayer *nishmat kol hai* (a third witness also cites it)[14] is interesting. This prayer is part of the *mussaf* service of the Sabbath; so perhaps as a child, Diego (Isaac) had been assigned to chant this prayer weekly, and in later life it became his favorite and best-remembered piece of Jewish liturgy.

Yet this nostalgia did not make Diego Arias Jewish, not even in secret, and certainly not in his own eyes. When speaking to the Jews (in Castellano's story) he addresses them as others. He does retain a warm spot for Jews and perhaps regrets that he can no longer share their religion—but he knows he can't, and does not try to change this situation. Jews, he intimates, like to complain of their situation, but fail to appreciate how much better off than Diego they are in some respects—above all, in being completely integrated in their religion and able to enjoy it without duality; it is as though, in practicing it, they had "the whole world in their possession." This starkly contrasts with Diego Arias himself, who possesses the world of political power and wealth—yet suffers from a spiritual deprivation incurred in his childhood, from which he has never recovered and knows he never will. He will not go back to being a Jew—this was completely out of the question for the mature Diego Arias, who has become basically irreligious, and resolved long ago to accept the Hispano-Christian social identity cast on him by his fate. But he feels estranged from Catholicism, which remains a foreign implant in him, although, as foreign, it has become part of his *self* and must continue to be so. In consequence, he chases the child he used to be prior to his worldly glory, rehearsing his favorite chants and prayers; but since he is unable to recapture that child, he shows sympathy for other Jewish children (such as young Jacob Castellano) who take part in the prayer, unaware that, one day, they will betray him to the Inquisition and, worse, will completely miss the nature of his person.

The Popularity of Adafina

Similar nostalgia and personal gratification explain Diego Arias's second major crime—his fondness of *khamin*, the typical Jewish dish. There is ample evidence he used to receive this Sabbath dish from Jewish providers and eat it with Doña Elvira. *Khamin* is prepared on Friday in order to avoid lighting a fire on Saturday, and continues simmering until it is consumed the next day. Ashkenazi Jews called it *tcholent* (from the French *chaud lent*: "slow-warm"), and the Sephardim called it *adafina*. In the records of the Inquisition, *adafina* was so popular a proof of secret Judaism that one gets the impression that the inquisitors liked it even more than the Jews did; and because the clerics spelled out its ingredients for the record, one is thankful to the "Holy Office" for an occasional Jewish recipe.

The inquisitors' meticulous concern with this dish highlights their bias and limitations in identifying secret Jews. *Adafina*, with its hearty ingredients and prolonged cooking, is indeed distinctive—not of Jewish cult, but of Jewish gastronomy. Not everyone who likes *adafina* keeps the Sabbath. Even today, secular and atheist Jews often eat this dish with relish—the food of their grandmothers, of bygone times, of the old country. Similarly, in consuming *adafina* a Marrano tells us more about his culinary tastes than his religious inclinations. It is well known that food preferences, especially for distinctive ethnic dishes, are the last customs to disappear in immigrant and other assimilating societies.[15] Food is the readiest object of group nostalgia, and the last bastion of resisting ethnic characteristics.

Anti-Feminism and Instrumental Saints

Deprecating Christianity was a further sign of Judaism on the Inquisition's list. Diego Arias's third crime was showing disrespect to Christian saints, to salvation, and to Jesus himself.

Once on a trip, Diego Arias's mule, startled by a saint's effigy set on the roadside, almost threw its rider off. An angry Diego Arias ordered his servant to pull the effigy out of the way and dump it in the bushes.[16] Jews regard the cult of saints' effigies as idolatry, so Diego's reaction could have arisen from a Jewish atavism. But not necessarily: it could have betrayed his religious indifference or skepticism, his irreverence toward occult symbols, or—as I think was the case here—Diego Arias tended to treat magical objects as utilitarian devices, to be discarded when dysfunctional. Diego did not see a real saint in the effigy: what he saw was a failed magical fetish. And although he credited magical objects with some degree of power (superstition is not attached to any particular religion, it can float freely between and outside religions), he looked scornfully upon that particular fetish because it botched its mission: instead of protecting him, the traveler, it almost caused him a serious accident—so, the hell with it! This reaction is very un-Catholic, but not necessarily Jewish. And the bad tempered arrogance it manifests is a fault of character, not of religion.

Was this a pattern of Diego Arias's conduct? Very probably, as another incident is reported in which he treated a failing saint with wrath. The witness was Diego's Jewish estate manager, Abraham Caragoza, whom Diego had ordered to construct a chapel for the use of the tenants living on his land. When work was nearly finished and Diego Arias rode to inspect the site, a heavy storm of hail broke out, so violent that he feared for his life. Finally making it to the site, Diego immediately inquired which saint was supposed to protect the chapel's visitors (checking for performance again!), and when he learned it was a *santa* (female saint), he exploded: "This old whore made me think I was going to die! . . . Get her the hell out of here, and put a *santo* (male saint) in her place!"[17]

Clearly, this was not so much a deprecation of saints as it was of females. In Diego's mind, women perform less well—even as saints. Nothing indicates that Diego denied the magical power of saints' effigies; quite the contrary, he believed in it: he tried to replace a defective fetish with a more effective one—a woman with a man.[18] On the whole, he treated Christian saints in the same possessive way one treats personal property. Diego Arias owns his saints and replaces them at will. He, the powerful official, is boss and master of his magical instruments, to which the saints have been reduced. This again is very un-Catholic, but far from being Jewish. It expresses the self-confidence or hubris of one who affirms himself in this world and is aware of his power alongside his limitations. He is human and needs protection, hence the use of effigies; yet he prostrates himself before no church. His worldly knowledge is also a possession, a source of self-assurance and confidence, which he owes to no superior authority.

The latter sentiment is recorded in yet another story. Once Diego Arias won a pile of precious coins in an auction, and a flatterer congratulated him: "What a fine profit you have just made, sir!" Diego Arias retorted: "I certainly do not have as much power as God, but in what concerns knowledge [of finances], I think I have as much as He."[19] The Inquisition, narrow as usual, interpreted this as Jewish blasphemy against Christianity. But even if said somewhat facetiously, these were the words of a confident man sure of his professional powers, worldly knowledge, and career: a Spanish renaissance man tracing the horizon of modernity. In later centuries, philosophers like Descartes and Leibniz claimed to know physics and mathematics the way God knows them; to Diego Arias it had been economics: in both cases, man, by using this-worldly reason, is no longer so helpless and inferior, but claims his world-confident place in the order of things.

Abraham Caragoza, the Jewish estate manager, plainly stated that Diego Arias "had no faith." His distance from both Judaism and Christianity alike is further demonstrated by the way Diego Arias spoke of his own death. In one testimony he wondered whether salvation exists at all, and what might lead to it. He knew, of course, the answers of Christianity and of the law of Moses, but believed in neither. Like many Conversos, he expected death to be final and remained this-worldly even in thinking of his death. He told the monk Alonso Henríquez he was pleased that his mortal remains would rest in the prestigious Merced monastery (a popular holy place in Segovia)—not because the monks' prayers could do him any good—on this he did not deceive himself—but because this popular place drew crowds who would recognize his tomb there. As for his soul, of which nobody knows anything, if by any chance it should have a future life and the monks' chants would not help it, then the Jews' prayers might, for behind the monastery there is a Jewish synagogue. . . .

This cynical clowning has a ring of truth. Its expression of skepticism and a split religious identity adds a distinctive brush stroke to the self-portrait of Diego Arias as an old Marrano—whose duality is very different from that of Antón de Montoro (in the poem to Queen Isabella). Unlike the humble poet, the arrogant royal minister makes no meek efforts to become assimilated. He boldly indulges his Jewish nostalgia, knowing and willing it to be merely a private gratification, which he insists on exercising although he has no intention of becoming Jewish again. Diego Arias had resolved to assume his Hispano-Christian identity but could not and would not realize it in full, so he gave it a personal, and therefore illicit (in the eyes of the Inquisition), version of his own, which was nourished by the lasting sense of deprivation incurred in his childhood.

And there, precisely, lay his offense. The attempt to personalize Christianity—to be Christian in one's own way—was incompatible with Catholic culture in fifteenth-century Spain, which was becoming intolerant and officially monolithic.

In the end, Diego Arias's life and duality are captured by the scene he drew himself, in which the jumbled Jewish prayer coming from the synagogue behind the monastery mingles with the stylized chants of the Merced monks, while Diego Arias lies in his grave—longing for the one, recalling the other, and listening to both with equal distance, disenchantment, and disbelief.

Elvira Goncález—A Protosecular Social Judaizer

A different relationship to Judaism is manifest in Doña Elvira Goncález, the bishop's mother and Diego Arias' first wife. It is a steadier, less distant relationship, scantily informed by Jewish culture yet more committed to Jewish affairs, and although less complex than her husband's, definitely dualistic. Born Jewish and named Clara, she was converted to Catholicism at age eleven but kept close ties with her Jewish relatives even as an adult. She visited them on Jewish holidays and on family occasions, sometimes staying for a whole week after a funeral or *brith* (circumcision). She enjoyed Jewish company, the distinctive atmosphere, and the traditional food. These family visits and her donations to Jewish causes were Doña Elvira's nontheological way of maintaining a link with a Jewish life that no longer was hers.[20] When she took part in the family's rituals during a visit there is no indication that she thereby expressed a living Jewish religious belief or intent: this was rather a form of social and family companionship—maintaining identitarian ties to a community she felt akin to. One of the significant charges against Elvira was that she used to "get idle" in the company of Jews during a Sabbath or holiday:[21] this nonact, an omission, became a positive deed in the eyes of the Inquisition (and perhaps her own), a form of active Jewish participation.

Charity was another way for her to keep a thread of Jewish loyalty without sharing the Jewish religion. (Even today Jewish charity is a secular, social way to maintain a Jewish communion.)[22] Six indirect inquisitory testimonies describe the wealthy Doña Elvira sending alms and oil to synagogues in Segovia, Avila, even Toledo. One gift was made on the eve of "the great fast" (*ayuno mayor*—Yom Kippur). Her donations evolved into a business operation. A nephew remembered Doña Elvira going over the accounts with her Jewish cousin, Jacob Melamed, who discreetly helped manage her charities. But not all her agents were as trustworthy. The jeweler Abraham Meme remembered that as a child his father took him to the Arias d'Avila home to offer textiles for sale. Doña Elvira took his father aside and gave him twenty or thirty *reales* several times over (intended for different recipients), saying: "Take this, Simoel Meme, to buy oil for the synagogue[s]; for what I give you reaches its destination, but the money I give Doña Luna does not get across."[23]

A strange scene took place on the eve of one Yom Kippur. Doña Elvira and her son Juan (the future bishop) convoked a group of Jewish notables to the Arias d'Avila mansion. Among them was Maestre Shemaya, chief of the Jewish *aljamas* in Castile and the king's physician. He was unpopular and came with his bodyguard. The scene was described by Shemaya's assistant, Simuel Nombroso:

> Elbira[24] and her son spoke to Maestre Samaya; after which all the Jews embraced Samaya before leaving the room, and each of them asked the other's forgiveness, so that these Jews remained friendly with Maestre Samaya. When they left . . . Juan Arias said aloud [to Shemaya]: "these clothes here are for the most needy, the rest should go to the synagogue of del Campo" which was under construction [the latter phrase seems to be Nombroso's explanation]. . . . Maestre Samaya took his leave . . . and on arriving home he put ten or twelve golden Enriques [pieces carrying King Enrique's image] on the table.[25]

What was this about? Clearly, a mixture of charity and inter-Jewish politics. Doña Elvira, the Conversa, and her son the future bishop, were mediating between rival Jewish factions and using the Jewish Day of Atonement to arrange for a truce between the state-appointed Jewish chief and his Segovian opponents. Meanwhile, mother and son handed out donations to Jewish causes—from the most needy to the affluent builders of a new synagogue, which gave them political clout. Juan Arias is seen here doing what he knew best—not Judaizing, but politicking. He surely did this for his mother's sake. To him, this filial service was doubtless a pastime. Not so to Doña Elvira, who was earnestly engaged in Jewish charity-cum-politics. Her involvement, a personal project, gave content to her life outside both religions; it compensated for her lost identity and impoverished religious existence. In that respect, Doña Elvira was the most Jewish-committed member of the Arias d'Avila family. She was not committed to Judaism as religion, but to something more visceral and confused, based on memory, kinship, a sense of tribal loyalty—and also, perhaps, on loyalty to the person she had been in the distant past, and which she still wanted to be in that past modality. Doña Elvira was a has-been Jew and, without trying to become an actual Jew, wanted this has-beenness to be her actuality, to be translated into present social and secular relations. This was the basis of her own special duality.

To accomplish this, Elvira needed to maintain intimate contacts with Jews who lived their Judaism as a *present* reality. This was possible in Spain as long as Jews were still living alongside the Conversos. In 1492, when the Jews were expelled, the Elviras of Spain and their male counterparts lost their peculiar kind of hold on Jewish identity and waned as a special phenomenon.

The Inquisition, in condemning Elvira as religious heretic, was narrow-sighted again. Doña Elvira's link to Jewish identity was basically social; it relied on shared social events, rites of passage, charities, politics, family ties, and ethnic background. In this significant respect Elvira González, unlike her husband and unlike her son, was engaged in a protosecular way of Jewish participation that anticipated forms of dualist Jewish identity in later centuries, including our own. Indeed, we might see in her a Marrano prototype of the postemancipation Jewish situation that today has structural cousins everywhere.[26]

In leaving this interesting lady, let us take a quick glance at the composite portrait that emerges from the prosecution and the defense in her case. The prosecutor made twenty-three charges of Judaizing, mostly of a social rather than religious nature. Doña Elvira loved *adafina* and Jewish weddings; she sent unleavened bread and lettuce to Jewish recipients on Passover; she gave charity to synagogues; she "idled together" with Jews on Saturdays; she talked a Jew out of his intention to convert; she ate meat on Lent; and she called two Jewish women to her bedside when she died.[27] The defense retorted that Elvira had always been an observant Catholic who went to confession every year; observed the mandatory Catholic holidays; gave charity to churches, monasteries, and the poor; did not keep the Sabbath; never said Jewish prayers; and died a Catholic and "not like a Jewess." Perhaps, except for a few inconstancies, both the prosecution and the defense were basically right.

Bishop Juan Arias d'Avila—Yet Another Spanish Exile

And what about the bishop? When chief inquisitor Torquemada finally issued a formal indictment against Juan Arias's deceased parents, the old bishop, then about eighty, protested vehemently. He challenged the Inquisition's methods and denied all charges against his parents. But when he saw that his pleas had no effect, he shocked the Spanish establishment by announcing his intention to appeal to Pope Innocent VIII in Rome.[28]

That was a dangerous strategy. The Spanish Inquisition was jealous of its autonomy. It was an intra-Spanish institution, not a papal instrument. The

Spanish monarchs, who initially had sympathized with the Converso bishop, now turned forcefully against him. Sometime in 1490, Bishop Juan Arias was himself indicted, accused of obstructing the work of the Inquisition. In the logic of the times, this amounted to being "hostile to Christianity"—that is, to the new kind of Christianity embodied in the Inquisition.[29] To make these political accusations more damaging, a charge of homosexuality was added.

When the bishop took his case to Rome, the angry Isabella and Ferdinand ordered their ambassadors to spy on Juan Arias in an attempt to get the Vatican to dismiss his appeal and remove the bishop. The perturbed bishop saw a flicker of hope when the unconventional Alexander VI mounted the Holy See. Yet no pope, however original, could politically afford to grant Juan Arias what he really wanted: a verdict implying that it was possible to be a faithful Christian while opposing the intolerant regime of inquisitorial Spain. So, inevitably, his case dragged on without resolution until the bishop's death seven years later, in 1497.

Those last years were the most pathetic of Juan Arias's life. In a way, like the Jews he saw being expelled in 1492, he too (the non-Judaizer who opted for assimilation) was irreversibly driven to exile by the New Spain. While perceiving himself as a Spaniard and a Christian, he had to live outside Spain, severed from his base and family, with a cloud hanging over his Christian credentials, and fighting against his own queen's envoys in a desperate attempt to secure a ruling that contradicted their deepest politics and the spirit of the new Spain.

It is obvious that this Marrano bishop was fighting not only for his clerical standing but for his hard-won identity—the Hispano-Christian identity, which was slipping away from him after a lifetime of hard effort to secure it. Juan Arias did not Judaize, not even in his father's whimsical, uncommitted way;[30] he spent a long career serving the politico-religious establishment of his country and had, in the past, used brutal means to clear himself of the suspicion of Judaism (by having sixteen Jews executed on false charges). By that act he meant to suppress his Judeo-Christian duality, but actually he made it all the more manifest (at least, to us today).

Yet while Juan Arias was moving so insistently toward Spain, Spain was irreversibly moving away from him. His suppressed duality turned his last years into a struggle against shadows he could not control—shadows within his family, himself, and the New Spain. Just as his father had lost his Jewish childhood, so Juan Arias had lost the Spain of his maturity, the Spain into which he thought he had succeeded in integrating. And although he was never convicted (which further symbolizes his case's lack of conclusive definition), he died in physical and mental exile, protesting against the duality cast upon him and, by that protest, reaffirming it.

PART THREE

The Growing Marrano Problem

8

Enrique the Impotent: Prosperity, Anarchy, and Inquisition on the Horizon

———————— ⮐ ————————

The Toledo affair of 1449 was a watershed event for the Conversos. During the latter half of the fifteenth century, amid uneven economic growth, political anarchy, and civil war, the Converso issue became one of Castile's pressing problems. Old and New Christians were engaged in conflicts that deteriorated into riots and pogroms, until the anti-Converso campaign assumed an official character with the founding of the Inquisition.

The process that climaxed in the Inquisition extended over the two decades of King Enrique IV's reign (1454–1474). Enrique was possibly the most maligned ruler in Spanish history. He was called tyrant, pervert, Jew-lover, Muslim-lover, madman, and impotent—and each epithet was accompanied by a torrent of elusive tales, almost all of them false. Actually, the unfortunate Enrique paid a high price for his father, King Juan II's, folly. At the end of his life, Juan sacrificed his able minister, Alvaro de Luna, to the wrath of the nobles, who had once again become unrestrained and insolent. Juan thereby bequeathed his son a crown that was too heavy for him to bear. But Enrique was also responsible for his many woes. A weak and unorthodox sovereign who despised regal pomp and honestly aspired to govern for his people's common good, Enrique alienated himself from the conventions of the court and from the concerns and lifestyle of the Spanish upper class. Many nobles regarded him as eccentric and untrustworthy—a feudal master who was jeopardizing the interests and political culture of the very class he headed. When their grumbling escalated into a true power struggle, the king's unorthodox inclinations were increasingly perceived as a threat, as faulty judgment, and soon even as heresy, perversity, and madness.

To better appreciate this background, which was decisive in the lives of the Marranos and conducive to the creation of the Inquisition, let us take a closer look at life in Castile.

Castile under Enrique

Times were difficult for king and country. Castile was undergoing rapid change, growth, and instability. The royal administration was inefficient, and the king was regarded as indecisive. As their power grew, the nobles created semisovereign estates for themselves and tried to extend their rule over the cities, which put up stubborn resistance.[1] Confronted with ambitious nobility and a weak central government, the cities organized the *Santa Hermandad* (Holy Brotherhood), an alliance for self-defense and crime fighting that soon developed into a military force capable of challenging other powers in the fractured realm. The cities became frequent scenes of strife and disorder. Violent struggles raged between rival grandee families (such as the clans of Ayala and Silva in Toledo), between Old and New Christians, and between the patricians and the restive lower classes. The plague—the enemy of minorities—also made a comeback and further fanned the flames of social discontent.

During the third quarter of the fifteenth century, Castile experienced a demographic recovery and rapid but uneven economic growth that led to friction and imbalances. A century after the Black Death, its population rebounded to 4.5–5 million, at a time when England's population was probably under 2 million. Agriculture remained the economic mainstay but shifted drastically from growing food to producing a raw material, wool. According to one estimate, there were five million sheep in Castile, one for every person. The wool industry was called the "daughter of the plague" because it required less manpower than standard agricultural activities. A surge in demand for wool in northern Europe further encouraged production. Eager to reap the fruit of this international demand, leading nobles and the Crown raised huge herds of sheep on their estates and reorganized their production methods.[2] Yet food production lagged behind demand despite progress in fishing techniques. There were periodic shortages of grain-based food (the main staple of the day), which led to soaring prices, hunger, and mounting discontent.[3] Great distortions were caused by inflation, which had raged in Castile since the start of the century. The price of grain doubled and then doubled again. Shortages were often addressed by importing grain from abroad but these costly imports did not always meet the need. The inflationary pressures were not properly understood; meanwhile, they destabilized the economy and reduced many people to ruin. The constant devaluation of money became physically visible as the edges of coins were cut or the percentage of the precious metals in coins was reduced.

As we saw in chapter 3, the Conversos played a far greater role in the rise of Castilian protocapitalism and urban bourgeoisie than did the Old Christians. Not only were Conversos present in most relevant industries but they were more likely than others to reinvest their profits in productive activities; and they viewed a person's worth as deriving from personal endeavors and economic success, whereas the Old Christian rich tended to invest—in capitalist terms: to *park*—their wealth in stationary landed assets or spend it on a lifestyle imitating the nobility. "The ideal of the fifteenth-century Castilian merchant was . . . to become an *hidalgo* and live off leasing his land," say the authors of *Historia de España*, who call this disposition "the triumph of the chivalrous ideal."[4] The historian Julio Valdeón Baruque argues more sharply that no bourgeoisie in the modern sense ever emerged in Castile: the rising nonagricultural sectors of the economy adjusted to the old feudal structures so the urban population they employed never became an agent of socioeconomic change and modernization.[5]

There was an exception to this rule: the New Christians. Because of their special situation—including their stigma of impure blood—the New Christians were able to develop a new economic ethos of labor, production, and wealth as legitimate goals. This gave them a relative economic advantage, but brought them into further conflict, emotive and normative, with Old Christian society. The threat they posed to the existing order did not stem only from their "contaminated" blood and former religion, but also from their new economic creed; that is, from the new secular value system that the Conversos had shaped. In this sense, too, they constituted a subversive minority within the old Hispanic society.

Burgos as Example

A quick glance at one city—Burgos—illustrates life in Enrique's Castile, the growing economic wealth together with instability and violence.[6]

The center of Burgos life was the great wool market. All the wool from southern Castile flowed into this place before going to the port of Bilbao to be shipped to Flanders or Rouen. The city was ruled by often-warring patrician families, including important Converso clans like the Santa Marías and Cartagenas (offspring of Rabbi Shlomo Halevi).[7] Emulating the nobles' lifestyle and values, many city oligarchs spent their profit on luxuries and large estates rather than reinvesting it in their business and production techniques. This typical Spanish phenomenon had a further motivation in Burgos: the local interest was to trade in wool, not produce or rework it, which made Burgos even slower than other cities in developing the rudiments of productive capitalism.

The older Burgos families, while fighting each other, resented the many new elements that arose among them: new rich, new nobles, and especially New Christians—some belonging to the same families. The older families' hostile reaction fanned the civil warfare that shattered Burgos under Enrique's shaky rule. The endemic crisis was worsened by the plague and an acute food shortage, one of the worst in the fifteenth century.

In consequence, Burgos experienced fourteen years of ongoing bloodshed (1460–1474). The populace fought against the patricians; the patricians fought among themselves; out-of-town nobles violently attempted to seize property in the city; and the new rich struggled against the established clans. The Conversos were twice involved in those clashes, both as members of one of the struggling classes and as a special group fighting for its existence and status against the hatred and prejudice of almost all other groups.

A similar picture was apparent in other Castilian cities. The failure of government and the sense that life was unstable removed the ordinary restraints from the human instincts of greed, lust for power, social bitterness, identity passions, and xenophobia—all those passions that fall under the purview of politics to restrain and rechannel in a useful and balanced way. But when the political regime itself is the problem, it cannot be counted upon to provide a remedy.

A historian of Toledo, Eloy Benito Ruano, summarized the quality of life during Enrique IV's reign: "Hardly a year passed during those two decades that was not marked by some drama or act of violence; the sum of these years looks like a long nightmare of fear, disasters, and cares."[8] Another scholar published a list of nearly thirty violent outbursts in Toledo, Burgos, Salamanca, Carmona, Bilbao, Seville, Alcaraz, Trujillo, Medina del Campo, Cordoba, Segovia, and so on—including six pogroms against Conversos. These figures support Angus MacKay's conclusions that the anti-Converso pogroms should be viewed as one aspect, albeit unique, of the general instability that plagued Castile during Enrique's years.[9]

Undermining the Regime and the Avila Farce

A special role in destabilizing the kingdom was played by the man who had been assigned to maintain its stability—Juan Pacheco. Pacheco was Alvaro de Luna's mistake. Luna, the great minister, had appointed Pacheco as tutor to young Enrique to help groom him for kingship and be his loyal adviser and confidant after he ascended to the throne—the same role Luna had played for Enrique's father. The crafty minister may have wanted to plant his own man at the future king's side, or perhaps the appointment was an aging statesman's attempt to create a successor in his own image, thus cloning himself and his own youth.

Either way, his design failed. Pacheco was practically Luna's antithesis. Young Alvaro de Luna had concealed his loyalty to King Juan behind a mask of cool detachment, and thus managed to survive the period of purges and intrigues against his royal master's men; whereas the more ordinary Pacheco feigned loyalty to Enrique while actually plotting against him. In return for his show of loyalty, Enrique showered Pacheco with offices, money, and powers, some of which he passed on to his brother and partner in intrigue, Don Pedro Girón. The king gave the brothers command of his fortresses—a major part of the royal military power—never suspecting that they would use this power against him.

Meanwhile a league of disgruntled nobles formed against Enrique. The league was led by the ambitious archbishop of Toledo, Don Alonso Carillo, in his drive to reach the pinnacle of power. Carillo made a secret pact with Pacheco and his brother. The conspirators planned to replace Enrique with his rival, King Juan II of Aragon, but a group of nobles from Aragon had turned against their king and invited none other than Enrique of Castile to be their sovereign (1462).[10] Enrique already saw the dream of a united Spain materializing under his scepter. But his advisers, especially the Pacheco brothers, argued that annexing Aragon would be hazardous and talked Enrique into accepting the mediation and judgment of King Louis XI of France. When Louis, who did not wish to see a strong united Spain on his border, ruled against Enrique's wishes, the Castilian sovereign did not immediately grasp what had happened; but when he learned that Pacheco and Girón had taken large monetary gifts from the French king, the pieces of the puzzle fell into place for him.

His disillusionment was fast, marked by disbelief and the pain of betrayal, but also by a sense of powerlessness because the brothers controlled the king's citadels. Therefore, instead of trying them for treason, Enrique was forced to make an accommodation. Pacheco and Girón retired from the king's service, soon to join his opponents. In their place Enrique appointed as chief councilor a courtier named Beltrán de La Cueva, who enjoyed the queen's favor and, gossip had it, also her bed.

Was this idle gossip? The lords of Castile did not think so. The king's sex life became a political issue of the first order. Pacheco and his cohorts, relying on their intimate familiarity with Enrique, declared that the king was impotent. Hence Princess Juana, the Infanta, could not be his daughter or the rightful heir to his throne. Juana, they claimed, was the queen's daughter by the traitorous minister Beltrán (traitors always accuse others of treachery). Repeated with relish among the Castilian ruling classes, this rumor spread around the country and has caught up by several historians as well. Wits of the day dubbed Juana *La Beltraneja*, after her presumed father. Today it is all but certain that the rumor was false. But the king's foes, led by Pacheco and Archbishop Carillo, exploited the gossip to declare that the legal heir to the throne was the child Alfonso, Enrique's half brother, and that next in line was Alfonso's minor sister, Isabella.

The league leaders demanded to take responsibility for the young prince and princess's education and "protection" from Beltrán's henchmen, who would stop at nothing to put the bastard Juana on the throne. Their aim, of course, was to gain control of a rival source of political legitimacy, and to obtain influence over the future king or queen. (As it turned out, their calculations proved short-sighted: Queen Isabella would dominate the nobility, not vice versa).

Exploiting the unrest in the kingdom, for which they were largely responsible, Pacheco, Carrillo, and the league leaders convened in Burgos in 1464, and sent Enrique a list of grievances—some not unfounded—calling for government reform. Their ultimate purpose was clear from their demands: to dismantle the Royal Guard (leaving Enrique vulnerable), dismiss Beltrán, and proclaim Alfonso heir to the crown.[11]

Some of the league's complaints targeted the Conversos in the king's service. The writers protested the appointment of "unsuitable people" to ecclesiastical offices; the impoverishment of the people by the king's tax collectors (many of them Conversos); the ruinous depreciation of the currency resulting from the policy of the Converso Diego Arias d'Avila, Enrique's top financier; and, in general, the king's close association with "Christians in name only," some of whom deny the afterlife "and claim there is no world but this world of ours in which man lives and dies like the animals" (as, indeed, Arias d'Avila believed—see previous chapter). By tolerating such people in his presence, they insinuated, the king was secretly a partner to their heresy.[12]

Aware of a genuine mood of distress seething in the country, Enrique sought a compromise. He agreed to sacrifice his daughter's crown, but not her reputation. So he agreed to appoint the eleven-year-old Alfonso as heir to the crown and turn him over to the guardianship of the nobles on condition that Princess Juana be recognized as his legitimate daughter and marry Alfonso when he matured. A joint commission was created to arbitrate all other demands and the king promised to accept its recommendations.

Within six weeks Enrique discovered that he had been betrayed again. The commission issued a report written in the nobles' spirit and opposing the king. Enrique discovered that two of his own men on the commission, including his secretary Alvar Gómez, had defected to Pacheco and the league. The furious Enrique rejected the commission's recommendations and the crisis came to a deadlock.

This was the background of the *Farce of Avila*, a political spectacle that led to serious consequences. On June 5, 1465, a group of high and low nobles, headed by Pacheco and Archbishop Carillo, assembled near the city of Avila to conduct a weird ceremony. They had built a podium with King Enrique's statue on it, and after reading a list of grievances and charges against the king they scornfully removed the stone crown from the statue's head and started smashing it into pieces while heaping invectives upon Enrique. Young Alfonso was then carried onto the podium to a flourish of trumpets and proclaimed king of Castile.

Thus began the civil war. Within five days Toledo had defected to the rebels, followed by Burgos, Seville, Cordoba, and other Castilian cities. But the revered primate of the Toledo cathedral, the Converso Francisco de Toledo, spoke out against the rebels: "No one has the right to depose a king, even a bad king," Don Francisco emphatically declared, "unless he is proved guilty of heresy."[13] As if taking their cue from that pronouncement, Enrique's foes spread the rumor that the king was a heretic, and a homosexual to boot. Enrique, however, also had considerable support, coming from the pope in Rome and from important loyalist forces, including most of the Conversos. But Enrique, as we shall see, failed to reward their loyalty and let them down in the Conversos' moment of need.

Toledo 1467: Anti-Converso Riots and Converso Dualities

The civil war set the scene for driving the Converso problem onto the streets. And widespread riots against them threw the patterns of duality that characterized Converso life into sharp relief.

The most famous violent confrontation occurred in Toledo on June 19, 1467.[14] The civil war was then two years old. Toledo was held by the boy-king Alfonso, but the city was divided between two rival families, Silva and Ayala; and the latter was strongly anti-Converso. Recalling how helpless they were in the events of 1449, the Conversos decided to prepare for self-defense. A new Converso generation had arisen, and it would take up arms. They organized a militia, gathered weapons (some say even a few cannons), and appointed the energetic young Fernando de La Torre as their commander. Understanding they could not win alone, they struck an alliance with a Silva chieftain, Don Alonso da Silva, Count of Cifuentes, who controlled several quarters in Toledo.

Apparently they were prepared and reasonably secure. But excessive initiative can work to one's detriment, especially when it is joined with bad luck.

The event that triggered the riots was almost trivial. The Converso Alvar Gómez de Ciudad Real, a former royal secretary (the one who had betrayed Enrique on the arbitration commission), now lived in Toledo as a senior judge and landowner, and was opposed by the Ayala clan. One day his Ayala foes, who controlled the cathedral, sent a Jewish tax collector to one of Gómez's estates to exact payment for the cathedral, and Gómez's manager, Escobedo, had the Jew beaten and locked up. The heads of the cathedral raised a wild protest.

"Scandal! Impudent conspiracy! Gómez must be punished!" Nothing indicates that Gómez was selected because he was a Converso, but the Conversos were certain of it and practically compelled the reluctant former official to join forces with them.

On Sunday, July 19, at the end of Mass in the cathedral, Alvar Gómez was flabbergasted to hear a priest proclaim an interdict against his man, Escobedo, and hint that Gómez himself might be excommunicated. Gómez burst into vocal protests but, realizing he was in the minority, agreed to turn Escobedo in for trial by the Ayalas. At that moment, according to Pedro de Mesa, the commander of the Converso militia, Fernando de La Torre, burst into the cathedral demanding that Gómez recant the agreement. Commotion, shouts, threats. Finally Gómez went back on his word and angrily left the cathedral with La Torre, both denouncing the misuse of a house of God as a political weapon.

Within hours the two were back at the cathedral, swords drawn, at the head of a company of Conversos. Two clerics were killed in the raid. Mesa reports that the invaders shouted: "Let them die! Let them die! This is not a church, but a conclave of villains!"[15] It seems the Conversos mounted this violent raid as a deterrent, to assert that the days of Pero Sarmiento were gone and, if attacked, they would defend themselves with arms.

The Conversos' outcry ("this is not a church") betrays a Converso mindset. They felt that the cathedral's sanctity was annulled by the Ayalas' using it as a secular instrument of power; yet in a Catholic religious psychology, sanctity is an objective feature residing in concrete objects even when they are abused. The Converso position reveals that, even if they did not Judaize, they had not developed typical Catholic reflexes since they lacked the instinctive, deep-seated reverence for a Christian cathedral as such. This is not to deny they were Christians. But they were new, dualistic Christians, capable of looking at a sacred Christian site with critical eyes and stripping its sanctity in their minds when it seemed called for.

This Converso duality gave their enemies a powerful weapon. "Come to save God's house," the slogan ran in Toledo. "Join us in defending the pure Christians against the bad Christians!" Within two days about one thousand recruits gathered in the cathedral. Lacking regular supplies and seeking an outlet, their existence posed a threat to the Converso quarters. The situation became explosive.

On July 21, the Conversos launched a preemptive strike intended to break the cathedral doors and disperse the force stationed inside. But the Old Christians repulsed the assault and burst out in counterattack. In the following days the battle raged in the Converso quarters, especially the Magdalena. In the heat of battle, the Old Christians started torching the homes of the Conversos street by street. Strong gusts of wind spread the flames. According to Mesa, about sixteen hundred houses burned, and we may assume that some people were burned alive. And since fire has no eyes, it probably claimed Old Christian victims as well.

The terrible conflagration tipped the scales against the Conversos. What began as a battle ended as a massacre. The Converso houses that survived the fire were looted by the mob during three days of anarchy and killing. The mob captured the two young commanders, Fernando and Alvaro de La Torre, and hung their naked bodies upside down before sending them by donkey cart to one of the city's squares, where they were kept on display for four days while members of the crowd mutilated them with daggers beyond recognition. Finally they were sent to the Jewish community and were buried near its cemetery. Whether they agreed or not, the Converso commanders were branded Jews both in life and in death.

But the bloody Toledo events also highlighted the difference between Jews and Conversos. Unlike the Jews, the Conversos had a claim on positions of authority in the city and society, and they were prepared to take up arms in their defense. This posture outraged the Old Christians not only as a rival interest, but because of its symbolic message. The Conversos' actions proclaimed: "We are an integral part of Hispano-Christian society and participate in its conflicts as such"—which was unimaginable for Jews. The Conversos saw this as proof that they were no longer Jews, while their enemies saw it as a sign that the eternal Jew, who can never change, was now trying to invade the Spanish Self and endanger it from within.[16]

Purity of Blood: Act I, Scene 2

No wonder the Toledo riots of 1467 raised again the specter of the blood purity regulations. The City Council reissued the *Sentencia Estatuto* of eighteen years earlier and applied it to church positions as well. Now, says Mesa, a Converso was forbidden to hold "either office or benefice" (*"ni oficio ni beneficio"*); he was barred from both secular and religious public offices. Mesa justifies the regulation by saying that Conversos were "Judaizing in many ways" and "buying offices for money."[17] But the regulation made no exception for Conversos who were faithful Catholics. Clearly it was blanket legislation based on blood, origin, and a rigid existential distinction between "pure" and "impure" Christians. It implied that Jews cannot change because Judaism is literally in their blood.

The Toledo city council knew it had revived a scandalous law that had been repudiated by the pope and the former king. In a bid for legitimacy, it sent a high prelate as envoy to Alfonso, requesting the child-king to endorse the exceptional Toledo legislation and pardon the perpetrators of violence against the Conversos. Alfonso had just survived a battle against his brother Enrique by the skin of his teeth.[18] But despite his weakened position, the boy-king spoke sharply to the envoy. "Sir, you have undertaken a disgraceful and dishonorable mission," the thirteen-year-old shot at the elderly prelate. "To ask of me that I approve such wicked acts?!" The stunned envoy apologized and said he personally deplored the action in Toledo, yet he knew that the city leaders intended to support Enrique if Alfonso rejected their petition. "They can do as they please," the boy-king replied with spirit. "I will not lend a hand to evil and hideous deeds."

In addition to the moral courage of a young prince, Alfonso's response apparently expressed his determination not to start his reign in weakness or to compromise with anarchy as Enrique had. After all, Alfonso claimed the crown on the ground that his brother Enrique lacked kingly virtues. He would not purchase his crown by yielding to the forces of disorder or accept the usurpation of power by riotous cities. Otherwise the country would ultimately turn against him as it had against Enrique.

In the end, Alfonso proved his noble spirit and Toledo defected to Enrique. The older king had made the political calculations and agreed to pay the price. Much like the famous French monarch who, years later, was to declare that "Paris is worth a Mass,"[19] Enrique undoubtedly thought that Toledo was worth one dubious law. The edicts he issued prohibited Conversos from holding positions in local government, the police force, and any other function regarding law and order in the city. And if such a post should be offered to a Converso, then, the king stated, "it is my grace and command" that he reject it.[20]

Enrique's statute was promulgated twice (in Ciudad Real, July 3 and 14, 1468). What the king actually did was to confirm, no less, the *Sentencia* of Pero Sarmiento that the pope and Enrique's father had condemned eighteen years earlier as abusive and scandalous. Now, for the first time, the principle of pure blood was laid down not by an illegal, wildcat declaration of a mutinous city, but in the name and under the seal of a Spanish monarch. That the signer did not keep his own law (Enrique was, and continued to be, surrounded by New Christians) does not change the historical importance and impact of his act.

In the years to come, the statutes of pure blood were to have only limited import. They were issued locally here and there but did not become a universal institution, and they carried limited weight in either the royal or ecclesiastical administration. Even the Spanish Inquisition at first rejected the principle of purity of blood. The Inquisition was officially based on the opposite principle, namely that Christianity depended on baptism as a sufficient and irreversible condition rather than on blood. The purity of blood regulations owe their full triumph to the sixteenth century, especially to the Counter-Reformation movement, when they became Spain's national policy and the Inquisition was appointed their watchdog (see "Back to Spain: Purity of Blood, Act II" in chapter 12).

Projects for Establishing the Inquisition: Oropesa and Espina

Despite his capitulation to Toledo's blackmail, Enrique himself never believed in the blood purity doctrine—to him it was a passing demagogic price he had to pay to shore up his throne. But he was worried by the Converso problem and aware of the danger to his kingdom from the widening gap between New and Old Christians. He therefore kept looking for a solution, and although he never found one, his ear was attentive to suggestions by others, suggestions he allowed to germinate but never actually put into practice.

Enrique knew there was truth in the allegations that many Conversos Judaized or abandoned all religion, and believed this to be the actual reason (and not just a pretext) for the animosity against the Conversos. So he concluded that in order to resolve the problem, it was necessary to put an end to the allegations.

But how? Since it was impossible to deny the truth, it was necessary to change it. The pope, as some advisers reminded Enrique, possessed a proven instrument for just that purpose: a mechanism for cleansing the country of heretics by investigation, exposure, punishment, and deterrence. Two hundred and fifty years earlier, it had done wonders in purging southern France (Languedoc) of the Cathar heresy. Since then it had sunken into dormancy; but it still existed officially in neighboring Aragon, though it had never had a foothold in Castile. Now is the time, Enrique was urged, to introduce an Inquisition into Castile and submit the heretical Conversos to its judgment.

So argued two monks who had the king's ear, though each spoke in a different voice. One, Alonso de Espina, was a Franciscan; the other, Alonso de Oropesa, headed the Hieronymite Order. Both were said to be Conversos, although this is uncertain concerning Oropesa.[21] But even if they were, this was where any similarity between them ends. Espina was bitter, fanatic, of a destructive temperament, an ill-wishing religious moralist for whom faith was a source of hatred, and piety a means to purge the world of ideological foes. Oropesa was an affable man of good will, free of rancor and hatred, admired for his honesty, open to people and friendly with the Conversos, whom he vigorously defended. Enrique, schooled in betrayal, placed his trust in Oropesa; he believed he could rely on his integrity (with good reason) and also (with less good a reason) on his judgment.

Alonso de Oropesa epitomized the paradox of certain liberals whose good intentions lead, if not to hell, then to its lobby. His goal was to restore the

Conversos' reputation in Castile. As simplistically as the king, and possibly with a measure of self-deception, Oropesa believed that the Converso problem was caused by a small minority of heretical Conversos who tainted the community as a whole. He therefore proposed a limited, yet credible and efficient, mechanism to investigate and prosecute the handful of criminals: this would clear of suspicion the great majority of innocent Conversos, and in punishing the minority, would send a message to the public that the actual culprits were taken care of and no popular action against them was either needed or allowed.

Oropesa argued heatedly that purity is a matter not of blood, but of a Christian way of life; and a way of life can be corrected by education, combined with some police work. The Inquisition he proposed was limited in scope and moderate in means. It should be run by the pope and his bishops, and concern all Christians, old and new alike, not just the Conversos.[22] Espina, on the other hand, envisioned a harsh, oppressive mechanism that targeted the Conversos as potential criminals and functioned in the tough, zealous, manly style of Spaniards rather than in the effeminate and indulgent manner of Rome, where gold and machinations could obtain a pardon for any sin.

In 1460 Espina published a tract entitled *The Fortress of Faith*, which contained, according to Baer, a programmatic draft of the later Spanish Inquisition.[23]

The king tended toward Oropesa's view, but Espina was the king's confessor and had Enrique as captive audience. After some wavering Enrique decided to test the waters. At the end of 1461, concealing his move from his own ministers (so he could retreat without losing face), Enrique asked Pope Pius II for authorization to appoint four inquisitors of his choice, headed by the pope's delegate (nuncio). Pius II hesitated to grant religious power to a secular ruler, but finally granted the essence of Enrique's request, although limiting his powers. But when the approval (given on March 15, 1462, in a special bull) arrived in Castile under great secrecy—even top ministers were unaware of it—Enrique had already changed his mind. Ignoring the powers granted to him, he nipped his own project in the bud.

Thus the Spanish Inquisition, in its first form, came into the world stillborn, in secret (like an unwanted child), and was buried in the graveyard of the royal archives. The Spaniards of the day knew nothing of it, and only modern historians discovered it had ever existed.[24]

King Enrique's character was exposed in this affair: having made a tough decision and started to act on it, he reversed his position before it was consummated and undid his own deed. Because he was reluctant to implement Oropesa's plan, he opened the way for the execution of Espina's sinister vision fifteen years later. And when that happened, Alonso de Oropesa, despite his intention, became, in retrospect, a cofounder of an institution he presumably opposed because he was one of the first to give currency and legitimization to the idea of the Spanish Inquisition. It must be said to Oropesa's credit that he tried to save the quasi-pluralist spirit of the old Spain from the fanatically monolithic currents represented by Espina. But the concession he made to these trends was so critical that in the end he actually lent a hand to their triumph.

One public figure came out most resolutely against Espina: Diego Arias d'Avila Castile's Converso finance chief. He was Espina's deadly enemy at court. But Espina shifted his efforts from the royal court to public opinion. Launching a broad propaganda campaign, he traveled and preached from city to city, with the help of Franciscan monks who joined his crusade and brought the mobile Citadel of Faith with them wherever they went, firing from its ramparts ammunition of hatred, rumors, libels, and legal proposals. Their message was twofold: expel the Jews from the land, and subject the Conversos to a grinding Inquisition.

King Enrique did not share Espina's aims and did not stop him. Perhaps he understood that the demons tormenting his confessor were born not only from Espina's personal complexes but from deep currents within the Castilian society, which was undergoing an identity change that Espina epitomized. Those crusades in the name of *purity*—purity of blood, purity of faith, purifying the land of the demonic Other that threatened the Spanish Self—obliterated the remnants of the partial pluralism that had characterized the older Spanish identity.

Pacheco's Return; Riots in Andalusia

In 1468 the boy-king Alfonso suddenly died, depriving the rebels of a legitimate leader. The weary Alfonsian coalition reached the verge of collapse. Enrique too was worn out by the long armed struggle and the failure of his kingly project. He who aspired to rule for the good of his subjects had brought them the hardship of civil war. Pressure on both sides led to an agreement. The rebel nobles would bow to the king's authority, and Enrique would recognize Princess Isabella as his heiress and reinstate Pacheco as chief minister. Princess Juana was forsaken. An official document referred to her as "the queen's daughter"—an insult, almost equivalent to the popular nickname *La Beltraneja*.

The agreement stipulated that Isabella could not marry without the consent of the king and certain nobles (who thereby would influence the next regime). But young Isabella flouted this prohibition by secretly marrying Prince Ferdinand of Aragon (see next chapter). Pacheco by then had assessed Isabella's strong character and realized he had no political future in her regime. So, in a move that was unusually opportunistic even for him, Pacheco shifted his allegiance to the lady whom he had always called a bastard. Princess Juana must inherit the throne after all! Thus he now pleaded with the weary, deceived, and momentarily surprised Enrique (only momentarily, because Pacheco could no longer really surprise him), whose view this had been all along.

Knowing that Isabella would not yield easily, Pacheco tried to reinforce his hand before she took power by capturing top fortresses in key cities, as he had done in his earlier confrontation with Enrique. To that purpose, said Palencia, he needed a climate of urban unrest, which his agents provoked by fanning the hostility against the Conversos.[25]

The riots that followed started in Cordoba and spread through smaller urban localities—La Rambla, Almodóvar, Montero, and above all, Jaén—to the gates of Seville. Andalusian Conversos suffered extensive casualties and damage. Adding to the previous riots—and their deep-seated roots—all this violence attests to one thing: the Converso question had become a prime social problem in Castile. This had already been the case when Enrique assumed the throne and it remained true—indeed, even more so—in 1474, when this peculiar and much-abused monarch passed away.

9

Ferdinand, Isabella, and the "True Inquisition"

When Alfonso de Castile, the half-brother and rival of Enrique the "Impotent," died in 1468, his claim to the throne devolved to their seventeen-year-old sister, Isabella. This maid was to become one of the greatest monarchs in Spanish history. Within a single generation Isabella, together with her husband, Ferdinand of Aragon,[1] brought the Middle Ages to an end on the Iberian peninsula and laid the political and cultural foundations of the new, united Spain, which was to become the world's greatest power in the next century. In the history of the Marranos, the two "Catholic monarchs" are remembered for two fateful events: they established the New Inquisition, and they expelled all the Jews from Spain. Those who remained had to convert to Christianity.

Isabella was a very religious woman—not in a grand spiritual sense, but in a pious and sectarian way. She had the skill of exploiting her religious devotion in the service of her political objectives. Her confessor since her days as the Infanta was a Dominican friar whose name—Tomás de Torquemada—would echo fearfully in history books. It is not quite clear who in their relationship was using the other: the shrewd queen or Torquemada, the future grand inquisitor. Either way, their collaboration left a lasting mark on Spain.

Isabella's first political decision, perhaps the most crucial of her career, was to choose a husband. By rejecting the hand of the widowed king of Portugal in favor of young Prince Ferdinand, heir of Aragon, she set the course of the Iberian Peninsula's future. Young Ferdinand was far more attractive than the aging Portuguese king—and so was Aragon. In contrast to Portugal's relative isolation, Aragon maintained close contacts with other European countries. What's more, the royal family of Aragon had Castilian roots and preserved its familial, feudal, and financial ties with Castile.

The effective cooperation between Ferdinand and Isabella, two ambitious monarchs who enjoyed a cosovereign status in each other's kingdoms, is almost matchless in European history. During their reign they shattered the power of the aristocracy (especially in Castile) and reduced the nobles from demikings of their castles and estates to semidisciplined vassals, and sometimes even to idle courtiers. The monarchs curbed the rights of the cities and, like Alvaro de Luna, intervened in the appointment of urban officials, making sure that the Crown's delegate *(corregidor)* sat on every city council, eventually becoming the real local authority. They subjugated the powerful military orders and took control of part of their immense wealth by declaring King Ferdinand the successor of every deceased head of a military order. They demanded and received from the pope the power to appoint bishops and used it to promote clerics from the lower classes, who were wholly dependent upon them. And to administer and execute their enhanced powers they chose professional officials *(letrados)* loyal to themselves, rather than relying on the self-seeking members of the nobility

The core of central Spanish bureaucracy was the royal councils, in which Converso and, at the second level, Jewish administrators played a significant role. But their roles were not symmetrical. Without deliberate planning, Conversos gradually took over the traditional functions that Jews had exercised in past royal administrations. This made the Jews far less vital to the realm and facilitated their expulsion at the end of the century.

Beyond restructuring the regime, the two Catholic monarchs instilled a new sense of purpose and pride in the country and drove the divided Spanish elite into more cohesive action. They conquered the kingdom of Granada, thereby completing the Reconquista. They established the national Spanish Inquisition, expelled (or partly converted) all the Jews, forcibly converted the Muslims in the south, sent Columbus sailing to India (and finding America instead), planted New Spain's flag in the New World and, with a single stroke of the pen, divided the entire globe between Spain and Portugal as zones of discovery and conquest. Not everything was preconceived or calculated; much was achieved by seizing opportunities as one thing led to another.[2] But by setting all these trends in motion, the royal couple laid the foundations of the glory of the new Spain—as well as of some of its later problems and notorious aberrations.[3]

The "True Inquisition"

The greatest of these aberrations was the *true Inquisition*. An ineffective papal Inquisition had existed in Languedoc (southern France) since the time of the Cathar heresy in the thirteenth century. From Languedoc it moved into nearby Aragon, though not to Castile, and in time became dormant. As the problem of the New Christians became acute, it was argued and believed in the young monarchs' circles that the new Spain, in order to forge its unity, needed its own state-run Inquisition and an ethos of purity and ethnic-religious homogeneity. Hence the strident demand to establish a *true* Inquisition—not a random and indulgent institution like the papal Inquisition in Aragon, but a severe and systematic disciplinary force, controlled by the Crown, that would cauterize every abscess of heresy in Spain. The new Inquisition must be centralized, efficient, and rigorous. It should spread its net over the entire land, preventing heretics from taking refuge through internal migration. Above all, it must serve the interests of Spain's civil government rather than the Spanish clergy or the intriguing papal court in Rome. By subordinating the ominous new tool—which could, and did, prosecute even bishops and cardinals—to their royal authority, Ferdinand and Isabella were to curb the autonomy of the Spanish clergy and make it more servile to the Crown.

Background

The Marrano community in Andalusia, especially Seville, was among the largest and wealthiest in Spain. It also contained many a covert Judaizer—a fact that supplied ammunition to the Conversos' enemies among the clergy and the burghers.

In 1477 Ferdinand and Isabella set court in Seville. Many Conversos became involved in court affairs, which fanned their rivals' envy. The fiercest and shrewdest of these enemies was Fray Alonso de Hojeida, abbot of a big Dominican center in Seville. He was to the Conversos in Andalusia what Ferrán Martínez had been to the Jews a century earlier. If Martínez watched the burgeoning synagogues in Seville with a jaundiced eye, Hojeida, and anyone else who surveyed the city from above, was now treated to a new sight. As a Hebrew source relates:

> In the city of Seville, an inquisitor said to the duke: if Your Grace wishes to know how the Marranos keep the Sabbath, let us go up the tower. They climbed the tower [the magnificent Giralda, which tourists still climb today], and he said: look around: here is a Marrano house, and there is another, and here are many others. You won't see any smoke coming out of these houses despite the harsh winter, because they don't light fire, as it is the day of the Sabbath.[4]

This anecdote mirrors an actual perception of the situation. We have seen that in the 1470s the Converso problem—not only in Andalusia but throughout Castile—became a major issue calling for action. The Conversos had multiplied in numbers over the years and could be found almost everywhere, sparking competition and opposition. They were involved in numerous street riots (even if mostly as targets) and entangled in the politics of the civil war. It was no secret that many kept Jewish rites, either as a residue of their past identity or because of a present resolution, and every sign of duality was interpreted as being subversively Jewish. Perhaps, as John Elliott holds, by then Castile had already more Conversos than Jews.[5] Yet with declared Jews (so the argument ran) you knew where you stood; not so with Conversos. Secrecy and hypocrisy were intrinsic to their existence, and as long as there was no policing mechanism to expose and purge them, they must all be classified as criminals, which was unfair to the sincere Christians among them. A society whose foundations are so corroded cannot endure. And rather than letting the mobs deal with them in the street, the harsh treatment they deserved should be orderly and legal.

During the court's residency in Seville, preaching campaigns urged the Marranos to repent and sincerely assume their Christianity. The more lenient clerics, believing in education, wrote a special catechism for Conversos to guide them in their new religion.[6] Yet Hojeida's party pleaded with the monarchs that no other remedy existed for the plague but fire. Within Isabella's circle, Hernán Pulgar, her diplomatic secretary, advocated a method of preaching and mass education, while Tomás de Torquemada, the queen's charismatic confessor, led the powerful clerical lobby that stressed the divine justice—and political benefits—inherent in an Inquisition. Both men were Conversos. Torquemada was to become the chief executor of the policy he advocated; Pulgar was dismissed from his post and became a historian and chronicler of Torquemada's deeds.[7]

Pulgar followed other famous Conversos, such as the Santa Marías and Cardinal Juan de Torquemada who, contrary to his nephew Tomás, demanded that Judaizers be reformed by education and persuasion.[8] The Conversos' foes replied that covert Judaizing was not due to poor instruction, but to willful choice. That was partly true: some forms of Judaizing resulted from choosing duality itself as an option—for example, when a person wished to remain essentially Christian even while maintaining residual Jewish components, or demanded the right to indulge in a passive, noneffective nostalgia, or hung on to a childhood memory, the affective reminiscence of a beloved figure or event in the past—without being immediately branded un-Christian. At the same time, Catholic instruction did eventually become decisive in shaping the Marrano mind and symbolism, even the mind of the Judaizers.

To pious Isabella, with her notion of royal authority, the idea of purging her country by fire through legal means looked desirable in itself; it could also add a dimension of sacred mission to the monarchs' new regime and set up an instrument of control that everyone, high and low, would fear. Still, Ferdinand and Isabella waited for the right timing. They were wary of making such an important decision without due preparation and public support.

On March 18, 1478, a young Sevillian noble visited the Jewish quarter of Seville for a secret rendezvous with his lover. Unfortunately (for himself and posterity) he mistook her room. This romantic mishap, usually a cause for comedy, produced tragedy instead. The straying lover entered a hall in which a mixed group of Jews and Marranos were conducting a strange ritual: it happened to be the Passover seder. When the surprised young man reported his discovery, a huge scandal erupted. This was the Catholic week of Easter, so Hojeida's followers blamed the New Christians for deriding the Savior's suffering and disparaging his sacrifice.

This interpretation is not altogether preposterous. The Jewish Passover shares certain symbols with the Christian Easter, especially the *matzo* with its Biblical link to the sacrificial lamb, which Christians see as Christ's body. Because of their proximity, these symbols also imply—and can be willfully made to express—the rivalry and mutual exclusion of the two religions in what concerns salvation, the messiah, the sacrificial lamb, etc. For a Marrano to eat the Passover matzo while shunning the Host can thus be interpreted as blasphemy and, with a stretch, even as a symbolic desecration of the Host.[9] But beyond the theological scandal, the fact that Marranos felt free to celebrate Passover so daringly caused a shock. Abbot Hojeida presented the incriminating evidence to Ferdinand and Isabella, who—prompted by the public outrage which they helped fan and exploiting the political opportunity it provided—chose the moment and made their move.

The National Inquisition

The Spanish monarchs now formally asked Pope Sixtus IV to authorize them to establish their own Inquisition in Castile. The pope's counterproposal—that his delegate, the papal Nuncio in Spain, would be given inquisitorial powers—contradicted the monarchs' political project and was adamantly rejected. Spain's new rulers would never create a policing and judicial system that answered to a foreign power, albeit Christ's deputy. The Inquisition was not meant to extend the pope's secular power but, on the contrary, to fortify the monarch's own regime by adding religious mission and zeal to it. Sixtus's role was to bestow this aura and mission upon the new, protoabsolutist state being built under their auspices.

Step by step, the pope capitulated. His court became a nest of manipulation and graft. The Spanish ambassador, Don Francisco de Santillana, relied on the Spanish Cardinal Rodrigo Borgia, later Pope Alexander VI (a prominent Renaissance figure notorious for his cupidity), while others—including Jewish lobbyists fluent in the game of Roman bribes—lobbied for the Marranos.[10] Sixtus IV first yielded, then reversed his position, all the while protesting the abuse of his original permits. In November 1478 he published the bull that laid the groundwork for the Spanish Inquisition.

Ferdinand and Isabella were authorized to appoint and, equally important, to dismiss, three inquisitors of their choice. The candidates had to be "over age forty, God-fearing, of good conscience and laudable lifestyle," as well as "masters or bachelors of theology, or doctors of canon law, or graduates who had passed rigorous examinations." The bull called upon the Spanish monarchs to also conquer Granada and convert the Moors. If Sixtus believed that by heaping together all those far-reaching missions he was casting an air of unreality on the Inquisition, he was wrong. Ferdinand and Isabella would realize all those goals without exception.

Meanwhile there were difficulties to overcome. Resistance to the Inquisition arose even among Isabella's loyalists: liberal statesmen; cities jealous of their powers; Converso agents operating at court and in Rome; and a few high prelates who thought the institution too radical, or a rival to their own authority. But Ferdinand and Isabella were now determined and, by 1480, were also secure on their thrones. In May they issued laws designed to isolate the Marranos from the Jews,[11] and four months later, on September 27, 1480, they launched the Inquisition's wagon of terror and torment on its three-hundred-year journey.

Two Dominican friars, Miguel de Morillo and Juan de San Martín, entered history as the first Spanish "inquisitor judges of depraving heresy." As the reason for the Inquisition, their letter of appointment states the need to purge the country of Judaizers, "evil Christians, men and women . . . who, after assuming the name and exclusive appearance of Christians, revert to the sect and superstitious and false faith of the Jews." The monarchs quoted the pope's directives, which they received on "a parchment stamped with [his] seal of lead and tied with colorful silk ribbons, as is customary in his court in Rome," and declared: "Therefore we, Don Fernando the king and Doña Isabel the queen, in our zeal for our Catholic religion, and wishing that our subjects live and be saved in it, and that all bad Christians be punished, and that all good and loyal Christians be proven innocent and free of stain,—we accept the mission and task set upon us by our most Holy Father."[12]

This was not the only case in which a political regime created a secret police and judiciary for the sake of its subjects' salvation but it was one of the more outstanding. Saving others' souls from sin is among the most violent favors that human beings do for their kin; it is an act of zealotry, the quintessence of intolerance. But Ferdinand and Isabella's concern for salvation had strong political motives. In worrying about their subjects' souls in the next world they were mostly concerned with their own power in this world, and with its religious halo and mission. But to maintain appearances they attributed the mission of pursuing heretics to the pope's will. It was the pope, they implied, who had ordered them to use their own discretion in acting on his behalf. The Spanish monarchs were the Holy Father's servants; they were obeying his will even while clipping his wings.

Actually, the pope authorized the monarchs to appoint and guide the inquisitors, but reserved for his own courts the power to hear appeals. Yet this power was hardly respected, and in 1507 it was abolished altogether.[13] The Spanish Inquisition thus became a national state institution; despite its need for nominal papal authorization, it was subject to the Crown and independent of Rome—indeed, a rival to Rome's authority.

First "Acts of Faith"

Seville was the theater of the Inquisition's first appearance. On Christmas 1480 the inquisitors Morillo and San Martín crossed the city gates. They were received with an impressive ceremony and mixed feelings by the aldermen, some of whom were soon to become their victims. As the inquisitors entered Seville, panic broke out and many Conversos fled to nearby towns and villages. The exodus provided the inquisitors with an opportunity to brandish the royal iron fist concealed beneath their Dominican gowns. On January 1, 1481, as soon as Christmas was over, they issued an order to all the Dons of the land, to "dukes, marquises, counts, *caballeros*, . . . commanders, and vice-commanders," to immediately identify anyone attempting to flee or hide "and to send them to us under arrest, well guarded, and at your expense." The two inquisitors invoked their dual authority, apostolic and royal, and they admonished the greats of the land, "for the first, second, and third time," to execute their instructions punctiliously, or they would be charged as accomplices to heresy, excommunicated, and stripped of their titles, and would lose the tributes their vassals owed them.

For two simple friars to issue such threats and commands to Spanish grandees, who several years earlier had almost deposed a king, signaled a sea change in Spanish politics. The language aimed at the nobles was even harsher than against the fugitive Conversos: Ferdinand and Isabella used the Inquisition as a tool for taming the nobility. In this way, the Inquisition essentially helped to forge the political might on which it subsequently relied.[14]

As fugitive Conversos returned to Seville—the Marquis de Cádiz alone, it was said, sent a few thousand Conversos back to the city[15]—the Inquisition began its work. Anyone who knew of acts of heresy was ordered to report them under penalty of excommunication. A few Conversos prepared an armed revolt, but again, a love affair foiled their plans. Their leader, Diego Ben Susan, had a beautiful daughter nicknamed *La Susana*. In a moment of weakness, she revealed the plot to her lover, an Old Christian noble (was he one of its targets?) who informed the authorities. The inquisitors acted swiftly.[16] Within a few weeks Seville's most prominent Conversos, including city councilors, were put to trial and found guilty; and on February 6, 1486, the first *auto de fe*[17] (Spanish: act of faith) was held in Seville. A public outdoor spectacle, it was a stylized mixture of horror, humiliation, brutality, and piety—one of the most renowned theatrical expressions of the Inquisition that became the model for years to come.

Six men and women, the more persistent and irreconcilable Judaizers, were burned alive. They marched to their death with triangular heretic's caps on their heads and dressed in sanbenitos—convicts' special robes with tongues of fire depicted on them, which had been designed especially for these spectacles and became their terrifying symbol for centuries. Other convicts wearing similar attire were paraded before the crowd in a humiliating procession, after which those who had confessed and repented were "reconciled" to the Church. The ceremony was presided over by Abbot Hojeida, the tireless campaigner, who had the honor of preaching a grandiloquent sermon to the odor of burning flesh. A few days later a second act of this public show was performed. The victims now included Diego Ben Susan, together with other Conversos with similar Arabo-Jewish names, such as *Abulafia* and *Ben-Adoba*. A wealthy Sevillian donated a large podium decorated with statues of the prophets to serve as the permanent site of the *autos de fe*—and was himself burned there some time later.[18]

From then on, such "acts of faith" were performed almost every month. By November 1481 about three hundred men and women had been burned alive, and on one occasion some fifteen hundred "reconciled" penitents were paraded before the crowd. The inquisitors burned not only living persons but the effigies of escaped convicts and the bones of dead heretics exhumed from their graves. This bizarre and startling action was intended to save the souls of the deceased in the next world. It also allowed the Inquisition to confiscate the convict's property from the heirs in this world.

The *autos de fe* in Seville became such attractive public spectacles that they competed with bullfights. People flocked to see them from all of southern Spain, sleeping in the streets the night before in order to secure a good spot for watching the holy horror show. To encourage attendance—for the sake of admonition, deterrence, and purging one's soul of evil intent—the clergy promised the audience points in purgatory: absolution as the prize of attendance.

Some voices were raised in protest. The Converso Hernán Pulgar, while still the queen's secretary, wrote the high Spanish prelate asking how was it possible to choose the path of fire when "there are at least 10,000 young women in Andalusia who have never left their parents' homes and who see the [Juda-izing] ways of their fathers and learn from them? To burn them all would be the utmost cruelty." The archbishop concurred. He too belonged to the liberal faction that tried to Christianize the Marranos by persuasion and instruction. But both men, the writer and the recipient of the letter, had already been over-taken by events.

Another liberal voice belonged to Fray Hernando de Talavera, a former Con-verso confessor of the queen who had taken personal risks in opposing the Inquisition and criticizing its methods—in vain. In later years, as the first Arch-bishop of Granada, Talavera opposed the Inquisition's entry to his town and tried to convert the Muslims by persuasion rather than force—but failed again. Cardinal Cisneros overruled his soft policies and the Inquisition started prying into his life. Only Rome's support saved him from trial.

Expansion beyond Seville

Following the early events in Seville, Pope Sixtus himself was shocked by the egregious cruelties and rebuked Ferdinand and Isabella on that account. Yet three days later he appointed new inquisitors—all Dominican monks—from a list recommended by the Spanish monarchs; and, quite in character for this vacillating pope, he extended the Inquisition's jurisdiction throughout Castile and León.

Torquemada

Among the new inquisitors, the name Tomás de Torquemada now made its first official appearance. Until then, Torquemada had been active behind the scenes. It was only in January 1482, at age sixty-one, that his meteoric public rise began. Within one and one-half years he was inquisitor general of all Castile and Ara-gon and over the next fifteen years, until his death in 1498, he was to burn nearly the number of persons that Pulgar had cited as absurd.[19] Torquemada's greatest mark, however, was left on the architecture of the Inquisition and on its secret methods. Down to minute details, he crafted a system that was to endure for centuries and spread as far as the Spanish colonies in the Americas,[20] Italy, and the Netherlands, and serve as a model for its younger sister, the Portuguese Inquisition.

Torquemada was one of the greatest early bureaucrats of the modern era, a herald of the modern phenomenon of tyranny by bureaucracy. If early modern

Spain displayed the rudiments of what was later dubbed totalitarianism more than did any other European monarchy, this was due primarily to the national aspect of the Inquisition and its dimension as "thought police." It spawned a secret espionage and judiciary apparatus that cast its net over the country and created a climate of fear and insecurity in the service of an official ideology. Torquemada was the organizational genius who designed and crafted this system. He gave it a solid pattern and stringent rules but also left leeway for local needs, and he set the guidelines for the future growth and preservation of his life's work. It was also Torquemada who insisted on the strictly legalistic character of the Inquisition and the imperative to meticulously record every detail, which yielded mountains of documents still waiting today to be deciphered. The Spanish Inquisition resembled modern dictatorships in this way, as well: Stalin's bureaucracy, eager to maintain an appearance of legality, recorded mountains of documents, and the Stasi, the secret police of Communist East Germany, left behind thirteen kilometers of shelves laden with personal files.

Like most despots who instill terror in others, Torquemada also lived in fear— of assassins, though none ever succeeded in harming him. Wherever he went he was accompanied by a private army of fifty cavalrymen and two hundred foot soldiers—a kind of Praetorian Guard of God and his fearless executor on earth. The pope loathed Torquemada's regime, but Torquemada did not depend on Rome. As long as the Spanish monarchs backed him, his rule was secure.

On a more personal level, Torquemada remains somewhat enigmatic. It is not easy to sort out his motives. His action suggests a penchant for extremes: absolute truth, merciless punishment, overweening organization, stylized cruelty, and the use of terror as a theologico-political instrument to control not only the public's behavior, but their emotions and inner thoughts as well. His zeal in targeting Judaizers could betray the classic insecurity of a Converso who over-affirms his Christian identity by persecuting those who digress from it, as well as those who refuse to share his immoderate ideal of purity. Torquemada's personal thirst for power cannot be dissociated from his fervor for the honor of the Christian God. And the religious culture of Catholicism, which holds that church hierarchy and organizations possess religious worth in themselves because they embody Christ's body and presence, provides a favorable terrain for merging bureaucratic passions with sincere religious fervor.

At the same time, the system that Torquemada constructed assumed a severity that strongly distinguished it from other Catholic life-forms and specifically characterized New Spain. Most religions stress piety and the fear of punishment; but in Catholicism these forces, especially the latter, are mitigated (one might say humanized) by the counter powers of atonement and absolution. Catholic absolution expresses recognition of the weakness of the will as human,

all too human. In Torquemada's system, absolution itself became a terrible punishment and deviance was regarded not as human but as demonic, to be utterly
expunged.

Torquemada's main crusade was directed at the Converso community, of
which, almost certainly, he was a self-denying descendent. His goal—to purge
Spain of Judaizers—required as an auxiliary the expulsion of the official Jews,
whose presence he saw as a permanent temptation and corrupting influence on
the Conversos. The Jews were guilty not so much of their own otherness as of
preventing the Conversos from erasing theirs. So the Jews had to go, and the
Conversos had to be crushed into submissive assimilation.

In following this policy, the inquisitor general implicitly agreed with his pro-
Converso uncle that racism was false. Blood and origin did not fully predeter-
mine a person's qualities. The Conversos' Jewish origin was stubborn indeed,
yet its influence could be erased—first by water (baptism), and then, should
that metaphysical act prove insufficient, by the rack and fire of the Inquisition.
Torquemada resorted to these radical methods precisely because he was not
a racist.[21]

The early Inquisition, though more ruthless and cruel, was different from
the one that evolved a century later because its practice was implicitly at odds
with the blood purity theory. In later times the Inquisition itself was made the
guardian of Spain's purity of blood, thus deviating from Christian doctrine and
the intent of its founding father.

Moving North

From Seville the Inquisition spread northward. Halfway to Toledo it held a
general rehearsal, so to speak, in Ciudad Real, where it burned and reconciled
many people in the course of two years.[22] But its high point was in Toledo,
Castile's largest, wealthiest, and most prestigious city, which also boasted the
strongest and most battle-scarred community of New Christians. Forty people
were burned alive in Toledo in 1488, along with one hundred corpses that had
been exhumed from their graves. Two years later, fire seared the bones of four
hundred dead heretics in a single day.

By 1488 the burned victims in Castile amounted to many hundreds (Pulgar says two thousand), and the reconciled—whose families were shamed and
ruined for generations to come—amounted to several thousand (Pulgar says
five thousand). The chronicler Andrés Bernáldez, who tended to defend the
Inquisition, claimed that the convicts' confessions testify "they were all Jews"
who saw themselves as the Children of Israel enslaved in Egypt, and declared:

"the fire is lighted . . . [and] will burn until it reaches the extremes of the driest woods."[23]

Alongside the Judaizers, Bernáldez cites another class of Marranos who were neither classically Jewish nor really Christian. They had worked their way up the social ladder to become scholars and intellectuals, accountants and secretaries, even nobles, canons, bishops, and abbots. Their sole objective, he said, was to flourish and spread, and they often caused harm to monasteries, monks, and nuns (remember Guadalupe).[24] Other commentators, too, spoke of Marranos who were heretics to all religions. A popular image circulating in Torquemada's milieu described the Marranos as hybrid creatures: neither Jews nor Christians nor Muslims, but chimeras resembling al-Burak, the horse of Prophet Muhammad who was composed of the traits of several animals.[25]

Other sources point out that this image had a solid basis in reality—that is, in the severed identity of many Marranos. Indeed, discounting the distorting effect of hostility, we can recognize in these allegations *the kind of Marrano that is of special interest to our study*: the Marrano who has no longer a definite religious identity, and whose split mind wavers between affirming a mixture of religions and repudiating them all.

Resistance in Aragon

Unlike the relative speed with which the Inquisition spread in Castile, resistance gradually arose in Aragon (and also in the Basque country).[26] Aragon was different from Castile. Political power in Aragon was not vested in landed feudal barons but held by an urban oligarchy of merchants (including Conversos). The proud Aragonese, who possessed a multitude of privileges and autonomies, could not swallow the semiabsolute power from Castile that threatened their historical freedoms. But King Ferdinand relentlessly imposed the royal Inquisition on his resentful countrymen with cunning and determination. In this he relied on his sharp legal adviser, Alfonso de La Caballería, who later was put to trial by the same Inquisition he had helped impose on Barcelona. These two men approached their mission very differently. Ferdinand was dedicated to Christianity both as a portal to salvation in the next world and as a power instrument in this world. Alfonso was an early secular technocrat, neither Jewish nor Christian in his beliefs, a man interested in solving legal and political problems for their inherent interest while promoting his career and personal life. (See his detailed portrait in chapter 6.)

The Aragonese resistance led to the assassination of an inquisitor and a confrontation between Ferdinand and the pope. A bastion of resistance was the city of Teruel, which expelled Torquemada's deputy and held on for a whole year, until the king sent his troops to subdue it.[27] Teruel's fall opened the way for other Aragonese cities—including Valencia—to grudgingly accept the new times.[28]

Bernáldez's prophecy was almost fulfilled. Two centuries later, the pyres were still burning throughout the Iberian Peninsula and in Ibero-America. In the early to mid-sixteenth century Judaizers ceased to be the prime target and were replaced by Alumbrados, spiritual seekers, and, later, Lutherans. Nevertheless, public burnings of Judaizers continued, and resumed their ferocity in several offensives in the seventeenth century. This shows the persistence not only of Torquemada's system, but also of Judaizing in its several dualistic forms.

Some historians explain the Inquisition as a mainly socioeconomic tool, destined to suppress a rival bourgeois group; but this reductionist view fails to recognize the genuine role of human passions, especially identity passions, and it substitutes a subsidiary role for a fundamental motive. Other scholars explain the Inquisition in purely religious terms, but this is too narrow. I think *identity passions* is a more adequate concept. These passions extend beyond the strictly religious sphere. They have a power of their own that cannot be reduced to other passions and interests, although it can be allied with them in several ways. The aggressive *We* which asserts itself by negating *Them*, the others, may occasionally focus on religion, but often religion is only one ingredient of a broader collective self-assertion in which ethnic, racial, cultural, and local components are at work. In late fifteenth-century Spain, the religious impulse worked in concert with other energies, political and identitarian, which flowed toward the creation of the new Spanish entity. The Inquisition helped create the impetus and fan the crusading sense of purpose that propelled the wheels of unified Spain. Religious imperatives operated in symbiosis with political forces to create the emergent Spanish sense of self—whose ingredients included the recognition of the role of the monarchy, of religious homogeneity, and later also of "pure blood," in forging the all-Spanish identity and shaping its historic-spiritual mission. In other words, religious drives were redirected by the Inquisition into political channels and became ingredients of broader identitarian passions. These passions, indeed, allied themselves with social and economic interests and became intertwined in numerous other conflicts—the struggles between old and new forms of life, between families, clans, and commercial rivals. But the fact that the socioeconomic camps were from the outset defined and divided according to identity lines—Old Christians against New Christians—indicates their affective and existential primacy.

For this and other reasons, it is mistaken to view the Spanish Inquisition as a medieval institution. In several important senses it came to express the spirit of the modern age. The True Inquisition was essentially a vehicle that carried Spain *out* of the Middle Ages by operating as a state institution in concert with the other forces that worked to centralize government and forge a uniquely Spanish national consciousness. It was far more efficient and overreaching than its papal predecessor due to the new organizational methods that built united Spain. It was also more severe and cruel,[29] and was marked by intolerant religious fervor and fanatic zeal, which were likewise features of early modern Spain, in contrast to the relative tolerance and *convivencia* that the Catholic monarchs abolished. Not only were some of the leaders of the True Inquisition emphatically not medieval in spirit, they typified the power of learning and innovation of the Renaissance. Torquemada created a protomodern system of central bureaucracy. His successor, Diego Deza was a learned intellectual, and the third inquisitor general, Cardinal Jiménez de Cisneros, introduced Renaissance studies into Spain, created the more progressive University of Alcalá de Henares, and printed a polyglot Bible in competition with Erasmus. At the same time, this Renaissance prelate forcibly converted the Muslims and burned their books.

Although the Inquisition instilled fear, even dread in the masses, the common folk were pleased to see the great of the land also in fear of the Holy Office. The realization that even the highest nobles, bishops, and archbishops were not immune to arrest and investigation made fear a social equalizer of sorts in Spain.[30] And it gave the commoners a sense of satisfaction to see their oppressors humiliated or anxious. This did not make the Inquisition popular, but attenuated some of its negative edge in the eyes of common folks.

In light of the horrific events of the twentieth century, one is led to conclude that a monolithic ideology that is mobilized in the service of the state and uses official violence to defend that ideology is characteristic of the modern era. If so, the Spanish Inquisition was a protomodern phenomenon. The Middle Ages had not seen such a combination of organization, bureaucracy, brutality, and monolithic zeal as that which powered Torquemada's Inquisition and continued, with ups and downs, to energize it for three more centuries. It is an illusion, spawned by the myth of historical progress (or its shallow interpretation), that the inclination for organized gruesome deeds diminishes as the level of political and technical civilization rises. Half a millennium before the twentieth-century concentration camps, the Iberian Inquisition, although it did not even come close to those recent horrors, had set an early modern precedent for what centralized organization, and a zealous ideological police state, can perpetrate.

Economic Interest and Spiritual Alienation

Also at work in the Inquisition were palpable material and social interests—the desire to destroy the economic standing of a rival group, to socially exclude the New Christians, or to confiscate their property, and thus sustain the Holy Office as an institution. Yet these interests do not constitute the prime and direct motive behind the Inquisition. The Inquisition embodied a highly self-alienated spirit, not because it concealed hidden economic interests but primarily because it gave a perverse expression to genuine spiritual interests. The self-righteousness and holy zeal in which people unwittingly encase their latent fears and cruelty, their hatred for the Other (which sometimes derives from self-hatred), the anxieties which uncertainty breeds in them, and their desire to find justification for the miseries of their existence, illustrate this sort of spiritual alienation. A longing for love, salvation, and eternal life can transmute into several perversions: envy and aggression, coercion and persecution, intemperate claims and demands, self-deception and masked frustration. By the same token, an authentic metaphysical anxiety can be transformed into a system of guilt and accusation—blaming the world or specific groups in it, whose very otherness justifies their victimization. These are some of the ways in which the holy perversity of the Inquisition expressed the self-alienation of the spirit, independent of all economic considerations.

Thus, different types of motives worked together, using and abusing each other according to circumstance. Some motives were inevitably economic, others had to do with a thirst for power and bureaucratic instincts, and all were underlain by an impossible passion and dream of identity that spurned all otherness, and used its persecutory exclusion of the Others Within as a tool for constructing an imaginary, though empirically real (that is, real in its consequences) official Spanish Self.

The Methods of the Inquisition

As the Inquisition spread through Castile and Aragon, Torquemada came to symbolize the united New Spain even more than the Catholic monarchs did. He was the only public official whose authority extended throughout the two kingdoms. His Council of the Inquisition (the Suprema) became a semi-independent organ that imposed its own system of laws and procedures on the two kingdoms through special policing and judicial powers.

The Suprema built the Inquisition as a consummate legalistic system. Legal casuistry, citing clauses and precedents, was amply used. Everything was recorded, documented and signed. An army of clerks and secretaries, all ranked in proper hierarchies, conducted the work at a grinding pace (except in the early years). The system nourished itself and, in time, produced its own legitimacy.[31]

Whenever the special court came to a city it declared a period of grace in which all heretics were required to confess. Faithful Christians were ordered, under threat of excommunication, to report every suspicious detail they knew. In this way the Inquisition transformed the entire population into potential informers. Witnesses were sworn to keep secret the content of their testimony and the fact they had given it.

To help informers, the Inquisition published a list of signs by which to identify Judaizers—an empirical definition of "who is a (secret) Jew." Did the person avoid pork or rabbit? Did he mumble a few words over a glass of wine (presumably a Jewish benediction)? Did she avoid food on the Great Fast (*Yom Kippur)* or, no less indicative, on Esther's Day? Were candles lit on Friday night? And did the men put on a fresh shirt on that night? Other signs, quite unknown in Judaism, included facing the wall at the moment of death and chanting Latin Psalms while omitting the *Gloria Patri*. We have already noted the irony of the Inquisition becoming a source of Jewish instruction (part of which was not really Jewish but distinctly Marrano: that is, dualist), and providing the converts a sort of catechism—a guidebook of what Judaizing was all about.[32]

Information was culled from every possible source. The testimony of eminent citizens was democratically admitted into evidence alongside reports by vagrants and prostitutes. In coming forward, some people were driven by religious devotion, others by hostility, fear of punishment, or thirst for revenge. In the idiom of the Inquisition—which, like all bureaucratic systems, developed a jargon of its own—a voluntary denunciation was called "clearing one's conscience."

Secrecy, the twin sister of fear, was a chief hallmark of the Inquisition and a source of its power. Accusation and arrest could strike a person as a sudden thunderbolt. The accusers' identities were concealed so they could neither be confronted nor cross-examined. The only way to undermine a testimony was by proving that the witness was a personal enemy. But how could the accused know who the witness was? Time after time, one finds the accused and their families in the grip of despair, compiling lists of enemies real and imagined, in the hope of hitting upon the informers. Those lists tell the story of complex human relationships: insecurity about friendships, gratuitous suspicions, love, betrayal, and deception among neighbors, relatives, and friends. And inevitably, they poisoned the texture of human interaction.

No less cruel and unjust was the practice of concealing from the accused the substance of testimonies against them. Prisoners were required to make full confessions, down to the last detail. Failing to do so, they were pronounced obstinate heretics or had their arrests drag on endlessly. But often the accused did not know what to say even when ready to confess. "Señores, why will you not tell me what I have to say? . . . Have I not said that I did it all?" pleaded Elvira del Campo while hanging from the torture rope during one dramatic interrogation. In response, the rope's pressure was cranked up another notch and no one came to her aid.[33] The rules required the accused to state the whole truth on their own, "voluntarily."

Torture was a stylized, legally controlled procedure. It was applied not only to the accused but also to witnesses suspected of holding out information. We mustn't imagine interrogation under torture as haphazard, a burst of brutality by an angry or impatient investigator. Torture was applied in an orderly, meticulous, almost ritualistic fashion. It followed strict rules and was performed in the presence of a court physician and inquisitors in their ceremonial robes. There were several levels of torture, and fixed guidelines for passing to the next level. Almost every step was recorded. Everything was organized, sanitized, legalistic.

A legal fiction maintained by the Inquisition was that it never executed its convicts. The Holy Office was driven by love and never shed blood: that messy task was left to the civil authorities. The euphemism for a death sentence by the Inquisition was: the convict is "released to the secular arm." The decision to release (hand over) a convict was accompanied by a plea for mercy, a ritualistic hypocrisy. Not all death sentences involved burning alive; convicts who, at the last moment, agreed to confess and repent their heresies earned the privilege of being garroted.

Those burned alive were, therefore, either martyrs for their Judeo-Marrano faith, or victims of false accusations insisting to the end they were innocent. And there were also "martyrs" who died as heretics to all religions. Yet the Inquisition saw them all as stiff-necked Judaizers. In clinging to their faith with absolute conviction and tenacity, they reminded the spellbound crowd of the courage and devotion of the early Christian martyrs. One bishop was so shocked by the resemblance that he proposed holding *autos de fe* behind closed doors. But his idea was doomed from the start. The outdoor *auto de fe*, with its public display of torment and rites of depersonalization and humiliation, was essential to the Inquisition's impact and a ritual-theatrical projection of its spirit.

Servants and family members were prized sources of information. The testimony of a wife against her husband, a brother against his sister, a father against his son was perfectly admissible. A confession was not accepted as complete—and the accused was held guilty of a new crime, concealment—until she turned in every last member of her family.

The Spanish Inquisition often provided the accused with defenders who served in good faith and tried to acquit their clients. But they had no access to the materials held by the prosecution and were not allowed to confront or cross-examine the secret witnesses, but only to send them questions in writing. So the defense was handicapped from the start. There was no correspondence between the defender's integrity and his effectiveness.

Jews, Marranos, and the Inquisition

Jews (while they still lived in Spain) were a coveted source of information. Jews were questioned as witnesses and sometimes tortured by the inquisitors to make them talk. Yehuda ibn Verga, chief rabbi of Seville, refused to inform on Marranos and died in prison. But such martyrs were rare. Quite a number of Jews did inform on Marranos. In some places the authorities got the rabbis to ban members of their community who refused to testify.

This collaboration is puzzling. Not all Jews acted under duress. This may indicate that they basically saw the Marranos as Christians, the progeny of Jewish apostates, and treated them with a mixture of suspicion and occasional sympathy. The rabbis debated the matter but most of them rejected the Jewishness of the Marranos.

What exactly did the witnesses report when telling the "truth" about a Marrano? Occasional quasi-Jewish acts do not necessarily indicate the intent to be Jewish. A Marrano, as we have seen, could participate in Jewish rites or eat Jewish fare because of habit or nostalgia, or because he has chosen duality without wishing to return to Judaism. Yet the inquisitors and their informants, like some modern scholars, concluded that the person was a secret Jew. The failure to grasp such acts in their complexity expressed an ideological or identitarian bias that was built into the very institution and projected into people's perception.

Still, one should avoid undifferentiated generalizations about the Holy Office. The Inquisition was no monolithic system: its methods changed with time, place, even case. As the decades passed, it gained a self-sustaining bureaucratic rigidity and periodically changed its severity and targets.

The Inquisition's pace also changed over time. In the early years it had operated swiftly, feverishly, with a sense of urgency. But from the sixteenth century onward its sense of inner time changed—as if its pulse had slowed down and its long breath extended over generations. By that time the institution was operating mainly through inertia. The accused could languish in prison for one, two or even five years, with very long intervals between interrogations. Most of the time, he had to live off his assets, which were dwindling due to neglect. If he failed to confess to a certain detail—which he had forgotten, or held out, or was innocent of—he was granted another chance to come clean. The Holy Office was patient; it worked on behalf of eternity and almost at that same pace.

A common, almost automatic, penalty was confiscation of the convict's property—or sometimes, more righteously, only the part he possessed "when he had started to Judaize." In consequence, silver and gold, houses and shops, vineyards and workshops, warehouses, and thousands of maravedis in cash flowed into the coffers of the Holy Office. In time several arrangements for dividing the confiscated property between the Inquisition and the civil authorities came into effect. Although the confiscations did not always cover the expenses (some poor defendants strained its budget), over the long term confiscations brought the Holy Office enough wealth to make it an economic force in its own right.[34] The resulting incentive to convict affluent Conversos served the interest of their Old Christian competitors, many of whom welcomed the Inquisition as a means to destroy the economic power and social ambition of their rivals. But it does not follow that the Inquisition was founded specifically for that purpose. The economic role of the Holy Office was subsidiary to its self-sufficient identitarian (and later bureaucratic) drives.

The Inquisition visited the sins of the fathers upon their children. The offspring of convicted persons, even if they were faithful Christians, lost their inheritance and were disgraced for several generations, forbidden to hold public offices or exhibit signs of honor and prestige. The outcome was to create a community of social pariahs and thus repress the Conversos not just as individuals but, more significantly, as families. Yet often they were nevertheless economically successful; and thus a typical hiatus was created between the Conversos' economic centrality and social marginality.[35]

Mariana's Complaint: Critique of the Inquisition

The sixteenth-century Jesuit reformer and historian Fray Juan de Mariana, an independent thinker, gave voice to the critics of the Inquisition:

> What especially surprised the people was that children paid for the sins of their fathers; that the identity of the accuser was not known, his name was not cited,

and he was not brought to confront the accused; and that the list of witnesses was not published—in sharp contrast to the ancient custom in other courts. Moreover, that sins of this kind warranted the death penalty was an innovation. And the gravest thing of all was that because of these secret interrogations, men were denied their freedom to listen and speak to each other, since special people in the cities, towns, and villages were assigned to report on everything that went on—a practice some deemed as most abominable and tantamount to death.[36]

In line with Mariana, modern historians tend to place the Inquisition's most negative aspect in its methods. But this legal viewpoint is too narrow; it singles out one important element from the constellation that makes the meaning of the whole. The Inquisition's methods must be viewed in relation to its scope, motives, and spiritual impact. In certain circumstances, every regime permits exceptions. It has not been uncommon for governments, then and today, to relax the rules of policing, evidence, and punishment in order to cope with some pressing crisis—an uprising, a war, terrorism, a serious crime wave, and so forth—and the principle of emergency decrees (even when their content is contestable) is admitted even in democratic states. But the Inquisition acted as if a state of emergency existed for three hundred years. An institution whose only possible justification lay in its exceptional nature became the most enduring force in the history of modern Iberia. And it spread its net to every corner of Iberia and its territories in Europe, America, Africa, and the far East,[37] creating a climate of relentless fear, insecurity, and suspicion, and providing a permanent temptation, and address, for spies and resentful denouncers. Its censorship tried to control literary and artistic creation.[38] Most important, the end that ostensibly justified all these measures—the goal that gave the system its underlying meaning and compounded the ignominious character of its single components—was to control people's inner thoughts, punish them for their beliefs, and thereby crush their emerging individual selves. Terror and humiliation were used to subdue personal conscience and drive people to conformity (or its outer fake shell) with an impossible dream of homogeneity that for them became a nightmare. Thus, the spiritual claims of the Inquisition amounted to the self-alienation of the spirit just as its claim to Christian love, though not an outright fabrication, had been—as Dostoyevsky masterfully showed in his portrayal of the grand inquisitor who would persecute Christ himself—a paramount example of perverse dialectical reversals.

Mariana notwithstanding, almost every separate element of the Inquisition can find a precedent, or near precedent, at some time or place. The confiscation of property has often been a corollary of political crimes. Death sentences (though not by burning, and not as punishment for religious belief) were even more common in civil courts, which also used torture (though for the Church, an institution standing for love, this was unnatural). Withholding witnesses' names had been practiced in the old papal Inquisition, in certain civil courts in Spain and southern France, and in medieval Jewish statutes against *malshinim*.[39] Only the exhuming and burning of bones was the Holy Office's original invention. But while most of these elements were not entirely new, their unique blend in the Inquisition—in the service of crushing free personality, the inner mind, and the emerging private sphere—as well as the extension of this unique blend into a ubiquitous omnibus system that cast its shadow on every walk of life, constituted an entirely new quality, greater than the sum of its parts.

The Holy Office owes its bad name to this unique quality, which cast its terrorizing effect on whole sectors of Spanish society at home and abroad and spread a net of espionage and intimidation that often penetrated personal relations and corrupted them. The Inquisition also owes its grim reputation to the interrelation of ideological extremism with official brutality practiced in the name of truth and love; to the urge to save the other's soul against his will by breaking him or her physically and spiritually through fear and humiliation; to the unholy mix of religious zeal with power politics; to the exceptional procedures which perverted the concept of justice prevailing at that time; and, in a prime place, to the spectacle of the *auto de fe*, which blended the other elements into a concentrate of dehumanized theatricality.

It was a theologico-political bullfight in which the fear of God and, no less, of his clerical and secular deputies, overwhelmed any feeling of pity for the victim and transformed that pity into dread and submission.

The *auto de fe* was not just a physical stage setting, as some see it. It perfectly expressed the gist of the institution's psychosocial content and its role in repressing and molding the people's spirit. The burning of heretics exemplified hell's fire on earth. It transformed the transcendent dread that Catholic education had instilled in the populace into a tangible earthly terror and, in the process, it was meant to cleanse the soul of sinful thoughts as well as the sins of pride and individuality involved in independent thinking. Spectators were immunized against the danger of thinking for themselves through a combination of horror, empathy, and cathartic discharge that reshaped metaphysical anxieties as potent this-worldly fright. In other words, the *auto de fe*, God's corrida, was a uniquely Iberian expression—metaphysical and political—of spiritual self-alienation.[40]

On a deeper symbolic level, the extravagant public character of the *autos de fe* signified that people's subjectivity—a potentially subversive power—was duly subdued and exposed to public control. Yet history has its ironies. In striving to crush people's emerging individual selves—to punish them for their private thoughts and who they intimately were—the Inquisition also helped cultivate the subjective free space it was fighting to crush. In the end, in going still deeper into the recesses of their minds, which the Inquisition tried to occupy and control, these people discovered *subjectivity* as an important domain, a power in which their singularity and personal autonomy were grounded—and they thereby discovered a principle that was to be advanced by the Enlightenment, later becoming a grounding force in modernity.

Another ironic reversal concerns the role of irony itself. Fear of the Inquisition and the restraints on speech and writing inadvertently cultivated a discourse of allusion and playing with words—and the art of irony in general, as it became embodied in the picaresque art of writing—Spain's gift to world literature, which plays with allusions and unveils existing masks while creating other masks.

The Inquisition was established explicitly to combat the Judaizing Marranos but history provided it with further objects of pursuit. In the second quarter of the sixteenth century the percentage of Judaizers decreased sharply, and the Inquisition started targeting religious reformers within Catholicism (most of them also Conversos), as well as Protestants, Moriscos, and of course witches and homosexuals—all in all, twenty-four types of enemies of God and the Spanish Crown.

No Jurisdiction over the Jews

One category is almost wholly absent from this list: the Jews. It is widely believed that the Inquisition persecuted the Jews—that it burned and imprisoned them because they were Jewish—but this is a misconception. Official Jews (those who were born Jews and never converted) were free to practice Judaism in Spain until 1492 and no court, civil or religious, could punish them for it. The Inquisition burned only bad Christians, mostly Conversos, but had no jurisdiction over Jews. The reason is that the Inquisition was based on canon law, which applies only within the Church. The Conversos were baptized Christians; the Jews were not. When Conversos Judaized they were heretics and traitors to Christ's church, to which they belonged willy-nilly; thus, it became necessary to purify Christ's body of their heresy. Whereas the Jews, who had murdered and mocked the Savior, remained outside the pale of his Salvation and, precisely therefore, also beyond the Inquisition's grip.[41]

This was not vain casuistry. The Inquisition was established to remove heresy not from the world, but only from Christianity. So not only Jews, but also Muslims,[42] Amerindians, and, under the Portuguese, Asian Indians and African blacks, were immune from Torquemada's courts. Not that the inquisitor general liked it: his attempts to extend his jurisdiction to the Jews were so inimical to a fundamental principle of canon law that they never took off.

Why, then, the common belief that the Inquisition operated mostly against Jews? Probably because many Marranos saw themselves as Jews and were seen as such by many non-Jews. Even today, historians sometimes call the Conversos Jews, either out of a Jewish-nationalist motive, or, conversely, because of anti-Jewish bias. Even so, the inquisitors did harm the Jews—not by prosecuting them, but by lobbying the government to expel them from Spain; and this the inquisitors did as a political pressure group, and not a judiciary authority. In a word: the Inquisition, as such, dealt with the Marranos; the Jewish problem required a different solution.

10

The Great Expulsion

Strictly speaking, there was no independent "Jewish problem" in late fifteenth-century Spain.[1] Jews were now seen as part of the Converso issue. They were resented not only as the traditional Other they had always been, but primarily as the main support of the new and unsettling phenomenon of the Other Within. As such, the Jewish presence in Spain acquired a further negative significance, especially in the eyes of religious leaders and the partisans of a single Spanish identity.

At the same time, Jews were no longer absolutely vital to the monarchs and the central government as they had been for centuries before. Their relative monopoly was shattered by Conversos, who preserved the same skills and occupations as the Jews and could replace them in finance and the central administration and were, also like the Jews, politically vulnerable and dependent on the crown. These functional Jews (so to speak) had the advantage of being officially brothers in Christ—though unreliable brothers, as long as the actual Jews were still around to corrupt and teach them how to Judaize.

Thus it was less what the Jews were in themselves, and more what their presence was perceived as doing to others—the Conversos—that finally spelled the doom of Spanish Jewry.

The Spanish expulsion was a momentous trauma in Jewish history, but far less so in Marrano history. The important changes for the Marranos were the elimination of Jews as a source of support for Judaizers, and the sudden surge in the overall number of converts of all sorts. But unlike the Jews who were uprooted and expelled en masse from their homeland of a thousand years, the Marranos stayed where they were, subject to an Inquisition that had already existed.

Few historical actions are as intentional and well planned as they appear to be in retrospect, in light of an emerging broader pattern that gives them ex post facto intelligibility, even a semblance of inevitability. Even determined rulers like Ferdinand and Isabella, who acted under a crusading drive, had to work through a multitude of contingencies and operate in a human way, that is, with limited foresight, information, and control. It may be exaggerated to assume that they had in advance a clear-cut idea of everything they wanted to accomplish. A good deal of what we call *intention* is buried under semiconscious drives, sensibilities, intuitive judgments, and passing momentary responses as they end up taking shape in action. Time and timing are of no less importance. It takes time for an action to mature, as it does for a project to crystallize in the mind; and picking the right moment for action (frequently under the pressure of rapidly changing, often surprising circumstances) is part of the talent of great statesmanship. The expulsion of the Spanish Jews, though perhaps a possibility mentioned or contemplated in the early days, was not a clear-cut plan or one that was decided on until much later. And far from being a simple idea to contemplate, it was contrary to basic interests and legal conceptions of the Catholic monarchs themselves.[2]

Jews had been living in Iberia for over a millennium (see part I). They had been tolerated (and used) by Christian Spain from the beginning of the Reconquista, a crusade that was directed not against them, but against the Muslims. As prominent jurists confirmed to the monarchs (themselves mindful of law and tradition), the Jews were long-standing royal subjects who could not be driven out arbitrarily. A compelling reason, such as having committed a major crime, was needed to justify such a move. Moreover, Jews had always been indispensable to the Crown as economic catalysts, financiers, and semiofficial administrators whom the Crown could trust to be more subservient than the ambitious nobles. True, the Catholic monarchs were bent on charging their reign with a crusading mission; but for that purpose, the Moors (politically) and the secret Marranos (religiously) provided better and more direct targets than did the Jews. Humble, weary of a century of blows and hemorrhage, politically feeble, and totally dependent upon the Crown whose legal "property" they were considered to be, the Jews seemed neither as worthwhile a target nor as intolerable a presence to the New Spain as did the arrogant memory of Muslim power (embodied in the refined palace of the Alhambra) or the malignant tumor of the Judaizing Marranos.[3]

And yet, argued Torquemada and other high clerics, how can you fight a malady if you tolerate those who nourish and spread it? Where do the reprobate Judaizers draw comfort and encouragement—and where do they get Jewish books, instruction, calendars for keeping their holidays—if not from the overt Jewish community that is scandalously allowed to exist alongside them? The official Jews contaminate the Converts, who contaminate Christianity—that is, the Spanish soul and sacred body. And since we are not allowed to convert the Jews by force, we must get rid of them through expulsion.

The argument was not devoid of logic, and Ferdinand and Isabella had an ear for it from the start. At first they agreed to a partial expulsion of Jews from Andalusia in 1483, a move that was urged (and cosigned) by the inquisitors, who wanted to facilitate their work in the region. In another strong measure, Jews throughout the country were segregated from the Christians and confined to Jewish quarters, following the early Visigoth model, but now the laws were better enforced.

All the while the monarchs persisted in protecting the Jews against illegal harassment and defended, even strengthened, the Jewish communal autonomy. In one document after another, Isabella came to the rescue of Jews whom rival townsmen tried to bar from settling down or practicing commerce. The Jews were her subjects—the queen proclaimed—and could not be harmed without offense to her royal self. It seems that Spanish burghers of that time, like some modern readers, confused Isabella's zeal against secret Judaizers with an all out anti-Jewish hostility. They also underestimated both monarchs' commitment to law, order, and effective governance.

Two opposite forces were at work, both emanating from a similar source. To bolster the authority of the new state, order and legality had to be cherished, which also meant respecting precedent and tradition. This played in the Jews' favor. Yet on the other hand, to provide impetus to the New Spain one had to go beyond tradition and negate it by using elements of tradition itself. *Radicalization* became the ruling phenomenon, in the dual sense of the word—taking an inflexible, unorthodox stance and grounding it in some element of one's own roots—an element that is blown up one-sidedly and, stripped of its historical context, is made to override and terrorize all the rest. That element (Hispano-Catholic uniformity) was actually a construct, a premodern national myth, and also a powerful theologico-political tool. If Spain is one, and if Spain is Christian, then the amalgam of creeds and peoples that had marked it should be deemed a symptom of sickness and decadence; and the practice that made it possible (patronizing tolerance) was a weakness of the Spanish spirit, a deviation from its destiny. Of course, tolerance and *convivencia* (coexistence) in the old Iberia should not be romantically exaggerated. It has never been an ingrained principle, only a practice. It existed, with fluctuations, as a form of grace rather than a basic right, and thus was itself only tolerated. The New Spain felt it could not afford to tolerate tolerance. The New Spain could come to its own only as *one*, pure and unyielding. It should complete the Reconquista not only on the battlefields of Granada, but also in its inmost soul.

The Inquisition, of course, played a major role in this radicalization of the social climate, mainly as its parent and partly, also, as its offspring. In dealing with the Jews, its logic was both direct and syllogistic. In themselves, Jews were undesirable aliens, anathema to the true faith. But the main argument for their expulsion was inferential: the Jewish problem arose, and had to be addressed, as a consequent and corollary of the Marrano problem.[4]

This argument eventually decided the monarchs. But not before the country was swept up in the victorious excitement of the fall of Granada, the last bastion of Muslim power in the peninsula, and not before Torquemada's Inquisition prepared the psychological stage by organizing a show trial to demonstrate the collaboration of Jews and Marranos in theologico-political crimes. Because the event was organized from the top it anticipated the show trials in the twentieth century, though its affective fiber was woven from more ancient myths and passions. The Jews who once had crucified Christ were now shown as continuing to do so symbolically, in concert with New Christians who were not only of their race but sometimes even of their family.

The "Holy Child" of La Guardia

On June 1, 1490, a Jewish-born Converso, Benito García, was arrested near the town of Asturga. He was a wandering craftsman, a washer of wool, just returning from a pilgrimage to Saint James of Compostela. In a hostel the previous night, drunkards had searched his bed and were shocked (they said) to find a piece of the Host, the sacramental bread. Heretic! Sacrilege! The outcry arose, García was summoned before the Episcopal vicar, an eager cleric who started by giving him two hundred lashes, then questioned him while he was immersed in cold water, then used a heavy rope to squeeze his aching limbs degree by degree. Later, in prison, García told an inmate: "They made me say more than I knew and enough to burn me."

What García was reported to have said was even more than what he actually was made to say. His questioning led to a series of arrests. Eleven men, six Jews and five New Christians (some from the same family), were accused of abducting a Christian boy from a street in Toledo around Christmas of 1488, then bringing him to a secret cave near La Guardia where they used him to reenact Jesus's crucifixion. First they inflicted injuries and abuses upon the child in the manner described in popular accounts of Christ's passion, then they nailed the child to a cross and cut out his heart. Two days later they met in the same cave again where they used the child's heart and García's piece of the Host to perform black magic intended to destroy the inquisitors and make Christianity perish and Judaism prevail. As the magic did not work, they decided to send García with his Host to a rabbi in Zamora, presumed to be more effective.

If there were grains of truth in the affair they were mostly banal. Benito García was a former Jew with qualms about his conversion to Christianity, which his pilgrimage to Saint James of Compostela did not attenuate. It seems the Host was of special significance to this simple craftsman as best symbolizing his religious doubts. He told a Jewish prison inmate that the Catholics "mix some dough with a little water and say it is God"—a traditional Jewish attitude, and a misgiving not uncommon among Christians of higher education than García. It cannot be excluded that some Jews or Marranos engaged in magic in order to alleviate a persecution or perform imaginary revenge on their foes. But the affair's explosive power derived from the story of the crucified child, an obvious fabrication combining a classic anti-Jewish libel (which survived into the twentieth century) with the ancient image of the Jews as deicides.

The "holy child of La Guardia," as the abducted child came to be known, remained nameless. He was never identified and no physical remains were produced. Nor was it ever established that a child was missing. In the absence of corpus delicti what counted most were written confessions and reports of the questioning. To get statements, ruse was used no less than torture. The chief Jewish defendant Juce (Yosef) Franco, was placed in a cell above Benito García and a hole was dug in the floor so the two could talk—and then be forced to report on each other. When Franco asked to see a Jew, a "Rabbi Abraham," who was actually a disguised monk, entered his cell. Franco asked him to pass a Hebrew message to the chief Jewish notable, Abraham Seneor, describing the nature of his accusations. This was written down and held against Franco as a confession.

Cunning, torture, psychological manipulation, and *agents provocateurs* finally produced the expected result. All defendants were found guilty and, in mid-November 1491, were burned in a spectacular *auto de fe* in Avila (a town, incidentally, with a 30 percent Jewish population), some in person and some in effigy. The verdicts were propagated throughout the country. Secret parts of the proceedings were released to an unusually large group of outsiders—professors, priests, and other opinion makers—ostensibly in quest of their advice (for example, asking "Is the Inquisition entitled to sentence Jews in this case?"),[5] but also as a propaganda move, to win over part of the learned elite to a cause it knew was not utterly kosher.

The Avila *auto de fe* and the earlier show trial, worthy of Stalin's propaganda machine, provided the climate—and the ostensible crime—necessary to expel the Jews. It also highlighted the fact that anti-Jewish policy was now organized from above, the result not of popular anarchy but, if anything, of excessive order. This policy enflamed and exploited public sentiment rather than merely responding to it. True, the populace had always resented the Jews and the burghers competed with them, but in the past a delicate balance had prevailed. Quite a number of nobles had, on the whole, always been favorable toward the Jews, while moderate and conservative-minded elements in the church, the intelligentsia, and the urban oligarchy itself, spurned radicalism. Now, with the nobility held in check by a strong and crusading Crown that used the edge of political radicalism to carve its own political route, a determined decision by the central government, especially if taken at the right psychological moment, was capable of upsetting and destroying the whole previous balance.

The Edict of Expulsion

This pivotal moment was provided by the La Guardia trial, followed by the conquest of Granada. Masters of timing and themselves susceptible to the significance of the hour—and to Torquemada's interpretation—it was as victors (*conquistadores*), in the shade of the magnificent Alhambra, that Ferdinand and Isabella examined a draft Edict of Expulsion penned for them by the inquisitor general. And then, after duly modifying and toning it down, they signed the historic document:

> Therefore we, guided by the counsel and vision of some of the clergy, the high and low nobility of the kingdom, and other men of science and conscience, and having thought of this at length, agreed to order all Jews and Jewesses to be expelled from our kingdoms, and no one of them should ever return.

Significantly, this move is explained by the same reason that led to the establishment of the Inquisition twelve years earlier: the need to combat the Conversos, "those bad Christians who Judaize and betray our Holy Catholic Faith." The Jews, the monarchs said, are committed to leading these bad Christians astray by all the means at their disposal; thus they commit "the greatest and most dangerous and infectious crime," for which innocent Jews must pay along with the guilty. The monarchs list the partial measures they have taken so far, including the segregation of the Jews and their expulsion from Andalusia—to no avail. Human nature being frail, and with the Devil, they complain, "always fighting against us," they see no solution but the radical one:

> And so we order all Jews and Jewesses of any age, living and inhabiting our kingdoms and possessions . . . that until the end of the month of July first coming in this year they shall leave our said kingdoms and possessions, together with their sons and daughters, their Jewish servants and maids and relatives, the small and the big, of any age, and shall not dare return to live in the places they used to live, neither by transit nor otherwise; under the penalty that . . . they will be condemned to death, and their property be confiscated in favor of our court and royal treasury. And these penalties will apply to them by the very act and law, *without trial, without a verdict, and without a[court's] proclamation.* (Italics added)

The harshness of these lines is somewhat mitigated by an offer of royal protection to the Jews until July 31 so that they would not be prey to a profiteering mob and could sell their property "in freedom and of their own will," as the text is ironically worded. Of course this provision was nearly meaningless. The Jews had to get rid of their property in a haste bordering on panic, and the edict prohibited them from exporting capital goods (gold, exchange bills), allowing only personal effects and merchandise to be taken out of the country.[6]

The Edict of Expulsion took the Jews by surprise. Signs of a gathering storm could be discerned earlier, but the timing was brutal and unexpected. Did not King Ferdinand, just one month prior to the expulsion, guarantee a loan made by the Jewish community of Saragossa, and express his interest in its continued existence? And four years earlier, did not the king impose a fine on the Aragonite Jews, payable in five to six years? Were not the taxes leased out to Jews in 1490 for a period of four years? Even the treaty of Granada's capitulation stipulated that its Jews could stay in their place. A younger contemporary, Niccolò Machiavelli, later praised Ferdinand's cunning and "charitable cruelty" in conducting the expulsion. Yet Ferdinand was no exemplary Machiavellian. Any prudent ruler would maintain an air of business-as-usual as long as no definite schedule was set for provoking a crisis that he may have been contemplating as a possibility, but had not actually set his mind to.

Ferdinand would reject Machiavelli's contention, said in his praise, that the Jews were deported in order to seize their money. He would rather agree with Pope Alexander VI, the greedy Borgia prelate, who was astounded to see monarchs ready to make financial sacrifices for the sake of their faith. The new Spanish radicalism was able to turn a blind eye on political expediency and material gain because it had loftier visions. It wished to infuse the country with unity by imposing a uniform identity on it—a single religion, culture, set of values, and later also "blood" that became a founding myth of imperial Spain. Meanwhile it took a stupendous toll in human suffering and folly.[7]

If, by 1492, the Jews did not clearly perceive the coming cataclysm, it was because they were hardly able to imagine (or face) its outcome. Jews were slow to identify the signals of a catastrophe of such magnitude, which threatened not just part of their life, but the total context of their existence—a complete uprooting of the community and the individual. Fear and hope breed self-deception, especially when the alternative seems blank and almost unthinkable. Partial suffering and persecution had become a way of life for Jews. It had educated them to phenomenal endurance and ingrained in them an almost atavistic strategy of survival. When a storm broke the immediate response was: bend, endure, dig deeper, cooperate, cut your losses, bribe, influence the authorities, extend self-help, hope, pray, and survive. But what about a total cataclysm? What about when a volcano threatens to erupt, cutting the whole earth from underneath your feet? Into what will you dig then? What is the right survival strategy in such conditions? Jews had little experience and no answers. They hardly were ready to envisage the possibility. Preemptive emigration? But where? And after all, why? Wouldn't it turn out well in the end, as it usually had in the past, with God's help? The sad, stubborn Jewish optimism, so crucial for the endurance of Jews in numerous ordeals, had proved tragically inapt and misleading in the rare volcanic cases when a *radical* solution was tried on their "problem." When signs of the coming earthquake were gathering, as Jews pathetically dug harder into a ground that was to slip altogether from underneath them, small wonder that self-deception was setting in and Jews clung to long-standing historical lessons that were now suddenly obsolete. In such approaching calamities—in Torquemada's time, or in pre–World War II Europe—Jews were by and large reluctant to believe, and therefore also slow to perceive, the writing on the wall.

A full month elapsed between the signing of the Edict and its publication. Perhaps the monarchs wished to minimize the period of transition, or were still attentive to Jewish petitioners like Don Abraham Seneor lobbying on the inside. Ferdinand and Isabella had relied on Jewish associates from early on. They confided to Jews a good deal of the finances of the country (to Abraham Seneor, Meir Melamed, Yizhak Abrabanel), military supplies (to Samuel Abolafia), the care of their private property (to Gento Silton) and even, in the early years, the care of their bodies (to Salomon Byton, physician to Isabella, and David Abenacaya, physician to Ferdinand).

First and foremost of these Jewish advisors was Don Abraham Seneor. Seneor had won Isabella's lifelong trust by his loyalty to her in the early uncertain days, when all was still at stake. Now holding the title of court rabbi, he presided over all the Jewish communal representatives in Castile.[8] He became so prominent in the kingdom's finances that even Torquemada dealt with him with a grudging sense of equality. (Once Torquemada asked and obtained from Seneor a reduction in taxes for the village of Torquemada, his namesake.) The Jews saw Don Abraham as their protector, as indeed he had been—except at the crucial hour. But if he, or any other Jew, believed that Isabella's friendship and trust for Seneor would be beneficial to their people, they were proven tragically wrong. No, Isabella did not want her old Seneor to be expelled—so in order that he could stay she pressured, almost forced, him to convert.

At age eighty, the betrayal by the distinguished Exilarch (head of the exile), as Jews dubbed him, was startling and demoralizing. Some defended his act as necessity, saying the queen had threatened to inflict even harsher penalties upon the Jews if Seneor did not convert and stay. Whether true or false, this is not an uncommon explanation. Ultimate betrayal has often been portrayed as a secret sacrifice, even as concealing a deep religious meaning. Yet Seneor was no Sabbetai Zevi (the impostor Jewish messiah of the seventeenth century who converted to Islam, whose followers explained his betrayal as a mystical secret predating redemption). He was a courtier, not a messiah, and if there is historical significance to his act it lies elsewhere. It throws into relief the declining self-confidence of the Jewish aristocracy and highlights the sudden inability of Jewish courtier-diplomacy to play its traditional role. For now arose a rather uncommon case in the Jews' history, in which the *central government itself*, rather than local authorities or a mutinous populace, decided to uproot the Jewish existence in the land and, what is more, had the effective power to execute its intent.

The Converso Effect

What made the Jews dispensable to the crown was the existence of Conversos that could replace them. The Conversos were politically vulnerable and almost as dependent on the Crown as were the Jews. As servants of the royal administration they were far more trustworthy than the nobles, and more learned. And many of them continued to practice the typical Jewish professions—finance, commerce, medicine, manufacture, and so forth. In these respects they were the Crown's "new Jews," replacing the actual Jews.

In addition, as soon as the Edict of Expulsion was published, in late April, Christian monks, especially Franciscans, started a conversion campaign among the Jews. Jewish preachers countered the offensive, offering nothing but tears and faith. But despite some impressive success, as in Teruel, they met with disappointing results overall. Town after town made known the names of Jews who changed their religion. Ironically, a measure intended to ease the Marrano problem injected a new influx of suspect Christians into the Spanish fold.

The Jewish Departure

Meanwhile most of the Jews were preparing to leave. In three months time they had to sever the ties of their former life without yet building another, leaving behind them friends, sometimes relatives, homes, property, a landscape, memories, smells and tastes, and the natural *habitat* of their language—the language itself they took with them into exile—and a thousand habitual patterns and rules for orientation that make up a person's anchorage in his or her milieu. And they had to sell their possessions in a rush, then try to smuggle the frequently meager returns out of a country that allowed them to take with them only personal effects and merchandise, but no capital.

And where should they go? France and England were closed: each had expelled its Jews in its time and kept the prohibition alive. The rest of western Europe, except for a few places in Italy, was barred to them. There was the sea, leading to shelter in the lands of Islam—Morocco, Turkey, and the rest of the Ottoman empire (Greece, Bulgaria)—but the sea led also into the hands of pirates eager to seize the goods and gold believed to be hidden in the boats, and into storms and cliffs, as legend mixed with reality tells us.

It was rather a *vincible* armada that took the Jews out of Spain. About one-third, perhaps up to one-half of the exiled Jews took to sea. As a contemporary chronicler (Bernáldez) suggested, this time God did not open the sea before them as he had for their ancestors. A safer route was by land—into neighboring Portugal, where King João II, for a price, had agreed to grant the exiles a two-year refuge, after which he would provide them with ships to leave. In fact, though not by design, the Portuguese refuge turned out to be a massive trap, as we shall see in the next chapter.

Legend has it that the last Jews left Spain on a single day, the ninth of Av (*tisha be'av*), the Jewish day of mourning over the destruction of their temple in Jerusalem. Actually, the July 31 deadline had occurred two days earlier. When *tisha be'av* arrived, Spain (except for a few Jews who had trailed behind and were jailed) was *Judenrein*.

A Conversa onlooker summarized the Jews' fate in one sentence: "*En ora mala vino el negro mal*" (On an evil hour came the black evil).[9] And a Catholic bishop described how Jews "were running around day and night like desperados" when the deadline to sell their homes and property expired, and how many accepted Christ's faith "in order not to deprive themselves of the fatherland (*patria*) in which they had been born."[10]

This bishop got it right. The Jews were, in fact, native Spaniards who for over a millennium had belonged to that country no less than anyone else on the peninsula. Their memories, territories, physical and mental horizons, their language, secular culture, links to the past and the landscape, their sense of time and the seasons, and of the flora and fauna were all part of the Hispanic experience. That a community was living by its own laws in Spain did not signify a radical seclusion or disunion in medieval times, when many semiautonomous groups—professional, regional, seigniorial—existed as integral parts of the system. Existentially, the Spanish Jews had no other country: their indigenous belonging defined them no less than did their *otherness*. In consequence, they were the Native Other (as I called them in chapter 2), not foreigners but a *different Hispanic tribe*. Now they were ruthlessly torn away from the country that they felt was their actual homeland, and in which their fathers' fathers have lived since antiquity—and thrust into the role of the "wandering Jew."[11]

The shock not only destroyed one of the greatest Jewish communities since ancient times, it also uprooted and disoriented the lives of innumerable individuals and families who saw the ground slipping from under their feet.

As the last shipload of Jews was leaving the port of Palos on July 31, 1492, it must have passed in view of the *Santa María* and two other ships lying at bay and due to set sail in the opposite direction three days later. On board were the captain, Cristobal Colón, known to posterity as Columbus, and a crew of Old and New Christians. They were looking for India, for gold, and for glory, and were backed by highly placed New Christians in the Castilian court.[12] As the curtain fell on the age-old Spanish Jewry, one of the freest, most prosperous, and culturally most glorious centers of Jewish life, what was to become its heir apparent half a millennium later was about to begin.

Some Jews Drifting Back

The departure of the Jews was harmful to the Spanish economy and administration for a while. But, as mentioned, departure was made possible by the availability of Conversos who could fulfill the Jews' traditional roles. In this respect, the Conversos were seen as non-Jewish Jews, aliens who were officially admitted to the Spanish self but remained other within in. And now, in one stroke, Converso numbers surged by a new wave of conversions, provoked not quite by coercion but by a cruel choice. Some of the departing Jews (such as Tomás Mendes [see note 6]), were unable to make it abroad and wished to return. Between 1492 and 1497 a thin but steady stream of defeated and demoralized Jews drifted back to Spain under the monarchs' protection.[13] They tried (and sometimes succeeded) to retrieve their property—a house, a shop, land, a vineyard, even the structure of a synagogue—or to collect old debts or get compensation from those who robbed them.[14] And, changing their names and religion, they joined the ranks of the new Conversos.

PART FOUR

Portuguese Marranism Takes Over

Who, if they're Portuguese, can live within the narrow bounds
of just one personality, just one nation, just one religion?
—Fernando Pessoa, "Portugal and the Fifth Empire"

11

Trap in Portugal

How many Jews left Spain? Exile statistics are a dangerous game. Plausible estimates range between 160,000 and 80,000. Taking 120,000 as a reasonable midpoint and assuming that only one-third of the exiled could find boats to leave in time, the rest taking the offer of João II for a paid temporary asylum in Portugal (see chapter10),[1] we get 80,000 as an estimated number of Jewish refugees—the more tenacious ones—entering Portugal.[2]

By autumn of 1492 Spain had about five or six million inhabitants, and no official Jews. Portugal had roughly one million inhabitants, and its rate of Jews in the population had more than tripled, jumping overnight from 3 to 4 percent to nearly 12 percent.[3]

Only six hundred families were permitted to settle in Portugal permanently. They were either among the wealthy or artisans in the vital industries of ship-building and metallurgy, then in great demand. All the others were admitted for eight months, paying eight Portuguese cruzados a soul for this temporary asylum. The local Portuguese Jews were mainly artisans but also had a prosperous financial class and a bright intellectual elite that contributed to the budding Portuguese Renaissance. Jews practically introduced printing into Portugal: all of the first eleven Portuguese incunabula are in Hebrew. As usual, Jews were also prominent in tax administration and medicine. But perhaps their most noticeable contribution was to the great discoveries that were then in the making. Active in the naval sciences—astronomy, cartography, geography—and in oriental languages, Jews were helping to lay the scientific foundation for setting sail into the unknown.

The royal astronomer and mathematician was Rabbi Abraham Zaccut (Abraão Zacuto), a Spanish refugee from Salamanca and a devout Jew. His short tenure in Lisbon was essential in drawing navigation charts that helped seamen sail for prolonged periods in unexplored waters. (Vasco da Gama, in just the first leg of his famous voyage, stayed ninety days in the open sea with no land in sight, three times longer than Columbus's whole trip.) Years earlier, Portugal had summoned the help of Jewish cartographers from the Spanish center for naval studies in Majorca. Foremost among them was the cartographer Hasdai Crescas, namesake (and possibly relative) of the philosopher.

Exploratory trips had already led the Portuguese down the western coast of Africa, through Zaire and Angola, to the exciting discovery that the western coast finally bends and turns northward again on the Cape of Storms, appropriately renamed the Cape of Good Hope. Upon such information the scientific headquarters in Lisbon, the NASA of the day, could launch a greater and more daring exploit—Vasco da Gama's discovery of the sea route to India.

Yet better knowledge sometimes curbs imaginative action. The superior quality of its science may have cost Portugal its access to America. When Columbus appealed to Lisbon for help (before turning to Queen Isabella of Castile), he was turned down by João II. Portuguese cosmographers knew that the world was round but estimated that it was much larger than Columbus supposed. The shorter sea route to India was still to the east, around Africa. They were right, and America went to Castile.

On the other hand, its cartographic skill may have secured Brazil for Portugal. It seems that Portuguese seamen had hit upon Brazil (which they took to be a big island) prior to the treaty of Tordesillas, in which Portugal and Castile boldly divided the unexplored globe between them—Castile taking the west and Portugal the east. João II, using diplomacy and bribes, succeeded in moving the demarcation line from 100 to 370 leagues west of Cape Verde. The new line, like the former, passed innocently from north to south through the middle of the North Atlantic; but when extended farther south, the line cut through the bulge of South America, leaving Brazil in the Portuguese sector.

João II did not live to reap the fruits of his preparations. This was left to his successor, Manuel I, "the fortunate king," as his people called him, "the king of spices," as an envious French monarch dubbed him. It was under Manuel that Portugal stepped into its golden age, establishing its power in India and far beyond, wresting the lucrative spice trade from the Muslims (and their Venetian middlemen in Europe), putting military pressure on the Muslim world from its rear, planting its flag in South America, and in the meantime, growing in wealth and in letters—and in official religious zeal.

The Birth of Portuguese Marranism

Watching from across the border, Ferdinand and Isabella could not suppress a sense of being defied, even of seeing their work partly undone, when João II offered the Jews asylum in Portugal. Of course, he did it only for money, but this just made the action even worse, especially since both parties, Castile-Aragon and Portugal, were still nourishing the vision of a unified Iberia to be issued from a matrimonial alliance between them. Would this mean that when the peninsula was finally united, it would again be diluted with Jews—when their expulsion was part of the same drive for Spanish unity?

True, when the eight-month deadline had elapsed, João supplied a few thousand Jews with seaborne transportation. But captains eager to get rid of their human cargo made them disembark at the first African port in sight—which did not make the prospect any more attractive to the remaining Jews in Portugal. João then took to cruelty, putting many Jews who failed to pay their fees in prison camps and sending a few thousand Jewish children to the equatorial island of St. Tomé, off the African shore. But the Catholic sovereigns did not cherish cruelty per se—and João's was ineffectual, which made it doubly objectionable. With reluctance the Spanish monarchs had to note that, after all, most Jews were permitted to stay in Portugal.

Manuel's Reign

When Manuel ascended the Portuguese throne he freed the captive Jews. But in abolishing a useless form of cruelty, Manuel was not implying that he was incapable of committing even greater ones for reasons of state. One of Manuel's first concerns was to take a wife—and through her, perhaps, a peninsula. To revive the prospect of Iberian unity, Ferdinand and Isabella had offered Manuel their eleven-year-old daughter, María. But Manuel wanted her elder sister, the sorrowful beauty Isabella (named after her mother). Young Isabella had already been married to a Portuguese prince, Dom Afonso, son and heir of João II, whose sudden death in a horse race had opened the way for Manuel to inherit his crown—and his widow. Manuel had possibly been in love, or a close semblance of it, with young Isabella since her first arrival in Portugal six years earlier; she, on the contrary, still mourned her dead lover and wouldn't hear of taking another. It is curious how political marriages sometimes assume a true romantic depth. But not in the eyes of the Catholic sovereigns. If, in their remote teens, they had shown a trace of this themselves, it was long forgotten. Pressed by her parents, and by priests who assured her this match would be pleasing to God, the unhappy young Isabella finally consented to the marriage, admitting that a princess's life was not her private affair, but dedicated to higher ideals.

And then her shrewd parents balked. This was again their sense of timing. With young Isabella assured, they could now bargain with Manuel; and judging him to be the more eager party (or to think himself as such) they were determined to press their advantage. No, they wrote to Manuel, their daughter couldn't possibly be queen in a country that swarms with infidels. Let Manuel first expel all Jews and Moors. Wouldn't he otherwise be defending the very opposite of what the marriage was supposed to incarnate?

Manuel had a stronger hand than he thought, but he misjudged it. Ferdinand and Isabella were rather eager to conclude the marriage. But they were more experienced and much the tougher bargainers. Now Manuel faced a dilemma. Only one life—that of Isabella's sickly brother, soon, indeed, to die—separated his would-be bride from inheriting the combined crowns of Castile and Aragon. That was a glittering, blinding prize. Additionally, deporting the Jews may also be pleasing to God—though not to some of Manuel's own jurists and councilors at court. It may, as they pointed out, also be pleasing to Manuel's Muslim adversaries in the Maghreb, who would be delighted to see Portugal lose this crucial segment of its population, which they would hasten to absorb. Manuel felt the unfairness of it all: It was easy for Ferdinand and Isabella to forego the Jews since they already had in their countries a class of New Christians that took over the traditional roles of the Jews in finance, administration, and learning. But Portugal? Portugal was just about to take off as a commercial world power and it had no New Christians at all. How could Portugal give up her Jews? But, on further reflection, wasn't the answer hidden just there? Let Portugal produce her own New Christians! If the problem was how to expel the Jews and yet keep them, would not holy water do it? Dom Manuel devised a two-stage plan.

> Judges, aldermen, attorneys, and good men, . . . feeling this to be for the service of God and our own service and for the welfare of our realm, . . . we have ordained that within a certain time all the Jews living in our realms must leave.

The time given to the Jews was ten months. That was stage one. The edict was published in December 1496. A week earlier Ferdinand and Isabella, duly notified, had signed their daughter's marriage contract. But they did not send the princess over to Portugal yet. Remembering João, they waited to see what would happen next.

Of the justifications given in the Portuguese Edict of Expulsion, only the first two were sincere, the third quite the opposite. Manuel acted "for the service of God" and certainly also for his own, but not for the good of his realm. There, on the contrary, he needed stage two to prevent his own action from taking effect. Advised by a Jewish apostate, Levi Ben Shem-Tov, Manuel ordered a mass capture of Jewish children in Evora and across Portugal. The children were to be taken away from their parents by force and converted. The aim of this new pharaonic decree was to compel the parents to follow. The only way for them to reunite with their children was under the Cross.

The resulting outcry and outrage were not confined to Jewish homes alone. Many Christian families, moved by the inhuman assault, helped to hide the Jewish youngsters. In the king's own council dissent was growing, led by the future bishop of Silves, Fernando Coutinho. A strange crossroads brought the Old Christian Coutinho and the ex-Jewish newcomer Shem-Tov into opposition.

Scenes of pity and heroism are reported by Christian witnesses, among them Coutinho. Some Jews, weeping and protesting, joined their children at the baptismal font. Others chose to "sanctify the Name of God." As at Masada and during the first Crusade in Germany, some Jewish parents—from the tenacious hard core of those who had refused to convert in Spain—reportedly killed their offspring to save them from what they deemed to be a harsher fate. It was heroic inhumanity, Abraham's unsolicited sacrifice. It uncovered a hard rock underneath the meek image of the Jew. But on the immediate calamity it had no effect, except as a transcendent escape. Manuel, in the end, had his way.

If baptism was earth and martyrdom heaven, then Jews seemed to be divided between them. But the truth was more complicated; otherwise, Portuguese Marranism would not have arisen. It was because they clung to heaven while choosing life on this earth that Portuguese Marranos emerged, incorporating the contradiction into their very existence. And, as one contradiction breeds another, it was precisely this form of existence that, rather than aborting the prospect of martyrdom, kept it constantly alive, even through later Inquisition and terror. While baptizing the Jews, the Portuguese authorities, foreseeing the needs of the future, forced the Jews by threat of death to dispose of all the Jewish books in the Lisbon synagogue, as a first step in erasing the memory of Judaism. But King Manuel, the royal businessman, found a more efficient and lucrative way (suggested to him by a New Christian adviser). The Jews possessed many valuable and precious books, some imported by the refugees from Spain. Manuel had the books confiscated and later sold many of them to Jewish congregations abroad, from Morocco to Cochin in India (1505).[4]

Along with the Jews, the Muslims were also ordered to evacuate Portugal. But no effort was made to convert them by force and they were treated on the whole with prudence, in order to avoid reprisals by Muslim countries.

The Jews had no country to protect them. What they got in May was a Protective Edict by Manuel who, using the carrot along with the stick, guaranteed converted Jews that no one would inquire about their sincerity during a transition period of twenty years. This was natural enough. How indeed could you expect—as Manuel explained to the pope, to the Spanish monarchs, and to the devout Christian in himself—that a whole community will change its heart overnight (as a result of an act of force), or will know what customs are practiced in their new religion? And yet Manuel's promise sounded, and might have been intended, as a tacit invitation to Judaize. To the ears of the hard-pressed, buttressed Jews, at the brink of despair and with almost no alternative, Manuel seemed to be saying: remain Jews under Christian cover—but remain.

Meanwhile Manuel had his mind on another embarkation. On July 7, 1497, he bade farewell to three ships and a supply vessel leaving Lisbon with the king's great hopes and aspirations. He was not to hear of them for another full two years, until their captain, Vasco da Gama, sent word that he had triumphed.

On the heels of Gama's departure, September was approaching—the official deadline for the Jews to leave Portugal. Manuel had no intention to let them go. He closed down all the ports of embarkation except Lisbon, and when twenty thousand Jews from other cities came to Lisbon to arrange their departure, he detained them all. Who said they were to leave? Let them rather try baptism! The Jews, thrown off balance, were herded into crowded quarters, deprived of sufficient food and sleep, and then hammered with pleas, threats, and lures by royal emissaries—among them another apostate—who used the tacit permission to Judaize as bait for conversion. Many succumbed. Others persisted, demanding to leave, but Manuel detained them until after the deadline had passed, then announced that since they had disobeyed his decree, they lost their liberty and were now his slaves. They could move nowhere—except to the baptismal font.

The Portuguese Expulsion thus turned into its opposite. In fact it was a massive imprisonment. Manuel's policy was consolidated in April 1499, when the king prohibited all New Christians from leaving the country and all Old Christians from buying their real estate or selling them bills of exchange (so they could flee). Lifted a decade later, the ban was to return with the Inquisition in the 1530s.

A small minority was, however, allowed to go. Among them, to Manuel's displeasure, was the royal astronomer Abraão Zacuto, who demanded and obtained that permission as a reward for his cartographic services to the sovereign and to Portugal's maritime exploits. If we are to accept Zacuto's testimony that, in 1492, "the main body of [Jewish] Castile entered Portugal," then the Spanish tragedy in Jewish history was really a Portuguese tragedy. From Spain the Jews were expelled, but in Portugal their "main body" was lost.

Portuguese Marranism lived on for centuries, however, and a few blazing splinters of it returned to open Judaism abroad in the sixteenth and seventeenth centuries, signaling the Jews' return to Western Europe and spreading new hopes and complexities wherever they went.

Shortly after the two semi-fictions, the expulsion and the conversion, Manuel married young Isabella. The ceremony was low key, as the bride's older brother was dying. When he died he left his wife pregnant. If she should bear a boy, then he—not Isabella—would inherit Castile and Aragon. She did bear a boy—stillborn. The royal Portuguese couple was now summoned to Toledo to be officially consecrated as heirs to the dual kingdoms. The grand prize was now in sight. Then young Isabella, the sad queen, died in childbirth. Brokenhearted, her parents held on to the baby, now the heir to Castile, Aragon, and Portugal—the future first king of Iberia. The Portuguese Cortes was displeased to have the baby brought up as a Castilian prince: that would mean Portugal would eventually be subdued by Castile, not united with her as equals. But the death of the royal baby at age two put an end to fears and grand hopes alike. Neither Manuel nor his heir would now rule over the whole peninsula. And the Jews were sacrificed to no avail—except the good of their souls (and perhaps the demographic balance of the country).

Manuel now married—after all—María, his dead wife's younger sister whom he had once rejected. María bore him an heir and nine other children. But the dual kingdoms of Castile and Aragon fell to her elder sister, Juana, later called "the mad Juana" who, after her mother's death, ruled Castile in name only, with her father Ferdinand acting as regent. When Ferdinand also died, both kingdoms went to Juana's famous son Carlos, soon to become Emperor Charles V. Charles did not need the Portuguese dominions in order for the sun never to set over his own; but it might have glittered more brightly had he had them. It was only under Charles's son, Philip II, that Portugal was united with Spain—indeed, annexed by force (the pretext going back to Manuel's marriage with María), to the annoyance of the Portuguese who, sixty years later, broke away and remained independent thereafter.

It was two years and two days after their departure that the first of Vasco da Gama's vessels approached the port of Lisbon. While the epopee was being told to the king, the great news resounded all over the country. It was Portugal who actually got to India! Columbus, by mistake, discovered a new continent, but Gama, by design, found the way to a most ancient one. No longer was Europe cut off from the riches and culture of the Far East by a hostile Muslim wedge. A new era was opening—as was realized not only by later historians but already by contemporaries, who lived the Renaissance without knowing its name.

Along with scars and memories, the ships were carrying samples from distant regions: scented wood, jewels, pepper, cinnamon, nutmeg, ginger, cloves. They also brought six Indians of a race hardly seen in Europe and, quite unexpectedly, a member of a race hardly seen in India—a Polish Jew. Brought as a child to Alexandria, where he grew up to become an expert in jewelry, the Polish Jew then traveled to the land of the Mongols and farther east before settling down in India. Vasco da Gama captured him trying to spy on his ships in the service of his employer, Adil Khan of Goa. Gama duly converted his Jewish prisoner and brought him as a present to the king.[5]

Manuel was delighted. The prisoner spoke a half dozen languages, none of them quite correctly, and seemed to know all about India and the Orient. He supplied the king with precious information and, possibly, a few mistakes. Anyway, the king marveled at this man, whom he saw as God-sent in more than a prosaic sense—a kind of divine sign that his actions were pleasing.

Jewish Assimilation in Portugal

With his mind turned to the seafaring adventures, Manuel paid less attention to the assimilation of the Jews. Officially converted yet relatively immune to prosecution for heresy, many Jews tried to remain Jews indeed, and most of their neighbors continued referring to them as such. With their synagogues closed or converted into churches, their Hebrew books confiscated or banned (except for medical books in Hebrew—the profession must go on), many converts continued to pray from memory and to keep Jewish holidays in deficient procedure, sometimes even on the wrong date. Meanwhile, on Sundays they would flock into churches, hearing Mass, taking communion, learning to pray in Latin, to practice Catholic rites, to confess—acquainting themselves with a whole new culture that they tried to reduce to a mere code of appearances. Some, indeed, attempted to identify themselves with these appearances, turning them into their new essence and struggling to reshape their personal identity through them. But even within this group, not many, as compared to the early Spanish Conversos, were eager to excel as bishops, theologians, and similar functions that put their new identity in self-assertive and proclamatory relief. Others— and, in the first decade, probably still a very large group—kept the essence and the appearance wide apart and in open contradiction, initiating themselves not only to the practice of Catholic customs but also to a subtler psychological art: using the confession as a means of concealment and taking the sacrament while annulling it at heart. The later slogan of nineteenth-century Jewish Enlightenment—"Be a Jew at home and a [universal] man outside"—applied to the first Portuguese Marranos, but with the crucial contradiction introduced by replacing *man* with *Catholic*, and under the menacing shadow of illegality.

Thus a dual system of life was taking shape; and its lines were bolder than known before. The first generation of Portuguese Marranism was different from that in Spain, where assimilation was faster and went deeper, and where the Judaizers slowly dwindled into a buttressed minority. In Portugal, at least in the first fifty years, Judaizers were more daring, sometimes almost sincere about their insincerity. And Portuguese New Christians, whether Judaizing or not, were generally a powerful, semiorganized community that manifested a good deal of in-group solidarity. With time it dealt independently with the king and even kept its own ambassador in the pope's court. Portuguese New Christians were impressive, first of all, in their relative numbers. Of Portugal's one million inhabitants, about 12 per cent were former Jews, most of them freshly converted in a single wave. (This is a prudent estimate: Portuguese and Jewish writers, perhaps for different reasons, tend to put the rate around 20 percent.)[6] Far more significant than total numbers is the rate of the New Christians in the urban population, where money, power, politics, learning, and trade were concentrated. Even in Spain before 1492, with five to six million people and a much lower rate of Jews, the Jewish population in most urban centers was over 10 percent and sometimes, as in Avila, it reached a solid 30 percent. Portugal had significantly fewer cities and relatively many more ex-Jews: small wonder they were soon felt—and resented—in many walks of Portuguese life, above all in international commerce.

It was a coincidence, full of consequences, that Vasco da Gama's discoveries were made parallel to the forced conversions of the Jews. With Portugal entering its global mercantile era, the New Christians did not have to rush into the centers of wealth and power as these centers were now moving toward them. They had only to modernize and expand their old Jewish roles in order to see themselves swayed into the center of a new system of international trade that they were helping to set up.

Portugal emerged from the fifteenth century a maritime power, but not yet a mercantile one. Located at the far end of Europe—which until that time was considered the farthest edge of the world—Portugal had taken no part in the trading experience of the great commercial centers of Italy and Flanders. Then suddenly she was in need of initiative and expertise even surpassing theirs. With the Indian and Atlantic oceans replacing the closed horizons of the Mediterranean as the major trading arena, what was needed were new techniques of trade and communication; new dimensions in volume, capital, risk taking, and the time span between investment and revenue; and new, sophisticated modes of exchange.

Like Spain, Portugal had its share of petty nobility, a poor crowd of *fidalgos* (nobles) too proud to be productive. As the proverb had it, they used to set a table "with many napkins and few courses," and looked down with disdain on anything smacking of work or commercial enterprise. The New Christians, as former Jews, were traditionally oriented toward commerce and finance, and free of the Iberian obsession with honor and quasinobility. As in Spain, they placed a high value on work, professional skill, and the clever manipulation of money and goods—qualities that won them a good deal of spite and moral hauteur from a society that, for the same reasons, needed them vitally.

They were also closely knit as a community. Less atomized and intimidated than the Spanish Conversos and manifesting stronger will power, they were able to better benefit from the Jewish custom of self-help and mutual support. For the same reason, in the eyes of the Old Christians they maintained the image and denomination of the foreigner—the Other Within—even more than their Spanish predecessors. In Portugal there was no period in which Old Christians were expecting the former Jews to sincerely assimilate before using their disappointment as a weapon in the social and economic struggle against them. And, while in Spain it took a half-century until the big anti-New Christian pogrom erupted, in Portugal it took less than a decade.

"New Christians or Jews": The Lisbon Massacre

It happened in April 1506. Lisbon was suffering from the plague, then a half year old, adding to the miseries of draught and lower-class famine. King Manuel ordered two additional cemeteries to be prepared and the city to be partly evacuated, himself taking the lead; but common folk had no alternative and wealthy burghers, too, were reluctant to move as trade was going on and the port was full of foreign ships.

Then the classic incident happened. Two independent sources, a German visitor stationed on a ship and the Hebrew chronicler Ibn Verga (then living as a Marrano in Lisbon, though absent from town) tell similar stories (as reconstructed by Yerushalmi).[7] On the night of April 17, a group of New Christians was apprehended while secretly celebrating the Passover seder and arrested. It was the wrong day for the seder, but they chose it either for the sake of concealment or simply because they had no Jewish calendars. The king was told the news and two days later the culprits were released. The populace, never reconciled to the Protective Edict, was bitter, looking for scapegoats, and spreading the rumor—not absolutely improbable—that bribes and mishandling were also involved.

Passover comes dangerously close to Easter—an age-old source of anti-Jewish explosion. On the very day the Judaizers were released (April 19, a Sunday), crowds were gathering in the Convent of São Domíngos when a miracle occurred—much needed and so comforting in the strained and suffering city. A crucifix in the chapel started emitting a mysterious inner light. Chroniclers differed on the nature of the miracle as skeptics differed on its explanation (one even suspected the effect was contrived) but there is no doubt about the outcome. Scenes of passion and devotion, nurtured by misery and hope, were taking place, representable to the modern eye perhaps by scenes from Fellini. But with so many New Christians in town, there almost inevitably was also a spoiler.

"How can a piece of wood do miracles?" asked a voice in the chapel, much too loud for the speaker's safety. "Put some water to it and it'll go out." Whatever the exact words—chroniclers differ about the quotation—they expressed the same rough Jewish common sense, resisting the Catholic sense of *mysterium* and insisting on calling super-rational phenomena by their earthly names, that we also met in Benito García, the Spanish Marrano, wondering that "a mixture of dough and water should be called God." Yet the unwise Lisbon skeptic was not arguing with a learned theologian; he was provoking an already emotional crowd and challenging what it cherished most at the moment.

The first to react was a group of women. They grabbed the unhappy blasphemer, dragged him out of the convent and, with the men helping, beat him to death and then dismembered his body. When his brother rushed to inquire and protest, he was also butchered. The two bodies were put to fire in the square, with the growing mob clamoring for death and burning of all the Jews.

Only a strong show of authority could have saved the situation from escalating into a major riot. But the local magistrate proved weak and, following a futile attempt to make arrests, practically ran away with his men. The angry crowd followed, shouting that since the king refused to punish the New Christians, God now must do so.

The work of God was assumed by two Dominican friars, one a Spaniard from Aragon who led the lower clergy in enflaming the mob. They were the catalysts that turned the incident into a major riot and massacre that raged for at least four days and ended in open revolt against the king.

The mob was frantic, running in all directions, killing any New Christian they met, pillaging, raping, breaking into houses, and carrying dozens, then hundreds, of dead corpses to the Praça de São Domíngos (Saint Dominic plaza) to be piled up and burned. Soon a work of charity was organized—giving money to buy wood for the burnings.

The breakdown of political authority was complete. With it collapsed the psychological barriers that make a political structure work. The horrors of those days were told in several accounts. The German chronicler, not very sympathetic toward the "New Christians or Jews," yet quite sober, said he would not have believed his own story had he not witnessed it. A Marrano survivor, Isaac ibn Faraj, told in a Hebrew letter how he salvaged from the flames the mutilated head of a friend in order to bring it to Jewish burial. Young girls and women were torn away from church altars where they futilely sought refuge. Pregnant women were dropped from windows to be pierced on the tips of spears. Women, we are told, were also numerous on the marauders' side, taking part in the physical carnage no less than the men.

Contemporary sources placed the number of New Christians massacred in four days as four thousand, possibly a gross exaggeration. But even accepting half that number, it is still enormous considering the demography of the time.

The German chronicler and other countrymen arrived at the Praça de São Domingos when a pile of four hundred cadavers was being prepared for burning, and contributed a hundred pfennigs each to pay for wood. They noted with satisfaction that, as it happened, *their* wood was used to burn the body of the single most hated New Christian in Lisbon, a prominent tax farmer and trader called João Rodrigues Mascarenhas, whom the German chronicler calls *das haubt allen juden* (the chief of all the Jews). Mascarenhas was in King Manuel's employ, collecting taxes at home and overseas, including Guinea and Gambia in Africa, and trading in new commodities, such as sugar, on behalf of the king. His execution was a highlight of the Lisbon massacre and a further affront and provocation to Manuel.

The pogrom, indeed, was not a purely religious affair but a true revolt of the populace against established authority and the king—a well-known pattern in Jewish history, which also started the Marrano problem in Spain in 1391. King Manuel was faltering. As Yerushalmi has shown, his first reactions to the revolt were hesitant, wavering between various courses of action and taking almost none. But when finally he found the power and the resolve to subdue the mutiny, he inflicted severe punishment on the perpetrators and also on those who failed to stop them. The two Dominicans were garroted and burned; others lost their lives and property, or part of it; and the city of Lisbon lost its governing Council of the Twenty-Four and its right to the title of "noble and always loyal city." (These rights, however, were restored a few years later; after all, an absolute monarch cannot break forever with the capital city of his kingdom.)

It is noteworthy that in all the major accounts of the Lisbon massacre, the New Christians are referred to as "Jews." The Dominican agitators demanded death to "the Jews"; Marrano sources (such as Ibn Faraj) call their folk "Jews" in a straightforward manner; and the German chronicler, in the title of his booklet, referred to them as "*newe christen oder iuden*" (New Christians or Jews), using *or* in the sense of equivalence, and in the text he refers to them simply as *iuden*. So do later scholars, from the French political thinker Jean Bodin (who used the Lisbon incident as an argument against forced conversions), to a recent British historian.[8] Each writer may have had his own reasons (or slips) for calling the Portuguese New Christians "Jews"; but it is noteworthy to find such convergence between the assailant, the victim, the witness, the philosopher, and the modern historian.[9]

Reality was more complex. The group that saw itself as Jewish from within was evidently smaller than the group of "Jews" as seen from without. Anti-Semites, especially, tend to see more Jews than do the Jews. Even among the Judaizers, their link to historical Judaism became questionable with time, as there were no professing Jews alongside them to teach, exhort, blame—and relate—to them. Exiled within an exile, they unwittingly started to form a special entity of their own, neither Christian nor Jewish, but fleeing from the first toward the second without really succeeding in either move.

At the same time, they sustained bonds of race, solidarity and common interest with the non-Judaizers within their larger group of New Christians, soon to be known as the Portuguese "Hebrew Nation" (*naçao hebrea*).

Opting for Duality: Marranism Becomes a Choice

The Lisbon massacre had another, more immediate aftermath that, in shaping the Portuguese "Nation," was even more important than the event itself.

On March 1507, following a year of negotiations, Manuel abolished the 1499 restrictions and granted the New Christians sweeping new freedoms. Now they could leave the country and return at will, take out money and exchange bills, and sell their immovable property to Old Christians. Emigrants were not considered outcasts. They could return when they wished and, in fact, kept their Portuguese affiliation and designation, thus helping to create a "Portuguese" trade community abroad. Even those who had emigrated illegally in the past were now pardoned and allowed to return.

There was only one reservation: emigrants should only go to Christian lands, using Portuguese ships—the Muslims, after all, were not only infidels but now also the economic archenemy of Portugal.

Manuel promised never again to discriminate against New Christians by subjecting them to special royal regulations. He kept the promise, with minor exceptions, until his death. This did not prevent local groups from discriminating against New Christians within their own jurisdiction. Sometimes Manuel intervened, but on the whole he could assure such liberality only in the central royal government. Meanwhile, to keep emigration under check, Manuel (in 1512, four years before it was to expire) extended by sixteen more years the guarantee against inquiries into the converts' sincerity. This, to the Conversos, was almost full emancipation. It won Manuel the title *King of the Jews* from his populace, without completely erasing his epitaph as *foe of the Jews* from Jewish books, which sometimes referred to him as "Pharaoh" and "Haman."[10]

Manuel's vacillation and ambivalence are comprehensible. The problem of the Jews had landed on Portugal as an abrupt, massive wave, when the country had no precedent experience in dealing with it on such a scale. Manuel was here facing the unknown no less than on the oceans. His general course was now set, but he had to navigate by trial and error, making rectifications as he went. His new decree was aimed to remove a contradiction from his former policy. The Jews were initially forced to stay in Portugal for mainly economic reasons. But how could they perform efficiently when the new conditions called for their worldwide role and presence if they were barred from travel and the free transfer of capital? The new measures were also calculated—with a risk—to rid the country of the most troublesome Judaizers while keeping the rest by granting them great opportunities and relative religious freedom.

If the king believed this package would avert a massive emigration, he proved right. But he did not leave everything to fortune. By permitting emigration only to Christian lands the king kept his finger on the valve. No Christian lands in Europe except for a few cities in Italy admitted professing Jews. If they wanted to openly return to Judaism, Marranos still had to take the roundabout and illegal route to a Muslim country and sever their Portuguese ties. This was a perfect possibility, but more taxing and complicated; it required a stronger incentive.

A stream of emigrants, indeed, followed. It included, among many others, Ibn Verga and Ibn Faraj. Not all the Marranos left to become Jews: some went as Catholics to foreign trading centers, including the newly discovered lands. But the majority remained in Portugal—a fact of capital importance in determining their future identity and self-perception.

Now, for the first time, living as a Marrano became a *choice*—though not in a positive way, but as acceptance of a fait accompli. The New Christians who remained in Portugal did not necessarily opt for assimilation. A large group rather chose duality—the contradiction inherent in their situation, which they began to get used to and which, as they witnessed, they could sustain almost with impunity. In a sense, they reiterated the pattern of choice implicit in their conversion: trying to cling to heaven and earth at the same time—seeking their earthly fortunes and abode in Portugal, and their salvation in the Law of Moses.

On the one hand they were former exiles, finally settled down in a promising economic landscape; on the other, they were ex-Jews wishing to keep their old faith—and practically able to do so, though in a concealed and interiorized way, which inevitably deviates from tradition. This combination now became *the content of their choice*—a passive choice no doubt, but still a preference in face of alternative courses.

There is an enormous psychological difference between the two forms of choice. The Marranos did not face an a priori choice between two alternatives, both abstract and unrealized; they already lived within one of them—and the question facing them was whether they were going to upset and revolutionize their lives in order to move to the other alternative. That many decided negatively did not mean they wanted to assimilate; but if so, then what they actually opted for, whether explicitly or not, was the duality (and duplicity) of the Marrano situation.

We must not, of course, assume that all had the same religious tension. Many may have kept their attachment to Judaism as an intimate secret, even as a dear possession that does not, however, dominate one's daily life and decisions; or as a memory of something that belongs to the past more than to the present and future. Others, contemplating departure, had put it off from one year to the next, confident that the option was still there—until the 1530s, when the legal doors were slammed again for many decades.

We must bear in mind that most of these men and women were former refugees who had already known exile and uprooting. Now that, after many ordeals, they had found anchorage and established a modus vivendi, free of persecution for Judaizing and facing attractive economic prospects, the drive to leave everything behind them and take to the wandering stick again was compelling only for a minority. The majority were divided roughly between those who assimilated or accepted Catholicism and those who opted for secret Judaizing as their specific way of life. Their failure to emigrate while the gates were open does not signify the sudden extinction of Portuguese Marranism, but rather its *final separation from Judaism* and its formation as a distinct (ethno-) religious phenomenon.

This also had a socioeconomic side. The 1507 decree lifted the last barriers from the New Christians' way to the highest ranks of Portuguese finance and overseas trade. Before long they attained prominence in foreign trade and virtually monopolized some of the new commodity markets such as sugar, and, to a lesser degree, they dealt in spices, rare woods, tea, coffee, and also in transportation of slaves. Many, perhaps most, were active in small trade, handicraft, and manufacturing; but their main contribution to the land—and the source of their great fortunes and political standing, though not popularity, in the realm—was foreign trade.

The social and economic role of the New Christians also helped to shape them as a group. It was not only an additional feature in them, but (like their origin and former religion) almost a defining one. In numbers they were between one-quarter and one-third of the urban population, and perhaps the largest subgroup within the commercial middle classes. In function they were the heart and motor of the new bourgeoisie. In appellation—that is, in the eyes of the others—they were the men of business *(homens de negócios)*, a term that needed no further elucidation in order to be understood. And all these factors formed parts of their collective self, of what constituted their uniqueness as a group. Moreover, the special way in which their identity was formed by the three ingredients of race, former religion, and socioeconomic role was in itself their first and most distinguishing singularity.

It also distinguished them from the Jews. The social and economic function was always additional to the Jews' identity; but in the case of the Portuguese New Christians, their socioeconomic role, as a group, was *constitutive* of their identity. They did not have a solid identity, in itself, on which to hang their broader activities as accidents. What they were was determined no less by the social function they fulfilled than by their race (or descent) and former religion, whether alive or not. Indeed, their identity was a fusion of all three, vague enough to allow for puzzling border cases, but also distinct enough to preclude being reduced to any single one of its ingredients.

Even in pure religious terms, the Judaizing New Christians were distancing themselves from the Jews. They did not circumcise their sons—the chief Jewish rite and sign of the Covenant with God; they committed "idolatry" by constantly practicing Catholic ceremonies; and they kept a shrinking minimum of Jewish cult, frequently in mutilated, distorted forms or mixed with Christian elements. In addition, they were cut off from the living community of the Jews, and this made great religious difference. Historical Judaism conceived of itself as living within an actual congregation. It was not an abstract system of ideas but a living practice, sustained by the real, historical community. The Marranos, inevitably, were placing the core of their religiosity in an interiorized belief, a subjective flame of the heart, lowering the value of overt ceremonial religious practice. This was incongruent with Judaism, for which all religious value and spirit must be embodied in a network of daily sacrosanct practices. Moreover, as we have remarked, the essence of the Judaizing Marranos' faith—that salvation lies in the Law of Moses—has a foreign ring to Jewish ears. It sounds like a Christian formula invested with a Jewish core.

Thus the religious life of the Judaizing Marranos had taken up a heterodox content. It was impregnated with Christian elements while missing essential Jewish ones. Small wonder that Jewish rabbis viewed the Marranos with ambivalence and growing estrangement. To outsiders, nearly all Portuguese New Christians were Jews; but to the Jews, even the Judaizers were questionable brethren: seldom accepted, always suspected, to be judged on the merit of each category of cases. Jewish leaders knew of course about the Marranos' Judaizing practices, but to many severe rabbis concerned with the *purity* of the holy congregation, that was exactly the problem: these practices were not strictly Jewish, nor performed by people who really opted for Judaism (since they remained in the "land of idolatry"). Though some rabbis were more lenient, suspicion and rejection had the upper hand.[11]

Rabbinical ambivalence toward the Marranos does not testify that the Marranos were mostly assimilated Catholics, as some historians believe.[12] What can be safely concluded from the rabbinical verdicts is the distancing of the Judaizing Marranos from the Jews—a distancing that in the sixteenth century, when Jews could no longer live in Spain or in Portugal, became also physical and geographic. Judaizing Marranos were still Jews by aspiration—by their persistent *esperanza*, much derided by Spanish playwrights—but they were not Jews in fact. Révah called them "potential Jews"[13] because a number of them later returned to open Judaism abroad. But if so, then they were no less "potential Catholics," since many ended by embracing a full-fledged Catholicism as their preferred identity. Moreover, even their aspiration to Judaism acquired a distinctly unreal nature. As demonstrated by their failure to emigrate, most Judaizing Marranos no longer yearned for Judaism as a concrete reality, but as an ideal, infinite dream. This is similar to the Jewish yearning for the Messiah, expressed in the saying, "next year in Jerusalem," which is also not pronounced with a concrete intention. Except for periodic messianic outbursts, Jews have educated themselves to wait for a messiah that *does not* really come. Of course he *will* come, there is no doubt of that, but not in our lifetime, only in the Messianic era, which is always deferred and projected beyond the present.

Manuel was succeeded by his son, João III, a lesser ruler governing for a longer period (1521–1557). At first João III renewed his father's assurances made to the New Christians in 1524. But secretly he ordered an investigation into their personal lives and habits. Information was gathered from parish priests inside and outside the confession cell. It depicted a picture of life under a mask that was often cast off at death. Many Marranos were more willing to live as Catholics than to die as Catholics. They accepted the sacraments of baptism and marriage, but at the point of death—a telling refusal—they shunned taking extreme unction, left no money to say Mass for their souls, and avoided burying their dead in church cemeteries. They were also reported to give charity only within their community, cut their attendance at Sunday Mass and practice the Passover seder ceremony.

To receive direct information the king employed a spy, a convert named Henriques Nuñes, dubbed *Firme-Fé* (firm faith). Masquerading as Judaizer, he won the friendship of Judaizing Marranos whose names he supplied to the king in 1527, together with a list of signs of Judaizing practices and suggestions for combating them. When his betrayal was discovered, Firme-Fé was ambushed and assassinated by two young New Christians, both clerics—a fact that corroborated his testimonies. The incident, which became a sensation, revived a long-standing demand to establish a Portuguese Inquisition.

David Reubeni—Cannons for the Messiah?

But now attention in Lisbon turned toward a dark-skinned Jew, all clad in white, who claimed to be a princely emissary from a distant Jewish kingdom in the desert. He spoke only Hebrew and Arabic. His name was David, and he belonged, he said, to the ancient Hebrew tribe of Reuben. His brother, King

Yosef, reigned over a segment of the mythological Ten Lost Tribes of Israel that had disappeared in antiquity.

According to Jewish legend, the Lost Tribes will reappear when the Messiah is about to come. So was the Messiah coming? Boldly mixing messianic and political allusions, the enigmatic messenger said his brother was planning a military expedition to conquer the Holy Land from the Turks. He had sent David to seek the alliance of Christendom against the common enemy.

A fantastic story, romantic and seemingly incredible, yet not totally outside the possible imagination of Renaissance Europe. This was the era of great novelties and explorations, when surprising new lands and peoples were being discovered, often by the Portuguese—so why not a forgotten Jewish kingdom in the desert? Europe itself had long cultivated the legend of the mysterious land of "Prester John" (Priest John), a Christian kingdom lurking in the mists of the pagan south; so a Jewish version of Prester John, though calling for caution, was not so outrageous to contemporary ears.

David Reubeni (as he was called) had gone at first to Rome, the capital of Christendom, and boldly demanded to see the pope. His audacity and pomp (and the help of Jewish lobbying and bribes) got him an audience with Pope Clement VII. The pope was not prepared to dismiss Reubeni's story offhand. The Ottoman Empire was a mounting threat. It was building the military might that would enable it later, under Suleiman the Magnificent, to conquer vast areas in central Europe, reach the gates of Vienna, and send its fleets to harass Christian shores and trade in the Mediterranean. The pope had reason for concern. He gave Reubeni letters of introduction to King João III of Portugal, piously explaining to the king that "there are times when God takes vengeance of his enemies by using his other enemies." The pope himself mixed *Realpolitik* with religious fantasy—a quintessential trait of the age—in giving David another letter, addressed to no other than Prester John!

Portugal had a distinct interest in having an ally who could outflank the Turks from the Southeast and threaten the trading routes from India that Portugal's rivals were using (passing through Aden to Suez and Alexandria). Four centuries later a comparable motive prompted England to send another romantic adventurer, Lawrence of Arabia, to conclude a similar alliance in the desert.[14] David Reubeni had been the Lawrence of *Jewish*-Arabia—or styled himself in a similar role. His demand was as prosaic as his story was fantastic: he wanted military hardware, especially cannons—state of the art European cannons, the formidable strategic weapon of those times. He was the first Jewish emissary to request advanced arms from a Western power.

Reubeni was received in Portugal with proper regalia as a foreign prince and diplomat and lodged in luxury. One can imagine the stir and sensation he created in the capital. Soon he became the newest social attraction, the subject of chatter and rumor, and also of suspicion and a sense of scandal. An avowed Jew honored as a celebrity when Judaism is forbidden in the land? For that very reason his figure fired the hopes and fantasies of Judaizing and assimilated Marranos. How could the Marranos not be excited on hearing that the Lost Tribes were being discovered and planning to reconquer the ancient homeland? Weren't they a lost tribe, too? And the fact that, of all places, Reubeni came to Lisbon held a special secret for them: he must have been sent to redeem them, the Iberian Marranos longing for a savior of their own. This was a necessary prelude to the larger Jewish redemption, and they, the Marranos, were chosen as the Jewish people's messianic avant-garde!

A wave of secret "reconversions" to Judaism followed, arousing the clergy's anxiety. In a memo to King João III, a high prelate complained that Reubeni has converted an innumerable crowd to the Jewish heresy. That was only partly true: Reubeni considered the reversions to Judaism a danger to his mission but he was unable to restrain the Marrano excitement.

David's problems compounded when Diogo Pires, a young Converso cleric with burning eyes, circumcised himself and, taking the Hebrew name Shlomo Molkho (invoking King Solomon), started a crusade to revive Iberian Judaism as prelude to the Messiah. Reubeni tried to distance himself from Molkho, who jeopardized his own mission. When danger was too close Molkho escaped to Italy, where he became Jewish in the open, studied Kabbalah, and enthusiastically spread the message of the coming Messiah. Meanwhile, negotiations between Reubeni and the Portuguese Crown produced no results. Many courtiers called him a fraud and a charlatan, though a few still supported him. Paradoxically, the improbable nature of his demand—to get cannons—lent him some credence. Had he asked for money or gold, he would have been dismissed earlier. But cannons? Cannons are heavy, they must be transported somewhere—and if so, someone was expecting them and had, indeed, sent him. (This argument, as we shall see presently, may work in a different direction.)

In the end the skeptics prevailed. Reubeni was expelled from Portugal and went to Italy. Now he openly assured Jews and Marranos that their ancient land was soon to be restored to them, and he joined forces with Molkho. The two placed their hopes on the Habsburg Emperor Charles V, the archenemy of Turkish power in Europe. But Charles was also the archenemy of Catholic heretics such as Molkho and the Marranos he incited. Against the advice of a wise Jewish courtier, the two crusaders made a rash appeal to the emperor, which ended in disaster. Molkho was arrested and committed to the flames as a heretic (becoming a famous Marrano martyr), and David was sent in chains to Spain, where his traces disappear.

Who, in the end, was David Reubeni? Some Jewish historians hailed him as national hero.[15] Others dismissed Reubeni as a scheming operator and adventurer. Could he not have been, at the same time, a Jewish political dreamer and a self-seeking adventurer? A key element to his mystery is whether he operated on his own, and if not, who did he mean to serve? Who were his clients, so to speak? Certainly not a Jewish king in the desert. But why not a more mundane power?

The nearest clue to the enigma could lie in the nature of Reubeni's request: cannons. Suppose he had gotten those cannons—what would he have done with them? Presumably, he would have pretended to be shipping them to his "brother" in the desert, but actually ship them elsewhere. And who, at that time, was eager to possess more cannons—advanced, up-to-date European-made cannons—if not the same Ottoman Empire that Reubeni pretended to oppose? Ottoman military tactics relied on the massive concentration of artillery; so the Turks needed cannons, always more and more advanced cannons. What better cover for a pro-Turkish agent than promoting the anti-Turkish scheme of capturing Jerusalem from the Sultan?[16]

Furthermore, Reubeni's messianic dreams, supposing he had such, could best be served by asking the Turks to allow Jewish settlement in Palestine as part of his reward. As a Jew, Reubeni had no reason to help Europe against the Ottomans. The Ottoman empire had been generous to the Jews, granting the Spanish exiles a haven and allowing Jews to live in peace in its empire, while Iberia was persecuting the Jews and most of Western Europe was closed to them. Supposing that Reubeni had a Jewish commitment in addition to seeking gain, it made no sense for him to help the powers that persecuted the Jews, and to endanger the Jewish communities in the Turkish empire that protected them.[17]

Sensing the rising Ottoman interest in Palestine (Suleiman the Magnificent was to rebuild the walls of Jerusalem), Reubeni might have dreamed, as part of the deal, to arrange for Jews to settle in Palestine—not against the Ottoman Empire's will but rather under its protection. This idea was not outlandish. Later in the century it surfaced again when the Marrano Juce Miques (Don Yosef Nasi), a financier and adviser to the Sultan, obtained permission for Jews to emigrate to Palestine and settle at first in Tiberias. The experiment failed, but it proves the idea had been in the air for quite a while, especially among Marranos.

My hypothesis, though demystifying, does not make Reubeni any less fascinating. He remains extraordinary in his fantasy and daring in his resplendent style and in the grand sting he had presumably concocted. And it certainly does not diminish his messianic impact on the Portuguese Marranos. Highly aroused and bitterly frustrated, they were now facing their most dramatic struggle—the battle over the establishment of the Inquisition.

12

Portuguese Inquisition, Pure Blood, and the "Nation"

---~⇒~---

The Battle over the Portuguese Inquisition

The battle over the Inquisition started in Portugal in 1531. The country was governed by João III, and Manuel's extended period of grace was nearing its end. The New Christians suffered from the hatred of the populace and the lower clergy; they had powerful enemies in court, led by Queen Catalina (who was, like the king himself, a grandchild of Ferdinand and Isabella), and they were envied by burgher competitors. Unlike in Spain a century earlier, the New Christians were also resented by many in the Portuguese nobility and upper clergy who were unable to come to grips with Portugal's new mercantile role, which the New Christians symbolized and embodied—and with their own image as reflected to them from this new role.

The Portuguese elite suffered from an agonizing conflict of identity. Reality and self-image were a world apart. In reality, in the sixteenth century, the Portuguese king had become the single most important merchant in the world. His agents and soldiers, mostly of noble origin, engaged in heavy trading and money lending on their own, especially overseas. So did even clerics and the religious orders who, like the Jesuits, financed their missionary activities by business dealings, sometimes including the slave trade. Opposite this reality was the Portuguese value system which continued to look down with contempt and a sense of guilt upon such "impure" activities. The Portuguese version of the cult of purity—of blood, class, and occupation—may perhaps be partly traced to this contradiction between life and value, reality and an abstract ideal.

Against this background the need arose for aliens, a kind of inner foreigners on whom to project the despised new attributes that one was shocked and reluctant to recognize in oneself. Aliens by race, the New Christians were aliens also by occupation, incarnating everything foreign to what the Portuguese elite still wanted to see as its true image. In this way the New Christians helped the Old Christian elite to perform an act of imaginary purification based on self-deception. They satisfied a psychological need no less than an economic one, and by way of the latter. It was *they*, not *we* who were the *homens de negócios*—a term that stuck specifically to the New Christian group. In that, the New Christians helped Portugal both become a trading power and conceal the fact from herself.

From the start, Portuguese commerce involved many foreigners—Italian, German, and Flemish merchant-bankers. But starting in the second half of the sixteenth century, these were surpassed by Portugal's *own* foreigners, the New Christians.

Portugal had a religious interest in assimilating the New Christians. Three decades (so far) of religious laxity had encouraged them to engage in Judaizing, religious doubt, and other heresies. This had to be stopped. But here again irony prevailed. When the Inquisition was finally set in motion, its pressure emphasized the New Christians' alienness and enhanced their solidarity. Thus persecution, although it broke in some the will to Judaize, fortified it in others. It is hard to say whether the Inquisition produced more Jews than it suppressed, but it certainly was effective in both ways.

The pressures to establish the Inquisition were fueled by the king's financial troubles. Various dealings caused the king's expenses to rocket even higher than his trading revenues. An Inquisition, the king estimated, would appease not only God, the populace, the clerics, and his wife Catalina, but also his treasurer; confiscations would serve as an indirect mechanism of taxation—admittedly harsh, but certainly also pious and just. (This was not the pope's view, who specifically prohibited the king from using the Inquisition as a pump for money.)

It took sixteen years of exceptional diplomatic battle to establish the Inquisition in Portugal, and another decade to consolidate its work.[1] An earthquake in Lisbon in 1531 signaled the opening shot. The populace blamed the New Christians for having invoked the wrath of God, and several theologians and intellectuals seriously debated this thesis. João III saw here a proper moment for asking the pope for permission to start his own national Inquisition in Portugal. When, after some hesitation, Pope Clement VII appointed an inquisitor, he only started a long series of conflicting bulls in which, in a back-and-forth movement, Clement and his two successors suspended, revised, renewed, and annulled their own actions. Even on his deathbed, Clement renewed a Bull of Pardon to the New Christians, which he had already once issued and once suspended.

The prime mover of these vacillations was the power and money of the New Christians. As soon as the first secret dealings between the king and the pope were leaked, the New Christians organized to fight for their life and future. Before long they had their own "ambassador" in the Vatican, a certain Duarte de Paz, who stayed ten years in Rome and became influential in the Roman curia, opposing a major European monarch who was none other than the monarch of those whom he served. Paz's many resources and few inhibitions had made him particularly fit to deal with the Renaissance papal court, renowned for its corruption and intrigue. With shrewdness, vigor, and heaps of New Christian gold, Paz paved his way into the chambers of leading cardinals and became a formidable opponent to the official Portuguese ambassador in Rome. The latter, exasperated, wrote back to João III how "truly repulsive" it was to watch the "gentlemen of the curia" treat Paz as their equal. But, the ambassador adds bitterly, these princes of the Church are but "common merchant[s]" who trade their conscience for their worldly interests.

Renaissance Rome was not only corrupt. It was also the site of new humanist ideas, with jurists and theologians who despised the spirit of the Spanish Inquisition; and Paz knew how to gain advantage from them, too. He used feeling, argument, and gold wherever each was appropriate, and frequently together.

Among the prelates bought off by the New Christians were two successive Papal nuncios in Lisbon. The post was crucial as it represented the Holy See's authority in Portugal.

The New Christians' official claim was that they were faithful Christians and the king of Portugal was only after their money. But to sound more credible they took another line, backed up with other means of persuasion. How can you expect some New Christians not to have deviated when they or their fathers were forced to convert against their will? What their situation called for was Christian clemency, not inquisitorial vengeance.

The Christian clemency they obtained had the form of a special Bull of Pardon, which granted the Marranos amnesty for all previous offenses against the faith, thus taking the wind out of any inquisitorial tribunal. The Bull of Pardon now became the pivot of the battle, suspended and renewed as the pendulum swung.

On one occasion, Clement VII went as far as to declare the original conversion of the Jews void since it had been done by force. This had a sensational implication: the new Christians were not subject to canon law (and could still live as Jews). But this radical move went too far and could have no issue.

If humanist ideas and Renaissance corruption worked in the New Christians' favor, the Counter-Reformation finally turned the tide against them. In 1536 Emperor Charles V intervened on behalf of João III, his brother-in-law. Charles was the most powerful monarch on earth. He was also the defender of Catholicism against the Lutheran onslaught. The imperial troops were stationed in Italy and Charles's generals had once sacked Rome itself. How could Rome refuse the emperor's request when all he asked was that the faith be defended on yet another front?

On May 23, 1536, the Portuguese Inquisition was irrevocably—though at first only lamely—established. Besides Judaizing it also had to fight Lutheran and Moorish (Muslim) rites, without forgetting sorcery, bigamy, and sodomy. The published signs of heresy included fasting during Ramadan and possessing a Portuguese translation of the Bible (a Lutheran danger); but this did not conceal the major target. To appease the New Christians, the Inquisition was barred from confiscating property for ten years and had to follow normal civil procedures for three years.

An Inquisition without inquisitorial procedures is a toothless tiger, a *corrida* without a matador. Three years passed without much action. Then one morning in 1539, Lisbon awoke to see its main churches covered with ludicrous posters. "The Messiah has not yet come," they declared, "Jesus is not the Messiah."

Provocation? Authentic exclamation? A Marrano named Manuel da Costa confessed under torture to having committed the abomination and was duly burned. Events now started rolling. The king got his brother, Dom Enrique, appointed inquisitor general. He was a man with the passion needed for the job and shortly after, in 1540, the first "Act of Faith"—henceforth called, in Portuguese, *auto da fé*—was held in Lisbon. The New Christians shifted strategy: now they were fighting to curb the powers of an Inquisition they knew was there to stay. Their new envoy in Rome, Diogo Antonio (Durate de Paz had meanwhile left the scene, gravely wounded in an attempt on his life) won his greatest victory in 1544, when the pope froze the action of the Inquisition and suspended all pending verdicts. Furious, João III, expelled the papal nuncio, who then excommunicated the inquisitors.

Peace returned only three years later, after Portugal grudgingly accepted the pope's condition for resuming the work of the Holy Office in 1547. All former convicts were pardoned; procedures, for a while, were moderated; and the right to confiscate property was again postponed for a decade.

The Portuguese Hebrew Nation

Thus a full half-century (1497–1547) elapsed between the Jew's conversion by force and the operation of something resembling a regular Inquisition in Portugal.

This half-century of relative freedom from prosecution was crucial in shaping the features of the New Christian community—or "Nation," as it became known—both in religious and in socio-economic terms. Most Portuguese Marranos had been among the more tenacious Spanish Jews whom Portugal had converted by force, but practically allowed to Judaize for fifty years without an effective Inquisition. As a result, Portuguese Marranism emerged stronger, more deeply rooted and much better organized than in Spain, and far more prominent in the urban population. So much so that a "Portuguese" designation eventually stuck to the New Christian Nation as a whole, especially abroad.[2] And when Judaizing was dwindling in Spain, Marrano immigrants from Portugal (where the Inquisition by then had become harsher) revived it in the early seventeenth century.[3]

The battle over the Portuguese Inquisition testifies to the New Christians' influence, wealth, and, especially, group cooperation. They dealt with the pope as if they were a world power. When losing a battle, they shifted strategy and continued. They drew support and money also from Portuguese New Christians abroad. (Among their contributors were the famous matron, Doña Gracia Mendes-Nasi, and her nephew, Don Yossef Nasi.) That difficulties arose in fund-raising is normal. The wonder is that, nevertheless, in generation after generation well into the seventeenth century the New Christians succeeded in raising huge sums for their collective defense and bargaining, even when they had no official congregation and no formal authority over their members—not even a shred of what the Jews had possessed in the old *aljamas*.[4]

The extinct Jewish *aljama* now made place for a looser New Christian entity—their Nation. Henceforth, and for two and one-half centuries to come, the New Christians constituted a kind of separate caste, a social (rather than religious) denomination that their struggle against the Inquisition and their later collective bargaining with the royal authorities helped to mold. Loosely grouping Judaizers and non-Judaizers, it was called "the (Portuguese) Hebrew Nation," known abroad also as "the Portuguese Nation," and sometimes simply as "the Nation." The term *Nation* was not used then in our modern way. Derived from *nativity*, it indicated a shared origin or community of birth, which could be local, regional, or ethnic.

University students from the same birthplace were thus called "a nation," as were Venetians or Genoese overseas and New Christians in both Iberia and abroad. Although called "Hebrew," this nation did not necessarily signify the Jewish people. It constituted a separate loose entity whose members were both Judaizers (or Marranos returning to Judaism abroad) and willing Christians who remained Catholic even abroad, or who lost interest or faith in any religion. They were connected by three main links: a common "impure descent"; the stigma or suspicion of Judaizing that hostile others attached to them; and to a lesser but decisive degree, by shared economic concerns. They were united by a common dual interest: religious freedom and free trade. Yet they were divided in other ways. They differed over strategies of defense—how to ward off intolerance and persecution—and over the interpretation of their collective identity.

Ironically (to the dismay of the Old Christians), the term *Portuguese* was often understood outside Portugal as meaning "Jew"—the presumption being that a Portuguese abroad must be a trader, and a trader was usually a New

Christian (whom foreigners, too, kept calling "Jew"). Another implication was that Portugal swarmed with Marranos and had become "Judaized" as a nation.

Each subgroup within the broader Nation wanted the group to be marked by its own colors. Yet both Judaizers and non-Judaizers faced an impasse. The Judaizers were cut off from the Law of Moses to which they aspired. Although in their hearts they accepted the designation of Jew that their foes imposed on them, they were unable to realize it in their actual lives and to make it acceptable to the practicing Jews abroad, their aspired-to brethren. The non-Judaizers were no less in a catch. Fleeing from their origin and former Jewish identity toward assimilation and emancipation in Christian Portugal, they lost the former without quite gaining the latter. They were branded, stigmatized, readily persecuted, and sometimes burned for that with which they no longer identified in their hearts—although, as an objective situation, they had to acknowledge it as their lot. The split between their being and their consciousness was, therefore, no smaller than the one that characterized the actual *anussim* (forced converts).

Implied in this ambivalence is the view (which Marranos shared with Old Christians) that the Jewish bond is broader than indicated by observing the Jewish religious cult. Menasse ben Israel, the Amsterdam ex-Marrano author and rabbi, in describing a group of Jews found in China, significantly called them "Jews by nation and religion." The small word *and* is revealing. It implies that in the Marrano experience, the "Nation" was broader than religion and called for a separate category. Rabbi Menasse is not making a programmatic statement here but speaking offhand—which lends his wording particular significance.

The triple basis of the New Christian Nation consisted of their "impure" Hebrew descent, coupled with a Judaizing image (sometimes true, sometimes false, and never truly Jewish), and with an economic role that distinguished their elite as "men of business affairs." It was a remarkable fusion of ethnic, religious, and commercial features. Marrano merchants used their familial or communal ties with other Marranos on three continents as a special trading asset—indeed, as a relative economic advantage. And in their collective bargaining with the authorities, Marranos at the end of the sixteenth century offered the Crown large sums of money in return not only for amnesties and religious concessions to Judaizers, but also for trading monopolies and other economic privileges. At one time, the New Christians agreed to annul the Crown's debt to them and add 675,000 cruzados in cash for a package of rights that included a monopoly over the king's pepper from India, salt taxes, and playing cards. And shortly thereafter, they paid the king a higher sum for releasing several hundred prisoners of the Inquisition and getting the pope to pardon all the pending charges against

Judaizers.[5] It was a peculiar mixture of pepper and faith, salt and the Messiah, that characterized the New Christians' dealings as a semiorganized group.

Economic and Identitarian Passions: The New Christian Bourgeoisie

There is a view that the Inquisition was merely a tool in the hands of the traditional classes in Portugal to destroy the incipient bourgeoisie, which was largely New Christian.[6] Like many oversimplifications, this theory has immediate attractions, but it fails to capture the genuine identitarian passions behind the Inquisition. In addition, even when seen as a socioeconomic player, the New Christian bourgeoisie was no less needed than resented. As such, it was allowed to flourish while, at the same time, being harassed and exploited—and even as a precondition for this exploitation. New Christians, moreover, were resented partly *because they were needed* and partly as an independent object for resentment. The class struggle against them was not only material. We have seen that it also had a psychological significance, as the struggle of the Portuguese elite to maintain a desirable image of itself while also responding to the new economic realities. In both ways, the New Christian bourgeoisie was absolutely necessary. Portugal needed its "Jews" to do the work it considered dishonorable, and to take the blame and pay the price for what they were and what they did.

The Inquisition was used to levy this price—moral, personal, and pecuniary. But it was not meant, and could not be allowed, to destroy the class of its victims. On the contrary, with time it developed a healthy interest in their survival, and even their prosperity, on which—through confiscations—the Inquisition thrived.

Of course, there were special interest groups that wanted the New Christians destroyed. But this went counter to the generalized Portuguese interest which, as the New Christians themselves knew, assured them a backbone of security in the midst of turmoil and harassment.

It is, in any case, a fact that the Inquisition did not break the New Christian bourgeoisie or stop its socioeconomic rise. The pinnacle of Marrano wealth was reached well after the Holy Office had learned to speak Portuguese. This should not be surprising: the inquisitors were serving a national institution, subject to an absolute monarchy that represented the state's overall interest. That the monarchy itself became an economic player was not surprising in a state that was moving from medieval fragmentation toward protomodern unity and absolutism. It was a sign of the new times that the notion of national interest became meaningful at all, embodied as it was in the special interest of the Crown, which at once acquired a universal significance. So the Inquisition could not be permitted to destroy the New Christian bourgeoisie; its persecution of the New Christians was severe, but economically measured, plucking the fruit without destroying the tree.

The Inquisition's economic role was secondary and ancillary. To reduce its whole import to the socioeconomic uses that were made of it is like understanding the love story of Romeo and Juliet in terms of the peace it might have brought Verona. Besides the new Christians, the Inquisition also persecuted Moriscos, Black Africans, Native Americans, and Asian Indians, none of whom belonged to the incipient Portuguese bourgeoisie. They were more likely to be found in hard labor plantations and slave camps, traded as commodities by that same bourgeoisie (including New Christians)—and by the Crown, the nobles, and the religious orders. This should remind us that identity passions, and the religious and racial prejudice they breed (and also the rarer drives toward benevolence and moral recognition), have their own mental specificity that should be admitted as such, without making it subordinate to mere economic interests.

Rigors of the Inquisition

When it finally worked in full steam, the Portuguese Inquisition became even harsher and more inhuman than the Spanish. Gathering wealth and power, it grew to become a state within a state. It reigned supreme over all other courts, civil and ecclesiastical, and answered to the king alone. And since Portugal was much smaller than Spain, its Inquisition was also more efficient, capable of exercising tighter control over the country.

The Inquisition operated from three permanent centers—in Lisbon, Evora, and Coimbra. (A fourth was later added in Goa, India—to prosecute, and often burn not only Judaizers, but Hindus and other Asians who relapsed to their pagan ways after converting to Christianity.)[7] The paper trail that this politico-religious secret police left behind could form a small mountain. Though many records were destroyed (in 1820, when the institution was abolished), there still remain 36,000 files, which scholars from Alexander Herculano to Israel Révah, to Anita Novinsky, Elias Lipiner, Nathan Wachtel, and many others have been laboring to study and publish. These records contain a story of horrors, intimidation, torture, humiliation, and distorted evidence and procedures.

In a conservative estimate, the Portuguese historian Oliveira Marques (who devotes only a few dry pages to the Inquisition in his two-volume *History of Portugal*), suggests that a minimum of 20,000 persons were condemned in the first 140 years of the tribunal's effective operation (1543–1684), and at least

1,400 were sent to the flames. The actual numbers may run higher since many records perished and those in existence have been studied only in part. Moreover, the higher figures must be complemented by thousands who languished in their cells and died before trial, or went mad, or were finally released for lack of proof. But even so, the terrible social and moral price that the Portuguese Inquisition exacted is not commensurate with its numbers.

Though its main effort targeted New Christians, the victims of the Inquisition also included over time various other outsiders—homosexuals, witches (often meaning nonconformist women), bigamists, and Portuguese Protestants. Its overall impact is summarized by Boxer:

> As an engine of persecution, the Portuguese Inquisition was regarded as being more efficient and more cruel than the notorious Spanish Inquisition. . . . People brought before these tribunals were never told the names of their accusers, nor given adequate information about the charges secretly laid against them. Blandishments, threats, and torture were freely used in order to extort confessions of their real or alleged guilt, and above all, to induce them to incriminate others, beginning with their own families. . . .
>
> The families of those arrested on suspicion were mostly turned out into the street forthwith and left to fend for themselves. The methods adopted by the Inquisition for collecting evidence placed a premium on the activities of informers, talebearers, and slanderers. Private grudges could be paid off merely by denouncing a man for changing his shirt, or a woman her shift, on a Saturday. Consequently mutual mistrust and suspicion permeated much of Portuguese society for over two centuries. Last but not least, the spectacle of the "New" Christians being slowly roasted to death in the autos-da-fé gave most onlookers much the same sadistic satisfaction as did the public executions . . . in contemporary England.[8]

Ironically, the harsher Portuguese Inquisition drove some Marranos to seek refuge in Spain, the land of its parent Inquisition. This Marrano emigration to Spain had also a commercial reason: to gain access to Spain's trading networks and sources of silver in Mexico and Peru. The emigration grew stronger and was facilitated after 1580, when Portugal was annexed by king Philip II of Spain.

Disaster and Sebastian Messianism

Philip exploited a particularly low moment in Portugal's history. In August 1587 the whole Portuguese army was wiped out and young King Sebastian was killed and his body mutilated in the battle of *Ksar el Kibir* (Morocco). The debacle was due to an ill prepared and pathetically mismanaged campaign, which the rash and visionary young king insisted on commanding in person. Sebastian had been haunted since childhood by the desire to conquer Morocco; this was a divine mission to him, a kind of Christian *Jihad*, extending the Reconquest to the infidel's homeland. Sebastian invested a great fortune and all his political authority in this vision. He crossed the Mediterranean accompanied by the flower of the Portuguese nobility and many aspiring youths (among them Conversos),[9] and led them in a disastrous expedition, that looked more like an erratic *happening* than a professional military operation. Of his army of seventeen thousand, only a few hundred escaped. The rest were slain by the Muslims or taken prisoner. The king's dead body was found the next day, disfigured almost beyond recognition.

Was this Sebastian, people wondered? No, the rumor started to roll: the king is alive! Sebastian must be hiding somewhere in the desert, or living as a prisoner under cover, and would return! The rumor fired the grieving people's imagination and soon became a popular legend. Sebastian's follies were forgiven, and the pathetic, enthusiastic, tragedy-stricken youth emerged as a mythological national hero, eventually penetrating the popular psyche, even among the elite.

One who did not share this myth was Philip II of Spain. Political as ever, Philip realized the opportunity and claimed the Portuguese crown for himself. Philip based his claim on being, through his mother, a descendent of King Manuel I, whose dream of a unified Iberia he now reinvoked. There were more legitimate claimants than Philip, but none possessed his ultimate reason—the strongest army in Europe.

In 1580, Portugal became part of the Spanish crown and remained so for sixty years.

During this period of "captivity," the Portuguese sense of separate identity (later called "nationalism") rose to high levels. The nobles resented the Spanish rule and many townsmen felt constrained and humiliated by it. A fervent belief in Sebastian's mystical return was spreading in high and low circles. Sebastian became a symbol, a dream, a messianic hope, in which religion, nation, and imperial vision were mingled. Soon a prophet was found to foster the myth. A cobbler-poet called Bandara had written mystical verses (*trovas*) that announced the arrival of a savior-king on a white horse who would redeem not only Portugal, but the whole world, and this was now interpreted as referring to Sebastian's return.[10] A few impostors claiming to be Sebastian appeared, but were duly exposed. As in Judaism, Portuguese messianism was based on a promise for the future, not on the Savior's actual arrival. Even when Portugal was liberated in 1640 not all Sebastians (as believers were called) hailed the new king, João IV, as the fulfillment of their hopes. Many continued to crave a higher, loftier, more distant redemption, for which Sebastian henceforth stood.

There can be no doubt that Marrano mentalities contributed to this myth. New Christian Marrano messianism combined the age-old Jewish craving for Zion with the Marrano yearning for liberation from Christian captivity. Both these threads were later turned into Christianity itself and, past it, infused into specific forms of Portuguese patriotism, nationalism, and empire building that lasted for centuries. (Even in the twentieth century they still affected Portuguese intellectuals, right-wing political visions, and writers such as the poet Fernando Pessoa.)[11]

In late eighteenth century a foreign diplomat serving in Lisbon was quoted as saying: "What can you expect of a nation one half of which looks out for the Messiah, and another half for Dom Sebastian who has been dead for nearly two centuries?" This is witty but not quite exact. The two groups, the New Christians and the Sebastians, were not separate parts of the Portuguese nation, but largely overlapped. Sebastianism, which is indeed special to Portugal, was partly shaped by Marrano messianic impulses, and bore their mark even when it no longer aimed at Jewish or Judaizing objectives. Sebastianism allowed Marranos to pour a Jewish mentality and pattern of yearning into the inner Portuguese fold. It illustrates a phenomenon we have been studying all along—the transfer of a pattern from one sociocultural domain to another, in which it assumes different contents but maintains it distinctive character.

In this view, there is a strange kinship of legacy between the two adventurers, King Sebastian and David Reubeni. An offshoot of the same messianic fervor that had fired Judaizers in Reubeni's days had shifted direction and now inspired the larger Portuguese scene. Its objective was no longer Jewish, but Christian— and at times neither Jewish nor Christian, but national, patriotic, and imperial.

Of course Sebastianism had other local sources as well. Yet one wonders what it would have been without the Marrano input. Even Bandara, its early prophet, may not have been an Old Christian. His cryptic prophecies used secret numerical combinations, as in Jewish Kabbalah, and relied on the book of Daniel, a Marrano favorite. His Messiah was a king, as in Judaism (but not in Christianity), and while redeeming Portugal he would also recall the Ten Lost Tribes of Israel, at which time all Jews would convert to Christianity. This may suggest a New Christian author, not a Judaizer, but one who poured his Jewish-messianic drives into a new politico-religious vision of Christian Portugal.[12]

Pure and Contaminated Portuguese Blood

There is a belief that Portugal, unlike other European powers, has not been afflicted by racial prejudices and policies. Yet facts are quite different.[13]

For several centuries Portugal had been haunted by the specter of "contaminated races," which threatened to impair its purity and honor. The term *raças infectas* recurs in official Portuguese documents until the late eighteenth century, and the concept of "purity of blood" (*limpeza* or *pureza de sangue*) was central in Portuguese experience at home and abroad. In their naval explorations the Portuguese encountered a vast world of non-European races, strange in appearance, heathen in religion, and no doubt, they believed, humanly inferior even when baptized. And in their own homeland the Portuguese confronted another "contaminated race," the huge wave of New Christians of Hebrew blood, far greater in proportion than Spain ever knew.

As in Spain, racial legislation served the Portuguese to continue discrimination against the ex-Jews even after religious barriers were lifted in principle. It was the Iberian Old Christians who first taught the Jews that what they were was not determined by religion alone. (The second lesson came after the modern Jewish emancipation and in recent existential anti-Semitism.)

Anti–New Christian discrimination had been practiced since the first days of the conversion, even when it still contradicted Manuel's policies. In a kind of affirmative action policy, Manuel had to force municipal councils to assign the ex-Jews a special quota of seats. The struggle over the Inquisition put new life into the racial practices; but they became a universal policy only after the annexation of Portugal by Philip II of Spain, the king who had made the Spanish *limpieza* a royal institution.

Back to Spain: Purity of Blood, Act II

Philip II affected the lives of Portuguese Marranos in other ways too. It was under him that the statutes of purity of blood became official in Spain before being extended throughout Iberia and its colonies.

At this point we may turn back, for a while, to Spain. The center of events is again Toledo, centering around Juan Silíceo, a high prelate risen from the rural poor.[14] Charles V had appointed him Archbishop of Toledo—the highest religious post in Spain—in recognition of his skills, and in order to create a healthy division between the great of the land. (He also made Silíceo a tutor to Prince Philip, his heir.) The other priests and canons of Toledo, who were mostly of noble origin, resented this appointment. But Silíceo had an advantage: like all simple commoners, his blood was "pure." This could not be claimed by his main rival, a respectable dean of the chapter named Pedro del Castillo, who had descended from kings on one side of his family and from converted Jews on the other. From both sides of his family, Castillo embodied everything the new archbishop loathed—and symbolized the situation of other Converso members of the upper clergy, who were also Conversos.

Haunted by his plebeian origin, Silíceo turned it into a weapon and a principle. His opportunity came when a Dr. Juan Martínez presented him with letters from the pope appointing Martínez as canon in Toledo. Silíceo discovered that Martínez's father had been a Converso charged with Judaizing who had escaped abroad, and probably returned there to open Judaism. Should such a man's son be canon in Toledo, the most important Christian center after Rome? In a letter to the pope, Silíceo warned against turning Spain's prime church into a synagogue and added: No horse trader would accept a horse without checking his blood and race—why should the Archbishop of Toledo act otherwise?

When the pope annulled Martínez's appointment, Silíceo rode on his success and passed a decision in the Toledo chapter stating that because of Toledo's pre-eminence in Christendom, all candidates to office must prove their purity of blood. Excepted were only those already holding office, a strategy used to split the opposition.

The protest that broke out against Silíceo was as stormy as it was inefficient. His rival, Castillo, argued contemptuously that since Toledo was so important, its authority should be protected by barring priests of low origin, or who hold lesser degrees (such as Silíceo). If these haughty words remind us of Alonso de Cartagena, it is because they express the same ideology of patrician Conversos. Yet Silíceo too could rely on Don Alonso. Once you allow discrimination based on origin, you are already using the concept of blood. Silíceo claimed that all Christians were equal in view of their salvation in Jesus, but not in view of offices and honors.

The ratiocinations over this question continued for many years after the laws of *limpieza de sangre* came into broad use. Theologically they were scandalous, for they violated basic Christian principles. If only it could be argued that Conversos had no soul—as was said of American Indians! But that was unfortunately impossible. Even Jews had souls, let alone Conversos, whose baptism brought their souls into communion through Jesus with all other Christians. Bad conscience and bad faith thus dominated this debate—and yet the racial statutes gained hold in practical life. In 1555 the new pope, Paul IV, gave his official consent to the un-Christian regulations, and a year later they were ratified by the new Spanish king, Philip II (who had formerly resisted Silíceo's pressure, as did many Spaniards in high office). Ignatius Loyola, the founder of the Jesuit order, called the king's decision a "whim," and proud members of the military orders refused to testify in blood purity inquests; but Philip, now adamant, used his royal powers to force them to cooperate. In thus obliging his former tutor Silíceo, Philip consoled himself that "all heresies in Germany, France, and Spain were spread by descendents of Jews."[15]

The statutes universalized and gave impetus to a practice that had already been widely in effect. Henceforth, candidates to public offices and honors, either religious or civil, were subject to scrutiny as to their origin and blood. Many aspirants lived in fear that an obscure Jewish ancestor would be unearthed in their past and disgrace them or ruin their hopes for a career. (One of many who were required to produce a certificate of pure blood was young Miguel de Cervantes, the future author of *Don Quijote*; and like others, his certificate was probably fraudulent.) There were several mathematical categories of impurity—from full New Christian to one-half, one-quarter, one-eighth, and one-sixteenth measure of impure blood in a person's veins; and we hear that as late as 1860, the test of pure blood was still demanded in order to enter the Spanish military school.[16]

Portugal Again

Following its annexation, and especially after 1588, this racist arithmetic became the law in Portugal as well. Those who had Hebrew blood in the third, and sometimes even in the seventh degree, were usually excluded from church and civil posts carrying honor. Of course, policies varied in time and place and exceptions existed all the time; but on the whole, the upper clergy, the royal administration, the municipal government, the three prestigious military orders, and later, to a lesser degree, also university teaching, were hard to enter and almost closed to New Christians. The rules left to New Christians mainly commerce, manufacturing, and finance—and thus encouraged, rather than suppressed, the rise of a New Christian bourgeoisie. Colored and other non-European races suffered even more than the ex-Jews (and sometimes at their hands). African Blacks were sold as slaves even when baptized; in their case, too, holy water could not purify their blood.

It was only in the 1770s that Count Pombal, then prime minister, abolished the Inquisition and annulled the blood purity policies. "His Majesty does not distinguish between his vassals by their color, but by their merit," declared Pombal, reiterating classic New Christian ideology. There is a story that when the Inquisition proposed to force all New Christians to wear white hats, Pombal appeared in the royal court the following day with three white hats: one for himself, one for the inquisitor general, and one for His Majesty himself. (A similar story could have been told, but wasn't, even in the times of Torquemada and Ferdinand the Catholic; yet times had changed.)

Abolished together, the Inquisition and the blood purity laws expressed a similar spirit and complemented each other in practice. But there were great differences between them in theory.

Theoretically, the Inquisition acted only against sinning Christians. The *limpeza*, on the other hand, discriminated against brothers in Jesus, whether they were sinful or faithful, solely for belonging to the group of contaminated races. This was in flagrant violation of fundamental principles of Christianity; but life and passion were stronger than theory, and eventually prevailed.

Another difference in theory was that the official intent of the Inquisition was to assimilate the New Christians. It had set out to forge one faith and a single nation. That it ended up enhancing the alien feature of the New Christians and producing almost as many Judaizers as it abolished was an ironic result, not included in the original intention. The *limpeza*, on the contrary, was anti-integrationist and discriminatory *from the start* and in its very ideology. Its whole raison d'être was based upon rejection—that is, upon the tacit assumption that the assimilatory work of the Inquisition was either insincere or doomed to fail—and that, religious fraternity notwithstanding, Portugal's impure races must be kept apart. Thus, the blood purity laws, even more than the Inquisition, contributed to splitting Portugal into two distinct societies—almost, indeed, into different nations.

Here again we look into a deep structure of Jewish history, using as our prism not full-fledged Jews, but Marranos. Although their religious definition as Jews had been washed off by baptism, they were not rid of objective Jewish attributes and designation, now attached to blood and descent. Their Jewishness took on an *existential* dimension. Or rather, the existential dimension was there all along, but now, severed and released from the religious context, it surfaced into clarity.

This seems to indicate that existence and religion are separate moments in Jewish history. During the Jewish middle ages—roughly between the conclusion of the Talmud (circa fifth century) and the French revolution—the Jews have been marked by an almost complete overlap—some call it symbiosis—between the Jewish people and their rabbinical religion. But in certain marginal cases—the Karaites, the Marranos, the presecularists—the overlap shifted and a fissure occurred between those two components of the Jewish identity, indicating that the symbiosis was actually a historical linkage of two separate elements that are not necessarily and essentially the same.

Of course, this could be visible only in situations of crisis and challenge, so it became manifest, not in ordinary Jews, but in a marginal group such as the Marranos, in whom the socioethnic component of their identity proved more stable than the religious, which was ambiguous (and wavering) in more than one way.

There was another opposition between the Inquisition and the rules of *limpeza*. The *limpeza* forced the Jewish designation upon the Marranos, while the Inquisition denied their right to adopt it. Thus, even if Marranos wished to accept the denomination of Jewish attached to them through *limpeza*, they were not permitted to do so. The Inquisition denied a person the right to be what the purity of blood rules said he could not escape. This left the Marrano suspended in the air. No identity could be supported by him as integral and coherent. In what concerned him, the opposition between *limpeza* and the Inquisition had complementary effects. It helped produce the typical Marrano situation as an inner exile, a person of unstable identity and, partly in a metaphorical sense, a new wandering Jew.[17]

PART FIVE

New Christian Religions and Spanish Culture

This part's title uses the plural ("New Christian Religions") for two reasons. The religious forms that distinguished the Judeo-Conversos branched off into a Judaizing variety and a Catholic variety; and each of these varieties diverged in some degree from its normative cultural model. In other words, both were unorthodox. The Judaizing Marrano religion diverged from rabbinical Judaism in many of its practices and, especially, in being confined to the private individual sphere and the inner heart, in contrast to rabbinical Judaism that stresses community, commandments, and cult. And the Christian variety dissented from Catholic orthodoxy by shaping itself as a "religion of the interior," and discovering new religious territories inside the believer's subjectivity.

In chapter 14 our attention will shift from the Jewish dimension of the Conversos to the role they played within the Hispano-Christian culture of the Golden Age. But before turning there, we should take a closer look at the religion of the Judaizing Marranos.

13

A Judaizing Marrano Religion

For forty years Portuguese ex-Jews lived free of an Inquisition, and another decade had passed before the Inquisition became effectively operational. We have seen how this half-century had shaped their Nation. Economically, it allowed them to penetrate into the Portuguese high commerce and finance and to establish the Marrano bourgeoisie, which, despite the Inquisition, had flourished until the eighteenth century and spread globally around the world. And in a religious sense, those five decades created a Portuguese variety of the mixed "Marrano religion" already known from Spain, a religion that was Judaic in aspiration but Christian in many fundamental components. The Portuguese brand of Marranism was much more widespread and persistent than the Spanish, since Portuguese Marranos had been originally the more tenacious Jews who preferred to leave Spain rather than convert, and because of the long period after the forced conversion in Portugal in which they lived free of an Inquisition.

Portuguese Marranism spilled back into Spain through Portugal's sixty-year annexation to the Spanish crown, from 1580 to 1640. As Portuguese Marranos reemigrated to Spain they helped revive the flame there, as well. What, then, was the profile of the Judaizing Marrano religion in Iberia?

Generalizations are impossible. Given the need for secrecy and the absence of books by which to transmit a common tradition, many improvised varieties of Marranism prevailed throughout the centuries. Given this diversity, every picture of Marrano practices and beliefs must be considered partial and, in many cases, local. Nevertheless, some prayers have persisted for centuries, such as those of Belmonte, which clearly originated (at least in part) in the sixteenth century. And there are several typological patterns that recur in different times and places due to the Judaizers' distinctive situation and shared basic phenomenology (even where no shared memory was maintained or transmitted).

Actually there seem to have been *several* Marrano religions (in the plural), distinguished by local conditions and religious orientation. All were dualistic, shaped as a mixture of Jewish and Christian elements in different measures and orientations; and the crucial question—the dividing line—was: which of the two religions commanded the person's will and intent? Marranos oriented toward the Law of Moses were further divided between those who kept a more or less faithful set of Jewish rites and prayers, however fragmented and impoverished, and those whose customs were mostly peculiar to the Marranos (as in Belmonte) and contained hardly any known Jewish precedent. Then, as in the monastery of Guadalupe, there was a brand of Marrano religion oriented toward Christianity. Those converts wished to find their salvation in the Cross but did so in heterodox ways, spiritual and internalized, that bore the marks of their Marrano past. Taking themselves to be truly New Christians, they promoted a new brand of interiorized Christianity that they valued as deeper and more authentically religious.

The present chapter centers on Jewish-oriented Marrano religion (the religion of the Judaizers). It draws on studies that employ materials from rabbinical responsa (written rulings on submitted questions) and the records of the Inquisition, which contain verbatim accounts of Jewish-Marrano prayers, chants, beliefs, rites, and even recipes for the Sabbath meals.[1] And then there is the surprising compilation of Marrano prayers and customs discovered in the twentieth century in northern Portugal (see the epilogue).[2]

A Judaizing-Marrano Theology?

There was, first of all, a basic theology of Judaizing Marranos, meager but persistent. At the heart of this theology stood the belief that salvation lies only in the Law of Moses, and that the Messiah, who is not Jesus, is yet to come. These simple, fundamental articles of faith are echoed persistently in the records. They have been repeated hundreds of times in the minutes of inquisitorial proceedings, in torture rooms, in confessions of faith among intimate friends, in the secret initiation of sons and daughters, and on the stakes of the *auto de fe*. Salvation was in the Law of Moses, and Jesus is not the Messiah: this is the whole doctrine in a nutshell, the hard core of Marrano theology as encountered everywhere. It is not a Jewish way of speaking, yet its content is Jewish. Concern with the problem of salvation (even the word itself) is somewhat strange to the Jewish tradition; and certainly alien to Judaism is the emphasis on salvation as the foremost religious issue. The noted historian I. S. Révah was so discomfited by the insistent recurrence of this un-Jewish sounding formula that he concluded that the "persecuted had accepted it from the inquisitors." Yet we must not explain away this crucial dissonance, which is essential to Marrano phenomenology and constitutes an integral part of the special religious consciousness of the Judaizers, a consciousness whose Jewish core was planted into a generally Christianized body of concepts and symbols.[3]

Other important items in the Marrano theology revolved around the unitary and indivisible nature of God. God was one—this was the Jewish message to the world; so he could not be three. The Incarnation and the Host were objects of mockery and disbelief. ("I saw God, but he did not see me," said one Converso of the holy bread.)[4] Along with the Trinity, both ends of Christ's life were denied—his virgin birth and his redeeming death. Catholicism was considered idolatrous. This was due to the deification of a human being—a created thing—and to the Catholic dependence on images. Images were anathema to Judaism, at least in theory; but the Marranos had a further reason to rebuff images—namely, appearances—since their whole existence deprecated outer appearances while cherishing a hidden religious truth. To them, not only was God invisible, but so was their own religious heart. What were they always rejecting in their heart if not the Catholic appearances they were forced to put on, the images of images? And what did their special experience teach them, if not to value the invisible essence of things and disavow their appearance?[5]

And yet, having been raised in a Catholic culture saturated with vivid images, the Marrano mind was molded by that which they shunned in principle; as if a screen of original sin was built into their consciousness and ran parallel to the original sin of conversion, which it symbolized.

Antonio Homem, a Judaizing leader preaching in secret, reduced the essence of his religion to rejecting images and keeping the Sabbath. This illustrates another feature of the Marrano religion—its relative poverty of content, a poverty for which many Judaizers compensated by intensity and a sense of sacrifice: indeed, through a built-in danger that atoned for a built-in sin.

Alongside its typical duality, Judaizing Marranism became a religion of bare essentials:

- Seeking salvation in the Law of Moses rather than the Church;
- Hoping for a twofold Messiah, to redeem them from their "Egypt" (meaning Iberia, "the land of idolatry") and to redeem the Jews from Exile in general;
- Shunning images;
- Praying to the true, invisible, unitary God, *Adonay* (or *Dio*, rather than *Dios*, which sounded plural to them);
- De-Christianizing the Old Testament and reappropriating it as their own;
- Trying to keep some fragmentary customs of the Sabbath, together with a few other Judaic rites, unwittingly—and almost inevitably—distorted and mixed with Catholic concepts.

This is a rather scanty doctrine. But what this mutilated closet religion lacked in diversity, it compensated by intensity, secrecy, and the sense of belonging to a select, semimystical fraternity that held the true key to salvation. Typically, Judaizing Marranos knew themselves to belong to this elect group without fully knowing what it was. They were ignorant of most of the detail of the Law of Moses and, for obvious reasons, could not fully observe even what they did know.

In a curious but not surprising psychological shift, what came to matter in their religion was, above all, belief itself, the bare knowledge that they possessed an intimate metaphysical secret that distinguished them from others as an elect group. Practice fell into the secondary level of religious life, while secret knowledge became the crux of their religious consciousness. Moreover, this esoteric knowledge was no less important than the meager set of rites they did practice. And that was already a shift away from Judaism, which stresses practice more than pure belief.

Initiation

When was a Marrano boy initiated into the family secret? Here was the crucial dilemma: should the parents risk their child's salvation by waiting too long, or risk the family's security by revealing the secret too early? Decisions varied, but a preferred target was the age thirteen, the age of Bar Mitzvah, when Jewish boys, too, are initiated to religious maturity. A Marrano in Mexico told the Inquisition: "When he was thirteen years old, Doña María de Rivera, his mother, called him, and when alone in the house . . . told him how the law of our Lord Jesus Christ, which he followed, was not good, and that [he should follow] the Law of Moses . . . because it is the true, the good, and the necessary Law for his salvation."

The profound moment when a person discovers she is not who she thought she was, or who she ought to be, projects new light on a person's past and future and can invoke a sense of guilt and a call for forgiveness. In lighting her first Friday candles, a young Marrano girl, recently initiated into Judaizing, says: "O Lord, [until now] I have not known how to keep your Holy Law [the Torah]; but now that I know, please give me strength and consolation, so I can keep your Holy Law . . . and grant me that which I do not know how to ask for: salvation for my soul, and Grace."

Blessed naiveté: at the moment of joining the secret fraternity—and true religion—the girl asks God to forgive her former ignorance and promises to observe the "Holy Law" of Moses, by which she hopes to attain the Christian high prize—Grace and her soul's Salvation.

Notice that these dualities are not simple mixtures. They manifest a recurring structure in which a Catholic conceptual framework is charged with a

Judaizing content and intent. The resulting conflict between form and content expresses a rebellion against one's real conceptual foundation and an attempt to reverse its meaning; yet inescapably, the attempt also reaffirms the Catholic meaning of the system by using it as the defining religious framework. Thus the duality is not an accidental aggregate of elements, but manifests the deep structure of the phenomenon.

Ignorance and Loneliness

Keeping the girl's promise was very difficult. Most Marranos did not know what was required by the true religion they had entered, and their ignorance could last for a lifetime. One Marrano prayer from Braganca that was used in funerals addresses the deceased in words that capture the Marrano lot in strange simplicity:

> You shall come to the Valley of Yehoshafat [near Jerusalem], and there you will find a lion [the Devil, as other versions of this prayer say]. If he asks you for a sign, give him money [the reciter passes a coin over the deceased body]; if what he wants is meat, give him bread [he passes a piece of bread over the dead body, perhaps invoking the Catholic equation of bread and flesh]; and if he asks, what is your faith? Tell him it is the faith of Moses, and that he should let you pass free and unhindered to the place to which God summons you.
>
> And if he asks, who has given you the [word unclear], tell him you were a Hebrew living in this world, and *if you did not do more of what is good [in God's eyes], it is only because you did not know what more to do.*[6]

This strange text with its touching finale reflects the loneliness of the Judaizing Marrano who cannot fulfill his own religion, of which he knows only fragments. So having lived as secret Hebrew in a hostile world, he dies without having satisfied either the Christian God or the Jewish; and his most sincere apology, by which he hopes to chase away the devil, is that he had tried his best to be a Jew but couldn't because he "did not know what more to do."

The Sabbath

Receiving the Sabbath was an intimate in-house occasion for Judaizing Marranos. On Friday night the men put on clean white shirts to greet the holy day in purity, and the mother lit "the Lord's Candles," which were later hidden in a cupboard or a cellar. More dangerous—because it involved public exposure— was abstaining from work on Saturday, so Marranos used various devices to feign work, or to work sporadically. Some men went to the countryside to be less observed. Some women, on the contrary, sat conspicuously at the window pretending to work the loom, which they actually did when a stranger went by, then let off after he passed. But such tricks were limited, and not working at all was impossible. So Judaizers had to compromise and work part of the time, a sin that some sought to expiate by refraining from eating meat on Saturdays. This was a rather Catholic reaction: observant Catholics abstain from meat once a week (on Fridays), and Catholic culture, through Confession, provides atonement for current religious sins. The habit became so entrenched that, centuries later, the Belmonte Marranos were surprised to learn that Jews did eat meat on the Sabbath.

Meat

Pork was a common fare in Iberia, as were rabbit, hare, and shellfish, all forbidden to Jews. Even beef and poultry are nonkosher unless slaughtered according to Jewish rites. The Judaizing Marranos' answer was again ritualized compromise: their religion was made of select islands of purity within a sea of transgression. On well-specified occasions (including before and after fasts) they abstained from meat altogether; at other times they ate everything and made sure they were observed. Such compromises produced Converso-specific dietary rituals, not universal as in Judaism, but varying locally and attached to definite occasions.

Major Holidays: Yom Kippur

Yom Kippur was the most revered day of the year. Four centuries of Marranos have known it under such names as *día puro* (the Pure Day, or Day of Purification) *ayuno mayor* (Great Fast) or simply *Quipur* (distorted into *equipur*, *antepur*, and *cinquepur*).[7] Efforts were made to celebrate this day in great solemnity. Judaizing Marranos wore light clothes, fasted, and recited all the prayers they knew. As in rabbinical Judaism, the Marrano holiday was devoted to the theme of pardon, but with a special Marrano edge. The day of purity was a moment of truth. As layers of pretense and beguiling were shed, the Marrano's soul stood as if naked before itself and its maker; and, conscious of the sin inherent in its dual mode of existence, begged *Adonay* to extirpate it—all while knowing that the sin must go on, and would go on. Thus, to the more discerning Marranos, a certain beguiling of self and God was built into their very moment of purification, making it, too, a moment of duality.

Seen from a different angle, *ayuno mayor* came to express a Marrano variation of the Christian theme of original sin. The Judaizing Marranos lived in a state of "fallenness" caused by their fathers' betrayal of Judaism. The brunt of this guilt passed to the children, who failed to emigrate from the peninsula when they could, and whose form of life—the Marranesque mode of existence—was marred by ongoing idolatry, duplicity, and failure to be Jews even when Judaizing. Such a sense of fallenness and guilt, which adheres to one's very existence (the rudiments of the consciousness of original sin) is a Catholic sensibility basically; but it fitted the Judaizing Marranos' situation and penetrated into their self-feeling, where it was buried under the humdrum of daily life, but emerged to the surface on special occasions, in particular on Yom Kippur, the greatest Jewish moment of the year.

The Jewish Kippur starts with the solemn prayer *kol Nidrei*, an awesome ceremony in which the congregation annuls all the vows and proscriptions previously made against sinners. In a Marrano version of that rite, the Judaizer disavows in advance "all the deeds I shall do in this imprisonment," and the sins committed because of "the cunning of my sense of self-preservation." This annuls, specifically, the *Catholic* vows and masks that the Judaizers must practice during the year in order to survive.

Another source of consolation was the memory that sin in Judaism is not ineradicable. Have not the greatest men and women of Jewish antiquity sinned and been pardoned? "Forgive us," one Marrano prayer entreats, "as thou hast forgiven King David who sinned with Bat-Sheba." (Her name is misspelled as *Bar*-Sheba, as in the Latin Bible, which the Marranos used). How could the sinning Marranos lose hope when King David, who was pardoned, begot the wise King Solomon from the same woman with whom he had sinned, and thereby established the dynasty from which the Messiah will issue? A Messiah born of sin was diametrically opposed to the Christian Messiah, born of virgin purity, but perfectly suited the Marrano psychology, situation, and hope.

Sometimes the fast began with the words: "This blood which I deprive of my body, I offer to you, so that my soul will be saved." This is unknown in Judaism, where human blood does not save—there is no Eucharist—and the highest religious goal is not to save one's soul, but to keep God's Covenant and commands.

The need for secrecy sometimes drove Marranos to sneak out of town and spend the fast out of sight:

> At the time of the grapes and figs, all the *confesos* of Barbastro went out to the orchards two by two, four by four, six by six ... they strolled up and down the orchards and did not work all day.... You could see in their faces they were nearly fainting, or dead. They did not eat all day long. They were formally dressed, but some were without shoes, just in their stockings.... They said Jewish prayers and they all hit themselves.[8]

A century and a half later, in Galicia, a Conversa witness testified how the defendant, her aunt Violenta Alvarez, had used the Kippur fast in 1599 to initiate her into Marrano Judaism:

> When it was night the prisoner [Violenta] took her to a field next to the house and said to her: "take care to fast today so our lord will grant you life." And . . . facing the setting sun, the prisoner uncovered her hair and recited prayers, one which she said was the prayer of the Star, and another of the Fast, and the witness said [repeated] the same words. And when they had finished she said: "Aunt, why are we praying?" And the prisoner replied: "You know that we worship one God alone, the God of Israel your people."[9]

Antonio Homem's trial provides a detailed description of a rare *public* Kippur ceremony: very Jewish in its intention and quite Christian in its performance. It took place in a large house with a whitewashed floor, a large candelabra hanging from the ceiling and candles burning on a table. Antonio Homem, says the report, "often took the part of priest." He performed rites, exhorted the people to keep to the Law of Moses. The public, all fasting and dressed in white, used the Christian Bible (the Vulgate) to recite Latin Psalms that expressed a Jewish-Marrano sentiment (Psalms such as "When Israel came out of Egypt," "On the rivers of Babylon," and "From the Abyss I called you, O God").[10] In those ancient Jewish poems the Marranos expressed their own, specific sense of exile and yearning for redemption. A few "priests of the Law of Moses," replicating a Catholic ceremony, dressed Homem in a long elegant garment and put "a sort of miter" on his head, decorated with golden plaque. There was an altar there, and incense, and painted images of Moses and of a Marrano martyr or saint "who had been . . . burned as a Jew." This elaborate semi-Catholic apparatus served as the setting for a devout, and highly risky, veneration of the Law of Moses—all while violating Moses's Law by having his picture as background.

Major Holidays: Passover

Second in importance to Kippur, Passover commemorates the Jews' liberation from Egypt. The Marranos, caught in their own Egypt, also prayed for liberation; and in the absence of a Haggadah (the ritual Jewish Passover text) they used the stories of the Old Testament and their own imaginations to produce popular chants and songs of Marrano authorship. One of these, a Portuguese "Song of the Water," recurs in both Brittes Henriquez's trial in the 1670s and the Belmonte collection compiled in the 1920s (see epilogue). So for at least 250 years it must have been a popular part of the clandestine Marrano Passover meal.

Where do you lead us, O Moses,
In this barren desert,
With neither bread, nor tree, no grazing for the sheep? . . .
Watch Moses with his staff
Striking the salted sea,
Dividing it into twelve rivers [for the 12 tribes of Israel],
And my people securely crosses
To the place God has ordered.

This chant is altogether Marrano, unknown to Jews.

The Passover meal was fashioned on the Old Testament. A lamb was roasted and consumed, together with unleavened bread (matzo). The ceremony was often conducted in symbolic haste, the participants holding sticks and standing ready to leave Egypt any moment. (The custom, as Roth noted, was a Marrano invention.) The matzoth were sometimes called "Holy Bread," a striking Catholic association.

While Jews were still living in Spain they would send Passover matzoth to the Marranos (and to Old Christians too, to confuse the authorities). With the Jews gone, the Marranos had to bake their own unleavened bread, and to do so under disguise. An important Passover item was the sacrificial lamb. Unlike the Jews, who usually make do with a token piece of lamb, Marranos were keen on roasting the entire animal, taking care not to break its bones.[11] And they ate it standing, as if ready to leave Egypt at any moment.[12]

Sources of Marrano Knowledge

In their dire need, Judaizing Marranos turned to the Christian Bible as a source of Jewish inspiration and information. Thus they read the Psalms and the prophets with a Jewish intentionality and as a Jewish text. When Catholics recite the Psalms they conclude with a *gloria patri*, which puts a Christian imprint on the Jewish original. Judaizers made a point of omitting the gloria patri, thereby re-Judaizing the text. To the Inquisition, this was sufficient to convict.

The Latin Vulgate also supplied literate Marranos with a stolen Jewish education.[13] They found in it stories of the Jewish patriarchs, God's covenant with Abraham, the exodus from Egypt, and above all, Moses receiving the Law on Mount Sinai. Poems in Portuguese were composed to celebrate the defeat of the Egyptian King Pharaoh—the same evil Pharaoh who persecutes the Jews anew in every generation, and whom Portuguese Marranos recognized in their own king and Inquisition.

Learning about themselves from Christian sources enriched the Marrano pantheon with heroes such as Saint Tobias, whom the Jews hardly know (and they do not have saints, anyway).[14] But most popular among Marranos were the biblical figures of Ruth, Esther, and the prophet Jeremiah. Ruth the Moabite had joined the Jewish people and eventually begot King David: this told the Marranos that barriers between Jew and Gentile were not absolute and hope of reunion was not irrevocably lost. Jeremiah lamenting the destruction of Jerusalem gave the Marranos a code text by which to lament their own plight under the Inquisition and the rule of idolatry. Above all, Queen Esther fired the Marrano imagination. Santa Ester was the Judaizing Marranos' sister and mother, their patron saint (a Christian concept), who best symbolized their destiny. Wasn't Esther the first Marrano? Isn't the Book of Esther written mystically (and thus covertly, as befits Marranos) about *them*? "And Esther did not reveal her nation and birth," says the Bible. Beguiling the world, concealing her true origin, and needing to break Jewish law every moment—at the Persian king's table, bed, and palace, where she could not keep rules set by Moses—did not Esther in the end save her people from destruction? And was this not a biblical premonition of the Marranos' own mystical destiny? Queen Esther—Santa Esther—in her symbolic matronage became the Marrano equivalent of Holy Mary, to whom devotion was offered and prayers were addressed.

No wonder that Esther's Fast, a very minor occasion in Judaism, became a principal Marrano ritual, whereas Purim, the holiday that follows Esther's fast with carnival and masquerade, was practically neglected by the Marranos. They needed no special occasion for masks, since they were wearing them all the time.[15]

Benedictions and Magical Formulas; Public and Inward Acts

Marrano prayers and benedictions were scarce, and rarely said in Hebrew. Some formulas were uttered inaudibly, in one's heart, and used to flatly disavow a Catholic ritual or holy object or place. When entering a church or taking part in Mass, a Marrano might murmur, or silently repeat in his mind, that everything there was worthless, anathema, and that *Adonay*—the One God—was alone king. Such disparaging formulas could persist in a family for generations, even after the family had become sincerely Christian. (See the preface.)

The silent inner abjurations of one's overt acts became quintessential in the practice of Judaizing—they encapsulated its meaning in a nutshell. They also had important consequences inside Christianity itself. Attaching an overriding value to inward acts and dispositions in contrast to outer ritual works became a main factor in generating the Spanish religion of the interior I shall discuss in chapter 15. Specifically, silent prayer was a hallmark of the new Spanish mysticism that culminated in Saint Teresa of Avila.

Marrano Liturgy and Chants

Gitlitz summarizes the changes that Marrano liturgy underwent after losing its written Jewish base and becoming oral: Its scope shrank; prayers became shorter and simpler (and, we may add, were often made to suit a particular person or occasion); Hebrew was replaced with Portuguese or Castilian (and sometimes Latin), though the name *Adonay* and a few other Hebraisms were preserved; and Catholic elements were fitted to serve the purpose of Judaizing.[16] Gitlitz gives as an example the Converso heads of family who sanctified the wine, then gave every member of the family a sip:[17] the Jewish *Kiddush* (ceremonial blessing over wine) espouses elements from the Catholic ritual while annulling its Eucharistic message. We have seen examples of this duality all along this book. And we find it again in the interesting file of Brittes Henriquez.

Brittes Henriquez was a young Portuguese Marrana whose entire family was destroyed by the Inquisition in 1674. Her father and two sisters died in jail, one of her brothers was burned alive, and another brother was sentenced to life in prison. Brittes herself was confined to a convent for life. In her cell she recited prayers and chants that express a Jewish-oriented devotion marked by Christian symbolism. The spies of the Inquisition took down her prayers verbatim.

> O great God, all-powerful,
> You who made the heaven and the earth,
> Who rule and govern the world,
> And who, as good shepherd [a typical Christian symbol],
> Lead the sheep back to their pastures:
> These lost, wandering sheep [the Marranos],
> Who had departed from the flock [from the Jewish faith]—
> Gather them, and let them not be harmed
> By another, foreign shepherd [Jesus].
> And I as a lost sheep,
> Who has forsaken thy herd,
> Call me back, O Lord, to thee,
> And give me life again [in Judaism, her true pastures]—.

....

Lend me help, and good things,
As thou hast promised Daniel
Of the coming of the Messiah,
Let it happen, O Lord, in our days.
Send us, by an angel,
The prophet Moses,
To lead us out of our bondage [forced Catholicism], Amen!

The prayer, clear and forceful, speaks for itself. The compelling sentiment is of a lost Jew (sheep) yearning to rejoin the source of her essence; yet the texture of her prayer naively illustrates the foreign pastures into which she strayed because it uses Catholic motifs and symbols to carry the anti-Catholic message.

Prayers on Herself, Locked in Her Cell

Although I cannot kneel [in the open]
And my eye does not shed waters [for fear of disclosure],
Only my heart [my inward silent truth] I humble before You,
Asking forgiveness and begging
That you relieve us from the Inquisition.

....

Grant me the faith of Abraham,
The toil of Jacob,
The patience of Job.

Excerpts from a Yom-Kippur Prayer

Lord of Lords, the infinite . . . give me knowledge of the truth [Judaism], and open my eyes and mind [to what I must do as Jew], so that my soul shall not forfeit its salvation [a Christian goal]. . . .

For the sake of thy holy Name [a Jewish formula], make the angels that accompany you pray for me [a Catholic request for mediation]; save me from judgment [by the Inquisition], from false witnesses, and *also from true witnesses* . . . save me, O Lord, as you saved Noah from the flood, Jonah from the fish, Daniel from the den of lions . . . and Saint Esther from the evil hands of Haman.

None of these prayers are known in Judaism. They reflect a specific Marrano experience, and they are typically Judaizing texts—that is, neither purely Jewish nor Christian, but the two combined in one of several ways in which Marrano's dualities existed. Note that the speaker typically asks God to open her eyes and instruct her in the ways of the true religion, of which she is ignorant. Judaizers were acutely aware of the gap between their Jewish will and lack of Jewish knowledge, between their commitment to the Law of Moses and what they actually knew about its meaning.

Were these texts composed by Brittes herself, or standard Marrano prayers? Probably the latter. And even if some were written by Brittes, she must have used established Marrano patterns and symbols—the allusion to the "good shepherd," the invocation of "Saint Esther," and the analogy between Daniel's lions' den and the Marrano predicament. Two and one-half centuries later, it is striking to find similar motifs—and dualities—among the Belmonte Marranos. The Belmonte prayers contain a special Marrano Paternoster (Our Father, addressed to *Adonay*, the Jewish God) and a Catholic-inspired Marrano confession. These and other texts, which neither Jew nor Christian has encountered in their prayer books, have traversed the centuries by oral transmission: they constitute a specific legacy of Judaizing Marranos that has survived not only the Inquisition but also its abolition, and is becoming extinct only today.

Unlike Brittes, some Marranos knew only a single prayer, clinging to it as a precious treasure, and some used straightforward Christian prayers, modified to express devotion to *Adonay*.

But Marranos did not only Judaize. Most of them accepted Christianity in various ways—some rather unorthodox. Therefore, the concept of Marrano religions (in the plural) should also include the *Christian* varieties of duality and dissent, to which we now turn.

14

New Christians at the Forefront of Spanish Culture

———————— ⇌ ————————

Just as the Marrano mind was invested with Catholic elements even when Judaizing, so the Catholic culture in Iberia was affected by the infusion of the New Christians. Ex-Jews abounded in learning, science, literature, and theology. In Spain much more than in Portugal, they also became high ecclesiastical figures and religious mentors and innovators. Some were not only ex-Jews but former Judaizers, with a history of secret worship in their families (and even in their own early biographies). This means they had learned to value the inward religion, of the intimate heart, as the essence of all religious life—a Marranesque attitude that was preserved when they became sincere Christians and frequently marked their new Catholic religiosity. Because of their Marrano background, they also carried with them an acute problem of identity, the need to find God afresh, and a potential for religious ferment and novelty.

Background

Spanish Catholicism at the end of the Middle Ages was predominantly formalistic and external. It was based on external ritual, church power, coercive scholasticism, and rigid hierarchy; and it suffered from extreme clerical abuses. The injection into Catholic Spain of ex-Jewish elements helped produce new forms of Christian experiences and devotion that alarmed the orthodoxy. Renaissance Spain, as a result, innovated a special brand of illuminist mysticism and manifested other forms of spiritual ferment and reform (and counter-reform), which aroused the Inquisition's suspicion and persecution. In the process, because their religiosity was grounded in interiority—as their former Marranism had been—these Judeo-Christians discovered the depth and importance of human subjectivity and of the inner self.

No less, ex-Jewish Conversos gave a powerful impetus to Spanish scholarship and literature, provoking some of the most original literary forms that made Spain's *siglo de oro*.

This Spanish "Golden Age" was not all gold. Spain was already bogged down in contradictions—between the practical economics of a global military power and its lofty sense of mission and, within that self-assigned mission, the contradiction between its transcendent craving and the human, all too human, greed for power, wealth, and self-gratification.

The infusion of Conversos heightened some of these trends and created new ones. The newcomers seized new economic opportunities, filled voids in the small bourgeois class, and tacitly challenged entrenched values. Manifesting an insulted thirst for status, they downgraded the value of birth and glorified individual achievement, which they understood both as personal virtue and as honest economic success. Their families' tendency to live inwardly and be more secretive and self-contained helped create an emerging sense of individuality and private life; and the mixture of Judaism and Christianity sometimes diminished their interest in religion altogether, replacing it with a growing concern for this-worldly secular affairs and even religious indifference or skepticism.[1] Yet at the opposite extreme from religious indifference—but manifesting the same Converso difficulty in accepting the religion of the majority in its prevailing form—other Conversos developed an exceptionally heightened religious tension. These Conversos rejected all forms of routinized and external religion. They searched for unorthodox ways of expressing a purer and more interiorized religiosity. Their quest found articulation in the various Spanish spiritual movements—the Alumbrados, the Hispano-Erasmians, the Avila mystics,[2] even the Jesuits and the Hispano-Lutherans—and it produced a rich and subtle phenomenology of the mystical mind and the inner religious experience. And this, more broadly, led to the discovery of human subjectivity and the inner Self, as a new area of exploration, and the basis for a new religious and secular culture.

All the while, Converso intellectuals were provoking a surge of cultural creativity in Spanish literature and scholarship—as authors, novelists, poets, and essayists, as well as members of a keen and growing reading public. This was the century following the invention of printing. Conversos were habitually more literate than the average Spaniard and, as readers, were particularly sensitive to the games of allusion and irony required in the semiunderground condition of the times. In this way, Converso sensibilities and a Converso-like spirit penetrated Spanish literature even beyond the direct works of Converso authors.

Turning away from the attractions of chivalrous adventure, from banal pastoral works and stories of courtly love, Spain gave Europe the vivid new literary genre known as *picaresque*,[3] with its knack for ironic realism, dual language, and allusion, and its aesthetic exploitation of the idea of an inverted underground world, opposing yet reflecting the official world in a game of crooked mirrors.

Spanish scholars since Américo Castro stress the weight of the Conversos in classic Spanish culture. The historian Angel Alcalá concludes that the majority of writers and mystics during the Spanish Golden Age stemmed from the Converso caste. They were predominant in sheer numbers and in creative innovation.[4] The impressive list he cites of Converso intellectuals (either proven or most probable), includes all the leading Alumbrados (illuminati, see below), most of the other spiritual reformers, the greatest humanists, the greatest mystics (including their towering figure, Saint Teresa of Avila); the best-known chroniclers; most physicians (the natural scientists of the time); all the Hebraists; a good many biblical scholars, and an unusually large number of fiction writers, including the founders of the picaresque novel.[5]

Unlike Castro, Alcalá argues convincingly (as Márquez Villanueva did before him) that the Conversos who created this culture were no longer Jews.[6] Less convincing is his other claim that the cultural prominence of these Conversos indicates that they had achieved "perfect assimilation" and integration in Hispanic Christianity, and even that their mode of life attained the "climax of Christian living."[7] Alcalá then qualifies this exaggerated claim—which other important Spanish scholars make even more strongly[8]—by suggesting that the perfect integration was in some measure only apparent, since these Conversos possessed the consciousness of belonging to a separate "caste," and their work betrayed bitterness and disapproval of the Spanish world they had joined. I certainly agree with the latter part; but if so, why hold on to the untenable notion of perfect assimilation[9]—rather than recognize that, on the contrary, these people were *not* full-fledged Hispano-Catholics but were *nonintegral* ones—alienated, disenfranchised, both belonging and not belonging, and unable to be identified with *any* established identity? Moreover—this is my main point here—it is precisely in this situation that one should look for the source of their unusual creativity. It was their *failure* to achieve perfect assimilation—their inability and even refusal to do so—that enabled these Conversos to manifest such extraordinary innovation within the Spanish fold, which they were, at the same time, both within and without.

In other words, the extraordinary cultural contribution of the Conversos indicates that, by necessity or choice, they were *unaccomplished* as Hispano-Catholics, people who dissented from the prevailing Spanish mold because they bore an irremediable duality even when becoming Christians (and often as the *price* or the condition for becoming Christianized).[10]

Roots of Converso Creativity

What, then, made the explosion of Converso creativity possible? As a first approximation, I suggest it was the ferment that arose from the unsolved dialectic between the Conversos' attempt to assimilate and the forces of rejection, external and internal, that made this project impossible to realize as simple integration. I am not referring to the whole Converso body, of course, but to an alert and sensitive subgroup within it, those who seriously attempted to become Christian Spaniards but felt unable to realize this intent except by dissenting from the socioreligious system they were joining. Thus a revaluation of entrenched values, social and religious, became both a need and a lever for their entry into Catholic Spain—and thereby prevented their full integration in it. (This factor worked independent of the exclusionary forces in Spanish society and in addition to them.)

Of special importance were sensitive Conversos whose families had Judaized in the past while being cut off from actual Jewish rites. These families had learned to place the origin of true religiosity in the inner heart rather than in external rituals; so when their offspring eventually decided to assume their Christianity, they found themselves at odds with the ceremonial character and external formalism of the dominant Catholic religion, which looked paradoxically too "Jewish" to them, too close to the religion they were trying to abandon. In addition, Conversos who had been stung by the stigma of "impure blood" fought back by disparaging the Spanish cult of birth and lineage, claiming that a person's honor depended on personal achievement and virtue. Thus, in both the social and religious spheres, these people could find their place in Catholic Spain only as reformers and nonconformists—an unsettling cultural force—and their assimilation had been conditioned from the start by the impossibility of full integration.

It is noteworthy that some of the most outstanding Converso innovators (such as the philosopher Juan Luis Vives, the religious humanists Juan and Alfonso de Valdés, and Saint Teresa of Avila, among others) had a long history of Judaizing in their families, and their next of kin—a father, a grandfather, an uncle, or the remains of a mother—were burned or humiliated by the Inquisition. These facts do not make Jews of Valdés, Vives, or Teresa: on the contrary, they were resolute Christians. But they were *different* Christians, expecting religion—as Marranos typically did—to express the inner self and heart rather than external worship. And they experienced unease and disquiet with regard to the prevailing modes and beliefs of Catholic Spain, which they wanted to improve—that is, reform.

Converso Reformers' Resemblance to Judaizers

The Converso reformers resembled the Judaizers in certain important structural respects: They dissented from the ruling form of religion; concealed their views from the world; treasured an internal truth and the private recognition of it (that is, a form of subjective conscience); and they often acted in networks and semifraternities. In all these respects the Converso reformers continued the experience of the Judaizers, and were possibly born from it. Yet again, the dissent of these Conversos did not serve to distance them from Spain, but rather enabled their entry into it. The Judaizers dissented in order to remain Jews, whereas these reformers dissented in order *not* to remain Jews, but to find a way, suitable to their condition, of becoming Spanish Christians—*New* Christians, as their appellation indicated. The designation of New Christians, which their foes used to derogate them, they themselves intended to fill with a positive, even superior, meaning. They intended a "New" Christian to mean a different and better Christian, more authentic than the veteran Spaniard.

This new meaning was made possible by the two typical Marrano claims: that the highest religious value is attained through the interior self, and that honor depends on personal achievement rather than birth. Each of these claims, and certainly their combination, allowed them to feel truly honorable and to find a source of Christian confidence and pride, compensating for the spurn and exclusion coming from the Old Christian society.[11]

The striking structural similarities between the Converso religious reformers and the Judaizers can be summarized in five essential points:

(1) *They all learned to place religious value in the secrecy of the inner self* (and thereby discovered its crucial role).

This is the single most important similarity. All the nonorthodox Spanish movements proposed a religion of the interior in some variety, thereby reiterating a basic pattern of the Judaizing Marrano experience while giving it different contents. Moreover, they discovered and further enriched the domain of subjectivity and the inner Self as emerging principles in the culture.

(2) *They all refused to assimilate into prevailing Christianity.*

This refusal defines the reformers while repeating a basic attitude of the Judaizers. Again, the pattern persists while its content varies. Judaizers refused to assimilate into Christianity under *any* form; the Converso reformers refused to assimilate into it in its *present* form. The refusal was internalized within the Christian sphere and assumed the shape of inner-Christian dissension and heterodoxy.

(3) *They all actively searched for an alternative way to salvation*, different from the conventional way preached and defended by the Church establishment.

(4) *They lived and communicated in the form of esoteric groups or fraternities.*

This Marranesque practice allowed them to separate their inner truth from public discourse, and, like the Judaizers, they had to devise strategies of prudence and disguised language.

(5) All Judaizers and most Converso reformers *insisted on their right to preserve certain Jewish traces within their new identity*—such as vestiges of food, style, taste, memory, behavior, and even doctrine.[12]

Some Marranos preserved these traces with a definite Jewish intent, while others, who resolved to become Christians, maintained these traces as personal nostalgia, or as claims to greater freedom in interpreting and living their Christianity.

The cardinal difference between the Christian spiritual seekers and the Judaizers resided in their intentionality. The spiritual seekers no longer wanted to be Jews. They thought of themselves as different Christians, better and more intimate with God. They wanted to realize their status as *New* Christians and change the meaning of the concept from a derogation to a sign of distinction.

Thus, the several forms of "internal" Christianity allowed New Christians to insist on personal conscience and subjectivity—their inherited Marrano specialty—as the locus of religious truth; to embrace the Cross without submitting to the alienating burden of excessive church mediation; and, by preferring silent prayer, to provide direct access to the deity, free of the rival claims and ceremonies of both religions yet allowing for *some* Jewish-derived elements to be expressed within a basically Christian way of life.

Of course, the identity ferment arising from the Converso situation needed auxiliary conditions to become creative. It found them in the cultural provocations and new proficiencies coming from Renaissance Europe, and in the Jewish tradition of literacy and intellectual alertness, which the Marranos preserved and channeled into different themes and concerns (as did assimilated European and American Jews in the nineteenth and twentieth centuries, as well).

15

A Christian Religion of the Interior

―――――――――――――――― ⚮ ――――――――――――――――

The Converso founders of the "Religion of the Interior" were partly mystics and partly disciples of Erasmus of Rotterdam, the great Catholic humanist. Both groups downgraded external cult and opposed the role of the church as a political power. The mystics ranged from crude seers (*beatas*) and radical illuminati (*Alumbrados*) to the most refined and sophisticated forms of Catholic mysticism. The Erasmians were (by and large) not mystics. They stressed inner piety, religious awareness, and spirit, but held on to reason and common sense and did not seek supernatural visions or union with God through mystical love.[1]

The *Beatas*

First there was the popular cult of the *beatas*. *Beatas* were charismatic women believed to possess supernatural powers and to stand in direct contact with the divinity. They would fall into ecstasy or trance, have visions of the upper world, foresee momentous events in the future, and give people inspired advice. Acting outside the religious establishment, the *beatas* were venerated by common people and also by members of the elite. Yet such direct access to the divine was not only a source of wonder and admiration. In a Catholic society trained in routinized worship and requiring the mediation of the church, it also provoked hostility and a sense of danger.

It is no accident that this unconventional religiosity was carried out mostly by women. Women were imagined to be less rational than men, more suggestive emotionally, and more susceptible to irregular experiences. Closer to reality, women were socially marginalized, unable to rise in the world through established venues. The Church allowed women to become nuns, saints, and martyrs, but not to hold positions of power in the community as priests, confessors, preachers, theologians (or inquisitors). Women were even forbidden to engage in serious study—to become learned in their own religion. Mothers superior, the highest female position in the church, were subordinate to male prelates and superior only to other females. The only recognized religious influence a woman could usually exercise was informal, confined to inside the home. Women oversaw the education of the young and helped maintain domestic and religious traditions (including secret ones, as among the Judaizing Conversos).

The *beatas* rebelled against this constriction. They came out into the open, to instruct and dispense their services in public—as mentors, counsel-givers, or alternative mediators to the divine world. It was, in a way, a reaction to the negative religious role assigned to women as "witches." The magical force attributed to the witch was transmuted into the benign, beneficent force of a *beata*. Yet in taking this way, the only available to them, on the outskirts of established religion, the *beatas* assumed the risks of their nonconformist position. They had to struggle against the suspicion that they spoke for the devil or were out to destroy the religious order, and fight for recognition from the official church. Hence their desire to attract many dignitaries as their visitors. For a while, indeed, some high prelates saw the *beatas* as the bearers of a new popular devotion and allowed them to operate and even flourish in Spain; but even then, their position remained precarious and basically transient.

The most famous of these popular seers was the *beata* of Pedrahita (by her actual name, Sister María de Santo Domingo.) The uproar she caused around 1509 proves that at that time she was a novelty. The daughter of a peasant with mystical inclinations, she was taught from early youth to mortify her body and to plunge into long meditations, mindless of her surroundings. Her fasts were so long that her digestive system was said to have shrunk. When meditating, she shut herself to the world and turned off her outer senses, allowing only inner stimuli to fill her mind with visions of another world. Like her contemporary, the Marrano *beata* of Herrera, whom we met in chapter 6, the *beata* of Pedrahita also visited heaven, where the Virgin showed her around. These visions occurred in full daylight as the *beata* abstracted herself from the world in deep contemplation, lying on the ground like a corpse, her extended hands frozen in the shape a cross. Thus she remained for hours.

When the *beata*'s soul returned to her body and the trance ended, she would report her experiences in an enchanting way that moved her audience to tears. Erotic metaphors abounded in her accounts. Here she was, just back from an intimate union with God, in whose arms she had been dissolved in love. She was Christ's bride, his elected spouse, and she lost herself in his bosom in infinite bliss. Sometimes she spoke as if she was Christ himself, so intimate was their union. When the Holy Virgin was showing her around heaven, sometimes she engaged in a gallant contest—who would cross a portal first? "The bride of so great a son should go first," the Virgin insisted; but the *beata* replied: "If you had not given him birth, how could I become his bride?"

Other *beatas*, many of Converso origin, did not fail to appear: Isabel de La Cruz, María Núñez, Francisca Hernández, Sister Francisca of Salamanca,[2]

Mother Marta of Toledo, and (to a certain extent) María Cazalla of Guadalajara, are among the names known today. And at least one *beata* (the one we met in Herrera in chapter 6) was not only a Conversa but also an active Judaizer who drove other Marranos to readopt the Law of Moses and announced their imminent messianic redemption.

The Alumbrados

A more doctrinal mysticism emerged with the so called Alumbrados (the illuminated ones). All their leaders and most of their known followers were Conversos. The Alumbrados flourished in the early 1520s and were repressed a decade later. Their movement was founded by two semi-intellectuals from Guadalajara, the *beata* Inez de La Cruz and the accountant Pedro Ruiz Alcaraz. Inez and Alcaraz, both self-taught, spelled out their mystical views in forthright, direct form. Their doctrine, which denounced conventional religion as meaningless, was as radical and daring as it was simplistic and blunt.[3]

The Alumbrados' goal was no less than union with God. This was to be attained through the practice of *dejamiento*, the self-abandonment of one's personal will to God, a kind of letting-go, which their foes, quite mistakenly, understood as licentiousness. The Alumbrados insisted that religious perfection requires the total renunciation of the will and intellect to God so that our love of him can unite with his love of us. God is nothing but this love. One must not imagine God as a separate substance emitting love, as if love were one of God's special acts, or properties; rather, God *is* his love, in the substantive sense of the word.[4] In Christological terms, this position identifies God with the Holy Spirit, but not with God's human Son. The Alumbrado religion thus marginalizes the Incarnation and the Trinity—two crucial issues which divide Christians from Jews. Incarnation and the Trinity, even the Church itself, hinder salvation because they impose a form of mediation on the individual soul; and mediation is a sign of religious imperfection, fit for inferior people who will never attain God's love.

Seen in this light, the whole edifice of the Catholic Church is at best an imperfect scaffold, which real believers must supersede. This applies to the church as a whole, as an organized institution, and to all forms of external worship, from sacraments and verbal prayer to benedictions, adorations, confessions, absolutions, pleas for divine help, and the cult of saints and images. The Alumbrados disdained the representation of God not only in sensual images, but even in the more refined theology that presumes to know or reach God through concepts, symbols, and dispositions drawn from this world. (This recalls the Jewish philosopher Maimonides.)[5] The Alumbrado renounced the world and shunned all the representations that trouble the soul through the senses, memory, the intellect, and above all—the will. In practicing *dejamiento*, the soul directs its self-effacing energy toward the attainment of absolute quiet, illumination, and fusion with God's love. Though the shutting of the senses may recall the trance of the *beatas*, there were no visions, no images, no explosive emotion. The Alumbrado's loving fusion with God was supposed to be loftier, purer, less agitated, yet even more exalted.

The dissenting Christianity of the Alumbrados thus owed essential elements to their Jewish or Judaizing origin—above all, the forthright rejection of images and the tacit underplay of the Incarnation. At the same time, if taken strictly, the Alumbrados would have become the first "Christians without a church" (to use a term made famous by Kolakowski),[6] before the radical protestant sects.

Having alienated most scholars and clergymen (including progressive ones), no wonder the Alumbrados found themselves isolated and politically vulnerable. On September 3, 1525, Inquisitor General Manrique signed an edict banning Alumbrado activity in Spain and listing all their "errors and novelties" (*novelty* is a bad word in a traditionalist society): forty-eight items in all. The edict is a treasure for historians studying the Alumbrado movement; for the movement itself it had been a political death sentence.

Political is a key word here. In doctrinal terms, the limits were blurred between the illegal Alumbrado position and the mysticism that became legitimate. The label *Alumbrado* was no less political than theological. It was used in the sixteenth century quite liberally—to stigmatize other kinds of spiritual novelty, related but different.

This lack of differentiation (as in the case of *Judaizer*) was not due to intellectual slackness alone. It was also a matter of policy. Some officers of the Inquisition must have been capable of more subtlety. But the Holy Office as an institution preferred to lump diverse phenomena together, so as to streamline its police work and preserve the ideological presumptions behind it. The intellectual sloppiness was institutional, rather than being a personal feature, which also made it permanent.

Converso Erasmians

Erasmus of Rotterdam was the most celebrated, and contested, humanist of the sixteenth century. His teaching inquired into the sources of Western Christian culture and the mentality of true religion—how it ought to be practiced and lived. This made Erasmus a Christian humanist and pre-Enlightener. To him,

Jesus's example was one of personal piety, not of ceremonial pomp and repressive dogma. He stressed inner human experience and worth, and this excluded the formality, the conformism, the arid scholasticism, and above all, the corrupting pursuit of power and wealth, which have plagued the Roman Church for centuries.

Erasmus's motto, *ad fontes* (back to origins), referred to several things at once: the origins of humanity; the sources of Christianity; God's original Word, and its text, the Bible; and the human heart and mind—the origin, to Erasmus, of true virtue, piety, religion, and civilization itself. Piety, a virtue arising from a person's heart, was the chief value to him, more important than dogma, ceremonies, liturgy, and formal church hierarchy.

Erasmus's attack on the abuses of the Church and plea for spiritual reform produced strong echoes in Europe. Martin Luther, among others, was deeply influenced by Erasmus's critique. But Luther was a fighter, a world-changer who dared split the Christian church—Christ's own body. Whereas Erasmus, in several ways Luther's master, was a man more of irony than action and a staunch defender of Christian unity, under the same papal Rome he so cuttingly criticized. In the end, the triumphant Luther censured Erasmus as a traitor to his own idea, while Rome banned his works posthumously.

Marcel Bataillon has famously shown that Erasmus's reception was more intense in Spain than elsewhere in Europe, and that it had been overwhelmingly driven by Conversos. The two facts must have been related. If Spain in the early sixteenth century was ripe for religious innovation, part of the reason was the presence of Converso clerics and intellectuals concerned with their unsettled identity as New Christians. Their need for a different kind of religion—indeed, of religiosity—made them attentive to the foremost Catholic innovator, who pointed to a new Christianity.

What in particular in Erasmus's writing appealed to Conversos? A major factor was his critique of external cult, and the role of the Church as a power structure. No less, Conversos were attracted by the link he established between interiority and religious freedom; his praise of the practice of dissimulating a precious interior so as not to expose it to profane eyes; the importance of irony; and, not least, Erasmus's tacit attack on the Inquisition and his outspoken stand against forced conversions.

The Erasmian movement spread in Spain in the early decades of the sixteenth century. At first (in the 1520s) the movement flourished, using the tactics of a semisecret fraternity (like the Marranos) and shielded by a letter from Emperor Charles V that declared its legitimacy. But in the next decade, as its conservative foes grew stronger, the Erasmian movement became a target of the Inquisition. Surviving until midcentury, it was brutally repressed by the

Counter-Reformation, which banned Erasmus's works altogether. Yet Erasmianism continued simmering in the underground and left a lasting mark on the Spanish cultural scene far beyond its official disappearance.

Some of the outstanding names in the Spanish Renaissance were Converso Erasmians. And they often came in families: the Valdés brothers, the Vergara and the Cazalla siblings, and the Coronel brothers (descendents of Don Abraham Seneor). Following are a few very brief sketches.

Juan de Valdés

Juan de Valdés (like his brother Alfonso) was a leading humanist of the Spanish Renaissance. The brothers must have known, and perhaps loved, their maternal uncle Fernando de La Barreda, who was burned as Judaizer by the Inquisition.[7] Yet to the Valdés brothers Judaism was no longer an option. They ardently wanted and felt themselves to be Christians, though in a way of their own, distinct from the Orthodox routine. As a teenager Juan was exposed to the Alumbrado preaching of Alcaraz, but later he came under the influence of Erasmian thinkers at the university of Alcalá. These encounters were surely not accidental. A restless, inquisitive young Converso does not "happen" to come by such unorthodox influences: ready for them, he actively seeks them out.

Juan de Valdés's best known work—*Dialogue on Christian Doctrine*—was a combination of mask and daring talk. The book's title sounds like ordinary instruction in church rituals and dogmas. Actually Valdés, the New Christian whose uncle was burned as Judaizer, was not teaching the prevailing Christian doctrine, but its far-reaching reform—how it *ought* to be understood and practiced. In so doing he assumed his definition as "new" Christian, and called upon everyone else to become new in this manner—namely, as spiritually reformed Christians.

Valdés's message was "living faith." It was not a cognitive attitude—a *belief*—but a powerful inner experience of trust in God's presence. Mere belief in biblical stories he considered "dead faith," found also among thieves and villains. Living faith consisted of absolute confidence in God, not in believing unproven stories and propositions. Valdés did not say that biblical stories were false; he accepted them but minimized their religious value.

It is striking that Valdés hardly spoke of Christ as an object of living faith. Time and again we hear it is God himself we must love and adore. The crucifixion is not even mentioned, except as a routine part of the credo.[8] This stunning silence seems to echo the Jewish criticism of the Trinity and the difficulty

Jewish Conversos had in accepting it. No less, it challenged a core principle of Catholicism—the required mediation of Christ, Mary, the saints, and the Catholic Church in approaching God.

Beside this daring silence there was also daring talk. Valdés played with fire in downgrading the commands of the Church and such pillars of Catholic life as confession, ritual prayer, church tax (the tithe), and the Church's worldly wealth. Valdés's *Dialogue* is put in the mouth of a high prelate conversing with a wise monk and an ignorant one. At a certain point the ignorant monk, exasperated, explodes: "You frighten me with all these utterances, so new and unreasonable!" Yet the wise monk tells the prelate in parting: "If all prelates followed your example, there would surely be another Christian life."

Another Christian life was precisely the goal Valdés was personally seeking for himself and others. But he was too imprudent. When he was arrested by the Inquisition, his friends were able to get him out the first time; but when he was summoned a second time, Valdés fled to Italy. There, under the name Giovanni Valdeso, he spread his ideas to the Italian aristocracy, including a member of the grand Gonzaga family. A Judeo-Spanish Converso with an unsettled identity, he was now telling Rome itself what its religion ought to be.

Juan Luis Vives

Juan Luis Vives is one of the two best known Spanish philosophers of the Renaissance.[9] A European-minded humanist, the younger friend of Erasmus and Thomas More, he was born to Judaizing Marrano families on both his father's and mother's sides. When he was an adult and already famous, the Inquisition burned his father as a Judaizer and exhumed and burned his mother's bones on similar charges. Vives, however, had parted from his Judaizing father at age sixteen and resolved to accept Christianity. But he could do so only as a dissenter and reformer, so he preferred living outside Spain, mostly in Spanish Flanders, and never returned to Spain again.

Vives's acceptance of Christianity was primarily an act of will, an identity choice rather than a fideistic change of heart. In casting off his family's tradition of Judaizing, Vives became a philosophically oriented Christian—critical, rational, empirically minded—rather than a fermenting religious person. Opposing the dominant scholastic culture, he gained fame by his free, elegant style and prolific work, which called for reform in all areas, not only religious but secular as well—in philosophy, education, society, and international politics. The latter issue made him one of the early Europeans, similar to Erasmus. But Vives's reasons had to do with his several split identities as a Converso.

Vives deprecated the Spanish value of birth and lineage. He mocked scholastic philosophy, argued against mechanical learning and education, opposed Spain's imperial designs, and, a European before his time, advocated an all-European peace (*concordia*). He called for moderate toleration inside states and spoke against the forced conversions of Jews, Muslims, and American Indians. All of this set him against both the emperor and the Inquisition; so, to be on the safe side, he preferred living away from the homeland, in which he felt equally in exile. (When offered the prestigious and well-paid post of professor in Alcalá de Henares, he turned it down.) This ambivalence was characteristic of his person, existence, and sense of self.

Vives was the only Erasmian of renown who had been raised by Judaizing parents, seen martyrdom in his immediate family, and said no to both. This experience gave him a Converso perspective of his own and a voice unlike that of other Conversos. His spiritual disquiet was not primarily religious but more philosophical and social (sometimes bordering on skepticism).[10] And his drive for reform, because it concerned the semisecular areas mentioned above, was addressed more to "Christendom," understood as a civilization, than to Christianity in the strictly religious sense.

Vives was also the most prudent among the Erasmians. His sense of exile was internal. It was not attenuated by the fact that his exile was self-imposed. In a famous letter to Erasmus he complained: "We live in difficult times, in which we can neither speak, nor keep silent." The dictum captures not only his situation, but the language that Conversos often had to adopt, an equivocal language that keeps silent even while speaking.

The Vergara Siblings

The university chair that Vives declined was offered him by another Erasmian Converso, Dr. Juan de Vergara, a distinguished humanist, preacher, historian, classicist, and man of the world. Vergara got his brother Francisco, a leading Greek scholar, appointed to the university, and the two brothers' expanding influence turned Alcalá into a major Erasmian center.

Their sister, Isabel de Vergara, though less learned, was so captivated by Erasmus's translated works that she studied Latin—a rare thing in a woman—in order to have access to those Erasmian texts that were considered too daring to render in Spanish. Such feminine scholarship was then viewed with mistrust. Social custom saw it as a sign of pride, even revolt.

No less daring, though in a different way, was Juan's half brother Bernardino Tovar. "A serious humanist and tormented intellectual,"[11] his search for an intuitive mode of religion, free of convoluted speculation, got him dangerously involved with charismatic mystics and *beatas*. Between 1525 and 1530 he was active in the illuminist movement.[12] Then, denounced by a devious *beata*, Tovar was jailed by the Inquisition.

His half-brother, Juan Vergara, took up Tovar's defense. For two years the brothers exchanged secret letters written in invisible ink. But in the end, the overconfident Vergara walked into a trap set by the Inquisition. At first he was accused of obstructing justice, and then of heresy. Vergara denied the charges, but his defense collapsed when a former Erasmian associate testified to having heard him speak against the sacraments. On December 21, 1535, Vergara abjured "with vehemence" in a well-staged *auto de fe*, of which he was the main star. His sentence was lenient—confinement to a monastery for one year. When he came out, Spanish Erasmianism everywhere was struggling for its life.[13]

María Cazalla

The daughter of rich Converso burghers, María Cazalla's early religious life was as frustrating as her marriage.[14] Nothing she did as a Christian touched her heart. She went to Mass like everyone else, but experienced the service as a meaningless social routine. She could not understand why one must visit a church in order to communicate with God, and why she had to address him in obscure Latin formulas. During confession, which was a deep spiritual event for her, she suffered from the confessor's superficial attitude and mechanical actions, so, half joking, she once suggested that the humdrum confession itself should be her atonement.

María was drawn to the Erasmian circle by her brother, the Converso bishop Juan de Cazalla, himself a leading Erasmian figure. María organized private meetings to promote Erasmus's ideas among the local Converso bourgeoisie around Guadalajara. María's nonconformist, semianarchistic effervescence found in Erasmus a more solid—and legitimate—religious framework and articulation. A charismatic woman, wherever she went she radiated a preference for interior religion over works and acts of cult.

In 1530 the Inquisition put María Cazalla on trial as an Alumbrada. María protested, quite rightly, that this negative stigma "is commonly attributed to every person who lives a little more withdrawn" and manifests some Christian purity. Her defense was that she was an Erasmian, and Erasmus had never been censured by the church. María was tortured but stuck to her guns. In the end her strong character prevailed and she was found guilty of minor heresies only. Yet her sentence, though light, was tailored to hit where it hurt most. Candle in hand, María Cazalla was forced to perform in a grand ceremonial Mass—to her, a most mechanical ritual—in which she had to kneel down at the altar, fix her eyes on the Host, and recite the Ave Maria and the Paternoster seven times each. For someone of her religious sensibilities, this was worse than an ordinary *auto de fe*.

Even after the ban against Erasmus, a special Hispano-Erasmian spirit continued to stir in Spain's mental underground. It was a counterculture adapted to Spain's situation and contesting its official values, both religious and secular. Hiding behind the secular critique of *hidalguía* and *pure blood*, and largely nourished by Conversos, its voice often spoke from the picaresque novels and the work of Cervantes. As such, the covert form of Erasmianism was part of the Spanish reality in the sixteenth and seventeenth centuries, even though it could not appear in public but—like Erasmus's *Praise of Folly*—had to speak in the language of irony and allusion.

Osuna as Bridge to Teresa

The simplistic mysticism of the Alumbrados was superseded by the mystical theology of the Converso monk Francisco Osuna. Osuna's follower, Saint Teresa of Avila, became the greatest mystic of Spain, and her own disciple and partner, Saint John of the Cross (Juan de La Cruz), is Spain's towering mystical poet.

The mystical theology was opposed to the prevailing scholastic theology. God was not an object of knowledge—certainly not the kind of dogmatic knowledge promulgated by the ruling scholastic schools—but of love, and, ultimately, union. To reach God the soul must sink deep into itself and be purified of all thoughts of created things. The lover of God must be free of sensation, desire, and rational reasoning; she or he must transcend all particular forms of life, thought, and wish, and plunge in silent concentration into that "dark night of the soul" (the title of Juan de La Cruz's best-known poetic collection), from which God alone might respond to his love. Ceremonies and vocal prayers are of equally little use. What matters is the heart; and the heart, in order to find its religious intensity and depth, must be liberated from external distractions like speech and ritual.

Yet, Osuna insisted, this does not lead to nothingness, but rather to supreme being and totality. Our *thinking nothing* is also *thinking all*, for in it we think nondiscursively of Him who by wonderful eminence is everything.

Osuna did not deny Christ's incarnation or divinity. Although a Converso, he was a Christian mystic, not a secret Judaizer. But he did deny the created, empirical side of God (that is, Christ's body and humanity) a role in mediating the soul's way to God as infinite. This may smack of a Marrano-like refusal to admit Christ into the center of religious life. Yet the underlying intention was not to Judaize, but to abandon Judaism together with ordinary Christianity in favor of a new, spiritual Christianity.

This was true in particular of Converso intellectuals with a Judaizing history in their close families, such as Valdés, Vives—and Saint Teresa of Avila, Spain's greatest mystic.

Teresa of Avila: The Patron Saint of the Interior Mind

Teresa de Cepeda y Ahumada—later known as Saint Teresa of Avila (1515–1582), the patron saint of Spain—was one of the great explorers of the Renaissance, yet she never set foot outside Spain. Her most important journey was inward. In searching for a new authentic Christianity this remarkable Converso daughter, whose father and grandfather had been humiliated by the Inquisition as Judaizers—more than any Westerner since Saint Augustine, and before Freud (and Pessoa)—discovered and explored the inner mind. Here was her privileged territory, the spiritual El Dorado in which Teresa was to find her true self, her real worth and religious fulfillment—and do so by her own mental effort, against the hard obstacles set by the established, and masculine, Church.

Teresa of Avila created a powerful synthesis, not free of contradictions, between Spain's main "internal" spiritual tenets, and she passed it on to the rest of Europe. Her several faces and masks were linked by her attempt to penetrate as deeply as possible into the "Interior Castle" (the title of her major book), into the far recesses of the divine presence as revealed in the layers of her own mind; and, thereby, to encounter and unite with God as a reality identical with her own deeper self.

It was obvious to Teresa that a complex goal like hers could not be realized by the immediate linear leap suggested by the Alumbrados, nor by the crude and naive sensual visions of the *beatas*. These early mystics practiced a hasty and superficial love of God, which was therefore inauthentic; in Teresa's vocabulary, it was a love full of "infidelities."

Teresa's shunning of popular public mysticism did not result from political prudence alone or from shyness. The reason was different: like her Judaizing Marrano ancestors, Teresa understood the essence of religion to lie within the mind, and the mind is each person's own. It cannot be replaced by someone else's mind or properly exhibited in the public arena. This interior universe,

Teresa held, is also the true domain of religion and the mystic's authentic arena. It is here—and not in outer worship, however important it may be for other reasons—that one's love of God can assume significant shapes—various, complex shapes—and eventually be consummated. The inner universe is private and singular, but also vast. When penetrating into it, a large and diverse inner landscape opens up to the mystic, who must travel and explore its receding horizons on her road to God's grace and union.

This road crosses the ineffable: regions that defy verbalization and cannot be properly explicated either by the intellect or the imagination, so they must elude the public sphere altogether. All we can turn to are allusive metaphors and allegories, which sound hollow when used in ordinary general discourse because they miss their intended target. But on privileged occasions, when the metaphors are realized within the intimacy of a well-prepared singular mind, they might take on a living meaning and serve as useful mystical signposts.

Teresa's insistence that the mind escapes public exposure also contained a political statement—a far reaching one. Her claim opposed the practices of the Inquisition by challenging the intellectual assumptions behind them. The Inquisition assumed that by systematic investigation and torture it can lay bare a person's inmost soul, which could then be exposed and punished in public (in an *auto de fe*). Teresa, on the contrary, recognized and hailed the existence of deep mental recesses that no public investigation (or torture) can expose, and that only their owner has the right—and the task—to discover and work out internally. In this respect, the whole Avila mysticism (which was dominated by Converso intellectuals)[15] presented a powerful antithesis to the Inquisition. The antithesis was, of course, implied, not spelled out in so many words—but isn't this the way in which Spain's underground contention usually worked? In the next century the same anti-inquisitorial implication resonated in the early European Enlightenment (Spinoza, Locke), fueling its arguments for religious toleration (and Spinoza, too, was the son of Marranos).[16]

Teresa, however, made heroic efforts to remain, or appear to be remaining, in the fold of church obedience and hierarchy. This ironclad principle taxed, and enhanced, Teresa's powers of self-restraint, diplomacy, and irony, adding a measure of Marranesque dissimulation to her discourse and demeanor.

The Marrano Daughter

In 1488 the Inquisition first entered Toledo. Juan Sánchez, a wealthy Converso cloth merchant, hastened to use the "grace period" (when Judaizers could confess without severe punishment) to confess of the Judaizing practices that ran in his family from generation to generation. In the following *auto de fe*, Sánchez marched in public with his young sons, including the six-year-old Alonso, wearing the shameful sanbenito, to the sneers of the mocking crowd. This humiliation was repeated six more times on different Fridays, after which father and sons were "reconciled" to the church. Their sanbenitos were hung in the parish church, a family stigma for generations to come.

Juan Sánchez would be Saint Teresa's grandfather, and little Alonso was to be her father.

From then on, the Sánchez sons' prime concern was to go out into the world and make it as Catholic Spaniards. Judaism had proven to be a social shame and a life-threatening political sin, so it had to be erased from their lives. The family adopted their mother's Old Christian name, Cepeda, and moved north to the city of Avila, where they tried to pass as Old Christian *hidalgos*. Yet their Jewish origin was widely known, and the secret of their *auto de fe* burst into the open with great scandal when Teresa was a young child.

Following that crisis, each member of the family tried to "de-Judaize" himself in a different way. And all their ways resounded in Teresa.

1. *Grandfather Juan Sánchez* did not (or could not) renounce his residual Jewish feelings, but he allowed no outward trace to betray their existence following the *auto de fe*. This, no doubt, deepened the Marranesque duality that marked his entire life, including the message—which inadvertently passed to Teresa—that what is truly valuable in religion is unspoken and lies inside the soul.

2. *Teresa's father, Alonso de Cepeda,* resolved to completely obliterate his Jewish background and expel it even from his memory. In conforming to the rules and mores of the Old Christian society, his ambition was to become a Christian like everyone else—to merge into the Catholic fold and climb its social ladder. Teresa received from him the unflinching assurance of her Catholicism and the powerful will to penetrate the Christian world. Yet to her this called for a nonconformist attempt to deepen and reform the Christian experience itself—by penetrating into its hidden spiritual heart, which was veiled from all ordinary Christians, Old or New.

3. *Teresa's uncle, Pedro de Cepeda,* manifested a third attitude.[17] Whereas Alonso strove to be Christian like everyone else, Pedro thought of himself as a better Christian, purer and more exigent than most. A wealthy man-of-the-world who later in life renounced his fortune and lived in semiseclusion while searching for a more meaningful religiosity, Pedro, like his famous niece (whom he influenced), felt he could be Christian only on condition of higher spirituality.

It was following a visit to her uncle Pedro that Teresa resolved to devote herself to religion; and it was Pedro who introduced her to the Converso mystic Osuna. The copy of Osuna's work that uncle Pedro gave her became Teresa's comfort and companion during the long years she spent, as she said, "in the [spiritual] desert."[18]

Those years were lonely and trying indeed. Only in her early forties did Teresa feel that she had reached her goal and come into her own. She described a moment of explosive joy, lucidity, and light, which her biographers call a "conversion." Yet no sudden event was involved here. The breaking of that light was made possible by the long trajectory of trials, joys, falls, discoveries, regressions, hopes, and anxieties that preceded it. Teresa did not discover her America by simply hitting a shoreline and calling "earth!" She crystallized and reappropriated what she had been exploring during many years of spiritual work.

Journey to the Inward Castle

The mature Teresa made a momentous—and paradoxical—effort to put into words that which she knew as fundamentally unutterable. The steps in the mystic's ladder to God depend on different forms of mental prayer and self-recollection *(recojimiento)* by which the soul exits the world and enters into its subjective, interior domain; and there alone can it reach the supernatural. As such, self-recollection is superior to acts of devotion.[19] Prayer does not become truly spiritual until it is silent, interiorized, and personal.

A master of nontrivial simplification, Teresa in her autobiography likened the stages on the mystic's itinerary to different methods of watering a garden (or the soul).[20] A soul that resolves to become "the servant of love" breaks the garden's primary ground; but then irrigation is needed. At first small quantities of water are provided by hard labor, drawn manually from a well. At the second stage, a lifting arm is used to draw more water with less toil. Next, a running stream supplies steadier and far ampler watering; and finally, profuse rain saturates the garden with ease and abundance. The deceptive simplicity of her images stands for a rich spectrum of mental movements, which become more complex as the soul advances. I cannot here describe those stages in any detail.[21] But I can illustrate their complexity by pointing out that even the stage of union (with God), which most mystics view as their final destination, is only a midway station in Teresa's long and oblique itinerary.

When the soul is out of itself in the state of union, it suddenly surges into great heights, like a huge tongue of flame bursting from a fire, or a giant eagle kidnapping the soul and flying with it to majestic heights. This creates an experience of sublimity, leading to sweet, painless suffering during which Teresa remembered herself as "flooded with tears without pain." Her description suggests that the whole human being, and not only the soul as opposed to the body, attains elevated existence—a rather unorthodox view for a Catholic.

Teresa as a (New) Christian Mystic

Since Teresian mysticism transcends ritual and ceremonial prayer, what makes it specifically Christian (or New Christian)? First, Teresa admitted of Christ's divinity and that he superseded the Law of Moses. Secondly, she humanized Jesus as bridegroom and mystical lover. And more generally, Teresa maintained that mysticism required a historical framework and tradition, which in her case could only be the Catholic. Catholicism provided the supernatural map from which Teresa's mystical adventure drew its terms and symbols, its orienting signposts, and no less important—the confining boundaries necessary to keep mysticism from becoming shapeless and anarchic. Yet at the same time, Teresa's "inward religiosity" set out to overhaul the historical framework that legitimized it. So, with all her radicalism, Teresa became a consummate "reformer from within": the disruptive forces of mysticism had to be restrained by the same historical tradition they were meant to transform. What could be more New Christian in intent (and more Marranesque in content)?

In the last part of her life, Teresa became an activist and reformer within the church. She created the monastic order of the "barefoot" Carmelites, and, traveling throughout Spain, founded no less than seventeen reformed monasteries in twenty years. Her goal was to educate an avant-garde elite that would lead a spiritual reform in the monastic world and, through it, in Catholic life as a whole. Her relentless activity—and being a woman—won Teresa powerful enemies. An exasperated superior, Father Sega, described her as a "restless, unstable, disobedient, and intractable woman," a not altogether unbefitting portrayal.

In all these respects, Saint Teresa of Avila was both an unwavering Catholic and a challenge to existing Christianity: a new kind of Christian, restless and passionate within her serenity, maintaining a split self even in the state of union; and journeying to God over and above the church, although she needed the church to exist—and to change—for that same purpose. This made her the patron saint, not only of the subjective mind, but of a *new* Christian—and the *New* Christian—way leading to it.[22]

Luis de León: A Converso's Song of Songs

A special place in this gallery belongs to Fray Luis de León, poet, theologian, biblical scholar, humanist, polemicist, and the leading Spanish Hebraist of his time. Luis de León was a Converso on both his parent's sides and a committed, though not submissive, Christian who looked for the origins of his devotion in the mystical poetry of the Hebrew Bible. This was an audacity, indeed an offense, which cost him a long period in the cells of the Inquisition. Today he is hailed as one of Spain's great figures of the Renaissance.[23]

Born in 1527 in Belmonte, near Cuenca, young Luis de León became an Augustinian monk and a professor of theology in Salamanca University (where his statue greets visitors today). As a biblical expert he had a particular passion for the *Song of Songs*—the favorite of mystics—and translated it to vernacular Castilian. This violated the Church's interdiction against vernacular translations of the Bible (a policy that was bolstered by the struggle against Martin Luther). Fray Luis claimed that the Latin Vulgate—the sacrosanct "Catholic Bible," recently reinforced by the Council of Trent—contained not only outright errors but, no less important, many infidelities to the spirit and nuances of the Hebrew original. Yet these elements are of essential importance in poetry, especially religious poetry. His goal, he said in his introduction, was to recapture the fine nuances missed by the Vulgate by finding the closest Castilian idioms that could express them. Thereby he was acting as an Erasmian humanist, going back to the original sources of the Word—and also as a Converso, seeking the deep truths of his Christianity in the mystical antecedents of his Hebrew ancestors. It was, we might say, the (possibly not fully aware) homecoming of the Converso—not outside Christianity, but within it.

This, and the envy of conservative colleagues, was sufficient for Fray Luis's arrest. He was never told who had denounced him, and remained unaware for a long time of the nature of the charges. Ascetic by temperament, he turned his long confinement into a spiritual journey, concentrating, cultivating his mind in solitude, writing personal poems, and drafting a book of "Christ's Names."

One of his poems on leaving jail reads:

> Here envy and lie
> Had locked me.
> Blissful the humble state
> Of a sage retiring
> From this evil world,
> Who with a poor table and house,
> In the delightful field,
> Passes his life in solitude
> Neither envied nor envious
> Measured only with God.[24]

Fray Luis's poems express a yearning for the purification of the soul through the discovery of its spirituality and interiority—leading to ultimate peace and oblivion.

> How peaceful is the person's life
> Who flees the world's vain noise,

> And follows the hidden path
> Trodden by the few sages
> Who have [ever] been in this world.[25]

Trained in scholastic theology, Luis de León sought to overcome its bareness by transforming its concepts into mystical images that transcend their own sensual substrate. This led him to poetry (and music), as a medium of spiritual elevation that serves theology by superseding it. Poetry can transform theological ideas into images and feelings that enable the soul to forget its earthly knowledge and desires, to surge above the world and beyond conceptual discourse. And music (as he wrote in an ode to Salinas, his musician friend) can be so attuned to the heavenly spheres that the soul discovers its true nature in these spheres and, regenerated, becomes oblivious of everything terrestrial and sensual.

> O blissful faint!
> O Death that gives life!
> O sweet oblivion!
> Let me remain in your repose
> And never be restored to this lowly, vile sense.[26]

This craving for "sweet forgetfulness" contrasts with the turmoil and "vain noise" of the world in which Fray Luis, a frequently agitated person, was actually involved as polemicist and reformer in the time of the Counter-Reformation.

In December 1576, after four and one-half years in jail, the tribunal found Fray Luis guilty of rash imprudence and ready for the rack. But the *suprema* in Madrid declined to ratify the verdict. Nine days later Fray Luis was released without a conviction, only a warning, and reinstated as professor in Salamanca.[27] When resuming his teaching, he famously began the first lecture with the words: "As we said yesterday. . . ." His long ordeal has shrunk into an instant, a mystical nonexistent, absorbed into Luis's person and intertwined with it.

Luis de León celebrated a minivictory a few years later when he was appointed to the Chair of Holy Scripture at Salamanca. But a spirit like his could not avoid some more friction with the Inquisition, which did not end in a trial. When appointed to a commission to correct the Latin Vulgate he refused to take part, arguing this would distance the Vulgate from the Hebrew original even more. His published writings (later collected in six volumes) included *The Perfect Married Woman*, a Christian-humanist guidebook that made him popular also among lay persons. But when he died in 1591 (at age sixty-four), his personal poems remained quite unknown; only the poet Francisco Quevedo published them in the next century.

16

Picaresque Antiheroes

A particularly distinct echo of the Converso experience resounds from the picaresque novel, a literary form that early modern Spain bequeathed to the rest of Europe.[1] It is significant that both the Conversos and the picaresque novel were specifically Spanish creations. The Spanish picaresque novel flourished in the sixteenth and into the seventeenth century. In its strict form, every story is narrated in the first person, as a fictional autobiography—or an ironic confession—by someone of base or dishonorable origins.[2] Born into the lower echelons of the social order, the narrator (known as *picaro*) conducts his life on the fringes of society, or outright among the underworld. Sometimes, however, the picaresque story is narrated in the third person or takes a dialogue form (as in Rojas's *La Celestina* and Cervantes's *Dog's Colloquy*). Because they revolve around the protagonists' base life and origin, all Spanish picaresque works reveal a hidden, officially forbidden universe which people of "good standing" and *honra* (social prestige) are not supposed to know, or to have any dealings with. Vividly, with astounding realism for the period, the reader is led into a world of rogues, beggars, servants, prostitutes, and petty criminals. We are introduced to their lingo and customs, values and forms of social intercourse—and to their unsavory, forbidden, yet alluring stories.

Picaro versus *Hidalgo* (or *Honrado*)

The picaro is the anti-*hidalgo* (and more broadly, the anti-*honrado*). He embodies almost everything held in contempt by the ruling Spanish values. Above all, he is invariably of base or impure extraction. In that he opposes the Spanish idea of *honra* and makes implicit fun of it. He is also roguish and deceitful, prone to using his inventive mind to devise schemes for surviving and enjoying his crude existence against major odds. This, of course, was part of the picaro's charm and success as a popular hero. Taking delight in the adventures of this rogue gave many readers a refreshing, if imaginary, sense of liberation. It also enabled them to transform their own protest against ruling social norms—especially *honra*, pure birth and social standing—into a form of aesthetic pleasure.

The picaresque literature manifested a special use of language, typical of esoteric (and oppressed) minorities, which can also be called "the language of the Marranos." Not much was explicitly said. Messages were passed by hint and allusion (sometimes crude, sometimes subtle and complicated), using dual meaning, jokes, quips, side stories, and fables, or attributing to people features and events that draw their significance from a covert layer of meaning. The picaresque genre thus provided ample opportunity for writers—and even more so for readers—to indulge in the chase after unsaid meanings and esoteric hints that only the initiated could grasp and enjoy.

Although the Marrano situation is not uniquely linked to the picaresque literature, it is highly relevant to it.[3] The picaro often speaks in the voice of the Converso, especially when recounting his origins, or attacking the ideals of *honra* and pure birth. The picaresque universe expresses an underground feeling and state of mind with which Marranos could symbolically identify. A group of allegedly "impure" newcomers, seeking—and lacking—actual integration in the host society (and sometimes concealment from it), New Christians could recognize their lot grotesquely reflected in the vicissitudes of their brother-in-impurity, the picaro. Converso readers would easily identify their "base (Jewish) extraction" and "impure blood" ironically reconfigured in the picaro's autobiography. Independently, they would recognize the duality of their own life expressed in the picture of a world behind the scenes, veiled by social conformity.

If there is an ideological message recurring in the picaresque literature (including Rojas's *La Celestina* and Cervantes's *Quijote* and several novellas), it is the challenge against the values of pure blood, descent, and nobility, and the stressing of what a person achieves by personal endeavor. A person's true value, the picaresque works tell us, is not dependent on the brute fact of his or her origin, but on what he has done and created himself, for which he can and ought to take responsibility. In that, the picaro plays a dual anti-hidalgo role: first, he is the opposite of the hidalgo *within* the dominant culture, and second, he (or rather, his author) attacks this very culture and its basic values.[4] In the first role he represents a Converso lot, and in the second he voices a distinct Converso ideology.

The picaresque use of language—the dual-talk characteristic of oppressed groups and minorities—drew from Marrano linguistic habits, and at the same time helped to develop their special linguistic sensibilities, the talent for ironic equivocation and reading between the lines. Moreover, there is a hidden ironic sense in which the picaro's first-person description of life in sin is a grotesque mirror image of a typical confession to the Inquisition.

The duality and equivocation in the picaresque work is not only logical, but also aesthetic. Not all readers enjoy the work in the same way. Though all would probably relish peering into an unknown world in which fleshy and robust things are going on behind the scenes, a sophisticated minority will take extra pleasure in piercing verbal masks, recognizing winks, ironies, and false moralism, and deciphering allusions to current situations. These include, in particular, the subculture arising from life under the Inquisition, and the various Marrano dualities abundant in Spanish society.

The typical picaresque situation is therefore created, I suggest, by the tension between these two drives—to tear the mask that covers reality, and to use other masks in doing so.

It follows that, even to the initiated, the picaresque mask of irony is *clear but not transparent*: we know it exists, but must decipher its particular instances, which often elude the alert reader, too. Readers must become amateur detectives and develop a special "ear," they must listen to nuances, detect the unsaid within (or opposing) the said, and often construct a counterstory within the one being told. But, unlike actual detectives who look for a hidden truth, the picaresque novel offers no perfect truth on either level. Its actual message—all the way to Cervantes[5]—is that truth, at least in Spain, no longer exists, or cannot be recognized in any pure form. Truth and mask have so penetrated each other that it is their interrelation, rather than any allegedly pure state, that, in different ways, marks life on all levels.

The Picaro as Semi-Converso

Four distinctive picaresque features stand in remarkable parallel to the Marrano situation: the narrator's lowly extraction and suspected "impure" blood; his being doomed to social exclusion, no matter what he or she (there were also *pícaras*) does for survival or ascent; the ubiquity of a covert real world opposing the Spanish normative world; and the unrelenting rebuke of hidalgo values and applause for personal achievement. All four were typical of the Marranesque experience, and are also the axes around which the original picaresque stories in Spain (as possibly distinguished from later English and French varieties) essentially revolve.[6]

The picaresque universe expresses an underground feeling and state of mind, with which Marranos could symbolically identify. In contrasting the official social values with a concealed reality behind them, the novels abound in specific hints invoking the life and psyche of Conversos. A group of allegedly impure newcomers, seeking integration in the host society (and sometimes concealment from it), New Christians could recognize their lot grotesquely reflected in the vicissitudes of their brother-in-impurity, the picaro. The picaro even often speaks in the voice of the Converso, especially when recounting his origins or attacking the ideals of *honra* and pure birth.

In addition to the features I mentioned, there is a strong *formal* analogy between the picaresque equivocations and the equivocal way in which Marranos had to mold their discourse. The Marranos had to live under a linguistic mask, and the picaresque use of language—that dual-talk characteristic of oppressed groups—drew from Marrano linguistic habits, which allowed insiders to communicate by code, hint, and metaphor while excluding outsiders from the game. Reciprocally, the picaresque literature helped to further develop Marranos' special linguistic sensibilities and talent for ironic equivocation and reading between the lines, which had first arisen out of a necessity for survival but acquired, with time, an added aesthetic value, enjoyable for its own sake.

We already noted that Spanish authors during the Golden Age were predominantly Conversos;[7] we should add that the small reading public also contained a relatively high number of Conversos. Golden ages are not a multitude phenomenon. During the Spanish *siglo de oro*, only one-fifth of the population could sign their names properly, and only a scant number of those read books. The usually literate Conversos, heirs to a Jewish tradition that their social roles helped maintain, were far more abundant among the readership than in the general population. And all Spanish readers and writers, whether New or Old Christian, were familiar with the pervasive Converso situation and sensitive to its traps and complexities.

As space permits us here to take no more than a brief glimpse into the rich and complex world of the picaresque, here are a few examples from the two founding novels of the genre, *The Life of Lazarillo de Tormes*, and *Guzmán of Alfarache*, and from certain episodes in Cervantes.

Lazarillo's Progress: *Válete por ti*

Like its first antihero, Lazarillo de Tormes, the picaresque genre was born an orphan. It had no definite date of birth, no solid lineage, and no known father. It burst into existence as a surprising novelty, its tongue hidden in its cheek. No one had ever read a work of fiction written this way. People even wondered (for a while) whether this could be a true autobiography. But, of course, it was fiction, and so refreshing. Success was immediate. But who was the author of *Lazarillo de Tormes*, the first "official" picaresque novel?[8] Certainly an intellectual, as most scholars believe; seemingly a humanist—an Erasmian reformer—and, judging by the content of his social criticism, undoubtedly a Converso. His origin and heterodox views were reason enough to desire anonymity.

Erasmianism was then being persecuted, and New Christians were held in constant suspicion.

While Américo Castro had spoken of the author's "Jewish line" (*estirpe judaica*),[9] Márquez Villanueva made an important modification: there is no Jewish content in the *Lazarillo*, but a distinctly Converso one.[10] The book contains an unforgiving satire of *honra*, a "corrosive attack" on hidalgo ideals, and shows hostility[11] toward organized church life—though no outright heresy. On the contrary, the anonymous author's anticlerical ardor can only be understood within a Christian framework, however heterodox.

Lazarillo's preface[12] is a mixture of irony and candor. At first ironizing on the theme of *honra*, the author then becomes straightforward: he has written *Lazarillo* in order that those who inherited noble estates will consider how little of it was their own due, since fortune has been partial to them; and how much more was achieved by those who, against fortune's opposition, have rowed with force and dexterity and landed in safe port.

This is a clear anti-hidalgo manifesto. It downgrades birth as the grounds for honor and standing and praises a person's own achievement as the true source of worth. In short—a Converso ideology. In the next chapter, Lazarillo's mother resumes the same Converso ideology in the three words she uses to bid farewell of her son: *válete por ti* ("help yourself," or "make yourself worthy by your own means"). Lazarillo's story would be the ironic realization of her exhortation.

Clear Converso hints also accompany Lazarillo's father's lot. The miller who used to pinch the contents of his client's sacks (the Converso who used to dissent from established norms?) was "persecuted for justice" (Matthew 5:10), "confessed and did not deny" (John 1:20), and after being "cast out" (in an *auto de fe*?), was sent to die in Christ's name fighting the infidel (was burned in Christ's name to save his heretical soul?). These ironic quotations from the New Testament boldly liken the delinquent father to a Christian martyr and invoke the lot of a Converso victim of the Inquisition who, although socially cast out, must be residing in God' glory because, says Lazarillo, the Bible promises: "Blessed are those who are persecuted for justice, for the kingdom of heaven is unto them."

This startling and funny reading of Matthew is not new; it comes from the *Celestina*, where it had been applied to the torture and execution of Parmeno's mother, a rather likable witch; and Conversos surely used it subsequently as a subversive proverb condemning the Inquisition.

It is the double equivocation in the phrase *por justicia*[13] ("for justice") that made this subversive reading possible. *Por* can mean both *by* and *because of*; and *justicia* can point to either the authorities of justice, or to a personal quality of justice. As a result, a person could be seen as persecuted either for reasons of justice (justly), or for being just (unjustly). The Spanish power structure favored the first reading; the Conversos—and Lazarillo and all marginals—preferred the second.[14]

We lack space to accompany Lazarillo in his peregrinations, but a few scenes may be mentioned.

His first master is a blind old rogue for whom Lazarillo serves as his eyes in the physical world. This master initiates the boy to human conniving and betrayal in the best pedagogical way—by practicing it himself. There is even an initiation rite. The old man lures Lazarillo to put his ear to a stone statue of a bull that, he promises, "makes a curious noise," and when the boy complies, the master smashes his head against the bull's horn. Lesson: never be so gullible, so trusting! "A blind man's boy must know more than the Devil!" he shouts, laughing. The bleeding and betrayed Lazarillo feels that his childhood is over. "I awoke from the child's simplicity in which I was sleeping." Now that he had learned to trust no one, he finds himself absolutely solitary and must consider "how I shall learn to help myself" (*cómo me sepa valer*).

Who else in Spain during the Inquisition felt so lonely, unable to trust anybody, and required to rely upon themselves alone, if not the Marranos? And what, in this literary context, does "knowing to help myself" allude to, if not Lazarillo's mother's Converso advice?

God's Face in Bread

Lazarillo's constant struggle against hunger becomes most intense under his next master, a priest so stingy that his house is clean of even dry leftovers of food. He locks all his food in a large wooden trunk and keeps a strict record of every item. Lazarillo is desperate. His only relief comes from funerals, where he shares in the crumbs of the burial meal; whenever an ailing person is blessed, Lazarillo silently prays for his death—so he can eat. Like a Marrano, he annuls in his heart what his lips are saying. He also wishes for his own death to come, but "it never came, although it was always within me."

It is the Host—Christ's body—that ironically becomes Lazarillo's salvation, though not in the way a true Christian would expect—not as a spiritual power— but in its pure material side. One day a locksmith visits the house while the priest is out, and Lazarillo gets him to fit a key to the food trunk. As the illicit key turns, the gates of heaven open and "the face of God beholds me from the ark"—in the form of luring bread loaves, consecrated bread that the priest is using as food. Though Lazarillo thinks he is saved, he remembers that his master keeps a strict record of the chest's contents, and must devise a plan to save himself (*válete por ti!*) by his own ruse. Observing that the trunk is slightly cracked, he breaks the bread into little crumbs and persuades his master that the chest is invaded by mice. That no trap can catch those mice and no repair can stop them from entering the chest remains a mystery, until the real mouse is caught, beaten to the point of unconsciousness, and thrown back into the street.

The metaphor of the desecrated Host is of particular significance here. Using holy bread as ordinary food is sacrilege, of course; but hadn't the priest committed this sacrilege even before Lazarillo did? And isn't the Church, by its crude materialism, committing it symbolically all the time? The Host is originally meant to be spirit in matter, the ineffable God as flesh: in flattening that mystical equivocation to its material side only, Lazarillo reenacts what the Church itself is doing. There is no God in this church, so Lazarillo's Erasmian author tells us, except in bread—that is, embodied in crude matter and utility. Religion to most clerics is exhausted in power, money, and gain—so they, too, accept the Eucharist only from its material side. Despite his irreverent tone, the (presumably Converso) author is not an atheist. Whatever he may think of the Host as dogma—and even if he entertains some doubts about its theoretical validity—he is offended by its desecration in practice. Both the picaro and the pope degrade God's incarnate body by using it for worldly purposes only. But, whereas for the starving Lazarillo it is perhaps natural to see nothing in the Host but physical food, for the Church to take this attitude is a depravity.

The Hungry Noble

The book's critical climax—and its most famous episode—is reached with Lazarillo's short tenure under the hungry *escudero* (nobleman, hidalgo). This walking parody of Spain's official ideals roams the streets of Toledo impeccably dressed, elegantly postured, speaking with grace, behaving with poise, carrying a high quality sword in his belt and not a single marevedi in his purse. He puts on a whole array of appearances "in order to save his dusky honor (*negra honra*)," says Lazarillo. Although he has not eaten for the whole day—indeed, for several days—he goes out into the street and picks his teeth with a straw, as if he had just enjoyed a luxurious meal. Using small lies and short-lived pretexts, he tries to conceal his true situation also from Lazarillo. But soon the boy discovers that his new master is not only penniless and unable to sustain himself, but their roles are reversed. Instead of finding himself a master who can feed him, it is up to Lazarillo (who alone can afford begging) to feed his starving master by granting him a few scraps of the food he collects in town as mendicant, all while pretending this is not happening. As the proud hidalgo graciously accepts the picaro's shoddy gifts, he pretends, with the boy's complicity, that he is consuming those scraps not for sustenance, but as a refined gastronomical experiment.

Just as Lazarillo's clerical masters represent the hollowness of external religion, so this grotesque *escudero* symbolizes the hollow secular ideal of *hidalguía*. Spain at the time swarmed with poor hidalgos refusing to work: their numbers and poverty resulted from the nature of this craved-for ideal, which was unproductive and could not be generalized without crippling society. The narrator uses this familiar phenomenon to portray the essence of the coveted hidalgo state—as being vacuous inside and built as mere facade. Similar thoughts run through Lazarillo's mind as he watches his master graciously walking toward the cathedral, his whole manner broadcasting satisfaction with his worthy self: "How many, Lord, have you spread in the world who, like him, are willing to endure for their dark [*negra*] *honra*, as they call it, that which they wouldn't suffer for the love of You?" This is one of the book's high points. The situation combines the two main picaresque themes—the pervasive mask covering Spanish life and values, and the antihidalgo ideology. Hidalgo ideals are vacuous both in themselves and because they become identical with the facade they project: the value of nobility, its very substance, resides in the appearance it assumes.

It is significant that, unlike his attitude to other masters, Lazarillo bears no grudge against the *escudero*, he neither hates him nor seeks to take vengeance on him, but pities him. That pity, the opposite of envy, helps the young picaro gain new insight into the widely coveted state of *hidalguía*. "God be my witness that to this day, when I meet someone of his kind, with that manner and pomp, I am chagrined by the thought that he is suffering like my own master had suffered." Thus, in the picaro's eye—which serves as our lens to a world behind the mask—the hidalgo ideal is destroyed, not only because it is incongruent with its enviable image, or linked to suffering for something hollow, but—ultimate shame—because it is made the object of pity by a picaro, the lowest and most dishonored of creatures.

Looking further, we see that the *escudero* is as much a victim of the value system he represents as are his opposite numbers—the picaros, the Conversos, the Moriscos, and all those of "inferior blood." When honor is placed in birth as its true source, personality shrinks to a minimum, indeed to zero, as the origin and carrier of worth. This makes for the familiar Spanish phenomenon of a person proud and satisfied with himself because he *is* himself, regardless of what he has *done* or *become*. His sense of merely being there, of sheer and contentless subjectivity, assures him a worth that he radiates for no other reason and is aggressively ready to defend. This attitude voids the self of all doing and becoming and identifies it with simple being. As generator of value, the Self is thereby made almost null, reduced to an inert fact called "blood," and graded in those terms. There is surely some self here, but it has no self-generated content by which to sustain and justify itself; in other words, it is empty. And because this empty self is all the hidalgo demeanor needs to justify itself, it actually derogates the self it wishes to extol. Lazarillo's New Christian ideology, however, seeks to break this iron-clad system and redefine honor so as to liberate not only those of impure blood, but the hidalgo as well.

Guzmán of Alfarache:
The Birth of the Picaro from the Death of Shame

The picaresque model assumed a final shape with *Guzmán of Alfarache*, the next founding novel of the genre. Of this lengthy classic we do have a birth certificate, complete with author's name and origin. It was written by Mateo Alemán, a Converso native of Seville, and published in Madrid in 1599 (part I) and 1604 (part II). Like *Lazarillo*, it is shaped as a fictitious autobiography of an "anti-honored" wanderer, but is far more elaborate, written in more profuse language, and more than ten times longer.

Mateo Alemán was a Converso ashamed of his origin and trying to conceal it. He was born in 1547 in Seville to Juana Enero and Hernando Alemán, a doctor who later served as surgeon of the royal prison. Alemán despised his father's medical profession as typically New Christian and refused to pursue it. In *Guzmán of Alfarache*, he refers to medicine as fit for "tailors' sons," by which he means the sons of Conversos who, barred from most other offices, cling to medicine as a typically Converso social ladder. The syndrome of Jews (and Conversos) interiorizing the social stain attributed to their stock and feeling incurably disgraced by it is well known in both Alemán's period and modern times. It explains, I think, Alemán's long homily against shame which, together with his attack on honor (of which shame is a condition), constitutes the main ideological drift in *Guzmán of Alfarache*.

Maurice Molho cites Alemán's several attempts to conceal his Converso origin. In presenting himself, Alemán omitted his mother's maiden name (Enero) because of its Converso ring. Sometimes he called himself "Mateo Alemán *de Ayala*," thus usurping a most prestigious Old Christian name. And he insisted that his father's ancestors had come from Germany (*Alemán* means "German"), implying that they were foreign Old Christians. (Guzmán, as we shall see, also makes a myth of his doubtful foreign origin.) Yet none of this tampering with his identity (which made him almost an impostor, like his hero) could erase the memory of the pyre on which one of Alemán's paternal ancestors was burned as a Judaizer in the time of Ferdinand and Isabella.[15]

The book opens with a dedication and two prefaces, "To the Vulgar" and "To the Prudent Reader." This immediately suggests a double audience and a dual voice, transmitting to the discerning reader things not intended for the vulgar. In a cryptic statement, Alemán says to the prudent reader: "I tell you much that I want to tell you; and leave out much unwritten, of which I write." In other words, even what he leaves unwritten is partly written between the lines.

Origin and Pilgrimage of Identity

Guzmán's whole itinerary, like Lazarillo's, is conditioned by the underlying attempt to overcome the problem of his origin. But whereas Lazarillo sought to do so by personal achievement, Guzmán is trying to find—or construct—a revised, higher identity for himself. In that he fails, and reluctantly accepts the partly deterministic nature of his lowly origin.

The story begins (a mark of the genre) with the description of Guzmán's "confused origin." His mother has an elderly spouse and a young lover, and when Guzmán is born, she convinces each of them that he is the father, so they both recognize the child as their own. Thus, Guzmán has two fathers, but isn't absolutely sure who had actually begotten him, or whether there hadn't been an obscure third party. Another reason for Guzmán's confused origin is his father's provenance. Assuming the younger man as the father, who was he? Guzmán places his paternal ancestors' origin in "the Levant," from where they moved to Genoa, and became "attached" (*agregados*) to the local nobility. Of their standing in Genoa he declares: "Although not natives of the place, I shall have to count them as such." It is to Genoa that Guzmán, since childhood, has looked upon as an ideal, a place in which to cast himself in a higher new identity. Genoa was his private Zion. Just as Jews and Marranos hope for return to their glorious origins in Jerusalem, so Genoa becomes Guzmán's place of redemption, in which to regain a presumed ancestral glory in addition to material relief. His wanderings in most of part I are structured as a pilgrimage to that city, even as a mock-messianic itinerary.

Guzmán also intimates that his paternal ancestors were ruthless money lenders, whose methods "hid the hands of Esau under the voice of Jacob."

What is Guzmán attributing to his father if not a Jewish origin? What European resident typically originated in the Levant? Who mixes but cannot integrate in a Christian city and society? Who, even when they "attach" themselves to the Christian elite (through apostasy, business ties, or an occasional marriage), must remain outsiders and will never be considered "natives" (as really belonging, or "Old Christians") except by a picaro's ironic verdict? Moreover, in the time of Shakespeare, the creator of Shylock, who were perceived as the worst money lenders in Italy (and therefore the world), hiding a "hand of Esau" under the literal "Jacob's voice?"

If those allusions are not enough, Guzmán goes on to attribute Judaizing Marrano behavior to his father. His mother had offered him a rosary with which the father had "to learn how to pray." Guzmán hastens to add "to pray in Castilian, I mean." But we know he is equivocating: his father, a Marrano, was learning to pray *like a Christian*. Guzmán's father manifested excessive external devotion, as many false converts did. Every morning he attended Mass on his knees, his hat raised up high. But evil tongues said (with "some foundation," Guzmán admits) that the man was using the hat to block his view of the ceremony and focusing his attention on the rosary so as not to hear the actual prayer in church. These were reputed Judaizing techniques.

Picaresque Semi-Asceticism

Driven by the passion to discover—or rather, revise—his origin, young Guzmán leaves his mother and, with no blind man to guide him, suffers through his own self-initiation. His life in sin does not produce actual gratification but a long sequence of privations and suffering, broken by temporary reliefs and unstable pleasures. As he leaves home he is more beaten than beating, exploited than exploiting, and hungry most of the time. In one episode after the other, his fellow hustlers and the rest of the world trick the hungry Guzmán into one trap after another. His successive privations look like a long *askesis*: the rogue's way is not far from its opposite, the ascetic's itinerary. The moral of the story is that one need not necessarily punish the picaro because his way of life does it already.

The only sin the picaro does not control is the "original sin" of his birth. This becomes a fate for him. From this perspective, the whole of world history can be seen as a picaresque tale emanating from an original Fall; and the actual picaros who, like Conversos, carry dishonor ("radical dishonor," in Molho's phrase) in their very being, specifically represent the falling side of humanity.

The Birth of the Picaro from the Death of Shame

Having endured his early woes, the hungry and aggrieved Guzmán considers turning back on his heels but is ashamed of what his mother and friends would say. Thus he learns the devastating power of shame. "How many things have

I seen lost because of 'I am ashamed'? How many maidens who ceased to be so? . . . how many fools ruined by guarantees they were ashamed to refuse?" The picaro is free of shame—that is, of the other's look and judgment—and this makes him free *simpliciter*. So Guzmán embarks on a long sermon denouncing social shame, together with its sibling, social honor.

This is the most important sermon in the book. Extended over three long chapters, it comes at a decisive moment—Guzmán's making of himself into a picaro— and expresses, albeit with some irony, one of the work's principal messages. The irony results from the fact that Alemán uses Guzmán's voice to say things that often sound out of character for his hero. Soon we realize that Guzmán's attack on shame does not challenge all normativity, for he approves of shame of oneself as a valid internal value. His forceful and persistent attack is directed against shame (and honor) in the external social sense, in which it depends on public conventions and the eye of the Other, and thereby alienates the Self. "It is of yourself you ought to have shame, so that you won't do vile and offensive things even in secret," Guzmán moralizes, almost like an Erasmian. As for shame in the common social sense, "Don't keep it as a dog at the door of your ignorance: give it a leash! let it run, trot away! For what you call shame is nothing but Necessity."

Shame is meaningless to a hard-nosed, confident picaro. Indeed, it is by renouncing shame that one becomes a picaro in the first place. This is also Guzmán's case:

> Seeing that I was lost, I started fulfilling the choice office of a picaro. The shame that in the past had stopped me . . . I lost on the road, as I was marching on foot and it was so heavy I couldn't bear it; or perhaps it was stolen together with my cape's head-cover. I started to harden up: Whatever was left in me of shame, I turned into uninhibitedness. . . . I understood that my former shame was lack of confidence.

His deliberate loss of shame is what turns him into a rogue: this is his investiture, his self-initiation as picaro. And with his shame gone, he hardens up and acquires self-confidence in his new role. But here Guzmán's voice starts running ahead of his creator's, for Alemán never succeeded in fully overcoming his shame of being a Converso. He knew, and argued from Guzmán's mouth, that this shame was unjustified, but was not as confident as his hero in rejecting it. Indeed, through his protagonist, Alemán is here pleading with himself. He too is part of Guzmán's intended audience.

But he also has bigger audiences and targets. One of those is no less than the Inquisition, which stands to lose much of its power if social shame is abolished. The greatest public or social shame in Hapsburg Spain was an *auto de fe*; second to it was a verdict of impure blood, and both were administered by the Inquisition. Thus, in repudiating social shame, the Converso Mateo Alemán (hiding behind the immoral Guzmán) threatens to undermine the effectiveness of two of the Inquisition's most fearsome weapons.

Genoa: Deception and Turning Point

Guzmán's itinerary is shaped from the start by a kind of Marrano *esperanza*—to find his redemption in Genoa. But when, after many adventures, he finally gets to Genoa, his presumed family does not recognize him and inflicts a burning humiliation on him. Hurt and disillusioned, he flees and continues his wanderings in Italy. But later he returns to Genoa disguised as a nobleman and takes revenge on his "family." He organizes a sting operation that robs them of a huge fortune, then disappears into a ship that carries him back to Spain, physically and mentally.

The ship's captain, a Florentine gentleman, has been persuaded to collaborate in the sting by the following argument: "I have no other honor than that which I inherited from my father . . . but since a traitor and enemy has stolen it, I live without it [honor] and *have to win it by my own hands and effort* [meaning here: by the sting]" (My emphasis). This is a cheerful equivocation and a major statement in the book. Guzmán is using the captain's traditional values (honor, requital) to declare a change in his own values. He lets the captain think that by *honor* he means *property*, when he literally means *honor*. Thus we get two messages in one. To the captain Guzmán says: "Since my father's inheritance was stolen and no one cares, I must avenge myself with 'my own effort and hands'; so please help me!" But to himself (and to us, his "prudent readers") Guzmán here is summing up his life's voyage and decides to change course. His tacit self-message reads: "Since Genoa has robbed me of the dream to find honor by revising my origin, I must now rely on my own efforts and deeds alone." It is as though Guzmán is telling himself in the voice of Lazarillo's mother: *válete por ti*. What had been Lazarillo's motto from the start becomes in Guzmán a life-changing resolution. This makes it part of the story's narrative core. From now on Guzmán practices the rogue's way for its own sake, with no higher goal in sight.[16]

In the end, Genoa turns out to have been a myth. Guzmán realizes the nullity of his attempt to construct a new origin for himself and reluctantly admits his inferior New Christian lot as inalterable. It can only be concealed and, within limits, fought against, but remains a crushing fact weighing down on whatever liberty he possesses.

Picaro versus Converso

The author, Alemán, did not follow Guzmán's example in Genoa. He did not give up hope for social integration, but emigrated to Spanish America to seek it there. Nor did Alemán renounce honor; he only demanded that it emanate from sources other than birth. In short, he was not a picaro. This should remind us that although in ironic exaggeration, the picaro embodies some of the Conversos' concerns and problems (blood, *honra*, hope, social exclusion, personal qualities versus birth status, the need for masks), they are two distinct figures. This is best illustrated in the distinction between Guzmán and his creator. The picaro is society's radical Other, the Converso is its Other Within.

The Hidalgo-Picaro of La Mancha

Was Cervantes of Converso origin? There are strong indications that he was, but they are not conclusive.[17] When trying to get a job in Rome as chamberlain to a Spanish prelate,[18] Cervantes was required to produce a certificate of pure blood, which he did. But this tells us little: such certificates were procured for a fee by operators making a living on Spain's racial prejudice. For our present purpose, what matters is Cervantes's awareness and state of mind, and there is no shred of a doubt that the Converso problem, with its pure blood aspect and the Inquisition at the background, was very much on Cervantes' mind—if not as a personal cloud hanging over his life, then as an endemic problem affecting Spanish life and culture in his time. Cervantes's work amply illustrates his awareness of the dialectic of suspicion and fear, hiding and concealment that the Converso problem provoked, and of the funny, often grotesque, situations it created.

Cervantes joins the picaresque authors in sniping at the sacred cows of Counter-Reformation Spain: the cult of *hidalguía* and pure blood; the life-constraining religiosity, which many people do not really observe, but pay lip service to; the drive for unity—or for religious and cultural uniformity—that is so wonderfully (and confusedly) refuted by life's diversity; the official culture of heroism undermined by a covert materialism (which, however, is not all that wrong). The result is a dual, inverted world and a web of contradictions in which one pole inextricably sends to the other.

Just as the picaro is the anti-hidalgo, so *Don Quijote* (the book, not the personage) is an anti-hidalgo critique; and the Knight of La Mancha, fighting the windmills on his bony Rocinante, is in this respect akin to the starving *escudero* in *Lazarillo de Tormes*.

Cervantes's full title reads: *The Ingenious Hidalgo Don Quijote of La Mancha.* It is the *hidalgo* in Don Quijote (and *hidalguía* in general) that is being satirized here, no less than this particular figure, the famous hidalgo-picaro from La Mancha. The critique of *hidalguía* wears in *Don Quijote* the ironic disguise of an attack against novels of chivalry—the extreme and by then worn-out literary offshoot of the system of hidalgo values. Cervantes's statement of purpose is thus his first ironic act. It was less dangerous to appear to be merely attacking some bookish, literary fashion than to challenge, as the book actually does, the core of Spanish social values. The most persistent voice in Spain demanding to replace the values of blood, lineage, and *hidalguía* with personal merit and achievement belonged to Conversos. So, by incorporating this issue into *Don Quijote*'s main concerns, Cervantes voiced a standpoint (and ideology) known to be linked especially to Conversos.

The Converso experience is embodied also in the aesthetic form of the *Quijote*. The book is shaped as an ongoing play of masks and the reversals of appearance and reality. Every other character is wearing a mask, or assumes a different appearance from what he or she is said to be in "real" conditions—to the point that reality and unreality are no longer well distinguished. In part II, even the line between the story and the outside world is blurred, as Don Quijote plays the role of a "real" figure in his own story. This amplifies the play of dual perspective and mask that is going on in the book from the start—with women being disguised as men, men as women, noblemen as shepherds, Moors as Christians, swindlers as pilgrims;[19] and of course, the petty gentleman Quijano/Quijada/Quesada as a medieval knight-errant, the peasant Sancho Panza as governor of an "island," and the Duke's men as his "subordinates." Objects in the real world (windmills, clouds, wine casks, a barber's bowl) also take on disguises and appear as what they are not, to at least one person in the story—the main protagonist.

Other problems of identity concern the author and his hero. The official author is not Cervantes but a fictional Moor, Cide Hamete Benengeli (Cervantes poses as his translator, so he has a different voice), and Don Quijote's actual name remains obscure—it could be Quijada, but also Quesada or Quijano.

Clues to the Inverted World

A recurring theme is the inverted world symbolized by "Mambrino's helmet"— the broken barber's basin that Don Quijote feigns to be the helmet of a legendary knight. Referring to the fact that no one but himself recognizes Mambrino's helmet in the basin, Don Quijote asks Sancho (and Cervantes tells the reader):

"Did you notice that in the itinerant knight's affairs, *everything is upside down*, the upper thing is low and the low is up?" (I, 25).[20] Here an ironic writer plants a clue for those who understand. As for the uninitiated majority, Don Quijote says a little later: "If Mambrino's helmet looks to most people like a common barber's basin, [if Cervantes's work seems univocal to them] so much the better, for they will not try to possess it [they will miss its dangerous allusions and won't try to unearth them]."[21]

First Adventures

Alongside the Conversos, the Inquisition also makes an early appearance in the story. Following his short first round of adventures, Don Quijote is carried back home beaten and shattered. To save his soul from further folly and his body from further beatings, a rigorous censorship and inquisition is performed on his library, complete with public burning (I, 6). The biblio-inquisitors are Don Quijote's friends, the local barber and priest, who, encouraged by his solicitous housekeeper, check his library to decide which books ought to be "released to the housekeeper's secular arm." The phrase *releasing to the secular arm* was the euphemism used by the Inquisition to signify a sentence of death by burning. The Holy Office, based on love, never sheds blood—that task was left to the secular authorities, to whom the culprit was "released." The pious self-deception involved in this approach was an inviting target for Cervantes's poignant but prudently phrased irony. The allusion to the "housekeeper's secular arm" clearly presents the library scene as a mock *auto de fe*. A still sharper irony awaits us later when we learn that the *auto de fe* has failed to save its object, and Don Quijote, refusing to be "reconciled" (to ordinary life), starts out wandering again—a "relapsed" knight errant.[22]

This is a key scene in the book, for it begins and underlies the main body of adventures. Henceforth Don Quijote is a *relapso* (a heretic [or Judaizer] who resumes his illicit activities after an *auto de fe*). Don Quijote is just as hooked on his chivalric (hidalgo) heresy against reality as other relapsos, who deserved and got the flames, were hooked on their religious heresies against the church.

Sancho's "Promised [Is]Land"

Cervantes's reproof of the blood-purity laws often rides on the issue of Sancho Panza's origin. The matter is first mentioned (in I, 20) by Cide Hamete Benengeli, the fictional "author" of the *Quijote* with whom Cervantes, as fictional "translator," sometimes plays games. Don Quijote is about to leave on a dangerous and lonely mission and assures Sancho he has provided for him in case he does not return; but should God bring him back safe, then Sancho "can be more than sure that the promised island will be his." With great emotion, poor Sancho bursts into tears and decides he will never forsake his master—until that affair is concluded. At this point the "author" remarks that Sancho's "honorable resolution" proves he "must have been well born, at least an Old Christian." Actually it was Don Quijote who acted nobly, whereas Sancho responded to his gesture with common utilitarianism and self-interest: he will not leave his master—until he gets his island! The non-noble nature of Sancho's response refutes the racist link between Old Christian blood and noble feelings that the fictitious author, echoing the major prejudice of Spanish society, tries to establish. The true author— Cervantes—denies such a link exists and makes fun of it by letting the fictitious author use the crude, self-serving Sancho Panza as his illustration. If Sancho is an untainted Old Christian, perhaps we should conclude that a noble disposition is *not* exactly guaranteed by an Old Christian origin.

But is Sancho indeed an Old Christian? Officially he is, yet his constant hope to attain his island—his promised island *(la prometida ínsula)*—sounds like a parody of the Judaizing Marranos' famous hope to reach the promised land, their redemption from religious servitude in Iberia. The structural similarity between the two hopes and the concept of a *promised island* that mimics a *promised land* is too outstanding to be ignored. Actually, Sancho's hope and its illusory fulfillment in part II, belong to the *Quijote*'s narrative plot, and thereby a Marranesque feature is planted in the book's underlying structure.

A little further in the story, Don Quijote portrays a poor knight errant— himself—rising to become duke, king, even emperor; but a cloud hangs over him: his origin, his blood. How will he persuade the king to give him his daughter if he cannot prove the merit of his lineage? His whole dialogue with Sancho now turns into an ironic discourse about the problem of blood purity that had haunted Cervantes personally, along with many other Spaniards. That the issue here is not just the cult of lineage in general, but specifically the anti-Converso laws that barred people of impure blood from public office and honors, becomes exceedingly clear in the following exchange between Sancho and Don Quijote.

—"By God," said Sancho, *"I am an Old Christian, and that is enough for being a count."* [my emphasis]

—"Quite enough," said don Quijote. "But it would not matter if you weren't [an Old Christian], for when I am king I can grant you nobility without you having to purchase it or earn it by service . . . and let gossips say what they will."

—"I swear[23] I will know what to do with my indignity [*litado*]," said Sancho.

—"You should say dignity [*dictado*, meaning title or office] and not indignity," said his master. (I, 21)

The language and content of this witty, allusion-packed exchange are those of the blood-purity statutes. "I am an Old Christian and that is quite enough for being a count" is, for the purpose of our study, one of the most significant quotations in the book. It is the sharpest mockery of the blood-purity statutes and a clear sarcasm in favor of its victims. And it links directly onto Sancho's fancy *esperanza*, his Marrano-like dream of the "promised island," which provides a narrative thread to the whole work, including part II.

Incidentally, the formula "let gossips say what they will" (or "let us not indulge in gossip") recurs also in the *Dog's Colloquy*, where it usually hints that Cervantes has someone specific in mind. By using this code phrase, Cervantes tells the alert reader: it is too dangerous or awkward for me to specify the person or social institution I am aiming at; so it is up to you to figure out who is intended. Thus the ironic admonition "let us not indulge in gossip" is actually a call to do precisely the opposite.

The Prisoners' Cortege

While master and squire are discussing their glorious future a procession of convicts approaches, linked by an iron chain (I, 22). Sancho observes that they are sent to do forced labor on the king's galleys, but Don Quijote only sees that "they are led where they do not wish to go," so he starts reflecting on the topic of coercion (and will), which becomes the underlying theme of this chapter, as its title also indicates.

Thereby, a Marrano subtext enters this scene. Marranos were coerced converts; they are also choice candidates for a procession of convicts—the *auto de fe*, which makes a new appearance here.

Don Quijote is scandalized by the thought that the king should coerce people against their will. "Can this be true?" he asks. "No," says Sancho, "these men are judged by law." "But they are coerced all the same ?!" "Yes," says Sancho, who must concede the obvious point. The question of whether these convicts *deserve* their punishment is disregarded by the "lunatic" Don Quijote (as it would be if one doubted the justice of the Inquisition, but were too prudent to say so): the issue of just punishment is too dangerous to invoke in inquisitorial Spain. Still, to maintain the necessary facade and make for a good picaresque story, Cervantes describes most prisoners as crafty villains—a thief, a debaucher, a briber, and so forth—but leaves out a few ambiguous cases.[24] Thus one is a melancholy lad whose crime, says a friend, is that he was a "canary," singing and playing. "What!" Don Quijote exclaims."Is playing and singing a reason for [arresting and] sending someone to the galleys?" The answer is known to any Converso who, at some time or other, has sung a Hebrew chant or prayer in nostalgia (as did Diego Arias d'Avila).[25] The allusion to the Inquisition is hidden here within another: "singing" in the colloquial sense of admitting a crime under torture.

The Sad Knight in His Cage

In its concluding chapters we see the poor, gentle, wise lunatic being ingloriously transported home in a cage led by his friends, the barber and the village priest. The frustrated Sancho himself has meanwhile become so deluded that he prods Don Quijote to escape and resume his adventures (I, 49). To the priest who lures Don Quijote home on false pretense, Sancho bitterly complains: "If your grace had not interfered, my master would by now have married Princess Micomicona, and I would be Count, at least" (I, 47). On hearing this, the barber explodes: "Have you joined your master's order of lunatics? You may as well join him in his cage! Damned be the hour when you were stuck[26] with his promises and with that island to which you so aspire!"

Sancho retorts:

> Nobody sticks anything into me [screws me], not even a king; and although I am a pauper, I am an Old Christian and owe nothing to no one; if I desire an island, others desire worse things. Everyone is the child of his deeds, and since I am a man I can become Pope, or at least governor of an island, for my master can gain so many islands there will be no one to give them to. (Ibid.)

This is a delightful pack of contradictions. Sancho boasts his Old Christian origin in the then-familiar voice of poor commoners who vaunted their lack of Jewish blood—and their hatred of Conversos—as an advantage over the higher classes who were unable to claim such distinction. Yet in the same breath, Sancho makes two explicit New Christian statements: first, "every man is the child of his deeds" (thus contradicting his claim to the governorship on the merit of his blood), and second, "because I am a man I can become Pope, or at least governor." The notion that being simply a *man* (rather than a hidalgo) suffices as basis for social ascent and high office was very daring and subversive for its time. In holding this protohumanist view Sancho again speaks like a Marrano, even while denying that he is one. Thus he speaks in the voices of both the Marranos and their worst enemies. What is significant is not that the famous squire contradicts himself—that is normal in Sancho—but that Cervantes uses a Marrano-related theme at each pole of this contradiction.

The "Promised Island" Made Good

It is in part II of the *Quijote*, published ten years later, that Sancho's Marrano-like hope (*esperanza*) for "the Promised Island" is finally fulfilled. A jesting duke, an avid reader of part I of *Don Quijote* who entertains our heroes and pretends to believe their fantasies, announces his intention to appoint good Sancho governor of "the Island of Barataria," as one of the duke's castles is rebaptized for the occasion.

In a speech full of (true) political wisdom, Don Quijote offers advice to the future governor (II, 42–43). (Don Quijote's lunacy, the author reminds us, concerns only his knighthood.) An important counsel inevitably refers to Sancho's blood and low birth. "Never try to conceal your origin," Don Quijote insists (II, 42), and "never get into argument about lineage"(II, 43). In other words, don't boast of your Old Christian origin as compensation for your lowly birth.[27] If you rely on good deeds and virtues, which are your own doing, "you won't have to envy lords and princes; for blood is inherited, whereas virtue is acquired—and virtue is more valuable than blood."

Thus Sancho, the self-styled Old Christian, upon realizing a Marrano-invoking dream, mounts his throne with the blessing of a New Christian ideology and advice.

The eleven chapters devoted to Sancho's tenure as governor of "Barataria" bring to a climax Sancho's improbable hope and expectation, and thereby establish this semi-Marrano pattern as a major element in the book's underlying plot. The hilarious details of Sancho's governorship lie beyond our scope here; to us, the episode is important because the Marranesque feature of Sancho's hope, established in part I, attains its mock fulfillment here, and thereby is confirmed as a structural pattern of the whole book.

A Donkey in Sanbenito

Toward the end of part II (68–69), the Inquisition comes back into the story in a vivid and caustic way. In a sudden unexpected raid, Don Quijote and Sancho are encircled and captured by a group of silent horsemen who refuse to give a reason for this abrupt arrest (exactly the procedure of the Inquisition). Then master and squire are taken to a nearby castle where a mock *auto de fe* takes place. A girl lies in the middle of the courtyard, flanked by candles and apparently dead. On a nearby podium the duke and duchess are seated amidst a crowd of spectators, accompanied by two stately figures (again, as in an *auto de fe*). Sancho is made to wear the dreaded sanbenito, the humiliating garb worn by convicts of the Inquisition, and to put on the head-cover that, Cervantes says explicitly, "penitentiaries of the Holy Office use to carry." Dressed in this apparel, the poor squire (his claim to having Old Christian blood notwithstanding) is subjected to grotesque beatings and pricking, applied in a ritual manner recalling the torture (or penance, or both) of the Holy Office. The goal is to bring back to life the beautiful Altisidora, who died of a broken heart when Don Quijote failed to return her love. The guilt-stricken Don Quijote prods Sancho to accept his "martyrdom" with patience, and the miracle occurs: fair Altisidora (actually a servant who got tired of lying motionless) rises from the dead to the public's cheers and applause.

This scene of "martyrdom" and "resurrection" is the equivalent of salvation in Cervantes's parody. The penance suffered in an *auto de fe*, including the burning of dead culprits' bones, was supposed to free the convicts from hell and help them go to paradise, just as Sancho's pains were to raise Altisidora from the dead.

The satire becomes darker when Sancho naively asks permission to keep his sanbenito and convict's hood as souvenirs. Yet in the end, Sancho (again naively) and Cervantes (not so innocently) take revenge on the repulsive trophy by finding the most proper place for it. In Don Quijote's final homecoming, as he and Sancho ride back into their village, the barber and priest are amazed to see Sancho's gray donkey's head crowned with a pointed convicts hood and the animal's body covered with a sanbenito, complete with the tongues of fire (II, 73). With the grotesque donkey-in-sanbenito entering the village, the curtain falls on the adventures of Don Quijote and Sancho Panza.

The sanbenito-clad donkey is therefore not an occasional joke, a passing episode, but a concluding statement. It raises the modest donkey to the same metaphorical level as Rocinante and Sancho Panza. Together, these metaphors add up to a strong Converso-inclined outlook. The bony Rocinante represents what is left of the worth and viability of *hidalguía*; the self-serving Sancho illustrates (among other things) that "pure" Old Christian blood is a meaningless criterion of merit; and finally, the striking image of the donkey in sanbenito represents Spain under the yoke of the Inquisition. It suggests that the true donkeys are the Spaniards who allow the Holy Office to put their country in a sanbenito. To this view, Cervantes's final statement in the *Quijote*, many Spaniards and almost all Conversos would subscribe.

PART SIX

Dispersion and Modernity

In this part we turn to two related topics: the Marrano cosmopolitan Dispersion, and the ways in which the Marrano experience anticipated, and possibly accelerated, certain main features of modernity.

17

Marranos Globalized:
The Networks, the "Nation"

The Marrano Archipelago

The Marrano experience was not confined to Iberia alone. From early on, despite recurrent prohibitions, Marranos had been emigrating outside the peninsula. Some crossed the Pyrenees to nearby France, others set base in northern Europe or the Mediterranean basin, or sailed as far as Lima in America and Goa in India. By the middle of the seventeenth century they had created a worldwide network of Hispano-Portuguese settlements, an archipelago of islands partly interacting with their environment, into which Marranos imported their Iberian languages, culture, customs, commercial links, and skills, together with their specific Marrano disquiet and split identities.

What drove them to emigrate? Beyond the evident reasons—persecution by the Inquisition, new economic opportunities, or the sense of being personally shut in—there was also the Renaissance spirit of venture and exploration. Marranos were Iberians to the bone. They belonged to the great maritime empires whose daring ventures broke the confines of the known world. Spanish and Portuguese explorers were discovering new lands, peoples, foods, products, and ocean routes, thereby extending the European imagination far beyond the confines of the closed, locally bound medieval mind. This stirred even greater excitement and wonder than our modern travels to the moon and, eventually, Mars.

Already in 1492, Marranos had backed Columbus's mission and were present on his ships. It is not impossible that the first European who set foot in the new continent of America was Luis de Torres, Columbus's Marrano interpreter who, as Cecil Roth suggests, may have tried his Hebrew on the native Indians.[1] A generation later, converted Jews took part in Hernán Cortés's expedition to Mexico. Two of them were later punished by the Inquisition, not for their betrayal of the Aztecs, but of Jesus. Meanwhile, Iberian Jews started creating commercial agencies in other parts of Europe. About 1512, the ultrarich Mendes family was already operating in Antwerp, where it built a commercial empire whose famous heiress, Doña Gracia Mendes-Nasi, eventually escaped to Istanbul, and together with her nephew, Juan Miques (alias Don Yosef Nasi, alias Duke of Naxos), played a major role in Jewish international politics. Less sensational cases of foreign settlement continued throughout the sixteenth century.[2]

It was mainly as international traders that Marranos participated in the new spirit of venture and expansion. The prominent French historian, Fernand Braudel, speaks of the "age of the great Jewish merchants."[3] Actually, the Marrano global presence reached its zenith in the second half of that century, after which, declining but active, it lasted to the end of the eighteenth century. With ups and downs, this remarkable phenomenon roughly covered the entire period of early modernity, from the discovery of America to the French Revolution. During its peak (around 1680), ships owned by Marranos were sailing all the major maritime routes, linking Europe to America, the Levant, Africa, India, East Asia (Indonesia, China, the Philippines) and over the Pacific Ocean to America again. They carried all the new products that Europe had discovered in America—cocoa, tobacco, and, above all, cane sugar, the new hit of world trade. They also carried older lucrative cargoes such as spices, textiles, metals, silks, grains, salt, lumber, diamonds—and slaves.[4] Like other merchants, Marranos even traded with enemy countries in time of war: this was the mercantilist era and trade was a separate affair, aloof from ordinary politics and morality.[5]

Trading in the New World was a hazardous business, quite different from the conservative, somewhat sedentary practices that give the word *merchant* its boring sound. By crossing the pale of the Old World, traders went out into a global cold. They could no longer rely on the relative reassurance of familiar routes and practices. World trade lacked important instruments that make it safer and streamlined today. There was no central banking system and no reliable mechanism of foreign exchange; insurance was in its infancy, and no agreement existed about the law of the seas. Each maritime power claimed parcels of the ocean to itself and followed a naval code of its own. International law was nonexistent, merely an incipient idea in the mind, not surprisingly, of a Dutch scholar, Hugo Grotius, who advocated free navigation to all.[6] Under those anarchic conditions, traders operated in a rough environment. Their treasured investment was at the mercy, in addition to the usual storms and pirates, of faraway swindlers, disloyal debtors, covetous local authorities, military blockades, and, in Iberia, confiscations by the Inquisition. Often the ship owners and captains had to practice contraband, diplomacy, and espionage to save their venture.

Trust: The Rarest Commodity in the World

It was imperative to tame those hazards, and Marranos, because of their in-group ties and loyalties, had a special advantage in this respect. Spread around the trading world (their settlements were almost always located near a seaport or large river), Marranos formed partial networks that provided a measure of confidence and stability to members of the network and their associates. A Marrano in Amsterdam could serve another Marrano in Bordeaux, Brazil, Hamburg, Curaçao, Porto, or the Philippines, as a relatively dependable correspondent, honor his letters of exchange, cash or accept his IOUs in payment or collateral, swap or barter cargoes with him, conceal his true identity when necessary, and bail, ransom, or bribe his ships out of trouble in foreign ports.

Thus, beyond sugar and pepper, beyond cocoa and tobacco and the other modern goods—the Marrano networks provided the rarest commodity in that world—*trust*.

Of course, the personalized nature of this system ruled out a single, overall network. There was a plurality of partial Marrano networks that occasionally crossed-linked.[7] And there were, expectedly, conflicts and tricks played between Marranos. The system knew frictions and partly depended on chance. But it gave the Marranos a distinct relative advantage over their competitors.[8]

Premodern Globalization

In pure business terms, the Marrano networks created the first, albeit fragmented, premodern model of economic globalization. Unlike other traders, the Marrano system was not confined to a particular zone or empire, but cut through all the empires and trading spheres of that era—Spanish, Portuguese, Dutch, English, French, Venetian, Ottoman (the "Levant"), and northern European. In that respect their system was truly global. Yet the Marrano model was premodern—not because it was thin or small (models usually are), but because the Marrano networks lacked streamlined coordination, and their system was based on personal and qualitative foundations rather than quantitative and impersonal ones. A distinctive characteristic of modern globalization is the anonymity of capital movements and exchange, and of the mechanism that guarantees them. Modern money has no personality; it drives itself, so to speak, as does the overall system, while name-bearing persons and institutions are practically the system's servers or functionaries. Not so in the Marrano networks, wherein trust was personalized, quantities depended on the quality of relations, members were linked by clan or "Nation," and the question of *who is who* was often more important than *how much*.

"Blood" as Asset: The Secularized Basis of the "Nation"

It can be said that the Marrano world traders managed to convert the distinctive "blood" that was attributed to them from liability to asset. The Jewish origin that barred their way to honored occupations in Iberia became a trump card in the field of international commerce. "Impure blood" could, after all, be good for business! The reliance on ethnic links signified a basic secularization of the Marranos' group ties. What basically united them was not necessarily religion, but their shared origin and common Converso experience and predicament (and this was coupled by similar life conditions in a dispersed archipelago of islands of their own, marked by their imported cultural features). Purely religious divisions, although they sometimes led to bitter fights within a community and even a family, did not necessary set a barrier to commercial partnership. The same trading network could include secret Judaizers in Seville or Mexico, assimilated Catholics in Antwerp or Toulouse, openly practicing Jews in London or Curaçao, perhaps a maverick convert to Calvinism, and any kind of wavering, agnostic, or freethinking Marrano. In consequence, even though individuals could be and remain personally religious, the *social* link and framework that united them—the Nation, as Marranos were known everywhere—was basically secularized (see also chap. 12).

The secularization of these links does not mean that religion had no role in creating the special relations between Conversos, but that its role was neither primordial nor necessary. We have seen comparable patterns in earlier generations. Remember Doña Elvira, wife of Diego Arias d'Avila, who used to participate in her Jewish clan's holidays, politics, and family events, while remaining Catholic and having no Jewish intent. In such cases of "social Judaizing," as we called them, the ethno-historic link took precedence over the religious.[9]

Diaspora or Constellation?

The Marrano Dispersion is often called a "diaspora," but the term is misleading. A diaspora implies there is a center, and one's identity somehow revolves around it. Iberia was neither the actual nor the normative center of the Dispersion. Spain and Portugal were *parts* of the system rather than its core. Marranos abroad could hardly view Iberia, with its two Inquisitions and ingrained racist policies, as the heart of their identity or the object of a nostalgic "myth of return."[10]

More appropriate to the Marrano Dispersion, I think, is the image of an archipelago—a system of separate but linked islands—or perhaps better, a constellation—a group of large and small stars with varying degrees of brightness, forming a loose system without an organizing core.[11] Over the decades and centuries, shining stars in this constellation dimmed (Antwerp, Ferrara, Dutch Brazil), other stars shone with great luster—Amsterdam, Livorno, Salonica—while new suns joined the system (Hamburg, London, Curaçao), followed by comets and satellites from Mozambique to Danzig—and, sprayed as star dust in between, were individuals or families operating in dozens of places around the globe.

Apart from their Marrano mentality, they all shared a kind of lay émigré culture. Marranos in Holland, Germany, India, and the Bahamas spoke Portuguese, read and wrote in Spanish, and emulated the elegant Iberian civilization and its often ceremonious manners (which gave the *Sephardim* a sense of superiority over the coarser *Ashkenazi* and Levantine Jews and, in some places, also over the non-Jews). Yet these were all the shadows of Iberia, not its substance. This was a basically alienated culture, secluded in social islands and maintained by émigrés and dissenters. In partial analogy, Jewish refugees from Nazi Germany often clung to their German culture while being estranged from the German polity and nation. The difference is that most of the German-Jewish exiles eventually integrated into their host societies in Israel and the United States, whereas the dispersed Marranos clung more persistently to their separate identity and lay Iberian heritage, which, in its diminished émigré form, had become a constitutive mark of their Nation. As a result, unlike other émigrés, they had no homeland to look back to, but had their émigré situation as homeland.

A Commercial Mirror-Image of Judaizing

Although Iberia was part of the constellation, it sometimes provided a hub for complex transactions. In a street in Lisbon known as *Nueve-des-Marchands*, "letters of exchange can be honored in any European currency," said a contemporary.[12] Some transactions were illegal and had to be secret because they involved heretical New Jewish *relapsos* or foreign enemies of the crown. A Marrano in Seville would serve as covert intermediary to a kinsman in Hamburg exchanging goods with another Spanish Marrano on their way to a trusted associate in Peru. Or, during the Spanish-Dutch war, an Amsterdam Marrano would hide behind a straw agent in Madrid—and behind false papers, aliases, and even fake ship names—to conduct business in the Spanish Empire. A clandestine business culture evolved in consequence, a commercial mirror image of the religious practice of Judaizing. And as in Judaizing, practitioners developed the spirit of secret semifraternity.[13]

To fool the Inquisition, Marrano traders used multiple identities. "Everyone has three different names!" a Spanish royal agent wrote in exasperation.[14] An Amsterdam Marrano would use his Jewish name at home and his Spanish or Portuguese name in his business abroad. Samuel Yahya of Hamburg was Alvaro Diniz, Moshe Abensur was Paulo Millão, Jacob Rosales was Immanuel Boccario, and Abraham and Isaac Seneor (Hamburg magnates who supplied the Swedish royal court) were known in Stockholm as Diogo and Manuel Tixeira.[15] The Marrano duality was thus stamped with a duality of names, Hebrew and Hispanic, one expressing the Jewish persona, the other the cosmopolitan persona; and the point is that none was the "true" or "actual" name. Even among Judaizers and New Jews, the Hispano-European name was no less the person's own—perhaps even more indicative of his actual life. There was neither similitude nor a possible hierarchy between the two identities—the Marrano was both of them, alternately and at once.

The "New Jews"

Although the Nation included emigrants of different religious and irreligious tendencies, its most conspicuous members (and best known to historians) were those who founded Jewish synagogues and congregations abroad. In so far, the Marrano Dispersion marked the return of the Jews to Western Europe after centuries of banishment. England had expelled its Jews in 1290, France in 1306 and again 1394, and most German and many Italian cities did so during the fifteenth century. Then Spain abolished Jewish existence in 1492, and Portugal in 1497. By 1500, Western Europe was nearly empty of Jews. Yet in the following centuries, Marrano emigrants were openly reverting to Judaism not only in the Ottoman Empire, the Jews' traditional haven, but in European cities like Venice, Ferrara, Hamburg, Amsterdam, and London. Under thin cover, Jewish congregations also arose in forbidden areas like Spanish Flanders and the Bordeaux region, where the authorities had commercial reason for looking the other way.[16]

A new phenomenon arose—the New Jews—formerly New Christians who returned to their forebears' religion after several generations of living as Catholics in Iberia. In returning to Judaism, their mental baggage and actual life were still imbued with Christian concepts and symbolism. They hardly knew what Judaism—The Law of Moses—actually meant. Also, many had formerly expressed religious doubt, indifference, or universalism, or drifted toward a this-worldly orientation. Thus, in becoming New Jews after having been New

Christians, they remained "New" in any case, and once again were not quite at home in their assumed culture and identity.[17]

The New Jews included ordinary people as well as persons of great wealth and famous intellectuals. Many, though not all, reconverted to Judaism because of religious and identitarian motives. Others joined a Jewish congregation mainly because it offered social or economic advantages: they sought admission to a commercial network, or needed a familiar milieu in which to operate. As a result, some New Jews practiced the Jewish cult externally, as a new kind of Marranism—or, as do many Jews today, observed Jewish law and custom as part of an assumed *social* identity. Nor did all emigrants convert to Judaism when they were able to: some chose to remain Christians even in relative freedom, or did not care for any established religion.

Solidarity among New Jews produced institutions that provided part of the social ground to their Nation's identity. Such was the *dotar*,[18] an organization to provide dowries to poor brides across the Dispersion. Its social importance went far beyond what its limited name and purpose might suggest. As a semi-secular communal structure that operated in several "Portuguese" communities and was open to applicants from other communities, its identity-building role recalls that of modern philanthropic Jewish organizations.[19]

A Crack in the Experience of Tradition

The religious picture of the New Jews was varied and quite complex. But, without verbalizing this to themselves, many who emigrated to free areas seem to have shared a new experience and attitude toward tradition: It was they who made the choice. They could remain Catholic, return devotedly to Judaism, join a Jewish congregation without religious conviction, or engage in any other partial or syncretistic religious activity: whatever the content of their choice, it cracked the self-perpetuation of tradition. Tradition was no longer an organic system enveloping a person's natural growth, but a value that the individual chooses as his or her context of meaning, thereby manifesting a certain autonomy vis-à-vis tradition in general. In this and other ways we shall discuss, new kinds of duality arose in the Marrano Dispersion, some anticipating basic features of modernity.

Different Degrees of Attachment (and Indifference) to Judaism

The New Jewish leaders grieved over those who remained Christian but did not despair of them. They considered them Jews-by-obligation, potential Jews whose duty it was to rejoin the fold, and who might one day do so. At the same time, using various sanctions, they campaigned inside the congregation against members who refused to be circumcised—the foremost sign of the Jewish Covenant—or had traveled periodically on business to Iberia, "the lands of idolatry," and lived there in sin as Christians.[20] This campaign indicates that, in practice, the *parnassim* (lay leaders) recognized de facto different degrees of attachment to Judaism. But while accepting ambiguity and wavering—that, after all, was natural to Marranos—they could not tolerate outspoken dissentions that appeared to threaten the fragile identity-in-becoming of the new Jewish congregation. In such cases, the leaders could be ruthless, as they were with the famous dissident Uriel da Costa and the philosopher Baruch Spinoza.[21]

This rigor marks a tension (one of several) within the broader Nation, between its interest in religious freedom for the community and its denying the same freedom to individuals within it. "The Jewish Inquisition," as the disciplinarian action of the Amsterdam leaders (which included rabbinical inquest and spying) was called polemically by some later historians, is an exaggerated appellation that, nevertheless, highlights an interesting dialectical feature, the residual influence of Iberia on its own fugitives and opponents.

The orthodoxy of the New Jewish congregations was thus rather special. The Orthodox Jewish tradition was not adopted in all its dimensions, and what was adopted was often observed with leniency and in a special mood and style. During the long Middle Ages, the Jewish rabbinical religion, based on the Talmud, had practically superseded the Bible. Its actual substance is not the Law of Moses but the law of the rabbis. Yet in most Jewish-Marrano congregations, the religious culture became basically biblical, linked to the stories, metaphors, and fables of the Jewish Bible, while the Talmud remained marginal. No wonder that Marrano rabbis were called uncreative and mediocre,[22] and that Karaite heresies (which rejected the Talmud and postbiblical teachings) arose periodically among the New Jews (and were rigorously suppressed).[23] The Bible strongly affected their *lay* culture, too. It was expressed in poems, pictures, and popular plays, it inspired personal names, was reflected in tombstones (the Marrano cemeteries in Ouderkerk, Holland, and Altona, near Hamburg, are fascinating examples),[24] and affected daily idioms and forms of speech. This Bible-centered culture was due in large part to the Marranos' *Christian* background: their long-time image of Judaism as "the Old Testament" and "the Law of Moses"; their need in Iberia to rely on the Latin Bible as their source of Jewish contents; and, of course, their lack of Talmudic rabbinical instruction and tradition.

In a subtler and less conspicuous departure from orthodoxy, the Jewish Marranos did not quite share to the view of rabbinical Judaism that the life of learning per se—plunged in the ocean of Talmudic hermeneutics and ratiocination—is superior to a life of commerce and worldly affairs. The Marrano traders appreciated sophisticated learning, but embedded in a practical context; and they respected their rabbis as practical guides in the art of being a Jew, rather than as the great Talmudic scholars they were not. In so far as Marrano traders resolved to become Jewish again, the rabbis were there to tell them how. And herein also lay the rabbis' main source of authority—in the last analysis, it derived from their congregates' will to be what they set out to become, namely, Jews. This was a new phenomenon in Jewish life—resulting from the crisis of conversion that broke its continuity, and from the fact that, for these New Jews, Judaism reemerged as a matter of personal choice and will rather than the habitual self-perpetuation of a tradition.

In their lifestyle, the New Jews allowed themselves more freedoms than traditional Jews, an easier, more relaxed approach to aesthetic pleasures and expression, including plastic images, and a more responsive cultural intercourse with the non-Jewish civilization around them. Religion was important, but not the overpowering center of life. It did not dominate their daily existence in the way of the Ashkenazim. The religious commands were there to *define an identity* rather than domineer and control; and they marked an alternative way to salvation—a Jewish alternative, replacing the Catholic and competing with the Lutheran, as well.

Dispersion Lands: Snapshots

The Marrano Dispersion had lasted for more than three centuries and spread around the globe. In the following pages we shall take a few glimpses into this phenomenon through a selection of several times and places, beginning with Italy in the fifteenth century.

Ferrara

Rare among Italian states, Ferrara in northern Italy had opened its gates to Jewish exiles after the Spanish expulsion. Situated on the Po River facing the Adriatic Sea, it wanted to compete with neighboring Venice and Ancona in the trade with the Levant; and its liberal rulers, the dukes of Este, resented Spain and stood in conflict with the pope's territorial ambitions. A generation later Duke Ércole II took a bold step. He offered Iberian New Christians, many of whom he knew were secret Judaizers, unheard of religious and commercial freedoms in Ferrara, including the right to settle as open Jews, no questions asked about their past. For forty years (1530–1570) Ferrara flourished as the first substantial, and open, Jewish-Marrano center in Europe and the world.[25] Rising economically, it also served as hub to Spanish and Portuguese refugees who returned to Judaism in Ferrara—the men getting circumcision and rudimentary Jewish instruction,[26] the women learning (or relearning) how to keep a kosher home, before they moved on to further destinations. Even the celebrated Doña Gracia Mendes-Nasi returned to Judaism in Ferrara and resided there for some time with her family, sponsoring literary works while preparing to transfer her immense fortune to Turkey.

Not all the dukes of Este were able or willing to defend the Marranos. With the rise of the Counter-Reformation, Alfonso II bowed to pressures by Rome and abolished many Jewish privileges. In 1583 three Ferrara Marranos were sent to trial in Rome, where the Inquisition burned them as heretics on the Campo dei Fiori, the same spot where it burned Giordano Bruno, the maverick pantheist Italian philosopher, seventeen years later. A visitor laying a flower at Bruno's statue that adorns the piazza today is unaware that, indirectly, he or she is also honoring Yosef (Abraham) Saralvo, alias Gabriel Henriques, whom the Marranos of Ferrara worshiped as "the Holy Martyr."[27]

Jewish Ferrara declined when the city came under the rule of the pope's legate. All professing Jews, Italian and Iberian, were driven into a ghetto under his vigilant eye, and many Marranos drifted away in search of better havens. Although a Sephardi congregation persisted in Ferrara for several centuries, its short-lived glory had gone. The Marrano torch in Italy now passed to Livorno and Venice.

Livorno (Leghorn)

When, in 1547, Cosimo I of Tuscany invited New Christians to settle in Pisa and Livorno (a languid coastal township that rose to greatness with the newcomers), could he foresee the role Livorno was to play in Jewish-Marrano history? The first fifty years were slow. The Livorno Marranos were practically required to put on a mask of obedient Catholicism; their only protection was a promise that if found out, they would be tried by the duke's lenient court rather than the Inquisition.[28] And in Pisa they wore a double mask, passing "as the Levantine Jewish Nation"—that is, both Turkish and Old Jewish—while being neither.[29]

Then came the "Livornina" in 1593, an edict addressed to "all foreign merchants" but tailored specifically for New Christians. Let them come, the duke's message went, let them practice Judaism—return to it, if they so choose—pray in a synagogue and enjoy juridical autonomy. This was the founding act of Jewish-Marrano Livorno, and it was renewed every twenty-five years. By 1650, despite the plague, the New Jewish population had grown more than ten-fold;[30]

soon after, it became the main Jewish-Marrano center in Southern Europe. Commerce thrived, and the port of Livorno had become a principal junction in the Mediterranean, linked to the northern commercial webs through Marrano Hamburg and Amsterdam. Culturally, Livorno boasted a few intellectuals—Elie de Montalto stands out as example—and a solid educational system. Every child had to attend school (Talmud Torah), and could continue in a religious college (Yeshiva) or, in some cases, get a doctorate at the university of Pisa. As elsewhere in the Dispersion, the *Kahal* (congregation) was governed by a self-perpetuating oligarchy of lay *parnassim*, more powerful than the rabbis.[31] And charitable organizations, besides assisting the poor, provided members of the community with a social structure that helped buttress the Nation's lay identity.

Venice

Venice had opened its gates to practicing Jews only in 1516, by creating the famous Ghetto Nuovo and locking the Jews nightly behind its gates. This "legalization" did not apply to Marranos reverting to Judaism because the Church considered them criminal renegades. Yet Venice wanted Iberian emigrants in order to gain access to the new commercial networks run by Iberians and to cope with Portuguese competition that undercut its traditional markets. The circle was squared by doubling the Marranos' external mask. By a treaty with Turkey in 1524, foreign merchants were allowed to operate in Venice only if they came from the Levant—that is, from Turkish dominions—so Spanish and Portuguese Marranos started settling in Venice by passing not only as non-Jewish, but also as Levantine. A witness told the Inquisition how it worked: refugees from Portugal went to Ferrara, got circumcised, then traveled east and returned to Venice wearing Turkish turbans. These "Turks" spoke fluent Spanish and Portuguese, but not a word of Turkish.[32]

This dual Marranism continued for more than a half-century. Protests by the pope were to no avail. The fiction was supported by high Venetian leaders because it allowed them to hang on to the two options of mercantilism and religious zealotry as if undecided, while actually preferring a mercantilist *raison d'état* to zealous piety. And Venice was much stronger than Ferrara in coping with Rome. In 1589, when the Ferrara Marranos were deep in crisis, the Venetian senate acted in the reverse direction. Prompted by an indefatigable Jewish-Marrano lobbyist, Daniel Rodriga, the senate issued a charter authorizing all New Christians—whether they came from the Levant or the *Ponent* (the West)—to settle in the republic and practice Judaism, no questions asked about their past, provided they lived in the ghetto and wore a distinctive yellow Jewish hat.

Venice had been traditionally reluctant to allow foreigners to operate in its port and the concessions now given the Marranos were unprecedented in its annals.[33] Sensing its coming decline, the veteran trading republic was eager to access the new commercial spheres that competed with it, and to reap other benefits from the Marrano skills and connections, even if that meant defying the pope at the height of the Counter-Reformation.

The charter was valid for ten years, after which it was renewed for another ten years, and another, and so forth. On the whole, it was renewed periodically for two full centuries, until 1797[34]—a remarkable combination of precariousness and stability. Its immediate effect was to create a vibrant Jewish-Portuguese community in the Venetian ghettos, alongside the Italian, Levantine, and Ashkenazi Jews.[35] The Portuguese Jews considered the other Jews embarrassingly backward and kept apart from them. The Jewish-Marranos' congregation had its own rabbis, lay officers (*parnassim*), governing council (*Maʾamad*),[36] schools and printers, as well as great merchants, elegant men of the world, painters and sculptors, and fascinating Renaissance intellectuals who were open to the new world of secular learning and lifestyles.

In retrospect, the Marrano ferment was successfully, if somewhat unstably, contained within the boundaries of normative Judaism—a *renewed* normative tradition, which did not simply mimic the old but assumed its own colors. Venice became a powerhouse of a new form of Jewish life, setting the institutional model for Portuguese-Marrano communities elsewhere, notably in Amsterdam; and its experience with the dualities of Marranism created a mold for reeducating New Christians in later generations.

Venice demonstrates the self-building circularity of the Marrano World Wide Web. Their networks spread as Marranos emigrated to localities where other Marranos had already been operating, or to their vicinity and dependencies; at the same time, the first Marranos had been admitted to those places because an international Marrano network had already existed, to which local authorities wanted to accede.[37]

Finally, the fact that Jewish-Marrano Venice set the pattern of social and religious organization for all other parts of the Dispersion helped concretize the social dimension of the Nation and gave an institutional backbone to its distinct character.

Northern Europe: New Jewish Amsterdam

Portuguese New Christians started settling in Antwerp in 1512 and soon made it a bridgehead and hub for Portuguese Marranos emigrating abroad. When

Antwerp declined during the Netherlands' war of liberation, Hamburg superseded it as the Marrano capital of the north. But as Amsterdam burst into the commercial center of Northern Europe, it became the new haven for Marranos, gaining the reputation of "The New Jerusalem in the north."

Like any major metropolis or nation, Jewish-Portuguese Amsterdam had its own founding myth, indeed, several of them. In one story, a ship of rich Marrano emigrants wandered in the Baltic Sea until they landed in Emden, a German port near the Dutch border. A local rabbi, Uri Halevi, redirected the emigrants to Amsterdam and pointed out a spot where they should meet him. He then rushed on land to join the refugees personally and help in their discreet settling in Amsterdam, not knowing he was planting the seed of the greatest Jewish-Marrano community of the Dispersion.[38]

Another founding story takes us to a private home in Amsterdam where Jacob Tirado, a captain of the early emigrants, was leading a Jewish ceremony in the Spanish language. The chants exceeded the prudent level of decibels and the suspicious neighbors summoned the authorities, saying a secret Spanish conspiracy was going on against the state. Tirado, who could not speak Dutch, was fortunate to find a Dutch officer who understood some Latin and, better still, was willing to understand the irony of the situation—that the "Spanish agents" were actually exiles and dissidents opposing Spain's policies.[39]

The Tirado anecdote conveys the early Dutch understanding of the distinctive value that Iberian Marranos held in store for them, given the Netherlands' incessant war of independence from Spain (1581–1648), and its rise to world prominence as a trading power. Neither side could miss the palpable analogies. Dutch and Marranos were being emancipated from Catholic oppression and harsh Spanish servitude; both were rising in global business, and expecting to expand more; and both embodied religious plurality and opposed Iberian intolerance and the Inquisition.[40] That Marranos should seek to lay anchor in Holland, and that Holland should seek to ride on the Marrano world web and Iberian profile, was a match pronounced in heaven (the non-Catholic part of it).

Fully legalized, the Portuguese Jewish community in Amsterdam saw its first upsurge in the 1620s. When Portugal broke free of Spain in 1640, a new wave of Portuguese Marranos hit the Dutch shores. A portion of the newcomers remained Christian but the largest and strongest Marrano group were the New Jews. The union in 1636 of their three founding congregations signaled the community's rise to prominence. By midcentury it counted about twenty-five hundred members (three thousand in 1700).[41] It was a proud, rich, and elegant community, cultivating letters, education, refined manners, and the arts. Many engaged in trading ventures in Asia, America, and the Levant, ran other businesses with links abroad, and operated in the Amsterdam stock exchange—the goods-oriented Wall Street of the age.

A brand plucked from the fire, the Jewish-Marrano community of Amsterdam became a diadem of gold. Half a century after the Tirado episode, its self-confidence was sufficient to confront a powerful figure like Peter Stuyvesant, the governor of New Amsterdam (today's New York), who was about to expel a shipload of Marrano refugees from Brazil who had found asylum in Manhattan. Responding to pressure by the Jewish-Portuguese *parnassim*, the regents of Amsterdam forced Stuyvesant to reverse his decision. The first Jewish settlement in North America thus owes its beginning to the first modern Jewish lobby acting on behalf of Jews abroad, the New Jews of Amsterdam.

Following the 1648 pogroms in Poland and the Ukraine (the "Chmelnitzky riots"), Ashkenazi Jews also started coming to Amsterdam; but the New Jews, although supplying them with basic help, kept apart from the poorer and less educated Polish Jews. The Portuguese New Jews also differed from the rich Dutch burghers, whose urban culture was often marked by a Calvinist severity unknown to the Marranos, and who lacked their Iberian decorum and extra refinement. Ironically, though not surprisingly (since a lay culture can bear the marks of a religion left behind), the Marranos in Holland embodied the Catholic way of life of the Southern European well-off classes, with their freer, more lavish and stylized forms and more indulgent mores.

The Jewish Marranos spawned a network of Jewish reeducation, publishing, and printing that, together with their wealth and glamorous lifestyles, won Jewish Amsterdam the appellation *The New Jerusalem*. A number of Marranos maintained an open, if sometimes ambivalent and even polemical, dialogue with the market of European ideas spreading in the non-Jewish world, but most of the community's effort was invested in Jewish reeducation. Innovation was rare and rather suspect. The Amsterdam leaders, as elsewhere in the Dispersion, were mainly concerned with revitalizing the extant Jewish religion and dressing it in Spanish and Portuguese so that Marranos whose minds were imbued with Christian concepts and symbols could recapture the lost religion of their fathers. This required a great deal of originality and imagination working in the service of conservatism—rebuilding the old fences of normative Judaism rather than transforming them. The rabbis' success was quite remarkable, given the complex and ambivalent Marrano experience they had to cope with; but it was a partial victory that paid the price of imposed conformity (often threatening and using the ban [*herem*] as a tool).[42] The more innovative figures and cases had to be repelled as heterodox and even banned as heretical. As a result, innovation existed either clandestinely within the community—creating silent dissidents and "New Marranos" among the New Jews—or on its excluded fringes and outside it.

Such were the cases of the philosopher Baruch de Spinoza, of Uriel da Costa, of Juan (Daniel) de Prado, and of other unnamed rationalist dissenters (see next chapter). But, as Gershom Scholem has argued, the former Marrano experience also explains the singular zeal with which ex-Marrano Amsterdam received Sabbetai Zevi, the self-styled Jewish Messiah who enflamed the Jewish world in 1666.[43] Having been liberated from their Iberian "Egypt" and gathered in a Dutch semi-"Jerusalem," the Marranos experienced a miniredemption of their own, which convinced them that the wider redemption of the Jews was not a foggy hope for the future but a historical possibility in one's own lifetime. Their disappointment when the Jewish Messiah converted to Islam was as great as their enthusiasm had been at the outset. In the following years they invested their energies in their own Jerusalem-in-exile, symbolized by the splendid Portuguese synagogue they inaugurated in 1675, an Amsterdam landmark to this day.

The Second Benjamin's Travels

At this point I ask the reader's permission to change the narrative voice. Suppose that around 1670, an adventurous young Marrano in Amsterdam—call him Benjamín López Tudela—persuades his wealthy grandfather to send him on a touring mission of the Marrano Dispersion, and that some fragments have been found of the old man's briefing and Benjamín's letters from the road.[†]

You must know, Benjamín, that people of our Nation live not only in very different places, but under different conditions as well. Worst of all are the conditions in the Lands of Idolatry where the two unholy Offices calling themselves Holy cruelly punish the slightest sign of Judaism, sometimes by burning. They keep a net of spies and informers not only there but, as you know, also here in Amsterdam, and in Venice, Ferrara, Antwerp, and elsewhere, so they can lay their hands on us, or try to get us back to their Jesus, or confiscate our ships and goods when discovered under their jurisdiction. This is why I use the alias Diego Henríquez in all my commercial dealings with the Peninsula. Still, many of our Nation there—including Antón Rodrigo de Tudela, your second cousin in Seville, and his wife's uncle, old Diogo Pereira in Lisbon, and members of their families, too, not only deal with us and other foreign Jews in secret, but try as much as they can, God help them, to keep some of the mitzvoth [commandments] of Moses' Law, our Santa Fe [Holy Faith], God forgive them for their remaining

---

[†] Though the viewpoint in the following texts is that of the fictional writers, the facts are historical. *Names marked by asterisk (*) refer to actual historical figures.*

transgressions as we, who have gone through the same trials in my late father's time—when I grew up as child in Avila—must understand and forgive.

Then, my dear boy, there are places in which the hand of the *malvados* [evil ones], although harsh and cruel when it strikes, is not striking all the time. They need us, they want our business, they make deals with us, so they often look the other way, pretending we are good Christians—just as we also pretend. Such is the situation in some Spanish dominions abroad, especially Antwerp, which used to be a great center of our Nation before this glorious city of Amsterdam took its place, God protect its Regents, who were so tolerant—and smart—as to allow us to set up our *Kahal Kadosh* [congregation] here and to live freely as Jews. I shall not pretend that we created Amsterdam's affluence; I know we had been attracted to it by its already rising prosperity. I also know that people tend to exaggerate our economic power and influence—by the way, I have nothing against this; it helps us open doors and frontiers. Yet there is a fair amount of truth in it. For, I ask—could this splendid city of Amsterdam have prospered as much as it did without us? Did we not, with our contacts abroad, our drive and subtlety in business, our methods and routes of exchange, our knowledge of foreign places and tongues—did we not amplify, multiply, spur Amsterdam's commerce in the Indies, the Levant, the Baltic, the sea of China?[44] I know first hand, being associated with the West India Company, the high opinion which the Company's directors have of us Sephardi merchants—how vital they think we are to their success in those parts![45] Was not your own father, his soul rest in peace, charged by the Company with settling more Jews in the island of Curaçao, to broker Amsterdam's commerce with Spanish America without being dependent on the Peninsula? Did he not go to Jamaica and Surinam, to extend the Dutch sugar plantations there? I hope you won't think me arrogant—or vengeful, though what's wrong with a little sweet vengeance, after all we had suffered from the hands of Spain and Portugal?—when I feel gratified that our persecutors have lost so much from our departure, while their enemies made many gains.

Yet no one seems to draw the lesson. Watch how the French are harassing the Calvinist merchants they call "Huguenots": in the end they will lose them, to their great disadvantage.[46] As for the Spaniards and Portuguese, they continue to prefer the Inquisition to good business. I know—you want to say that the Inquisition itself is good business? Bah! All they know is to confiscate other people's property—steal the riches that already exist. Did they ever create one Florin of new riches? Did they help others create it? And what is this damned nonsense of "pure blood"? The Spaniards know that Jew and Moor exist inside their veins, in their mind and blood stream, inside whatever makes a Spaniard what he is today. But they want to forget and deny this truth to themselves and mask it to the world, so they invented its opposite, this idol of *limpieza,* for which they put innocent people to shame, poverty, and exile. But God is just: this senseless policy works against them. They raise their chin in barren pride (just like that hungry *escudero* of whom I read in some sad and funny Spanish book),[47] worshiping idle nobility and looking down on worldly work and commerce—not on its fruit, this they pluck with greedy hands; but since they must, after all, get involved in coarse commerce, they do it with a divided heart—and shrinking coffers, which they have been wasting on their wars; so every now and then their government goes bankrupt, and everyone sees they are in decline.

In my youth the Spaniards called Holland a rebel state and barred it from trading with Spain and its colonies. So we had to trade in secret, like smugglers (some would say: like "Marranos")—calling ourselves by fake names, sailing under false flags, using German ships owned by merchants of our Nation in Hamburg, and collecting our profits in Antwerp.[48] Today we deal more freely with Spain and Portugal, and no longer depend on their ports as before, because of the trading stations we have meanwhile set up for ourselves in the West Indies, which you will be visiting with God's will.

Speaking of the Indies—the inquisitors are more erratic in America than in Iberia, less consistent in suppressing our Jewish Santa Fe, though rigorous when they do. Life is more lax in the Indies, more adventurous, so the pores in the net of the Inquisition are large enough to give our Nation some respite. But of course you must be careful there. Quite recently, Francisco Botello* and Diego Gómez* were burned alive in Mexico's Plaza Mayor before 40,000 spectators;[49] and in Brazil, suspects are sent to be tried in Lisbon.[50] Yet quite often, the authorities are ready to close one eye.

In France they close almost both their eyes. Our Nation there lives mostly near the Spanish border—in Bayonne, Bordeaux, Peyrehorade, St. Jean de Luz and other places near the foot of the Pyrenees.[51] This allows them to have direct links with Spain while being sheltered from its tyranny. Officially they are "Portuguese," but everyone knows that many pray to the God of Israel. If you are properly introduced—I shall give you letters to André López* in Bayonne, my onetime associate, who will also re-supply you with money—you will find that everywhere in that region there is a *Kahal Kadosh* [Jewish congregation], unseen yet not quite secret, with its synagogue, rabbi, *parnassim* [regents], even the same charities we have here in Amsterdam, like our *dotar*, the Society for Providing Dowries to Orphans. And as in Amsterdam and the rest of our Dispersion, it is not the rabbis but the lay leaders who hold the top authority. You will find that André López* actually runs the *Kahal* of Bayonne.

Even so, their life is precarious. Lately in Rouen, on the river Seine, Diogo d'Oliveira* and other Portuguese leaders had to be ransomed for a gigantic sum, 250,000 livres, after being denounced as Jews to the local council. Much earlier—

I was 32, and sent to Rouen on business by my father—the merchant Gaspar de Lucena* was tried by the French for living as a Jew. The Spanish Inquisition arrested Lucena's relatives in the towns of Seville, Lima, Mexico, and Cartagena of the Indies, yet other relatives of his continued to operate as Jews in Rouen itself, and in Bordeaux, Antwerp, Ferrara, Midlburg, and London[52]—imagine how dispersed this family has been! Of course, many of our people also have relatives scattered over the lands, but usually not as many, and not all of them observe the Holy Law of Moses. Some are stubborn Catholics, some are half-Jews, mixed families, wavering persons. . . . Even inside the *Kahal* there are people who are not sure what their true religion is, or have no religion at all, like that young man we had to expel fourteen years ago here in Amsterdam—Baruch,* son of the late Michael d'Espinoza,* who had studied in Keter Torah*—your own yeshiva, Benjamin—and today, I am told, lives in Den Haag and has just published a dangerous book without his name on it.[53]

From Rouen, through Le Havre, you cross the channel to London on the Thames. England had been a gray zone for us for a long time. In the times of Queen Elizabeth, a few members of our Nation living as Christians in London served the English as sources of information about Spain. A certain Hector Núñez* even supplied Lord Walsingham* with information about the preparations of the Great Armada.[54] But such services can be double edged. Núñez's successor was Doctor Rodrigo López,* who became Queen Elizabeth's personal physician. His enemies in court, especially Lord Essex,* denounced him as a Spanish double agent; they even accused him of trying to poison the queen. Poor López was sentenced to death. Before his execution, he cried out in protest: "God is my witness that I loved the queen no less than I love Jesus Christ!" But some of his listeners laughed and said he "spoke like a Marrano" to his last gasp![55]

Conditions started changing twenty years ago, when the Cartwrights,* Englishmen living in our city whom you may remember as child, petitioned the new Puritan rulers in London to permit Jews to settle in England. The English have not seen an overt Jew in three hundred years, except on the stage, in a play about some frightful Jewish money lender in Venice. But the Puritans, who had killed their king Charles, believed they were bringing in no less than the Kingdom of God on earth, in which the second coming of their Messiah Jesus was to be expected, and the Jews had a role to play in the Puritans' messianic scheme. Of course, the English also wanted the benefit of our commerce and connections. So a big debate started in England on the Jews, and more petitions were presented, one of them by our own great scholar, Menasse Ben Israel,* who sailed to London to convince Oliver Cromwell in person.

You know that Menasse, like my father, had been born a Catholic in Portugal; his name was Manoel Dias Soeiro. As a Jew in our city he was respected by Christians around Europe because of the breadth of his knowledge. Foreign dignitaries paid him a visit, and the painter Van Rijn,* who lived near the Jewish quarter, was his friend and drew up his portrait.[56] Menasse too saw the Messiah—*our* Messiah—as being on his way. He believed that the lost Ten Tribes of Israel were being discovered among the new races found in America, and that was a sign of the coming Messiah. Another sign he saw in our Nation's exodus from the Lands of Idolatry. Menasseh told the English Puritans that according to the Bible which they revere, the Messiah will not come before the Jews were dispersed everywhere[57]—so they must be admitted to England too! Cromwell's counselors favored another argument. According to their belief, Jesus's second coming must be preceded by the conversion of the Jews of their free will; and where could the Jews find true Christianity if not in Puritan England?

Cromwell convened a Conference in Whitehall, but the matter was left hanging because of opposition from short-sighted English merchants fearing our Nation's competition. Good Menasse died several years later, not knowing he had actually won, because Cromwell started to admit Jews anyway, and the Second King Charles, who rules England today, made this policy official.

By the way, in Cromwell's last years, when Spain and England were at war, the authorities confiscated the ship of Antonio Robles,* a London man of our Nation, saying he was an enemy subject. Robles asked the court to declare that people like himself are neither Spaniards nor Portuguese, but Jews protected by English toleration. The judges returned Robles' ship, but refused to make the declaration he demanded, saying that in the end they were unable to decide what his nation and religion actually were. Perhaps, as I heard a scholar say,[58] the English were unfamiliar with secret Jews; but I suspect that had they been familiar with our kind, their confusion would have been even greater!

Today our Portuguese Nation lives openly in England, rising in its commerce as England does in the world. Not all are openly Jews. I am sad that some of my Portuguese associates prefer to live as Christians even in England, where they can be Jews if they so wished. But I know that many of them can be trusted even more than some of our Jews over here. As for the heart, only God sees into it.

[*Author's note*: At this point the records break and we lose the old man's voice. But the fragments contain scraps of Benjamín's letters to his grandfather from the road].

Here Vera Cruz in New Spain, 10th day of March 1671

To my revered master and grandfather, God prolong his life:

I stopped in Vera Cruz for several days before going inland to the city of Mexico. The sea was the roughest since my arrival in the Indies. But my welcome here was pleasant, as it had been in Curaçao, where I encountered some distant relatives. Recife in Brazil had been much colder to me. Dutchmen are not too welcome there, and some people still remind you of the role which members of our Amsterdam community—whom they call Portuguese traitors—had played when the Dutch captured Brazil to exploit its sugar [1630].[59] I now can better understand why, after the Portuguese reconquered Brazil [1654], they expelled our kin with such vengeance. I remember as child the arrival in Amsterdam of the poor refugees from Pernambuco with their grim rabbi, old Isaac Abohab,* who was the first rabbi in the New World. Now I've learnt that some refugees fled into the Brazilian forest, where they mingled with the natives and have been known ever since as "the Dutch."[60] Although they became Catholic again, they maintain some Jewish rites, like burying their dead in shrouds. As for the shipload that fled to Nieuw Amsterdam in the northern Indies and settled in the island of Manhattan, I hear they are building a synagogue there called She'erit Yisrael*; it is located on a street near the Wall which Governor Peter Stuyvesant* built to protect the town against the Indians and the English.[61] I don't think I shall visit this place, though, because it may soon come under English siege again, and in any case it is of minor importance to our Nation.

Curaçao is another story altogether. It is a like a capital city for us in the Indies. The harbor is splendid; our people here grow steadily in numbers, and start to equal the Dutch in navigation, even in ship building and armaments, and in other naval crafts that we Jews have rarely practiced. A fleet of several dozen ships owned by Jews crisscrosses the seas of the Antilles [Caribbean] and the Americas; some of them have Hebrew names from the Bible, like "Zebulun and Isaschar"; and many have Jewish captains or navigators.[62]

I am glad to see that Jewish Curaçao has become a regional power, the cornerstone of our trade with the Americas, as you, Senhor grandfather, and my late father of blessed memory, and other Amsterdam *parnassim*, had planned.[63] Further islands in this region—English Jamaica and Barbados, Dutch Surinam, French Martinique—are satellites dominated by Curaçao, which some already call "the Amsterdam of the Antilles."[64]

One more word on Brazil. While the Dutch ruled this colony, some New Christians remained firmly Catholic, so they were allowed to stay in Brazil when the Portuguese returned. Today we find among them solid partners in the sugar trade. Meanwhile a flow of new immigrants from the peninsula keeps coming to Brazil. The place has become a hub through which people of our Nation spread also to Mexico, Lima, Rio de la Plata [Argentina], the Antilles, and the rest of the Americas.[65]

These people include secret Jews, and also half and quarter-Jews. In Rio de Janeiro I found that some of them use the house of Miguel Cardoso* as synagogue. Senhor Cardoso allowed me to take part in one such occasion, after

I delivered a message to him from his nephew who had visited Amsterdam (remember the blond youth* from Brazil I once introduced to you?) which contained signs known only to the two of them.[66] I also discovered that the registrar Pedro da Costa* ties a colored ribbon to his back whenever he wants to transmit a covert message to other New Christians, calling them to prayer or to a secret meeting.

I was also puzzled to discover that a pious fraternity named Our Lady of Ajuda, meets on Saturdays outside the city of Rio to celebrate the feast of our Queen Esther. These people are not cheating; they truly respect the Christian Saint whose name they bear, but revere our Queen Esther as a greater Saint and as their secret patron.[67] I know the Inquisition will call them Jews, but shall we? Are they Jews of another kind, or heretical Christians, or what? I am neither a rabbi nor a theologian or philosopher to answer this question. But I see such people—such double heretics—all the time. . . .[68]

Here Mexico [City] in New Spain, 1 day of April 1671
To my revered Senhor abuelo, God prolong his life:
I arrived safely in this chief city of New Spain. This land is so diverse it dazzles you. The foods, the plants, the smells and colors are all so different from what we are used to. The language of Castile mingles with many local lingos, and there is a sense of tense ambition here, even wildness in the air. Old Spain is present here with an imposing cathedral in the Plaza Mayor, crosses and monasteries everywhere, haughty armed Spaniards (but also many poor and picaros), and, of course, the Inquisition. This is no land of a single god, however, nor of a single law or tongue, or food; and there is a constant drive to impress the Spanish ways upon the locals, among whom are many colorful heathens— and no overt Jews.

But there are many secret Jews—there always have been here, ever since the famous Carvajal family was wiped out in the flames almost a century ago. People still remember Luis Carvajal El Mozo, whose religion required not only faith, but sincerity too, so he ended in martyrdom, which he desired and obtained. But some of his admirers say in low voice he was wrong to deny the secrecy and concealment that has become our Nation's life's necessity and second nature. . . . The Inquisition's last outbursts which occurred here in 1649[69] and 1659 had greatly damaged our local networks; and although the Inquisition itself has many holes in its net, nobody knows when it will strike again.[70] Meanwhile, small secret communities practice our Law of Moses not only in the city of Mexico but also in Puebla, Oaxaca, Vera Cruz, Guadalajara, Queretaro, Pachuca, and of course Taxco, the center of silver.

Trade goes on with east and west, and silver is on everyone's minds—silver mined, minted, treated, used as collateral, silver quarreled and fought about, silver shipped to Seville, smuggled to England, and used in trading with the Asians. But most of the silver goes of course to Seville. People are also making a profit in this new stuff, cocoa, which is so bitter you need the other new stuff, sugar, to make it the delicacy it has become. Some merchants import African slaves, which they buy from their Arab or Portuguese captors and sell here, or ship further to Lima: I hear that a man from Guinea costs 500–600 pesos in Lima and only 270–300 pesos in Cartagena.[71]

In addition to trading with the Old World, quite a few of our Nation look westward—to what in Amsterdam we call the East. Goods are shipped to China and Manila, indirectly to Batavia in Java or to Nagasaki in Japan; and some ships even get as far as Goa, from where the merchandise—or its worth in capital, since the goods themselves have been exchanged more than once—might continue to Portugal and Spain, and return here to Mexico after circling the world which God has made round possibly for this purpose.

Still, not all our people in New Spain are "homens de negocios," as we are often called in Portuguese. Many work as artisans, physicians, scribes, public officials, even priests; and there are more Jewish poor in this land than one sees in Amsterdam or Italy. I reckon the reason is that our *parnassim* in Europe encourage poor refugees to go to the New World, and give them money for the road.

The diversity of this land also affects religion. The strange idols of pagan cult are still more prevalent here than crosses, or they exist in the same place together with a cross. The heathens are persecuted in order to save their souls, as the priests now say. This is a change from a hundred years ago, when the Indians were killed or let to perish by disease because many believed they had no souls. As for our own people, they too are persecuted to save their souls—above all, from being other than the rest. Difference, variation, is the great enemy here, yet it exists all over the place.

Unfortunately, some of our rabbis at home are also shocked by variation. They refuse to recognize as Jews some brave people who take great risks and even give their lives for the Law of Moses (I must say that the Inquisition is much more generous in granting the title of "Jew"!) On the other hand, I know about people here who keep certain customs in secret, to which no rabbi or priest would give his blessing. They want to remain Catholic, though not in the severe way imposed by the Inquisition; and the fact that others call them "Jews" does not make them Jews in their own eyes. So on both sides there are people in our Nation who are at variance with what they are meant by others to be. Why this fear of variety? Why should we use the words heretic, dissenter, so quickly and so negatively, each in his own camp and under his banner? I sometimes wonder if in so doing, we do not accept the basic teaching of our worst enemy, the Inquisition. But I dare not go on with my thoughts. I know, revered abuelo, I shouldn't.

The labels by which we are called are quite confusing. "New Christian" means here a Jew, and "Portuguese" means New Christian, hence a Jew, but it also means a man of affairs, a businessman; so "Portuguese" amounts to a Jewish businessman, yet one who may not be an actual Jew in our rabbis' eyes. . . . And our Nation is sometimes called Portuguese, sometimes Spanish-Portuguese, sometime the Hebrew Nation, and often simply "the Nation" without further adjective. My head turns from all these appellations. But I am no logical scholar in search of definitions; my travels taught me how elusive that is which we are, yet how kindred all the names are by which everyone tries to describe us, and fails, but not completely. I also learned that, in our particular Dispersion, there is more to being Jewish than a synagogue. This is not quite true of those other Jews who have never known forced conversion and Inquisition. I suppose that the people who call us "Hebrews" have realized we have something else in common than a law and religion. (But what is it, I wonder?)

Here Thessalonica in Greece, under the Great Turk
To my beloved and revered grandfather in the great city of Amsterdam:
It has been a while since I had written to you, and I ask for your indulgence. In the meantime I have received your good news through Manuel Rodrigo in Istanbul, where I spent more time than I had planned, because of some local Portuguese Jew who offered me a deal that might have interested our family, a link to his trade in Alexandria in Egypt, where spices from India are still arriving through Arab traders using the old route of the Red Sea. I was tempted by the idea and continued negotiating, until I realized that this gentleman was also trying to marry his daughter to me as part of the bargain. So the deal fell off and I found myself with one friend less in the Levant.

Thessalonica must be the greatest Jewish city of the world. A French traveler staying in my inn—a certain Count de La Magdeleine*—said to me that Thessalonica is the Rome of the Jews,[72] and I see what he means. Jews make up the large majority of the population here, and their number is ten times greater than in Amsterdam. They are not as wealthy as we but are doing well, and are treated fairly by the Turks, who consider them inferior but let them live in peace.

The harbor of this splendid city contains up to three hundred ships, and its walls are three miles long.[73] Water is supplied by pipes from the mountain, a half day's walk away. There are nine Turkish baths, ten great mosques—seven of them had been Greek churches before—and a few dozen Jewish synagogues. The Jews live by fabrics—different kinds of fabrics and rugs that they weave, design, dye in a variety of delicate colors, always keeping the secrets of their art to themselves, and which they ship in great quantities to the rest of the Mediterranean. They even pay most of their taxes to the Great Turk in fabrics. (In recent years the Jewish fabric business has suffered competition from English wool, but it is still a formidable operation.) The fabric market is the most agitated in town. The place bustles with people, animals, colors, shouts, grimaces, and smells. Five languages are spoken there at once—Spanish, Greek, Turkish, Portuguese, and Italian. Peddlers try their luck in the streets, while rich merchants chase them away from their shops, and summon the coffee servers to pour their clients a cup—yes, grandfather, coffee is a great favorite in the Levant; the Turks fell for it long ago, and we in Amsterdam must take notice and exploit this opportunity.

Our Portuguese Nation is a mere fraction of the Jewish population here. Most of the Jews in town descend from the exiles who had left Spain in the time of Doña Isabel and Don Fernando. At that time, Thessalonica accepted more Jewish exiles than any other city, except Istanbul. Those Spanish Jews are so dominant in their tongue and customs they have turned the older Greek Jews into Sephardim too, as they have also done elsewhere in the Levant.[74] Us Portuguese they consider a different kind and also as repentant, because we had committed idolatry by living as Christians, whereas their ancestors have never left the old Faith.

Today there are no less than five Portuguese congregations here, each with its own rabbi, synagogue, school, and Hascamot [bylaws]. Your trading agents, the Buenos* and the Mirandas,* belong to KK [congregation] Portugal, nicknamed *kalabaça* [pumpkin*]; my younger friends the Amarillios* are members of KK Evora, labeled aroz [rice*]; while KK Lisbon, labeled *mangrana* [pomegranate*] is split in two because of old rivalries. Nor should we forget the congregation founded by Doña Gracia Nasi, which is aptly named after her Liviat Hen (Grace, Beauty [Hebrew]).

Just as we have a colony in Curaçao, so the Jews of Thessalonica established an offshoot in Safed, in the Holy land. The fabric business in Safed has meanwhile collapsed, but the city flourishes in mystical Kabbalists, similar to those who had bred that false Messiah Sabbetai Zevi, who has recently fooled the whole Jewish world—and most of all, us in Amsterdam!—and now is wearing a Muslim's cap. In Thessalonica he is still a cause of turmoil over him, many accuse others of following him in secret, which is true of a small number only, a sect known as Dunmeh. Meanwhile, the scandal has paralyzed the printing of Jewish books in Thessalonica, which has been a major center of Jewish publications alongside Venice and Amsterdam, so perhaps some good may arise to our business from this matter.

My plans for the last part of my trip are now set. With God's help and your permission, I will soon—

[*Author's note:* At this point the fragments end. Did Benjamín plan to go further to Alexandria, and from there to Rhodes, Ragusa (Dubrovnik), Ancona, Piedmont, Toulouse, Biarritz, Paris, Frankfurt, and Danzig before returning home? Or was he about to move on from Egypt to Mozambique, Albuquerque (in the Persian Gulf), Goa, Batavia (Indonesia), Manila and Macao (Portuguese China)? Perhaps he planned to go to Iberia, crisscrossing the peninsula from Seville to Trás-os-Montes, and from Oporto to Burgos? We do not know. But we do know that if he had such intentions, he would have met Marrano traders in all these places, all speaking his language and relating to the same fluid entity, which everyone called the "Nation" though no one was able to fix and define it.]

The "Nation" Revisited

The term *Nation* derives from nativity, common birth (or common birthplace, birth-group, and so on); and prior to the advent of modern nationalism, such ethnic and indigenous connotations had determined the use of the concept. At the University of Padua in Galileo's time, students were officially divided into the nations of Naples, Siena, Ancona, Arrezo, Urbino, and so on, alongside those of France and Spain; and Genoese, Venetian, or northern German merchants living in foreign ports used to form their own nations in those places. The Portuguese Hebrew Nation, too, was based primarily on the Marranos' ancestral and ethnic attributes and their derivatives. But in determining their group image, either in the eyes of the world or in their self-perception and inner experience, this common descent was almost inseparably colored and reinforced by other elements.

First, the Marranos' common birth was laden from the start with the shared Iberian experience of conversion and persecution, the experience of New Christians facing the threat of the Inquisition and coping with social ostracism and hostility due to their origin. Therefore, what distinguished them as Nation was not just their blood, but its putative impurity—not only their biological origin but the social exclusion and stigmatization attached to it. In other words, their natural ancestry and nativity was infused from the outset with history—their own, specific historical experience as the Other Within.

In addition, these Marranos all spoke Portuguese (and sometimes Spanish), and shared a common Iberian culture and linguistic affinities. Although rejecting some of Iberia's fundamental values, they retained much of the Iberian mores and cultural heritage—albeit in an alienated, émigré form—and took it wherever they went, to all the islands of their archipelago, as part of their own group identity.[75] This made them a unique, nonconformist brand of Iberians who, in casting away the violent Iberian dream of religious uniformity, had shed the religious dimension of their Iberian culture altogether and maintained it as a secularized, lay culture—of which they were rather proud, and which gave their Nation a sense of superiority and sharp separation from non-Iberian Jews and Gentiles alike.

A third characteristic of this Nation was the merging of its ethnic descent with its economic role. The socio-economic activity of the trading Portuguese helped determine their peculiar group character. It was not an additional feature but, we might say, a *constitutive* trait that participated in shaping their identity no less than did their common descent and erstwhile religion. Just as the term *the Nation* was grasped immediately as referring to New Christians, so the term *men of affairs* (*homens de negocios*) was commonly understood as directly referring to them.[76] It was a code word based, no doubt, on stereotype, but the stereotype relied on a solid basis of fact. Most Portuguese abroad were traders, and most were New Christians. The Marranos' commercial role became part of their collective self, of what made them into a separate group (at least, in the perception of others, and thereby, to a large extent, in their own perception). Moreover, the special way in which their identity was constituted by all three ingredients—race, former religion, and economic function—was in itself their most unique and distinctive feature. In this they differed from ordinary Jews. In ordinary Jews, their economic role had always been additional to their identity; whereas in the Portuguese Marranos' case, it participated in building their very group identity. We might say the Marranos' group identity fused those elements together in a way that was vague enough to leave room for undetermined border cases and zones, but was sufficiently distinct to bar its being reduced to a single one of its ingredients.

A further important characteristic of the Nation was that the links uniting it were largely secularized, in the sense that they did not depend on religion as a necessary condition. As we have seen, differences in cult and faith did not prevent a person from belonging to the same network or nation; quite the contrary, a typical feature of this Nation was the mix of different religious elements, manifested both horizontally (between various members of the group) and vertically (within the same person). Not only was the Nation divided into different forms of cult and confessional fidelity, but the individual's very religious identity was often ambiguous, split into several shades and expressions.[77]

At the same time, all members of the Nation had a common Jewish descent and were often explicitly called "Jews" by others, regardless of the religion they were practicing. From the inside, too, Judaism as memory, as an ineradicable self-perception (either welcome or discomfiting, or both), or as a challenge, and in some cases, a living reality, remained a typical trait of the Nation. They all knew where they came from and what it had cost them historically. The old religion existed for many of them only in the personal past tense, as lingering echoes and remnants (often in distorted form) that they wished to shed, repress, repair, play with, indulge in nostalgically, or adopt as their own and live by, knowing the price tag attached to their choice. To those who emigrated to free countries, Judaism presented itself as a freshly reconstructed religious framework to which, if they chose—it was now their choice, rather than a habitual perpetuation of tradition—they would adhere in several degrees of commitment and/or indecision, and which even its devotees practiced not without duality, due to their mental baggage as former Catholics.

Because of the above, and their experience of persecution in Iberia, another prominent feature of the Nation was the Marranos' strong antithesis to the ruling religious order. Whether they returned to Judaism, remained Catholic, secretly Judaized (which often involved a Judeo-Christian mixture), converted to Calvinism, or became skeptical of any religion, they required the possibility, if not the right, of being what they were *regardless of the state's governing religion*. In other words, they were early moderns in their seeking not only free trade but—in the *same* package—also free religion. The pluralism, syncretism, and religious ambivalence that in Iberia were considered illegitimate and persecuted by the religious police of the regime, were of paramount importance to this Nation and essential in its constitution.

Their common descent and conflict with the Inquisition produced a measure of solidarity, sometimes even a special intimacy, between New Christians of different circles, similar to the solidarity sometimes found between observant, secular, and traditionalist Jews today. Of course, as among the Jews, it was an incomplete solidarity, laden with inner conflict and mutual blaming.[78] Yet these phenomena do not nullify the concept of solidarity, they only modify its romantic halo and give it a more dialectical and realistic image.

The Portuguese Nation was indeed distinguished from the Jewish people. Reuven (Robert) Bonfil notes that Jewish-Portuguese Marranos were closer to the Christians than to the other Jews in their general culture and civil behavior.[79] Their unique consciousness, he adds, the sense of being a separate "semi-nationality," was above all due to their socioeconomic role, and also to the cultural (identitarian) desire to preserve their own customs and mores.[80] In particular, they kept rigorously apart from the Ashkenazim, whom they thought awkward and less cultivated. The solidarity they did show them was rather normative and formal, based more on rabbinical rules than on their own heart's call and demand.[81]

Paradoxically, all these uniquely Portuguese features helped develop the Marranos' *cosmopolitan* consciousness. In being so different wherever they went; in having a foreign "nativity" attached to their name but no actual metropolitan country they could naturally claim (Iberia was no longer viewed by them in this way); in living in scattered places on the sole basis of interested tolerance, without an established natural right and the indigenous "roots" of the local population, they had to fall back on their *own* worldwide Nation as a social entity, and for anchorage and support in a precarious world. Foreigners without an actual metropolitan fatherland, they made their Nation into a fatherland, a cosmopolitan one; and this enhanced their cosmopolitan outlook, which had already existed because of their global networks and worldwide economic role.

This early cosmopolitanism had not yet been considered the political sin it became under high European nationalism in the nineteenth and early twentieth centuries. The victims of the romantic nationalist glorification of "organic roots" were not the Marranos, who by then had dwindled out, but the politically emancipated Jews of the nineteenth and twentieth centuries. But in the seventeenth and eighteenth centuries a cosmopolitan outlook was still treated as legitimate, at times even as a desirable utopia, and the Portuguese Marranos were among those embodying it, for good or bad.

18

Marrano Mosaic II: Wanderers, Martyrs, Intellectuals, Dissenters

―――――――――⟿―――――――――

The Marrano Dispersion was so rich in characters—wanderers, bourgeois, poets, revolutionaries, rabbis, *conquistadores*, martyrs, messianic dreamers, and heretics to all religions—that no single volume can do justice to their fascinating variety. Instead, here are a few semi-random sketches, all related to the theme of Marrano duality.

Wanderers and "Converso-Picaros"

Alongside the established bourgeois families, the Marrano Dispersion also had another face—the wandering Marrano, the unsettled, disquieted, or unfortunate type who roamed not only between geographical places but between roles, masks, cultures, and religions. This phenomenon of "Converso-picaro"[1] existed in Iberia prior to the Expulsion, but gained new traits in the Dispersion. Several monographs, classic and new, record the varieties of this phenomenon.[2]

One early case was Bartolome Gaillego. He was born Jewish as Ben Menahem, he converted at age six to Christianity in Sardinia (then a Spanish colony), and we find him as an adult in North Africa (Fez and Oran) doing small trade, commuting between Muslim and Jewish communities, and acting as Jew among the Jews. Later he turned up in Spain (Talavera), where he had Converso relatives and acted there as Christian; but the Inquisition arrested and tried him for praising Islam. Unable to settle down even in prison, he performed a rare feat and escaped. His further wanderings are unknown. But it is clear that he had wandered between the three religions while believing in none. He was, in his way, a popular anthropologist of religions—observing from outside their relative peculiarities and advantages, and confused about his own position and identity.

Another picture—small panorama—is drawn by Eva Alexandra Uchmany's study of the Nieto family in the sixteenth century.[3] She tells the story of Ruy/ Yaakov Nieto, brought to Jewish Ferrara as a boy by Portuguese Judaizing parents, who soon died. He grew up in the streets, and as adult went as a Christian to Portugal to get help from his uncles—one a Judaizing international merchant trading with Brazil and Goa, the other a heretic interested in politics, who died in Morocco with King Sebastian during Sebastian's disastrous mission there. With his uncles' financial help, Ruy started a flourishing business in Ferrara, trading with the Levant. He married and had a legitimate son, Diego/Yizhak, in addition to two older illegitimate sons who had accompanied their uncle to Morocco. These sons were taken as prisoners to Turkey, where their father succeeded in ransoming them through a brother-in-law who had emigrated to Istanbul.

For a while it looked as if the former picaro boy had turned bourgeois. But the loss of one of his ships sent him and Diego/Yizhak back to the streets—not of Ferrara, where his debtors were chasing him, but to Iberia again—Madrid, Lisbon, Braga, Porto, and Seville. They met all sorts of "men of the Nation," covert and overt, some locals, others who emigrated back to Spain for commercial or identitarian reasons, a few keeping homes in both Spain and abroad. This gallery of Marrano characters, and its scale of attitudes toward both religious cultures, makes the core of Uchmany's fascinating story. In the end, father and son sailed to Mexico, where they met the fervent Judaizer Carvajal (see next section) and ended in the cells of the Inquisition. Diego/Yizhak claimed he had been born a Jew, and hence he was no heretic to Christianity. He was forced to take his oath before the Inquisition "by the God whose name is spelled Y,H,V,H" and, having convinced the court, got a light sentence. But Ruy had no such excuse, and seems to have died in jail.

Marrano Martyrs

The Inquisition's work in the Iberian colonies left a trail of convicts and martyrs who died for their faith, and deep dualities. They hardly conformed to orthodox or "normative" Judaism (some even denied the afterlife, and the exclusive truth of the Mosaic religion), but chose a stiff-necked loyalty to something in which they felt their choice and self-perception were inseparably embodied.

The Carvajals

Don Luis de Carvajal y de La Cueva (1539–1590) was an ambitious Marrano admiral and conquistador. Serving King Philip II, he conquered for him the vast northern territory of New Spain, stretching to San Antonio in today's

Texas. This colonial exploit won him the hereditary title of Governor of the Kingdom of New León—and many enemies in high places. A Christian by resolution, Governor Carvajal was unable to fully realize his project of assimilation because he was surrounded by Judaizers on all sides: not only his mother, but also his partly estranged wife, his favorite sister, her husband, and most of their children (who probably replaced in his heart the children he never had himself). Standing out among these children was his beloved nephew, Luis de Carvajal Junior (*el Mozo*), a young intellectual and poet whom the older Carvajal named as his heir to the governorship.

The inquisitors refused to believe that the governor was unaware of all the Judaizing going on around him. They were probably right: awareness has many veils, and one of them, self-deception, is an escape from hard dilemmas. Insofar as the governor did have suspicions, he chose to reveal them only to his private confessor and not to the inquisitors, as he was required to do. This was a grave offense: at the moment of test, an officer of the Crown proved more attached to his heretical kin than to the lords of his adopted religion. Carvajal's proud claim that he "had been too busy fighting the Chichimeca Indians," left the inquisitors unimpressed. Carvajal was convicted of harboring heretics, deprived of his titles and property, and sentenced to a year in prison, during which he died.

Luis el Mozo *and His Circle*

The governor's nephew, Luis de Carvajal *el Mozo* (Junior), was born to parents whose passion for the Law of Moses far exceeded their knowledge of it.[4] They passed this ardor to six of their children, above all Luis Junior. One of Luis's brothers fled Mexico and became a rabbi in Thessalonica; the other became a Dominican monk in Mexico. Luis himself, in his search for what he took to be his ideal identity, became a private investigator—of the customs and contents of Judaism. Luis, his charismatic mother (Doña Francisca Núñez de Carvajal), and his three sisters practiced Judaic rites quite daringly—until they were exposed and convicted of heresy. In their first trial they lost most of their property and were sentenced to wear sanbenitos for long periods of time, before being "reconciled" to the church. Any further Judaizing would send them to the flames.

Caution above all, demanded their exasperated spouses, especially Antonio Cáseres, Luis's brother-in-law, married to his sister Catalina. Cáseres was a Marrano on four sides who preferred prudence to devotion. When the Inquisition arrested the Carvajals for the first time, Cáseres loaded a ship in Acapulco and sailed—fled—to China and the Philippines. After harrowing adventures, in which he escaped mutiny and death, became involved in political intrigue, was arrested twice, sentenced to death, released, lost and recaptured his merchandise, and changed ships, he returned to Mexico with a load of Asian goods, of which the scrupulous Inquisition duly confiscated "the part belonging to his wife Catalina." In Mexico, Cáseres kept away from his "reconciled" wife, although he discreetly supported her and their daughter. He continually warned Catalina and Luis that their way would end at the stake.

The conflict between the brothers-in-law was inevitable. They were as different as two Judaizing Marranos could be. Cáseres was an ordinary Marrano, Luis an extra-ordinary one. Cáseres was worldly, prudent, and secretive; Luis was intellectual, mystical, and recklessly sincere. Cáseres argued that the Marrano situation entailed compromise and discretion. A pure heart cannot be truthfully projected outside; it must bounce back to itself in compromise, and possibly in guilt. That, to Cáseres, was the Marrano condition, perhaps the human condition. Yet Luis insisted on purity and sincerity as conditions for being what he was. He was ready to conceal his actions (to a point), but not to refrain from performing them. A Judaizing Alumbrado (he actually called himself "Lumbroso," the illuminated), Luis Carvajal demanded to assert himself through his actions (meaning ritual actions) rather than bury his deep beliefs inside a heart that compromises its purity by censoring its own expression.

There was no way Luis would not be caught. He was a tragic figure from the start. Perhaps unavowedly, he sought martyrdom knowing that under the political conditions into which he was born, this was the inevitable price of purity and openness.

Cáseres vehemently objected: this was madness. A practical businessman, he opted for life rather than tragedy, and for ordinary reason rather than the sublime. He too considered the Marrano Law of Moses important, but not the center of his existence. His goal was to see his family traverse the hard times; and he knew that perfection was for the dead.

In the end, Luis's way prevailed and the family perished. Luis Carvajal *el Mozo*, his sisters, and his mother were burned alive as *relapsos* in a grand *auto de fe*. Cáseres himself, engulfed in the tide, was sentenced to life imprisonment.

This tragedy was not without an ironic side: *Luis Carvajal died for a religion quite estranged from rabbinical Judaism*. His religion rested on the Bible, on mystical experiences, and on a short list of theological dogmas and Judaizing practices. Rabbinical Judaism is not centered on the Bible, but on the Talmud and the rabbinical literature around it. The Bible's authority is nominally admitted, but is superseded by layers of Talmudic interpretations and ramifications and is allowed to exercise its influence only through them. Stripped of these protective layers, even the Bible *in itself* is viewed with suspicion, as a possible source of Sadducee or Karaite heresy.

In addition, Talmudic culture helps restrain the bursting forces of mysticism that were important in Carvajal's religiosity. And the rabbis, with few exceptions, do not take as much interest in abstract theological dogmas as do Catholics—and as did Carvajal.

Luis de Carvajal had almost no other sources by which to give content to his Jewish intent than the Bible—the *Christian* Bible, which he studied through the eyes of Catholic-Marrano scholars.[5] He also relied on a Spanish translation of Maimonides's "Thirteen Articles of Faith," a bare-bones summary of Jewish beliefs that is far less central to Judaism than the *credo* is to Catholicism. From such eclectic sources, and lacking the crucial input of the Talmud, Carvajal had to carve out the content of the Law of Moses, by which he had resolved to live—and die. As a poet following the Hispano-Catholic mystics of his time, he composed mystical liturgy through which the Marrano soul could approach union with the God of Moses. He was a mixture of quasi-biblical Jew, Jewish Alumbrado, semi-Karaite, and Christian-inspired scholastic; and he became a martyr of a religion in which most rabbis would have felt strangers. At the same time, and rather inadvertently, Luis shaped for himself and other Marranos a new kind of Judaism: rudimentary and lacking public legitimation, but quite innovative and heterodox—the first in modern Jewish history.[6]

Francisco Botello, Unorthodox Martyr

In the *auto de fe* of November 19, 1659, Francisco Botello was burned alive in Mexico's Plaza Mayor.[7] The rainy weather did not deter a huge crowd from gathering to watch the thrilling show—forty thousand people, says a chronicler,[8] cramping the plaza and nearby streets. The chronicler called Botello "the most obstinate Jew whom the Holy Office has punished for centuries." Until the last minute, and for long years before, the inquisitors had pressured him to admit Jesus and avoid the flames but he refused. His motto was: *"One has to be what one is, and to die remaining what one is."*[9]

Who exactly was Botello, and what did he know about what he thought he was? For most of his life he had been a wanderer in Spain and Mexico, moving between places and occupations at a dazzling pace. At age forty-two he settled down and married María de Zárate, an Old Christian innkeeper, against the fierce opposition of her family.[10] Most of Francisco's relatives had been humiliated and reconciled by the Inquisition, whereas María's maternal family claimed the ancestry of no less a Jew-hater than Archbishop Juan Silíceo, the architect of the "pure blood" legislation (see chapter 12). But María loved Francisco, and in the Romeo-and-Juliet situation—and tragedy—that followed, was ready to espouse her lover's cause more than Shakespeare's heroine did.

Their happiness lasted for eight years. In 1642, Botello, already suspected, was arrested for the first time. A spy overheard him conduct a conversation in the inn, in which the Law of Moses was praised. Francisco persisted in refusing to make a full confession and recant, so his incarceration lasted six years. During that time he gained instruction in the revered Law of Moses, which he considered to be his defining identity. Just as criminal prisons today are often schools of crime, so the cells of the Holy Office had sometimes functioned as a covert college of Jewish studies—teaching the impoverished, Catholicized, unorthodox Judaism of the Marranos.

Though Botello was steadfast as a Jew (whatever he understood by that term), he respected Christians who professed their *own* religion. His belief in authenticity was linked to religious universalism: everyone should be faithful to what they are and be saved in their own way. Botello did not die an enemy of Christ, but of intolerance.

When put to torture he refused to make a full confession, knowing this might compromise María and send his already "reconciled" relatives to the flames. In agony, Botello shouted and protested, invoking God, the Virgin, and the Devil—but he persisted. The Inquisition took down his cries. "Ay, ay, God help me, I already told the truth! Ay ay, I am dying, I can no more"—thus for two and one-half hours. Then the inquisitors gave up. Botello's first ordeal ended in the *auto de fe* of 1649, in which he was "reconciled."[11]

If he relapsed now, he would be burned. This was clear to Francisco, to María, and also to José de Zárate, the disgruntled young man who six years later denounced Francisco again (and also María). José was the natural son of a mestizo servant whom María had practically adopted, but anger, ambition, and envy turned him against María when she refused to allow him to marry her niece. José realized he would never be accepted by the family because of his birth. But why was Francisco, with his equally "impure blood," María's chosen and beloved? José told the Inquisition that Francisco had secretly converted María to Judaism. The charge seems a blow-up of José's envy of Francisco. His evidence was confused. He recalled that as a child María used to pray without making the sign of the cross. She recited her Catholic prayers "so as to praise only the God of Abraham, Isaac, and Jacob, and nothing else." At that time she also abstained from pork and rabbit. José and others saw her light a candle in front of a tapestry with the icons of Moses, King David, and Saint Jerome on it, pretending to honor the latter but actually intending the former. All this, as

Nathan Wachtel comments, can be explained by love and empathy for her jailed husband who was suffering because of his attachment to Jewish-like symbols, rather than by actual apostasy.

Perhaps this empathy caused María to adopt her husband's tolerant (and thus scandalous) viewpoint on religion. "God did not want man's free will to be forced," she said in his defense, "but wanted each one to follow the Law he prefers."[12] To this heretical statement of toleration she added a grain of Botello's religious universalism: "God the Father was not angry of those serving God the Son, nor was the Son angry with the servants of God the Father." María knew only too well that Botello could not demand of her to abandon Christianity. His influence on her barred apostasy rather than encouraging it.

The prosecutor in Botello's second trial described Botello's use of classic Marrano tricks to avoid participating in Mass, or looking away from the Host during Adoration. At first Botello tried to discredit his accusers; he even asked to be served pork in his meals, but it was discovered that he dumped the pork into the latrine. In the end he gave up on active defense. As the awesome need to choose between recanting and the stake was coming near, he tried to evade it by feigning to be mad. Perhaps he actually experienced hallucinations. He continued to behave extravagantly even after he was resigned to dying by fire—to be what he was—but now it resulted from a wild sense of liberation. Marrano prudence was cast away; the inhibitions of reason were the adversary now, instruments of self-alienation. At last Francisco Botello did not have to calculate, to pretend; now he was able to be what he was publicly—in the open and on the most conspicuous stage in the Hispanic world.

But what exactly did he die for? Not so much a religious creed—certainly not the rabbinical Judaism of which he had scant knowledge and a meager, distorted practice—but an identity that precedes its detailed attributes, his own identity as he perceived and willed it, in its relation with a broader origin or group, the Nation, and (as Wachtel suggests) memory. In Botello *the will went ahead of knowledge, and self-fidelity preceded its content.* In this he resembles other Marranos, including certain Judaizers, and anticipated the more secular form of Jewish identity known in later generations.

Botello was burned together with a relative, seventy-year-old Diego Díaz. When a priest admonished them for making signs of encouragement to one another, Díaz retorted: "Father, isn't it good that we exhort each other to die for God?" The old man, unlike Botello, used a Marrano double language to the end.

María, meanwhile, had gone through a grueling session of torture—her cries and groans cover several pages of Holy Office records[13]—after which she was cleared of apostasy by a vote of four to three. But she was severely punished for her actual dissent—for the modest attempt, driven by love rather than ideology, that she made at religious freedom. In the *auto de fe* in which her beloved husband was burned, María too marched as penitent, watching the horror. Then, shattered, penniless, childless, and estranged from her family, she was confined as a worker in a monastic hospital, from which she sought for years to be liberated. But when her request was finally granted, she reconsidered and withdrew it: she had nowhere to go.

Fernando de Medina: Martyrdom as Paradox

Botello's unorthodox Jewishness and self-struggle were magnified in the sharp reversals and paradoxes in which another martyr, Fernando de Medina, assumed his Jewish fidelity under inquisitorial pressure. Medina went much farther than Botello in relativizing religion. A religious universalist, semiatheist, and Judaizer all at once, his problem was not on the order of theology, but of personal loyalty—*faithfulness to where he came from and who his people were*; in other words, to the Nation. This became the only stabilizing power capable of overcoming his otherwise changeable attitude and confounding contradictions. And it emerged principally in jail, following an initial weakness in facing himself and the inquisitors.

Fernando de Medina was born in 1656 as Moisés Gómez, son of Abraham and Sara Gómez, in the Marrano "gray zone" of southwest France (Peyrehorade), where Judaism, though forbidden, was practically tolerated but was more lax and diluted than in Livorno and Amsterdam.[14] In his first depositions to the Inquisition, Fernando volunteered the fatal information that he had been both circumcised and baptized. (This duality deprived him of the defense of being a full-fledged Jew, and thus outside the Inquisition's jurisdiction.) At age twelve, Fernando clandestinely followed his father and brothers to Madrid, where they assumed Christian names and manners while secretly Judaizing (and where the boy probably was circumcised, which indicates a fervent Jewish attachment).[15] Now called Fernando de Medina, he spent the next decade working in different cities for the royal monopoly of tobacco, but lost all his money and was twice jailed for debt. During that time he was involved with a network of Judaizers and tried to observe Jewish holidays, though not always on the correct date.

In 1687 he tried his luck again in Mexico. Four years later he was arrested on charges of Judaizing in Spain and the New World. At first he cooperated with the Inquisition and seemed ready to make a clean breast; then he became erratic and arrogant, insulting the inquisitors and contradicting himself time and again. "He is confused and unable to fix himself on anything," the clerk wrote. The inquisitors thought he was feigning madness, but his turmoil seemed real.

Time and again he made confessions then retracted them. All the signs indicate he was experiencing deep guilt—for talking, for incriminating others, possibly for his own disorder in what he believed. In one remarkable session he poured out the names of dozens of Judaizers he had known in Spain but refused to sign his own statement: "These are my friends!" he shouted, "I denounced my friends! Am I crazy to sign this paper?" He then tried to destroy it.

With long interruptions, the procedure against Medina lasted eight years. At one point he seemed determined to openly identify himself as a Jew. He prided himself on being of "the Jewish Nation," invoked Abraham, Isaac, and Jacob as his true ancestry, and derided Christ's claim to be the Messiah. When found in his cell wearing a blouse that represented a *talit*, he told the jailers he wasn't a Christian but a Jew, and that Judaism was the purest and best religion.[16]

Significantly, Medina did not say Judaism was the *true* religion because on that he had doubts. It turned out in the interrogation that Medina doubted God's existence and denied the afterlife. "The soul is the mind, and when the body dies, the mind also dies and disappears," he flatly stated. This was remarkable for a person facing martyrdom. In another session Medina reiterated that he did not know if God exists, while reaffirming at the same time that he was a Jew. The confounded clerk noted that Medina was talking "beside the point" and "feigns not to understand." But it was the clerk—and the inquisitors—who did not understand the new phenomenon before them: adherence to a people and historical identity that is free of a specific theology.

Repeatedly in his prayers Medina invoked the Jewish patriarchs but never mentioned God. His agnosticism did not disqualify religion; it only relativized and moralized it. Religions were good for *this* world, not the next; and salvation consisted in a morally virtuous life here and now. "He thought there is nothing but the present," the clerk reported, "that no sin exists beside doing wrong to others, and that the good should be rewarded in this life." It was from this inner-worldly moral viewpoint that Judaism was purer than Christianity. The perplexed clerk commented that Medina "mixes different errors, some coming from the Jewish faith, others from the absurdities of the atheists." But actually Medina mixed many more positions, each characteristic of some Marranos. In him all the contradictory modes of being a Marrano that we analyzed in chapter 5 were curiously united. He was simultaneously a Judaizer, a skeptic, a religious universalist, an agnostic, and an adherent of Marrano this-worldliness (which I called elsewhere "a philosophy of immanence"). And he was absolutely unable to condemn Judaism, as the inquisitors demanded that he do. He clung to his historical culture and lineage not in mere nostalgia, but as a willed belonging, an ongoing adherence to the nation founded by the Jewish patriarchs, which his own parents and ancestors had continued. This gave him, in the last analysis, his anchorage in the universe, a possible sense for his existence and, no less, the expiation of whatever sense of guilt and betrayal he had experienced because of his early inglorious vacillation in front of the Inquisition and his own destiny.

Marrano Intellectuals

Botello and Medina were no intellectuals; but the Marrano Dispersion did boast poets, natural scientists, philosophers, and essayists of different intellectual levels, alongside the religious popularizes and messianic agitators. And several Marrano centers organized literary and musical clubs, dignified as *academias*. Most of their culture was brought from Iberia, or depended on it; and when they became New Jews, they "Iberianized" this new experience by casting it into Spanish and Portuguese forms of language, mentality, custom, and style. In the next pages we shall meet a sample of these intellectuals and their spectrum of dualities.

Enemy Brothers: The Cardosos

For a Marrano family to be split between Judaizers and faithful Catholics was common enough. A rarer sight was Marrano siblings who chose to restore their Jewish selves outside Iberia, yet clashed bitterly over what kind of Judaism to adopt. Such was the case of the Cardoso enemy brothers, Fernando and Miguel.[17]

Born around 1603, Fernando Cardoso had a meteoric career in Spain. At age twenty-two, he held a chair at the University of Valladolid. Several years later he penetrated into the elegant, literary and political circles of Madrid and its royal court. A physician and man of science, Dr. Cardoso also tried his hand at poetry and was admitted to the circle of Lope de Vega, the literary prince of the time.

At the height of his career, Fernando Cardoso underwent a change. He delved into his suppressed Jewish past and identified with it. The records show that, at least since the mid-1640s, he was secretly active as propagandist of the Law of Moses. As Yerushalmi shows, he too drew the content of his Judaism from Christian sources, such as the Latin Bible and the church fathers.[18]

Meanwhile, Fernando's younger brother Miguel, his junior by twenty-three years, finished his studies of medicine and Catholic theology (which marked him for life), and joined his brother in Madrid. At first Fernando was upset by Miguel's penchant for light music and chasing women, but soon he was able to stir in Miguel the same Jewish sentiment that animated him. In 1648 both Cardosos broke with their life in Spain and returned to open Judaism in Italy. They were circumcised in Livorno and got their Jewish reeducation in Venice, the capital of Jewish-Marrano learning. Miguel became Abraham (also Abraham-Mikhael) and Fernando became Yizhak.

The brothers differed in temperament as well as age. Yerushalmi calls Yizhak "calm, methodical, always in control of himself," whereas Abraham was "an ecstatic, a visionary, always turbulent."[19] Yet each brother's Jewish path was markedly, if differently, stamped by his Hispano-Catholic education. Yizhak remained attached to the rational, semischolastic philosophy of his upbringing; whereas Abraham effervesced over the grand eschatological prospects of Jewish mysticism, especially in its Lurian version. His approach to Kabbalah had a Catholic subtext; it betrayed Christian themes and drives, which Abraham reintegrated into his New Jewish experience. Thus, he believed that Catholic mysteries such as the Incarnation and the Trinity were falsifications of original Kabbalist ideas, so in adopting Jewish mysticism in the unconventional way he did, Abraham was tacitly setting a Christian vision right and restoring it to authenticity. When Sabbetai Zevi, the Jewish messianic pretender who stirred the whole Diaspora, made his appearance, Abraham Cardoso received him as the true messiah—the one Jesus was supposed to have been—and remained his fervent devotee and ideologue even after Sabbetai's humiliating conversion to Islam.

This issue, more than anything, destroyed the brothers' bond forever. From Egypt and Tripoli, where he had moved, Abraham flooded the Jewish world with tracts and letters arguing that a deep secret was hidden in Sabbetai's apostasy. The true Messiah must undergo suffering and humiliation (a Christian theme again), so Sabbetai's apostasy was the utmost degradation, which fulfills his messianic destiny! Moreover, he wrote, Marranos should be the first to know that redemption must be attained through sin and transgression, as Queen Esther, their idol, also testifies. An apostate Messiah is a powerful vindication of the Marranos' own sins and plight.[20]

To his brother's rationalist ears this antinomistic theology sounded as hollow sophistry. Yizhak despised Kabbalah and called it "foolish," as absurd as alchemy and astrology.[21] In Sabbetai Zevi he saw a traitor and charlatan, and he condemned his brother's defense of the apostate as treason to embattled Judaism. Yizhak launched a public campaign to stop his brother's heretical propaganda and caused Abraham to be chased away by most Jewish communities. Yet secret Sabbetians everywhere saw him as their guide. As his boldness grew, Abraham made several predictions of the day of Jewish redemption, which turned sour. One of the dates he set for Sabbetai's reappearance was 1706. But in that year Abraham himself died, killed by a relative over a matter of money.

Still, Abraham/Miguel was the more original brother. That Yizhak/Fernando was more conventional, a member of the cultural establishment wherever he went, is seen in his *Philosophia libera*, the 1673 tract he published in his old age. The book was published during the most innovative period in modern philosophy and science; yet Yizhak Cardoso basically echoed the conventional wisdom of Spain in his youth. Not only was Descartes' philosophical revolution practically ignored, Yizhak Cardoso even rejected Copernicus's and Galileo's pictures of the universe, in favor of the ancient Ptolemaic cosmology to which his Spanish teachers—and the Inquisition, too—had adhered.

Yizhak Cardoso's text is fresher and bolder in *The Excellences of the Hebrews*, a combative apologia for the Jews that draws on gentile and Jewish sources in responding to libelous stereotypes against the Jews and praises their qualities. By this apologetic work, Yizhak Cardoso contributed to a specifically Marrano genre of Jewish authorship, just as his brother created a Marrano kind of Jewish messianic theology. In both cases, Jewish-Marrano culture in the Dispersion is seen as distinct from the Orthodox rabbinical literary tradition.

Jewish-Marrano Poets

Working alternately within Catholicism, Judaism, and the no-man's-land between the two, Jewish-Marrano writers produced a distinct voice in poetry and religious expression.[22] The best known poets were João Pinto Delgado (ca. 1585–1653), Antonio Enríquez Gómez (ca. 1600–1663), and Miguel de Barrios (1635–1701). Their literary style depended on Spanish writers of the Golden Age, but thematically their poeticized experience was mainly drawn from the Marrano condition.

João Pinto Delgado chose a life of Jewish ambivalence and concealment infused with Hispano-Portuguese culture. He moved between Lisbon and Rouen (France), where an unofficial New Jewish community was operating. In Rouen, Delgado published his main works, among them three long poems on the Biblical figures closest to Marranos' hearts—Queen Esther, Ruth the Moabite, and the prophet Jeremiah in his lamentations. Esther was the "first Marrana," who in the end saved her people; Ruth, a foreign convert, ended up begetting King David; and Jeremiah wrote the lamentations on the Judean exile, which Marranos read as referring to their own. (This again points to the biblical culture of Jewish-Marranos.) Although not great art, Delgado's stanzas were read with poetic tension by his audience because they made the biblical metaphor actual in terms of their present. "O City . . . I no longer know you now," Delgado's Jeremiah says to the city of Jerusalem, here representing Judaism:

no Judaizing Marrano will fail to recognize his own lack of Jewish knowledge in these words. And when Delgado aptly exclaims: "Your sons in their despair have gone silent," what could be more Marrano-like than this silence?[23]

In other stanzas mystical tones arise, influenced by the Spanish mystics of the time and, like them, using the biblical *Song of Songs* as reference.[24] The beloved Shulamit (the poet's soul) has betrayed her lover (God), and in losing the mystical tower he had built for her, she cries, "I myself was lost." Now the soul hopes for a miraculous fire that will consume its enemies (meaning Christianity, but also meaning its own sins in betraying Moses) and allow the soul to ascend to God again. "For when like a dove [a Christian symbol] I lift myself up to heaven, the net would not detain me here." This is not a happy ending, however, but a dialectical story; in order to overcome its symbolic exile, the soul must spring the "net" that detains it in Iberia and, like Delgado, go into physical exile.

In another personal poem Delgado writes:

> So send, O Lord, into my night
> A ray of your divine light,
> And in the desert,
> Within the loving fire's light
> Let it call me. There,
> Unaffected by worldly memories . . .
> My soul rises blissfully to behold
> Your glory, in which, by miraculous effect,
> The sovereign object transforms
> My being into himself.[25]

This is a mystical poem in the style of Saint John of the Cross and Fray Luis de León, but a Jewish heart is implanted into its Christian body. The desert is Moses' desert, and the "loving fire," a typical image in Spanish mysticism, refers to Moses' burning bush. The prisoner of "tyrannical servitude" is at once the Jewish people and the poet's soul, because of its Catholic upbringing (and thus, unavoidable betrayal). Delgado knows that his "Egypt" is not only Iberia, but resides in his own mental baggage wherever he goes.

Miguel (Daniel Levi) de Barrios. In 1665, a book of Spanish verse about life, love, beauty, reflection, anecdote, and a lot of social flattery was published in Brussels. The author of this *Flor de Apolo* (Apollo's Blossom) was Miguel de Barrios, a Spanish cavalry captain and an aspiring socialite in Brussels, the capital of Spain's government in the low countries. Few people knew his secret—that he was, at the same time, a circumcised member of the Jewish-Portuguese community in Amsterdam, where he kept a wife and three children and used to travel periodically.

This extraordinary arrangement lasted for twelve years. In 1674, Barrios settled permanently in Amsterdam as an open Jew, calling himself Daniel Levi de Barrios, and remained there until his death in 1701. He lived by his pen, producing heaps of verse of all kinds, some of it distinctly religious. Barrios was too bohemian for the Marrano bourgeois community, too much of an outsider and nonconformist. Even his lax Judaism was too jealous in one respect—he remained faithful to the pretender-messiah Sabbetai Zevi even after the latter's conversion to Islam. So he often stood in conflict with the Jewish oligarchs. He did not dare leave the congregation. Where would he go? In Spain and Brussels he could speak Spanish but there was the Inquisition, and in gentile Holland Barrios lacked contacts and the necessary language and social skills. So the Jewish community that was his refuge also became his prison and he died there in misery.[26]

Philosophers and Dissidents

The Wise Master of Eyquem: Montaigne

The Spanish Marranos in the region of Bordeaux gave France not only big traders, but also its brightest writer of the sixteenth century. Michel de Montaigne, landlord of Eyquem, was born in 1533 to a wealthy Christian merchant and to his Converso wife, Antoinette López, whose family had settled in southwestern France some time earlier. This was the time of the early Reformation. Montaigne and his father were Catholic, while his ex-Jewish mother and two of his brothers were Protestants. Thus Montaigne grew up in a family marked by the presence and traces of three religions, two of them opposed to the ruling order. His mother incorporated both a Marrano background and its not unnatural shift to the Reformation; so in choosing to be Catholic, Montaigne rejected his mother twice. Yet her impact must have played a part in the relaxed and skeptical way in which he assumed his Catholicism.

Montaigne matured into the wars of religion that tore the French body politic. But he never became a fervent adherent of any religious persuasion. While Frenchmen slaughtered each other for the same God, differently approached, Montaigne kept a clear head, advocating tolerance and emitting prudently the sense that all sects had something relative in them. Characteristically, Montaigne supported the Protestant King Henri IV in his decision to reconvert to Catholicism in order to pacify France and secure his kingdom. Henri's famous dictum,

"*Paris vaut bien une messe*" (Paris is well worth a Mass), is generally interpreted as cynical; yet to Montaigne it was politically and morally wise. No religion in the world was worth the destruction and mass killing it generated, or the disintegration of the body politic, a result that always breeds barbarism and suffering. The "Paris" that was worth a Mass signified the restoration of a central government, of a unified political community, and the citizens' peace and chance of well being; and that, to Montaigne, must overrule theological differences.

Encouraged by Montaigne, Henri IV's move signaled the deconfessional-ization of the French state as such and anticipated the future emancipation of politics from religion.[27] Whether or not Montaigne had acted as Marrano, a Marrano (of a certain kind) would have acted like Montaigne.

In that he was akin to a later philosopher of Marrano origin, Baruch Spinoza, who, like Montaigne, transcended all three historical religions. Yet in other ways, Montaigne's intellectual attitudes were almost opposite to Spinoza's. Spinoza sought to replace revealed religion with a rigorous system of reason that manifests the same absolute truth that religion vainly claims. Montaigne, skeptical by temperament and prudent in method, was sufficiently ironic to shun this ideal. Though he doubted the specific claims of all revealed religions,[28] he accepted Christianity not as truth, but as a fact of civilization, a basic European given (this form of acceptance is also Marrano-like), and turned his real attention from dogmatic scholasticism to personal reasoning and examined experience. These he made his only guide to wisdom, for wisdom was this-worldly to Montaigne (again a Marrano-like attitude), the fruit of individual self-reflection and observation of the human world, rather than derived from religious dogma or timeless philosophical generalizations.

The result were his celebrated volumes of *Essays*, which launched a new genre in Western literature. Nothing similar had been written before. The French term *essai* means trial, and Montaigne, indeed, wrote as an experimenter, an explorer describing with ease and fluency the human comedy as he encountered it, and tried to draw a reasoned sense from his reflections on society and the inner mind. Unlike rationalist philosophers who seek rigor and demonstration, Montaigne used reason in an observational mode, informed by concrete situations from his own experience and by the wisdom of ancient pagans.

Montaigne claimed neither divine grace and inspiration nor an indubitable "natural light." He recognized the diversity of the human world and did not try to systematize it. For these and other reasons he was called a skeptic, yet he did not doubt the sagacity of his own reflections or their value for others. He was simply aware that wisdom, in being this-worldly, is also finite and temporal, so he was reluctant to give any views, including his own, the cachet of an absolute eternal truth.

When Henri IV ascended the throne he offered Montaigne the post of senior counselor, but Montaigne turned it down. He had long before retired from his public career (he had been mayor of Bordeaux and member of its high court) to his estate of Eyquem, to reflect peacefully and write and polish the *Essays* (and possibly enjoy the wine which, known today as Chateau d'Yquem, is still one of France's best). His individualism and worldly search for wisdom, his early, and dangerous, preaching of tolerance, his opposition to forced conversions and torture (and hence, to the Inquisition), would surely put him in spiritual alliance with many New Christians. That his New Christian ancestry was causally responsible for these positions is hard to prove, but its relevance is even harder to dismiss.[29]

Gabriel (Uriel) da Costa

A shattering event occurred in 1640 in the Portuguese-Jewish community of Amsterdam.[30] Uriel da Costa, a famous maverick and rebel who had twice been banned by the community, humiliated in public, and lived bitterly in forced isolation, put a bullet through his head. The dramatic event brought to a climax the itinerary of a dissenter within Catholicism who had turned reformer within Judaism, and finally sought to become a "universal man," but failed in all these endeavors.

Born a New Christian in Porto, Portugal, young Gabriel da Costa had studied Catholic canon law and risen to become church treasurer. But he was disaffected with the hiatus between Catholicism and the original biblical spirit of religion. He continued—and radicalized—the Converso intellectuals we met in chapters 14–15, who could endorse Christianity only by becoming dissenters within it. But young Costa went further. His semi-Erasmian move, seeking to retrieve the pure origins of the Gospel, finally led him outside Christianity altogether and back to a form of Judaism. The true word of God lay in the Bible, and the true Bible was the Old Testament, the law of Costa's Jewish ancestors. In a moving autobiography attributed to him, Costa recounted his itinerary but failed to mention that he used to practice Judaism in secret, as did his mother.[31] This fact, discovered by a modern scholar, might indicate that young Costa had been aware from the outset that Judaism, too, was no longer purely biblical, but contained rules and beliefs that the Bible denied or did not recognize. Yet Costa, I think, believed and expected that, unlike ossified Iberian Catholicism, the New Jewish experience outside Iberia was sufficiently fresh and flexible to allow for a spiritual renewal and reform of Judaism, based on the original Bible.

Thus Costa was a Marrano from beginning to end. His dissent inside Christianity arose from a Marrano unrest and duality; and his answer focused on another Jewish-Marrano experience rather than on orthodox Judaism. To many he looked like a Karaite; but the sources of his Jewish heresy were different, fully anchored in the Marrano situation.

When the Inquisition targeted his town of Porto, Costa and a few family members fled Portugal. It was only in the Dispersion that he fully realized how far away rabbinical Judaism was, not only from the Bible, but also from the Crypto-Jewish practices Costa had followed in Portugal. Costa became an official Jew in Amsterdam but soon his religious disenchantment took over again, now directed against contemporary Judaism, which he found no less distorted than Catholicism and even more fraught with external rituals—hundreds of religiously irrelevant minutiae by which the rabbis had shrouded the true meaning of God. Moreover, the rabbis followed the Christians in requiring belief in the immortality of the soul—a false dogma that not only reason, but the Bible itself rejects.

Costa had pressed the latter point already in Portugal. But he expected the New Jewish experience in the Dispersion to be more flexible and amenable to reform, and precisely herein lay his tragic mistake. He failed to realize that the Marrano immigrants could not reconnect with the rest of the Jews and forge and solidify their inner congregations unless they accepted, at least superficially, the rabbinical religion, which indeed was initially very foreign to them—and that, therefore, they would have to denounce and expel reformers like himself. His ideal Judaism was just too spiritual, too rational to serve the sociological needs of historical and communitarian integration.

The clash was inevitable. The Portuguese Jewish community banned Costa, and he, not knowing Dutch and unable to make a living outside the Jewish community, lived for years in isolation and misery. Finally he broke down and recanted—externally, without changing his views. Now he was "reconciled" to the community and lived as a Marrano among ex-Marranos. But soon the believer in religious authenticity found it impossible to dissimulate (like Carvajal, his opposite number and martyr), and a new conflict arose. Costa was banned a second time. He stood his guns for seven more years, until he recanted again. In a Jewish-Marrano version of public humiliation—a kind of a Jewish auto da fé—Costa was required to prostrate himself at the door of the synagogue and was lashed thirty-nine times. Before his suicide he wrote his personal story—*Exemplar of a Human Life*—composed in semi-picaresque style, but projecting self-pity rather than irony. By that time he had turned deist, believing in a universal God who interferes little in worldly affairs. Thus he moved beyond all historical religions.

Costa's quest for religious authenticity had first made him a reformer within the Catholic fold. When he crossed to Judaism, he did so from within Christianity. His mistake was to expect that Judaism in the Marrano Dispersion would lend itself to a purifying reform, toward its biblical origins. He did not realize that Marrano Judaism needed the solidifying effect of the same historical tradition he hoped to overcome. In colliding with the historically determined shape of Judaism, the frustrated Costa discovered—and disavowed—the historical face of all revealed religions, going beyond them toward a religion of reason. But his attempt to live as a universal man, outside of all links of belonging, was premature and proved disastrous. Lacking the mutual assistance of others like him, Costa was unable to survive in isolation, neither practically nor in an inward sense.

Dr. Juan (Daniel) de Prado

A particularly complex personage among the Marrano heretics of the Dispersion was Dr. Juan (Daniel) de Prado, an older friend of Spinoza who was also banned by the Amsterdam community.[32] Prado was a Spanish New Christian who turned to the Law of Moses while studying medicine and theology at the university of Alcalá de Henares. Later he boasted to a relative that he did so by his own choice, on the sole basis of his personal learning and judgment. Thus from early on, Prado manifested the early modern tendency for relying on one's personal thought and judgment in most important matters, including the sacred teaching of tradition.

During the academic year 1635–36, Prado met and fraternized in Spain with a younger man, Balthazar Orobio de Castro, who studied the same subjects. The two young men made a pact of clandestine Judaizing. Prado, while practicing medicine, organized semi-Jewish rituals and persuaded other New Christians to adopt the Law of Moses. In 1650 he led a conspiracy to frame and discredit an informer of the Inquisition and smuggled encouraging letters to Judaizing prisoners. However, five years later he was banned by the Amsterdam community as a heretic to Judaism. How is this to be explained?

We know that early doubts had already fermented in Prado's mind in Spain. He had told Orobio de Castro that, at bottom, all religions recognize the same God, which is Aristotle's first cause. Religions differ only politically, in how they order the life of the community, but this is not what salvation depends upon. Salvation depends exclusively on knowing God, so every man can be saved while following his own religion. Some historians conclude that Prado was acting as a Jewish believer while being a heretic at heart. Perhaps, but why should a person masquerade as Jew when he perceives Judaism to be both risky and unnecessary for his salvation? A possible answer is: because he considers underground Judaism important for other things he values, more this-worldly things such as brotherhood, authenticity, pride of origin, or opposition to authority. That Prado had such dispositions is shown in his unusual demand later in Amsterdam—to remain a member of the Jewish community despite his religious dissension. We should, however, be careful not to attribute to Prado more rationality, and greater control of his contradictory drives and personas, than his case warrants. It is more plausible to impute the ambivalence to Prado's own mind.

The masks that Prado wore did not conceal an integral inner self posing as something else to the world; they reveal a duality that prevailed in his very inner Self. Struck by Prado's paradoxes, Orobio tersely chided him for having been "a fake Christian and a true Jew where you could not be a Jew [in Spain], and a fake Jew where you could be truly Jewish [in Amsterdam]."

As I have suggested elsewhere,[33] in leaving Iberia, Prado moved from Judaism as an existential and fraternal condition to Judaism as a normative and doctrinal system. In Spain it was a reality of men and women sharing a common fate and fighting for their special kind of existence. Now, in Amsterdam, Judaism posited itself as a system of norms, rules, and mandatory beliefs that Prado was required to accept as a condition of his reentry into historical Judaism, but to which he, as an individual stressing personal judgment, could not assent. As the pressing necessities of an underground brotherhood no longer existed, his doubts burst into the open, leading to his friendship with the younger Spinoza—and their ban by the Jewish community.

While Spinoza accepted his severance from the community, Prado appealed his ban. His demand confronted the community with a problem no one had faced before. Here was a Jew who refused to sever his ties with them and yet was a heretic in his beliefs. Was it possible to maintain within the historical community of the Jews a person who denies basic religious beliefs and commandments? Unwittingly, Prado set himself in the role of the first unorthodox Jew. Just as in Iberia, Judaism to him was primarily a fraternity, a social network and fidelity, so now again he tried to break the tie between orthodox religion and participation in the community of Jews. He did not do it as a conscious project; he simply acted out his own perceptions and drives—and his personal contradictions. But thereby he foreshadowed the broader modern problem of nonreligious Jewishness. From the other side of the inquisitorial divide—so did also Francisco Botello whom we met earlier: in that protomodern problem, which history rather than ideology must decide, the banned heretic and the Judaizing martyr landed in the same spot.

Baruch Spinoza, the Emblematic Jewish Heretic

Baruch (Bento, or Benedictus) Spinoza was born in 1632 to parents who had been New Christians in Iberia, as were most of the members of his Amsterdam Jewish-Portuguese community. His brilliant performance at the religious college (yeshiva) Keter Torah—where he gained the world-class expertise in the Bible that later served him as founder of secular biblical criticism—would have destined young Baruch for the rabbinate, as Saul Levy Morteira, his chief teacher, must have hoped. Yet in the end, Rabbi Morteira found it necessary to anathemize Spinoza in harsh and terrible words, for Spinoza's unorthodox and searching mind became deeply dissatisfied with Judaism and Christianity alike. Spinoza took a far more radical step than most former Marranos in the Dispersion: while they typically passed from one particular religion to another, or mixed the two, Spinoza transcended the whole universe of historically revealed religion as such. Instead, he looked to philosophy for supplying an alternative system of irrefutable truth and ethical guidance, grounded in the natural power of reason rather than the supernatural lights of prophecy and revelation, which he considered the effects of the imagination. Moreover, young Spinoza expected philosophy to provide not only knowledge and ethics, but a religion of reason by which to find salvation, or something parallel to it, not in the afterlife, but in this world—in a perfected personal state attained in this life.

At first, however, all the philosophy he was able to set his eyes on was contained in old Hebrew books by Jewish philosophers such as Maimonides and Hasdai Crescas. These works did not figure in the official curriculum of the yeshiva (Rabbi Morteira used to say: "Whoever does philosophy is an evil sinner [*rasha*])," so young Spinoza had to seek them out wherever he could. In reading these texts—which sometimes sound daring to orthodox ears—Spinoza must have stressed ideas that, in context, would still be considered legitimate, yet taken in themselves might undermine religious certainties.

It was only in his twenties that Spinoza studied Latin (in private), and gained access to Descartes and the New Philosophy of the age. He adopted Descartes' conceptual apparatus and part of his method but rejected the Cartesian dualism of mind and body, God and world. God is identical with the world; he is not the world's creator, but resides eternally in the world's infinite totality. The mental and physical domains are two complementary aspects of the same overall divine entity. There is no free will: God's laws are inscribed not in the Torah or the Christian scriptures, but in the immutable and necessary laws of nature, to which there is no exception. And human virtue derives from our natural desire for indefinite existence, guided by true understanding—both of which are natural powers. Spinoza had thus formulated what might be called a "philosophy of immanence": the conviction that the natural world is all there is, and that human civilization in all its aspects—knowledge, ethics, law, political legitimacy, private and social emotions, true freedom, love of God, even salvation—is derived exclusively from this world and can be attained only within it.

No wonder such views, even in their embryonic stage, scandalized the New Jewish congregation: they threatened its volatile cohesion-in-the-making. Advised by Morteira, the *parnassim* (aldermen) banished Spinoza and damned him with the harshest words found in the Amsterdam records. "Cursed be he by day and cursed by night, cursed in his lying down and cursed in his waking up . . . and may the Lord's wrath and zeal burn upon him." Spinoza's older friend Prado was banned a year later and for a while the two kept together, each searching in his own way. Informers told the Spanish Inquisition (which kept a vigil eye on the Dispersion, too) that the banished friends believed the soul dies with the body, and "there is no God except philosophically." This report is quite accurate, though in very different ways. Prado's philosophical God was a separate entity existing outside the world, in the traditional mode of the Deists; Spinoza's God was the world itself, in its unity and infinity—a strictly immanent deity.

The Calvinist establishment also denounced Spinoza; yet he was able to find a supportive milieu among the radical Protestant sects of Holland and later was supported by some liberal Dutch burghers. He lived modestly, supported by a fellowship from a friend and by designing and polishing optical lenses, then a high-tech art and science. When offered a professor's job in Heidelberg Spinoza refused, fearing to compromise his independence. His many enemies dubbed him "Jew and Atheist," a vilifying combination of two of the worst adjectives in the Christian vocabulary. His name was anathema to most European circles, and remained so for over a century after his untimely death in 1677 at age forty-five. It was only in the late eighteenth century that his revolutionary ideas became a major issue on the agenda of European philosophy, affecting a host of thinkers, artists, and scientists who helped shape the modern intellectual climate, from Kant and Goethe to Hegel, Heine, Nietzsche, Darwin, Freud, Bergson, Einstein, Sartre, Bertrand Russell, Davidson, and Deleuze, among many others.

One can recognize in Spinoza several attitudes and mental patterns that are typical of Marranos and that, transported from the context of religion to this-worldly philosophy, make him "a Marrano of Reason." (1) Spinoza manifested on a grand scale the intellectual unrest that generated religious skepticism in many Marranos, and, in some, also produced a new confidence and trust in rationality. (2) Similar to Judaizing Marranos, Spinoza's life ran on two planes, inner and outer, covert and overt; his inward truth opposed the dominant religion(s) of his society, yet this inner truth was no longer Judaism, but the universal religion of reason. (3) Spinoza often needed to use equivocal, dual language—which to most Marranos was a life's necessity, and which Spinoza developed into a special art. (4) His was a dual career: like many Marranos we met in this chapter, Spinoza's life divided in two parts (periods), though he did not move into Judaism but into a life of reason outside the historical creeds. (5) His search for an alternative road to salvation was typically Marrano; but whereas the Judaizers declared that salvation was not in Jesus but in the Law of Moses, Spinoza said that salvation lies neither in Moses nor in Jesus or any other revealed religion, but in the "intellectual love of God" based on rational understanding. (6) While Marranos stood in *existential* opposition to the Inquisition, Spinoza expressed this opposition philosophically, in demanding freedom of thought and expression, and in stating—contrary to the Inquisition's project—that any attempt to totally control the inward human thinking is doomed to fail. Thereby he became the philosopher of toleration, and a founding father of political liberalism.

Finally, like Judaizing Marranos adhering to their truth, Spinoza had the will and character to cling fast to his new truth even against ban, defamation, isolation from his family and friends, and anathema by the Calvinist establishment. After his expulsion he withstood pressure by his gentile friends to convert to Christianity; he probably saw this as an act of betrayal—both of his new inner conviction, and of his Jewish kin, who continued being burned for their faith in Iberia and Spanish America.

Spinoza complained of the identity created by post-exilic Judaism between faith in the rabbinical religion and partnership in the Jewish people. After the destruction of their ancient state, the Jews transformed their religion into a mobile fatherland, which they take with them wherever they go. Religious observance became a political condition of being part of the Jewish people. Spinoza considered this identity an aberration, a fundamental flaw of Jewish life, but had, in his time, no remedy to offer. The notion of secular Jewishness, which distinguishes between religious belief and belonging to the historical community of Jews, was still unthinkable at the time, although Spinoza foreshadowed it—not consciously, but in his case.

This, indeed, became the foremost feature of Jewish modernity. In several ways Spinoza was a forerunner of European modernity, and within it, of the modern Jewish situation, the topics we shall explore in the last two chapters.

19

Marranos and Western Modernity

Apart from their mixture of identities, the Marranos in Iberia have been marked by a dissonance between their economic weight and socio-cultural fragility. Despite their positive role in the middle and higher urban strata, they carried a negative stigma of alienness and innate dishonor that marginalized them socially; as the Other Within, their dialectic of exclusion-within-inclusion undermined their anchorage in the ruling social ideology and opened their minds to divergent possibilities. The Iberian Marranos thus failed to manifest the compact sociocultural solidity and rootedness typical of a bourgeoisie. Ambiguity, unrest, social discomfort, a measure of deracination, and inner fissure were rumbling under the insincere façade of social solidity and acceptance. From here arose a tacit culture of irony and passive doubt and also of active inner dissent—attitudes and ideas that the social conservative must find utterly inconceivable, and therefore condemn as scandalous, the product of corrupt judgment and even madness.

Immigrants carry their baggage in their heads more than in their trunks. When Iberian Marranos went abroad, they brought with them the whole range of unorthodox attitudes that had been stored in their minds for generations. Besides the Law of Moses, Marranos were involved in inward Christianity, ecumenism, universalism, deism, syncretism, some Calvinism, and religious pre-Enlightenment. Some were skeptical of any religion's claim to be the bearer of truth or ground of meaning, so they treated religion as merely a necessary social convention, an institution to which one belonged in a politically organized society (not unlike today in America). A great many, even when believers and regardless of their affiliation, manifested an individualistic and this-worldly orientation that focused its energies on personal achievement in this world rather than on salvation in the next.

Indeed, the whole mental geography of Marranism we have toured in previous chapters was exported with the Dispersion and came into contact with other societies across the globe. The Marrano experience was thus, in a sense, globalized and set on a cosmopolitan course.

Summary of the Argument

It has long been recognized that a significant relation must have existed between the Marrano phenomenon and Western modernization. But the idea has been floating in general fashion mostly, without much analysis and detail, or by stressing only a few relevant points. In what follows, I shall address the issue more broadly, by breaking it into specific ingredients and checking the matching patterns, or correlations, they present. My approach is *descriptive* and *analogical* rather than causal and linear. Although direct linear causes must have been at work, they are hard to isolate and even harder to measure. Moreover, they carry no weight in isolation, and never work alone. Localized causes are effectively relevant only within a broader structure or process that the researcher's questions and perspective delineate—indeed, only thus are they recognized and articulated as causes in the first place. Therefore our primary attention must be given to broader trends and structures and to the *matching* patterns that, quite surprisingly, they often reveal.

Looking back at the story and analysis in the previous chapters, we note a wide scale of attitudes and patterns of the Marrano experience that pre-illustrate or anticipate main features and claims of Western modernization. Here is a partial list:

- Cultural and religious restlessness;
- The breakdown or mixture of legitimizing traditions;
- Being at variance with accepted social modes, values, and routines;
- Religious skepticism and heterodoxy;
- The rise of a secular urban culture;
- Rationalism and universalistic tendencies;
- A search for a different way to salvation—either *within* religion or *instead* of it (that is, in a secular way);
- An emphasis on this world rather than the next as the center of one's existence and attention;
- A new system of values, honoring a person for initiative and achievements, rather than because of his or her origin and descent;
- Opposing religion's role as a coercive power system, and as a political instrument of the state;
- "privatizing" religion, both as a matter of one's inner home and mind;
- The demand for new (proto-modern) freedoms—the freedom of trade (including in the international space) and the freedom of a person's inner forum of conscience and belief;

- Antithesis to the political theology of the Inquisition, which used early modern tools of social organization to bring a premodern, basically medieval, outlook to its radical climax;
- The needs and demand for toleration, religious plurality (no state religion), free speech and thought.
- The discovery of subjectivity and the inner mind;
- The construction of the *Self* and personal conscience (which become the bearers of worth and, eventually, rights);
- The discovery or construction of private life (the private sphere, distinguished and sheltered from the communal public sphere).
- Valuing novelties; curiosity and openness to a changing world;
- A strong emphasis on international trade and global economic activity, superseding local differences;
- Relative cosmopolitanism, and interest in new widening horizons—both geographical and anthropological;
- A widening view of human civilization, sensitive to differences as well as to common features, thus creating a broader concept of *humanitas* than is possible in a closed indigenous society;
- Special appreciation for the acquisition of knowledge and intellectual assets, both as end in themselves and as levers for personal advancement;
- New aesthetic sensibilities, including the emphasis on irony and self-irony, linguistic allusions, and games of equivocation.

Each of these features can be read in a dual perspective: all are illustrated in some distinctive Marrano experience we have met, and all invoke recognizable trends in the rise of Western modernity. So a significant match between the two springs to eye. What took place on the macro-European scale in the matter of modernization and secularization had been prefigured by microforms of life and mind that Marranos experienced in Iberia and exported into their Dispersion. Did Marranos also play a role in *generating* those trends? Here, for reasons I mentioned above, the answer is more difficult. The scale of the Marrano phenomenon was too restricted to have played a determinative causal role. But it may not be excessive to assume that, at certain junctures, Marranos served as catalysts in modernizing trends that had already begun without them, or joined the process as a contributing factor, or helped prepare the ground by undermining the solidity of the existing state of affairs and pointing to its possible mutation. Historical transformations are intricate enough to allow for more complex kinds of participating agents than simple linear causes and effects suggest.

Thus, in saying that Marranos prefigured future modern forms of life I do not mean merely a passive anticipation: the prefiguring became a prodding, a temptation—the constructing of possibilities that ceased to be outlandish or mad, but were illustrated as pregnant in the existing situation and thereby became conceivable, even partly expected and worth trying.

Further Elaborations

The rest of this chapter elaborates on selected areas drawn from the list above. Every heading discusses some essential aspect of Western modernization that, at the same time, also recalls or alludes to pertinent varieties of the Marrano experience. My aim, as before, is to highlight analogies and kinships between the two. I shall devote more space to the relevant features of modernity than to the corresponding Marrano references, which have been abundantly worked out throughout this book.

Religious Freedom and Free Trade

The modern era emphasizes religious freedom and free trade. The Marranos incarnated both these demands, even as mutually linked. Marranos of all shades required religious freedom; they carried its message wherever they went and thus became the early bearers of the idea of toleration, which was a lubricant on the wheels of modernity. One of them, the philosopher Baruch Spinoza, gave this principle one of its first modern groundings (thereby influencing Locke, Bayle, Voltaire, Mendelssohn, and others). Although religious freedom was never officially granted the New Christians, they endeavored to possess it informally, and in the end seized it as a matter of illicit and secret fact. As we have seen, the New Christians practiced a de facto religious pluralism in which Judaizing, deism, syncretism, and the rejection of all religions coexisted alongside orthodox and dissenting Catholicism.

Of course, this underground pluralism had no chance of being legitimized in inquisitorial Iberia, which was based on the opposite political theology. So the Conversos periodically appealed to their governments for "amnesties"—a kind of civil "indulgences," for which they paid mammoth sums of money (actually, bribes). But when they emigrated overseas they embraced whatever level of religious freedom the local conditions permitted and used it to the utmost.

Religious freedom entailed freedom of conscience. Initially this had been understood as freedom of religious conscience; but even as such it already implied a wider message—namely, that the individual person had a privileged inner domain, which should be immune to control by the state, the church, and external social forces. Subsequently, the same realization—of the normative status of human subjectivity, in which the individual is master, and where his or her dignity and claim to further rights are rooted—was secularized and broadened into a pillar of Western modernity.

Freedom of trade, another pillar of western modernization, was no less vital to the Marranos. A caste of international business people that settled along the major trading routes of the world, the Marrano networks had to cope with innumerably varied laws, customs, tariffs, currencies, privileges, monopolies, and other vested interests. While their primary goal was to remove these obstacles from their own way, the Marranos drove and gave voice to a broader claim that transcended the protective national policies of contemporary governments. Later, of course, free trade gained a more powerful lobby and public voices—for example, among British politicians and scholars (such as Adam Smith) and their American offshoots; but there was a difference. Most of these advocates were concerned with their own nations' wealth and influence no less than the protectionists they opposed; whereas the Marranos, whose Dispersion had no normative center, came closest to genuine cosmopolitanism in matters of trade (as in other matters, too).

The two demands, free trade and free religion, were practically inseparable in the complex identity of the Jewish-Portuguese Nation, especially in the Dispersion.[1] Unlike traditional Jews, the identity of the Portuguese New Christians did not precede their socioeconomic function but was partly constituted by it— alongside their race, birth, typical dualities, and the awareness that an "inward mind" distinguished many of them. The "globalized" Marrano networks did not usually or necessarily pry into their members' religious beliefs and worship. A global network could include open Jews, open Christians, secret Judaizers, and tacit religious skeptics and atheists—as long their loyalty could be trusted in an ethnic and commercial way. To this extent the Nation was basically, if ambivalently, secularized (in the sense of transcending purely religious commitments), and maintained a noteworthy measure of toleration, opposing the spirit of the Inquisition.

Yet on the other hand, *inside* the New Jewish congregations no such level of toleration could prevail. Although the New Jews maintained more liberal and open lifestyles than mainstream Jews, in the end they recognized that normative Judaism was the only common denominator by which they could organize a cohesive community. Furthermore, the Marranos were children of their time: originating in inquisitorial Iberia, they were unable to completely shed its spirit even when they set out against it. Thus we saw them treat intolerantly the publicly outspoken heretics among them, including rationalists, Karaites, deists, and the philosopher Spinoza.

Individualism: The Modern Subject and the Rise of a "Modern Will"

The fact that already in Iberia many Conversos had been confused about both religions until they lost interest in any religion, and that in joining the Catholic mainstream and conventions, some were mainly interested in advancing their worldly career, indicates a nonreflective, existential form of secularity that had arisen among them. Less preoccupied with the hereafter and with life before God, such people placed the most important value on themselves as individuals—their private life, person, family, worldly career, personal achievements, and worth. From here arose an early form of individualism—in a sense, of protomodernity—that emerged on the Spanish and European scene together with the Conversos.

Modern individualism was not a self-evident phenomenon. It was due to the individual's emerging and *affirming* itself as such after having been submerged in the nonreflective social convention and its routinized roles and duties. Converso reality participated in the rise of the modern individual in several ways: through the ambivalence it showed toward the normative power of tradition; the discovery of the inner Self; the appearance of personal conscience; the role of worldly careers, stressing the Self's achievements and self-realization in this life; and the emphasis on personal will as a person's center of identity (see below). In all these ways the Converso experience contributed to the construction of the modern *subject*, but at the same time also split and fragmented its unity. The subject that emerged in Marranism was surely individualized, but not in the unified, harmonious way dreamt of by classic modern philosophers.

The emergence of the particular individual in Marranism was partly due to the crucial role the *will* played as the center of the Marrano's identity. Carl Gebhardt's famous definition of the Marranos—"Catholics without faith and Jews without knowledge, yet Jews by their will"[2]—applies (in what concerns the will) not only to Judaizers but to *all* the inner dissenters among the Marranos. All had positioned the individual in tacit defiance not only of the social environment, but also of important layers of their own inner minds that, through upbringing and acculturation, had been shaped by the Catholic conformity that they opposed. And since they refused to accept themselves as such, they challenged these elements inside themselves by the bare force of will. This will—to view and define oneself as someone other—was certainly abstract, removed from the person's real situation and mental constitution; but for that reason it had to be forceful and resolute; and in taking over the center of one's identity, it paved a specific way in which the individual could arise as a separate entity, detached from routine immersion in traditional society and its lore.

In this way the Marrano mind contributed to initiating the "modern will."[3] At first this will lacked the typical modern urge—to shape a new world in its own image. But subsequently it did contain the demand to reform the world—especially in matters of religious freedom, toleration, free trade, the abolition of binding state religions, and the creation of a cosmopolitan-inspired model of life.

Discovering the Inner Self

A major feature of the Marrano experience was the discovery of subjectivity and inwardness. In most of its forms, Marranism involved a hidden personal truth in which life's deeper meaning and motivation were rooted, a truth that must be concealed from the world and worked out in private. Thereby, the Marrano mind turned back into itself from the outer world, affirming—indeed, discovering—its inward sphere as the true domain of its Selfhood, open only to self-observation—and to God (when one believed in him). This important experience was shared not only by Judaizers (although they present its paradigmatic case), but by all Marrano groups whose inner consciousness was sharply at variance with the ruling tradition and social ideology, including the "spiritual seekers" and those I called "Marranos of reason." In chapter 15 we met several forms of the "interior religion" developed by Conversos who could not accept Christianity except through an inward, personal form of religiosity. So they plunged in different ways into the inner Self in search of authentic piety, a personal religious conscience, the truly divine, and the highest union with God.

Saint Teresa and other Converso mystics, such as Francisco Osuna, Juan de Avila, Juan de La Cruz, and Luis de León, discovered in their interiors a new terrain for exploration, no less vast and mysterious—and dangerous—than the geographical horizons then opening before travelers. And the nonmystical Juan Luis Vives, using reasoned introspection (a new approach then), became a founder of the rational psychology of the passions.

In both ways, the mystical and the rational, a new cultural entity—the inner Self—was discovered, and at once also constructed as a special domain, a separate category and human potentiality.

The precise links between discovery and construction are not crucial to the present analysis. But whether as discovery, construction, or both,[4] the explication of human subjectivity and the notion of the Self became a cornerstone in the culture of modernity.[5] It was used as an anchor of knowledge and ethics, to criticize received traditions, to ground individual rights and freedoms, and to achieve the goal of personal self-determination, with everything it entails.

Marranos—the "Modern Subject"

We might restate the above in a different way. In premodern times, a person's identity did not express that person's interior and mental constitution, but mostly the external parameters that defined his or her social existence. People's identities were derived from their immersion in a solid tradition and the social body that embodied it. Of course even this was not an integral identity; yet it was to a large extent rooted in and firmly held together by fixed externalities. This semi-integral identity cracked in the modern situation. The process of modernization led to an individual whose identity was often split between several partly opposed internalized ingredients, without integration between them. Moreover, the Self as an individual domain, with its own interior space, emerged as a key modern concept. All this was illustrated and anticipated in the varieties of the Marrano situation as described in this book, while also constituting a major pattern of the modern condition as such.

A number of historical factors contributed to this result. Among them: the breakdown of traditions and their justifying or legitimizing authority; the rise of a secular urban civilization, the state's central power (which placed all citizens in direct relation to itself, without the mediation of intermediary groups), a technological and bureaucratic civilization, and a global market system; and of course, the waning of religious feeling and belief, together with a dual separation of religion—from other spheres of life (law, the state, education, economics, science, and so forth), and from the individual himself. By this I mean that religious affiliation was relegated to a limited, well-defined area in the individual's world, which had meanwhile been filled with other, worldly interests, and by a secular perspective on life and on the question of salvation (I shall summarize this issue in the last section of this chapter).

The modern situation produced a Marrano-like, partly self-alienated subject whose identity was plural and nonintegral from the start. This individual (not the only modern kind, but typical and current) emerged from the outset as split in three ways: (1) between different traditions (old and new, rural and urban, religious and worldly, communal and universal, homeland and adoptive land, and the like); (2) within each tradition—between its substance and its breakdown; and (3) between his or her self-conscious individuality and the conflicting impersonal forces that affect the person on all sides, threatening to dominate the singular I; yet this I is unable to give itself content and concreteness without partly adopting these forces, and at the same time negating and transcending—or confusing—them even as they are adopted.

In this way the process of modernity produced the self-conscious individual, and in the same act undercut his or her reality since it did not form the individual as an actually singular entity, but as a composite of ingredients, none of which determines one's complete and unified identity. This is not necessarily a complaint. As a matter of fact, such complete or integral identity exists nowhere. People imagine it because they need stability and desire continuity, but they blur or conceal the real situation from themselves—which explains the relative weight of conservatism persisting in modern societies despite all their changes, and partly because of them.

On the dialectical other side of that coin—modern individualism has always allowed for, and even supposed, the individual's identification with some abstract universal element (such as human and civil rights, or the worth of the human person as such), while empirically, individualism became associated with the modern mass society, in which individuals became partly emancipated and at once also estranged, unable to feel at home in that society and make it the terrain for genuine self-realization. Thereby, individuals' emancipation—and very constitution—involves their partial alienation from themselves and the broader society, which is another reason why the individual is created neither as *actual* nor as truly free.

G.F.W. Hegel, a philosopher of modernity who recognized this problem from early on, believed it could be remedied by negating and elevating the phase of abstract enlightenment into a universe of a historically embodied ethics (*Sittlichkeit*). The different stages of this ethico-political sphere, culminating in a concrete system of rights, can endow the individual with public recognition and rights without abolishing the specific historical nature of his or her existence, and allow the individual to be constituted as *actual* through dialectical self-identification with the universality of reason as embodied in history. Though Hegel's direction has merit, his optimism can no longer be shared. Modernity has its price, which can neither be abolished by a retreat from it, nor by a harmonious utopia projected into the future; it is the price of human finitude recognizing itself—and its limited autonomy—as such.

Effects of Universal Rights, Popular Sovereignty, and the Nation

The split identity caused by modernization is due not only to the uprooting of people from their native cultures through urbanization, mass immigration, proletarization, and the opening of global and cosmopolitan horizons. Even native groups rooted in a single place and culture were affected, because the world around them had changed in ways that forced their identity to split, too. For example, the modern state issued from the French Revolution transformed the peasants and small urban artisans and tradesmen into participants—even constituents—of new abstract entities called "Nation" and "the sovereign people." It superimposed on them not only a political culture based on universal rights and popular sovereignty, but also an all-national language (modern French, high German, modern Italian, and so forth), which they were required to use in public and in all acts of participation in the state—administration, army, education, and the like. This national language opposed their native dialect just as the Nation opposed and superseded their local identities. Thus, even without moving physically into the cities, they were uprooted from their original culture. A structural split arose between the private and the public, the home culture and the world outside; and since it was built in their situation, it created a *duality in their very identity*—between the inner and outer circles of life that build one's particular identity. Thereby, too, the marranesque paradigm with its dual face of the inner and outer prefigured the wider and more fundamental modern situation.

Philosophical Consequences—Split Identity as Freedom

Philosophers after Hegel (and also before, such as Herder) speak of the fracture that modernity introduced into the human Self. But the remedies usually suggested are not better or more effective. Nostalgia for an allegedly lost unity triggers an illusory romantization of the past that is no less problematic than the present condition and, moreover, conceals this fact from itself. And most demands for authenticity generate expectations of an integral personality free of contradictions, and even free of unresolved tensions and dissonances, which often lead to repression and to acute internal conflict, self-deception, and the coercion of others. In their extreme manifestation, the demands for an integral or authentic personality (in the sense of a complete self-identity) lead to a social and political fundamentalism that imposes on the actual person an illusory pattern of official, allegedly ideal, unity and purity that rests on self-deception—as was illustrated in early modernity by Habsburg Spain, and, in different forms, by latter-day movements of mass mobilization.

Nationalism was among the several modern ideologies seeking to subdue multifaceted individuals under an umbrella of uniformity said to hold their essential substance and to command their total and undivided allegiance. It is no accident that in Western parlance, the person's "identity"—a concept originally pointing to that which constitutes a *singular* being as such—is commonly understood as designating the person's *collective* group: not the Me, but the We. In speaking and acting in its name, the self-appointed owners of this We tend to attribute its content (in their interpretation) to the willing or unwilling individuals as their "true selves," which they are therefore bound to assume and serve without qualms. Otherwise—if the person has more concerns and partial allegiances than this—it is supposed that he has illicitly split and betrayed his Self. This false construal of self and identity makes it legitimate to take possession of others because they resemble us in *some* respect, regardless of the actual weight a person attaches to that resemblance, and irrespective of whatever other concerns, dreams, and loyalties, however partial and conflictual, he or she may entertain.

Hence a political link between the imagined notion of an "integral" self and the sociopolitical repression practiced by ethnic and religious identity groups, as well as by modern ideologies and revolutionary causes, whether they are in power or oppose the ruling power.[6]

Liberalism, the traditional guardian of individual rights and self-realization, has propagated an inflated notion of personal autonomy that is constantly called into question by the reality of atomized mass societies and their inherent forces of bureaucracy, technology, the market, and mass communication. As a result, the very notion of individual freedom is often denounced today as a liberal invention. The failure of certain liberal dreams does not undercut the reality and moral worth of singular individuality, however; it only calls for a better, more sophisticated and dialectical understanding of what it means. In particular, the relation of singular individuals to the broader contexts of meaning and value—by which, indeed, their very singularity must be nourished if they are to *become* actual individuals—should be conceived as plural and diverse, consisting of several strata, choices, roles, and allegiances that are neither total nor uniform, and do not necessarily link up into a coherently knit Self. Such constituents, even when substantial, are still partial and fragmented, and what holds them together (either consciously or not) is the *will* with its several choices and projects, rather than a formal logical function or the famous Kantian "unity of self-consciousness."

The latter is an important modern notion that was construed dogmatically by Kant and his direct disciples, who did not recognize the full depth of human finitude and the merely partial coherence of which a human mind (and being) is capable. Fichte argued that the unity of self-consciousness must necessarily break down if the mind contains an inner contradiction or unresolved tension—a claim that was based on a priori logic rather than phenomenological insight and observation. In contrast, Hegel—who understood that contradictions and tensions, and thereby an inner dialectic, are *constitutive* of human consciousness as such—in the end conceived of these contradictions as capable of being reconciled within a higher synthesis or totality, which led him back to the illusions of dogmatic reason. In the last century, however, the sciences, art, literature, and psychology, as well as philosophy, made us realize that human selves are not necessarily coherent and unitary in their functioning and constitution; yet even as such they can manifest a significant singular identity by which they are distinguished, even if this unity is "narrative" or historical rather than epistemological, and is based on the various practical projections of a self-asserting *will* (or desire) rather than a cognitive principle. Thus the severed, dissatisfied modern self resurfaced and reasserted itself through the works of modern writers and artists from Kafka, Duchamp, Joyce, and Musil to Freud, Sartre, and Derrida. At bottom, these works project the modern self's inner split and alienation as its true or *authentic* state.

Whether synchronically or over time, a human self is capable—and should be allowed—to operate on several planes at once without fully coherent unification, and to balance different choices and allegiances without allowing any one to take over as the compelling identity or "true self." Therefore, the *non*-integral identity that the Marranos throw into sharp relief, and that many others—from the Inquisition to modern nationalism and other ideologies, as well as fundamentalist communities—view as devious, illicit, illogical, or immoral, should rather be recognized as *a basic human freedom*. And, given our rights-based democratic culture (which, despite its justified malaise, is still the best defense of individuals)—it should be defended, on both the political and the social plane, as a specific human right.[7]

Marranos and "Postmodernity"

It may be argued that in so far as Marranism decenters the subject's identity and splits its unity into a number of nonharmonious ingredients, it prefigures the so-called postmodern situation even more than the modern. But what is called postmodernity is not really a new era, but a late reactive phase within modernity itself that sharply explicates some of its dilemmas and calls for rectifying its flaws, not by reversing the process of modernity but by offering alternate routes within it. Some of these dilemmas concern the effects of cultural diversity, mass immigration, alienation, and the rights of minorities, which links them to the problems of pluri-identity that the Marranos embody.

The so-called postmodernists stress a form of relativism and skepticism; they undermine stable identities, cherish irony, and view reason as subject to power interests and subconscious drives; they insist that identity is mediated by difference and that human particularity evades all general definitions; and they place the marginals, the Others, the peripheral elements, at the focus of their attention. Yet many such features were already active in modernity, the result of the breakdown of solid traditions, and expressed in works by Kafka and Musil, in Picasso's art, in existentialist thought, and previously in Nietzsche's attempt to clear the world of the shadows of the dead God. It is an error to equate modernity with a stable, regimented rational order, or with the ideas of progress, or with Marxist reason: these throw into relief certain trends of modernity at the expense of others.

In one of its main aspects, the "postmodern" perspective of modernity reflects the situation of immigrant or minority cultures existing on the barely legitimate margins of society and demanding a share in the center, which determines what is accepted and legitimate (thereby becoming pluralized and decentered). Similarly, the Marranos had undergone a sort of "inner immigration"—the forced religious conversion that made them, as minority, the Other Within—after which the Marranos evolved on the fringes of social prestige and legitimacy. At a later stage they also exercised actual emigration—their Dispersion; and in the end their peculiar pattern of cultural transfer and pluri-identity has become today an accepted and even normative form of late-modern existence.

Some multicultural trends today encourage the return to ethnocultural "roots" as a way to constructing one's identity. Yet the identity of an individual and his or her group affiliation are not the same. An individual identity cannot be derived from the attribution (or self-attribution) to some group to which the person is said to "belong." At most, such belonging is only a partial ingredient in a person's existence, which always involves other elements as well, none of which constitute the person's singular identity, and which may well be disharmonious or even mutually opposed to one another.

For this reason (among several), contemporary attempts to return to ethnic and cultural roots often prove merely artificial, because they contradict people's actual life conditions. Retreating from the impersonal cold of modernity to the reassuring shelter of tribal, religious, and other "complete" premodern loyalties is liable to run up against a dialectic similar to that of the Judaizing Marranos, who remained Christians in most practical and mental respects, so what they considered their true essence conflicted with the actual substance of their lives. Such attempts, then or today, do not recapture the lost identity but usually result in a torn, unrealized state of nostalgia, and thus in a new form of severance. The lost essence becomes past; it can no longer be retrieved, although a strong and abstract will can sometimes incorporate a few elements of this past into the present, as most Judaizing Marranos did.

On the other hand, it may be that all one wishes is to include some elements of one's tradition within the nonintegral subjective present (even calling them by the misnomer *roots*, yet meaning something lighter, less encroaching, more detached and localized—a factor of memory that is not reified into an inert "essence" that is meant to dominate the person). Then those elements will function as an identity ingredient that is not only legitimate, but deserves recognition by others as part of the late-modern ethical context. But it makes all the difference in the world whether these elements are recognized as only ingredients—significant but not dominating—of a nonintegral identity, or as determining its totality. The first enriches our view of humanity, the second is a prelude to oppression (of the Self and of others).

Dual Language as a Medium of Historical Change

The creation of the modern subject required the use of dual language. We have seen how crucial this form of language was for the Marranos; similarly, it was an essential lubricant on the wheels of modernization. The imperative of prudence—and the need to legitimize and make effective the talk of change—produced several characteristic forms and levels of rhetoric, based on hints and allusions, which addressed separate audiences in the same phrase or body of discourse. In inquisitorial Iberia, this was a necessity even for those who had little to hide, because suspicion and denunciation could hit anyone. Moreover, the fact that intimate thoughts were considered in Iberia the domain of the state's jurisdiction and could be declared a grave offense made almost everyone, Converso or not, dependent on some masked behavior. Using verbal masks was a necessity of life that soon developed into an art, a science, and an aesthetic pleasure. Spanish literature in the golden age and beyond revels in equivocation; sometimes using it in dead seriousness and sometimes exploiting its comic and ironic possibilities to the utmost.[8] This is the poetic transformation of a mode of writing that had primarily arisen as a condition of life.

Equivocal language was equally used in the dynamics of change. Any new ideas that arose in Spanish minds, Converso or not, had to assume a cloak of legitimacy by sounding to be what they were not—aligned to the ruling convention. Much of this discourse was ironic in its deep structure (though not always in its mood) because its inner message was opposed to its surface appearance and undermined it.

In perfecting the uses and modes of equivocation, the Marranos set a linguistic pattern that played an indispensable role in the process of European modernization. Ever since the Renaissance, Western Europe had undergone transformations that destabilized the frameworks of traditional life and belief and generated changes in government, religion, social mores and subjective feeling. Most of these transformations had evolved under the surface long before they gained social legitimacy; so for a long time they had been considered scandalous and heretical, unfit to appear in the public space. In order for historical change to mature, it was imperative that the gap between the covert and open levels be bridged by a high dosage of equivocal discourse; more broadly, there was an objective need for masks, both linguistic and behavioral.

My thesis is that the major transformations characterizing modernity would not have been conceivable without the mediation of ironic, evasive, equivocal (and plurivocal) language that served as bridge between the pregnant new processes working under the surface and the overt, normative sphere. The extent of this need changed with place and circumstances, but its existence became a recurrent pattern. Hence we can say that some measure of marranesque element was indispensable in that evolution: the creators of modernity often had to act like quasi-Marranos.

The Enlightenment in particular manifested this need—Hobbes and Spinoza, Hume and Shaftesbury, Diderot and Mandeville, Locke and Montaigne, the Deists, the materialists, possibly Boyle, even Kant (on religion) and Descartes (on his intended project), and a multitude of lesser figures and mediators found it necessary to revert to various techniques of masked writing.

Vital in repressive regimes, dual language made its return to the twentieth century in a totalitarian state such as the USSR, and in a democratic state in crisis, such as the United States during McCarthyism. In both these (unequal) cases, dual language had a *defensive* function primarily. Hence, we should further distinguish between two different functions of equivocal discourse, defensive and offensive, or static and subversive. The first is exhausted by the imperative of prudence; the second combines prudence with a drive for transformation.

Skepticism and Rationalism

Religious skepticism, and the claim that there is only this world and this life to worry about, had already appeared in Iberia during the first Marrano generations. Of course its voice was heard only in hushed private conversations, and—by aesthetic transformation—also in literary works, the underground culture, and Iberian forms of linguistic equivocation. But in those forms it recurred with a surprising consistency which, in the subterranean layers of the individual mind, planted some of the main heretical ideas of modern times. This is evidenced in the records of the Inquisition for over two centuries, and between the lines of some of the classic works of Spanish literature.[9]

In this dialectical way, the forced conversions, which first had seemed a victory for intolerant religion, created a situation under whose surface rumbled heterodox, secular, individualist tendencies (all in initial stages) that tacitly opposed the official Spanish culture, although they lacked the power to overturn it. This heterodox spirit was barred by the Iberian Inquisitions and Counter-Reformation from penetrating the private and moving into the public sphere. But in the Western Dispersion the same irreverent ideas were able to work with less fearful consequences; so the Conversos' contribution to modernity seems to have been less equivocal in the broader European scene than in their native lands.

Even so, it was easier for a Marrano to appear openly as a Jew in the Dispersion than as a heretic: *atheism* was a bad word and a cause of sanctions. While Marranos returning officially to Judaism in Livorno, London, or Amsterdam could freely set up synagogues, the skeptics and heretics among them, although their voices became more daring, needed to express themselves with much more prudence, using equivocal language to hide their most irreligious views. As for those who felt unable to become Jews again, they had the alternative of assimilating into the group of educated Europeans among whom there already existed deists and freethinkers. In joining the ranks of these dissenters, the Marranos again penetrated into the fertile margins where the intellectual ferment and some of future European movements were stirring.

Secularization Trends

Many topics in this chapter add up to the de facto production of a secular culture of life. And, in fact, Marranos were involved in many early forms and levels of secularization prior to others. This is perhaps their most noteworthy—and comprehensive—anticipation of modernity.

Secularization, a rather complex concept, indicates a set of processes rather than a static and uniform result. It does not have a single form, but has taken several shapes in different cultures and places, and assumed different levels and degrees in each of those places. Nor is it a finished phenomenon, but a variety of ongoing historical trends, working both locally and cross-culturally, expanding or receding as the case may be. However, with all its notorious complexity (which today is the object of renewed debate),[10] the concept of secularization can, for our purposes, be dissected into several varieties that, explicitly or in embryo, recall typical phenomena in the Marrano experience.

In all its varieties, secularization indicates some degree of transition from a culture with a religious core to a secular culture. As must be stressed from the outset, this does not necessarily involve atheism (denial of God's existence), or agnosticism (denial of the possibility of knowing whether God exists), or even deism (denial of God's involvement in the affairs of the world), though it can. The primary forms of the concept are: decentering of religion; emancipation of important areas of life from religion's control; fading of the Sacred; loss of trust in traditional mediating vehicles that link a person to the divine; and doubt and the waning of belief. All of the above also gives rise to: self-assertion of individuality vis-à-vis established traditions; revaluation of social values; and an implicit or explicit "philosophy of immanence."

The Decentering of Religion

In its primary sense, secularization means that religion loses its place at the center of daily concerns, and its power pales as the justifying source in the life of the individual and the social body. The affairs of the current world—the *saeculum*—acquire value and importance of their own. Individuals do not see their life on earth as chiefly a passage or preparation for the next world; and they do not draw the vindicating sense of their existence from living before God, serving his will, or sharing in his Church. The world—this world, and human action and achievement in it—is no longer experienced as a flawed reality, certainly not as temptation, but becomes legitimate for itself.[11]

This mutation has several degrees. One of its radical forms is expressed in the Marrano saying that was heard and recurred for centuries: "There is only living and dying in this world, what lies beyond it I do not know." In milder forms of secularization, religion no longer hovers over people's daily existence and does not directly determine the value of their action or the legitimacy of their institutions. Receding to an implied, rather uncertain metaphysical background, religion is invoked mainly on well-defined occasions—holidays, rituals, family events, *rites de passage*—and these are often reduced to social habit primarily, symbolic gestures of belonging, or statements of participation in a community. Well known in modernity, this phenomenon was illustrated among the "social Marranos" we have met since the fifteenth century in Iberia and the Dispersion.

The metaphysical meaning of religious events either diminishes to a low threshold (from where, in rare personal moments, it may reawaken in the form of dim memory, suppressed nostalgia, or a blank question); or for those who maintain a more significant degree of religious belief, the transcendent dimension of life becomes a dimension only, instead of being life's defining totality. In that and other senses, religion becomes a private affair, its level of meaning and intensity depending on the particular individual mind.

Emancipating Worldly Domains

Seen from the public sphere, secularization entails that central institutions and areas of life become emancipated from religion's control. Politics is grounded in reason rather than grace; economic activity follows its own business logic, free of religious restrictions (banking interest, religious taxation); the state is refounded on the citizens' this-worldly interest and will, rather than on God's will embodied in the monarch; natural science, not without struggle, strives to follow its immanent criteria and methodology despite church censorship and the guidelines of Revelation; personal morality and public ethics are rebuilt on worldly foundations (such as self-interest, benevolence, universal human reason, or the natural drives of survival); and philosophy, no longer the maidservant of faith, restructures itself (with certain compromises) on independent foundations. Even the religious mind, by going through competing new forms, becomes open to variety, and thereby to tradition-shattering trends that enhance enlightenment and semisecular tendencies from within religion itself.[12]

Marranos, as we have seen, have taken part in most of these trends, especially in those concerning economic activity, personal values, learning, and the demand for religious liberty and plurality.

The Fading of the Sacred

A further aspect of secularization involves the fading of the sense and experience of the sacred attached to objects, people, and events in the world or outside it, and of any mystical significance attributed to our world. As Hegel put it, the thread of light that linked everything to its meaning in heaven is cut off.[13] Sources of meaning and justification flowing from the beyond dry up, and the universe, in people's experience, is no longer saturated with the transcendent light that endowed nature itself with a certain supernatural halo. This *désenchantement*[14] leaves the universe a prosaic domain, even a metaphysical desert and "vale of tears," that can be filled only with human projects as its source of meaning and vindication. This typically modern experience is strongly expressed by Marranos as early as the fifteenth century, starting with the agnostic Marrano Fernando de Rojas in his classic play *La Celestina*.[15]

Given its various forms and degrees, secularization has often been working within or on the fringes of religion itself, and even nourished by religious reformist drives. On the other hand, one of its several competing offshoots has been *sacralization*, the transference of religious terms and absolutes to some worldly object or ideal (including political and historical utopias, or a "*religion* of reason"). Yet such resacralization is opposed by other, more radical forms of secularization that reject secular absolutes no less than religious ones.[16]

The Breakdown of Mediating Channels to the Divine

The personal experience had an institutional counterpart. Religious people usually depend on mediating institutional and symbolic liaisons by which to relate to the beyond: the Church, the Torah, organized prayer, traditional rites, the holy congregation of worshipers, the periodic ritual, and other mediators that, in their historical particularity, transmit religious meaning to the individual religious person. It is not faith in a supreme deity that makes up the core of historical religions, but rather their divergent mediating symbols and institutions. Likewise, the process of secularization is primarily marked by the erosion of those mediating bridges, the vanishing trust in their truth or effectivity.[16]

Part of the reason for that erosion (only part, but an important part) was the breakdown of the Catholic Church's monopoly as a single mediator. Alternative ways to salvation, to the divine, to the meaning of life—arose within and outside religion, some gaining political legitimacy as new religious denominations, while others remained vacillating, generating new dissent and experiment. The new plurality produced some ardent new parochialisms, yet also opened the way to religious universalism and deism, doubting the claims of any single religious mediator, and freedom to choose which religion to follow, if at all, and to what extent.

This book has shown that Marranos, with similar diverse results, had known a plurality of alternative ways to salvation prior to the Christian Reformation and independent of it. Their wandering between religious and secular mediators of meaning was specific to their condition; and insofar they prefigured (perhaps even as catalysts) some of the major tenets in European modernization.

Doubt and the Waning of Belief

The weakening or waning of religious belief is, of course, another recurrent feature of secularization. People come to doubt or deny the veracity of Biblical stories, religious dogmas, miracles, prophecy, the afterlife, or the worth of prayer and ritual, all the way to God's involvement in the affairs of the world and his very existence. Such doubts or negations can apply to three levels: the very idea of a supreme power; its involvement in the affairs of the world; and the particular beliefs, rites, and institutions that constitute and distinguish a specific historical religion. It seems clear that *some* degree of decline in religious belief was necessary for the process of secularization to take effect in its other senses.

For religion cannot be decentered, lose its grip on other domains of life, or allow for such things as personal conscience, unless a significant measure of religious disbelief is already at work, piercing the compactness of premodern religious forms.[17] And this presupposes the subversive power of self-consciousness, affected with doubt, searching, and seeing alternatives.

This activity had been going on among Marranos since the fifteenth century as an underground power outlawed by the state and persecuted by the Inquisition. When, centuries later, it gained legitimacy and became characteristic of the modern West, the Marranos were already in decline—a marginal group at the end of its vigor, soon to be engulfed, and their cosmopolitanism superseded, by the nation-state, a modern feature they did *not* prefigure.

Secularity and the Recognition of Individuality

From the senses of secularization already discussed another results: the self-assertion of personal choice and judgment. We have already discussed this modern trait in another context; now we shall look at its intersection with the secular.

Secularization involves the demand of the individual Self to experience, interpret, confirm, or otherwise judge whatever is presented to him or her as a binding tradition or cultural vindication; in other words, to be able to identify himself or herself in it or, when this proves impossible, to dissent and depart from it. The appearance of this demand already indicates that an individual Self has emerged from the enveloping culture, and that self-consciousness, with its peculiar capabilities and demands, its power of negation and pressing need for recognition, has already become active. The need for recognition—by others, by the law, by social and political institutions—is the key factor by which the virtual, tentative, self-proclaiming emergence of the individual can turn into actuality. Historically, endowing the individual with explicit legitimacy, even priority, required radical ideas (for their time) and great upheavals such as the Reformation, the Enlightenment, the French Revolution, and its several aftermaths. In the case of the Marranos, however, the individual Self was discovered and constituted *without proper social recognition*; therefore, it still lacked solidity and positive actuality, although it was effective in a subversive and critical way.

The Self as Worldly Interest

The secular interest invested in the world is not only material or utilitarian. Though driven by self-interest, the Self that owns this interest is pursued also for its own sake; it seeks to assert, project, and achieve itself in the world. This is the secular form of the modern drive often called self-realization. The person's worldly pursuit is not simply directed toward the acquisition of external objects—goods, powers, honors, and social recognition. Partly through those, it aims at the person himself, his itinerary in being, the mark he leaves on the world (and receives from it)—and the way the Self emerges from this relation with the world. This is a drive toward Selfhood, toward the accession of values and achievements related to the Self, which are to be attained in this life rather than the next. We may say that in thus projecting and asserting itself as a goal, the early modern Self was discovered and constituted in the first place.[18] In chapter 7 we met an early Marrano example in Diego Arias d'Avila, whose irreligious, self-directed attitude was so unfamiliar at the time that it was confused with Judaizing.

This is where Max Weber's celebrated theory of modernity proves too narrow. Weber's analysis focused on the Calvinists, who were so oppressed by a stark doctrine of predestination that they tended to interpret their worldly (economic) success as a sign that God had elected them to eternal salvation. For them, as Weber would affirm, economic success did not in itself realize the Self's goal; that goal remained metaphysical and depended exclusively on God's unfathomable decision to elect them. By contrast, in much of the modern secular experience, the Self (a) achieves realization through its own initiatives; and (b) finds its satisfaction as a Self in its worldly career, which practically replaces salvation in another world. Only this break between the metaphysical and the worldly allows us to understand the striving for Selfhood as a modern goal; yet Weber's Calvinist model does not account for this crucial factor, whereas the Marrano model does. If there is nothing but "living and dying in this world," then the Calvinist's anxiety does not arise and self-realization replaces metaphysical salvation as the individual's goal.

A Revaluation of Social Values

Given the above, secularization also requires a radical revaluation of social values. Opposing the foundations of traditional society, it demands that people be valued and honored not because of a status conferred on them by birth, or by some metaphysico-religious ordination, but on account of their personal efforts and achievements—material, intellectual, or moral. This new ideology expressed the needs of the nascent bourgeoisie and entrepreneurial class; and as the present book has amply shown, it found its most persistent voice in the Marranos. Marranos had a dual reason to propagate this principle, not only because they were forming the backbone of a new urban bourgeoisie but because, at the same time, they suffered from the prejudice of "impure blood," which fixed their hereditary stigma as static and irrevocable. No wonder that almost all Marranos, whatever their religious and other differences, pressed for the new values both in the open and in the underground culture: together with the claims of free trade and free religion, this was the most important common feature uniting all the Marranos and defining their wider Nation. The secular Marrano Self thus asserted itself by turning into the world.

An Implicit Philosophy of Immanence

One way to characterize much of the above is to say the Marrano experience gave rise to an explicit and, more frequently, implicit "philosophy of immanence." By this I mean an approach to life and the world that focuses on the existing empirical universe as the whole scope of one's concerns and resources. It is not necessarily a reflective position, but it can be articulated philosophically by saying there is no room for an effective supernatural perspective of a world beyond. The transcendent domain is either inexistent or not effectively present. The immanent world defines the whole horizon of being; it is also the sole valid source of values, meanings, moral standards, and political legitimizations: these can only derive from the human will, mind, and civilization. Moreover, every salvation to which humans can aspire—meaning also emancipation, freedom, perfectibility, and the like—must also be achieved in this world and derived from its resources. This kernel idea can be construed in many divergent ways, as modern thought illustrates; and the idea or life feeling that these divergent constructions encapsulate has had one of its early sources and beginnings in the Marrano experience.

Before concluding this chapter, let us remember that Marranos were not only restless, but cosmopolitan in attitude; they came into contact with diverse circles of European society, especially the literate and influential. The more dissenting among them found their way into the underground intellectual sphere, where subversive pre-Enlightenment attitudes were stirring, and from where, at times, a greater mind emerged to give these attitudes constructive shape. Even by merely being there, present among other Europeans, and equipped with their peculiar mental and cultural baggage, the Marranos set an example of something yet unclear but different, partly alarming, perhaps also enticing, that became possible and was taking shape. Thus, they not only anticipated in micro form what went on later on the larger European scale, but may have enhanced processes that had started independent of them.

20

Marranos and Jewish Modernity

———————————— ⤳ ————————————

Anticipating the Modernization of the Jews

The Marranos anticipated not only major aspects of Western modernity, but of Jewish modernity as well. Y. H. Yerushalmi has indicated important analogies between postemancipation Jews in Germany and the Marranos.[1] The present chapter further develops this theme and links it to other related issues. I have in mind not only the modernization of the Marranos themselves (for instance, in the New Jewish Dispersion), but also the modernization of other Jews, especially Ashkenazi Jews in the nineteenth and twentieth centuries, with whom the Marrano saga manifests some interesting links of analogy and precedent.

Jewish modernity is characterized, among other things, by the following traits:

- *Political emancipation:* Jews attain legal and political rights and status equal to that of other citizens; as such, they enter the host society.
- *Paying a price for emancipation:* Jews are required to deny being a separate people and renounce membership in a nation of their own; at the same time, fear and hatred of Jews persist and are shifted toward the category of the Jewish race.
- *No single model of Jewishness:* No mandatory single model of being Jewish is available any longer; religious reforms and a widening secularization compete with traditional and neo-Orthodox Judaism for the shared Jewish identity.
- *A rift between the religion and the people:* A rift emerges between the Jewish religion and the Jewish people, shattering the close bond that had held these two elements together throughout most of the Jewish Middle Ages (and, in different form, since the time of Ezra the Scribe).
- *European influence:* A trend of *Haskalah,* or cultural enlightenment and Europeanization, penetrates traditional Jewish communities.
- *Assimilation:* Modern Jewishness links up with other cultural circles (and with other political interests), creating various forms and degrees of assimilation.

- *Split identity:* A twofold, split, or "hyphenated" Jewish identity becomes common, raising structural questions and various readings of the question: "Who is a Jew?"
- *Existential Jewishness:* A fundamentally modern split occurred between the Jews' special attributes and their bare existence. This led to an existential hatred of Jews that, together with the secularization process, strengthens the perception and the reality of what may be called an existential Jewishness.

Most of these developments reveal a structural similarity with some significant phenomenon in the Marrano experience, a phenomenon that is intensified and reframed in new historical circumstances.

Political Emancipation and Its Price

At the end of the eighteenth century, signs of openness to European learning and culture appeared among German Jews in the shape of *Haskalah*, the movement of Jewish Enlightenment. But the decisive and, in fact, the constitutive event of Jewish modernity was the legal and political emancipation of the Jews following the French Revolution. Until then, Jews in France had had a right to settle only in a few isolated areas; then, all at once, they became citizens sharing equal rights with the rest of the French population and emerging Nation. The Napoleonic wars, which spread and institutionalized the spirit of the Revolution, brought the tidings of Jewish emancipation to other places as well. During the nineteenth century, political equality was eventually granted to Jews in most of Western Europe. Jews became an integral feature of most layers of urban society, except for the peasantry and the high aristocracy; they poured their renewed energies into the circles of European economy, law, politics, media, the arts, and academia. Like the Conversos in Iberia, they absorbed in various degrees the culture of the host society and became involved in all the European cultural and political movements (especially liberalism, nationalism, and socialism) that criticized the existing order and tradition, and they strove for reforms and even revolution.

In all these regards, the Jews' entry into modern European society resembled the patterns of the first Conversos' entry into Iberian society. Yet Jews in the modern West were not obliged to convert. The price they were required to pay was different.

"To the Jews as individuals—everything; to the Jews as a nation—nothing." This was the battle cry of the Jews' friends and the slogan of the French Revolution, which Napoleon implemented. The Jews attained emancipation by virtue of the principle that all human beings are equal. They deserved equality not as Jews, but as individuals participating in the general body politic, as the republic's citizens-to-be. The state they were joining was modern and fundamentally Jacobean. It had, at least in principle, no room for halfway groups mediating between the individual and the political government. Therefore, Jewish legal autonomy—the cornerstone of medieval Jewish existence—had no place in the new state constituted in France. The French Revolution established a centralized modern political state in which every individual belongs to the civic, political *people* and relates directly to the national government. Ethnic groups or "nations," urban guilds, the aristocracy, the priesthood, the various regions, local loyalties—no longer possessed a recognized status in the new body politic. The state's authority purportedly relied on a "general will" involving direct citizen participation, and its unity transcended the multiple groups and interests within it.

In this way, the French Revolution established not only political freedom and legal equality but, through them, also a new concept of nation. Henceforth, only one inclusive nation existed, the one built from all its equal citizens, and only a political people existed, embodying the nation's sovereignty. The nation-state that was thereby created could not tolerate loyalty to any nation other than the French. Hence the "republican" opposition still persisting in France today (although it shows signs of weakening) to displays of ethnicity and multicultural politics.

As the price of entering the French nation, then, Jews were required to give up their existence as a separate nation and, in fact, their peoplehood. This was a decisive renunciation, not merely of a name or word, but of a fundamental feature of the Jews' historical identity. Until then, the existence of a Jewish people, in the sense of an *ethnos* or *genos* that also has a special religion, had been obvious and widely accepted. Jews had referred to themselves from antiquity as "the people of Israel" (*am Israel*), and Gentiles used to speak of the "Jewish nation." From now on, in a single stroke, the concepts of a Jewish nation or people became illegitimate, in about the same way that formerly, in Iberia, the Jewish *religion* had become illegitimate for those Jews who, by converting to Christianity, had known a kind of pre-emancipation

The difference stemmed from the changing times. The civilization of late medieval Iberia was religious (Catholic). People were equal only in the sense of being brothers in Christ; in every other respect they lived in a rigidly hierarchical society. Therefore, Jews could become equal to the rest of the population only by sharing its Catholicism through conversion. Whereas in the nineteenth and twentieth centuries there reigned in Europe a secular national civilization, which Jews had to join in order to be considered equal; hence, they had to renounce their separate nationality and assume the motherland's nationality as their only one.

Yet the Jews, to themselves and to others, had always been "the seed of Abraham" and not merely "Frenchmen of the Mosaic religion." In their historical-mythological memory as embodied in the Bible, they had, as Israelites, been members of a single people prior to sharing the same religion. For many centuries the Israelites had "worshipped foreign gods" (practiced idolatry), which means that the people and the religion had not been the same; rather, the people had fought against the very religion it had given itself. The Jews did not fully accept their religion before the Persian era (sixth to fourth century B.C.), perhaps under the influence of the Babylonian exile. Only afterward, following Ezra and later the Pharisees, did the Jews come to see their religion as inextricably linked to their ethnic people. Ezra excluded the Samaritans and other inhabitants of Palestine (including the descendants of the Kingdom of Israel) from both the religion *and* the people, paving the way for a purist perception of the boundaries of Judaism as a fusion of *ethnos* and ritual. This policy was relaxed under the Hasmoneans, who converted many foreigners to Judaism, as did Jewish leaders across the Roman Empire; but Ezra's policy returned even more stringently with the rise of rabbinic Judaism, partly because of its struggle against Pauline Christianity.

Paul's disciples created a multinational (universal, or "catholic") religion that viewed itself as "the *spiritual* people of Israel," thus severing religion from the original ethnic Israel. According to Pauline doctrine, participation in the genuine religion of Israel (Christianity) established a people of believers whose ethnic origins were diverse and irrelevant. This spiritual people inherited God's election of Abraham's seed while the ethnic Jews were banished to the margins of history.

The rabbis saw this as an attempt to usurp the Jews' identity, a threat to their survival and mission among the nations. So they became even more steadfast in teaching that God's election and covenant were inseparable from the actual Jewish people, Abraham's seed. Rabbinic Judaism, which ruled supreme from the conclusion of the Talmud (around the sixth century A.D.) to the French Revolution—the period we might call "the Jewish Middle Ages"[2]—insisted that the Jewish religion and the actual Jewish people (as *ethnos* or *genos*) are mutually constitutive, and therefore inseparable. On these grounds, rabbinic Judaism refrained from proselytizing as long as the exile continued: the nations of the world would acknowledge the Jewish truth only at the end of days, when the Jewish mission would come to an end through its completion.

Thus, during the long centuries of the Jewish Middle Ages, neither Jews nor Gentiles doubted that the Jews were a people in the empirical, and not merely the spiritual, sense. European discourse too, in its natural use, labeled them a nation because this is how their actuality was perceived. Now the Jews were required to renounce this actuality—not just the *word*, but one of the two concrete elements of their historical identity—and, as it were, divest themselves of it as the price of their political liberation. This historical concession became deep-rooted in Jewish life in the liberal West and is expressed in its current idiom. For most Western Jews today, their Jewishness is defined solely by religion. Therefore, when their religious belief wanes, they experience an unsolved problem. Some hold on to Jewishness as a social framework. Others return to the concept of ethnic Jewishness that, at least in the United States, has acquired some legitimacy in light of the multicultural American experience while maintaining the distinction between *ethnos* and nation. The nation remains political and American; the *ethnos* (or, peoplehood) is perceived as one of several cultural identities, anthropological and historical, existing within the nation. In this way, a quasi-Marrano element returns to modern Jewish identity, which—like the Conversos, though differently—cannot claim integral unity, but becomes marked by duality and internal plurality. (The similarity is in the mixture of identities; the important difference is, of course, between willingness and coercion: contemporary Jews have a choice.)

Thus a partial but outstanding structural similarity exists between the Conversos' entry into Iberian society and the modern period. In both cases, Jews were required to renounce a basic ingredient of their historical identity as a condition for emancipation. The Iberian kingdoms "liberated" the Jews at the price of their religion: this conformed to the necessities of those times. The European states emancipated the Jews at the price of having them renounce their nationhood. *Like the Marranos, Jews in the modern liberal West were forced to make a major identitarian concession.* And they had to endorse a Christian (Pauline) political theology that uses religion as a separate, universal category severed from any specific link to a definite historical group.

The Second Price of Emancipation

The analogy goes further. After a period of successful penetration, social promotion, and partial assimilation, western European Jews started to encounter strong social resistance, sometimes venomous and violent, as did the Conversos five centuries earlier. Within a single generation both groups discovered they had remained the *Other* and the stranger; the pattern of being the Other Within is typical of Jews in modern Europe no less than of the Iberian Conversos. And then in both cases a new kind of Jew-hatred arose—now directed not against the Jewish religion, or against the Jews as the Messiah's deniers who caused his crucifixion, but against the Jews in their existential origin and very being. Racial prejudice proved to be far deeper than any official, ideological fraternity. Christian ideology had made all Christians, including forced converts, brothers in Jesus. Modern liberal ideology made all members of the political people— and all members of ethnic groups such as the German, the Polish, the Magyar, or the French—partners or "brethren" in the sovereign nation. Yet both then and now, the official ideology failed to hold its ground against profound and negative identity passions; and these passions, when no longer able to deny the Jews' participation and very being on grounds of their era's universal principles (Christianity then, liberalism later)—turned to blood and race to justify their position. In this respect, the Iberian statutes of blood purity anticipated the events that engulfed European Jews half a millennium later.

To sum up: political equality involved, in both cases, paying two prices. One was a major identitarian concession—in Iberia, renouncing the Jewish religion, and in the modern West, renouncing allegiance to the Jewish people or nation. The second was the appearance of a new anti-Jewish hatred, particularly fierce and venomous, which I call *existential* because it focuses not on religion but on a feature that cannot be cast off ("blood" or "race").

The Breakdown of the Single Pattern of Being Jewish

Another basic feature of the modern Jewish situation is that no single pattern for being Jewish exists any more. The processes of secularization and religious reform compete over the shared Jewish identity against traditional religion and the new (*haredi*) Orthodoxy that arose in response to them. This is a fundamental change with respect to the Middle Ages, which the Marrano situation had also prefigured several centuries earlier. In the Jewish Middle Ages, any attempt at difference or deviation, such as Karaism, obstinate Sabbateanism, or Frankism, ended in expulsion outside the Jewish pale. By contrast, the modern period is marked by a broad spectrum of Jewish modes of being, most of which do not express an exclusive or full Jewish existence—if such fullness ever existed—but a complex and multifaceted situation in which the Jewish component is intricately linked to other spheres of one's existence. The general division of Jews into such categories as religious, secular, orthodox, traditionalist, national, existential, social, and assimilated (in various senses and degrees) is still short of describing the multiple combinations that exist in reality. The comprehensive characteristics of Jewish modernity are plurality and complexity: not only are there various forms of Jewish life, but the Jewish ingredient in each individual is often woven from personal combinations of life which make the person different from others even within the same group.

A similar Jewish pattern prevailed among the various Marranos. It likewise included plurality, personal complexity, and several divergent or incomplete forms of Jewishness (and assimilation). In Iberia and the Dispersion we have met new unorthodox modes of Jewish, half-Jewish and quasi-Jewish existence, incompatible with normative rabbinical Judaism. They included Christian Jewishness, nostalgic Jewishness, social Jewishness, selective Jewishness (observing only some commandments), and a Jewish form that emphasized descent and historical solidarity over and above religion. And when Conversos in the Dispersion founded overtly "New Jewish" communities, they also diverged from the usual Jewish profile, cleaving to the Bible more than the Talmud and observing Jewish ritual alongside a rich Iberian and cosmopolitan culture.

However, the Marranos' nonuniform Jewish identity did not claim to be a legitimate positive principle, as nonuniform Jewishness claims today. In this respect, what was seen as an anomaly for its time has become the normal condition in another, later time.

The Split between the Jewish Religion and the Jewish People

The modern Jewish era is characterized by a split between the Jewish people and their religion. Jews no longer are necessarily religious in one of the traditional forms, or at all. The processes of secularization and religious reform put masses of Jews at a distance from the traditional rabbinic religion, while *Haskalah* offered them an alternative path for shaping a different Jewish persona, fundamentally cultural and social. As a result, Jewish reactions to modernity range from neo-Orthodoxy to several forms of Jewishness that do not depend on religious faith or observance. Not all who became estranged to religion assimilated into the European nations: many refused to do so, or failed in their assimilation because of resistance from the host societies, or because of the modern, existential anti-Semitism that no longer depended on religion. A new historical phenomenon emerged: nonreligious Jews who are nevertheless considered Jewish by themselves and by the outside world. As these Jews required a non-Pauline (nonreligious) definition of their Jewishness, some explicitly proclaimed themselves to be an ethnic and historical nation. Thus Jewish nationalist movements emerged, both Zionist and Diasporist anti-Zionist, mainly in Eastern Europe but also in the West. Although influenced by European nationalism of the nineteenth and twentieth centuries, Jewish nationalism largely resulted from the inner needs and contradictions of the modern Jewish situation. The Jewish nation that they heralded, whether it was to be realized in Palestine or in the Diaspora (Bund, Dubnowism, Territorialism), was perceived as offering a secular path, unbound by religious commandments, for continuing Jewish existence in the modern period.

The main alternatives often cross or develop secondary directions. Many secularized Jews in today's United States choose to remain within a Jewish social framework (with or without a religious attribute); and some observe certain religious customs and laws although they have little or no religious faith—much as Iberian Conversos used to "Judaize" for social or nostalgic reasons. In another example, Jews who had abandoned religion have often also rejected Jewish nationalism, yet consider themselves Jews nevertheless, as Freud, who called himself a "godless Jew," famously said, while Isaac Deutscher (and, differently, Jacques Derrida) regarded themselves as "non-Jewish Jews." A modern Jewishness was created, one that is concerned with its new meaning and will not renounce it, even when incapable of defining it unequivocally. What could be more Marrano?

The Marranos prefigured the modern Jewish condition not only in their mixed identity but also because, with them, the age-old linkage of the Jewish people and orthodox religion was shattered. In part this was due to the non-Orthodox ways in which Judaizers clung to their variants of Jewish identity, but also to the attitude of the host society, which regarded the assimilated Marranos as fundamentally Jewish—in their stock, or "blood." (Another reason was that, in the Dispersion, Marranos considered themselves linked to a broader Nation through their ethnic and familial ties, and those who practiced the Jewish religion tended to do so in unconventional ways.)

Such Marrano "anomalies" allow us to glimpse into a deep structure of Jewish history and see that the longtime link between the people and the religion is not a timeless metaphysical essence, but a historical situation; it had come into being through certain conditions, lasted for a long era, was cracked on certain occasions (as by the Marranos), and broke down in modern times. The very long period in which the people and the religion had been in close overlap made us lose sight of the fact that they are not identical, but two separate elements. The Marrano saga shifted these components slightly apart; it disturbed the perfect overlap that made them look identical, and allowed an observer to peek into the duality at the bottom. This duality had prevailed in antiquity, when the Israelites rejected their normative religion; it was submerged by Ezra and again by rabbinical Judaism, and resurfaced in the last two centuries as a crucial condition with which Jewish modernity has to grapple and come to terms.

Of course, the concept of *people* should not be understood here in the sense of a modern *nation*. Nationality is a conscious voluntary phenomenon, whereas historical membership in a people, at least at the basic level, can be determined by nonvoluntary and nondeliberate elements such as descent, labeling by the social environment, competition, and hatred (anti-Semitism), and also by the person's positive sense of connection and belonging, even when it lacks explicit intentions or a clear explanation. When the basic belonging is determined by involuntary elements of which the individual is aware, and particularly when it is reinforced by a hostile external world, a Jewishness is constituted that might be named existential. The individual has then to determine her attitude toward it—how, if at all, she interprets it further, beyond its given facticity, and whether she accepts, affirms, rejects, or escapes from her Jewishness (and where to).

Intellectuals such as Sigmund Freud and Jacques Derrida articulated this attitude in characteristic ways. Derrida considered himself a non-Jewish Jew and a kind of Marrano. He identified in his Jewishness all the marks of the dualities and disintegrated identity that his philosophy ascribed to the human condition in general. Freud, who called himself a "Godless Jew" and also rejected Jewish nationalism, said that, nonetheless, he is a man "who has never repudiated his people, who feels that he is in his essential nature a Jew and who has no desire to alter that nature. If the question were put to him: 'Since you have abandoned all these common characteristics of your countrymen, what is there left to you that is Jewish?' he would reply: 'A very great deal, and probably its very essence.'"[3] Both Freud and Derrida knew and suffered personally from anti-Semitism; the existential element of their Jewishness is unmistakable, as is their Jewish self-perception.

For better or worse, a Jewish self-perception was also shared by many modern Jews who converted to Christianity for social reasons (again, like some Marranos). The poet Heinrich Heine, though a young atheist, became a Lutheran in order to "gain a ticket to society," but continued to consider himself Jewish in deep and complex ways that resound in his work (and even more in his letters); in older age he embraced the Bible as a Lutheran, no less than as Jewish book. The writer Franz Werfel felt attraction to Christianity, or to some middle area between it and Judaism, but remained a secularized and wavering Jew. The philosopher Ludwig Wittgenstein regarded his Jewish origin as a wound and an oppressive shame; and being a kind of secularized Catholic, he even felt obliged to "confess" his Jewishness as if it were a burden of guilt. Even Theodor Herzl, the founder of political Zionism, had first proposed to overcome anti-Semitism through mass conversion. Herzl had only scant knowledge of Jewish traditions, and after he became a Zionist, he envisaged the future *Judenstaat* (State of the Jews) as a German-speaking branch of liberal Europe.

Jews who refused to convert have assimilated in varying degrees into European culture. Some continued to do so even after the Holocaust. The cultural historian Victor Klemperer, a nonreligious and anti-Zionist Jew who survived the war living in Nazi Germany, had endorsed the ideas of the French Enlightenment and German civilization. At first he despised the Nazis as "un-German" and regarded himself as the true German. But the Holocaust made him aware of his inalienable Jewishness, and after the war he was active in Communist East Germany. The philosopher Theodor Adorno, though deeply shattered by Auschwitz, returned from the United States to Germany after World War II because he felt this was his true language and culture; he became a leading teacher and social critic in postwar Germany. His colleagues Herbert Marcuse, Hannah Arendt, and Hans Jonas remained in the United States, from where they spread their social and political theories. Jews have had a prominent presence in all the movements striving for social reform in the last two centuries, a topic we shall resume later.

Jewishness Combined with Other Spheres of Identity

A salient pattern of the modern Jewish condition is the combination of Jewishness and other circles of culture and identity. It is rarely a harmonious combination. Often it is marked by unrest and dissonance—a pattern that the Marranos anticipated, and that is so familiar today that no further evidence is required. Most readers know some examples—from their personal encounters, from the available information, and often from themselves. Modern Jews are Jews who have more than one tradition. They have assimilated into modernity and incorporate its features in several ways in their lives and identity. They take part in different communities, roles, affiliations, and so forth, that play a role in who they are or become without dominating their identity. These spheres of identity are not without tensions and contradictions, they do not necessarily harmonize, and are often linked together only by the person's choice and will, the will to recognize certain factually given and optional elements as constitutive of one's Self.

Some speak in this context of a *hyphenated identity*, but the hyphen metaphor could be misleading. Apparently the hyphen links and unites, but in practice it also separates and splits. The result is a tension that remains unresolved for the most part, two (or more) poles coexisting without real harmony and held together by an act of will and by the human talent for playing multiple roles. Furthermore, the hyphen suggests a dividing link between two components, each of which is complete in itself; yet in practice, we would need many hyphens to describe the modern Jew, and a modern person in general; and each component between those hyphens, rather than being complete within itself, is affected by their mutual relation, so that an inner fissure occurs within each as a result of its coexistence with others.

To be a modern Jew is not simply *Jew + modernity*. It is not a mechanical addition of two closed components. The Jewishness connected with the modern condition cannot be the same Jewishness it had been before or without it.[4] Modernity is not an integral essence to which an integral Jewishness can be added. Modernity itself is disjoined and decentered; it generates a plurality of life-spheres that are neither complete nor exhaustive; and it requires us to frequently pass between different functions and symbolic systems by which we act, or that give meaning to our actions, or justify different types of claims we make or accept. A person living in modernity does not use the same system of meanings for every issue, but tends to cross over between such systems according to the matter at hand, not necessarily in a conscious and deliberate mode, but as part of the flow of life.

Of course, it does not follow that every dissonance and contradiction should be accepted as desirable. On the contrary, wild contradictions are better reduced and held in check. A distinction seems, therefore, necessary between a profound and blatant inner conflict that might break or paralyze the personality, and a situation of tension and inner dissonance that may even prove creative or, at least, allow the subject to embrace and hold together the many facets of its multi-leveled person and to identify itself, in various degrees, in all of them. Although this fertile domain defies rigorous definition, it is here, rather than at the extremes, that an answer could be found.

Haskalah *and Assimilation*

Jewish modernity was partly driven by the *Haskalah* movement, which sought to transform the self-enclosed Jewish mode of life, engrossed as it was in the struggle for survival, and confining its intellectual energy to Jewish religious studies. *Haskalah* called on the Jews to break the self-imposed barriers that separated them from Europe's culture, science, aesthetics, and lifestyles; abolish their separate dress and idiom; reverse the negative attitude toward the body and nature; cultivate manners; and introduce European Enlightenment into Jewish minds and quarters. Most of this had been practiced as a matter of normal course by the former Marranos. The New Jews from Iberia did not need the special impetus of *Haskalah* because they had brought it with them from Iberia. Their communities were open to the Euro-Iberian culture and beyond; their rich lifestyles were modeled after the Iberian elegant fashion; they manifested a positive attitude to aesthetics and the arts; boasted a number of scientists and Renaissance men of letters; and conducted an intellectual dialogue with Christian dignitaries and scholars.

Should the Marranos then be seen as anticipating *Haskalah*, the movement that promoted Jewish modernization? Not quite: the difference outweighs the resemblance. The founders of *Haskalah* saw themselves as bearers of a new message aiming to *transform* the Jewish world, whereas the former Marranos carried their Iberian culture with them as a legacy and reminder of their former existence. Their émigré culture continued and replicated what had been going on in their countries of origin. In this sense it was conservative and past-oriented. By contrast, for the *maskilim* (promoters of the *Haskalah*) European culture was groundbreaking and future-oriented. They had not been born into it, but acquired this culture as an intentional project, with the goal of transforming Jewish life as a whole. The Marrano New Jews did not try to transform the lives of other Jews. They secluded themselves in "Portuguese" congregations and cultivated a sense of cultural superiority (including toward the Sephardi exiles). The new thing in their lives was not European culture, but Judaism. They absorbed the rudiments of their new religion from veteran Jews, but did not spread their own European culture among those other Jews.

And yet there is a deeper analogy between the *maskilim* and the Marranos—though not in the Dispersion, but in Iberia. The motto of *Haskalah*: "Be a Jew at home and a man when you go out." This dualistic approach divides the human being into two personas. It splits a person's life into two distinct spheres—inner and outer, intimate and overt, private and public—quite as Marranos had done. At the immediate level, the slogan of *Haskalah* says: Judaism should be restricted to private life; in the public space, when functioning in the broader culture, Jews should act and appear as "universal human beings." (The latter phrase actually refers to Europeanization, and even—in Moses Mendelssohn's circle—Germanization.) Here, then, was a specific Jewish formula that, on one hand, resembles a Marrano strategy, and, on the other, expresses a modern liberal idea—namely, that religion is a private matter. To Iberian Marranos this separation was considered a deadly sin punishable by the Inquisition, and it had to be practiced clandestinely, while in modern Europe it became a right, and even an inherent duty. What had been forbidden to the Marranos was now not only permitted, but demanded of modern Jews. Religion, said liberal Europe, must remain private; but as such, it is an unshakable right of the modern subject, whose private world must be recognized as exclusively its own, immune to censorship and official control. This is a radical antithesis to the principle behind the Inquisition, which no one had embodied more distinctly than the Marranos.

The privatization of religion also means its exclusion from compulsory public institutions. Religion becomes a voluntary choice, and no legitimate ground is recognized for imposing a religion by law or coercion. This principle too was what the Marranos embodied in their actual lives. What was their secret Judaizing if not a voluntary choice? And what was their religion if not a private religion—the most private possible, involving concealment, secrecy, and mortal danger?

In a word: the Marranos were the first, among Jews and Europeans alike, to illustrate and embody the principle that religion is private and a matter of choice, long before these subversive ideas became legitimate in Western Enlightenment culture.[5]

Yet another Marrano-like element resonates in the famous motto of *Haskalah*. Shifting Judaism to the personal realm also implied playing it down, as if there was something embarrassing in it that warrants concealment. Many *maskilim* were in fact ashamed of flaws in the Jewish way of life. They hoped that removing these flaws would reveal the beauty and vision hidden in Jewish culture, and what it had to offer to the modern world. Yet shame is a source of complexes and contradictions; so the tendency to play down one's Judaism existed together with the hope to eventually unveil its beauty to the world.

Assimilation Reconsidered

The Marranos' experience further demonstrates the impossibility of sustaining a duality of the inner and outer without the one affecting the other: and this, too, recurred in the Ashkenazi *Haskalah*. Introducing the Jews to scientific novelties and the ideas of the Enlightenment could not be an innocuous addition. Jewish modernity brought the outside world into the inside, creating religious doubt and disenchantment with traditional forms, and often casting inner Jewish contents, such as prophetic ideals, into the ways in which European Jews joined the modern world (see below).

This involved several modes of assimilation. In current Jewish discourse, *assimilation* has taken a narrow and often negative connotation, similar to *Hellenization* with regard to antiquity. In both cases the negative ring is inappropriate because it assumes the total and necessary renunciation of Jewish identity. Actually, Hellenism in antiquity was the "universal" culture, and several Jewish tendencies arose (and competed) in relation to it from the Hasmonean leaders to Philo and his flourishing Jewish Alexandria, and even to many rabbinical sages who created the Mishnah and Talmud: all were *Jewish* life-forms, and all were affected by Hellenism to some extent. Similarly, in the nineteenth century, European culture and science came to be perceived as "universal" culture, in which a civilized human being could not afford *not* to take part, and thus must assimilate it to a certain extent. The assumption was that one's humanity would not be complete, but would remain partial and fragmentary unless one shared in certain universal values and attributes that transcend one's particular group (in this case, Judaism). The paradox, of course, was that in order to be a "whole" human being the person had to split—between the public and the private, the Jew and the European, and so forth. This may indicate again that there is no whole or integral human subject. Even if a person does complement that which is felt to be missing in their identity, he or she does not thereby necessarily attain harmonious integration of all its elements—which again is highlighted by the Marranos.

Religion as Semi-secularized Culture

Finally, the motto of *Haskalah* seems to accept the demand that Jewishness be shaped as religion only. This was how it was interpreted in Germany and later in the United States. In Eastern Europe, and today in Israel, Jewishness also assumed nationalist colors. Meanwhile the contemporary picture in the West has become more complex. Many Western Jews today view religion itself, along with its rites and customs, as primarily cultural factors, the signposts of a semi-secularized Jewishness they wish to maintain in their private lives or as the linchpin of communal organizations. Being "Jewish at home" is thus sometimes interpreted as an ethnic or cultural connection rather than necessarily a theological one. The rapport of these phenomena to the varieties of the Marrano experience can hardly be missed.

Negating Adherence: Modern Jews and the Change in the World

In chapters 14 through 16 we explored the influence of Marrano descendants on Spanish Renaissance culture, particularly in movements of religious reform. Since Iberian civilization was then fundamentally religious, the reforms of religion championed by these converts meant reforming the very foundations of culture. In addition, the Marranos also pushed for secular social changes (not mediated by religion) by advocating various liberties and, especially, claiming that a person's worth must derive from individual achievements rather than origin at birth. On these counts, the Marranos' similarities with modern European Jews are surprising. In both cases, the rapid penetration into non-Jewish society was associated with a prodigal drive for achievement and success, an emphasis on learning and research—a fundamental Jewish trait—and a striving to excel in everything that matters to the host society. As a result, modern Jews and Iberian Conversos gained noticeable influence both economically and in the field of ideas, letters, learning, and communication. Furthermore, in both cases there also was a radical, innovative minority that vigorously attempted to change the society they were entering, as a condition for their very ability, moral and mental, to join it.

Here we see a recurring pattern. When modern Jews—or earlier Conversos—enter into non-Jewish societies as formally equal members, a good number of them try to "mend the world" by becoming active reformers. They pour their intellectual and moral energies into new social and civilizing projects that often translate (and universalize) the ancient Jewish prophecy into contemporary ideals that extend far beyond the Jewish context. In the nineteenth and twentieth centuries, Jews filled the ranks of social and political movements that pursued universal moral visions like liberalism, socialism, communism, or the liberation movement of European nations, which they eagerly joined. While in Spain in the sixteenth and seventeenth centuries, Erasmianism—a pre-Enlightenment movement—promoted Renaissance humanism through and beyond its religious message.

This is a phenomenon we might call *negating adherence*: the inability to endorse a given group or society in a straightforward way, leading to the demand to transform and reform it, to create something better in its place. Thus a Converso enters Ibero-Christianity, and a nineteenth century Jew leaves the Jewish ghetto and enters European civilization and German or Polish society, not as these actually are, but as they ought to be in accordance with a higher ideal, a better shape that does not exist in reality. These kinds of newcomers will press for reform, and even revolution, of the society they are joining—as a condition of their very ability to join it. Yet they do not really have an alternative—the Converso cannot return to Judaism and the modernizing Russian Jew will not return to the shtetl; so their demand for reform acquires extra pressure and urgency. Often, though not always, the ideal underlying the reform is unconsciously nourished by an ancient Jewish moral vision that has been universalized (or even secularized), by which those reformers would have amended Judaism itself if it remained their concern—yet their concern had shifted to the larger society, and even to "humanity" at large. In both the Converso reformer and the Jewish socialist revolutionary—say, Vives and Trotsky—the drive to change the world involves a conscious and determined transcending of the Jewish sphere, possibly a latent Jewish spiritual source, and the universalization of an older vision—reshaping the world in patterns that fit the society that these reformers want to join and to transform.

But the reformers were a minority. The Marranos also prefigure the masses of modern Jews who sought, without full success, complete assimilation within the host nations. Just as some Conversos were the fiercest propagators of Orthodox Christianity, so many modern Jews competed over who was the more patriotic German, Frenchman, and the like. In a typical anecdote, Sami Groniman, a German rabbi's son who turned secular Zionist, was sitting in a café watching a schoolteacher addressing a group of boys. Repeatedly Groniman overheard phrases such as "patriotism," "the German eagle," and "the glorious Kaiser" coming from the group, so he concluded it must be a Jewish school—and he was right. "Patriotic phraseology," he remarked, "was then [before World War I] heard in Jewish assemblies more than in [German] soldiers' societies."[6] French and Hungarian Jews weren't much different. Their nationalism combined hard assimilation with a touch of progressive activism (since nationalism was then an antitraditional force.) This typical compromise, under different circumstances, had existed also among Marranos who assumed their Christianity and conformed to the ruling ideology with determination, yet slightly, in varying degrees, also revised it.

Purity of Blood: Existential Anti-Semitism and Existential Jewishness

The split between religion and Jewish existence is also evident in the secularization of the "Jewish problem." A new racial hatred of Jews, which might be called *existential anti-Semitism*, arose and spread in the nineteenth century. Hatred of Jews had persisted for two millennia; but the anti-Semitism that developed in the wake of the emancipation, the Enlightenment, nationalism, Jewish assimilation, and European political romanticism, is a fundamentally modern and secular phenomenon.[7] The new anti-Semitism shifts the classic hate and mythological fear of Jews from the religious to the existential plane. Jews provoke fear and hostility neither because they rejected the Savior or are blamed for his death, nor because of any act or belief related to their religious rituals, but because of their very being Jewish; and this is an existential stigma which no baptism or assimilation can redeem. Jews who had maximally assimilated into European society, even converted to Christianity, continued to be seen as fully Jewish by the secular anti-Semites who, to justify their continued negation of the Jew, shifted its ground from religion to the semibiological concept of race.

We have seen a parallel development in Iberia. After the Jews' conversion had emancipated them in principle, hatred of them could no longer be anchored in religion, so the doctrine of blood purity was devised as a ground for discriminating against and persecuting the converts. "Blood purity" in Iberia, like "race purity" in modern Germany, implies that Jewishness is not contingent on the individual's beliefs, actions, consciousness, self-perception, or on any attribute or predicate; instead, it inheres in the person's *bare existence*, stripped of all qualities. The Jew is a "featureless person" whose Jewishness defines his primary being or pure self outside of any qualities. As that Spanish royal counselor is aptly made to say in *Shevet Yehudah*: "Know, my lord, that Judaism is one of those diseases that have no cure" (see chapter 4, note 5).

Modern racist theory provides a convenient popular channel that diverts the anti-Jewish venom from the religious to the existential plane. But race theory is an outward apparel. I think the concept of existential anti-Semitism captures better the core of this phenomenon, which the muddled doctrine of a Jewish biological race expresses in vulgar terms. Biology serves a dual purpose: to insist on the unchangeable nature of Jewishness, as being an ontological fact, and to dress up passionate hatred and prejudice in scientific garb. As anti-Semitism was labeled the "socialism of fools," so racism may be labeled "the science of fools." And yet, racism articulated an entirely new historical situation, and a new mode of factual Jewish belonging that no Jew can dismiss or abolish by a subjective act of choice or change of consciousness: first, because the non-religiously based attribution of Jewishness is imposed from outside, and second, because a Jew could not reject this attribution as irrelevant without self-deception. Existential anti-Semitism thereby lays the ground for an existential Jewishness, which is neither religious nor nationalist, but precedes both as bare existential and historical factum that a person cannot deny without self-negation and self-deception. It is not accidental that unwilling modern Jews hated themselves as Jews: such self-hatred only confirms that there is no escape from being Jewish (for if such a possibility existed, those people would have succeeded in evading Judaism and would have had no reason to hate themselves).

Existential Jewishness can be left as just that, or the person may choose to give it further attributes—religious, nationalist, communitarian, cultural, and so on. But none of these Jewish shapes—which depend on basic choices since they can be assumed or renounced—can rightfully claim the allegiance of an existential Jew who refuses any further qualification. In other words, an "existential" Jew can choose to join some more saturated Jewish forms—religious, cultural, national—but none of these has a right to impose its "we" on him or her or recruit him or her to its cause.

An existential link transcending religion was anticipated by the Conversos' peculiar use of *Nation* (not meant in the modern sense). This vague but stable concept of a shared Hebrew Nation was constituted from elements that gave primacy to descent (blood), and to how the outside establishment regarded the Converso group and related to its members. Paraphrasing Spinoza[8] one could argue that the Inquisition and persecution that paradoxically helped the Jews survive also helped the Marranos trace the outer boundaries of their Nation. And what persisted within those boundaries was not only a covert "Mosaic religion," but a broader and more complex kinship, historical and existential.

The Holocaust and Existential Anti-Semitism

The twofold historical shift we described earlier and called "existential"—in anti-Jewish hatred, and in Jewish belonging—lies at the background of the genocide of the Jews in World War II. The Holocaust brought existential anti-Semitism to its terrifying culmination, yet also to its logical conclusion. If Jewishness is an affliction that stains the Jew's very existence, if it cannot be remedied either through assimilation or conversion, then the only solution is "the Final Solution." As soon as Jewishness is defined as inseparably attached to the individual's bare being, the effective way of removing it is to deny the Jews' *being*—to annihilate them physically. This is the dark logic of this position. Of course, in order to carry out this logic a special historical situation was necessary—the revolutionary moral nihilism of the Nazis, the fog of total war, and a leader driven by black racial Messianism, a Hitler. But this was not an outburst of the same classic hatred of Jews that had existed for centuries; it was not a terrifying further step in the same direction. The fact that Jews were actually negated—systematically murdered in their real bodies—reflects the radically new condition of the Jew vis-à-vis the anti-Semite. This condition continues to be part of the fundamental conditions of existence for modern Jews today as well, although anti-Semitism had become illegitimate in the public discourse of the West after the Second World War (but survived in private, and is now re-emerging in public, too). Accordingly, the existential link of Jews continues, in its amorphous way, to be there factually also today, preceding any interpretation that might be given it, and superseding all attempts to repress or ignore it.

Clearly, there is no similarity between the Nazi horror and the Inquisition. The latter, harsh and inhuman, did not engage in genocide and did not seek it. But from the viewpoint of *the victims' methods of survival*, there was an instructive similarity between the Nazi persecution and the Spanish Expulsion, in that both were organized *from the top*, by an effectively ruling central government, a fact that completely upset and confounded the classic Jewish strategies of survival used in pogroms originating locally and mostly from below. As for the role of Christian authorities in both periods, it is true that Catholic prelates on several occasions displayed hypocritical piety while allowing local pogroms to occur—events they considered illegitimate, yet tolerated as a political necessity, and sometimes even encouraged as contained local events that are part of life. Moreover, since the time of Philip II the politicized Church tolerated the "pure blood" regulations, a theological aberration (indeed, heresy) that denies the equal value of baptism, and allowed the Inquisition, a Christian agency, to administer this un-Christian policy. And yet, the Church as institution could not and did not subscribe to systematic murder as an ideology or global policy. Thus, the consequences of existential hatred for Iberian Conversos, though grave, were restrained by the same culture, however problematic, that had produced the aberration of "pure blood" in the first place. In Nazi Germany, with its wild revolutionary climate and the moral anarchy it spread in the masses—and in those countries that collaborated with the Nazis—such effective barriers did not exist, or were washed away. Even some important Christian organizations, both Protestant and Catholic, supported the anti-Semitic policies. During the war, some high-ranking Christian leaders allowed Nazi deportations to take place without effective protest.[9]

In summary, the underlying feature of the modern Jewish condition is the rupture or separation (in several degrees) between Jewish religion and Jewish existence. This separation explains not only existential anti-Semitism and the Holocaust, but also existential Jewishness, and diverse other modern phenomena like Jewish nationalism, assimilation, secularization, Zionism, the non-orthodox religious movements, and the resumption of Jewish sovereign politics in the state of Israel. All these phenomena would have been impossible without assuming some measure of separation, as well as of conflict, between the Jewish religion and Jewish existence. But this is not an entirely new condition: a previous instance existed among the Marranos. They were the first to personally experience the separation between Jewish religion and Jewish existence, thereby anticipating a phenomenon that, although not essential in their own times, became essential half a millennium later.

In this perspective, what happened to the Conversos in the confines of the Iberian experience as an *exceptional* phenomenon in their times prefigured the *fundamental* condition of Jews everywhere in modern times.

Epilogue

Present-Day Marranos

Part I: Belmonte

Cecil Roth's book on the Marranos (1932), the only available synthesis so far, ends with an epilogue telling the story of a Marrano community that had survived in Northern Portugal, in the regions of Beiras and Trás-os-Montes. Their main concentration was around the town of Belmonte. In 1917 Samuel Schwarz, a Polish Jew recently settled in Portugal who worked as a mining engineer near Belmonte, was looking for supplies for his mine. A Belmonte merchant warned him against doing business with one of his competitors, saying he was "a Jew." The puzzled and aroused Schwarz wondered what the man meant. Was he using "Jew" as an anti-Semitic adjective standing for "cheat"—or did he refer to an actual Jew? Further inquiries revealed that the region of Belmonte was full of presumed *Judeos* who practiced Jewish-like rites in semisecrecy. Most of them were simple provincial folks who knew little about the outer world and absolutely nothing about other Jews. For a long time they resisted Schwarz's advances and suspected his motives. His worst argument in trying to gain their trust was that he, too, was a Jew: this was final proof that he was an impostor and spy, since no Jews existed any more in the world except them! This belief, which may have helped sustain them, indicates that these Marranos identified "Jews'" with their own mixed and clandestine situation, to the point of appropriating the whole appellation.

Schwarz noticed that the Belmonte Marranos (like other Marrano groups we met in this book) were guided by "priestesses" or female "rabbis," who preserved and transmitted their religious tradition; so he tried to convince these women by reciting Jewish prayers to them. In vain: the *Judeos* did not recognize any Jewish prayer as their own. Everything sounded foreign to them, including the strange language, Hebrew, in which these prayers were recited. Finally, the exasperated Schwarz pronounced the quintessential formula of Judaism: *Shema Yisrael, Adonay Elohenu Adonay ehad.* The word *Adonay* is the holiest in Marrano liturgy, the true name of the one-and-only God; so, each time Schwarz uttered this word, the women covered their eyes in piety. At last the leading lady declared: "This man is really and truly a Jew, for he calls the name of *Adonay*."

Once admitted into their trust, Schwarz devoted several years to compiling the Marranos' chants and prayers, which he published in 1925.[1] Ironically, sixty years later, on my visit to Belmonte (1985), I found that Marranos were using Schwarz's book in photocopy as their prayer book. Inadvertently, the scholar had turned their oral tradition into written lore and provided their religion with its canonical book.

The irony is double since nothing was farther from Schwarz's original intention. A secular supporter of Zionism, Schwarz had hoped that the Marranos would renounce their hybrid religion and convert to official Judaism (while keeping only a few token customs as mere folklore) as a sign of their "return" to the nation. Not all Jewish notables in Lisbon liked this plan. Some opposed it for fear of creating an aberrant religious sect, or rousing a counterwave of anti-Semitism in Portugal;[2] others simply looked down on the Judeos as socially and culturally inferior. Yet a drive to reconvert these Marranos had taken off, and persisted until World War II.

Its fervent spokesman was a decorated hero of World War I, Captain Arthur de Barros Basto, who took the Hebrew name Ben Rosh. In 1923 he founded an open Jewish community in his hometown of Oporto. With help from Sephardic groups abroad he launched a propaganda campaign that made him known in Portugal as the "Apostle of the Marranos." He published a journal (*HaLapid*, the Torch) and, in 1938, opened a synagogue for ex-Marrano converts. But strong opposition arose. A prominent renegade in an ultraconservative Catholic land, a sworn republican in Salazar's semifascist state, and much too radical a Jew for the insecure Jewish establishment to swallow, Barros Basto was defamed, banished from the army, and resisted on all sides. His many enemies won him a few attributes of a martyr but also curbed his influence. The moderate Schwarz, at first his admirer, became his strong opponent.[3] By midcentury both men saw their hopes come to meager results.

Roth's account ends a bit earlier, in the early 1930s. Before we take the story further, here is what a traveler at that time might have reported about Belmonte:

The Belmonte Judeos are all officially Catholic. Their main stages of life (rites of passage) occur under the sign of the Cross. They are all baptized, and none is circumcised. They marry in church with a priest's blessing, and are buried in a Catholic cemetery, a cross usually marking their grave. Yet they hardly go to church on Sundays or other Christian holidays. Every Friday night they light candles to honor the Jewish Sabbath, and hide them inside a closet or a fireplace. Their most sacred events of the year are Passover and Yom Kippur. They celebrate these holidays in their own Marrano way, using their special rites and liturgy, which are neither Jewish nor Christian, though inspired by both these religions.[4] Most of them commemorate the biblical Queen Esther, the Marrano patron saint.[5] All these occasions are celebrated in privacy and jealous secrecy, which has become part of their sacred ritual, although it is no longer a life-saving necessity.

It is typical of the Marranos that they have no collective forum. Each family prays on its own, in separation from the others. Because of this familial structure—and the women's roles and responsibility inside the house—it is the women who keep the tradition and teach the young; men are often ignorant of important chants and prayers. The Marranos do not eat *kosher*, but make sausage without pork and burn the lard through the chimney to fool the neighbors. Their duality is expressed not only in the mixture of Christian and Jewish elements in the same rite, but also in using parallel rites for the same occasion. Before marrying in church, the bride and bridegroom are married "properly" at home by a Marrano wise woman. After they fast a day or two, the toes on their right feet are tied together by an unused (virgin) strip of linen (*linho*), and the marrying wise woman (usually old) says a Marrano benediction that constitutes the marriage bond.[6] In places north of Belmonte there is also a kind of Marrano "baptism" to replace circumcision: the grandmother holds the newborn up and, saying a Marrano formula, applies vegetable oil to its temples and chest (thus making the movement of a partial cross!). When later the family goes to church for the Catholic baptism (or for a wedding), some Marranos whisper: *"Nesta casa entrei / Nem pau, nem padre, nem pedra adorarei"* ("Into this house I have entered / But neither wood, nor priest, nor stone shall I adore").[7]

Post-Salazar

The climate of oppression, censorship, and harsh conformity that reigned during Salazar's long dictatorship (1936–1968) set Portugal into closure and a kind of inertia, which also affected the Marranos. Though open Judaism was legal and accepted—Salazar even helped Jewish refugees to escape Hitler—proselytizing was seen in a bad light. The Marrano community diminished, not by conversion to Judaism but by absorption into Catholic society.

With the return of democracy in the 1970s, Portugal opened to the world again, and the Belmonte Marranos started getting new visitors: scholars trying to document their community; photographers wishing to present them to the world; and people with more intrusive agendas who sought to "free" the Marranos of something they considered flawed or deformed about them—namely, their own dualistic identity. Jewish activists encouraged the Marranos to convert to "normative" (that is, Orthodox) Judaism, and some superficial Israeli politicians even wanted them to emigrate to Israel—as if this fulfilled their destiny or true essence.

The Marranos were confused and divided by the intrusion of an assertive Jewish presence into their intimate world. While many, especially the parents, were keen to preserve their ancestral identity with its dualist character and semisecretive way of life, there was another, mostly younger, group who wished to become Jewish in the allegedly "right way."

A Visit to Belmonte

I visited Belmonte in the autumn of 1985, before these developments had taken full effect. My wife Shoshana and I drove up from Lisbon a few days after Yom Kippur, accompanied by young José Ruah, son of the president of the Lisbon Jewish community, Dr. Joshua Ruah, who was in the Marranos' trust and graciously arranged for us to be admitted.[8] We arrived late on Friday night, and immediately encountered several distinguishing marks of this community. Our hosts, Abilio Morão Henriques and his wife Amélia, apologized that they could not offer us a warm meal, only bread, cheese and fruit, because they never cook on Friday. But tomorrow, they promised, we shall enjoy Amelia's best dishes, cooked on Saturday! This is how they confuse the Christians: on Friday they keep the Sabbath, on Saturday they work and light fire. Of course, they admitted, no Christian is really fooled by this any more; all know what is going on. So why do they continue to dissimulate? The (utilitarian) reasons they gave at first did not sound very convincing, or quite coherent; but as the conversation went on—and in further talks with Marranos over the next two days—the final answers converged on one theme: this is their revered tradition, the way their ancestors have always kept their religion, and this is how it should be. In other words: secrecy had become important to the Marranos as a *religious* value. The mask had acquired ritual meaning in itself, and duality was now practiced for its own sake.[9]

Before showing us to our room our hosts gave us a tour of their spacious house. At the far end we entered a storage area with brooms, canned food, and the like. On a shelf in the corner, a cluster of small oil-lamps projected their glitter to the ceiling. Amélia explained these were the candles she had lit earlier that evening. "There are fifteen of them," she said, "one for the Sabbath, one for *Adonay*, and the rest for the souls of deceased relatives." What do the candles do to the souls of the deceased?—"They lighten them up!" Without our asking, Amélia started singing some of the prayers she used in lighting candles.

When done, she pronounced the names of God, Moses, and the Hebrew patriarchs while making a curious and interesting gesture. With three fingers she touched her lower chest, saying "Adonayoo," her middle chest, saying "Moyzes," her upper chest, saying "Abraham," her forehead, saying "Isaac," and finally she kissed her fingers saying: "Y Jacob." It looked like she was crossing herself—in a Jewish-Marrano manner.

Back at the table, the conversation turned to how the family had recently celebrated Yom Kippur and what they do on Passover. In a clear, chanting voice, Amélia treated us to a sample of Marrano prayers for both these holidays ("not from Schwarz," she insisted, but directly from her own mother). When she sang of the crossing of the Red Sea—a distinct Marrano ceremony—we saw her cover her eyes as the words "*adonayoo! adonayoo!*" came ringing from her lips. Digging into a chest, Abilio took out several stone-hard pieces of Passover bread that had been baked twenty-six years earlier when he and Amélia got married, and kissed the blackened pieces before showing them to us. Why keep these relics all this time?—"So that God will protect us." When we asked about Sukkot, the upcoming Jewish holy day, we met with a blank gaze. Clearly, they had not heard of it. Do they keep any other holy day? Well, they fast one day on Christmas![10]

Until that time Raphael, their only son, had kept silent. But when we asked how the family felt about the attempts to reconvert them, he made a few poignant observations. In Belmonte, he said, there are two schools of thought, one believing in Marrano Judaism (his term), while the other prefers Orthodox Judaism. With empathy and understanding Raphael expounded the viewpoint of those Judeos who cling to their ancestral form of life, Marrano Judaism, which is, he held, as legitimate as the Orthodox Judaism from which it differs. At this point his father, Abilio, turned to José, our Lisbon companion and translator, with a rhetorical question: "Are all Jews in Lisbon orthodox [meaning observant]?" A good question, I remarked, and Abilio continued: "So what difference is there between Joseph Ruah, a nonreligious Orthodox Jew, and myself, a nonorthodox Marrano Jew?"[11]

We left the question hanging. But after Raphael's speech, we were surprised to learn that he had been speaking for his father rather than himself. He personally did not believe that Marrano Judaism had a future, and would accept—indeed, seek—to be converted by a rabbi and marry a non-Marrano Jewish girl. (We were to hear this wish from other young men too, though not all.)

The next day our host took us to meet some relatives and acquaintances. The word got out that we were from Israel, and people turned back in the street to look at us. Some accompanied us to the store of Antonio Morão Henriques, where a vivid conversation was started by our questions. Suddenly all fell silent: an old woman, a gentile customer, entered the store. We were shown into an inner room, better concealed from outsiders, and asked to wait until she left. While taking notes, my eye fell on an engraving hanging on the wall that showed an elegant French lady, nineteenth-century style, with a large necklace and heavy curls, who looked quite regal. A reverent Marrano hand had struck out her French name (Stephanie something) and wrote instead: *Rainha Santa Ester* (Queen Saint Esther). The French beauty was promoted to represent the Marrano patron saint.

A young man, Antonio José Henriques Vaz, aged twenty-nine, took us to an outdoor restaurant for lunch. Speaking of the trend to reconvert, he expressed his preference for the Marrano prayers and traditions and said the demand that he go through a special ceremony in order to count as Jew insulted him. Antonio confirmed that his life as Judeo was mingled with Christian elements (he even, with some embarrassment, took us to see the Cross on his father's grave), but insisted that this is who they are, this is their reality, and people are sometimes more complex than meets the eye.

Another young man, also called Henriques (names revolve in circles in this endogamous community, where people have intermarried for centuries, so often they look physically cumbersome and suffer sometimes from genetic and mental problems), made this comment to us: "The Jews in Israel practice the religion of Israel, we practice our religion." He added: "And our religion is more intense because we sacrifice more for our Judaism!"

Here are further excerpts from our talk with him:

—I am a Jew. I had felt proud when [Catholics] had called me that [in derogation]. And when they realized I was not insulted, they stopped.

—And today?

—Today this does not happen any more. I am a Portuguese citizen with equal rights.

—So you practice your Judaism in the open?

—No, only secretly at home.

—Why?

—To avoid criticism. This is a Catholic country.

—But you say you are a free Portuguese citizen?

—The Catholics know what we are doing, they know the dates of our holidays, and they criticize and mock us for that.

—So it is social pressure that makes you hide?

—No, it is the mockery.

—But why be affected by it, since you are not doing anything shameful?

—[*Insistent*] What we do is *secret* Judaism. The Catholics know this, they know we do Kippur, Passover, they also know what we are doing—but they have never seen it.

—So that's what's important to you?

—Precisely.

—I mean, what matters is not to be seen by outsiders?

—Exactly so.

—Your secrecy is then part of your religious tradition?

—Yes, this is how we have been taught.

—By whom?

—By our ancestors.

—And if tomorrow all Catholics will turn super-liberal and no longer mock you,
 would you still continue to practice in secrecy?

—Yes, personally I would.

The next day Antonio took us to a young Marrano couple who had at first been reluctant to see us, but finally invited us to their home, a modern middle-class house. When noticing my tape recorder, their thirteen-year-old daughter nervously signaled her mother, who asked that I not use it. They would answer some of our questions if I promised I was not a journalist. The first thing they told us was that all they knew about their tradition came down in the family through women.[12] The wife had learned it from her mother and was already teaching the little she knew to their daughter. As the tension abated they showed us the secret cupboard in the kitchen where they kept their Sabbath oil candles, and even their bedroom, where a cross hung over the bed near a picture of Saint Esther, and they described to us their "Jewish" marriage ceremony, with the strip of linho linking their toes.

—Were you also married in church, by a Catholic priest?

—Yes, but only pro forma.

—Was there a large crowd in church? Catholic guests?

—Yes, in the same way that Jews attend Catholic weddings.

—Have you also been baptized?

—We were, including our daughter, but today I would no longer have baptized
 her.

—Was there any Jewish ceremony at home before baptism?

—No, none. [*They clearly weren't aware of the "Jewish baptism" mentioned
 above.*]

—Did you know that the Jews have the custom of circumcision?

[*Blank faces. They ask: "What is circumcision?"*]

—Did you think that all the Jews practice the same way as you?

—Yes, more or less [*said the wife (the husband kept silent)*]. Though last year my
 sister went to Lisbon and was surprised to see it was different there.

It became evident that this couple, although quite educated and well-to-do, were faithful to the appellation of Jews without knowing anything of a Judaism other than their own. Even of their own tradition, to which they clung with insistence, they only had an impoverished notion. Even so, the distinctive features of secrecy and duality were as clearly demonstrated in them as in far better-informed Marranos.

Again the issue of dissimulation arose, and again the final answer was: "This is the tradition," "This is how our fathers used to do it." The pragmatic, utilitarian motive has been long lost. Duality and secrecy have became important in their own right, as Marrano values per se ingrained in their religion. (As we saw in the book, this had already occurred centuries before.)

The next day I was given a book by a local Jewish-Portuguese scholar, Amilcar Paolo, that contains Marrano chants and customs beyond those of Schwarz.[13] One of them in particular caught my eye. It was a *romance* about the biblical Judah and his widowed daughter-in-law, Tamar. Originally this must have been an anti-Jewish satire; but the Belmonte Marranos turned it into a jovial, bona fide Purim chant they were still singing in 1985. Such reversals— in both directions—were common in Marrano history (see the episode with SAKESTESAKSENU in the preface). In our host's view, too, the Marranos had created a religion sui generis. But he predicted that it would disappear within twenty-five years because "the young are getting out of it."

We left Belmonte impressed by these Marranos and their ingrained dualities and their ritualized double life, still opposing the inside and the outside, mixing images from both religions, and continuing to practice secrecy even when it is no longer necessary—for it had become a defining structure of who they are. I knew of the forces already working to change them, but did not predict some of their ironic results.

Later Developments—Marranos under the Star of David

A couple of years later, in 1987, six younger Belmonte Marranos started a vigorous movement to convert their fellow Judeos and establish an organized Jewish congregation where none had existed before. These "young Turks" relied on outside Jewish bodies in seeking "to impose a measure of unity and discipline" on their traditionally individualistic fellow-Judeos,[14] and, though dividing the community, their main goals had been achieved. By the mid-1990s, an official Jewish congregation had been set up, a synagogue built, dozens of Marranos—probably the majority—had converted,[15] and foreign rabbis were coming intermittently to Belmonte to instruct, supervise, perform Orthodox rites, and start implanting Jewish law (*halacha*).

Some of the Marranos resisted conversion; but for those who converted, prayers had become radically different (and were said in Hebrew, a language they don't understand) and a network of new Jewish rules had been added to their lives. The rites of passage also changed. Marriages were now performed by a rabbi, not a Marrano wise woman. Burials were conducted in the Jewish way, with David's Star replacing the cross on Marrano graves. Many babies and, less often, adults were circumcised. Moreover, when relatives wanted to bury as Jew a man who has resisted conversion in life, they had him circumcised after death and buried under a Jewish name. Thus the movement in favor of conversion and against Marranism gave rise to a new peculiar Marrano rite (and also, ironically, to a posthumous new form of forced conversion).[16]

This irony was not isolated. As time went on, it became manifest that the Marranos' traditional patterns of behavior were too deeply ingrained to be effaced by the change. Rather, the old forms of life—duality and secrecy—survived the act of conversion and surfaced again under the Star of David. The growing pressure (and number) of Jewish laws, which they experienced as foreign, caused converted Marranos to defy Orthodox Judaism just as they had defied Christianity in the past, and to conceal the truth about their transgression from their supervising rabbi (who, in this respect, took the role of the Catholic priest or "inquisitor"). Thus the converts became Marranos again, now in relation to Orthodox Judaism. As Molho puts it: "In the past the Marranos were hiding from the Christians and the Inquisition . . . now [in 1997] they hide from the rabbis of normative Judaism."[17]

The mask, so it seems, is the most difficult thing for a Marrano to shed—and not only when it serves to conceal transgression. On a deeper level of the Marrano mentality, religious acts *as such*, whether lawful or illicit, must be concealed from the outer world; and the outer world, in some cases, includes a supervising rabbi who becomes too inquisitive. The Marrano shuns interrogation, defies supervision, and believes that religion is, by nature, a concealed and intimate affair between the person and her or his God.[18]

Duality, too, survived the act of conversion and persisted as a Marrano pattern. Converts who observed the new Jewish rites were known to hang on to older Marrano practices. Thus men returning from synagogue on Friday night would sit to table, their heads covered with a Jewish Orthodox *kipa* (yarmulke), and continue the celebration by chanting Marrano prayers to the tune of the woman of the family. Women opposing conversion, who most of the time pray in private according to their own custom, could nevertheless be sometimes seen in the synagogue. In all such cases, the deeper pattern to which those Marranos cling (or revert) is *duality*: no longer a coupling ambivalence of Judaism and Christianity, but of Orthodox Judaism and Marranism. The content has changed, the structure rests the same.

Less obvious, yet distinct, traces of the Marrano experience that survived until today have been lately discovered in New Mexico (United States) and given rise to several books.[19] Other places with contemporary Marrano traces are Sicily[20] and the Spanish island of Majorca, where the descendents of Jews are called Chuetas.[21] Majorcan Marranism had suffered cruel blows between 1675 and 1691[22] but, enfeebled and diminished, its descendents survived into modernity.[23]

Part II: Other Present-Day Marranos

This part is extremely short for it shifts the burden of the epilogue to the reader.

Beyond the "official" Marranos we surveyed in the book, Marranism in a more metaphoric or analogous way exists today everywhere in the world—everywhere, that is, where old compact identities collapse. The reason can be immigration, urbanization, globalization, and any other pertinent "-ation." The contemporary person is characterized by a cluster of identity marks that are not necessarily coherent, and whose inevitable tension is sustained by the self-referring act of the person who wills or intends (whether consciously or not) to hold them together and to hold himself or herself together in and through them. In many cases, two such identity ingredients are dominant—for example, in immigrants from Italy to the United States, from the Caribbean to the United Kingdom, from Tunisia to France, from Mozambique to Cape Town, and so on. But many cases manifest three or more cultural spheres coming into play, and, of course, our identity anchors are not distinguished only by ethnic and geographical zones, but also by social roles, types of interests, professional communities, and the like, insofar as these are internalized and gain a deep personal significance. Contemporary intellectuals, novelists, and poets have provided us with ample evidence to the ubiquity of such "Marranesque" structures of identity, together with their typical patterns of difference, self-Otherness, and unrest. Each of us today knows such phenomena, when not from personal experience, then from our near periphery, our reading and movie going, our exposure to the world in other ways. So, counting on this widespread experience, the author of this book asks to take his leave here, and to leave it to readers to complete this part of the epilogue in their own way, as best they can.

Trends in the Literature

The large Converso literature is marked by several trends and polemics, some quite emotional. This appendix can only map some of these trends briefly.[1]

Since much of the scholarship has been written within a national/cultural context, there have been differences between Spanish and non-Spanish (especially Jewish) scholars, and heated controversies inside each of those circles.

Most of the Spanish discussion was part of the debate over Spain's national identity and its image of itself (*ser de España*). The discussion was not aimed at a phenomenology of the Conversos in themselves (this, when discussed, as by A. Domínguez Ortiz and F. Márquez Villanueva, was ancillary), but at the role Conversos occupy in determining the Spanish national "essence," or the structure of Spain's history and identity. Similarly, most of the Jewish debate was conducted from the vantage point of nation-building historians working to cultivate and interpret a modern Jewish consciousness and identity. In both cases, historians were fulfilling an ideological role that modern national movements, and post-Hegelian historiographic schools, have associated with the writing of history since the nineteenth century.

It should go without saying that whatever criticism may be implied in some of the following summaries concerns the scholars' interpretative scheme; it is not intended to detract from their often immense contributions to knowledge through shedding light on important documentary treasures and significant issues and events.

The Inner-Spanish Debate

From its inception to the first half of the twentieth century, modern Spanish historiography paid little or no attention to the Conversos, except in dismissive or negative terms. It was as if, shunning their troubling presence in the Spanish social and cultural body, scholars continued to reject the Conversos theoretically—to exclude them from the very concept of Spain—as the Spanish

---

[1] Regrettably, there is no room to mention everything important, so this survey must be illustrative only.

state had excluded them socially and legally in the sixteenth to eighteenth centuries.

The Spanish historical ideology in late nineteenth and early twentieth century was embodied in the figure of Marcelino Menéndez y Pelayo (1856–1912) and his dominant school. Menéndez Pelayo combined an impressive range of literary and historical knowledge with ardent national-Catholic pleading in the service of the *patria* (fatherland).[2] As a rising star he was close to the integrist right that saw medieval Catholicism as "cosubstantive" with the Spanish nation and inherent in everything truly Spanish; he even applauded the Inquisition as "the daughter of the genuine spirit of the Spanish people."[3] The Spanish "essence" was ancient and pure of Semitic elements; it was forged by a cross between Roman antiquity and Catholic Christianity, and has manifested itself in the heroism and suffering of the Spanish nation, which evangelized half the world. Those who did not share this sacred spirit he denounced as "heterodox" (meant pejoratively).[4] Muslims, Jews, and Conversos obviously had no homeland in this metaphysical concept of Spain and were relegated, as merely negative elements, to the marginal outskirts of its history.

Menéndez Pelayo's successor, Ramón Menéndez Pidal, continued that general line, which persisted until well after World War II. Claudio Sánchez-Albornoz (1893–1984, a distinguished anti-Franco exile) still insisted that Spain owed nothing positive to Moors and Jews. Rather, the vital core of what is Spanish—the fusion of the Visigoths with pure Catholicism—had resisted their harmful effects and reemerged almost intact with the Reconquista:[5] as if the long Muslim centuries, the penetrating Arabization, the great Berber influx, the cross-cultural intercourse during the Reconquest itself, and a millennium of Jewish presence had all been a bad dream that deserved to be forgotten. In this context, the Converso offshoots of the Jewish presence looked even less relevant.

Yet there were signs of change. A new Journal, *Sefarad*, has since the 1940s encouraged works on Jewish Spain, and F. Cantera Burgos published pioneering microstudies on Conversos. Even more important, the French Hispanist Marcel Bataillon published in 1937 his classic *Erasme et l' Espagne*, which stressed

---

[2] For a sharp portrayal of him, see Carolyn P. Boyd, *Historia Patria: Politics, History, and National Identity in Spain, 1875–1975* (Princeton, NJ: Princeton University Press, 1997), 99 and passim.

[3] *Revista Europea* 8, September 24, 1876; quoted in Boyd, *Historia Patria*, 102.

[4] Marcelino Menéndez y Pelayo, *Historia de los heterodoxos españoles* (Madrid: 1880–1881; reissued in Buenos Aires, 1945–1946 and Santander, 1946–1948, 3rd ed. Madrid, 1978).

[5] Claudio Sánchez-Albornoz, *Spain: A Historical Enigma*, 2 vols. (Madrid: Fundación Universitaria Española, 1975). For a (surprisingly sympathetic) review of his views, see Miguel Angel Ladero Quesada, "¿Es todavía España un enigma histórico? (Releyendo a Sánchez-Albornoz)," in *Lecturas sobre la España histórica* (Madrid: Real Academia de la Historia, 1998), 317–341.

the primacy of Conversos in the Spanish spiritual movements of the sixteenth century;[6] later Bataillon realized the Conversos' centrality also in shaping the picaresque literature as an ironic response to the blood purity policy.[7] Bataillon's impact on Spanish and other scholars cannot be exaggerated.[8] But the actual revolutionary was Américo Castro (1885–1972).[9]

Castro reversed both the factual picture and its evaluation. What made Spain unique in Europe was not its crusade against Muslims, Jews, Conversos, and Moriscos, but rather the incorporation of these groups into Spain's historical self. The truly Spanish identity was shaped not in antiquity but after the Muslim conquest, when the Christians, reduced to one "caste" among others, interrelated with the Muslims and the Jews within a mutual *convivencia* (coexistence) that was both cooperative and conflictive. By the same logic, the events that destroyed *convivencia*—the Reconquest, the expulsion of Jews and Moriscos, the blood purity laws—were forms of Spain's self-alienation and low points in its history.

Some of Castro's value statements may be debated; but his basic historical picture was almost therapeutic, in that it tore a veil of repression and self-concealment from many Spanish eyes and minds. And like any attack on repression, it provoked a furor of opposition and resistance. Castro backed his theory with extensive historical and literary materials (his other innovation was using literary works to complement historical sources).[10] His reinterpretations were often convincing and even ingenious, but sometimes exaggerated or too speculative even for his followers. Castro was open to revisions, but ardently defended his main thesis, notably against Sánchez-Albornoz. Their famous polemic eventually allowed Castro to turn the tide.[11]

Castro took special interest in the Conversos, whom he saw as fully integrated in the Spanish nation. So did Antonio Domínguez Ortiz (1909–2003), who also recognized the Conversos' importance but, he said, independent of

[6] Marcel Bataillon, *Erasme et l'Espagne* (Paris: E. Droz, 1937; Geneva: Droz, 1991); Spanish expanded edition: *Erasmo y España* (Mexico City: Fondo de Cultura Económica, 1966).

[7] Marcel Bataillon, *Novedad y fecundidad del "Lazarillo de Tormes"* (Salamanca; Madrid: Anaya, 1968); Bataillon, *Le roman picaresque* (Paris: La Renaissance du livre, 1931); Bataillon, *Pícaros y picaresca* (Madrid: Taurus, 1969).

[8] In the present book, chapters 15 and 16 bear Bataillon's mark.

[9] Especially in Castro, *España en su historia: cristianos, moros, y judíos* (Buenos Aires: Editorial Losada, 1948); translated into English as *The Structure of Spanish History* by Edmund L. King (Princeton, NJ: Princeton University Press, 1954); and Castro, *La realidad histórica de España* (Mexico: Ed. Porrúa, 1954).

[10] As in Américo Castro, *De la edad conflictiva: El drama de la honra en España y en su literatura* (Madrid: Taurus, 1961, 1963).

[11] There is already a literature on this polemic. See, for example, José Luis Gómez-Martínez, *Américo Castro y el origen de los Españoles: Historia de una polémica* (Madrid: Editorial Gredos, 1975).

Castro's broader assumptions.[12] In several works[13] he studied the Conversos as a distinct "social class"; investigated the issue of pure blood; and stressed the Conversos' vulnerability, disquiet, and marginality, which led to their different values (or, "mentality"): opposing conventionalism, valuing interiority and personal achievement, and disparaging birth and external *honra*. He concentrated on assimilated Conversos, not on Judaizers, and paid little attention to their Dispersion outside Hispanic lands. On the whole, he told an inner-Spanish story, without the Jewish and the cosmopolitan dimensions.

Domínguez Ortiz criticized Castro for underrating economics and using literature as history; yet, said an admirer of both, together they "knocked down the Menéndez Pelayo myth of Spain's monolithic unity."[14]

In 1962, Julio Caro Baroja published a three-volume history of the Jews in modern Spain.[15] (By Jews he meant also Conversos, a misnomer that probably arose from the dubious equation: Conversos = Judaizers = Jews.) The hard core of this uneven work is a study of sixteenth- to seventeenth-century inquisitorial trials; in addition, it covers the main events of Spain's persecution of Jews and Conversos, until the "final repression" of 1721–1725. In conflating Jews and Conversos, Caro Baroja seemed intent on telling a single, unified story: Spain's violent—and failed—attempt to eject its "Jewish" element. In the end, the author suggested—to the dismay of many of his countrymen—that "the typical [modern] Spaniard would be . . . the result of an explosive mixture of the characteristic 'Gothicism' of the 15th century with 'Judaism.'"[16]

Despite the change of tone, part of the Spanish scholarship before the demise of Franco's regime remained forgiving or apologetic of the Inquisition. And in 1957, a Catholic polemicist wrote a two-volume study of the Tortosa Disputation, attacking Baer's account of it and arguing that Gerónimo de Santa Fe was right and had proven his case.[17]

---

[12] F. Márquez Villanueva, "Hablando de Conversos con Antonio Domínguez Ortiz," in *La clase social de los conversos en Castilla en la edad moderna*, by Antonio Domínguez Ortiz (Granada: Universidad de Granada, Servicios de Publicaciones, 1991).

[13] Ibid.; Domínguez Ortiz, *Los judeoconversos en España y América* (Madrid: ISTMO, 1971); Domínguez Ortiz, *Los judeoconversos en la España moderna* (Madrid: MAPFRE, 1992).

[14] Márquez Villanueva, "Hablando de Conversos con Antonio Domínguez Ortiz." This, we may observe, is their importance to Spanish history, not so much to the history of the Conversos per se (which resists identification with any single national entity or context).

[15] Julio Caro Baroja, *Los judíos en la España moderna y contemporanea* (Madrid: Arión, 1962).

[16] Ibid., 3:266, epilogue. That much of this epilogue lacks rigor and tosses around old-fashioned stereotypes about peoples' "national character" does not detract from the overall importance of the work's contribution.

[17] Antonio Pacios López, *La disputa de Tortosa* (Madrid and Barcelona: Consejo Superior de Investigaciones Científicas, Instituto Arias Montano, 1957).

Francisco Márquez Villanueva, a follower of Castro and Bataillon, made a crucial contribution to Converso studies both through specialized studies and by reflecting on the field's basic concepts and orientation.[18] He criticized the simplistic application to Conversos (by inquisitors and scholars alike) of labels such as *Jew, Protestant,* and even *Judaizer.* He stressed that many Conversos condemned for Judaism were actually heretics to all religion, and that a subgroup among the Judaizers was distinctly Marrano rather than Jewish. Like Domínguez Ortiz, he strongly objected to focusing attention on Judaizers, whose numbers and historical importance—to Spain—he downplayed.[19] The historically significant Conversos, to him, were fully integrated into orthodox Catholicism, yet became nonconformists or "heretical" to the Spanish system's formalism, intolerance, and Inquisition. Such "Spaniards of Jewish origin" produced Spain's first intelligentsia and generated an outstanding cultural creativity that went in two directions—toward a mystical/spiritual Christianity, and toward a rationalist/heretical denial of religion.[20]

Other scholars joined and produced momentum. Eloy Benito Ruano studied the anti-Converso agitations, especially in Toledo, and how the "Converso problem" replaced the "Jewish problem" in Castile.[21] Angel Alcalá reinterpreted the Expulsion and the Inquisition and continued the focus on the assimilated Conversos' role in sixteenth-century culture. Carlos Carrete Parrondo, in addition to particular studies on Conversos (including on Judaizing priests and nostalgic Judaizing), published several volumes of inquisitorial records from Salamanca,

[18] In a number of essays, including: (1) "The Converso Problem: An Assessment," in *Collected Studies in Honor of Américo Castro's Eightieth Year,* ed. M. P. Hornick (Oxford: Lincombe Lodge, 1965), 317–333; (2) "El problema de los conversos: cuatro puntos cardinales," in *Hispania Judaica: Studies on the History, Language and Literature of the Jews in the Hispanic World,* ed. J. M. Solá Solé et al. (Barcelona: Puvil, 1980), 1:51–75; (3) " 'Nasçer e morir como bestias' (criptojudaísmo y criptoaverroísmo)," in *Los judaizantes en Europa y la literatura Castellana del siglo de oro,* ed. F. Díaz Esteban (Madrid: Letrumero, 1994), 273–293; (4) "Hispano-Jewish Cultural Interactions: a Conceptual Framework," in *Encuentros and Desencuentros: Spanish-Jewish Interaction throughout History,* ed. C. Carrete Parrondo et al. (Tel Aviv: Tel Aviv University Projects, 2000), 12–25; and (5) "Sobre el concepto de judaizante," in *Encuentros and Desencuentros,* 519–542. More recently, he collected his Converso studies in a book, *De la España judeoconversa—doce estudios* (Barcelona: Ediciones Bellaterra, 2006).

[19] Yet he recognizes their existence, and strongly opposes Netanyahu and Saraiva, who deny it. See the discussion later in this appendix.

[20] Márquez Villanueva inherited many of Castro's virtues in a less speculative mode, including the use of literature and the art of reading between the lines. And, like Castro, he discussed the broader phenomenon of the Conversos within the partial horizon and interest of "Spanishness." This is the main difference between his work and the present study, which otherwise shares and is inspired by many of Márquez Villanueva's astute insights.

[21] E. Benito Ruano, *Los orígenes del problema converso* (Barcelona: Ediciones El Albir, 1976), 85–92; E. Benito Ruano, "Del problema judío al problema converso," in *Simposio Toledo judaico* (Toledo, Spain: Publicaciones del Centro Universitario de Toledo, 1973), 2:7–28.

Segovia, Soria, and Almazán.[22] Other Spanish scholars worked on the records of Valencia (Ricardo García Cárcel); Aragon (Encarnación Marín Padilla); Almagro and Albacete (Juan Blázquez Miguel); Granada (María Antonia Bel Bravo); Murcia (José Martínez Millán); and the Basque country (Iñaki Reguera), to cite but a few. And Miguel Angel Ladero Quesada, a social historian, contributed traits to the Conversos' social profile, their professions, and their presumed numbers.

Of course, much of that work interrelated with research by non-Iberian scholars (Sicroff, Révah, MacKay, Gilman, Dedieu, Beinart, Benassar, Kamen, Elliott, Haliczer, Kriegel, Henningsen, and others) and with growing research in Portugal and the Americas.

Jewish Scholarship

Jewish scholarship in the nineteenth century took an interest in the Conversos (the so-called crypto-Jewish among them) mainly as a romantic saga of Jewish fidelity and martyrdom, and as aftermath to the greater story of Jewish Spain.[23] Serious scholarly attention started in the twentieth century and was incorporated into general histories of the Jews, such as Simon Dubnow's in the 1920s and Salo Baron's in the 1950s and onward. In 1932 Cecil Roth published the first historical synthesis, *A History of the Marranos*, as well as several monographs of famous Marrano families (such as *The House of Nasi*). And, using inquisitorial records and Schwarz's 1925 study of residual Marranos still living in Portugal (see the epilogue), Roth also published his pioneering study "The Religion of the Marranos" (1931–1932). This started an intriguing (and methodologically difficult) research into Marrano rites and customs that has culminated (so far) in David Gitlitz's rich and extensive *Secrecy and Deceit* (1996).[24]

A new chapter opened with Yitzhak (Fritz) Baer's *History of the Jews in Christian Spain*[25] (preceded by two volumes of documents).[26] A meticulous researcher

---

[22] C. Carrete Parrondo et al., eds., *Fontes iudaeorum regni castellae* (Salamanca: Universidad Pontificia de Salamanca, 1981, 1985, 1986, 1987).

[23] Both trends are embodied in the converted poet Heinrich Heine, a Marrano descendent through his mother and a kind of "Marrano" in his own person, who in youth had been a founder of Jewish studies in Germany, and who in old age glorified the Hispano-Jewish legend in his poetry.

[24] David M. Gitlitz, *Secrecy and Deceit: The Religion of the Crypto-Jews* (Philadelphia and Jerusalem: Jewish Publication Society, 1996).

[25] For Baer, "Conversos and Jews were one people, united by bonds of religion, destiny, and messianic hope"; and as for the Conversos, "Most of them practiced Jewish religion in secret, and some did so openly" (*A History of the Jews in Christian Spain* [Philadelphia: Jewish Publication Society, 1961], 2:424).

[26] For the collection of documents, see Y. Baer, *Die Juden im christlichen Spanien: Urkunden und Regesten* (Berlin: Akademie für die Wissenschaft des Judentums, 1929–1936), 2 vols.

with strong theoretical commitments, Baer studied the first century of Conversos (1391–1492) as a chapter in Jewish history and from the standpoint of Jewish history as he conceived it. In a later essay, *Galut* (Exile), Baer described the Jews' Dispersion as a fall from their "natural place," which deprives them of vital support until they return to their place of origin. The Conversos (*anussim*) were likewise, to him, Jews severed from their main stock, the victims of (a) an inexorably rising Spanish anti-Semitism, and (b) a failing Jewish leadership, detached from the true folks and "corrupted" by rationalist philosophy. Baer claimed that most of the Conversos observed Jewish laws and remained an integral part of the Jewish people.

Despite their apparent opposition, Baer's historiography is closer to the main Spanish historians than meets the eye. Both schools (including Castro and his disciples) approach the Conversos by appropriating them to their own national viewpoint and hemisphere; and both interpret the historian's role as serving the national identity. On a deeper level, Baer and his Spanish counterparts owe much of their metahistory to German Romantic (and also *völkisch*) views and to post-Hegelian schools that tend to treat historical entities, such as peoples and nations, as possessing a semiorganic core and/or an evolving distinctive Self.[27]

I remarked in the preface that Baer's declarative inclusion of the Marranos in the Jewish people sounds like a "secular rabbinical ruling." To give it empirical substance, Baer's followers in the "Jerusalem School,"[28] especially Haim Beinart, investigated a great many inquisitorial records. Beinart's seminal study of Ciudad Real concludes, in Baer's spirit, that "a picture emerges of a people [the Marranos] which continued to live as the Jewish community had done, even after the latter were expelled from Spain and all contact between them and Conversos had ceased."[29]

---

[27] The polemical tone of disagreements between certain Jewish and Spanish scholars, which prevailed despite—or because of—their deeper common ground, can be clearly sensed by juxtaposing two bibliographic surveys: (1) Domínguez Ortiz, "Historical Research on Spanish Conversos in the Last 15 Years," in *Collected Studies in Honor of Américo Castro's Eightieth Year*, ed. M. P. Hornik (Oxford: 1965), 63–82; and (2) Yosef Kaplan, "The Problem of the Marranos and 'New Christians' in Historical Research of the Last Generation," in *Studies in Historiography*, ed. Moshe Zimmermann et al. (Heb., Jerusalem: Shazar Center, 1987), 117–143. The latter essay describes Jewish and Spanish scholars as two camps divided by a "barrier" (133).

[28] Baer was a founder of what is called the "Jerusalem School" in historiography. See, among others, David Myers, " 'Between Diaspora and Zion': History, Memory, and the Jerusalem Scholars," in *The Jewish Past Revisited: Reflections on Modern Jewish Historians*, ed. David N. Myers and David B. Ruderman (New Haven, CT: Yale University Press, 1998), 89–98.

[29] Haim Beinart, *Conversos on Trial: The Inquisition in Ciudad Real*, trans. Y. Guiladi (Jerusalem: Magnes Press, 1981), 2.

However, Beinart's findings—also in Trujillo, Guadalupe, Herrera, and more, as well as outside Spain—do not warrant such a sweeping statement. They certainly established that Judaizing had existed as a significant phenomenon, but not that it was universal or even dominant, as he and Baer would think. Beinart's interpretation of his data is too concomitant with the standpoint of the Inquisition, which saw a secret Jew, or the will to be one, in fragmentary signs that do not necessarily warrant this (or, often, any other) univocal conclusion. Like others in the "Jerusalem school," Beinart is not attentive enough to distinctly Marrano dualities, which cannot be simply reduced to either Judaism or Catholicism (like the Marrano *beata* of Herrera; see chapter 6).

With some qualifications, this has been a current line in Jewish scholarship. Israel S. Révah (1917–1973) was a major force in Converso studies. Focusing mainly on Portugal and its Dispersion, he plowed through mountains of inquisitorial archives (arguing that they should be accepted generally as reliable) and made important discoveries and observations, including about heresies among Marranos (and new facts about Spinoza and Uriel da Costa). Révah defined the Marranos as "potential Jews," by which he meant (1) they had a basic Jewish commitment, (2) they lacked Jewish knowledge and opportunity to practice, and (3) certain Marranos later transformed into *actual* Jews in the Dispersion.[30] Révah's definition is subtler than Baer's, but likewise ascribes a Jewish-teleological essence to the Marranos. Révah's concept of "potential Jew" implies that to be a Marrano is to have Judaism as one's *telos* and destiny, in other words, to be a Jew in a state of privation—which points back to Baer.

Yosef H. Yerushalmi, in addition to a classic monograph on Cardoso (see chapter 18), produced enlightening essays on a variety of Marrano issues, including Marranos' deriving Jewish knowledge from Christian sources and perspectives, the difference between the Spanish and Portuguese Marrano experience, and the formation of the Nation.[31] A reflective historian, Yerushalmi also went beyond the Marrano issues at hand to reflect on wider, recurring structures of Jewish history—for example, how the trauma of 1492 became creative of a modern Jewish historical consciousness; how anti-Converso laws and blood policies anticipated the situation of emancipated Jews in nineteenth-century Germany;

---

[30] Israel S. Révah, "Les Marranes," *Revue des études juives* 118 (1959–1960): 29–77.

[31] For example, in the introduction to Yerushalmi, *From Spanish Court to Italian Ghetto* (New York: Columbia University Press, 1971); and in essays such as Yerushalmi, "The Re-Education of Marranos in the Seventeenth Century" (Third Annual Rabbi Louis Feinberg Memorial Lecture in Judaic Studies, Jewish Studies Program, University of Cincinnati, March 26, 1980); and others (see next note). Most of Yerushalmi's Marrano-related essays are collected in the French volume *Sefardica: Essais sur l'histoire des juifs, des marranes et des nouveaux-chrétiens d'origine hispano-portugaise* (Paris: Chandeigne, 1998).

and how the Lisbon massacre of Conversos in 1506 encapsulated a recurrent trap for Jews caught between royalty and populace.[32]

Albert Sicroff wrote the classic study on the statutes of "purity of blood" that still serves as a matrix for this issue,[33] as well as discerning studies on several heterodox types of Converso monks in Guadalupe.[34] Henry Kamen wrote one of the most debated books on the Inquisition and its effects, which serves as a common reference also to his critics.[35] Angus MacKay assessed the creation and evolution of the Conversos in often telling ways.[36] John Edwards addressed pertinent queries that arise from particular cases discussed in his articles.[37] Maurice Kriegel's critical essays, especially on Spain's attempt to delegitimize the Conversos' very existence (rather than integrate them), proved that original thinking is compatible with a more traditional "Jerusalem" affinity.[38] Stephen

[32] On these three issues, see Yerushalmi, *Zakhor: Jewish History and Jewish Memory* (Seattle: University of Washington Press, 1982); Yerushalmi, *Assimilation and Racial Anti-Semitism: The Iberian and the German Models* (New York: Leo Baeck Institute, 1982); and Yerushalmi, *The Lisbon Massacre of 1506 and the Royal Image in the Shebet Yehuda* (Cincinnati: Hebrew Union College, 1976).

[33] Albert Sicroff, *Les controverses des statuts de "pureté de sang" en Espagne du XV au XVII siècle* (Paris: Didier, 1960).

[34] Albert Sicroff, "Clandestine Judaism in the Hieronymite Monastery of Nuestra Señora de Guadalupe," in *Studies in Honor of M. J. Bernadete: Essays in Hispanic and Sephardic culture*, ed. Izaak A. Langnas and Barton Sholod (New York: Las Americas, 1965), 89–125.

[35] Henry Kamen, *Inquisition and Society in Spain* (London: Weidenfeld and Nicholson, 1985); revised and expanded edition: *The Spanish Inquisition: An Historical Revision* (London: Weidenfeld and Nicholson, 1997).

[36] A reprint collection of his studies is included in Angus MacKay, *Society, Economy, and Religion in Late Medieval Castile* (London: Variorum Reprints, 1987).

[37] Including: Edwards, "Religious Faith and Doubt in Late Medieval Spain: Soria circa 1450–1500," in *Past and Present* 120 (Aug. 1988): 3–25; Edwards, "Race and Religion in 15th- and 16th-Century Spain: The 'Purity of Blood' Laws Revisited," in *10th World Congress of Jewish Studies, 1989* (Jerusalem: Avraham Harman Institute of Contemporary Jewry, Hebrew University of Jerusalem; and World Union of Jewish Studies, 1993), 159–167; Edwards, "Bishop Juan Arias d'Avila of Segovia: 'Judaizer' or Reformer?" in *Cultures in Contact in Medieval Spain: Historical and Literary Essays Presented to L. P. Harvey*, ed. David Hook and Barry Taylor (London: Kings College, Medieval Studies, 1990), 71–86.

[38] Kriegel's expected volume on the Conversos is still awaited. Meanwhile, several of his published essays complete the views expressed in his seminal article, "Entre 'question' des 'Nouveaux-Chrétiens' et expulsion des Juifs: La double modernité des procès d'exclusion dans l'Espagne du XVe siècle," in *Le Nouveau Monde: Mondes nouveaux*, ed. Serge Gruzinski and Nathan Wachtel (Paris: Éditions de l'École des Hautes Études en Sciences Sociales, 1996). The Conversos, Kriegel argues, were resented because they broke established social roles and forms of status, and because most of them had fluid, undetermined identities that provoked fear and repulsion. The Inquisition's role was not to reeducate and integrate them into Catholic society, but rather to delegitimize their existence in Spain and block the process of their acceptance. Kriegel sees here a preview of the postemancipation anti-Semitism in modern Western Europe. See also Kriegel, "The 'Modern' Anti-Semitism of the Inquisition" (Heb.), *Zemanim* 41 (1992): 23–33; Kriegel, "El Edicto de expulsión: Motivos, fines, contexto," in *Judíos, sefarditas, conversos: La expulsión de 1492 y sus consecuencias*, ed. Angel Alcalá (Valladolid: Ambito, 1995), 134–149; and Kriegel, "La liquidation du pluralisme religieux dans l'Espagne des rois catholiques: Limites et efficacité de l'approche 'intentionnaliste,'" *Temas Medievales* 4 (1994): 35–45.

Haliczer debated with Kriegel (and others) on the reasons for the Expulsion and the question of the monarchs' intentionality.[39]

How Jewish Were the Marranos?

At the opposite pole from Baer stands Benzion Netanyahu. In an early work often quoted,[40] Netanyahu argued that almost all Spanish Marranos assimilated into Christianity in the fifteenth century. Judaizing was a negligible phenomenon already by midcentury, before the Inquisition came in. The Inquisition was established not to fight the almost inexistent Judaizers, but to destroy the social standing of the sincere converts who formed a new urban bourgeoisie by calling them Judaizers and fabricating charges to prove it. Thereby, the Inquisition reignited the extinct movement of Judaizing and, rather than abolishing Judaizers, produced them for a while. Netanyahu relied on rabbinical sources, most of which treat the Marranos as non-Jews. He dismissed the Inquisition's records as untrustworthy because they were motivated by nonreligious interests (not noticing, as Yerushalmi remarked, that many rabbinical rulings, too, were determined by social rather than religious considerations, such as helping to solve family problems).[41]

Netanyahu's thesis found support from the Portuguese historian A. J. Saraiva, who applied a similar thesis to Portugal.[42] (Formerly, it had been voiced by the nineteenth-century historian of the Portuguese Inquisition Alexander Herculano.)[43] Similar revisionist views are held by Ellis Rivkin,[44] H. P.

[39] Stephen Haliczer, "The Expulsion of the Jews as Social Progress," in *The Jews in Spain and the Expulsion of 1492*, ed. Moshe Lazar and Stephen Haliczer (Lancaster: Labyrinthos, 1997).

[40] Netanyahu, *The Marranos of Spain, from the Late XIVth to the Early XVIth Century, according to Contemporary Hebrew Sources* (New York: American Academy for Jewish Research, 1966; 3d ed., updated and expanded, Ithaca, NY: Cornell University Press, 1999).

[41] In *From Spanish Court to Italian Ghetto*, 25. Moreover, even rabbis who rejected the Marranos on purely religious grounds did not necessarily imply that they were assimilated Christians. It was enough that the Marranos Judaized in ways that were too dualistic for an Orthodox rabbi to tolerate.

[42] A. J. Saraiva, *Inquisição e Cristãos Novos*, 3d ed. (Porto: Editorial Inova, 1969), and many later editions. Saraiva sees the inquisitorial trials as a monumental fraud, designed to destroy the New Christians who constituted the rising bourgeois class in Portugal. The "return" to Judaism in the Dispersion was also mainly motivated by economic interests plus the need to escape the Inquisition. New Christian "Judaism" was the result of inquisitorial persecution rather than its cause.

[43] Alexander Herculano, *History of the Origin and Establishment of the Inquisition in Portugal*, trans. J. C. Branner (New York: Ktav, 1972).

[44] Ellis Rivkin, *The Shaping of Jewish History: A Radical New Interpretation* (New York: Charles Scribner, 1971), chapter 6, "The Rise of Capitalism." Rivkin offers a Marxian view parallel on many points to Saraiva's.

Salomon,[45] and less categorically by Norman Roth.[46] Yet the thesis failed to convince except a small minority. Meanwhile, Netanyahu worked on his magnum opus, *The Origins of the Inquisition*[47] and, to support his erstwhile view, turned this time to texts by assimilated Converso intellectuals, such as Bishop Alonso de Cartagena (see chapter 4) and Cardinal Juan de Torquemada (chapter 6), who expressed strong personal and group dedication to Catholicism. There is no evidence, however, that these members of the elite represented the mass of converts.

Today the revisionist thesis is widely seen as exaggerated. The large majority of scholars converge on the view that a certain degree of Judaizing had been a historical reality, though they differ on how it should be defined and interpreted. "To deny there were Judaizers would be like denying the light of the sun," said Márquez Villanueva.[48] And most Jewish historians agree. This includes scholars from Graetz and Dubnow to Baron, Cecil Roth, Baer, Scholem, Beinart, Révah, Yerushalmi, Sicroff, and Gitlitz, among many others.[49] Even so, the revisionist school caused other scholars to be more prudent and sophisticated in dealing with inquisitorial evidence. And its insight that the Inquisition boosted Judaizing (a view shared by Spinoza and by contemporary Spanish critics of the Inquisition)[50] is pertinent to appreciating the intricate dialectic of this phenomenon.

[45] Herman P. Salomon, introduction to *A History of the Marranos*, by Cecil Roth (New York: Schocken Books, 1974). See also Herman P. Salomon, "Review of David M. Gitlitz, *Secrecy and Deceit*," *Jewish Quarterly Review* 89, nos. 1–2 (July–October 1998): 131–154.

[46] Norman Roth, *Conversos, Inquisition, and the Expulsion of the Jews from Spain* (Madison: University of Wisconsin Press, 1995), 12. Roth only denies the Conversos were part of the Jewish people.

[47] Netanyahu, *The Origins of the Inquisition in Fifteenth-Century Spain* (New York: Random House, 1996).

[48] Although he objects to placing this fact at the center of interest. F. Márquez Villanueva, "Ideas de la 'católica impugnación' de fray Hernando de Talavera," in *Las tomas: Antropología histórica de la ocupación territorial del reino de Granada*, ed. J. A. Gonzáles Alcantud and M. Barrios Aguilera (Granada: Diputación Provincial de Granada, 2000), 13–32.

[49] Still, critical caution is needed. Gitlitz, for example, puts his counter-Netanyahu conclusion in the following terms: "Crypto [that is, secret] Judaism and a strong Jewish identity were very real phenomena among many New-Christians" (Gitlitz, *Secrecy and Deceit*, 81). The uncontestable phenomenon, however, was Judaizing, which does not necessarily signify "secret Judaism" or "a strong Jewish identity," but had a broader spectrum of manifestations. On the Marranos' kind of Jewishness, see also Moshe Lazar, "Scorched Parchments and Tortured Memories: The 'Jewishness' of the Anussim (Crypto-Jews)," in *Cultural Encounters: The Impact of the Inquisition on Spain and the New World*, ed. Mary Elizabeth Perry and Anne J. Cruz (Berkeley and Los Angeles: University of California Press, 1991), 176–206.

[50] As Maurice Kriegel has shown in a richly documented lecture, "Spinoza's Views on Jewish Survival: Their Historical Context," presented at the "What Enabled the Jews to Survive in History" conference, Jerusalem Spinoza Institute, January 4–7, 2005.

Both Baer and Netanyahu, I think, had a tacit ideological (indeed, Zionist) agenda, Baer providing the modern national Jewish consciousness with heroes and martyrs, Netanyahu implying that Jewish life in the Diaspora is fragile and prone to assimilation. Yet both views, from their opposite perspectives, are too unilateral and miss the fertile complexity of the Marrano phenomenon.

If I may add my own viewpoint, I think we need to supersede definite and clear-cut determinations, including those of Baer, Netanyahu, and the Spanish post-Castro school, and recognize that the Marrano story draws most of its interest and significance from its *inherent dualities and ambiguities*, and from the fact that it breaks integral identities and transcends any single culture. To apply a modern national outlook (or any other definite determination) to the Conversos distorts their complexity and misses their phenomenological interest. I first expressed this viewpoint in *Spinoza and Other Heretics*, volume 1, and spelled it out in several later papers and lectures.[51] A similar approach, it seems, is being adopted in a few other studies.[52]

The Dispersion

The Dispersion of the Marranos—their cosmopolitan dimension—was low on the priority list of Spanish scholarship. But Portuguese and, especially, Jewish scholars were far more interested. In the early mid-twentieth century, Salo Baron, Cecil Roth, Herbert Bloom, and I. S. Révah, among others, laid a ground for a history of the Dispersion, which expanded considerably in the later part of the century due to the flourish of Jewish history in general and also to a special

---

[51] Including: Yirmiyahu Yovel, "The Jews in History: The Marranos in Early Modernity," in *Zionism and the Return to History: A Reevaluation* (Heb.), ed. S. N. Eisenstadt and M. Lissak (Jerusalem: Yad Ben-Zvi, 1989), 211–248; Yovel, "Converso Dualities in the First Generation: The Cancioneros," *Jewish Social Studies* 4, no. 3 (1998): 1–28; and Yovel, *The New Otherness: Marrano Dualities in the First Generation. The 1999 Swig Lecture, September 13, 1999* (San Francisco: Swig Judaic Studies Program, University of San Francisco, 1999). See also my review of Netanyahu, *The Origins of the Inquisition*: Yovel, "Marranos in Struggle" (Heb.), *Sepharim*, Ha'aretz Weekly Book Review, 14 Aug. 1996.

[52] Gretchen D. Starr-LeBeau, *In the Shadow of the Virgin: Inquistors, Friars, and Conversos in Guadalupe, Spain* (Princeton, NJ: Princeton University Press, 2003), which supports my view that the Inquisition, for its own institutional reasons, rigidified the Conversos' fluid identities and dualist religious practices into hard definitions; David L. Graizbord, *Souls in Dispute: Converso Identities in Iberia and the Jewish Diaspora, 1580–1700* (Philadelphia: University of Pennsylvania Press, 2004); and Charles Meyers and Norman Simms, eds., *Troubled Souls: Conversos, Crypto-Jews, and Other Confused Jewish Intellectuals from the Fourteenth through the Eighteenth Century* (Hamilton, New Zealand: Outrigger Publishers, 2001), preface.

ethnic interest in "Sephardic studies."[53] Several lines of research developed: (1) individual studies of persons or families: Y. H. Yerushalmi (Cardoso), Alexandra E. Uchmany (Nieto), Nathan Wachtel (numerous cases), Gershom Scholem (Herrera), Martin A. Cohen (Carvajal), and others; (2) studies of "Hebrew-Portuguese" congregations, their structure, and their typical conflicts: Gerard Nahon (southwest France), Yosef Kaplan (Amsterdam and London), Myriam Bodian (Amsterdam), Brian Pullan (Venice), Henry Méchoulan (Amsterdam), David Katz (London), Jacob Marcus (North America), and so on;[54] (3) the broader Nation and its international links and commercial networks: Jonathan Israel, Myriam Bodian, Yosef Kaplan, D. M Swetschinski; and (4) the Conversos and the Inquisitions in Latin America. The latter is a vast field stretching from José Toribio de Medina in the nineteenth century (on Lima, and today's Chile and Argentina) to Antonio Baião and António Domínguez Ortiz, to Anita Novinsky, Elias Lipiner, Arnold Wiznitzer, Nachman Falbel,[55] T. Neumann Kaufman[56] (on Brazil), Seymour Liebman, Martin Cohen (Mexico), Boleslao Lewin (Mexico, Lima), Nathan Wachtel (Mexico, Brazil, Chile), P. Castañeda Delgado and P. Hernández Aparicio (Lima), and more recently Guibovich Pérez (also on Lima).[57]

Most of these studies are social and cultural. Economic studies, though crucially important for this commercial Nation, have been too few (though sometimes, like that by Jonathan Israel, excellent). A closer collaboration of economic and social historians could shed more light on this peculiar fusion of global commerce, blood-parentage, and unorthodox ideology and religion known as the Nation.

---

[53] The concept of Sephardic studies is not without problems when applied to Marranos. The primary sense of *Sephardim* ("Spaniards") refers to Spanish Jews, including the exiles, who *never converted* and whose choice and historical experience were completely different from those of the Marranos—indeed, quite opposed. The Marranos who later emigrated from Iberia were so distinct from the exiles that they usually set up their own congregations separate from those of the exiles. In addition, many emigrant Marranos remained Catholic or irreligious and did not join any Jewish congregation. So one cannot simply conflate all members of the Nation into a single (Jewish) entity called "The Sephardim" or assign them a common "Sephardic heritage."

[54] To illustrate the abundance: over two dozen authors working on the Iberian Dispersion collaborated in the volume edited by H. Méchoulan, *Les juifs d'Espagne: Histoire d'une Diaspora, 1492–1992* (Paris: Liana Levi, 1992).

[55] Nachman Falbel, *Estudos sobre a comunidade judaica no Brasil* (São Paulo: Federação Israelita de São Paulo, 1984).

[56] Tânia Neumann Kaufman, *Passos perdidos, história recuperada: a presença judaica em Pernambuco* (Recife, Brazil: Editora Bagaço, 2000).

[57] Pedro Guibovich Pérez, *En defensa de Dios: Estudios y documentos sobre la Inquisición en el Perú* (Lima: Ediciones del Congreso del Perú, 1998).

Regarding religion, the studies of converts in America draw an ambiguous picture. Some stress the phenomena of Jewish fidelity, even martyrdom (Liebman, Lipiner, Wiznitzer), while others (Novinsky, Cohen, Wachtel) stress the Marranos' distinctness from Jews, their semisecularity, or their religious heterodoxy. Wachtel's work, in particular, admirably shows how, paradoxically, both pictures (of the martyr and the heretic) could apply to the same persons, who died as martyrs not of traditional Judaism, but of a Marrano identity—and memory—of their own.[58]

Controversies over the Inquisition

No other subject is as widely treated and as hotly debated. A bibliography of this topic alone would contain hundreds of items.[59] A common debate concerns the Inquisition's goals and raison d'être: were they *religious* (crushing Judaizing and other dissent), *political* (serving the centralized state, subjugating the great of the land), *social* (abolishing the *convivencia*), *economic* (repressing a rising urban bourgeoisie), *psychological* (legitimizing, even sanctifying, xenophobic hostility and superiority), *pecuniary* (amassing riches through confiscations), *bureaucratic* (promoting the institution's own dynamic and interests), or some other reason?

Each of these has its supporters; yet no single answer will do. The controversy over the motives and practices of the Inquisition can make sense only when limited in time and place; and even then, it would be hopeless to provide an adequate generalization that captures the varieties of the institution. Apart from its lasting main institutional body and structure (which did manifest surprising persistence), there was no *essential core* to the Inquisition, no single hidden function or goal embodied in all its manifestations.

At the same time, almost all the roles scholars have attributed to the Inquisition have been, at some time or place, a real aspect of its actual functioning. A primary drive around which they revolved and which nourished their energy was supplied by the passions related to identity, difference, and otherness. To these, other drives were infused in varying degrees—political, theological,

---

[58] In addition to his outstanding collection of subtly analyzed cases and captivating personal stories (Nathan Wachtel, *La foi du souvenir: Labyrinthes marranes* [Paris: Editions du Seuil, 2001]), see Wachtel, "Frontières intérieures: La religiosité marrane en Amérique hispanique (XVIIe siècle)," in *Passar as Fronteiras*, ed. Rui M. Loureiro and Serge Gruzinski (Lagos, Portugal: Centro de Estudios Gil Eanes, 1999), 111–132.

[59] For some of these debates, see chapter 9 and its notes, especially notes 2, 14, 19, 20, 29, 30, and 33.

social, economic, and lay-ideological. And of course, personal greed and institutional need played their part too, as did local interests of power and career, sporadic sadism, occasional compassion, a sense of personal mission, and an aberrant love of God.

Another debate is on whether the functions which the Inquisition is said to have served were conscious goals from the outset. This question is hard to settle and not essential. Institutions are set up for one goal and soon fulfill another, they change, they adapt to new purposes and situations, they grow offshoots, and they develop their own dynamics and intrainstitutional interests (and hence, perspectives), especially when spread across many lands and several centuries.

Another debate—over the credibility of the Inquisition's records—is also a question that cannot be answered wholesale. It is safe to assume that a certain number of informants were defamatory and vindictive, and that inquisitors sometimes fabricated charges and whole cases. But it would be absurd on that account to totally reject the Inquisition's records, or to suppose a grand conspiracy that went on, unexposed, for centuries. Abuses and machinations exist in many legal records, including those of today's democracies: this calls for vigilance, not wholesale dismissal.[60] The Inquisition's vast records hold a wealth of near-verbatim utterances that sound bona fide in their crude simplicity and many small details that ring true—details that no bureaucrat could make up— so a generalized presumption of falsity cannot hold water.

The main problem is the distortion not of fact, but of the conceptual schemes by which the facts were understood. Many records call for critical deconstruction, for the exposure not so much of intentionally fraudulent constructs but of ideological bias and misconceptions built into the notions and categories that the inquisitors employed. I used this approach in chapter 7 to distinguish between three dualist stances (in the Arias d'Avila family) that were all branded as Judaizing by the Inquisition. This illustrates a broader problem. The Inquisition discovered Judaizing everywhere because it looked for it everywhere, and because it interpreted as Jewish every deviation by a Converso from orthodox conduct or thinking (sometimes including even deism or the denial of all religion). This institutional bias was built into the system. It was stronger than individuals and, once internalized, could easily be translated into a bona fide attitude of individual inquisitors, who were unable (or not allowed) to perceive the phenomena before them in any other way.[61]

---

[60] Dedieu ("The Archives of the Holy Office of Toledo as a Source for Historical Anthropology," 158–189) is one of several voices trying to show that a trustworthy critical reading is possible.

[61] Sometimes the Inquisition issued rules whose logic implied an unconscious recognition of duality. Thus, priests were prohibited from giving absolution to a Converso who confessed that he had "Judaized" by performing an act on the "Jewish list." (Personal communication from Charles

For other debated issues, readers can refer to bibliographic essays such as Lawrence, "The Inquisition and the New Christians in the Iberian Peninsula"; and Bujanda, "Recent Historiography of the Spanish Inquisition (1977–1988)."[62]

Amiel of the Collège de France.) This assumes that the guilty Judaizer is enough of a Catholic believer to feel punished by the denial of absolution; so he is not a secret Jew. His case is not one of Judaism, but of dualism.

[62] Bruce A. Lawrence, "The Inquisition and the New Christians in the Iberian Peninsula—Main Historiographic Issues and Controversies," in *The Sephardi and Oriental Jewish Heritage*, ed. Issachar Ben Ami (Jerusalem: Magnes Press, 1982); Jesús M. de Bujanda, "Recent Historiography of the Spanish Inquisition (1977–1988): Balance and Perspective," in *Cultural Encounters: The Impact of the Inquisition in Spain and the New World*, ed. Mary Elizabeth Perry and Anne J. Cruz (Berkeley and Los Angeles: University of California Press, 1991), 221–247. The titles of Bujanda's subsections give an idea of the content of his essay: "A Better Knowledge of the Inquisitorial Sources," "A More Serene, Complete, and Critical History," "A Politico-Religious Tribunal," "An Institution with Religious and Social Control," and "An Organism of Cultural Repression."

Notes

Preface

1. A similar story is attributed to the late Prof. Michael Bruno (a former chancellor of the Bank of Israel and vice president of the World Bank) after he returned from a short visit to Spain (reported by his colleague Prof. Giora Hanoch).

2. Yirmiyahu Yovel, *The Marrano of Reason*, vol. 1 of *Spinoza and Other Heretics* (Princeton, NJ: Princeton University Press, 1989).

3. In his *Philosophy of Right*; implicitly in *The Science of Logic*, trans. A. V. Miller (Atlantic Highlands, NJ: Humanities Press International, 1989); in *The Phenomenology of Spirit*, trans. A. V. Miller (Oxford and New York: Oxford University Press, 1977); especially in *Preface to the Phenomenology of Spirit*, trans. Y. Yovel (Princeton, NJ: Princeton University Press, 2005); and in his historical lectures, including *Lectures on the Philosophy of Religion: The Lectures of 1827*, ed. Peter C. Hodgson, trans. R. F. Brown, P. C. Hodgson, and J. M. Stewart (Berkeley and Los Angeles: University of California Press, 1988).

Chapter 1. Sefarad, the Spanish Jerusalem

1. S. W. Baron, *A Social and Religious History of the Jews*, 2d ed., rev. and enlarged (New York: Columbia University Press, 1952–1983), 3:34.

2. Tartesus, on the mouth of the Guadalquivir, was an important realm and port that eventually fell to the Phoenicians in 500 B.C. Its identification with Tarshish is accepted by some, contested by others.

3. Baron, *A Social and Religious History of the Jews*, 3:34; Yosef Haim Yerushalmi, "Le judaisme sefarade entre la croix et le croissant," in *Sefardica: Essais sur l'histoire des juifs, des marranes et des nouveaux-chrétiens d'origine hispano-portugaise* (Paris: Chandeigne, 1998); Alfredo Mordechai Rabello, *The Jews in Visigothic Spain in Light of the Legislation* (Heb.; Jerusalem: Shazar Center, 1983), 118.

4. Scott Bradbury, ed. and trans., *Severus of Minorca: Letter on the Conversion of the Jews* (Oxford: Clarendon Press, 1996).

5. That occurred when the Carolingians took over from the Merovingians.

6. E. A. Thompson, *The Goths in Spain* (Oxford: Clarendon Press, 1969), 53–54. See also Baron, *A Social and Religious History of the Jews*, 3:35–36. The code in question is the Lex Romana Visigothorum, which Alaric II set up for his Roman subjects, segregating the various communities, including the Jews, under different systems of law.

7. Many are recorded in the decisions of the various Toledo councils of bishops, which served as parliaments; see Karolus Zeumer, ed., *Leges Visigothorum*, rev. ed. (Hannover: Hahn, 1973), pt. XII, 426ff., 481ff. Quoted in S. W. Baron, " 'Plenitude of Apostolic Powers' and Medieval 'Jewish Serfdom,' " in *Yitzhak F. Baer Jubilee Volume*, ed. S. Ettinger, S. W. Baron, B. Dinur, and I. Halpern (Heb.; Jerusalem: Historical Society of Israel, 1960).

8. A similar manifesto, called the *placitum*, and containing the same provisio about pork, had been made to King Chintila by an earlier generation of converts; it seems to have been a formalized, humiliating ritual Conversos were recurrently forced to undergo. See E. A. Thompson, *The Goths in Spain*, 186; Baron, *A Social and Religious History of the Jews*, 3:42.

9. In later-date inquisitorial Spain there was a further, nontheological reason for holding this view: the dominant classes wished to socially discriminate against the Jews even after their conversion. Whether such a factor was at work in Visigoth Spain is harder to determine, because of the very different social conditions and scarcity of relevant data.

10. This is how H. V. Livermore understands it, in *The Origins of Spain and Portugal* (London: Allen & Unwin, 1971), 253–254.

11. On the following period, see Eliyahu Ashtor, *The Jews of Moslem Spain*, 3 vols. (Philadelphia: Jewish Publication Society, 1973–1984). On Jewish Spain under all medieval regimes, see Norman Roth, *Jews, Visigoths, and Muslims in Medieval Spain: Cooperation and Conflict* (Leiden: Brill, 1994). The latter book quotes Jewish responsa literature as a source on Jews in towns, commerce, agriculture, slave ownership, and so on.

12. There were Jewish communities in France and Italy, but they were small, and Italian Jews consider themselves different from both Sephardi and Ashkenazi. See H. H. Ben Sasson, *On Jewish History in the Middle Ages* (Heb.; Tel-Aviv: Am Oved, 1969), 1–21; see also Baron, preface to vol. 2 of *A Social and Religious History of the Jews*, also part 4, and beginning of chap. 19.

13. See Joseph Lecler, *Histoire de la tolérance au siècle de la réforme* (Paris: Albin Michel, 1994), 104; quoting P. Charles, "L'islam," in *Histoire générale comparée des religions du Baron Descamps*, ed. Edouard Eugène François Baron Descamps (Brussels: L'Edition Universelle, 1932), 653–654.

14. Lecler, *Histoire de la tolérance au siècle de la réforme*, 104.

15. Thomas F. Glick built a statistical model of that process, explaining how the existence of many converts already greatly accelerates the process. See Glick, *Islamic and Christian Spain in the Early Middle Ages* (Princeton, NJ: Princeton University Press, 1979), 35.

16. Ibid.

17. Arabization is to be understood as a cultural, not demographic phenomenon. In *Jews, Visigoths, and Muslims in Medieval Spain*, 44–45, Norman Roth stresses that the majority of Spanish Muslims were Berbers (they kept coming from North Africa during the eighth through twelfth centuries), rather than Arabs. Some of them faked Arab credentials to get more prestige.

18. After a short while he built himself an out-of-town palatial campus called Madinat a Zahra. But practically, this too was Cordova.

19. Philip K. Hitti, *History of the Arabs: From the Earliest Times to the Present*, 10th ed. (London: Macmillan, 1970), 525.

20. Ibid., 526.

21. Ashtor, *The Jews of Moslem Spain*, 1:275, based on Muhammad Imamuddin, "Historia económica de España en la época omeya," *Revista de la Universidad de Madrid* 5 (1956): 351.

22. Thus Hisdai himself reports in the letter to the Khazar king. See Ashtor, *The Jews of Moslem Spain*, 210; Baron, *A Social and Religious History of the Jews*, 3:156.

23. The story, whether true or not, is told by the philosopher Averroes in his middle commentary on Aristotle's *Poetics*. See S. M. Stern, "Shtei Yediot Hadashot al Hisdai ibn Shaprut" (Heb.), *Zion* 11 (1946): 141–146; my translation. Ashtor, *The Jews of Moslem Spain*, 1:182.

24. There are two versions of the Talmud, the "Jerusalemite" (or "Palestinian"), third to fifth century A.D., and the "Babylonian," third to sixth century A.D., of which the latter is far more dominant. Both have a similar Mishna but not the same Gemara.

25. By the twelfth-century Jewish writer Rabad—Abraham Ben Daud—in his *Sefer Ha-Qabbalah* [The Book of Tradition], a critical edition with translation and notes by Gershon D. Cohen (Philadelphia: Jewish Publication Society of America, 1967).

26. Ibid., 66.

27. As Ashtor confirms twice (*The Jews of Moslem Spain*, 1:241; 3:96), though he does not draw the same conclusion.

28. Though Hisdai's own letter is generally accepted as genuine, perhaps with interpolations.

29. D. M. Dunlop, *The History of the Jewish Khazars* (New York: Schocken Books, 1967), 241–243. See also A. Koestler, *The Thirteenth Tribe* (New York: Random House, 1976), 113.

30. William M. Watt, *A History of Islamic Spain* (Edinburgh: University of Edinburgh Press, 1965), 99.

31. See also Ron Barkai, "Reflexiones sobre el concepto 'El Siglo de Oro' de los judíos en España musulmana y su significación contemporánea," *El Olivo* 14 (1981): 19–28.

32. *Nagid* can be rendered as *chieftain* or *governor*—the chief of the Jews.

33. "Kingdom" (*malkhut*) is also an allusion to one of the ten emanations in Kabbalah, whose connotation is "the congregation of Israel." So Ibn Gabirol's semi-Plotinian God is endowed from the outset with a Jewish characterization through the language of Kabbalah. This cannot be done in the same way when writing in Arabic or Latin.

34. A Neoplatonic treatise modified by Aristotelian and other motifs, *fons vitae* was reidentified as Ibn Gabirol's work by Shlomo Munk in Paris, in 1845. See Isaac Husik, *A History of Mediaeval Jewish Philosophy* (New York: Atheneum, 1969), 63.

35. Watt, *A History of Islamic Spain*, 101.

36. אהה ירד/עלי ספרד/ רע מן השמים

37. Hayim Schirmann, *History of Hebrew Poetry in Christian Spain and Southern France* (Heb.; Jerusalem: Magnes Press, 1997), 1:387, poem 156.

38. Ibid., 1:577, poem 253.

כבודי במקומי—ואם אשפיל שבתי/ ולא אבחר מקום כקלים בגאונם/ אשר המה חושבים היותם ראש מושב/ והמושב להם יכסה עלבונם./ **אני הוא המקום והמקום אתי**/ והמה המקום ימלא חסרונם!

39. But as we shall see, this was also a familiar disposition among the later Marranos, contesting Spain's view of external honor.

40. Watt, *A History of Islamic Spain*, 113.

41. יסיתוה זרים באלהים אחרים/ והיא במסתרים תבכה לבעל נעורים.

42. The common ("Christian") calendar is solar, whereas Jewish and Muslim calendars are lunar, and thereby shorter; but the Jews adjust the difference by adding seven extra months in every cycle of nineteen years. The five-hundred-year period allegedly granted by the Prophet Muhammad was to start with the *hijra* (622), so it ended in 1122 according to the Jews and in 1007 according to Muslims.

43. The latter seems to be the case; see David Corcos, "On the Nature of the Al-Muwahiddun's Attitude toward the Jews" (Heb.), in *Studies in the History of the Jews of Morocco* (Jerusalem: Rubin Mass, 1976), 319–342. Corcos reports the evidence for both views and argues for the second.

44. Although the origin was in North Africa—whose Jews suffered equally harshly—the impact on Spain was unmistakable, and became, like so many other foreign influences and intervention, a genuine element of Spanish history.

45. Schirmann, *A History of Hebrew Poetry*, 1:628, poem 287.

46. In some of his letters he plays with verse, but on the whole he was unpoetical; his imagination proved vivid only as interpreter—when reading the Bible allegorically.

47. According to the entry on Maimonides in Al-Qifti's biographical dictionary (in a summary made in 1249 by Al-Zawanzani), all Jews and Christians under Abd al-Nu'min's reign were ordered to accept Islam, or depart without their property. Those who had few assets and family ties departed, whereas those who saved their families and property dissimulated Islam, while hiding their infidelity. Maimonides was one of the latter. Later on, after settling his financial affairs, Maimonides emigrated to Egypt and resumed practicing Judaism openly. When a Muslim scholar, who had known Maimonides in Spain, accused him of renouncing Islam after having accepted it—an offense punishable by death—Maimonides was saved by his Muslim patron, who denied the binding force of coerced conversions. The reliability of Al-Qifti's account is contested and defended by different scholars. A generation later, the Muslim scholar Ibn Abi Usaibia presented a somewhat different version of the story. According to Ibn Abi Usaibia, Maimonides converted in North Africa rather than in Spain, engaged in Muslim law, and learned the Qur'an by heart. This testimony is also contested. For an account of the ongoing scholarly debate on Maimonides' alleged conversion, see Herbert A. Davidson, *Moses Maimonides: The Man and His Works* (Oxford and New York: Oxford University Press, 2005), 9–10. See also Mordechai Akiva Friedman, *Maimonides, The Yemenite Messiah and Apostasy* (Heb.; Jerusalem: Ben-Zvi Institute and the Hebrew University of Jerusalem, 2002), 31–37.

48. Moses Maimonides [Moshe ben Maimon], "Epistle on Conversion or a Treatise on Martyrdom" (Heb.) in *Epistles*, ed. M. D. Rabinowitz (Jerusalem: Rav Cook Institute, 1981), 64–65. A minority view, such as Herbert Davidson's, maintains that this epistle is not authentic.

49. A letter describing his overcharged day (with some intentional exaggeration—to deter the recipient from coming to visit him) has been preserved. See Joel Kraemer, "Two Letters of Maimonides from the Cairo Geniza," *Maimonides Studies* 1 (1990): 96–97. See also Davidson, *Moses Maimonides*, 63, mentioning four separate letters, written between 1191 and 1199, in which Maimonides alludes to his "time-consuming medical obligations."

CHAPTER 2. RECONQUEST AND REVIVAL: THE CROSS IS BACK

1. Angus MacKay, *Spain in the Middle Ages: From Frontier to Empire, 1000–1500* (New York: St. Martin's Press, 1977), 37.

2. Angus MacKay, *Society, Economy, and Religion in Late Medieval Castile* (London: Variorum Reprints, 1987); Jonathan Ray, *The Sephardic Frontier: The Reconquista and the Jewish Community in Medieval Iberia* (Ithaca, NY: Cornell University Press, 2006);

Mark D. Meyerson, *Jews in an Iberian Frontier Kingdom: Society, Economy, and Politics in Morvedre, 1248–1391* (Leiden: Brill, 2004), esp. chaps. 1–2.

3. Edward Cheyney gives the number of a hundred cities, though he must have considered as "cities" also very small places, perhaps because *fueros* (special rights and exemptions) were given to tiny settlements during the early Reconquest. See Edward P. Cheyney, *The Dawn of a New Era, 1250–1453* (New York: Harper & Row, 1962), p. 65.

4. Thus, though I accept the importance of the socioeconomic struggle of the cities against the Jews, I do not see it as the single or even a predominant cause. Identity passions, religious zeal, and social bigotry against the Jews as "radical others" have played no less decisive a role in the movement against them.

5. Y. Baer, *A History of the Jews in Christian Spain* (Philadelphia: Jewish Publication Society of America, 1961), 1:220.

6. Of course loyalty and impartiality are not the same, especially when the king himself is party to an ongoing struggle. Yet officially, the king was above the baronial competition, so those loyal to him were nominally supposed to represent the more "universal" standpoint.

7. The Muslims too were Others, but they had an enemy Muslim empire behind them.

8. Baer, *A History of the Jews in Christian Spain*, 1:153. Baer's English translator rendered it as: "I have never seen a man defend a wrong cause so well." On Nachmanides, see Moshe Halbertal, *By Way of Truth—Nachmanides and the Creation of Tradition* (Heb.; Jerusalem: Shalom Hartman Institute, 2006). On the conditions of Aragonese Jews at that period, see Yom Tov Assis, *The Golden Age of Aragonese Jewry: Community and Society in the Crown of Aragon, 1213–1327* (London and Portland, OR: Vallentine Mitchell, 1997).

9. Baer's title for chap. 7 of his *History of the Jews in Christian Spain*, vol. 1.

10. For a vivid picture, see Barbara Tuchman, *A Distant Mirror: The Calamitous 14th Century* (Harmondsworth, Middlesex: Penguin Books, 1979).

11. An official complaint to this effect was filed by the Cortes of Valladolid in 1351. Quoted by Benzion Netanyahu, *The Origins of the Inquisition in Fifteenth-Century Spain* (New York: Random House, 1995), 95n12; of course, by then conditions had greatly worsened because of the Black Death.

12. Actually, all three explanations (including the natural and the theological) have been attempted by scholars; see A. López de Meneses, "Una Consecuencia de la Peste Negra en Cataluña: El Pogrom de 1348," *Sefarad* 19 (1959): 93–131.

13. David Nirenberg, in a study of medieval patterns of violence against minorities, sensibly concluded that periodic violence against Jews—at least in the period he studied, before the Black Death—was part of an ongoing balance of relations between unequal communities within the framework of an accepted basic coexistence. The bursts of violence were not necessarily signs of radical intolerance or an open-ended downhill movement, but rather were part of the way the balancing system worked. See David Nirenberg, *Communities of Violence: Persecution of Minorities in the Middle Ages* (Princeton, NJ: Princeton University Press, 1996). Of course, this delicate balance was effective as long as the magnitude of the violence did not break the system itself or draw radical impetus from new sources. Such a breakdown occurred in 1391; and part of the new impetus that helped gather the storm may have come from the demonization of the Jews following the Black Death.

14. For a detailed and absorbing account of Martínez's struggle with the establishment, see Netanyahu, *The Origins of the Inquisition in Fifteenth-Century Spain*, 129–148.

15. The king's rebuff—and the Jews' complaints that provoked it—are published in J. Amador de Los Ríos, *Historia social, política y religiosa de los judíos de España y Portugal* (Madrid: Turner, 1984); quoted in Netanyahu, *The Origins of the Inquisition in Fifteenth-Century Spain*, 131–148.

CHAPTER 3. POGROMS AND MASS CONVERSIONS

1. As explained in the preface, in this book I use the terms *Marranos, Conversos,* and *New Christians* interchangeably. Some scholars draw distinctions among these three terms, but using separate definitions has proven unsatisfactory and often confusing. Following Révah, Roth, Netanyahu, Yerushalmi, and the French school, I have chosen to use the three terms synonymously and, if necessary, to add an adjective or a modifier.

2. Hasdai Crescas, "Rabbi Hasdai Crescas Gives an Account of the Spanish Massacres of 1391," in *A Treasury of Jewish Letters*, ed. Franz Kobler (New York: Farrar, Straus and Young, 1952), 1:272–275.

3. See Benzion Netanyahu, *The Origins of the Inquisition in Fifteenth-Century Spain* (New York: Random House, 1995), 159.

4. Y. Baer, *Die Juden in christlichen Spanien: Urkunden und Regesten* (Berlin: Akademie für die Wissenschaft des Judentums, 1929–1936), 1:440.

5. See Angus MacKay, "Popular Movements and Pogroms in Fifteenth-Century Castile," *Past and Present* 55 (1972): 33–67.

6. I am using the modern word *pogrom*, which became current in describing these events, because it applies to a violent and injurious mob attack against a peaceful minority.

7. The allusion is to the biblical text telling of Abraham's near-sacrifice of Isaac.

8. Y. Baer, *A History of the Jews in Christian Spain* (Philadelphia: Jewish Publication Society of American, 1961), 2:104–105.

9. This phenomenon recurred in all waves of conversion. See, among others, David M. Gitlitz, "Divided Families in Converso Spain," *Shofar* 11, no. 3 (1993): 1–19.

10. In Jewish law a childless widow must either marry her late husband's brother (she is called his *yebama*), or be ritually released by him, in which case she can marry anyone else. The releasing ceremony is known as *halitsa*.

11. An *aguna* is an undivorced woman whose husband is missing and there is no proof that he died. These women were unable to remarry.

12. Baer, *A History of the Jews in Christian Spain*, 2:133.

13. Baer himself was, of course, a highly intellectual German Jew. As a moderate Jewish nationalist, his interpretation of Spanish Jewry was perhaps partly meant to educate and draw a lesson for modern German and European Jews of his day. But his romantic belief in "simple people," his sweeping dismissal of philosophy as a peril for Jews, and the claim that acculturation in a gentile civilization is another peril to Jewish survival (one can make a case for the opposite thesis—that partial acculturation was a condition for the success of Jewish survival)—are too ideologically laden to count among the better products of this distinguished historian.

14. As he himself seems to have done. There is strong evidence that the Maimon family had nominally and insincerely converted to Islam under duress in Morocco, ruled by

the fanatical Al-Muwahiddun, but annulled the conversion when emigrating to Egypt shortly after. (See chap. 1.)

15. See Heim Beinart, ed., *The Marranos in Christian Society and in Jewish Society: Seminar Sources* (Heb.; Jerusalem: Department of Jewish History, Hebrew University, 1976), 139–148.

16. Cecil Roth, "A Hebrew Elegy on the Martyr of Toledo, 1391," *Jewish Quarterly Review* 39 (1948): 142.

17. The contribution was blind, not conscious: there was no "black teleology" working behind the scene. (I concur with those who, like David Nirenberg, criticize an ex post facto view of inevitably gathering shadows.) Yet even without teleology, contingent events sometimes accumulate into patterns, and these can create springboards or "cranes" that facilitate their further development, even if this occurs (as in Darwin) without an overt or covert plan.

18. The following is based mainly on Baer's detailed description and analysis of the records of the Disputation. For a partisan Christian attempt to rebut Baer—and also the Jewish rabbis of the time—and to justify Gerónimo and Pope Benedict, see Antonio Pacios López, *La disputa de Tortosa*, 2 vols. (Madrid and Barcelona: Consejo Superior de Investigaciones Científicas, Instituto Arias Montano, 1957). On the event, see also Ram Ben-Shalom, "The Disputation of Tortosa, Vicente Ferrer, and the Problem of the Conversos according to the Testimony of Isaac Nathan" (Heb.), *Zion* 56 (1991): 21–45.

19. Baer, *A History of the Jews in Christian Spain*, 2:181.

20. This, based on a Talmudic saying, is Maimonides' essential doctrine of the Messiah.

21. In a close study of one Jewish community (in Morvedre, near Valencia), Mark Meyerson has shown that, for the Jews there, "the century between 1391 and 1492 was not simply a gloom-filled parenthesis; it was instead an era of remarkable resurgence," which the author even calls a "renaissance." Mark D. Meyerson, *A Jewish Renaissance in Fifteenth-Century Spain* (Princeton, NJ: Princeton University Press, 2004), 3.

CHAPTER 4. CONVERSOS: THE OTHER WITHIN

1. This is a rough order of magnitude. Marrano numbers are very tricky to estimate. Netanyahu's figure of 200,000 (out of a presumed 600,000 Jews) seems exaggerated (Benzion Netanyahu, *The Marranos of Spain from the Late XIVth to the Early XVIth Century, according to Contemporary Hebrew Sources* [New York: American Academy for Jewish Research, 1966], 248). The number of Spanish Conversos around 1480 is estimated by Domínguez Ortiz at 225,000 (Domínguez Ortiz, *Los judeoconversos en la España moderna* [Madrid: MAPFRE, 1992], 43), which seems more reasonable (as David M. Gitlitz says in *Secrecy and Deceit: The Religion of the Crypto-Jews* [Philadelphia and Jerusalem: Jewish Publication Society, 1996], 74). Assuming that the number had roughly doubled since 1415, we get 100,000 (as an order of magnitude, not an actual figure) for the first two waves of conversion.

2. Maurice Kriegel has studied the issue in detail, also (and especially) for Portugal, following Alexander Herculano's work. It seems that several cardinals opposing the establishment of an inquisition held a more realistic definition of forced conversion, by which many, if not most, Conversos were not to be considered legally Christians. But this was the minority view and lost the argument.

3. Or so it was understood in Spain, reiterating a principle that the Visigoths had established a millennium earlier; see chap. 1.

4. For a complete version of the decrees, see Y. Baer, *Die Juden im christlichen Spanien: Urkunden und Regesten* (Berlin: Akademie Verlag, 1929), vol. 2, nos. 264–270.

5. Also: "Know, my Lord, that Judaism is one of the diseases for which there is no cure." See Solomon ibn Verga, *Shevet Yehudah* (Heb.), ed. Y. Baer (Jerusalem: Bialik Institute, 1947), section 64, p. 129.

6. As we shall see, this concept is not homogeneous—it covers several kinds of attitudes toward Judaism, from an ardent (though hardly fulfilled) wish to remain Jewish or to return to Judaism, to residual Jewish gestures performed without such intent, to a dualistic demand to be able to combine elements of one's former Jewish identity with one's (now accepted) Christian identity. The problem has methodological and conceptual aspects that will arise in the course of our story, and as I shall argue, nearly all these forms were dualistic in some manner or mode. Several writers use the term *Crypto-Jews* as synonymous with the broader phenomenon of "Judaizers," but this conflation can be misleading. It implies the (often ideological) judgment that all Judaizers were essentially Jews, thus obliterating their distinctive dualities. Yet many Judaizers had neither the resolve, nor the commitment, nor the self-image of a "Jew in hiding."

7. Quoted in Simha Asaf, "The *Anussim* in the Responsa Literature" (Heb.), *Zion* 5 (1933): 19–60.

8. Carlos Carrete Parrondo et al., eds., *Fontes iudaeorum regni castellae* (Salamanca: Universidad Pontificia de Salamanca, 1985), 2:8, no. 442.

9. On the rabbis' attitude toward the Marranos, see Asaf, "The *Anussim* in the Responsa Literature"; and Moisés Orfali Levi, *Los Conversos españoles en la literatura rabínica* (Salamanca: Universidad Pontificia de Salamanca and Universidad de Granada, Federación Sefardí de España, 1982). Netanyahu (*The Marranos of Spain*) famously used the rabbis' majority view, which denied the Marranos' Judaism, to argue that all or most of the Marranos assimilated to Christianity. Yosef Hayim Yerushalmi (*From Spanish Court to Italian Ghetto: Isaac Cardoso: A Study of Seventeenth-Century Marranism and Jewish Apologetics* [New York: Columbia University Press, 1971], 25) pointed out that the rabbis' attitude to the Marranos was usually determined by the need to solve painful practical problems in split or broken families, even by bending some facts or flexing abstract principles.

10. See, among others, Julio Caro Baroja, *Los judíos en la España moderna y contemporánea* (Madrid: Arión, 1962), 2:15; and Miguel Angel Ladero Quesada, "Los Judeoconversos en la Castilla del siglo XV," *Historia* 16, no. 194 (June 1992): 39–51.

11. See Maurice Kriegel, "Ferdinand le Catholique, fils de Palomba: Les juifs et l'alliance royale," in *Le temps de l'Etat: Mélanges en l'honneur de Pierre Birenbaum*, ed. B. Badie and Y. Déloye (Paris: Fayard, 2007).

12. Albert Sicroff, *Les controverses des statuts de "pureté de sang" en Espagne du XVe au XVIIe siècle* (Paris: Didier, 1960), 28–29.

13. Angus MacKay, "Popular Movements and Pogroms in Fifteenth-Century Castile," *Past and Present* 55 (1972): 45. MacKay quotes from Alonso de Cartagena, "Instrucción del Relator," in *Defensorium Unitatis Christianae: Tratado en Favor de los Judíos Conversos*, ed. Manuel Alonso (Madrid: Escuela de Estudios Hebraicos, 1943), 345.

14. Quoted in Benzion Netanyahu, *The Origins of the Inquisition in Fifteenth-Century Spain* (New York: Random House, 1995), 1138.

15. Luna's relation to the Marranos is described in detail ibid., 238–252.

16. Linda Martz describes the formation of such urban bourgeoisie by following several Converso families from the fifteenth to the seventeenth centuries. See L. Martz, *A Network of Converso Families in Early Modern Toledo: Assimilating a Minority* (Ann Arbor: University of Michigan Press, 2003).

17. Ladero Quesada, "Los Judeoconversos en la Castilla del siglo XV." See also Miguel Angel Ladero Quesada, "Judeoconversos andaluces en el siglo XV," in *La sociedad medieval Andaluza: Grupos no privilegiados* (Jaén: Diputación Provincial de Jaén, 1984), 22–55.

18. In Toledo, 60 percent; in Seville, 77 percent; in the Badajos area, about 50 percent.

19. In Toledo, 30 percent; in Cordova, 49 percent.

20. In Toledo and Cordova, 15 percent; in Badajos, 30 percent.

21. In Cordova, 15 percent; in Toledo, 13 percent; and in the rural areas, 10 percent.

22. In Toledo and Cordova.

23. In Toledo, 8 percent; in Baena, 6 percent; in Cordova, 2 percent.

24. Francisco Márquez Villanueva, "Conversos y cargos concejiles en el siglo XV," *Revista de Archivos, Bibliotecas y Museos* 63 (1957): 503–540.

25. The classic study of the blood purity policies, which the Toledo mutiny of 1449 had started, is Sicroff, *Les controverses des statuts de "pureté de sang" en espagne du XVe au XVIIe siècle*. For the full Spanish version of the Sentencia-Estatuto, see E. Benito Ruano, *Los orígenes del problema converso* (Barcelona: Ediciones El Albir, 1976), 85–92.

26. Even so, some scholars of the period supported it, such as Marcos García de Mora, in a memorial to the Holy See (see E. Benito Ruano, "El Memorial contra los conversos del bachiller Marcos García de Mora," *Sefarad* 17 [1957]: 314–351; and see further analysis in Netanyahu, *The Origins of the Inquisition in Fifteenth-Century Spain*, 486–511). On the other hand, the theological incongruence was so strong that even the Inquisition, in its early period, had problems with the notion of purity of blood. It took a full century before the Inquisition became the watchdog of "blood purity" in addition to religious orthodoxy. See my discussion of Torquemada's theology in chap. 9. See also Henry Kamen, "Una crisis de consciencia en la edad de oro en España: La Inquisición contra 'Limpieza de sangre,' " *Bulletin hispanique* 88 (1986): 321–356.

27. A similar position was held by the late Cardinal Lustiger, archbishop of Paris, who had been born a Polish Jew and converted to Catholicism at age fourteen. I had the privilege of discussing this with him in private, evoking the Marrano precedent of Cartagena. Father Lustiger confirmed that this was approximately his sense too, but insisted that it was a privately held position ("je ne veux pas créer une secte aberrée").

CHAPTER 5. THE NEW OTHERNESS: DUALITY IN MANY FACES

1. An earlier version of this chapter served as the basis for Yirmiyahu Yovel, *The New Otherness: Marrano Dualities in the First Generation. The 1999 Swig Lecture, September 13, 1999* (San Francisco: Swig Judaic Studies Program, University of San Francisco, 1999).

2. Carlos Carrete Parrondo et al., eds., *El tribunal de la Inquisición en el Obispado de Soria (1486–1502)*, vol. 2 of *Fontes iudaeorum regni castellae [FIRC]* (Salamanca: Universidad Pontificia de Salamanca, 1981), no. 12. These records represent a typical Castilian city in late fifteenth century. Hereafter, references to this source are indicated by volume and item number, thus: *FIRC*, 2, no. 12. I thank María Alexandra Tortoreli and Diego

Ulstein for help in sorting this material. Eliezer Moav (Roszenbaum) made perceptive use of this source in his master's thesis, written under Prof. Alisa Meyuhas Ginio at Tel-Aviv University. See Eliezer Moav (Roszenbaum), "Between Jews and Christians in Spain from the End of the 14th to the 16th Century: Conversos Wavering between Two Opinions" (Heb.; M.A. thesis, Tel Aviv University).

3. Yirmiyahu Yovel, "Converso Dualities in the First Generation: The *Cancioneros*," *Jewish Social Studies* 4, no. 3 (1998): 1–27.

4. For other classifications, see José Faur, "Four Classes of Conversos: A Typological Study," *Revue des études Juives* 149 (1990): 113–124; and David M. Gitliz, *Secrecy and Deceit: The Religion of the Crypto-Jews* (Philadelphia: Jewish Publication Society, 1996), 82–90.

5. For example, *Cema Ysrael; Oye Ysrael* ("O Israel, hear"—the most sacred popular Jewish formula); *Adonay abre los mis labios* ("O God, open my lips to tell thy glory"—the most current Jewish prayer). See Haim Beinart, *Conversos on Trial: The Inquisition in Ciudad Real*, trans. Y. Guiladi (Jerusalem: Magnes Press, 1981), 256. Also, *alabado se Adonay* ("blessed be *Adonay*") (ibid., 258).

6. Ibid., 251. In addition, Beinart published *Records of the Trials of the Spanish Inquisition in Ciudad Real* in four volumes, covering 1483–1485, 1494–1512, and 1512–1527 (Jerusalem: Israel National Academy of Sciences and Humanities, 1974, 1977, 1981, 1985). Some of the Ciudad Real records were studied with attention to other types of converts than "crypto"-Jews by María del Pilar Rábade Obradó ("Expresiones de la religiosidad Cristiana en los procesos contra los judaisantes del tribunal de Ciudad Real/Toledo, 1483–1507," *La España medieval* 13 [1990]: 303–330).

7. The appellation exists today. On a visit to Belmonte (see epilogue) I saw an engraving of a French matron with her name "corrected" to *Rhaina Santa Ester* ("Queen Saint Esther").

8. Beinart, *Conversos on Trial*, 223.

9. Ibid., 265n118.

10. Ibid., 267.

11. Actually, *Dios* is also singular (from the Latin *deus*), but that was overlooked.

12. Ibid., 289.

13. Beinart, *Conversos on Trial*, 226.

14. Ibid., 229.

15. Though some progress has been made in the last decade, with orthodox women trained as rabbinical pleaders in religious courts.

16. The leading role of women in keeping and transmitting Marrano traditions was studied by Renée Levine Melammed. See Renée Levine Melammed, *Heretics or Daughters of Israel? The Crypto-Jewish Women in Castile* (New York: Oxford University Press, 1999); Renée Levine Melammed, "Women in (Post-1492) Spanish Crypto-Jewish Society: Conversos and the Perpetuation and Preservation of Observances Associated with Judaism," *Judaism* 41, no. 2 (1992): 156–168; and David Nirenberg, "A Female Rabbi in Fourteenth-Century Zaragoza?" *Sefarad* 51 (1991): 179–182. For the role of women in twentieth-century Belmonte, see reports by Sara Molho and me in the epilogue.

17. Samuel Schwarz, *Os Christaõs-Novos em Portugal no Século XX* (Lisbon: Empresa portuguesa de livros, 1925), prayer 8a.

18. As the epigraph to her book *Heretics or Daughters of Israel?* Renée Levine Melammed uses a quotation from Mary Elizabeth Perry, a writer on the Moriscas (secret

Muslim Conversas), who said that the main struggle between Moriscos and Catholics did not take place in the battlefield, but inside the home, carried on by the oppressed women who performed the daily subversive work against the establishment and for their subculture. These words are apt for the Judeo-Conversas, too.

19. See Yosef Hayim Yerushalmi, "Marranos Returning to Judaism in the Seventeenth Century: Their Jewish Learning and Mental Preparation" (Heb.), in *Jewish Studies in a New Europe: Proceedings of the Fifth Congress of Jewish Studies* (Copenhagen: C. A. Reitzel, 1969), 201–202; and Yosef Hayim Yerushalmi, "The Re-education of Marranos in the Seventeeth Century" (Third Annual Rabbi Louis Feinberg Memorial Lecture in Judaic Studies, University of Cincinnati, March 26, 1980).

20. For more details, see chap. 13. For further written sources used by Judaizers in Portugal, see Claude B. Stuczynski, "Between the Implicit and the Explicit: Books and Reading Techniques among the Marranos in Portugal during the Sixteenth Century" (Heb.), in *Sifriot VeOsfei Sefarim: The 24th Conference on History* (Jerusalem: Shazar Center, 2006), 161–162.

21. Netanyahu conjectures that, despite the rabbis' overall negative attitude, many Jewish commoners were more indulgent toward the Judaizing Marranos (Benzion Netanyahu, *The Origins of the Inquisition in Fifteenth-Century Spain* [New York: Random House, 1995], 208). Maybe some were; yet most people tend to follow their religious leaders, even when they are less dogmatic. The rabbis' attitude toward Marranos is summarized in Simha Asaf, "The *Anussim* in the Responsa Literature" (Heb.), *Zion* 5 (1933): 19–60; and Moisés Orfali Levi, "Establecimiento del estatuto de limpieza de sangre en el monasterio de los Jerónimos de Guadalupe," in *Actas de las Jornadas de Estudios Sefardíes*, ed. Antonio Viudas Camarasa (Cáceres: Universidad de Extremadura, Instituto de Ciencias de la Educación, 1981), 245–250.

22. Beinart, *Conversos on Trial*, 274n161. The same occurred with another Conversa, María Gonzales (ibid.).

23. Ibid., 274n162.

24. Cross-confessional trends do exist today, but they remain a well-intentioned "dialogue" with little substance. Even when syncretic-looking phenomena are seen in mixed marriage ceremonies in the United States, this is mostly due to the secularized atmosphere prevailing in the couple's social environment. Basically, the three monotheistic religions are unable to renounce their particularistic claim to truth.

25. Carrete Parrondo et al., *FIRC*, 2:71, no. 132.

26. Ibid., 2:161, no. 387.

27. Ibid., 7:29, no. 40. Quoted in Moav (Roszenbaum), "Between Jews and Christians in Spain," 124.

28. C. Carrete Parrondo, *Hebraístas judeoconversos en la universidad de Salamanca (siglos XIV y XV)* (Salamanca: Universidad Pontificia, 1982); quoted in Moav (Roszenbaum), "Between Jews and Christians in Spain," 51.

29. Partly, in our case, because one can no longer want them as a reality (this is unlike nostalgia for one's own past, or youth, where the will plays no role).

30. There can be no doubt that, numerically and also phenomenologically, assimilation was the dominant trend, though not the exclusive one. Judaizing was not unrelated to assimilation; rather, the two dialectically strengthened one another through the mechanisms of guilt, nostalgia, reaction, and polemics. And when Spanish society started persecuting the Conversos, the reaction sometimes strengthened the Judaizing

instinct and even provoked a "return" to Judaizing in assimilated families. In this respect, anti-Converso persecution helped both to suppress Judaizing and to encourage it.

31. This phenomenon did not get much attention, perhaps because the category was lacking. But see Rábade Obradó, "Expresiones de la religiosidad Cristiana," esp. 314. For quite a different variety of "Christianizer," see my analysis of Bishop Juan Arias d'Avila in chap. 7.

32. It will also serve as a corrective to the often confusing use of the term *Judaizer* in the literature, both by inquisitors and by modern scholars.

33. Yirmiyahu Yovel, *Spinoza and Other Heretics* (Princeton, NJ: Princeton University Press, 1989), vol. 1, attributes a rudimentary philosophy of immanence to certain Marranos, and shows how this attitude was systematised philosophically by Spinoza; vol. 2 follows the adventures of the concept of immanence in philosophers after Spinoza.

34. Francisco Márquez Villanueva, "The Converso Problem: An Assessment," in *Collected Studies in Honor of Américo Castro's Eightieth Year*, ed. M. P. Hornick (Oxford: Lincombe Lodge Research Library, 1965), 327.

35. J. Cabezudo Astrain, "Los Conversos aragoneses según los procesos de la Inquisición," *Sefarad* 18 (1958): 282. Quoted in Moav (Roszenbaum), "Between Jews and Christians in Spain."

36. For a more extended discussion, see chap. 19.

37. This basic idea—the denial of the afterlife, and often of all transcendence, and focusing on this world as all there is—is typical of Conversos of different heterodox and agnostic kinds, in all generations, from late fourteenth-century Spain to seventeenth-century Mexico and Jewish Amsterdam. In the records of Carrete Parrondo et al., *FIRC*, vol. 2 alone it recurs a dozen times.

38. Lucien Febvre, *The Problem of Unbelief in the Sixteenth Century: The Religion of Rabelais* (Cambridge, MA: Harvard University Press, 1982). In arguing this, I concur in Edwards's dissent from Febvre's thesis. See John Edwards, "Religious Faith and Doubt in Late Medieval Spain: Soria circa 1450–1500," *Past and Present* 120 (August 1988): 3–25. Even if strong atheism—denying God's existence under any interpretation—was rare, it did exist among Conversos, together with its other connotations: denying transcendence, revelation, providence, the afterlife, divine justice, and the binding force of tradition, while locating life's real interest, and even the search for meaning and redemption, in worldly matters.

39. In a convincing and fine-tuned study, Heinrich Fichtenau affirms the existence of atheists, among other heretics, in the eleventh and twelfth centuries. See Heinrich Fichtenau, *Heretics and Scholars in the High Middle Ages, 1000–1200* (University Park: Pennsylvania State University Press, 1998).

40. In Yovel, *Spinoza and Other Heretics*, vol. 1 (esp. chap. 2).

41. I do not thereby adhere to the fashionable view that there is only context and no text—or nothing beyond the text. I assume that reading between the lines, as is required by the social and literary context of these texts, can point to concealed extratextual reality, which the text equivocally or ironically both hides and reflects. Accordingly, I use (in this book, chap. 15, and in other works) literary texts such as the *Cancioneros, Celestina, Don Quijote*, and the picaresque novels as signs pointing to what lies beyond them.

42. He added: "I believe we are born in order to die." Paradise means "to have the needs of this world," and hell is "where the poor reside." Deism often combines religious dissidence with social awareness.

43. Or derision, scoffing.

44. Fernando de Rojas, *La Celestina*, ed. Bruno Mario Damiani (Madrid: Cátedra, 1982).

45. For the full analysis of the *Celestina* along these lines, see Yovel, *Spinoza and Other Heretics*, vol. 1, chap. 4. An enlarged version is included in my manuscript "The Mystic and the Wanderer: Conversos in Spain's Golden Age Culture."

46. I discussed these recurring patterns (with special attention to Marranos who returned to Judaism) in *Spinoza and Other Heretics*, vol. 1. See also chaps. 17 and 18 in the present book.

47. At least not in Castile. In Aragon there was a branch of the old Papal Inquisition, but it was fairly inactive and did not really endanger the Conversos.

48. The nostalgia is only half-justified, since even the best periods of toleration maintained the supremacy of one religion—either Islam or Catholicism—over the other two.

Chapter 6. Marrano Mosaic I: Places, Persons, Poems

1. The "mosaics" in this chapter (as also in chap. 7) are fragments or parts of longer essays, or original chapters, I had written previously on these subjects.

2. In this I subscribe to the views of Castro, Bataillon, and Márquez Villanueva.

3. I analyzed the heretical Marranism of the *Celestina* in "Marranos in Mask and the World without Transcendence: Rojas and *La Celestina*," in *Spinoza and Other Heretics* (Princeton, NJ: Princeton University Press, 1989), vol. 1, chap. 4.

4. Albert A. Sicroff, "The Jeronymite Monastery of Guadalupe in 14th- and 15th-Century Spain," in *Collected Studies in Honour of Américo Castro's Eightieth Year*, ed. M. P. Hornick (Oxford: Lincombe Lodge Research Library, 1965), esp. 409–411. Previous historians of the monastery quoted by Sicroff are Siguenza, Talavera, Revuelta, and Highfield. The defense of the monastery's practices was framed by Fray Juan de Serrano, then the prior, who in 1428 sent a memo to Pope Martin V.

5. Y. Baer, *A History of the Jews in Christian Spain* (Philadelphia: Jewish Publication Society of America, 1961), 2:353.

6. The records of this investigation were studied by Albert A. Sicroff and reported in a major article: Albert A. Sicroff, "Clandestine Judaism in the Hieronymite Monastery of Nuestra Señora de Guadalupe," in *Studies in Honor of M. J. Bernadete: Essays in Hispanic and Sephardic Culture*, ed. Izaak A. Langnas and Barton Sholod (New York: Las Americas, 1965), 89–125. For Sicroff's sources, see his notes 9 and 11. Previous mention of such events is found in Baer, *A History of the Jews in Christian Spain*, 2:338. A more recent study of Guadalupe (which I did not have at hand when writing this chapter) is Gretchen D. Starr-LeBeau, *In the Shadow of the Virgin: Inquisitors, Friars, and Conversos in Gaudalupe, Spain* (Princeton, NJ: Princeton University Press, 2003). This book, through its study of the town, monastery, and Inquisition of Guadalupe, shares and supports my view that the Inquisition, for its own institutional reasons, rigidified the Conversos' unstable identities and dualist religious practices into hard binary definitions. (Further illustrations are found in this chapter and the next, on the Arias d'Avilas; for the theoretical argument, see chaps. 5 and 9.) The regular Inquisition's work in Guadalupe had previously been discussed in Fidel Fita, "La Inquisición en Guadalupe," *Boletín de la Real Academia de la Historia* 23 (1893): 283–343. And the application to the monastery, years later, of the "blood purity" regulation is described by Moisés Orfali Levi,

"Establicimiento del estatuto de limpieza de sangre en el monasterio de los Jerónimos de Guadalupe," in *Actas de las Jornadas de Estudios Sefardíes*, ed. Antonio Viudas Camarasa (Cáceres: Universidad de Extremadura, Instituto de Ciencias de la Educación, 1981), 245–250.

7. Although the figure is fictional, the report is based on a critical reading of the records as reported by Sicroff.

8. Sicroff, "Clandestine Judaism," 91n6; subsequent references to this source will appear parenthetically in the text. This monk was an active Judaizer, later burned at the stake.

9. See the realization of this "prophesy" in chaps. 14–15.

10. Actually, this affair occurred after 1478, but may be included here because it is indicative of the same situation.

11. Antón de Montoro, *Poesía completa*, ed. Marithelma Costa (Cleveland: Cleveland State University, 1990), 70. Subsequent references to Montoro's poems will appear parenthetically in the text. For Montoro's works, see Francisco Cantera Burgos and Carlos Carrete Parrondo, *Cancionero de Antón de Montoro* (Madrid: Editora Nacional, 1984).

12. This information comes from Montoro's enemy, a poet known as Commander Román, who in a hostile exchange with Montoro wrote: "although today you are Antón / in the past you were Saul." See Cantera Burgos and Carrete Parrondo, *Cancionero de Antón de Montoro*, 327.

13. A Hispanized expression, from the Hebrew *mazal* (luck), here given a Spanish form. *Desmazaldo* has the ring of a colloquial translation of the Hebrew *bish-mazal* (unfortunate).

14. For further illustration and analysis of Marranos dualities expressed in their poems (including other Montoro poems), see Yirmiyahu Yovel, "Converso Dualities in the First Generation: The *Cancioneros*," *Jewish Social Studies* 4, no. 3 (1998): 1–27. See also Cristina Arbós Ayuso, "Los cancioneros castellanos del siglo XV como fuente para la historia de los judíos españoles," in *Jews and Conversos: Studies in Society and the Inquisition*, ed. Yosef Kaplan (Jerusalem: World Union of Jewish Studies, Magnes Press, 1985), 74–82. Unlike Arbós Ayuso, to me these texts reveal the history not of the *judíos*, but of the Marranos as a special kind.

15. The records were published in Bernardino Llorca, "La Inquisición española y los conversos judíos o 'marranos,' " *Sefarad* 2 (1942): 113–151. Quoted in S. W. Baron, *A Social and Religious History of the Jews*, 2d edition, rev. and enlarged (New York: Columbia University Press, 1952–1983), 13:319n31; and in Haim Beinart, ed., *The Marranos in Christian Society and in Jewish Society: Seminar Sources* (Heb.; Jerusalem: Department of Jewish History, Hebrew University, 1976), doc. 14, 103–122.

16. Phrases in quotation marks are taken from her confession to the Inquisition at age eighty-plus.

17. The houses were probably a gift for Donosa's marriage and/or childbirth, and were financed either by the mentor herself, who was anxious to preserve her quasi-daughter's Jewish ties, or through funds raised from other Jews and Judaizers.

18. Perhaps she also wanted to dissociate herself from Queen Catalina, who issued the anti-Jewish laws that had led to Donosa's conversion.

19. We may generalize and say that only a dualist can make the "no harm" argument. For a nondualistic believer, this claim is plainly untrue, since there certainly is harm in turning to a rival savior or religion. The God of Moses would consider it a grave, punishable sin if one turned to Christ in parallel worship. Hence the inherent illegitimacy of

syncretism in the three monotheistic Hispanic religions. Also, the "no harm" argument does not move people to turn anywhere. Donosa—or any Jewish Converso—would hardly consider turning to Muhammad or Buddha.

20. *Que no sientes tu dolor*—this is logically impossible, but poetically effective. A probable interpretation: Montoro is not always aware of the sorrows involved in his situation as Converso—sometimes he too represses them, as Juan Poeta *always* does; but now he is in a lucid mood and will sadly describe them.

21. Literally: "*ynviolata permaniste*"—you have remained unviolated. Montoro, and those like him, accepted the Christian dogma of Mary's virginity, which Jews reject as absurd.

22. *Y nunca juré al creador*—swearing "to" is a somewhat curious expression. Montoro's enemy, Commander Román, precisely accuses him of *jurar al Dio*. This has two compatible interpretations: (1) addressing God directly, as do the Jews; and (2) calling God vaguely "the Creator" (or, worse, "Dio" in the singular), as do Judaizers who wish to avoid the seeming plural form "Dios."

23. Literally: the knots (*los nudos*) of the passion. The beads of the rosary and the stations of the Cross are both intended here. There also seems to be a further allusion to the Jewish Haggadah here: usually, the events of the Exodus from Egypt are told at Passover, but here tells instead of the stations of the Cross, commemorating Christ's passion.

24. Those remnants could be either (1) the Jewish guilt of having sent Jesus to his death, which the Conversos are made to bear; or (2) the remnants of their own Jewish self (and behavior), which many Conversos have not totally erased. Perhaps Montoro alludes to both at the same time.

25. In the Talmud (Treatise *Berachot*, chap. 1, *Mishna* 5), and in the Passover Haggadah following it, it is explained that Ben Zoma changed this custom and started telling the story of the Exodus at night, as is still done in the seder ceremony.

26. We must not take these statements as strictly biographical; they are poetic constructions, and the "self" they portray is a generalized Converso one. Montoro personally was more ambiguous. Also, the number sixty is surely only an approximation. Montoro is using it as a poetic paraphrase rather than a precise statement of his age.

27. *Puto* today means "queer" (pejorative for homosexual), but that was not the meaning then. Perhaps the idea of prostitution was linked in popular invective to the Marrano situation—having converted for utility, sacrificed a high personal value for gain.

28. *Agora señor Antón, / porque me temporizastes, / yo vos otorgo perdón / d'aquel que crucificaste.*

29. I owe the latter point to my wife, Shoshana Yovel.

30. I follow here Baer's conclusion, as I do in the general portrait of Pedro de La Caballería. See Baer, *A History of the Jews in Christian Spain*, 2:276–277. See also Manuel Serrano y Sanz, *Orígenes de la Dominación Española en América* (Madrid: Bailly-Bailliere, 1918), 189 and passim.

31. Baer, *History of the Jews in Christian Spain*, 2:372–373.

32. Ibid., 2:378–379.

33. Ibid., 2:375.

34. Juan Alfonso de Baena, *Cancionero*, ed. José María Azáceta (Madrid: Consejo superior de investigaciones científicas, 1966), poem 142. My emphasis.

35. This was suggested to me by Moshe Meller, a former assistant who was delightfully enthusiastic about these poems.

36. I do not exactly attribute to the author the intention as phrased here in present-day idiom, but claim that his text lends itself to this reading. Of course, there is a certain breach of communication between us and the author, due to the historical and cultural distance. But this reservation applies to any reinterpretation without necessarily disqualifying it. The question remains: Does the text allow such a reading, even a modern paraphrase, if we remember that it involves a transformation of meaning, which is more an analogy than a straight citation? If only the analogy can find an anchor in the text, and as long as we are aware of its existence, it can illuminate something crucial in the text that another reading, which clings to the past idiom only, will miss or obscure.

37. Devalued? Or are the "new ones" the New Christians?

38. Literally: "for they [do] not work on the Sabbath."

39. Reading *nescia* as *necia*.

40. His *talit*, in Spanish *sudario* (which rhymes with Çidario). Hence the executor's name is actually "Jacob *talit*."

41. I cannot leave the pair Alvarez/Semuel without making a speculative remark. Alvarez's attack against both the living and the dead renegade makes one wonder whether the writer and his target, two Conversos named Alfonso, might not be dialectically one. In other words, Alvarez is also satirizing *himself*: he writes about his own possible or actual self as a Converso who shares the same situation; and thereby Semuel, his victim and enemy, is Alvarez's alter ego. Of course, this conjecture is hard to prove, but at least other scholars recognize the possibility that Alvarez too was a Converso (so does Adolpho Castro, as reported in Francisco Cantera Burgos, "El Cancionero de Baena: Judíos y conversos en 61," *Sefarad* 27 [1967]: 89).

42. See Benzion Netanyahu, *The Origins of the Inquisition in Fifteenth-Century Spain* (New York: Random House, 1995), 431–434, for a discussion of the evidence, and cf. pp. 435–449 for a detailed survey of Torquemada's work. Torquemada's partly Jewish origin is also mentioned by the Converso chronicler Pulgar, and in a *Memorial* to the Holy See by Marcos García de Mora, written around the events of 1449 (E. Benito Ruano, "El Memorial contra los conversos del bachiller Marcos García de Mora," *Sefarad* 17 (1957): 314–351), which Netanyahu considers a decisive corroboration (*The Origins of the Inquisition in Fifteenth-Century Spain*, 486–511). In Américo Castro's view (*The Structure of Spanish History*, trans. Edmund L. King [Princeton, NJ: Princeton University Press, 1954], 530), Torquemada was definitely of Converso origin.

43. In attributing a nonracist view to the Cardinal in the context of the times, however, one should be careful. If pressed hard, Torquemada would probably agree, as most people then would, that some peoples or races are higher than others; but he would deny that the difference survived the act of conversion—that baptized Jews (or blacks, or Muslims, or Asians) could never be good Christians. It was, we might say, an antiracist view limited to the confines of the Christian fold. Baptism was the great equalizer. But this Marrano ideology was still very advanced for its time—more than Cartagena's.

44. Baer, *A History of the Jews in Christian Spain*, 2:338.

45. Incidentally, the Judaizing Conversos in the city of Guadalupe seem to have acted as an "organized community" (Baer, *A History of the Jews in Christian Spain*, 2:337), and visits by Jews to instruct them were common. Two of these visitors, Mose Arovas of Trujillo and another Jew from Medellín, used to stay with a Converso woman married to an Old Christian butcher; when her husband once brought home a cross, she treaded on it and threw it into the latrine; and after her son was baptized, she hastened

to wipe the oil off his forehead. The evidence against her was given by her own daughter, as sometimes happened in "mixed" families. A broader view of Jews and Conversos in Guadalupe is given in Starr-LeBeau, *In the Shadow of the Virgin*.

46. There was a curious report about Nogales trying to send a Converso novice to join a Judaizing group as a spy. Sicroff speculates that this was a pretext—a prudent way of approaching the young man, whom Nogales actually wished to join the group "not as a spy but as a regular member" (Sicroff, "Clandestine Judaism," 121). This intriguing possibility is, unfortunately, unsupported by the scant evidence Sicroff brings to make Nogales appear as a full-fledged Judaizer. It is equally possible that Nogales was excluded from that group precisely because they knew of his dualities, and that he wished to know for himself what was going on in a milieu that both attracted and repelled him.

47. Ibid., 104.

48. Ibid., 91n7.

49. This is what Márquez Villanueva may have meant in saying that intellectually restless Conversos "moulded to their pleasure the Order of the Hieronymites." See Francisco Márquez Villanueva, "The Converso Problem: An Assessment," in *Collected Studies in Honour of Américo Castro's Eightieth Year*, ed. M. P. Hornick (Oxford: Lincombe Lodge Research Library: 1965), 328.

50. The story is based on the records of Inez's trial. See Haim Beinart, "The Prophetess Inez and Her Movement in Her Native Herrera," in *Pirke Sefarad* (Heb.; Jerusalem: Magnes Press, 1998), 2:543–591; and other essays on Inez exerting influence beyond her region. Beinart's conclusion stresses the "strong excitement that seized the *beata's* followers in expectation of redemption." My analysis focuses on their *duality*, and the Christian framework of the Judaizing core intent.

51. On the role of Elijah in Marrano Messianism, see John Edwards, "Elijah and the Inquisition: Messianic Prophecy among Conversos in Spain c. 1500," *Nottingham Medieval Studies* 28 (1984): 79–94. On the *beato* Melchior, see below.

52. According to a Talmudic saying, the sole difference between this and the Messianic world will be "the [Jews' liberation from] the yoke of the Nations"; upon which Maimonides built his basically political theory of the Messiah (*The Laws of Kings* in *Mishne Torah*).

53. Marcel Bataillon, *Erasme et l'Espagne* (Paris: E. Droz, 1937; Geneva: Droz, 1991). More on Melchior in my manuscript "The Mystic and the Wanderer: Conversos in Spain's Golden Age Culture."

CHAPTER 7. THE ARIAS D'AVILAS: HIDDEN JEWS OR MARRANO DUALISTS?

1. This chapter is based on a longer (unpublished) analysis of the inquisitorial records concerning members of the Arias d'Avila family accused by the Inquisition that I did in the late 1980s. Its purpose is (1) to illustrate three different kinds of Marrano dualities—wavering among nostalgic Judaism, social Judaism, and Christianity, and between this-worldly skepticism and atheism; and (2) to illustrate how the complex notion of "Judaizing" was misused by the Inquisition, has been misunderstood by some modern scholars, and should be critically "deconstructed." I am thankful to my then assistant Diego Ulstein for his help in working with these records, although our conclusions somewhat differ. See also pertinent points in Eleazar Gewirth, "Elementos étnicos e históricos en las relaciones judeo-conversas en Segovia," in *Jews and Conversos: Studies in Society and the Inquisition*,

ed. Yosef Kaplan (Jerusalem: World Union of Jewish Studies and Magnes Press, 1981), an essay that reinforces the notion of "social Judaism" that I used in discussing Elvira. For other interpretations of this family, see note 4 in this chapter.

2. See Yirmiyahu Yovel, "Converso Dualities in the First Generation: The *Cancioneros*," *Jewish Social Studies* 4, no. 3 (1998): 11. See also Cristina Arbós Ayuso, "Judíos y conversos: Un tema tópico en la poesía medieval," in *Encuentros en Sefarad: Actas del Congreso Internacional "Los Judíos en la Historia de España"* (Ciudad Real: Instituto de Estudios Manchegos, 1987).

3. The records of the Arias d'Avila family's trial were published in Carlos Carrete Parrondo et al., eds., *Fontes iudaeorum regni castellae* [FIRC], vol. 3, *Proceso inquisitorial contra los Arias d'Avila Segovianos: Un enfrentamiento social entre judíos y conversos* (Salamanca: Universidad Pontificia de Salamanca, 1986). Incidentally, this rich source was unavailable to Baer, who said that there was no knowledge of Diego Arias's attitude toward "his fellow Jews." The lack of this knowledge did not keep Baer from calling (or pronouncing) Diego Arias a "Jew," however. See Y. Baer, *A History of the Jews in Christian Spain* (Philadelphia: Jewish Publication Society of America, 1961), 2:282–283.

4. John Edwards, using the same *FIRC* records, has shown convincingly that the bishop cannot properly be called a "Judaizer"; see John Edwards, "'Bishop Juan Arias d'Avila of Segovia: 'Judaizer' or Reformer?" in *Cultures in Contact in Medieval Spain: Historical and Literary Essays Presented to L. P. Harvey,* ed. David Hook and Barry Taylor (London: Kings College, Medieval Studies, 1990), 71–86. (The present chapter's title echoes Edwards's title by applying a similar query to the more complex cases of the bishop's father and mother.) On the other hand, David Gitlitz supports the view that Diego—and even the bishop—secretly leaned to Judaism. See David M. Gitlitz, *Los Arias d'Avila de Segovia: Entre la sinagoga y la iglesia* (San Francisco: International Scholars Publications, 1996).

5. The following will also illustrate how the inquisitorial process worked, and how it might be critically assessed and sometimes, as here, "deconstructed."

6. Carrete Parrondo et al., *FIRC*, 3, no. 16.

7. A sanbenito is the humiliating body cover that repentants were made to wear in an inquisitorial *auto de fe.*

8. Carrete Parrondo et al., *FIRC*, 3, no. 25.

9. Ibid., 3, no. 219.

10. Ibid., 3, no. 77.

11. Ibid., 3, no. 111.

12. His testimony has other problems too: it was recast with a heavy hand by the inquisitorial clerk, who put it, as usual, in his own words, but this particular clerk was more ignorant of Jewish affairs than usual. Also, the incident is said to have taken place in "the Goncález house," which may mean either the d'Avila house (Doña Elvira was née Goncález), or the house of Doña Catalina Goncález, Elvira's mother, who was also among the accused.

13. As distinguished from the small *talit* (*talit katan,* worn permanently under one's garment).

14. Anillo Yuce [Yosef], on January 9, 1491.

15. Sometimes, indeed, it disappears first—in those who are actively ashamed of their old identity or rush toward assimilation—but it is still strongly kept by others; and even the assimilated, or their offspring, often return to it in the next generation as an object of nostalgia.

16. Juan de Duration, May 26, recalling a story he heard from Diego Arias's servant; Carrete Parrondo et al., *FIRC*, 3, no. 33.

17. Ibid., 3, no. 123.

18. As in the former episode—one wonders whether we have a pattern here, or two versions of a single story—Diego Arias handled the fetish instrumentally, checked its performance and utility, and censured it when it failed.

19. Carrete Parrondo et al., *FIRC*, 3, no. 151.

20. So, unlike her husband, perhaps *adafina* was a kind of identity mark for her, and not just a nostalgic pleasure.

21. Carrete Parrondo et al., *FIRC*, 3, nos. 81, 124.

22. On the modern role of philanthropy in semisecular Jewish identity, see Derek Penslar, "Modern Jewish Philanthropy," in *Philanthropy in the World's Traditions*, ed. Warren F. Ilchman, Stanley N. Katz, and Edward L. Queen II (Bloomington: Indiana University Press, 1998), 179–214; and Derek Penslar, "Philanthropy, the 'Social Question', and Jewish Identity in Imperial Germany," *Leo Baeck Institute Yearbook* 38 (1993): 51–73.

23. Carrete Parrondo et al., *FIRC*, 3, no. 89.

24. This is how her name usually appears in the records (B and V are often interchanged in old Spanish records, as are Z, C, and S).

25. Carrete Parrondo et al., *FIRC*, 3, no. 231.

26. See also Gewirth, "Elementos étnicos e históricos en las relaciones judeoconversas en Segovia." This study stresses the socioethnic links between Jews and Conversos of different sorts (anticipating the "Nation" of later generations), and mentions Elvira's case (and that of the other Arias d'Avilas) as an illustration.

27. Carrete Parrondo et al., *FIRC*, 3, no. 232.

28. Ibid., 3, no. 253, Diego 29.

29. In a similar way, under Stalin devout Communists were accused of "anti-Sovietism" and "counterrevolution."

30. His youthful help to his mother in reaching a political arrangement among Jewish leaders and handing out charity was precisely that—a diplomatic and PR service, assisting his mother in her social interests. His loyalty was to her, not to the Jewish religion.

CHAPTER 8. ENRIQUE THE IMPOTENT: PROSPERITY, ANARCHY, AND INQUISITION ON THE HORIZON

1. Detailed in Julio Valdeón Baruque, *Feudalismo y consolidación de los pueblos hispánicos (siglos XI–XV)* (Barcelona: Labor, 1980); Julio Valdeón Baruque, *Los conflictos sociales en el Reino de Castilla en los siglos XIV y XV* (Madrid: Siglo Veintiuno, 1975); and Asunción Esteban Recio, *Las ciudades castellanas en tiempos de Enrique IV: Estructura social y conflictos* (Valladolid, Spain: Secretariado de Publicaciones, Universidad de Valladolid, 1985).

2. See Manuel Tuñón de Lara et al., *Historia de España* (Barcelona: Labor, 1991), 152ff.

3. For further details, see ibid., 150–156.

4. Ibid., 154–155.

5. Valdeón Baruque, *Feudalismo y consolidación*, 54; quoted in Recio, *Las ciudades castellanas*, 15.

6. The following is based on Carlos Estepa Díez et al., *Burgos en la Edad Media* (Valladolid, Spain: Junta de Castilla y León, Consejería de Educación y Cultura, 1984), and source materials mentioned there.

7. On the various branches of this clan, their control of Burgos and other cities, and their role in religion, society, culture, and the army, see Francisco Cantera Burgos, *Alvar García de Santa María: Historia de la judería de Burgos y de sus conversos más egregios* (Madrid: Instituto Arias Montano, 1952).

8. E. Benito Ruano, *Toledo en el siglo XV: Vida política* (Madrid: Consejo Superior de Investigaciones Científicas, Escuela de Estudios Medievales, 1961), 84. Also see E. Benito Ruano, "Del problema judío al problema converso," in *Symposio Toledo judaico* (Toledo, Spain: Publicaciones del Centro Universitario de Toledo, 1973), 2:7–28.

9. In Angus MacKay's seminal article, "Popular Movements and Pogroms in Fifteenth-Century Castile," *Past and Present* 55 (1972): 33–67. Norman Roth criticizes MacKay but practically rephrases his view: the general politico-economic circumstances encouraged the hostility toward New Christians, which had its separate (in my terms, identitarian) sources, to erupt into violent riots. New Christians were, so to speak, the "usual suspects," the first expected targets. Norman Roth, "Anti-Converso Riots of the Fifteenth Century, Pulgar, and the Inquisition," *En la España medieval* 15 (1992): 367–394. See this essay also for further points on the riots in Toledo—1449 and 1467—and Andalusia.

10. Castile and Aragon were two separate kingdoms until the joint reign of Isabella and Ferdinand. Enrique's father was Juan II of Castile; his rival was Juan II of Aragon.

11. In analyzing the importance (explicit and implicit) of the Conversos in this letter, I follow Benzion Netanyahu, *The Origins of the Inquisition in Fifteenth-Century Spain* (New York: Random House, 1995), 756–757. The document is included in *Colección Diplomática—RAH, Memorias de Don Enrique IV de Castilla* (Madrid: Fortanet, 1835–1913), 2:331–336.

12. If Pacheco too was a Converso, as Domínguez Ortiz believes, this would add an ironic line to his figure. Antonio Domínguez Ortiz, *Los judeoconversos en España y América* (Madrid: ISTMO, 1971), 19.

13. Quoted in Benito Ruano, *Toledo en el siglo XV*, 91.

14. The description in this section primarily follows Eloy Benito Ruano's. See ibid., 93–110; and E. Benito Ruano, *Los orígenes del problema converso* (Barcelona: Ediciones El Albir, 1976). An early account had been given by Amador de Los Ríos, based on two sources: (1) Palencia's chronicle, which uses contemporary testimonies and is marked by biases and imprecision characteristic of this writer; and (2) the report of Pedro de Mesa, a *canónigo* of Toledo, in a letter to a "Gran señor" in that city written shortly after the riots (August 17), which is fresher and more direct, but manifestly anti-Converso. Benito Ruano mentions a third, anonymous source that was uncovered in 1960. Benito Ruano bases his own account mainly on Mesa's report, whereas Netanyahu (*The Origins of the Inquisition in Fifteenth-Century Spain*, 771–793) makes extensive, albeit consistently critical, use of Palencia as well. Incidentally, Baer based his description in *A History of the Jews in Christian Spain* on the sources published in F. Baer, *Die Juden im christlichen Spanien: Urkunden und Regesten* (Berlin: Akademie für die Wissenschaft des Judentums, 1929–1936), vol. 2, no. 321. Consequently there are differences between him and Roth, who relies on Amador de Los Ríos, *Historia social, política y religiosa de los judíos de España y Portugal* (Madrid: Turner, 1984).

15. "¡Mueran, mueran, que no es ésta iglesia sino congregación de malos y de viles!"

16. For Toledo's role as a special scene of conflicts concerning Jews, see Juan Blázquez Miguel, *Toledot: Historia del Toledo Judío* (Toledo: Arcano, 1989).

17. Quoted in Benito Ruano, *Toledo en el siglo XV*, 100.

18. Known as the second battle of Olmedo.

19. Henry of Navarre, later Henry IV of France, who fought as a Protestant in the religious wars but agreed to return to Catholicism as a condition of his ascending to the throne in Paris.

20. Baer, *Die Juden im christlichen Spanien*, vol. 2, no. 321.

21. Espina is widely believed (except by Netanyahu) to have been a Converso; Oropesa is also considered a Converso by Márquez Villanueva, Benito Ruano, Domínguez Ortiz, and others.

22. Benito Ruano (*Los orígenes del problema converso*, 75–77) goes so far as to characterize Oropesa's proposal as a model of a "nonprejudiced" Inquisition, a well-meaning oxymoron.

23. Baer, *A History of the Jews in Christian Spain* (Philadelphia: Jewish Publication Society of America, 1961), 2:283–284. See also Alisa Meyuhas Ginio, "De bello iudaeorum: Fray Alonso de Espina y su Fortalitium fidei," in C. Carrete Parrondo et al., eds., *Fontes Iudaeorum Regni Castellae* (Salamanca: Universidad Pontificia de Salamanca, 1998), vol. 8.

24. V. Beltrán de Heredia, "Las bulas de Nicolás V acerca de los Conversos de Castilla," *Sefarad* 21 (1961): 35, 44–45. Quoted in Netanyahu, *The Origins of the Inquisition in Fifteenth-Century Spain*, 738n54.

25. Palencia loathed King Enrique and contributed to his negative image, but generally defended the Conversos. His claim that Pacheco caused the new anti-Converso riots is too simple. The social dynamite was already there; Pacheco could only accelerate its explosion into violence.

CHAPTER 9. FERDINAND, ISABELLA, AND THE "TRUE INQUISITION"

1. The couple's Spanish names, Fernando and Isabel, have been Anglicized here to accord with widespread common usage.

2. The question of preconception is widely debated (by Haliczer, Kriegel, Kamen, and others). Kriegel's assumes that there was a certain consistency in the motives of the Catholic monarchs regarding the destruction of religious plurality in Spain, but no master plan prepared in advance. See Maurice Kriegel, "La liquidation du pluralisme religieux dans l'Espagne des rois catholiques: Limites et efficacité de l'approche 'intentionnaliste,'" *Temas Medievales* 4 (1994): 37–39. I tend to think that there was a clear drive for royal power and a vaguer, derivative, and more confused goal of "unification" (administrative, ideological, religious, etc.) that responded to circumstances without a guiding blueprint.

3. The studies of their reign are numerous. See, for example, Joseph Pérez, *Isabel y Fernando, los Reyes Católicos* (Madrid: Nerea, 1988); Henry Kamen, *Crisis and Change in Early Modern Spain* (Aldershot, Hampshire, UK, and Brookfield, VT: Variorum, 1993); and, more recently, Miguel Angel Ladero Quesada, *La España de los reyes católicos* (Madrid: Alianza, 2005). For Pulgar, see note 7 in this chapter.

4. Solomon ibn Verga, *Shevet Yehudah* (Heb.), ed. Y. Baer (Jerusalem: Bialik Institute, 1947), 129.

5. John H. Elliott, *Imperial Spain, 1469–1716* (New York: New American Library 1966), 95. Elliott presumes that there may already have been three hundred thousand Marranos, compared to some two hundred thousand Jews.

6. Haim Beinart, *Conversos on Trial by the Inquisition* (Heb.; Tel-Aviv: Am Oved, 1965).

7. On Pulgar, see Francisco Cantera Burgos, "Fernando del Pulgar and the Conversos," *Sefarad* 4 (1944): 295–348. For his chronicles, see Fernando del Pulgar, *Crónica de los reyes católicos* (Madrid: Espasa-Colpe, 1943).

8. See his short portrait in chap. 6.

9. On the links between the Passover matzo and the Host, and their role in the Jewish-Christian debate (including the charge of "desecrating the Host"), see Israel Yuval, *Two Nations in Your Womb* (Heb.; Tel Aviv: Alma, Am Oved 2001).

10. The Spanish Marranos were not sufficiently organized to form their own lobby in Rome, as Portuguese Marranos later did. See chap. 12.

11. Y. Baer, *A History of the Jews in Christian Spain* (Philadelphia: Jewish Publication Society of America, 1961), 2:325.

12. Bernardino Llorca, *Bulario pontificio de la Inquisición española* (Rome: Pontificia Università Gregoriana, 1949), 48–49. Cited in Haim Beinart, ed., *The Marranos in Christian Society and in Jewish Society: Seminar Sources* (Heb.; Jerusalem: Department of Jewish History, Hebrew University, 1976), 75.

13. Among the rare cases taken to Rome were those of Alfonso de La Caballería (see chap. 6) and Bishop Juan Arias d'Avila (see chap. 7). But neither was procedurally an appeal; rather, both men took their defense to Rome on their own.

14. The vast literature on the Inquisition includes, beside monographs, also discussions in broader histories, and many inquisitorial records published, quoted, paraphrased, and analyzed in other works. An older classic is Henry Charles Lea, *A History of the Inquisition of Spain* (New York: Macmillan, 1906–1908), written by a Protestant critic. A century earlier, Juan Antonio Llorente became the semiofficial historian of the Inquisition in his *Historia crítica de la Inquisición española* (Madrid: Hiperión, 1980). An inner-Catholic view is expressed also in Bernardino Llorca, *La Inquisición en España* (Barcelona: Labor, 1954). See also Bernardino Llorca, "La Inquisición española y los conversos judíos o 'marranos,' " *Sefarad* 2 (1942): 113–151. Three more recent collections are: Angel Alcalá, ed., *The Spanish Inquisition and the Inquisitorial Mind* (New York: Columbia University Press, 1987); Joaquín Pérez Villanueva, ed., *La Inquisición española: Nueva visión, nuevos horizontes* (Madrid: Siglo Veintiuno de España, 1980); and Joaquín Pérez Villanueva and Bartolomé Escandell Bonet, eds., *Historia de la Inquisición en España y América*, 3 vols. (Madrid: Centro de Estudios Inquisitoriales, Biblioteca de Autores Cristianos, 1984–2000). Other Spanish scholars discussed the subject within the framework of their wider historical work (including Américo Castro, Antonio Domínguez Ortiz, Julio Caro Baroja, Francisco Márquez Villanueva, and others). Of the more specialized studies in the last generation, see Henry Kamen, *Inquisition and Society in Spain* (London: Weidenfeld and Nicholson, 1985); and its revised and expanded edition: Henry Kamen, *The Spanish Inquisition: An Historical Revision* (London: Weidenfeld and Nicholson, 1997); Jean-Pierre Dedieu, *L'administration de la foi: L'Inquisition de Tolède, XVIe–XVIIIe siècle* (Paris: Casa de Velázquez, 1989); Antonio Domínguez Ortiz, *Autos de la Inquisición de Sevilla: Siglo XVII* (Seville: Servicio de Publicaciones del Ayuntamiento de Sevilla, 1981); Bartolomé Benassar, ed., *L'Inquisition espagnole: XV–XIX siècle* (Paris:

Hachette, 1979); Bartolomé Benassar, "Patterns of the Inquisitional Mind as the Basis for a Pedagogy of Fear," in *Inquisición española y mentalidad inquisitorial*, ed. Angel Alcalá (Barcelona: Ariel, 1984); Gustav Henningsen and Charles Amiel, eds., *The Inquisition in Early Modern Europe: Studies on Sources and Methods* (Dekalb: Northern Illinois University Press, 1986); and works by Beinart, Kriegel, Haliczer, and García Cárcel cited elsewhere in notes to this and other chapters.

15. Cecil Roth, *A History of the Marranos* (Philadelphia: Jewish Publication Society of America, 1932), 47.

16. They also acted with resolve, as indicated by the language of the order I quoted. This is in contrast to Baron's assessment that, from the outset, the court behaved "rather cautiously." S. W. Baron, *A Social and Religious History of the Jews*, 2d ed., rev. and enlarged (New York: Columbia University Press, 1952–1983), 13:27.

17. This is the original Spanish term for what was later called in Portugal "auto da fé." I shall mostly use the Spanish term, except when dealing with Portugal.

18. Cecil Roth, *A History of the Marranos*, 43–44.

19. To get this number, we should add to the various estimates regarding Seville in the first seven years (until 1488) the other parts of Castile and Aragon, and another eleven years of intensive inquisitorial activity, including the burning of corpses.

20. Boleslao Lewin, *La Inquisición en hispanoamérica: Judíos, protestantes, y patriotas* (Buenos Aires: Paidós, 1967). Also see notes 50 and 69 in chap. 17. The older work on the Inquisition is: José Toribio Medina, *Historia del tribunal de la Inquisición de Lima (1569–1820)* (Santiago, Chile: Fondo Histórico y Bibliográfico J. T. Medina, 1956); José Toribio Medina, *Historia del tribunal del Santo Oficio de la Inquisición en Chile* (Santiago, Chile: Fondo Histórico y Bibliográfico J. T. Medina, 1952); and José Toribio Medina, *Historia del tribunal del Santo Oficio de la Inquisición en Cartagena de las Indias* (Santiago, Chile: Elzeviriana, 1899).

21. This goes beyond his person. Albert Sicroff sees the early Inquisition as fighting for a religious, not an ethno-racist agenda. See Albert A. Sicroff, "Spanish Anti-Judaism: A Case of Religious Racism," in *Encuentros and Desencuentros: Spanish-Jewish Cultural Interaction throughout History*, ed. C. Carrete Parrondo et al. (Tel Aviv: Tel Aviv University Publishing Project, 2000). So does Henry Kamen, in "Una crisis de conciencia en la edad de oro en España: La Inquisición contra 'limpieza de sangre,' " *Bulletin hispanique* 88 (1986): 321–356. Another opponent of the blood laws was Ignatio de Loyola, the founder of the Jesuit order, whose deputies and followers included many Conversos. See Antonio Domínguez Ortiz, *La clase social de los conversos en Castilla en la edad moderna* (Granada: Universidad de Granada, Servicios de Publicaciones, 1991), 70.

22. The trials of Ciudad Real are analyzed in rich detail in Beinart, *Conversos on Trial by the Inquisition*, now a classic. The book establishes genuine cases of Judaizing, but often interprets signs of ambivalence as intent to live as Jews.

23. Cantera Burgos, "Fernando del Pulgar and the Conversos," 297; quoted in Norman Roth, "Anti-Converso Riots of the Fifteenth Century, Pulgar, and the Inquisition," *En la España medieval* 15 (1992), 367–394.

24. Quoted in Beinart, *Conversos on Trial by the Inquisition*, 21.

25. Baer, *A History of the Jews in Christian Spain*; Nicolás López Martínez, "Libro llamado Alboraique," in *Los Judaizantes catesllanos y la Inquisición en tiempo de Isabel la Católica*, ed. Nicolás López Martínez (Burgos: Seminario Metropolitano de Burgos, 1954), 391–404.

26. Miguel Angel Pallarés, *Apocas de la receptoría de la Inquisición en la zona nororiental de Aragón (1487–1492)* (Monzón, Huesca: Centro de Estudios de Monzón y Cinca Medio, 1996); Iñaki Reguera, *La Inquisición Española en el país Vazco* (San Sebastian: Texertoa, 1984).

27. Henry Kamen, in his influential *Inquisition and Society in Spain*, uses the Aragonese resistance to illustrate a continued pluralism in Spanish society. Yet Aragon's resistance seems to have been aimed less against the intolerance and exclusionary policies of the Inquisition than against its excessive centralized (and Castile-centered) power.

28. The tribunal of Valencia had later to do not only with Judaizers but with Moriscos (Christianized Muslims) living in the area, and still later with Lutherans and other dissenters. Its well-documented archives were studied in Stephen Haliczer, *Inquisition and Society in the Kingdom of Valencia, 1478–1834* (Berkeley and Los Angeles: University of California Press, 1990); Ricardo García Cárcel, *Orígenes de la Inquisición española—El Tribunal de Valencia, 1478–1530* (Barcelona: Ediciones Península, 1976); and Ricardo García Cárcel, *Herejía y sociedad en el siglo XVI—La Inquisición en Valencia, 1530–1609* (Barcelona: Ediciones Península, 1980).

29. I am referring not to the subjective measure of cruelty, whereby some individuals have always been more sadistic than others, but to its objective significance, for example, the degree of organization and efficiency of a system created to inflict suffering.

30. Kamen's view that the Inquisition did not affect the daily lives of Old Christians underestimates the immense shadow of fear and suspicion that the Inquisition projected on individual life, high and low. The mystery of its shadowy power, secret operations, and grim prisons; the danger of sudden, false, or vindictive accusation and arrest; the examples of the greatest men fallen and humiliated; and the widespread poisoning of human relations by mutual suspicion and mistrust—all of these produced a cumulative life-experience that lasted for generations, a psychological yoke that cannot be sufficiently recognized and appreciated by a functional analysis of the institution per se. In this respect, Benassar is more convincing in speaking of the culture (or "pedagogy") of fear created by the Inquisition (see his "Patterns of the Inquisitional Mind as the Basis for a Pedagogy of Fear"). One can see this culture mirrored also in the forms of discourse that evolved in life and literature, such as irony overcoming fear and expressed as dual language.

31. Presumably this legalism—combined with the cathartic *autos de fe*—had the benefit of preventing street mob action against the Conversos in later years in Spain. If so, this would also mean that the Inquisition with both its instruments—the formal legalism and the public shows of *auto de fe*—substituted itself for mob outbursts as their stylized legal sublimation, and as such embodied the same spirit in a permissible form. A similar argument is made by Stephen Haliczer, who maintains that the Inquisition gave an official stamp to the ancient fears of the Jew as demon, and transferred this demonology to the Conversos, too. See Stephen Haliczer, "The Jew as Witch: Displaced Aggression and the Myth of the Santo Niño of La Guarda," in *Cultural Encounters: The Impact of the Inquisition in Spain and the New World*, ed. Mary Elizabeth Perry and Anne J. Cruz (Berkeley and Los Angeles: University of California Press, 1991), 146–155.

32. See chaps. 5 and 13.

33. The harrowing scene (recorded verbatim by the clerk) is given at length in Cecil Roth, *A History of the Marranos*, 111–116.

34. Although the economic interest of the Inquisition is evident, it was far from being its raison d'être. Rather, once in existence, the Inquisition was hungry for resources to finance its operations and, where possible, to grow in influence through affluence. This was not easy to achieve. Studies show that often the local Inquisition's expenses surpassed the income from confiscations, as in Valencia in early years. See Ricardo García Cárcel, *Orígenes de la Inquisición española*; and García Cárcel, *La Inquisición* (Madrid: Anaya, 1990). On the general issue, see José Martínez Millán, "Structures of Inquisitorial Finance," in *The Spanish Inquisition and the Inquisitorial Mind*, ed. Angel Alcalá (New York: Columbia University Press, 1987). But the pressure of these interests often led to abuse and manipulation. When the father of Juan Luis Vives, the Converso humanist, was burned as Judaizer, the Inquisition confiscated his property down to the last maravedi. Vives and his sisters appealed, arguing that part of the money had been the dowry of their dead mother, Blanca Vives March, and should be returned. The ever-legalistic Inquisition started a posthumous trial against the deceased Doña Blanca, found her, too, guilty of Judaism, and confiscated her dowry a second time, this time for good.

35. Even more important in creating this gap were the "purity of blood" rules.

36. Mariana wrote with the verve of the Jesuit reformer he was. Elliott (*Imperial Spain*) treats his book critically, and Llorca disputes the huge number of inquisitors Mariana cites for the early years (seventeen thousand). Only Américo Castro unhesitatingly accepts Mariana's statements. See A. Castro, *España en su historia: Cristianos, moros y judíos* (Barcelona: Editorial Crítica, 1983), 521.

37. By the "Iberian" colonies, I mean also the Portuguese Inquisition, which followed the Spanish one; see chap. 11.

38. Edward Peters, *Inquisition* (Berkeley and Los Angeles: University of California Press, 1989), chap. 7. Also Tomás José Pardo, *Ciencia y censura: La Inquisición española y los libros científicos en los siglos XVI y XVII* (Madrid: Consejo Superior de Investigaciones Científicas, 1991).

39. This limited "Jewish Inquisition," probably adopting the papal model, was designed to combat the *malshinim* (Jews who supplied adverse information to the authorities), who posed the greatest threat to the Jewish autonomous congregations in the Middle Ages.

40. For other views on the Inquisition, see the sample of works mentioned in previous notes (esp. 14, 29, and 33) and the appendix.

41. Except in special cases, such as blasphemy, or when a Jew attempted to convert a Christian, in which case Jews could be prosecuted.

42. As distinguished from Moriscos, that is, baptized Muslims in southern Spain.

Chapter 10. The Great Expulsion

1. This chapter is written from the viewpoint of Marrano, not Jewish, history; hence its relative brevity and minimal detail.

2. See Stephen Haliczer, "The Expulsion of the Jews as Social Process," in *The Jews in Spain and the Expulsion of 1492*, ed. Moshe Lazar and Stephen Haliczer (Lancaster: Labyrinthos, 1997), and earlier work. Halizcer argues that the Catholic monarchs had no clear vision of what they wanted; their policy "emerged from a messy combination of conciliation, compromise, and brute force rather than the rational calculation and long-range planning that historians have tended to ascribe to it." This is a reasonable

corrective to a simple-minded view of the monarchs as working according to detailed master plan that they meticulously executed. But Haliczer's corrective only describes the nature of politics in general. The lack of a master plan does not exclude the possibility that Ferdinand and Isabella had a long-range purpose: to subject the realm to a strong Crown and create a more centralized and streamlined government, served by new ideological and political tools (such as a Catholic crusade and an Inquisition). Whether the monarchs had planned the Expulsion ahead or were drawn into it by circumstance and escalation, in the end they succeeded, here too, in mobilizing the forces of the moment, including political and identitarian emotions, in the service of their vision of the New Spain.

3. Maurice Kriegel, in a series of articles, attributes a long-term plan to expel the Jews—not to the monarchs, but to the inquisitors, whose goal was independent of that of the Crown. See Kriegel, "La liquidation du pluralisme religieux dans l'Espagne des rois catholiques: limites et efficacité de l'approche 'intentionnaliste,'" *Temas Medievales* 4 (1994): 39. See also Kriegel, "The 'Modern' Anti-Semitism of the Inquisition" (Heb.), *Zemanim* 41 (1992): 23–33; and Kriegel, "Entre 'question' des 'Nouveaux-Chrétiens' et expulsion des Juifs: La double modernité des procès d'exclusion dans l'Espagne du XVe siècle," in *Le Nouveau Monde, Mondes Nouveaux*, ed. Serge Grunzinski and Nathan Wachtel (Paris: Éditions de l'École des Hautes Études en Sciences Sociales, 1996), 469–490. Kriegel argues that the Inquisition did not seek to solve a religious problem, or to integrate the Conversos, but rather to block their social advance and to eliminate the Jewish presence in Spain; and that it succeeded in imposing its objectives on the state. Kriegel sees here an early version of "modern anti-Semitism," an anti-Jewish policy that in both cases follows the Jews' political semiemancipation and is aimed not against the Jews' religion but against their very social presence. Kriegel makes an important point about the analogy between postemancipatory attitudes in early modern Spain and in modern Western Europe (see chap. 20), but I think his thesis fits the "purity of blood" policies better than the expulsion of the Jews or the action of the Inquisition. For further views and assessments of the Expulsion, see Haim Beinart, *The Expulsion of the Jews from Spain* (Oxford and Portland, OR: Littman Library of Jewish Civilization, 2002); Edward Peters, "Jewish History and Gentile Memory: The Expulsion of 1492," *Jewish History* 9 (spring 1995): 9–34; Henry Kamen, "The Mediterranean and the Expulsion of the Spanish Jews in 1492," *Past and Present* 119 (1988): 30–55; Joseph Pérez, *Isabelle et Ferdinand, rois catholiques de l'Espagne* (Paris: Fayard, 1988), 354–365; Pérez, *Historia de una tragedia: La expulsión de los judíos de España* (Barcelona: Crítica, 1993); Norman Roth, *Conversos, Inquisition, and the Expulsion of the Jews from Spain* (Madison: University of Wisconsin Press, 2002); Luis Suárez Fernández, *La expulsión de los judíos de España* (Madrid: Editorial MAPFRE, 1991); Yom Tov Assis and Yosef Kaplan, eds., *Jews and Conversos at the Time of the Expulsion* (Heb.; Jerusalem: Shazar Center, 1999); Lazar and Haliczer, *The Jews of Spain and the Expulsion of 1492*; Angel Alcalá, ed., *Judíos, sefarditas, conversos: La expulsión de 1492 y sus consecuencias* (Valladolid: Ambito, 1995); and Erna Paris, *The End of Days: A Story of Tolerance, Tyranny and the Expulsion of the Jews from Spain* (Amherst, NY: Prometheus Books, 1995).

4. Like some scholars, I tend to give credence to the to Edict of Expulsion's claim that its goal was to remove the Jews from helping the Conversos to Judaize. Kamen and others see this as a religious issue only; Kriegel believes the goal was to abolish the old Spain of *convivencia* and thus was social and exclusionary (see previous note). I view the two

as partial aspects of a more fundamental motive I call identitarian: to create, or impose, a "unified" identity—social, religious, ideological, and eventually ethnic—on the newly becoming Spanish state. The concept of an identitarian drive (seeking a unitary identity) also fits better the long-term developments of which the Jewish expulsion was one chapter (the others were the establishment of the Inquisition, the conversion of the Muslims, the blood purity policy, and the expulsion of the Moriscos).

5. Normally it was not (see end of the previous chapter); but this was a thundering exception, justified by the religious blasphemy involved in the alleged crime.

6. The personal effects taken by one Jewish exile might illustrate an ordinary load. This man, Tomás Mendes, hired a cart driver for 1,800 maravedis to carry his family to the Portuguese border. At night the driver robbed him and took all his belongings. The demoralized Jew returned to Spain, converted, and sued the robber for the contents of his cargo: six new copper plates, a double bed, a large bag full of new shirts (his own, his wife's, and his children's), three overcoats, two sheets made of grayish cloth, "and various other things." See Haim Beinart, *The Expulsion of the Jews from Spain* (Oxford and Portland, OR: Littman Library of Jewish Civilization, 2002), 246.

7. This toll included: forced conversions, brutal expulsions (of the Jews in 1492, and of the Moriscos in 1609); centuries of intermittent inquisitorial persecution in Spain and its colonies; and the "statutes of the purity of blood," the first racial laws in Europe, applied to former Jews, Muslims, blacks, Amero-Indians, and Asians. Indirectly, the toll extended to the civil violence and civil wars that tore Spain in later centuries, belying the notion that uniformity imposed by force can create a unified nation. Even today, the unresolved problem of the Basque, Catalan, and other "inner minorities" who resent the unified Spanish state can be seen as a fruit of the same historical mistake that confounded unity with imposed uniformity.

8. On Seneor as "court Jew" and communal leader, see Eleazar Gewirth, "Abraham Seneor, Social Tensions and the Court-Jew," *Michael* 11 (1989): 169–229.

9. C. Carrete Parrondo et al., eds., *Fontes iudaeorum regni castellae* (Salamanca: Universidad Pontificia de Salamanca, 1987), 4:24.

10. C. Carrete Parrondo, *El judaísmo español y la Inquisición* (Madrid: Editorial MAPFRE, 1992), 29–30.

11. For a noted Hispanist's assessment of the expulsion made during the time of another catastrophe (in 1941), see Marcel Bataillon, "Peregrinations espagnoles du juif errant," *Bulletin hispanique* 43 (1941): 116.

12. See, among others, María del Pilar Rábade Obradó, "Los judeoconversos en la corte y en la época de los reyes católicos" (PhD diss., Universidad Complutensa, Madrid, 1990).

13. The protection was offered in royal ordinances (November 1492, and then again in 1493 and 1494) that also set the conditions for return. Beinart, *The Expulsion of the Jews from Spain*, chap. 7.

14. Ibid., appendix to chap. 7, gives a list of Jews who succeeded in doing this between 1492 and 1498.

CHAPTER 11. TRAP IN PORTUGAL

1. Rabbi Abraham Zacuto, the Portuguese royal mathematician, states, in *The Book of Lineage or Sefer Yohassin*, trans. and ed. Israel Shamir (Tel Aviv: Zacuto Foundation,

2005), that "the main body of Castile entered Portugal." This is a major point for understanding the magnitude of later events.

2. Fifteenth-century sources give higher figures, in about the same order of magnitude. Bernáldez gives 93,000 estimated from official data in entry-posts between Spain and northern Portugal. Abraham Zacuto, the mathematician, gives 120,000. Among modern scholars, Roth estimates 100,000; Livermore 60,000; Azevedo 120,000; and Baer 100,000–120,000. Some Spanish writers give differing numbers for the overall Jewish population in Spain. Dominguez Ortiz estimates their number as 200,000–250,000, Suárez Fernández, checking tax records, revised an earlier estimate of 372,000 down to 100,000. For a more detailed review, with references, see Gitlitz, *Secrecy and Deceit*, 74.

Although these estimates are quite tricky, I shall err perhaps no more than others by offering the following distribution:

Jews in Spain before the expulsion—160,000;
Remaining and converted Jews—40,000;
Went into exile—120,000;
Crossed into Portugal—80,000.

3. Assuming 40,000 original Portuguese Jews plus 80,000 newcomers.

4. Claude B. Stuczynski, "Between the Implicit and the Explicit" (Heb.), in *Sifriot veOsfei Sefarim: The 24th Conference on History* (Jerusalem: Shazar Center, 2006), 161–162. The paper discusses sources about Jews at the Marranos' disposal.

5. See Elaine Sanceau, *Good Hope: The Voyage of Vasco da Gama* (Lisbon: Academia Internacional da Cultura Portuguesa, 1967), 164–167.

6. Thus for Azevedo, Baer, and Kayserling there were about 190,000 New Christians in a population of one million. A lower estimate—but still an impressive figure (120,000)—results from using the figure of 80,000 refugees entering Portugal from Spain, plus about 40,000 local Jews, minus a small number of departures from Portugal (including exiles who converted in Portugal and returned to Spain to claim their property there).

7. See Yosef Haim Yerushalmi, *The Lisbon Massacre of 1506 and the Royal Image in the Shebet Yehuda* (Cincinnati: Hebrew Union College, 1976), on which this section is based.

8. H. V. Livermore, in *A New History of Portugal* (Cambridge: Cambridge University Press, 1966).

9. A rare parallel concerning Spanish Conversos is Caro Baroja's discussing them as part of the history of the "Jews" in Spain (see appendix). But this is rather an exception.

10. Only once is he is called "a benevolent king" (מלך חסיד)—by Ibn Verga, author of *Shebet Yehuda*. Yerushalmi (*The Lisbon Massacre*, 2) finds it equally curious that Ibn Verga passes over in silence the forced conversions of 1497 in which he himself had accepted baptism. (Later he returned to Judaism abroad.)

11. The issue is summarized in Asaf, "The *Anussim* in the Responsa Literature" (Heb.), *Zion* 5 (1933): 19–60. More material is in B. Netanyahu, *The Marranos of Spain*, 3d ed. (Ithaca, NY: Cornell University Press, 1999). See also Moisés Orfali Levi, *Los Conversos españoles en la literatura rabínica* (Salamanca: Universidad Pontificia de Salamanca and Universidad de Granada, Federación Sefardí de España, 1982).

12. Netanyahu, *The Marranos of Spain*, 4, for example; António José Saraiva, *The Marrano Factory: The Portuguese Inquisition and Its New Christians*, trans., revised, and augmented by H. P Solomon and I.S.D Sasson (Leiden: Brill, 2001).

13. I. S. Révah "Les Marranes," *Revue des études Juives* 118 (1959–1960): 29–77.

14. By then India was a British colony, and the Suez Canal, which the British wanted to secure, had been dug in the Egyptian desert.

15. The *Encyclopedia Hebraica*, in an edifying tone and on scant evidence, states that behind the outer face of the worldly courtier there hid "a pious Jew observing all the commandments hard and light, mortifying himself six days and nights weekly, a [genuine] Jewish person feeling chosen by Providence to announce the approaching redemption to his oppressed and coerced people." "David HaReubeni," in *Encyclopedia Hebraica* (Tel Aviv: Massada, 1976), vol. 12. The body of the article, by the historian Shmuel Ettinger, does not warrant this pious nationalist conclusion.

16. I am not suggesting that Turks had actually sent Reubeni; more likely, he acted on his own initiative, counting on Istanbul to make a deal later. The Ottoman Empire controlled enough deserts in which to receive the shipment (pretending it was "King Yosef's" territory).

17. If the same question were to be asked in Lisbon, Reubeni would answer that his desire to conquer the Holy Land by force made him a natural enemy of the sultan. The breadth of Reubeni's ambition, and the more fantastic elements of his story, paradoxically made him sound more credible.

CHAPTER 12. PORTUGUESE INQUISITION, PURE BLOOD, AND THE "NATION"

1. The story is told in great detail in Alexander Herculano's work, now a classic: *History of the Origin and Establishment of the Inquisition in Portugal*, trans. J. C. Branner (New York: Ktav, 1972). For later works on Portuguese Marranos, see Meyer Kayserling, *História dos judeus em Portugal*, trans. Anita Novinsky (São Paulo: Livraria Pioneira, 1971); and Salo Baron, *A Social and Religious History of the Jews*, 2d ed., rev. and enlarged (Philadelphia: Jewish Publication Society of America, 1952–1983), vol. 10, chap. 14. See also A. J. Saraiva, *Inquisição e Cristãos Novos* (Porto: Editorial Inova, 1969).

2. Julio Caro Baroja, *Los Judíos en la España moderna y contemporánea* (Madrid: ISTMO, 1978), 2:50, quoting a memo of the time.

3. Though numbers remain a tricky business, let us note that an anti-Converso economist of the seventeenth century, Murcia de la Llana, claimed that 70,000 Conversos crossed from Portugal into Spain, of which 40,000 were living in Madrid alone, and none did manual work; they all dealt in money in one way or another. This hostile picture, with its inflated numbers, nevertheless indicates the visibility and the strong impact the Portuguese Marrano reimmigration had on Spanish life, especially during the government of the Conde-Duque de Olivares. (This source is mentioned in Caro Baroja, *Los Judíos en la España moderna y contemporánea*, 2:48, and J. Lúcio de Azevedo, *História dos christãos novos portugueses* (Lisbon: Livraria Clássica Editora A. M. Teixeira, 1975), 462–463.

4. Their self-governed communities in Spain, sanctioned by the civil government (see the preface).

5. In another deal, the New Christian lobby offered Madrid (Spain was then ruling Portugal) a package of 800,000 cruzados—600,000 for halting the Inquisition's right to confiscate the Judaizers' property and permitting them to emigrate, and another 200,000 for the right to trade with Portugal's colonies. And a later deal liberalized the rules of emigration, enabling Judaizers and non-Judaizers alike to turn their Nation into a world-trading Dispersion (see chap. 17).

6. Its better-known proponent is A. J. Saraiva, *Inquisição e Cristãos Novos* (Porto: Editorial Inova, 1969).

7. On the Goa Inquisition's treatment of New Christians, see, among others, Alisa Meyuhas Ginio, "The Inquisition and the New Christians: The Case of the Portuguese Inquisition of Goa," *Medieval History Journal* 2, no. 1 (1999): 1–18.

8. C. R. Boxer, *The Portuguese Seaborne Empire* (New York: A. A. Knopf, 1969), 267–268.

9. For example, Domingo Hernandes, a politically involved Converso and probably indifferent to religion, who hoped to make a career in court, and was slain together with the king in Morocco. He was the uncle of Ruy Díaz Nieto, the wanderer—a kind of Converso picaro—who is the protagonist in Eva Alexandra Uchmany's study of the Nieto family: *La vida entre el judaísmo y el cristianismo en la Nueva España, 1580-1606* (Mexico City: Fondo de Cultura Económica, 1992). See more details in chap. 18.

10. Eliyahu (Elias) Lipiner, "Der Shuster fun Trancasa un der Shneider fun Setubal" [The Cobbler from Trancasa and the Tailor from Setubal], in *Tsvishn maranentum un shmad* [Between Marranism and Apostasy] (Yiddish; Tel Aviv: Verlag Y. L. Peretz, 1973).

11. As late as the twentieth century, important intellectuals such as the poet (of Converso origin) Fernando Pessoa still indulged in its mysteries. See "Portugal and the Fifth Empire," in *The Selected Prose of Fernando Pessoa*, ed. and trans. Richard Zenith (New York: Grove Press, 2001), sec. 5–8.

12. A similar pattern is known from Spain. For example, the enigmatic *beato* or seer known as Fray Melchior, sketched by Marcel Bataillon in *Erasme et Espagne* (Geneva: Droz, 1991), 62–70. Melchior was a heterodox New Christian seer who painted the picture of an approaching apocalypse in strong Jewish colors, yet his goal was to establish a new Christian realm rather than to reinstate the old Jewish one. The same seems to apply to Bandara.

13. The myth has been spread by the former Salazar regime in its attempt to remain the last colonial power in the world. See Boxer, *The Portuguese Seaborne Empire*.

14. The following is based on Albert Sicroff's classic study, *Les controverses des statuts de "pureté de sang" en Espagne du XVe au XVIIe siècle* (Paris: Didier, 1960).

15. Ibid., 138n184. For a more lenient view of the king's action, see Henry Kamen, *Philip of Spain* (New Haven, CT: Yale University Press, 1997), 83–84.

16. Sicroff, *Les controversess des statuts de "pureté de sang" en Espagne du XVe au XVIIe siècle*, 262n, quoting Henry Charles Lea, *A History of the Inquisition of Spain* (New York: Macmillan, 1906–1908). On the purity of blood, see, in addition to Sicroff, Pierre Chaunu, "L'Espagne du refus: Les statuts de pureté de sang," in *L'Espagne de Charles Quint* (Paris: Société d'édition d'enseignement supérieur, 1973), 2:469–525; Henry Méchoulan, *Le sang de l'autre ou l'honneur de Dieu: Indiens, juifs, morisques dans l'Espagne du siècle d'or* (Paris: Fayard, 1979); Charles Amiel, "La 'pureté de sang' en Espagne," *Annales du C.E.S.E.R.E.* 6 (1983): 27–45; John Edwards, "Race and Religion in 15th- and 16th-Century Spain: The 'Purity of Blood' Laws Revisited," in *10th World Congress of Jewish Studies, 1989* (Jerusalem: Avraham Harman Institute of Contemporary Jewry, Hebrew University of Jerusalem; and World Union of Jewish Studies, 1993), 2:159–166; and Juan Ignacio Gutiérrez Nieto, "El problema de la limpieza de sangre en la España de San Juan de la Cruz," in *Simposio sobre San Juan de la Cruz: Ponencias*, ed. María del Carmen Bobes Naves et al. (Avila: Mijan, 1986), 33–60.

17. Needless to say, this characterized the phenomenology of the group, not every single individual.

CHAPTER 13. A JUDAIZING MARRANO RELIGION

1. Neither of these sources is free of bias. The Inquisition was prone to stereotyped interpretations and to framing the testimonies in its own clichés; and the rabbinical responsa were often written with a pressing practical agenda of the day in mind. But when read with critical attention, these sources can supply precious information. The founding work on the religion of the Judaizers is Cecil Roth, "The Religion of the Marranos," *Jewish Quarterly Review* 22 (1931–1932): 1–33, abridged in the chapter that bears the same title in Cecil Roth, *A History of the Marranos* (Philadelphia: Jewish Publication Society of America, 1932). The richest survey of Judaizing Marrano customs to date is David M. Gitlitz, *Secrecy and Deceit: The Religion of the Crypto-Jews* (Philadelphia and Jerusalem: Jewish Publication Society, 1996). This volume thematically organizes a huge number of Marrano customs, prayers, expressions of belief, and the like, drawn from the scholarly literature that is based on inquisitorial and other records (including twentieth-century Belmonte and other places in Portugal—see the epilogue). Other works—by Révah, Baer, Beinart, Amilcar Paulo, and (for the Americas) Liebman, Marcus, and Wachtel—add much to the picture. A particularly interesting compilation of prayers comes from the inquisitorial file of Brittes Henriquez (Lisbon, 1674), published as an appendix to Samuel Schwarz, *Os Christaõs-Novos em Portugal no Século XX* (Lisbon: Empresa portuguesa de livros, 1925).

2. Schwarz, *Os Christaõs-Novos em Portugal no Século XX*. See also Amilcar Paulo, *Os Judeus secretos em Portugal* (Porto: Editorial Labirinto, 1985); and a series of studies published by the magazine *HaLapid* (the organ of the re-Judaizing Marranos in Portugal) under the title "Tradições Crypto-Judaicas" in 1928, 1929, 1932, 1934, and 1937. Although some of these rites and texts are clearly ancient, others must have evolved in later centuries. See also J. M. Pedrosa, "La bendición del día y Dios delante y yo detrás: Correspondencias cristianas y judías de dos oraciones hispanoportuguesas," *Romanistisches Jahrbuch* 45 (1994): 262–270.

3. Unlike Révah, Gitlitz recognizes that for the majority of Judaizers who rapidly have lost familiarity with Jewish belief and observance, "Judaism ceased to be an autonomous, self-referential system. Instead, Christianity became their common reference point, the template against which the crypto Jewish beliefs and practices were measured." Gitlitz, *Secrecy and Deceit*, 99. This explicit recognition of duality is not, however, expressed in the chapters Gitlitz devotes to observance, the bulk of his book. His emphasis remains on "secret Judaism" as the leading category.

4. C. Carrete Parrondo et al., eds., *Fontes iudaeorum regni castellae*, vol. 2, *El Tribunal de la Inquisición en el Obispado de Soria (1486–1502)* (Salamanca: Universidad Pontificia de Salamanca, 1985), 132. This is an original but mild form of irony; harsher mockery was even more common.

5. Gitlitz basically concurs with this. In chap. 6 he describes a "common core" of crypto-Jewish belief and spells it out in several "dogmas": (1) God is One; (2) the Messiah has not come, but is coming; (3) the Law of Moses is a condition for individual salvation; (4) [some] observance is required in addition to belief; and (5) Judaism is the preferred religion (Gitlitz, *Secrecy and Deceit*, 100–101).

6. This version of the text and ritual, reported in Nahum Slouschz, *Ha'Anusim BePortugal* (Heb.; Tel Aviv: Devir, 1932), differs from the version given in Paulo, *Os Judeus secretos em Portugal*, 145, which Gitlitz translates on page 285 of *Secrecy and Deceit*. I find the Slouschz version the more moving and telling. (The ritual and text were recorded in several versions both in Portugal and in America.)

7. Gitlitz, *Secrecy and Deceit*, 357.

8. Ibid., 359–360. From the testimony of a witness in the trial of an Aragonese Marrano, referring to events in 1469.

9. Ibid., 367.

10. *In exitu Israel de Egypto* (Ps. 114); *Super flumina babylonia* (Ps. 137); and *De profundis clamavi* (Ps. 130).

11. Of course, in Catholicism, the sacrificial lamb is Christ, and one is presumed to be eating Christ's flesh in the Eucharist. The Passover sacrifice is a dense symbolic web linking and opposing the two religions, and the Marranos lived, as it were, in its midst.

12. Gitlitz, *Secrecy and Deceit*, 387. See especially Luis Carvajal's description of his father's teaching.

13. Yosef Hayim Yerushalmi, "The Re-Education of Marranos in the Seventeenth Century" (Third Annual Rabbi Louis Feinberg Memorial Lecture in Judaic Studies, University of Cincinnati, March 26, 1980).

14. The reason is that the Christian Bible admits books, called "apocrypha," that the rabbis had rejected from the Jewish canon.

15. Many other Jewish holidays were lost to the Marranos: Pentecost was forgotten, Rosh Hashanah nearly so, and Sukkoth, though still remembered, was rarely observed. As for Hanukkah, the "holiday of candles," it waned away or was replaced by Natal on December 25—a derivative of Christmas.

16. Gitlitz, *Secrecy and Deceit*, 460.

17. Ibid., 454.

CHAPTER 14. NEW CHRISTIANS AT THE FOREFRONT OF SPANISH CULTURE

1. The Converso influences on this-worldliness, religious skepticism, and the emerging forms of private life, were hidden and indirect; they reverberate in multiple records of the Inquisition and between the lines of literary works. I discuss them separately in my manuscript "The Mystic and the Wanderer." In the present chapter I concentrate on the varieties of religious interiority and spirituality.

2. I use this shorthand term to denote the "high" mystical school around Teresa of Avila, from Osuna and Juan of Avila to Juan de La Cruz.

3. I use the term in both the broad and the narrow senses. The narrow sense is limited to works such as *Lazarillo de Tormes*, *Guzmán*, and so on, which are told in the first person by a lowly and "impurely" born picaro; the broader sense includes works that express a picaresque world and mood, but without conforming formally to the genre (such as Rojas's *Celestina* and Cervantes's *Don Quijote*).

4. Angel Alcalá, "El mundo Converso en la literatura y la mística del Siglo de Oro," *Manuscrits: Revista d'Historia moderna* 10 (January 1992): 91–118. Alcalá describes himself as a moderate follower of Castro, who, together with Marcel Bataillon in France, was the first to recognize the important part played by Conversos in Spanish culture.

5. Domínguez Ortiz, too, stresses the "abnormally high" number of Converso scholars and literary persons; see Domínguez Ortiz, *Los judeoconversos en España y América* (Madrid: ISTMO, 1971), 167; and Domínguez Ortiz, "Los judeoconversos en la vida española del Renacimiento," in *Estudios de historia económica y social de España* (Granada: Universidad de Granada, 1987), 163–178. And Márquez Villanueva writes, "The ever-increasing list of Conversos [in culture] reads like an honor-roll of the Spanish classics. . . . [I]t would be impossible to imagine what Golden Age literature would be without their creative activity" (F. Márquez Villanueva, "Hispano-Jewish Cultural Interactions: A Conceptual Framework," in *Encuentros and Desencuentros: Spanish-Jewish Interaction throughout History*, ed. C. Carrete Parrondo et al. [Tel-Aviv: Tel Aviv University Projects, 2000], 17). At the same time he claims, like Alcalá, that they underwent "complete assimilation," which is a conceptually problematic affirmation (see notes 9–10). See F. Márquez Villanueva, "Hablando de conversos con Antonio Domínguez Ortiz," in *La clase social de los conversos en Castilla en la edad moderna*, by A. Domínguez Ortiz (Granada: Universidad de Granada, Servicios de Publicaciones, 1991), 18.

6. Alcalá, "El mundo Converso en la literatura y la mística del Siglo de Oro," 97.

7. Ibid., 96.

8. Including A. Domínguez Ortiz and F. Márquez Villanueva, partly following A. Castro (see appendix).These scholars and their disciples often waver between their attempt to appropriate the Conversos as "perfect Spaniards" into a full-fledged national identity, and their recognition of the Converso intellectuals' dissent and inner distance from the Spanish world they had joined.

9. This notion is incongruent with the Conversos' exclusion, disquiet, fragile social situation, their life under constant suspicion, and the *refusal* of the ruling society to admit their full Hispano-Christian legitimacy—all facts that the same scholars accept and even stress.

10. Márquez Villanueva (in C. Carrete Parrondo et al., eds., *Encuentros and Desencuentros: Spanish-Jewish Interaction throughout History* [Tel-Aviv: Tel Aviv University Projects, 2000], 17) also made a dual statement about the Conversos: "little of what [they] did could be considered specifically Jewish," and *"most of them proudly considered themselves nothing but Spaniards and orthodox Catholics"* (my emphasis). Although the first statement is essentially true, the second does not follow. How can dissenting, alienated intellectuals be "proudly . . . nothing but Spaniards"? And how can heterodox Christian reformers be "nothing but . . . *orthodox Catholics*"? The intellectuals who fascinate Márquez Villanueva (and Domínguez Ortiz, and Alcalá, and me too) were *uncommon* Christians and *more* than simply Spaniards. The legitimacy of their "full Spanishness" was put into question by the veteran owners of that title, equipped with racial laws and a state police, while they themselves questioned the religious purity and worth of the old owners and their establishment. As such they did not belong to the Spanish Self—certainly not in its own time—but were the Spanish Other Within.

11. Another way in which a "New" Christian was construed as a better Christian was taken by those who became Catholic zealots and inquisitors. Castro attributes to them a "theocratic" Jewish mentality that they invested in the unholy Spanish link of Church and State. In my reading, the excessive Catholic zeal and self-assertion of these people does not betray a Jewish trait but the specifically Converso syndrome of "identity-disquiet" (which, in their case, drove them to overcome the Jewish element in themselves by persecuting it in others). See also chap. 5.

12. For problems of doctrine, see the sections on Guadalupe and the Cancioneros in chap. 6, and the sections on the Alumbrados (Alcaraz) and Valdés in the next chapter.

CHAPTER 15. A CHRISTIAN RELIGION OF THE INTERIOR

1. This chapter is drawn from a far more detailed treatment of the same topic and figures in my book in progress, "The Mystic and the Wanderer: Conversos in Spain's Golden Age Culture."

2. Although Bataillon is in doubt, I shall assume these two Franciscas to be different persons. Sor Francisca of Salamanca is known from the reports about the *beato* Melchior, which describe her as *paupercula femina sed spiritu dei plena* ("a very poor woman but full of God's spirit"). See Bataillon, *Erasme et l'Espagne* (Paris: E. Droz, 1937; Geneva: Droz, 1991), 71. The last thing one could call the pampered and comfort-loving Francisca Hernández was *paupercula*.

3. On the Alumbrados see, in addition to Bataillon, Antonio Márquez, *Los alumbrados: Orígenes y filosofía (1525-1559)* (Madrid: Taurus, 1980). See also Angela Selke, "El illuminismo de los conversos y la Inquisición: Cristianismo interior de los Alumbrados: Resentimiento y sublimación," in *La Inquisición española: Nueva visión, nuevos horizontes,* ed. Joaquín Pérez Villanueva (Madrid: Siglo Veintiuno de España, 1980), 617–636.

4. I realize that my reading adds a conceptual or theological dimension to the Alumbrados' teaching that they may not have clearly intended; but there seems to be no other way of making sense of their doctrine, except as mere slogans. Mystical materials neither require nor warrant a mystical approach.

5. Though one wonders whether and how the Alumbrados could have had access to his ideas; for Maimonides wrote in Arabic and was translated into Hebrew. (Perhaps there was an oral source in their families, or the Alumbrados reached these views independently?)

6. Leszek Kolakowski, *Chrétiens sans église: La conscience religieuse et le lien confessionnel au XVIIe siècle* (Paris: Gallimard, 1969).

7. José C. Nieto, *Juan de Valdés y los orígenes de la reforma en España e Italia* (Mexico City: Fondo de Cultura Económica, 1979), 169.

8. As pointed out by Christine Wagner in her introduction to the French translation of the *Dialogue, Le dialogue sur la doctrine chretienne de Juan de Valdés: 1529,* trans. Christine Wagner (Paris: Presses Universitaires de France, 1995), 47.

9. The other is the scholastic philosopher Francisco Suárez.

10. Skepticism is too strong (and too definite) a position to attribute to Vives; his stance is perhaps better described as combining a lack of dogmatism, an openness to questions, and an abhorrence of pedantry. Noreña, who sees him as a relativist in matters of value and taste, links his attitude directly to his Judeo-Christian background— more precisely, to his being a "Jewish exile educated in Paris, the Low Countries, and Oxford." See C. G. Noreña, preface to *The Passions of the Soul: The Third Book of De Anima et Vita,* by J. L. Vives, trans. C. G. Noreña (Lewiston, NY: E. Mellen Press, 1990), 7; and also C. G. Noreña, *Juan Luis Vives and the Emotions* (Carbondale: Southern Illinois University Press, 1989). But Vives was no longer a Jew.

11. Angela Selke, *El Santo Oficio de la Inquisición: Proceso de Fr. Francisco Ortiz, 1529–1532* (Madrid: Ediciones Guadarrama, 1968), 56.

12. Bataillon, *Erasme et l'Espagne,* 373.

13. Further figures and a more detailed picture will be given in my "The Mystic and the Wanderer."

14. Her case is known from extensive records of the Inquisition published by Melagres Marin and discussed by Henry Charles Lea in *Chapters from the Religious History of Spain Connected with the Inquisition* (New York: Burt Franklin, 1967), 251–257; and by Bataillon, *Erasme et l'Espagne*, 192–193, 226–228, 509–513. The following portrait is based on a reinterpretation of these materials

15. The major figures of this trend, beside Teresa, were her mentors Francisco Osuna and especially Juan de Avila, and her followers and colleagues, Jerónimo Gracián and Juan de La Cruz. Osuna is accepted by most historians as Converso; so is Gracián; about Teresa and Juan d'Avila (who practically created a "Converso university" in Baeza) there is no possible doubt; the evidence about Juan de La Cruz is significant but not direct; his Converso background is mostly inferred from characteristics of his father's family and from his close association with Baeza University.

16. See my *Spinoza and Other Heretics* (Princeton, N.J.: Princeton University Press 1989), vol. 1, *The Marrano of Reason*. Actually, Locke in Holland sought and read Spinoza's *Theologico-Political Treatise* prior to writing his first *Letter on Toleration*.

17. He shouldn't be confused with a great uncle by that name mentioned in the inquisitorial records as a witness who had testified against Juan Sánchez.

18. On her encounters with uncle Pedro and Osuna's writings, see Teresa of Avila, *The Book of My Life*, trans. M. Starr (Boston: New Seeds Books, 2007), chaps. 3, 4.

19. Teresa of Avila, *The Interior Castle*, trans. Kieran Kavanaugh and Otilio Rodríguez (New York: Paulist Press, 1979), Fourth Dwelling Places, chap. 3.

20. See Teresa of Avila, *The Book of My Life*, chap. 11; for detailed exposition, see chaps. 11–21.

21. A fuller account will appear in the chapter on Teresa in my "The Mystic and the Wanderer," which also discusses Teresa's celebrated disciple and younger colleague San Juan de La Cruz (John of the Cross).

22. An extraordinary portrait of Teresa, blending history, philosophy, and psychoanalysis with a novelist's personal vision, is offered by Julia Kristeva in her recent *Thérèse mon amour* (Paris: Fayard, 2008).

23. On Luis de León, see Colin P. Thompson, *The Strife of Tongues: Fray Luis de León and the Golden Age of Spain* (New York: Cambridge University Press, 1988); and José Jiménez Lozano, *Fray Luis de León* (Barcelona: Ediciones Omega, 2000).

24. Luis de León, *The Unknown Light*, trans. Willis Barnstone (New York: SUNY Press, 1979), 42. I did not reprint the Barnstone translation but chose to render the poems more literally in English.

25. Ibid., 52.

26. Ibid., 46.

27. Manuel Fernández Alvarez, *El proceso de fray Luis de León*, Studia Zamorensia 1 (Salamanca: Universidad de Salamanca, 1980).

CHAPTER 16. PICARESQUE ANTIHEROES

1. This chapter is drawn from a broader and much more detailed treatment of the same subjects in my book in progress, "The Mystic and the Wanderer: Conversos in Spain's Golden Age Culture."

2. This is true of the original Spanish form of the picaresque novel; later, in France and England, these rules were not always observed.

3. Norman Roth rejects the collective attribution of a "Converso mentality" to writers and other figures, and demands specific research on each case. Norman Roth, *Conversos, Inquisition, and the Expulsion of the Jews from Spain* (Madison: University of Wisconsin Press, 1995), 158. Although I share this caution about essentialism, I find that attention to concrete cases does suggest that there have been distinct Converso uses of language and concerns with certain thematic issues close to their experience, which can be detected not only in specific works, but also in the picaresque genre as such.

4. Maurice Molho, similarly, speaks of "un-honor" and "anti-honor" as distinct categories. Un-honor is the lack of honor within the existing system; anti-honor is an attempt to uproot the system itself. Maurice Molho, introduction to *Romans picaresques espagnols*, trans. M. Molho and J. F. Reille (Paris: Gallimard, 1968).

5. I mean not only in *Dogs' Colloquy*, but even more in his classic *Don Quijote*, which is not a picaresque work but is inspired by the genre.

6. On some of these non-Spanish varieties consult Robert Alter's by now classic study, *Rogue's Progress* (Harvard University Press, 1965).

7. See chap. 14. This resembles the preponderance of Converso authors among the fifteenth-century satirical *cancioneros*, which preceded and, in a way, prepared the picaresque mode of speech. On the *cancioneros*, see Yirmiyahu Yovel, "Converso Dualities in the First Generation: The *Cancioneros*," *Jewish Social Studies* 4, no. 3 (1998): 1–28; and also Cristina Arbós Ayuso, "Los cancioneros castellanos del siglo XV como fuente para la historia de los judíos españoles," in *Jews and Conversos: Studies in Society and the Inquisition, Proceedings of the 8th World Congress of Jewish Studies*, ed. Yosef Kaplan (Jerusalem: Magnes, 1985), 74–82.

8. By "official" I mean that it fits the exact parameters of the genre, especially the fictional autobiography, rather than being written as a play (like *La Celestina*) or a third-person tale (like *Don Quijote*).

9. Américo Castro, *Hacia Cervantes* (Madrid: Taurus, 1967), 21, 140, and passim. Quoted in F. Márquez Villanueva, *Espirtualidad y literatura en el siglo XVI* (Madrid: Alfaguara, 1968), 104–105.

10. Márquez Villanueva, *Espirtualidad y literatura*, 104–110.

11. Márquez Villanueva says "indifference or antipathy" (ibid., 105), but these terms are not strong enough. (He himself speaks of the "acidity" of the anticlerical feelings in this work.)

12. I say "Lazarillo's preface" when actually it is the author speaking through Lazarillo in the preface. The distinction is significant (1) because part of irony's role is to make Lazarillo say "naively" something the author wants to convey through his (true or feigned) naiveté; and (2) because, more deeply, the two of them differ in that the picaresque author stands wholly against the culture of *honra*, whereas his picaro hero is partly a (negative) member of it. But to avoid repetition, I shall have to rely on the reader bearing this in mind while I continue to say "Lazarillo" even where I mean "Lazarillo's voice as used by the author."

13. Latin *propter iustitia*.

14. Another analysis of the equivocation, perhaps more correct from the standpoint of biblical scholarship, is to see that the early Christians were persecuted by the estab-

lished authorities (kingdom), yet were promised the kingdom of heaven. Later, when Christianity itself became the power structure, it had to twist the original meaning to suit its new position—as did also the Spaniards and the Inquisition. Thus, the Converso reading happens to be historically more accurate, though this is not the reason they chose it. From their standpoint, they were twisting the "true" meaning—the one established by the extant authorities and convention.

15. Molho, introduction to *Romans picaresques espagnols*.

16. Earlier works on satire and equivocation in that period include: Kenneth Scholberg, *Sátira e invectiva en la España medieval* (Madrid: Gredos, 1971); and Sanford Shephard, *Lost Lexicon: Secret Meanings in the Vocabulary of Spanish Literature during the Inquisition* (Miami: Universal, 1982).

17. For a balanced review of the evidence, see William Byron, *Cervantes, A Biography* (Garden City, NY: Doubleday, 1978), 10–32, and elsewhere in that book. See also Luis Landau, *Cervantes and the Jews* (Heb.; Beer Sheva: Ben Gurion University Press, 2002), chaps. 1–3.

18. The young Cardinal Giulio Aquaviva y Aragon. His luxurious style and almost evident homosexuality are described in Byron, *Cervantes*, 86–87, 231.

19. Luis Landau, afterword to the Hebrew trans. of *Don Quijote* (Tel Aviv: Hakibutz Hameuchad, 1994), 2:424.

20. Miguel de Cervantes Saavedra, *Don Quijote*, trans. Burton Raffel (New York: Norton, 1999). I quote by part and chapter number.

21. Of course, equivocation should not always have an exact parallel for every phrase, or else it will be too obvious, and hence dangerous or boring.

22. *Reconciliation* (to the church) and *relapse* (into heresy) were equally common terms in the Inquisition's glossary. *Relapsos* were those who were burned in person.

23. *Montas:* an ironic invective used to say the opposite of the thought one wishes to express.

24. The whole matter is overshadowed by the verse we have mentioned several times "Blessed be those who are persecuted for justice, for the kingdom of heaven is unto them," which served ironic writers since Rojas to attack the Inquisition. Cervantes is less bold but can rely on the reader's memory of those other works as background for his own allusion.

25. Of course, arresting such a person is an absurdity—which Don Quijote's naive (and Cervantes's equivocal) question throw into sharp relief.

26. *Empreñaste*; Sancho's response later uses this verb in its vulgar sexual sense.

27. As several Spanish prelates used to do, notably Archbishop Silíceo, who instituted the blood purity statutes under Philip II; see "Back to Spain: Purity of Blood, Act II," in chap. 12.

CHAPTER 17. MARRANOS GLOBALIZED: THE NETWORKS, THE "NATION"

1. See Cecil Roth, *A History of the Marranos* (Philadelphia: Jewish Publication Society of America, 1932), 272.

2. This famous family has been the subject of much historical and fictional writing. See Cecil Roth, *The House of Nasi: Doña Gracia* (Philadelphia: Jewish Publications Society, 1947); and Cecil Roth, *The House of Nasi: The Duke of Naxos* (Philadelphia: Jewish

Publications Society, 1948); and Catherine Clément, *La Señora* (Paris: Calmann-Lévy, 1991).

3. Which he compared to "the age of the Fuggers" (the great German bankers) and to the Genoese. Fernand Braudel, *The Mediterranean and the Mediterranean World in the Age of Philip II* (New York: Harper & Row, 1995), 2:823. More recently, a leading historian of the period stated: "Western Sephardic Jewry fulfilled a highly distinctive, and perhaps unique, set of functions throughout the maritime and colonial expansion of Europe from 1492 to the late 18th century" (Jonathan I. Israel, *Diasporas within a Diaspora: Jews, Crypto-Jews, and the World Maritime Empires (1540–1740)* [Leiden: Brill, 2002], 1).

4. The commerce in humans thrived on the need for cheap labor in American mines and plantations; and contemporary Europeans considered black people less human than Native Americans. The Marranos trading in slaves followed the conventions of the time and participated in the conventional brutality. That they missed the similarity between their own "impure blood" and the stigma of nonwhites was due to the immense class difference and to the special prejudice attached to "black." This seems to illustrate that compassion, the capacity to identify others as resembling us in some major respect, is often confined to a specific class or group. It is the problem of liberalism—in order to realize that we resemble others in our very humanity, we often unconsciously require them to be like us in some other way as well. Often, but not always, the opposite is illustrated by the Converso author of *Lazarillo de Tormes*, in the episode of the black baby, discussed in chap. 16 of this book.

5. On the importance of mercantilism in affecting Jewish (and Marrano) life, see Jonathan I. Israel, *European Jewry in the Age of Mercantilism, 1550–1750* (London and Portland, OR: Littman Library of Jewish Civilization, 1998); and Y. H. Yerushalmi, "Between Amsterdam and New Amsterdam—The Place of Curaçao and the Caribbean in Early Modern Jewish History," *American Jewish History* 72 (1982): 175–176. Israel shows that the predominance of this ideology favored a greater toleration of Jewish presence and activity. And Yerushalmi stresses that religious scruples became secondary for those believing that the true wealth of a nation depended on commerce, especially at a time when the economic image of the Jew shifted from the diabolical usurer to a catalyst of international commerce.

6. Hugo Grotius (de Groot), *The Free Sea* (Indianapolis: Liberty Fund, 2004).

7. Miriam Bodian, " 'Men of the Nation': The Shaping of *Converso* Identity in Early Modern Europe," *Past and Present* 143 (1993):48–76.

8. Daniel M. Swetschinski, "Kingship and Commerce: The Foundations of Portuguese Jewish Life in Seventeenth-Century Holland," *Studia Rosenthaliana* 15, no. 1 (March 1981): 52–74.

9. Miriam Bodian describes the "Nation" as maintaining solidarity "across national and religious boundaries" (Bodian, *Hebrews of the Portuguese Nation: Conversos and Community in Early Modern Amsterdam* [Bloomington: Indiana University Press, 1997], 132). See also Eleazar Gewirth, "Elementos étnicos e históricos en las relaciones judeo-conversas en Segovia," in *Jews and Conversos: Studies in Society and the Inquisition (Proceedings of the 8th World Congress of Jewish Studies Held at the Hebrew University of Jerusalem, August 16–21, 1981)*, ed. Y. Kaplan (Jerusalem: Magnes Press, 1985), 83–102. Gewirth's study is based on Segovia before the Expulsion, when Conversos of all sorts lived alongside openly practicing Jews and they all formed a socioethnic "network," and

the Inquisition, for most of the period, did not yet exist. No such situation existed later in Iberia, but years later it recurred in the Dispersion, in the form of the Nation.

10. In commerce, the Marrano world activity eventually bypassed Iberia, although for a while (before the Marrano centers in the Caribbean were set up), Lisbon and Seville provided hubs for important transactions.

11. I borrow the image from the philosopher Richard Bernstein, who used it to describe certain related trends in contemporary thought. See Bernstein, *The New Constellation: The Ethical-Political Horizons of Modernity/Postmodernity* (Cambridge: Polity Press, 1991).

12. See Anita Novinsky, "Juifs et nouveaux chrétiens du Portugal," in *Les Juifs d'Espagne: Histoire d'une diaspora 1492–1992*, ed. Henry Méchoulan (Paris: Liana Levi, 1992), 90.

13. In one of many examples, the Marrano trader de Mora in Livorno (a relative of the poet Antonio Enríquez Gómez) and another Marrano called Guimarães in Paris served as middlemen in the business deals between the Amsterdam merchant Shlomo Amari (alias Jorge Lopes Telles) and the Madrid banker Fernão Monesonos, the survivor of three inquisitorial inquests. See Carsten Wilke, *Jüdisch-Christlich Doppelleben im Barock* (Frankfurt am Main: Peter Lang, 1994), 221.

14. In a message from Gonzalo de Luna, Alcalde in Fuenterrabia, written in San Jean de Luz on November 2, which is quoted in Haim Beinart, ed., *The Marranos in Christian Society and in Jewish Society: Seminar Sources* (Heb., Jerusalem: Hebrew University, Faculty of Humanities, Jewish History Department, 1976), B, no. 29, p. 130.

15. Gabriel Zürn, "Les Séfarades en Allemagne et en Scandinavie," in *Les Juifs d'Espagne*, ed. Méchoulan, 235.

16. The Dispersion has been studied amply by scholars from I. S. Révah to Jonathan Israel and Yosef Kaplan. See Kaplan's collection of studies, *From New Christians to New Jews* (Heb.; Jerusalem: Shazar Center, 1997), translated into English as *An Alternative Path to Modernity: The Sephardi Diaspora in Western Europe* (Leiden and Boston: Brill, 2000); and Kaplan, *Hapzura HaSephardit HaMaaravit* (Heb., Tel Aviv: Ministry of Defense, 1994). See also Méchoulan, ed., *Les juifs d'Espagne*; and Gérard Nahon, *Métropoles et périphéries séfarades d'Occident* (Paris: Cerf, 1993). A much older classic in the field is Meyer Kayserling, *Biblioteca española-portuguesa-judaica*, renewed ed. (New York: Ktav, 1979).

17. For a phenomenological analysis of their mentality and situation see Yirmiyahu Yovel, *Spinoza and Other Heretics* (Princeton, NJ: Princeton University Press, 1989), vol. 1, *The Marrano of Reason*, chap. 2.

18. The *dotar*'s functions and implications are analyzed in Bodian, *Hebrews of the Portuguese Nation*; and in Bodian, "The 'Portuguese' Dowry Societies in Venice and Amsterdam," *Italia* 6 (1978): 55–61. See also I. S. Révah, "Le premier réglement imprimé de la 'Santa Companhia de dotar orfanes e donzelas pobres,'" *Boletim internacional de bibliografia luso-brasileira* 4 (1963): 668, 678.

19. On the identity role of Jewish philanthropy, see Derek Penslar, "Modern Jewish Philanthropy," in *Philanthropy in the World's Traditions*, ed. Warren F. Ilchman, Stanley N. Katz, and Edward L. Queen II (Bloomington: Indiana University Press, 1998), 179–214; and Penslar, "Philanthropy, the 'Social Question', and Jewish Identity in Imperial Germany," *Leo Baeck Institute Yearbook* 38 (1993): 51–73.

20. Mentioned by several scholars, including Yosef Kaplan, "The Travels of Portuguese Jews from Amsterdam to the 'Lands of Idolatry' (1644–1724)," in *Jews and Conversos*, 197–211; and Eva Alexandra Uchmany, *La vida entre el judaísmo y el christianismo*

en la Nueva España 1580–1606 (Mexico City: Archivo General de la Nación, Fondo de Cultura Económica, 1992). Uchmany's protagonists, the Nieto father and son, do just that and meet others who have done the same.

21. On Spinoza's ban, see, among others, Steven Nadler, *Spinoza's Heresy: Immortality and the Jewish Mind* (New York: Oxford University Press, 2002); and Nadler, *Spinoza: A Life* (Cambridge and New York: Cambridge University Press, 1999). For a different analysis of the ban, see Yovel, *Spinoza and Other Heretics*, vol. 1, chaps. 1, 3; the latter chapter also includes my interpretations of the intellectual cases of Juan de Prado and Uriel (Gabriel) da Costa. Prado's background has been studied mainly by I. S. Révah, in *Spinoza et le Dr. Juan de Prado* (Paris: Mouton, 1959). Costa has been variously studied by Carl Gebhardt in *Die Schriften des Uriel da Costa* (Amsterdam: M. Hertzberger, 1922); I. S. Révah in "Du Marranisme au Judaïsme et au deisme: Uriel da Costa et sa famille," in *Annuaire du Collège de France* (Paris: Collège de France, 1969–1970, 1970–1971, 1972–1973); J. P. Osier in *D'Uriel da Costa á Spinoza* (Paris: Berg International, 1983); and José Faur in *In the Shadow of History: Jews and Conversos in the Dawn of Modernity* (Albany: State University of New York Press, 1992).

22. This was the judgment not only of their non-Marrano colleagues, but of most modern historians as well, from Heinrich Graetz to Simon Dubnov and others.

23. Karaites (also new "Sadducees") were those who rejected the postbiblical legal tradition (the "oral law") and accepted only the (often literal) Bible. Such was in essence the case of Uriel da Costa, and also in a certain sense of Spinoza, who rejected both but favored the Bible as the basis for a popular moral religion. A group of later Marrano Karaites was discovered and banned in Amsterdam (Kaplan, *An Alternative Path to Modernity*, chap. 11).

24. For a description of Ouderkerk and how Marrano dualities are embodied in its tombstones—mostly through sculptured scenes from the Bible—see Yovel, *Spinoza and Other Heretics*, 1:54–57.

25. See Robert Bonfil, "Ferrare, un port sûr et paisible pour la diaspora séfarade," in *Les Juifs d'Espagne*, ed. Méchoulan, 295–303; and Renata Segre, "La formazione di una comunità marrana: I portoghesi a Ferrara," in *Storia d'Italia*, ed. Corrado Vivanti (Torino: G. Einaudi, 1996), 11:781–784.

26. Concerning circumcision in Ferrara, see the quotation from a witness in the next section on Venice; according to Segre, circumcising adults was not done frequently, however, because of the danger involved (Segre, "La formazione di una comunità marrana," 11:837).

27. In this view, Bonfil's title—calling Ferrara "a peaceful and safe haven" for the Sephardim, must be meant with irony. The phrase comes from the prologue and ending of *Lazarillo de Tormes*, and also from Samuel Usque, *Consolação às tribulações de Israel* (Lisbon: Fundação Calouste Gulbenkian, 1989).

28. Jean-Pierre Filippini, "L'Oasis' toscane," in *Les Juifs d'Espagne*, ed. Méchoulan, 306–312.

29. Their official name was "the Jewish Levantine Nation," where the appellation *Jewish* (*ebrea*) sounds as though it refers simply to Jews (such as the Levantines and the Ashkenazim), who were practically immune to the Inquisition. Yet the Pisa Marranos were neither Levantine nor old Jews, but western New Jews.

30. Filipini, "L'Oasis' toscane," 309. In 1601, there were only 134 Jews; in 1645, this number was 1,250 (in a city of about 15,000, to which non-Jews were attracted because

of its prosperity). In the second half of the century the number of Jews may have reached 3,000, and was second only to Amsterdam. Yosef Kaplan, *Hapzura HaSephardit HaMaaravit* (Tel-Aviv: Misrad ha-Bitahon, 1994), 40.

31. Eventually, the other Jewish groups came under the rule of the Portuguese *Ma'amad* (governing council)—a rare case in the Marrano Dispersion. (The common denominator was the pride or sense of superiority—another outcome of their lay Iberian culture.)

32. Benjamin Ravid, "Les séfarades à Venise," in *Les Juifs d'Espagne*, ed. Méchoulan, 284–294.

33. Ibid., 289

34. Ibid.

35. It was not free of problems, however, nor of the shadow of a local inquisition. Brian Pullan, *The Jews of Europe and the Inquisition in Venice, 1550–1670* (Oxford: Blackwell, 1983).

36. *Parnas* in Hebrew means "one who nourishes," hence an elder; *Ma'amad* means an elevated standing place.

37. In this way, because the early networks were anchored in Iberia, the peninsula played an important early role as generator of the Dispersion.

38. On the Amsterdam Portuguese community, see Yosef Kaplan, "La Jérusalem du Nord: La Communauté séfarade d'Amsterdam au XVIIe siècle," in *Les Juifs d'Espagne*, ed. Méchoulan, 192–209; Kaplan, "The Portuguese Community of Amsterdam in the 17th Century: Between Tradition and Change," in *Society and Change: Proceedings of the Second International Congress for Research of the Sephardi and Oriental Heritage*, ed. Abraham Haim (Jerusalem: Misgav, 1984); Kaplan, *Hapzura HaSephardit HaMaaravit*, 62–71; and Bodian, *Hebrews of the Portuguese Nation*. See also Henry Méchoulan, *Amsterdam au temps de Spinoza* (Paris: Presses Universitaires de France, 1990).

39. This type of irony, recurrent among exiles, is often tragic: in World War II, the French arrested anti-Nazi German refugees as enemy subjects (some were later captured and executed by the Nazi invaders); and the Roosevelt administration sent Jewish refugees back to Europe and to their deaths on the same pretext, and sequestered Japanese-American *citizens* after Pearl Harbor.

40. This did not prevent them from being often harshly intolerant of dissenters within their communities; the dialectic of being influenced by opposites and opponents was also at work here.

41. Marrano demography is special, in that the numbers almost always appear to be small when compared to the popular masses. This is not only because Marranos were a dissident minority. We should think of a Marrano family in the Dispersion in terms that resemble a business firm or economic enterprise (usually with links abroad) rather than simply as a household comprising a number of individuals. The space a Marrano community can occupy in a city is therefore defined by the economic growth and scope of that city. The Marrano poor, although always present, were held under control and encouraged to emigrate (mostly to the Indies).

42. The *herem* was not used for religious purposes in the narrow sense only, but mainly in the traditional function of a political instrument to keep the community cohesive and obedient to its semiautonomous institutions.

43. Gershom Scholem, *Sabbatai Sevi: The Mystical Messiah* (Princeton, NJ: Princeton University Press, 1973).

44. On Jewish Amsterdam's commercial activities, see Bloom, *The Economic Activities of the Jews in Amsterdam in the Seventeenth and Eighteenth Centuries* (Williamsport, PA: Bayard Press, 1937). And see Jonathan I. Israel, "The Economic Contribution of the Dutch Sephardic Jewry to Holland's Golden Age, 1585–1713," in *Empires and Entrepots: The Dutch, the Spanish Monarchy, and the Jews, 1585–1713* (London and Roncevert, WV: Hambledon Press, 1990), 417–447.

45. Israel, *European Jewry in the Age of Mercantilism*, 87.

46. The Huguenots were practically fleeing from France in 1685, after Louis XIV revoked the edict of Nantes, which had given them basic religious rights.

47. Anon., *Lazarillo de Tormes*. See chap. 16, p. 336 and passim.

48. See also Israel, *European Jewry in the Age of Mercantilism*, 88.

49. 1659. The event and names of the victims are actual. The number of spectators, given by the chronicler Rodrigo Ruiz de Cepeda Martínez, may be exaggerated (Nathan Wachtel, *La Foi du souvenir* [Paris: Seuil, 2001], 227n205).

50. On the Inquisition and the Conversos in Brazil, see Anita Novinsky, *Cristãos novos na Bahía* (São Paulo: Perspectiva, 1972); and on the eighteenth century, Anita Novinsky, *Inquisicão: Rol dos Culpados: Fontes para a história do Brasil (seculo XVIII)* (Rio de Janeiro: Expressão e Cultura, 1992); Elias Lipiner, *Santa Inquisicão: Terror e linguagem* (Rio de Janeiro: Documentario, 1977); and Elias Lipiner, *Tsvishn maranentum un shmad* (Tel Aviv: Verlag Y. L. Peretz, 1973).

51. On France, see Frances Malino, *The Sephardic Jews of Bordeaux: Assimilation and Emancipation in Revolutionary and Napoleonic France* (University: University of Alabama Press, 1978), chaps. 1–2; Gerard Nahon, "Communautés espagnoles et portugaises de France (1492–1992)," in *Les Juifs d'Espagne*, ed. Méchoulan, 111–132; Nahon, *Les "Nations" juives portugaises du sud-ouest de la France, 1684–1791* (Paris: Fundação Calouste Gulbenkian, 1981), chap. 6; Zosa Szajkowski, "Trade Relations of Marranos in France with the Iberian Peninsula in the Sixteenth and Seventeenth Centuries," *Jewish Quarterly Review* 50 (1960): 69–78; and Szajkowski, "Population Problems of Marranos and Sephardim in France from the 16th to the 20th Century," *Proceedings of the American Academy for Jewish Research* 27 (1958): 83–105.

52. I. S. Révah "Les Marranes," *Revue des études Juives* 118 (1959–1960): 29–77.

53. The philosopher Baruch (Benedictus) de Spinoza (see next chapter), expelled by the Portuguese-Jewish community of Amsterdam in 1656, published anonymously in 1670 his classic *Theological-Political Treatise*. (Incidentally, Spinoza's father was a *parnass* and a trustee of the *dotar*.)

54. David Katz, "Les Juifs d'Angleterre: Entre la réadmission et l'émancipation," in *Les Juifs d'Espagne*, ed. Méchoulan, 150.

55. That happened while Shakespeare was active in London, and some critics believe that it may have prompted *The Merchant of Venice*. See Anthony Burgess, *Shakespeare* (New York: Knopf, 1970), 136–137; and Stephen Greenblatt, *Will in the World* (London: Jonathan Cape, 2004), 273–277.

56. Rembrandt lived by the Jewish quarter of Amsterdam, knew Menasse, drew his portrait and illustrated one of his works.

57. Based on Deuteronomy 28:64 and Daniel 12:7. The argument is included in Manasseh Ben Israel, *La Esperanza de Israel*, ed. Henry Méchoulan and Gérard Nahon (Madrid: Ediciones Hiperión, 1987). The supposed discovery of the lost tribes, also

claimed in this book, was based on a report by the New Jewish Marrano Antonio Montezinos, who had explored the Andes.

58. Actually, this was suggested by David S. Katz ("Les Juifs d'Angleterre," 159), on whose work the section on London is partly based. See also Katz, *The Jews in the History of England, 1485–1850* (Oxford: Clarendon Press; New York: Oxford University Press, 1994); and Katz, "English Redemption and Jewish Readmission in 1656," *Journal of Jewish Studies* 34, no. 11 (1983): 73–91.

59. On Marrano settlement and life in Brazil see Arnold Wiznitzer, *Jews in Colonial Brazil* (New York: Columbia University Press, 1960).

60. Based on an oral communication by Nathan Wachtel, the French Marrano scholar, who had learned that such a group, now speaking Portuguese and bearing Portuguese names, still exists today under the appellation "the Dutch" inside the state of Rio Grande del Norte. Similar information about Brazilian "Jews in the jungle" was given by Tânia Kaufman of the University of Pernambuco. She reported on Marranos who showed up in her region, some returning to Judaism (Alan M. Tigay, "The Jewish Traveler: Recife," *Hadassah Magazine*, May 2001 [online: http://www.hadassah.org/news/content/per_hadassah/archive/2001/may01/traveler.htm]).

61. That first synagogue in North America can still be identified in the Wall Street area.

62. By the end of the seventeenth century, two hundred Jewish ships were in operation. Their names, owners, and Jewish captains are listed in Isaac S. Emmanuel and Suzanne A. Emmanuel, *History of the Jews of the Netherlands Antilles* (Cincinnati: American Jewish Archives, 1970), 2:681–746.

63. Curaçao's role as annex of Amsterdam and its hub to Ibero-America made it a "Disapora of a Diaspora" in that particular sense, too. See Jonathan Israel, *Diasporas within a Diaspora: Jews, Crypto Jews, and the World Maritime Empires (1540–1740)* (Boston: Brill, 2002), chap. 16. See also Frances Karner, *The Sephardics of Curaçao* (Assen: Van Gorcum, 1969); and Mordechai Arbell, *The Jewish Nation of the Carribean* (New York: Gefen, 2002).

64. Yerushalmi ("Between Amsterdam and New Amsterdam," 190), describes Curaçao as the freest Jewish community in the world at that time—even more than Amsterdam—and an early forebear of Jewish emancipation.

65. Nathan Wachtel, *La Foi du souvenir* (Paris: Seuil, 2001), 251.

66. See ibid., 259–261. The information comes from a spy reporting to the Inquisition in Lisbon. He was Domingos Pimentel, an Old Christian from Brazil who had been captured by Dutch pirates and brought to Amsterdam. In Amsterdam he met some fellow Brazilians, including the "blond" mentioned in the text, and another man he describes as "corpulent," who mistook him for a Marrano and spoke freely in his presence of their common acquaintances in Rio.

67. Ibid., 260.

68. As records of the Brazilian Inquisition in Lisbon and works by Wachtel, Novinsky, and others attest.

69. Seymour B. Liebman, trans. and ed., *Jews and the Inquisition of Mexico: The Great Auto de Fe of 1649* (Lawrence, KS: Coronado, 1974).

70. Actually, when this "letter" is dated, a new inquisitorial attack was in preparation, in which about one hundred persons were tried as Judaizers between 1672 and 1676

(Moshé Nes-El and Leonardo Senkman, "Histoire des séfarades du Mexique," in *Les Juifs d'Espagne*, ed. Méchoulan, 579).

71. Wachtel, *La Foi du souvenir*, 83. (The data apply to 1620–1630.) The slave trade required special permits.

72. Claude de La Magdeleine wrote this in his travel account, *Le Miroir Ottoman* (Basel: J. R. Genath, 1677).

73. From here to the end of the paragraph, the description is based on a report by the Turkish traveler and geographer Mustafa ben Abdalla Haji Halafa, writing in 1653. His text is published in Karl Braun-Wiesbaden, *Eine türkische Reise* (Stuttgart: Auerbach, 1876), 2:272–274.

74. Michel Abitbol, "Yahadut Zefon Africa aharei Gerush Sefarad," in *HaPezura HaYehudit HaSefardit aharei HaGerush*, ed. M. Abitbol et al. (Jerusalem: Zalman Shazar Center, 1992), 16–17.

75. Spinoza said of the ancient Jews that after their state was destroyed they packed their fatherland into their religion and laws and took it to their Diaspora; by paraphrase we might say that the "Portuguese" Marranos took their Iberian fatherland wherever they went in the form of a lay emigré culture.

76. Yerushalmi, *From Spanish Court to Italian Ghetto, Isaac Cardoso: A Study of Seventeenth-Century Marranism and Jewish Apologetics* (Seattle and London: University of Washington Press, 1981), introduction.

77. This has been vividly illustrated by several individual and group studies, notably by Uchmany, Wachtel, and Graizbord.

78. For one of many examples, see the case of Luis de Carvajal *el Mozo* and Antonio Cáseres analyzed in the next chapter.

79. Bonfil, "Ferrare, un port sûr et paisible pour la diaspora séfarade," 301.

80. Ibid. See also Kaplan, *Hapzura HaSephardit HaMaaravit*, 90. Elsewhere this author insists that the members of this Nation included diverse members such as "Marranos; Christians by choice and will; open Jews . . . who shed their former Christian veil, and irreligious people . . . rebels against Jewish tradition" (Kaplan, "The Problem of the Marranos and 'New Christians' in Historical Research of the Last Generation," in *Studies in Historiography*, ed. M. Zimmermann et al. [Heb.: Jerusalem: Shazar Center, 1987], 117).

81. Bodian, looking at the same phenomenon from the vantage point of Amsterdam, concurs: "Their attachment to relatives and commercial correspondents in the peninsula or in the New World were richer, more concrete, and more natural than their attachment to the 'Jewish people.' The term 'the Nation' evoked an entire world of vivid memories and feelings; in contrast, 'The Jewish people' remained a somewhat cerebral theological concept" (Bodian, *Hebrews of the Portuguese Nation*, 133). This entails that they were tied more to members of their Nation even when they were Catholics, or heretical, or uncommitted Jews.

CHAPTER 18. MARRANO MOSAIC II:
WANDERERS, MARTYRS, INTELLECTUALS, DISSENTERS

1. As I called it in *Spinoza and Other Heretics* (Princeton, NJ: Princeton University Press, 1989), 1:95.

2. In addition to works referred to in this section and the next, see the more recent study: David L. Graizbord, *Souls in Dispute—Converso Identities in Iberia and the Jewish*

Diaspora, 1580–1700 (University of Pennsylvania Press, 2004). Graizbord looks specifically at the "renegades"—who first re-Judaized and then returned to Catholicism—mostly in Iberia. The book stresses their torn minds and frequent ambivalence, their humiliations as twice repenters, their being viewed with distrust by both sides, and their outer and inner itinerant mode of life, traveling both physically (for business) and mentally.

3. Eva Alexandra Uchmany, *La vida entre el judaísmo y el cristianismo en la Nueva España, 1580–1606* (Mexico City: Archivo General de la Nación, Fondo de cultura económica, 1992). This is a description of Marrano wanderers—wandering both geographically and mentally—whose itinerary spans diverse places and situations in the Old and New Worlds, and a variety of Marrano types, all complex in different ways.

4. Carvajal's trials and story were studied by several scholars, including Seymour B. Liebman (*The Jews in New Spain: Faith, Flame, and the Inquisition* [Coral Gables, FL: University of Miami Press, 1970], 141–158; and *The Enlightened: The Writings of Luis Carvajal El Mozo* [Coral Gables, FL: University of Miami Press, 1967]); and Martin A. Cohen (*The Martyr Luis de Carvajal: The Story of a Secret Jew and the Mexican Inquisition in the Sixteenth Century* [Philadelphia: Jewish Publication Society, 1973]). On the rest of the Carvajal family and the trials of others related to them, see Uchmany, *La vida entre el judaísmo y el cristianismo en la Nueva España*; and Cohen, *The Martyr Luis de Carvajal*; as well as Alfonso Toro, *The Carvajal Family: Jews and the Inquisition in New Spain in the Sixteenth Century* (El Paso, TX: Western Press, 2002).

5. As did the Converso spiritual writer Luis de Granada, a copy of whose book Carvajal had given to a Converso relative in hiding (Uchmany, *La vida entre el judaísmo y el cristianismo*, 55). Uchmany's fascinating study highlights another fact of the Marrano Dispersion: the wandering Marrano, the unsettled, disquiet, or unfortunate type who roamed not only between geographical places but between roles, masks, cultures, and religions. The same phenomenon comes out vividly in Nathan Wachtel's equally fascinating *La Foi du souvenir: Labyrinthes marranes* (Paris: Seuil, 2001).

6. In that, as their Jewish counterpart, he resembled the Catholic-oriented Marrano reformers of the sixteenth century.

7. The following cases are based on Wachtel, *La Foi du souvenir*. Wachtel's gallery of cases testifies to the deep duality and nascent secularism of many Marranos, and their fidelity to an identity that was no longer necessarily religious.

8. Rodrigo Ruiz de Cepeda Martínez, in Jose Toribio Medina, *Historia del tribunal del Santo Oficio de la Inquisición en México* (Santiago, Chile: Elzeviriana, 1905). Quoted in Wachtel, *La Foi du souvenir*, 227n205.

9. Wachtel, *La Foi du souvenir*, 180.

10. On María de Zárate, see Wachtel, *La Foi du souvenir*; and Boleslao Lewin, *La Inquisición en México: Racismo inquisitorial. El caso singular de María de Zárate* (Puebla, Mexico: Editorial J. M. Cajica Jr., 1971).

11. Wachtel, *La Foi du souvenir*, 197.

12. Ibid., 206.

13. Ibid., 216.

14. Gerard Nahon, *Métropoles et périphéries séfarades d'Occident* (Paris: Cerf, 1993), 257.

15. Medina reported that the circumcision occurred "between ages 12 and 14" (Wachtel, *La Foi du souvenir*, 233). But by age twelve he was already in Madrid. So he was circumcised either shortly before leaving or afterward. The latter would indicate a rather fervent Judaizing.

16. Wachtel, *La Foi du souvenir*, 239.

17. On the Cardosos, see Yosef Hayim Yerushalmi's classic study *From Spanish Court to Italian Ghetto, Isaac Cardoso: A Study of Seventeenth-Century Marranism and Jewish apologetics* (Seattle and London: University of Washington Press, 1981).

18. Ibid., 276, 282–284. As Yerushalmi shows, even in old age, Fernando Cardoso continued to refer various Jewish citations to the Christian authors from whom he had initially learned them.

19. Ibid., 331.

20. On this, see also Gershom Scholem, *Sabbatai Sevi: The Mystical Messiah, 1626–1676*, trans. R. J. Zwi Werblowsky (Princeton, NJ: Princeton University Press, 1973).

21. Yerushalmi, *From Spanish Court to Italian Ghetto*, 332

22. Timothy Oelman, ed. and trans., *Marrano Poets of the Seventeenth Century* (Rutherford, NJ: Fairleigh Dickinson University Press; London: Associated University Presses, 1982), 31. This bilingual book contains long excerpts from the three poets. For a rhymed new translation of a Delgado poem, see *The Poem of Queen Esther by João Pinto Delgado*, trans. David R. Slavitt (New York: Oxford University Press, 1999). See also I. S. Révah, introduction to *Poema de la Reina Ester; Lamentaciones del profeta Jeremías; Historia de Rut y varias poesías (Rouen, David du Petit Val, 1627)* (Lisbon: Institute Français au Portugal, 1954), 120–159.

23. Oelman, *Marrano Poets of the Seventeenth Century*, 101–102.

24. Ibid., 104–105 (with minor changes).

25. Ibid., 122 (my translation).

26. On Miguel de Barrios, see Kenneth Scholberg, *La poesía religiosa de Miguel de Barrios* (Madrid: Universidad de Ohio-Edhigar, 1962–1963); and Scholberg, "Miguel de Barrios and the Amsterdam Sephardic Community," *Jewish Quarterly Review* 53 (1962/63): 120–159.

27. This is so, at least in principle, since the king's conversion did not outlaw Protestantism; on the contrary, Protestants were given an edict of rights and recognized as legitimate French subjects. In the next century, Louis XIV revoked those rights, but the idea of the separation of church and state was soon to take off theoretically in the philosophy of the Enlightenment, and was instituted in practice in several steps since the French revolution.

28. He did accept the basics of a natural religion, however, as seen in his "Apology of Raimund Sabonde" and other essays.

29. Causal links are elusive, but analogies and recurrent patterns are also significant. In several ways Montaigne, though distant from a Marrano upbringing and awareness, manifested Marranolike attitudes and preferences. He was beyond any revealed religion and accepted Catholicism externally, as a social-political necessity; he turned his attention to this world, where alone wisdom is to be found; he stood for tolerance and against all religious extremism; and he suspected nonreligious absolutes as well. Each of these attitudes is typical of certain Marranos, and their aggregation in a person of that origin is hardly coincidental.

30. The following section is based on the fuller analysis in Yovel, *Spinoza and Other Heretics*, vol. 1, chaps. 1–3.

31. This fact was discovered by I. S. Révah. Costa's autobiography, *Exemplar humanae vita*, was published years after his death by a Dutch liberal Calvinist who preached tolerance, harbored Locke when he took refuge in Holland, and debated Judaism in a

"friendly" way. The text, even if authentic, seems to include interpolations and omissions. See Carl Gebhardt, *Die Schriften des Uriel da Costa* (Amsterdam: Curis societatis spinozana, 1922).

32. For my detailed analysis of the case, see *Spinoza and Other Heretics*, vol. 1, chap. 3. For the basic documents on which this analysis is based, and I. S. Révah's own interpretation, see I. S. Révah, *Spinoza et le Dr. Juan de Prado* (Paris: Mouton, 1959). For other discussions of Spinoza's Marrano background, see, among others, Carl Gebhardt, *Spinoza* (Buenos Aires: Editorial Losada, 1977); Lewis Feuer, *Spinoza and the Rise of Liberalism* (Boston: Beacon Press, 1958); Steven Nadler, *Spinoza: A Life* (Cambridge and New York: Cambridge University Press, 1999); and Rebecca Goldstein, *Betraying Spinoza: The Renegade Jew Who Gave Us Modernity* (New York: Schocken, 2006). For Orobio, see Yosef Kaplan, *From Christianity to Judaism: The Story of Isaac Orobio de Castro*, trans. Raphael Loewe (Oxford and New York: Published for the Littman Library by Oxford University Press, 1989).

33. In Yovel, *Spinoza and Other Heretics*, 1:63–64, from which these two sections (on Prado and on Spinoza) are reprinted in part.

CHAPTER 19. MARRANOS AND WESTERN MODERNITY

1. See the relevant discussions of the "Nation" in chaps. 12 and 17.

2. Carl Gebhardt, *Die Schriften des Uriel da Costa* (Amsterdam: M. Hertzberger, 1922), xix.

3. I intend to devote a special study to the topic of modernity and the will. For a brief sketch, see Yirmiyahu Yovel, "Kant and the History of the Will," in *Kant's Legacy: Essays in Honor of Lewis White Beck*, ed. Predrag Cicovacki (Rochester, NY: University of Rochester Press, 2001).

4. No discovery is "bare" or naïve. It depends on some categorization, which presupposes a linguistic and social input. On the other hand, not all constructs are simple inventions; often they use elements and lead to areas that are encountered in the mode of discovery, and can be said to exist independent of one's goals and interests.

5. For a masterly account of this process—told from a perspective different from mine—see Charles Taylor, *Sources of the Self: The Making of the Modern Identity* (Cambridge, MA: Harvard University Press, 1989).

6. Incidentally, the adverse consequences of identity control in social, political, and (no less important) existential terms have been demonstrated not only in despotic systems, but also, in different and far milder forms, in democratic ones. Modern technological capitalism, for example, even when it is materially pleasing, is a source of existential oppression and self-flattening human regimentation. Here the shared metaphysical essence is the *market*, and the mandatory We is the abstract community of *consumers* (and of *communicants*, cogs in global networks that allegedly "unite" the species) to which all singular individuals are abstractly reduced and, in this alienated capacity, are recognized as "free agents" who are called on to play out their essential collective role, embodied in tacit imperatives such as "consume!" or "get connected!" (or "choose!" between often sham options). People are implicitly considered bad citizens, even failed human beings, unless they consume enough, or link electronically, or buy the right products that drive the market and keep "the Economy"—that self-sustaining construct of which we are microwheels—going.

7. This must be subject to shifting lines and limitations that the application of any right may involve because of other political fundamentals. In other words, a measure of conflict and incoherence must be equally recognized and allowed in a free society that must balance between various value-objectives and therefore must often, perhaps always, hold on to contrasting elements and live with passing circumstantial incoherencies, called compromises, that may look hypocritical to a radical critic.

8. As in Rojas's *La Celestina*, in the picaresque novels, in Cervantes and others, and in many social and theological writings.

9. I referred to some of those works in chaps. 14–15. A far more detailed analysis is in my manuscript "The Mystic and the Wanderer."

10. A more recent challenging voice is Charles Taylor's, in *A Secular Age* (Cambridge, MA: Harvard University Press, 2007).

11. Despite differences on other issues, I basically share Hans Blumenberg's view (in *The Legitimacy of the Modern Age*, trans. Robert M. Wallace [Cambridge, MA: MIT Press, 1983]) of the modern world as self-legitimizing rather than as drawing its legitimacy from the religion that preceded it. The product of secularization is not a transfer of the same authority under different cover, but its replacement by a new, immanent authority that asserts itself in lieu of the former (although, historically, the process to a large extent was nourished and assisted by religion's own novel varieties).

12. Like "natural religion," religious universalism and enlightenment, deism, religious liberty, and personalism (stressing individual conscience and consciousness).

13. G.W.F. Hegel, *Preface to the Phenomenology of Spirit*, trans. Yirmiyahu Yovel (Princeton, NJ: Princeton University Press, 2005), 78.

14. See also M. Gauchet, *The Disenchantment of the World: A Political History of Religion*, trans. Oscar Burge (Princeton, NJ: Princeton University Press, 1997).

15. For an analysis of this play, see Yovel, *Spinoza and Other Heretics* (Princeton, NJ: Princeton University Press, 1989), vol. 1, chap. 4; and Stephen Gilman, *The Spain of Fernando de Rojas: The Intellectual and Social Landscape of La Celestina* (Princeton, NJ: Princeton University Press, 1972).

16. Here I accept in large measure a point stressed by Michael Heyd in a workshop on Spinoza's *Theologico-Political Treatise* held at the Jerusalem Spinoza Institute.

17. It must, however, be stressed that the total collapse of religious belief was not a necessary condition of secularization. In Western Europe, religious affiliation waned only in the late twentieth century; while secularization as a process had long preceded it. In America, religious belief, although significantly shrunk, is still widespread, especially the belief in God as a transdenominational power, but also the affiliation with specific religious organizations or groups (which often serves as an identity mark and a social anchor rather than as a metaphysical principle). Some sociologists use these examples to contest the validity of the notion of secularization. But if we bear in mind the several meanings and degrees of the concept, and realize that for secularization to occur in those other senses, some decline in religious belief, though not its total collapse, is necessary, then we do justice to the complexity of the concept without impairing its fertility.

18. For a magisterial historical discussion of this drive in relation to modernity, see Charles Taylor, *Sources of the Self: The Makings of the Modern Identity* (Cambridge, MA: Harvard University Press, 1989).

CHAPTER 20. MARRANOS AND JEWISH MODERNITY

1. Yosef Hayim Yerushalmi, *Assimilation and Racial Anti-Semitism: The Iberian and the German Models* (New York: Leo Baek Institute, 1982). See also Maurice Kriegel's articles, which point to a parallel between two "postemancipatory" anti-Jewish movements. Kriegel, "The 'Modern' Anti-Semitism of the Inquisition" (Heb.), *Zemanim* 41 (1992): 23–33; and Kriegel, "Entre 'question' des 'Nouveaux-Chrétiens' et expulsion des Juifs: La double modernité des procès d'exclusion dans l'Espagne du XVe siécle," in *Le Nouveau Monde, Mondes mouveaux*, ed. Serge Gruzinski and Nathan Wachtel (Paris: Éditions de l'Ecole des Hautes Études en Sciences Sociales, 1996), 469–491.

2. Periodization in Jewish history is not easy. But it cannot be denied that modernity started later in the Jewish world than in Christian Europe (the *Haskalah* and the French Revolution both belong to late eighteenth century), and also that the typical sociology, normative texts (the Talmud and its ramifications), religious authority, congregation structure, and survival strategies that characterized the Jews in the Middle Ages were not settled before the middle of the first millennium (prior to that, the new Jewish culture that dominated later centuries was still in a process of becoming).

3. Sigmund Freud, preface to the Hebrew translation of *Totem and Taboo* (Heb.; Jerusalem: Kiryat Sefer, 1930).

4. Similarly, the Marranos' Jewishness could not be the same as that of traditional Jews outside the Marrano world.

5. This important analogy adds also to the matching patterns we saw in chapter 19 between the Marranos and Western modernization.

6. Sami Groniman, *Zikhronot shel Yekke*, trans. Dov Stock (Tel Aviv: Am Oved, 1946), 1:83.

7. Strictly speaking, using the term *anti-Semitism* to designate hatred of Jews in all ages is imprecise. The term *Semitism* relates to the theory of races, and as such expresses the secularization of the classic hatred of Jews. *Anti-Semitism* therefore denoted a specifically modern hatred of Jews; but since the term has come to have a generalized meaning, we should speak here of a "new anti-Semitism."

8. Spinoza apparently was the first who claimed that hatred of Jews preserves their historical existence. See Spinoza, *Theologico-Political Treatise*, end of chap. 3.

9. It is noteworthy that the fifteenth-century Vatican denounced Torquemada's excesses, and the pope did not hesitate to get into a conflict with King Ferdinand over their extension to Aragon. As for Torquemada personally, he did not espouse the "purity of blood" policy, which implicitly annulled the sacrament of baptism. Torquemada burned Judaizers—not Jews—because they betrayed their baptism, which was irreversible. But he believed that baptism *did* erase the Jews' Judaism and produced Christians, whose fate depended uniquely on their personal comportment, not blood.

EPILOGUE. PRESENT DAY MARRANOS

1. Samuel Schwarz, *Os Christaõs-Novos em Portugal no Século XX* (Lisbon: Empresa portuguesa de livros, 1925); translated into Hebrew as *Ha-notzrim ha-chadashim be-portugal ba-mea'a ha-esrim*, trans. Claude B. Stuczinski (Jerusalem: Dinur Center, 2005).

2. A particularly anti-Semite scholar attacking Schwarz was Mário Saa, in *A Invasão dos Judeus* (Lisbon: Imprensa L. da Silva, 1925), and elsewhere.

3. For a more recent biography of Barros Basto, see Elvira Azevedo de Mea and Inácio Steinhardt, *Ben-Rosh: Biografia do Capitão Barros Bastos: O apóstolo dos Marranos* (Porto: Edições Afrontamento, 1997).

4. See chap. 13.

5. See chaps. 5 and 13.

6. The tying of the toes, symbolizing union, together with the Marrano benediction, make up the performative act that creates the marriage bond. Catholics understand this bond as a metaphysical sacrament, while Jews interpret it as a contract before God. The Jewish bond is performed by the action of the groom, who places a ring on the bride's finger and says, "Hereby thou art wed to me"; but in Catholicism, creating the sacramental bond can be performed only by the priest. In this respect, the Marrano rite seems closer to the Catholic.

7. I heard and recorded this from a Marrano named Domingues, whose family lived in Meda, northeast of Belmonte, and had come there from a village near Lamego (Beiras). He said the anointing of the baby replaced circumcision, and "was a way of presenting it to God." Without this rite, the baby would not be expected to grow.

8. I also had been invited by members of a Marrano group I met when they visited the Diaspora Museum in Tel Aviv a half year earlier.

9. They did not put it in those exact terms, but spoke in a way that meant the same. David Augusto Canelo agrees; see Canelo, *O resgate dos Marranos portugueses* (Belmonte, Portugal: D. A. Canelo, 1996). Schwarz had reached a similar conclusion. Canelo also has an earlier work, *Os últimos criptojudeus em Portugal* (Belmonte, Portugal: Centro de Cultura Pedro Alvares Cabral, 1987).

10. Christians do not fast on Christmas, but rejoice; so this Marrano custom can be construed in two ways: (1) taking part in the greatest Christian holiday through unChristian means; or (2) a Marrano act of mourning Jesus's birth. (Historically, it could have started as the latter and later turned into the former.)

11. He meant, I take it, "Why should there be a difference?"

12. For the dominance of women in Belmonte (which, as we have seen, echoes a generalized phenomenon in Marrano history), see Maria Antonieta Garcia, *Judaísmo no feminino: Tradição popular e ortodoxia em Belmonte* (Lisbon: Instituto de Sociologia e Etnologia das Religiões, Universidade Nova de Lisboa, 1999).

13. Amilcar Paulo, *Os Judeus secretos em Portugal* (Porto: Editorial Labirinto, 1985). An earlier study is José Leite de Vasconcelos, "Cristãos novos de nosso tempo em Trásos-Montes e na Beira: Suas prácticas judaicas," in *Etnografia portuguesa: Tentame des sistematizacão* (Lisbon: Imprensa Nacional-Casa da Moeda, 1982), 4:162–253.

14. As stated by Joãn Diogo, one of the leaders who later became president of the new congregation. Quoted in Sara Molho, "Three Portraits of Marrano Leaders in Belmonte" (Heb.), online at www.mybelmonte.com/.

15. In 1997, their official number (by congregation records) was about eighty-five, though perhaps the actual number was higher. See Sara Molho, "Masks for Kippur, Masks for Passover: A Sociological Look at the Belmonte Marranos Today" (Heb.), in *Proceedings of the 12th World Congress of Jewish Studies* (Jerusalem: World Union of Jewish Studies, 2001), 264.

16. From a different angle, this posthumous rite might recall the Inquisition's custom of burning the bones of heretics as a way of salvation and absolution: in both cases, a radical religious act, performed in a metaphysical space, changes the destiny and/or identity of the deceased person.

17. Molho, "Masks for Kippur, Masks for Passover," 265–266.

18. Molho (ibid., 266) tells of a Marrano who had fasted on "Esther's Fast" as Jewish law requires, but refused to answer the rabbi's inquiry whether he did, claiming (to Molho): "This is between me and my God."

19. Stanley M. Hordes, *To the End of the Earth: A History of the Crypto-Jews of New Mexico* (New York: Columbia University Press, 2005); Benjamin Shapiro, "The Hidden Jews of New Mexico," *Avotaynu: The International Review of Jewish Genealogy* 5, no. 4 (1989): S4.

20. Sicily belonged to the Aragonese Crown during the Expulsion. Of Marranism in Sicily in the crucial years, see Nadia Zeldes, *The Former Jews of This Kingdom: Sicilian Converts after the Expulsion, 1492–1516* (Leiden and Boston: Brill, 2003).

21. Francesco Renda, *La fine del giudaismo siciliano: Ebrei marrani e Inquisizione spagnola prima, durante e dopo la cacciata del 1492* (Palermo: Sellerio, 1993); Angela Selke, *Los Chuetas y la Inquisición* (Madrid: Taurus, 1972). See also Baruch Braunstein, *The Chuetas of Majorca: Conversos and the Inquisition of Majorca* (New York: Columbia University Press, 1936).

22. Angela Selke, *Vida y muerte de los chuetas de Mallorca* (Madrid: Taurus, 1980).

23. For a more recently published study on Belmonte and Majorca, see Renée Levine Melammed, *A Question of Identity—Iberian Conversos in Historical Perspective* (New York: Oxford University Press, 2004), chap. 8.

Works Cited

Abitbol, Michel. "Yahadut Zefon Africa aharei Gerush Sefarad" [North African Jewry after the Expulsion from Spain]. In *HaPezura HaYehudit HaSefardit aharei HaGerush* [The Sephardi Jewish Diaspora after the Expulsion from Spain], ed. M. Abitbol et al. Jerusalem: Zalman Shazar Center, 1992.

Alcalá, Angel. "El mundo Converso en la literatura y la mística del Siglo de Oro." *Manuscrits* 10 (January 1992): 91–118.

———, ed. *Judíos, sefarditas, conversos: La expulsión de 1492 y sus consecuencias.* Valladolid: Ambito, 1995.

———, ed. *The Spanish Inquisition and the Inquisitorial Mind.* New York: Columbia University Press, 1987.

Alemán, Mateo. *Guzmán de Alfarache.* Barcelona: PPU, 1988.

Alter, Robert. *Rogue's Progress.* Cambridge, MA: Harvard University Press, 1965.

Amador de Los Ríos, J. *Historia social, política y religiosa de los judíos de España y Portugal.* Madrid: Turner, 1984.

Amiel, Charles. "La 'pureté de sang' en Espagne." *Annales du C.E.S.E.R.E.* 6 (1983): 27–45.

Anon. *Lazarillo de Tormes.* Madrid: Edición de Francisco Rico, Cátedra, 1992.

Arbell, Mordechai. *The Jewish Nation of the Caribbean.* New York: Gefen Books, 2002.

Arbós Ayuso, Cristina. "Judíos y conversos: Un tema tópico en la poesía medieval." In *Encuentros en Sefarad: Actas del Congreso Internacional "Los Judíos en la Historia de España."* Ciudad Real: Instituto de Estudios Manchegos, 1987.

———. "Los cancioneros castellanos del siglo XV como fuente para la historia de los judíos españoles." In *Jews and Conversos: Studies in Society and the Inquisition,* ed. Yosef Kaplan. Jerusalem: World Union of Jewish Studies, Magnes Press, 1985.

Asaf, Simha. "The *Anussim* in the Responsa Literature" (Heb.). *Zion* 5 (1933): 19–60.

Ashtor, Eliyahu. *The Jews of Moslem Spain.* 3 vols. Philadelphia: Jewish Publication Society, 1973–1984.

Assis, Yom Tov. *The Golden Age of Aragonese Jewry: Community and Society in the Crown of Aragon, 1213–1327.* London and Portland, OR: Vallentine Mitchell, 1997.

Assis, Yom Tov, and Yosef Kaplan, eds. *Jews and Conversos at the Time of the Expulsion* (Heb.). Jerusalem: Shazar Center, 1999.

Azevedo, J. Lúcio de. *História dos christãos novos portugueses.* 2nd ed. Lisbon: Livraria Clássica Editora A. M. Teixeira (Filhos), 1975.

Baena, Juan Alfonso de. *Cancionero.* Ed. José María Azáceta. Madrid: Consejo superior de investigaciones científicas, 1966.

Baer, Y. *Die Juden im christlichen Spanien: Urkunden und Regesten.* 2 vols. Berlin: Akademie für die Wissenschaft des Judentums, 1929–1936.

———. *Galut.* Trans. Robert Warshow. New York: Schocken Books, 1947.

———. *A History of the Jews in Christian Spain.* 2 vols. Philadelphia: Jewish Publication Society of America, 1961.

Barkai, Ron. "Reflexiones sobre el concepto 'El Siglo de Oro' de los judíos en España musulmana y su significación contemporánea." *El Olivo* 14 (1981): 19–28.

Baron, S. W. "'Plenitude of Apostolic Powers' and Medieval 'Jewish Serfdom.'" In *Yitzhak F. Baer Jubilee Volume,* ed. S. Ettinger, S. W. Baron, B. Dinur, and I. Halpern (Heb.). Jerusalem: Historical Society of Israel, 1960.

———. *A Social and Religious History of the Jews.* 2d ed., rev. and enlarged. 18 vols. New York: Columbia University Press, 1952–1983.

Bataillon, Marcel. *Erasme et l'Espagne.* Paris: E. Droz, 1937; Geneva: Droz, 1991. Spanish expanded edition: *Erasmo y España.* Mexico City: Fondo de Cultura Económica, 1966.

———. *Le roman picaresque.* Paris: La Renaissance du livre, 1931.

———. *Novedad y fecundidad del "Lazarillo de Tormes."* Salamanca and Madrid: Anaya, 1968.

———. "Peregrinations espagnoles du juif errant." *Bulletin hispanique* 43 (1941).

———. *Pícaros y picaresca.* Madrid: Taurus, 1969.

Beinart, Haim. *Conversos on Trial: The Inquisition in Ciudad Real.* Trans. Y. Guiladi. Jerusalem: Magnes Press, 1981.

———. *Conversos on Trial by the Inquisition* (Heb.). Tel Aviv: Am Oved, 1965.

———. *The Expulsion of the Jews from Spain.* Oxford and Portland, OR: Littman Library of Jewish Civilization, 2002.

———, ed. *The Marranos in Christian Society and in Jewish Society: Seminar Sources* (Heb.). Jerusalem: Department of Jewish History, Hebrew University, 1976.

———. "The Prophetess Inez and Her Movement in Her Native Herrera." In *Pirke Sefarad* (Heb.). Jerusalem: Magnes Press, 1998.

———, ed. *Records of the Trials of the Spanish Inquisition in Ciudad Real.* 4 vols. Jerusalem: Israel National Academy of Sciences and Humanities, 1974–1985.

Beltrán de Heredia, V. "Las bulas de Nicolás V acerca de los Conversos de Castilla." *Sefarad* 21 (1961): 22–47.

Ben Daud, Abraham (Rabad). *Sefer Ha-Qabbalah* [The Book of Tradition]. English and Hebrew. A critical edition with translation and notes by Gerson D. Cohen. Philadelphia: Jewish Publication Society of America, 1967.

Ben Israel, Manasseh. *La Esperanza de Israel* [Israel's Hope]. Ed. Henry Méchoulan and Gérard Nahon. Madrid: Ediciones Hiperión, 1987.

Ben Sasson, H. H. *On Jewish History in the Middle Ages* (Heb.). Tel Aviv: Am Oved, 1969.

Benassar, Bartolomé, ed. *L'Inquisition espagnole: XV–XIX siècle.* Paris: Hachette, 1979.

———. "Patterns of the Inquisitional Mind as the Basis for a Pedagogy of Fear." In *Inquisición española y mentalidad inquisitorial,* ed. Angel Alcalá. Barcelona: Ariel, 1984.

Benito Ruano, E. "Del problema judío al problema converso." In *Simposio Toledo judaico.* Toledo, Spain: Publicaciones del Centro Universitario de Toledo, 1973.

———. "El Memorial contra los conversos del bachiller Marcos García de Mora." *Sefarad* 17 (1957): 314–351.

———. *Los orígenes del problema converso*. Barcelona: Ediciones El Albir, 1976.

———. *Toledo en el siglo XV: Vida política*. Madrid: Consejo Superior de Investigaciones Científicas, Escuela de Estudios Medievales, 1961.

Ben-Shalom, Ram. "The Disputation of Tortosa, Vicente Ferrer, and the Problem of the Conversos according to the Testimony of Isaac Nathan" (Heb.). *Zion* 56 (1991): 21–45.

Bernstein, Richard. *The New Constellation: The Ethical-Political Horizons of Modernity/Postmodernity*. Cambridge, UK: Polity Press, 1991.

Blázquez Miguel, Juan. *Toledot: Historia del Toledo Judío*. Toledo: Arcano, 1989.

Bloom, Herbert. *The Economic Activities of the Jews in Amsterdam in the Seventeenth and Eighteenth Centuries*. Williamsport, PA: Bayard Press, 1937.

Blumenberg, Hans. *The Legitimacy of the Modern Age*. Trans. Robert M. Wallace. Cambridge, MA: MIT Press, 1983.

Bodian, Miriam. *Hebrews of the Portuguese Nation: Conversos and Community in Early Modern Amsterdam*. Bloomington: Indiana University Press, 1997.

———. "'Men of the Nation': The Shaping of *Converso* Identity in Early Modern Europe." *Past and Present* 143 (1993): 48–76.

———. "The 'Portuguese' Dowry Societies in Venice and Amsterdam." *Italia* 6 (1978): 55–61.

Bonfil, Robert. "Ferrare, un port sûr et paisible pour la diaspora séfarade." In *Les Juifs d'Espagne*.

Boxer, C. R. *The Portuguese Seaborne Empire*. New York: A. A. Knopf, 1969.

Boyd, Carolyn P. *Historia Patria: Politics, History, and National Identity in Spain, 1875–1975*. Princeton, NJ: Princeton University Press, 1997.

Bradbury, Scott, ed. and trans. *Severus of Minorca: Letter on the Conversion of the Jews*. Oxford: Clarendon Press, 1996.

Braudel, Fernand. *The Mediterranean and the Mediterranean World in the Age of Philip II*. 2 vols. New York: Harper & Row, 1976–1995.

Braunstein, Baruch. *The Chuetas of Majorca: Conversos and the Inquisition of Majorca*. Columbia University Oriental Studies, vol. 28. Scottdale, PA: Mennonite Publishing House, 1936.

Braun-Wiesbaden, Karl. *Eine türkische Reise*. Stuttgart: Auerbach, 1876.

Bujanda, Jesús M. de. "Recent Historiography of the Spanish Inquisition (1977–1988): Balance and Perspective." In *Cultural Encounters: The Impact of the Inquisition in Spain and the New World*, ed. Mary Elizabeth Perry and Anne J. Cruz. Berkeley and Los Angeles: University of California Press, 1991.

Burgess, Anthony. *Shakespeare*. New York: Knopf, 1970.

Byron, William. *Cervantes: A Biography*. Garden City, NY: Doubleday, 1978.

Cabezudo Astrain, J. "Los Conversos aragoneses según los procesos de la Inquisición." *Sefarad* 18 (1958): 272–282.

Canelo, David Augusto. *O resgate dos Marranos portugueses*. Belmonte, Portugal: D. A. Canelo, 1996.

———. *Os últimos criptojudeos em Portugal*. Belmonte, Portugal: Centro de Cultura Pedro Alvares Cabral, 1987.

Cantera Burgos, Francisco. *Alvar García de Santa María: Historia de la judería de Burgos y de sus conversos más egregios.* Madrid: Instituto Arias Montano, 1952.

———. "El Cancionero de Baena: Judíos y conversos en 61." *Sefarad* 27 (1967): 71–111.

———. "Fernando de Pulgar and the Conversos." *Sefarad* 4 (1944): 295–348.

Cantera Burgos, Francisco, and Carlos Carrete Parrondo. *Cancionero de Antón de Montoro.* Madrid: Editora Nacional, 1984.

Caro Baroja, Julio. *Los judíos en la España moderna y contemporánea.* Madrid: Arión, 1962.

Carrete Parrondo, C. *El judaísmo español y la Inquisición.* Madrid: Editorial MAPFRE, 1992. 2nd ed. Madrid: ISTMO, 1978.

———. *Hebraístas judeoconversos en la Universidad de Salamanca (siglos XIV y XV).* Salamanca: Universidad Pontifica, 1982.

Carrete Parrondo, C., et al., eds. *Encuentros and Desencuentros: Spanish-Jewish Interaction throughout History.* Tel Aviv: Tel Aviv University Projects, 2000.

———, eds. *Fontes Iudaeorum Regni Castellae [FIRC].* 8 vols. Salamanca: Universidad Pontificia de Salamanca, 1981, 1985, 1986, 1987.

Cartagena, Alonso de. "Instrucción del Relator." In *Defensorium Unitatis Christianae: Tratado en Favor de los Judíos Conversos,* ed. Manuel Alonso. Madrid: Escuela de Estudios Hebraicos, 1943.

Castro, Américo. *De la edad conflictiva: El drama de la honra en España y en su literatura.* Madrid: Taurus, 1961, 1963.

———. *España en su historia: Cristianos, moros y judíos.* 2nd ed. Barcelona: Editorial Crítica, 1983. (Earlier edition: Buenos Aires: Editorial Losada, 1948).

———. *Hacia Cervantes.* Madrid: Taurus, 1967.

———. *La realidad histórica de España.* Mexico City: Editorial Porrúa, 1954.

———. *The Structure of Spanish History.* Trans. Edmund L. King. Princeton, NJ: Princeton University Press, 1954.

Cervantes Saavedra, Miguel de. *Don Quijote.* Trans. Burton Raffel. New York: Norton, 1999.

———. *Novelas ejemplares.* Ed. Harry Sieber. 2 vols. Madrid: Catedra, 1991.

Charles, P. "L'islam." In *Histoire générale comparée des religions du Baron Descamps,* ed. Edouard Eugène François Baron Descamps. Brussels: L'Edition Universelle, 1932.

Chaunu, Pierre. "L'Espagne du refus: Les statuts de pureté de sang." In *L'Espagne de Charles Quint.* 2 vols. Paris: Société d'édition d'enseignement supérieur, 1973.

Cheyney, Edward P. *The Dawn of a New Era, 1250–1453.* New York: Harper & Row, 1962.

Clément, Catherine. *La Señora.* Paris: Calmann-Lévy, 1991.

Cohen, Martin A. *The Martyr Luis de Carvajal: The Story of a Secret Jew and the Mexican Inquisition in the Sixteenth Century.* Philadelphia: Jewish Publication Society, 1973.

Corcos, David. "On the Nature of the Al-Muwahiddun's Attitude toward the Jews" (Heb.). In *Studies in the History of the Jews of Morocco.* Jerusalem: Rubin Mass, 1976.

Crescas, Hasdai. "Rabbi Hasdai Crescas Gives an Account of the Spanish Massacres of 1391." In *A Treasury of Jewish Letters,* ed. Franz Kobler. New York: Farrar, Straus and Young, 1952.

Davidson, Herbert A. *Moses Maimonides: The Man and His Works.* Oxford and New York: Oxford University Press, 2005.

Dedieu, Jean-Pierre. "The Archives of the Holy Office of Toledo as a Source for Histori-cal Anthropology." In *The Inquisition in Early Modern Europe—Studies on Sources and Methods*, ed. G. Henningsen and J. Tedeschi. Dekalb: Northern Illinois University Press, 1986.

———. *L'administration de la foi: L'Inquisition de Tolède, XVIe–XVIIIe siècle*. Paris: Casa de Velázquez, 1989.

Delgado, João Pinto. *The Poem of Queen Esther*. Trans. David R. Slavitt. New York: Oxford University Press, 1999.

Domínguez Ortiz, Antonio. *Autos de la Inquisición de Sevilla: Siglo XVII*. Seville: Servi-cio de Publicaciones del Ayuntamiento de Sevilla, 1981.

———. "Historical Research on Spanish Conversos in the Last 15 Years." In *Collected Studies in Honour of Américo Castro's Eightieth Year*, ed. M. P. Hornik. Oxford: Lin-combe Lodge Research Library, 1965.

———. *La clase social de los conversos en Castilla en la edad moderna*. Granada: Univer-sidad de Granada, Servicios de Publicaciones, 1991.

———. *Los judeoconversos en España y América*. Madrid: ISTMO, 1971.

———. *Los judeoconversos en la España moderna*. Madrid: MAPFRE, 1992.

———. "Los judeoconversos en la vida española del Renacimiento." In *Estudios de histo-ria económica y social de España*. Granada: Universidad de Granada, 1987.

Dunlop, D. M. *The History of the Jewish Khazars*. New York: Schocken Books, 1967.

Edwards, John. "Bishop Juan Arias d'Avila of Segovia: 'Judaizer' or Reformer?" In *Cultures in Contact in Medieval Spain: Historical and Literary Essays Presented to L. P. Harvey*, ed. David Hook and Barry Taylor. London: Kings College, Medieval Studies, 1990.

———. "Elijah and the Inquisition: Messianic Prophecy among Conversos in Spain c. 1500." *Nottingham Medieval Studies* 28 (1984): 79–94.

———. "Race and Religion in 15th- and 16th-Century Spain: The 'Purity of Blood' Laws Revisited." In *10th World Congress of Jewish Studies, 1989*. Jerusalem: Avraham Har-man Institute of Contemporary Jewry, Hebrew University of Jerusalem; and World Union of Jewish Studies, 1993.

———. "Religious Faith and Doubt in Late Medieval Spain: Soria circa 1450–1500." *Past and Present* 120 (August 1988): 3–25.

Elliott, John H. *Imperial Spain, 1469–1716*. New York: New American Library, 1966.

Emmanuel, Itshac. "The History of the Jews of Saloniki" (Heb.). In *Zikhron Saloniki* (Heb. with articles in Ladino), ed. David A. Recanati. Tel Aviv: El Commmitato por la Edition del Livro sovre la Communita de Salonique, 5732 [1971 or 1972].

Emmanuel, Isaac S., and Suzanne A. Emmanuel. *History of the Jews of the Netherlands Antilles*. Cincinnati: American Jewish Archives, 1970.

Esteban Recio, Asunción. *Las ciudades castellanas en tiempos de Enrique IV: Estructura social y conflictos*. Valladolid, Spain: Secretariado de Publicaciones, Universidad de Valladolid, 1985.

Estepa Díez, Carlos, et al. *Burgos en la Edad Media*. Valladolid, Spain: Junta de Castilla y León, Consejería de Educación y Cultura, 1984.

Ettinger, Shmuel. "David HaReubeni" (Heb.). In *Encyclopedia Hebraica*. Tel Aviv: Mas-sada, 1976.

Falbel, Nachman. *Estudos sobre a comunidade judaica no Brasil.* São Paulo: Federação Israelita de São Paulo, 1984.

Faur, José. "Four Classes of Conversos: A Typological Study." *Revue des études Juives* 149 (1990): 113–124.

———. *In the Shadow of History: Jews and Conversos in the Dawn of Modernity.* Albany: State University of New York Press, 1992.

Febvre, Lucien. *The Problem of Unbelief in the Sixteenth Century: The Religion of Rabelais.* Cambridge, MA: Harvard University Press, 1982.

Fernández Alvarez, Manuel. *El proceso de fray Luis de León.* Aneyos de Studia Zamorensia, 1. Salamanca: Universidad de Salamanca, 1980.

Feuer, Lewis. *Spinoza and the Rise of Liberalism.* Boston: Beacon Press, 1958.

Fichtenau, Heinrich. *Heretics and Scholars in the High Middle Ages, 1000–1200.* University Park: Pennsylvania State University Press, 1998.

Filippini, Jean-Pierre. "L'Oasis' toscane." In *Les Juifs d'Espagne.*

Fita, Fidel. "La Inquisición en Guadalupe." *Boletín de la Real Academia de la Historia* 23 (1893): 283–343.

Freud, Sigmund. Preface to the Hebrew translation of *Totem and Taboo* (Heb.). Jerusalem: Kiryat Sefer, 1930.

Friedman, Mordechai Akiva. *Maimonides: The Yemenite Messiah and Apostasy* (Heb.). Jerusalem: Ben-Zvi Institute and the Hebrew University of Jerusalem, 2002.

Garcia, Maria Antonieta. *Judaísmo no feminino: Tradição popular e ortodoxia em Belmonte.* Lisbon: Instituto de Sociologia e Etnologia das Religiões, Universidade Nova de Lisboa, 1999.

García Cárcel, Ricardo. *Herejía y sociedad en el siglo XVI—La Inquisición en Valencia 1530–1609.* Barcelona: Ediciones Península, 1980.

———. *La Inquisición.* Madrid: Anaya, 1990.

———. *Orígenes de la Inquisición española—El Tribunal de Valencia, 1478–1530.* Barcelona: Ediciones Península, 1976.

Gauchet, M. *The Disenchantment of the World: A Political History of Religion.* Trans. Oscar Burge. Princeton, NJ: Princeton University Press, 1997.

Gebhardt, Carl. *Die Schriften des Uriel da Costa.* Curis Societatis Spinozanae. Amsterdam: M. Hertzberger, 1922.

———. *Spinoza.* Buenos Aires: Editorial Losada, 1977.

Gewirth, Eleazar. "Abraham Seneor, Social Tensions and the Court-Jew." *Michael* 11 (1989): 169–229.

———. "Elementos étnicos e históricos en las relaciones judeo-conversas en Segovia." In *Jews and Conversos: Studies in Society and the Inquisition,* ed. Yosef Kaplan. Jerusalem: World Union of Jewish Studies and Magnes Press, 1985.

Gilman, Stephen. *The Spain of Fernando de Rojas: The Intellectual and Social Landscape of La Celestina.* Princeton, NJ: Princeton University Press, 1972.

Gitlitz, David M. "Divided Families in Converso Spain." *Shofar* 11, no. 3 (1993): 1–19.

———. *Los Arias d'Avila de Segovia: Entre la sinagoga y la iglesia.* San Francisco: International Scholars Publications, 1996.

————. *Secrecy and Deceit: The Religion of the Crypto-Jews*. Philadelphia and Jerusalem: Jewish Publication Society, 1996.

Glick, Thomas F. *Islamic and Christian Spain in the Early Middle Ages*. Princeton, NJ: Princeton University Press, 1979.

Goldstein, Rebecca. *Betraying Spinoza: The Renegade Jew Who Gave Us Modernity*. New York: Schocken, 2006.

Gómez-Martínez, José Luis. *Américo Castro y el origen de los Españoles: Historia de una polémica*. Madrid: Editorial Gredos, 1975.

Graizbord, David L. *Souls in Dispute: Converso Identities in Iberia and the Jewish Diaspora, 1580–1700*. Philadelphia: University of Pennsylvania Press, 2004.

Greenblatt, Stephen. *Will in the World*. London: Jonathan Cape, 2004.

Groniman, Sami. *Zikhronot shel Yekke* [Memoirs of a Yekke (Yekke = Israeli colloquial expression for a German Jew)]. Trans. Dov Stock. Tel Aviv: Am Oved, 1946.

Grotius (de Groot), Hugo. *The Free Sea*. Indianapolis: Liberty Fund, 2004.

Guibovich Pérez, Pedro. *En defensa de Dios: Estudios y documentos sobre la Inquisición en el Perú*. Lima: Ediciones del Congreso del Perú, 1998.

Gutiérrez Nieto, Juan Ignacio. "El problema de la limpieza de sangre en la España de San Juan de la Cruz." In *Simposio sobre San Juan de la Cruz: Ponencias*, ed. María del Carmen Bobes Naves et al. Avila: Mijan, 1986.

Halbertal, Moshe. *By Way of Truth—Nachmanides and the Creation of Tradition* (Heb.). Jerusalem: Shalom Hartman Institute, 2006.

Haliczer, Stephen. "The Expulsion of the Jews as Social Process." In *The Jews in Spain and the Expulsion of 1492*, ed. Moshe Lazar and Stephen Haliczer. Lancaster, CA: Labyrinthos, 1997.

————. *Inquisition and Society in the Kingdom of Valencia, 1478–1834*. Berkeley and Los Angeles: University of California Press, 1990.

————. "The Jew as Witch: Displaced Aggression and the Myth of the Santo Niño of La Guarda." In *Cultural Encounters: The Impact of the Inquisition in Spain and the New World*, ed. Mary Elizabeth Perry and Anne J. Cruz. Berkeley and Los Angeles: University of California Press, 1991.

Hegel, G.W.F. *Elements of the Philosophy of Right*. Ed. A. W. Wood, trans. H. B. Nisbet. Cambridge: Cambridge University Press, 1991.

————. *Lectures on the Philosophy of Religion: The Lectures of 1827*. Ed. Peter C. Hodgson, trans. R. F. Brown, P. C. Hodgson, and J. M. Stewart. Berkeley and Los Angeles: University of California Press, 1988.

————. *The Phenomenology of Spirit*. Trans. A. V. Miller. Oxford and New York: Oxford University Press, 1977.

————. *Preface to the Phenomenology of Spirit*. Trans. Y. Yovel. Princeton, NJ: Princeton University Press, 2005.

————. *The Science of Logic*. Trans. A. V. Miller. Atlantic Highlands, NJ: Humanities Press International, 1989.

Henningsen, Gustav, and Charles Amiel, eds. *The Inquisition in Early Modern Europe: Studies on Sources and Methods*. Dekalb: Northern Illinois University Press, 1986.

Herculano, Alexander. *History of the Origin and Establishment of the Inquisition in Portugal.* Trans. J. C. Branner. New York: Ktav Publishing House, 1972. First published 1845–1859.

Hitti, Philip K. *History of the Arabs: From the Earliest Times to the Present.* 10th ed. London: Macmillan, 1970.

Hordes, Stanley M. *To the End of the Earth: A History of the Crypto-Jews of New Mexico.* New York: Columbia University Press, 2005.

Husik, Isaac. *A History of Mediaeval Jewish Philosophy.* New York: Atheneum, 1969.

Ibn Verga, Solomon. *Shevet Yehudah* (Heb.). Ed. Y. Baer. Jerusalem: Bialik Institute, 1947.

Israel, Jonathan I. *Diasporas within a Diaspora: Jews, Crypto-Jews, and the World Maritime Empires (1540–1740).* Boston: Brill, 2002.

———. *Empires and Entrepôts: The Dutch, the Spanish Monarchy, and the Jews, 1585–1713.* London and Roncevert, WV: Hambledon Press, 1990.

———. *European Jewry in the Age of Mercantilism, 1550–1750.* London and Portland, OR: Littman Library of Jewish Civilization, 1998.

Jiménez Lozano, José. *Fray Luis de León.* Barcelona: Ediciones Omega, 2000.

Les Juifs d'Espagne: Histoire d'une diaspora, 1492–1992. Ed. Henry Méchoulan. Paris: Liana Levi, 1992.

Kamen, Henry. *Crisis and Change in Early Modern Spain.* Aldershot, Hampshire, UK, and Brookfield, VT: Variorum, 1993.

———. *Inquisition and Society in Spain.* London: Weidenfeld and Nicholson, 1985. Revised and expanded edition: *The Spanish Inquisition: An Historical Revision.* London: Weidenfeld and Nicholson, 1997.

———. "The Mediterranean and the Expulsion of the Spanish Jews in 1492." *Past and Present* 119 (1988): 30–55.

———. *Philip of Spain.* New Haven, CT: Yale University Press, 1997.

———. "Una crisis de conciencia en la edad de oro en España: La Inquisición contra 'limpieza de sangre.' " *Bulletin hispanique* 88 (1986): 321–356.

Kaplan, Yosef. *From Christianity to Judaism: The Story of Isaac Orobio de Castro.* Trans. Raphael Loewe. Oxford and New York: Published for the Littman Library by Oxford University Press, 1989.

———. *From New Christians to New Jews* (Heb.). Jerusalem: Shazar Center, 1997. Translated into English as *An Alternative Path to Modernity: The Sephardi Diaspora in Western Europe.* Leiden: Brill, 2000.

———. "La Jérusalem du Nord: La communauté séfarade d'Amsterdam au XVIIe siècle." In *Les Juifs d'Espagne.*

———. *Hapzura HaSephardit HaMaaravit* [The Western Sephardi Diaspora]. Tel Aviv: Ministry of Defense, 1994.

———. "The Portuguese Community of Amsterdam in the 17th Century: Between Tradition and Change." In *Society and Change: Proceedings of the Second International Congress for Research of the Sephardi and Oriental Heritage,* ed. Abraham Haim. Jerusalem: Misgav, 1984.

———. "The Problem of the Marranos and 'New Christians' in Historical Research of the Last Generation." In *Studies in Historiography* (Heb.), ed. Moshe Zimmermann et al. Jerusalem: Shazar Center, 1987.

———. "The Travels of Portuguese Jews from Amsterdam to the 'Lands of Idolatry' (1644–1724)." In *Jews and Conversos: Studies in Society and the Inquisition*, ed. Yosef Kaplan. Jerusalem: World Union of Jewish Studies, Magnes Press, 1985.

Karner, Frances. *The Sephardics of Curaçao*. Assen: Van Gorcum, 1969.

Katz, David. "English Redemption and Jewish Readmission in 1656." *Journal of Jewish Studies* 34, no. 11 (1983): 73–91.

———. "Les Juifs d'Angleterre: Entre la réadmission et l'émancipation." In *Les Juifs d'Espagne*.

———. *The Jews in the History of England, 1485–1850*. Oxford: Clarendon Press; New York: Oxford University Press, 1994.

Kaufman, Tânia Neumann. *Passos perdidos, história recuperada: A presença judaica em Pernambuco*. Recife, Brazil: Editora Bagaço, 2000.

Kayserling, Meyer. *Biblioteca española-portuguesa-judaica*. Renewed ed. New York: Ktav Publishing House, 1979.

———. *História dos judeus em Portugal*. Trans. Anita Novinsky. São Paulo: Livraria Pioneira, 1971.

Koestler, A. *The Thirteenth Tribe*. New York: Random House, 1976.

Kolakowski, Leszek. *Chrétiens sans église: La conscience religieuse et le lien confessionnel au XVIIe siècle*. Trans. Anna Posner. Paris: Gallimard, 1969.

Kraemer, Joel. "Two Letters of Maimonides from the Cairo Geniza." *Maimonides Studies* 1 (1990): 96–97.

Kriegel, Maurice. "El Edicto de expulsión: Motivos, fines, contexto." In *Judíos, sefarditas, conversos: La expulsión de 1492 y sus consecuencias*, ed. Angel Alcalá. Valladolid: Ambito, 1995.

———. "Entre 'question' des 'Nouveaux-Chrétiens' et expulsion des Juifs: La double modernité des procès d'exclusion dans l'Espagne du XVe siècle." In *Le Nouveau Monde, Mondes Nouveaux*, ed. Serge Gruzinski and Nathan Wachtel. Paris: Éditions de l'École des Hautes Études en Sciences Sociales, 1996.

———. "Ferdinand le Catholique, fils de Palomba: Les juifs et l'alliance royale." In *Le temps de l'Etat: Mélanges en l'honneur de Pierre Birenbaum*, ed. B. Badie and Y. Déloye. Paris: Fayard, 2007.

———. "La liquidation du pluralisme religieux dans l'Espagne des rois catholiques: Limites et efficacité de l'approche 'intentionnaliste.' " *Temas Medievales* 4 (1994): 35–45.

———. "The 'Modern' Anti-Semitism of the Inquisition" (Heb.) *Zemanim* 41 (1992): 23–33.

Kristeva, Julia. *Thérèse mon amour*. Paris: Fayard, 2008.

La Magdeleine, Claude de. *Le Miroir Ottoman*. Basel: J. R. Genath, 1677.

Ladero Quesada, Miguel Angel. "¿Es todavía España un enigma histórico? (Releyendo a Sánchez-Albornoz)." In *Lecturas sobre la España histórica*. Madrid: Real Academia de Historia, 1998.

———. "Judeoconversos andaluces en el siglo XV." In *La sociedad medieval Andaluza: Grupos no privilegiados.* Jaén: Diputación Provincial de Jaén, 1984.

———. *La España de los reyes católicos.* Madrid: Alianza, 2005.

———. "Los Judeoconversos en la Castilla del siglo XV." *Historia* 16, no. 194 (June 1992): 39–51.

Landau, Luis. Afterword to the Hebrew trans. of *Don Quijote.* Tel Aviv: Hakibutz Hameuchad, 1994.

———. *Cervantes and the Jews* (Heb.). Be'er Sheva: Ben Gurion University Press, 2002.

Lawrence, Bruce A. "The Inquisition and the New Christians in the Iberian Peninsula— Main Historiographic Issues and Controversies." In *The Sephardi and Oriental Jewish Heritage,* ed. Issachar Ben Ami. Jerusalem: Magnes Press, 1982.

Lazar, Moshe. "Scorched Parchments and Tortured Memories: The 'Jewishness' of the Anussim (Crypto-Jews)." In *Cultural Encounters: The Impact of the Inquisition on Spain and the New World,* ed. Mary Elizabeth Perry and Anne J. Cruz. Berkeley and Los Angeles: University of California Press, 1991.

Lazar, Moshe, and Stephen Haliczer, eds. *The Jews of Spain and the Expulsion of 1492.* Lancaster, CA: Labyrinthos, 1997.

Lea, Henry Charles. *Chapters from the Religious History of Spain Connected with the Inquisition.* New York: Burt Franklin, 1967.

———. *A History of the Inquisition of Spain.* New York: Macmillan, 1906–1907.

Lecler, Joseph. *Histoire de la tolérance au siècle de la réforme.* Paris: Albin Michel, 1994.

Leite de Vasconcelos, José. "Cristãos novos de nosso tempo em Trás-os-Montes e na Beira: Suas prácticas judaicas." In *Etnografia portuguesa: Tentame des sistematizacão.* Lisbon: Imprensa Nacional-Casa da Moeda, 1982.

Levine Melammed, Renée. *Heretics or Daughters of Israel? The Crypto-Jewish Women of Castile.* New York: Oxford University Press, 1999.

———. *A Question of Identity—Iberian Conversos in Historical Perspective.* New York: Oxford University Press, 2004.

———. "Women in (Post-1492) Spanish Crypto-Jewish Society: Conversos and the Perpetuation and Preservation of Observances Associated with Judaism." *Judaism* 41, no. 2 (1992): 156–168.

Lewin, Boleslao. *La Inquisición en hispanoamérica: judíos, protestantes, y patriotas.* Buenos Aires: Paidós, 1967.

———. *La Inquisición en México: Racismo inquisitorial: El caso singular de María de Zárate.* Puebla, Mexico: Editorial J. M. Cajica Jr., 1971.

Liebman, Seymour B. *The Enlightened: The Writings of Luis Carvajal El Mozo.* Coral Gables, FL: University of Miami Press, 1967.

———. Trans. and ed. *Jews and the Inquisition of Mexico: The Great Auto de Fe of 1649.* Lawrence, KS: Coronado, 1974.

———. *The Jews in New Spain: Faith, Flame, and the Inquisition.* Coral Gables, FL: University of Miami Press, 1970.

Lipiner, Eliyahu (Elias). "Der Shuster fun Trancasa un der Shneider fun Setubal" [The Cobbler from Trancasa and the Tailor from Setubal]. In *Tsvishn maranentum un shmad* [Between Marranism and Apostasy] (Yiddish). Tel Aviv: Y. L. Peretz, 1973.

———. *Santa Inquisicão: Terror e linguagem.* Rio de Janeiro: Documentario, 1977.

Livermore, H. V. *A New History of Portugal.* Cambridge: Cambridge University Press, 1966.

———. *The Origins of Spain and Portugal.* London: Allen & Unwin, 1971.

Llorca, Bernardino. *Bulario pontificio de la Inquisición española.* Rome: Pontificia Università Gregoriana, 1949.

———. *La Inquisición en España.* Barcelona: Labor, 1954.

———. "La Inquisición española y los conversos judíos o 'marranos.'" *Sefarad* 2 (1942): 113–151.

Llorente, Juan Antonio. *Historia crítica de la Inquisición española.* Madrid: Hiperión, 1980.

López de Meneses, A. "Una Consecuencia de la Peste Negra en Cataluña: El Pogrom de 1348." *Sefarad* 19 (1959): 93–131.

López Martínez, Nicolás. "Libro llamado Alboraique." In *Los Judaizantes castellanos y la Inquisición en tiempo de Isabel la Católica,* ed. Nicolás López Martínez. Burgos: Seminario Metropolitano de Burgos, 1954.

MacKay, Angus. "Popular Movements and Pogroms in Fifteenth-Century Castile." *Past and Present* 55 (1972): 33–67.

———. *Society, Economy, and Religion in Late Medieval Castile.* London: Variorum Reprints, 1987.

———. *Spain in the Middle Ages: From Frontier to Empire, 1000–1500.* New York: St. Martin's Press, 1977.

Maimonides, Moses [Moshe Ben Maimon]. "Epistle on Conversion or a Treatise on Martyrdom" (Heb.). In *Epistles,* ed. M. D. Rabinowitz. Jerusalem: Rav Cook Institute, 1981.

———. *Guide of the Perplexed.* Trans. S. Pines. Chicago: University of Chicago Press, 1963.

———. *Mishne Torah.* Trans. E. Touger. New York and Jerusalem: Moznaim, 1986–2000.

Malino, Frances. *The Sephardic Jews of Bordeaux: Assimilation and Emancipation in Revolutionary and Napoleonic France.* University: University of Alabama Press, 1978.

Marques, António Henrique R. de Oliveira. *History of Portugal.* 2d ed. 2 vols. New York: Columbia University Press, 1976.

Márquez, Antonio. *Los alumbrados: Orígenes y filosofía (1525–1559).* Madrid: Taurus, 1980.

Márquez Villanueva, Francisco. "The Converso Problem: An Assessment." In *Collected Studies in Honour of Américo Castro's Eightieth Year,* ed. M. P. Hornick. Oxford: Lincombe Lodge Research Library, 1965.

———. "Conversos y cargos concejiles en el siglo XV." *Revista de Archivos, Bibliotecas y Museos* 63 (1957): 503–540.

———. *De la España judeoconversa—Doce estudios*. Barcelona: Ediciones Bellaterra, 2006.

———. "El problema de los conversos: Cuatro puntos cardinales." In *Hispania Judaica: Studies on the History, Language, and Literature of the Jews in the Hispanic World*, ed. J. M. Solà-Solé et al. Barcelona: Puvil, 1980.

———. *Espiritualidad y literatura en el siglo XVI*. Madrid: Alfaguara, 1968.

———. "Hablando de conversos con Antonio Domínguez Ortiz." Introductory essay to *La clase social de los conversos en Castilla en la edad moderna*, by Antonio Domínguez Ortiz. Granada: Universidad de Granada, Servicios de Publicaciones, 1991.

———. "Hispano-Jewish Cultural Interactions: A Conceptual Framework." In *Encuentros and Desencuentros: Spanish-Jewish Interaction throughout History*, ed. C. Carrete Parrondo et al. Tel Aviv: Tel Aviv University Projects, 2000.

———. "Ideas de la 'católica impugnación' de fray Hernando de Talavera." In *Las tomas: Antropología histórica de la ocupación territorial del reino de Granada*, ed. J. A. González Alcantud and M. Barrios Aguilera. Granada: Diputación Provincial de Granada, 2000.

———. " 'Nasçer e morir como bestias' (criptojudaísmo y criptoaverroísmo)." In *Los judaizantes en Europa y la literatura Castellana del siglo de oro*, ed. F. Díaz Esteban. Madrid: Letrumero, 1994.

———. "Sobre el concepto de judaizante." In *Encuentros and Desencuentros: Spanish-Jewish Interaction throughout History*, ed. C. Carrete Parrondo et al. Tel Aviv: Tel Aviv University Projects, 2000.

Martínez Millán, José. "Structures of Inquisitorial Finance." In *The Spanish Inquisition and the Inquisitorial Mind*, ed. A. Alcalá. New York: Columbia University Press, 1987.

Martz, L. *A Network of Converso Families in Early Modern Toledo: Assimilating a Minority*. Ann Arbor: University of Michigan Press, 2003.

Mea, Elvira Azevedo de, and Inácio Steinhardt. *Ben-Rosh: Biografia do Capitão Barros Bastos: O apóstolo dos Marranos*. Porto: Edições Afrontamento, 1997.

Méchoulan, Henry. *Amsterdam au temps de Spinoza*. Paris: Presses Universitaires de France, 1990.

———. *Le sang de l'autre ou l'honneur de Dieu: Indiens, juifs, morisques dans l'Espagne du siècle d'or*. Paris: Fayard, 1979.

———, ed. *Les juifs d'Espagne: Histoire d'une diaspora, 1492–1992*. Paris: Liana Levi, 1992.

Medina, José Toribio. *Historia del tribunal de la Inquisición de Lima (1569–1820)*. Santiago, Chile: Fondo Histórico y Bibliográfico J. T. Medina, 1956.

———. *Historia del tribunal del Santo Oficio de la Inquisición en Cartagena de las Indias*. Santiago, Chile: Elzeviriana, 1899.

———. *Historia del tribunal del Santo Oficio de la Inquisición en Chile*. Santiago, Chile: Fondo Histórico y Bibliográfico J. T. Medina, 1952.

———. *Historia del tribunal del Santo Oficio de la Inquisición en México*. Santiago, Chile: Elzeviriana, 1905.

Menéndez y Pelayo, Marcelino. *Historia de los heterodoxos españoles*. Madrid, 1880–1881; reissued in Buenos Aires, 1945–1946, and Santander: Aldus, 1946–1948. 3d ed., Madrid: Editorial Católica, 1978.

Meyers, Charles, and Norman Simms, eds. *Troubled Souls: Conversos, Crypto-Jews, and Other Confused Jewish Intellectuals from the Fourteenth through the Eighteenth Century*. Hamilton, New Zealand: Outrigger Publishers, 2001.

Meyerson, Mark D. *A Jewish Renaissance in Fifteenth-Century Spain*. Princeton, NJ: Princeton University Press, 2004.

———. *Jews in an Iberian Frontier Kingdom: Society, Economy, and Politics in Morvedre, 1248–1391*. Leiden: Brill, 2004.

Meyuhas Ginio, Alisa. "The Inquisition and the New Christians: The Case of the Portuguese Inquisition of Goa." *Medieval History Journal* 2, no. 1(1999): 1–18.

———. "De bello judaeorum: Fray Alonso de Espina y su Fortalitium fidei." In C. Carrete Parrondo et al., eds., *Fontes iudaeorum regni castellae*.

Moav (Roszenbaum), Eliezer. "Between Jews and Christians in Spain from the End of the 14th to the 16th Century: Conversos Wavering between Two Opinions" (Heb.). M.A. thesis, Tel Aviv University.

Molho, Maurice. Introduction to *Romans picaresques espagnols*, trans. M. Molho and J. F. Reille. Paris: Gallimard, 1968.

Molho, Sara. "Masks for Kippur, Masks for Passover: A Sociological Look at the Belmonte Marranos Today" (Heb.). In *Proceedings of the 12th World Congress of Jewish Studies*. Jerusalem: World Union of Jewish Studies, 2001.

———. "Three Portraits of Marrano Leaders in Belmonte" (Heb.). Online at www.my belmonte.com/.

Montaigne, Michel de. *Essais*. Ed. Pierre Michel. Paris: Gallimard, 1965.

Montoro, Antón de. *Poesía completa*. Ed. Marithelma Costa. Cleveland: Cleveland State University, 1990.

Myers, David. " 'Between Diaspora and Zion': History, Memory, and the Jerusalem Scholars." In *The Jewish Past Revisited: Reflections on Modern Jewish Historians*, ed. David N. Myers and David B. Ruderman. New Haven, CT: Yale University Press, 1998.

Nadler, Steven. *Spinoza: A Life*. New York: Cambridge University Press, 1999.

———. *Spinoza's Heresy: Immortality and the Jewish Mind*. New York: Oxford University Press, 2002.

Nahon, Gerard. "Communautés espagnoles et portugaises de France (1492–1992)." In *Les Juifs d'Espagne*.

———. *Les "Nations" juives portugaises du sud-ouest de la France 1684–1791*. Paris: Fundação Calouste Gulbenkian, 1981.

———. *Métropoles et périphéries séfarades d'Occident*. Paris: Cerf, 1993.

Nes-El, Moshé, and Leonardo Senkman. "Histoire des séfarades du Mexique." In *Les Juifs d'Espagne*.

Netanyahu, Benzion. *The Marranos of Spain from the Late XIVth to the Early XVIth Century, according to Contemporary Hebrew Sources*. New York: American Academy for Jewish Research, 1966. 3d edition, updated and expanded, Ithaca, NY: Cornell University Press, 1999.

———. *The Origins of the Inquisition in Fifteenth-Century Spain*. New York: Random House, 1995.

Nieto, José C. *Juan de Valdés y los orígenes de la reforma en España e Italia*. 1st Spanish ed. Mexico City: Fondo de Cultura Económica, 1979.

Nirenberg, David. *Communities of Violence: Persecution of Minorities in the Middle Ages*. Princeton, NJ: Princeton University Press, 1996.

———. "A Female Rabbi in Fourteenth-Century Zaragoza?" *Sefarad* 51 (1991): 179–182.

Noreña, C. G. *Juan Luis Vives and the Emotions*. Carbondale: Southern Illinois University Press, 1989.

———. Preface to *The Passions of the Soul: The Third Book of De Anima et Vita*, by J. L. Vives, trans. C. G. Noreña. Lewiston, NY: E. Mellen Press, 1990.

Novinsky, Anita. *Cristãos novos na Bahía*. São Paulo: Perspectiva, 1972.

———. *Inquisicão: Rol dos Culpados: Fontes para a história do Brasil (seculo XVIII)*. Rio de Janeiro: Expressão e Cultura, 1992.

———. "Juifs et nouveaux chrétiens du Portugal." In *Les Juifs d'Espagne*.

Oelman, Timothy, ed. and trans. *Marrano Poets of the Seventeenth Century*. Rutherford, NJ: Fairleigh Dickinson University Press; London: Associated University Presses, 1982.

Orfali Levi, Moisés. "Establecimiento del estatuto de limpieza de sangre en el monasterio de los Jerónimos de Guadalupe." In *Actas de las Jornadas de Estudios Sefardíes*, ed. Antonio Viudas Camarasa. Cáceres: Universidad de Extremadura, Instituto de Ciencias de la Educación, 1981.

———. *Los Conversos españoles en la literatura rabínica*. Salamanca: Universidad Pontificia de Salamanca and Universidad de Granada, Federación Sefardí de España, 1982.

Osier, J. P. *D'Uriel da Costa á Spinoza*. Paris: Berg International, 1983.

Pacios López, Antonio. *La disputa de Tortosa*. 2 vols. Madrid and Barcelona: Consejo Superior de Investigaciones Científicas, Instituto Arias Montano, 1957.

Pallarés, Miguel Angel. *Apocas de la receptoría de la Inquisición en la zona nororiental de Aragón (1487–1492)*. Monzón, Huesca: Centro de Estudios de Monzón y Cinca Medio, 1996.

Pardo, Tomás José. *Ciencia y censura: La Inquisición española y los libros científicos en los siglos XVI y XVII*. Madrid: Consejo Superior de Investigaciones Científicas, 1991.

Paris, Erna. *The End of Days: A Story of Tolerance, Tyranny, and the Expulsion of the Jews from Spain*. Amherst, NY: Prometheus Books, 1995.

Paulo, Amilcar. *Os Judeus secretos em Portugal*. Porto: Editorial Labirinto, 1985.

Pedrosa, J. M. "La bendición del día y Dios delante y yo detrás: Correspondencias cristianas y judías de dos oraciones hispanoportuguesas." *Romanistisches Jahrbuch* 45 (1994): 262–270.

Penslar, Derek. "Modern Jewish Philanthropy." In *Philanthropy in the World's Traditions*, ed. Warren F. Ilchman, Stanley N. Katz, and Edward L. Queen II. Bloomington: Indiana University Press, 1998.

———. "Philanthropy, the 'Social Question,' and Jewish Identity in Imperial Germany." *Leo Baeck Institute Yearbook* 38 (1993): 51–73.

Pérez, Joseph. *Historia de una tragedia: La expulsión de los judíos de España*. Barcelona: Crítica, 1993.

———. *Isabel y Fernando, los Reyes Católicos*. Madrid: Nerea, 1988.

———. *Isabelle et Ferdinand, rois catholiques de l'Espagne.* Paris: Fayard, 1988.

Pérez Villanueva, Joaquín, ed. *La Inquisición española: Nueva visión, nuevos horizontes.* Madrid: Siglo Veintiuno de España, 1980.

Pérez Villanueva, Joaquín, and Bartolomé Escandell Bonet, eds. *Historia de la Inquisición en España y América.* 3 vols. Madrid: Centro de Estudios Inquisitoriales, Biblioteca de Autores Cristianos, 1984–2000.

Pessoa, Fernando. "Portugal and the Fifth Empire." In *The Selected Prose of Fernando Pessoa,* ed. and trans. Richard Zenith. New York: Grove Press, 2001.

Peters, Edward. *Inquisition.* Berkeley and Los Angeles: University of California Press, 1989.

———. "Jewish History and Gentile Memory: The Expulsion of 1492." *Jewish History* 9 (spring 1995): 9–34.

Pulgar, Fernando del. *Crónica de los reyes católicos.* Madrid: Espasa-Colpe, 1943.

Pullan, Brian. *The Jews of Europe and the Inquisition in Venice, 1550–1670.* Oxford: Blackwell, 1983.

Rábade Obradó, María del Pilar. "Expresiones de la religiosidad Cristiana en los procesos contra los judaisantes del tribunal de Ciudad Real/Toledo, 1483–1507." *La España medieval* 13 (1990): 303–330.

———. "Los judeoconversos en la Corte y en la época de los Reyes Católicos." PhD diss., Universidad Complutense, Madrid, 1990.

Rabello, Alfredo Mordechai. *The Jews in Visigothic Spain in Light of the Legislation* (Heb). Jerusalem: Shazar Center, 1983.

Ravid, Benjamin. "Les séfarades à Venise." In *Les Juifs d'Espagne.*

Ray, Jonathan. *The Sephardic Frontier: The Reconquista and the Jewish Community in Medieval Iberia.* Ithaca, NY: Cornell University Press, 2006.

Reguera, Iñaki. *La Inquisición Española en el país Vazco.* San Sebastian: Texertoa, 1984.

Renda, Francesco. *La fine del giudaismo siciliano: Ebrei marrani e Inquisizione spagnola prima, durante e dopo la cacciata del 1492.* Palermo: Sellerio, 1993.

Révah, I. S. "Du Marranisme au Judaïsme et au deisme: Uriel da Costa et sa famille." In *Annuaire du Collège de France* (Paris: Collège de France, 1969–1970, 1970–1971, and 1972–1973).

———. Introduction to *Poema de la Reina Ester; Lamentaciones del profeta Jeremías; Historia de Rut y varias poesías,* by João Pinto Delgado. Lisbon: Institute Français au Portugal, 1954.

———. "Le premier réglement imprimé de la 'Santa Companhia de dotar orfanes e donzelas pobres.'" *Boletim internacional de bibliografia luso-brasileira* 4 (1963): 650–691.

———. "Les Marranes." *Revue des études Juives* 118 (1959–1960): 29–77.

———. *Spinoza et le Dr. Juan de Prado.* Paris: Mouton, 1959.

Rivkin, Ellis. *The Shaping of Jewish History: A Radical New Interpretation.* New York: Charles Scribner, 1971.

Rojas, Fernando de. *La Celestina.* Ed. Bruno Mario Damiani. Madrid: Cátedra, 1982.

Roth, Cecil. *A History of the Marranos.* Philadelphia: Jewish Publication Society of America, 1932.

————. "A Hebrew Elegy on the Martyrs of Toledo, 1391." *Jewish Quarterly Review* 39 (1948): 123–150.

————. *The House of Nasi: Doña Gracia.* Philadelphia: Jewish Publications Society, 1947.

————. *The House of Nasi: The Duke of Naxos.* Philadelphia: Jewish Publications Society, 1948.

————. "The Religion of the Marranos." *Jewish Quarterly Review* 22 (1931–1932): 1–33.

Roth, Norman. "Anti-Converso Riots of the Fifteenth Century, Pulgar, and the Inquisition." *En la España medieval* 15 (1992): 367–394.

————. *Conversos, Inquisition, and the Expulsion of the Jews from Spain.* Madison: University of Wisconsin Press, 1995.

————. *Jews, Visigoths, and Muslims in Medieval Spain: Cooperation and Conflict.* Leiden: Brill, 1994.

Saa, Mário. *A Invasão dos Judeus* [Invasion of the Jews]. Lisbon: Imprensa L. da Silva, 1925.

Salomon, Herman P. Introduction to *A History of the Marranos,* by Cecil Roth. New York: Schocken Books, 1974.

————. "Review of David M. Gitlitz, *Secrecy and Deceit.*" *Jewish Quarterly Review* 89, nos. 1–2 (July–October 1998): 131–154.

Sanceau, Elaine. *Good Hope: The Voyage of Vasco da Gama.* Lisbon: Academia Internacional da Cultura Portuguesa, 1967.

Sánchez-Albornoz, Claudio. *Spain: A Historical Enigma.* 2. vols. Madrid: Fundación Universitaria Española, 1975.

Saraiva, António José. *Inquisição e Cristãos Novos.* 3d ed. Porto: Editorial Inova, 1969.

————. *The Marrano Factory: The Portuguese Inquisition and Its New Christians.* Trans., revised, and augmented by H. P. Solomon and I. S. D. Sasson. Leiden: Brill, 2001.

Schirmann, Hayim. *History of Hebrew Poetry in Christian Spain and Southern France* (Heb.). Jerusalem: Magnes Press, 1997.

Scholberg, Kenneth. *La poesía religiosa de Miguel de Barrios.* Madrid: Universidad de Ohio-Edhigar, 1962–1963.

————. "Miguel de Barrios and the Amsterdam Sephardic Community." *Jewish Quarterly Review* 53 (1962/63): 120–159.

————. *Sátira e invectiva en la España medieval.* Madrid: Gredos, 1971.

Scholem, Gershom. *Abraham Cohen Herrera, Author of "Gate to Heaven": His Life, Work, and Influence* (Heb.). Jerusalem: Bialik Institute, 1978.

————. *Sabbatai Sevi: The Mystical Messiah, 1626–1676.* Trans. R. J. Zwi Werblowsky. Princeton, NJ: Princeton University Press, 1973.

Schwarz, Samuel. *Os Christãos-Novos em Portugal no Século XX.* Lisbon: Empresa portuguesa de livros, 1925. Translated into Hebrew as *Ha-notzrim ha-chadashim be-portugal ba-meaʾa ha-esrim* [The New Christians in Portugal in the Twentieth Century], trans. Claude B. Stuczynski. Jerusalem: Dinur Center, 2005.

Segre, Renata. "La formazione di una comunità marrana: I portoghesi a Ferrara." In *Storia d'Italia,* vol. 11, ed. Corrado Vivanti. Torino: G. Einaudi, 1996.

Selke, Angela. "El illuminismo de los conversos y la Inquisición, Cristianismo interior de los Alumbrados: Resentimiento y sublimación." In *La Inquisición española: Nueva visión, nuevos horizontes*, ed. Joaquín Pérez Villanueva. Madrid: Siglo Veintiuno de España, 1980.

———. *El Santo Oficio de la Inquisición: Proceso de Fr. Francisco Ortiz, 1529–1532.* Madrid: Ediciones Guadarrama, 1968.

———. *Vida y muerte de los chuetas de Mallorca.* Madrid: Taurus, 1980.

Serrano y Sanz, Manuel. *Orígenes de la dominación española en América.* Madrid: Bailly-Bailliere, 1918.

Shapiro, Benjamin. "The Hidden Jews of New Mexico." *Avotaynu: The International Review of Jewish Genealogy* 5, no. 4 (1989).

Shepard, Sanford. *Lost Lexicon: Secret Meanings in the Vocabulary of Spanish Literature during the Inquisition.* Miami: Ediciones Universal, 1982.

Sicroff, Albert A. "Clandestine Judaism in the Hieronymite Monastery of Nuestra Señora de Guadalupe." In *Studies in Honor of M. J. Bernadete: Essays in Hispanic and Sephardic Culture*, ed. Izaak A. Langnas and Barton Sholod. New York: Las Americas, 1965.

———. "The Jeronymite Monastery of Guadalupe in 14th- and 15th-Century Spain." In *Collected Studies in Honour of Américo Castro's Eightieth Year*, ed. M. P. Hornik. Oxford: Lincombe Lodge Research Library, 1965.

———. *Les controverses des statuts de "pureté de sang" en Espagne du XVe au XVIIe siècle.* Paris: Didier, 1960.

———. "Spanish Anti-Judaism: A Case of Religious Racism." In *Encuentros and Desencuentros: Spanish-Jewish Cultural Interaction throughout History*, ed. C. Carrete Parrondo et al. Tel Aviv: Tel Aviv University Publishing Project, 2000.

Slouschz, Nahum. *Ha'Anusim BePortugal* [Marranos in Portugal] (Heb.). Tel Aviv: Devir, 1932.

Spinoza, Baruch. *Ethics.* In *The Collected Works of Spinoza*, ed. and trans. Edwin Curley. Princeton, NJ: Princeton University Press, 1985.

———. *Theologico-Political Treatise.* Trans. Samuel Shirley. Leiden and New York: Brill Paperbacks, 1991.

Starr-LeBeau, Gretchen D. *In the Shadow of the Virgin: Inquisitors, Friars, and Conversos in Guadalupe, Spain.* Princeton, NJ: Princeton University Press, 2003.

Stern, S. M. "Shtei Yediot Hadashot al Hisdai ibn Shaprut" (Heb.). *Zion* 11 (1946): 141–146.

Stuczynski, Claude B. "Between the Implicit and the Explicit: Books and Reading Techniques among the Marranos in Portugal during the Sixteenth Century" (Heb.). In *Sifriot VeOsfei Sefarim: The 24th Conference on History.* Jerusalem: Shazar Center, 2006.

Suárez Fernández, Luis. *La expulsión de los judíos de España.* Madrid: Editorial MAPFRE, 1991.

Swetschinski, Daniel M. "Kinship and Commerce: The Foundations of Portuguese Jewish Life in Seventeenth-Century Holland." *Studia Rosenthaliana* 15 (March 1981): 52–74.

Szajkowski, Zosa. "Population Problems of Marranos and Sephardim in France from the 16th to the 20th Century." *Proceedings of the American Academy for Jewish Research* 27 (1958): 83–105.

———. "Trade Relations of Marranos in France with the Iberian Peninsula in the Sixteenth and Seventeenth Centuries." *Jewish Quarterly Review* 50 (1960): 69–78.

Taylor, Charles. *A Secular Age.* Cambridge, MA: Harvard University Press, 2007.

———. *Sources of the Self: The Makings of the Modern Identity.* Cambridge, MA: Harvard University Press, 1989.

Teresa of Avila. *The Interior Castle.* Trans. Kieran Kavanaugh and Otilio Rodríguez. New York: Paulist Press, 1979.

———. *Libro de la Vida.* In *Obras Completas,* by Santa Teresa de Jesús. Madrid: Biblioteca de Autores Cristianos, 1977.

———. *Moradas del Castillo Interior.* In *Obras Completas,* by Santa Teresa de Jesús. Madrid: Biblioteca de Autores Cristianos, 1977.

———. *Teresa of Avila: The Book of My Life.* Trans. Mirabai Starr. Boston: New Seeds Books, 2007.

Thompson, Colin P. *The Strife of Tongues: Fray Luis de León and the Golden Age of Spain.* New York: Cambridge University Press, 1988.

Thompson, E. A. *The Goths in Spain.* Oxford: Clarendon Press, 1969.

Tigay, Alan M. "The Jewish Traveler: Recife." *Hadassah Magazine,* May 2001. Online at www.hadassah.org/news/content/per_hadassah/archive/2001/may01/traveler.htm.

Toro, Alfonso. *The Carvajal Family: Jews and the Inquisition in New Spain in the Sixteenth Century.* El Paso, TX: Western Press, 2002.

Tuchman, Barbara. *A Distant Mirror: The Calamitous 14th Century.* Harmondsworth, Middlesex: Penguin Books, 1979.

Tuñón de Lara, Manuel, et al. *Historia de España.* Barcelona: Labor, 1991.

Uchmany, Eva Alexandra. *La vida entre el judaísmo y el cristianismo en la Nueva España, 1580–1606.* Mexico City: Archivo General de la Nación, Fondo de Cultura Económica, 1992.

Usque, Samuel. *Consolação às tribulações de Israel.* Ferrara, 1553; Lisbon: Fundação Calouste Gulbenkian, 1989.

Valdeón Baruque, Julio. *Feudalismo y consolidación de los pueblos hispánicos (siglos XI–XV).* Barcelona: Labor, 1980.

———. *Los conflictos sociales en el Reino de Castilla en los siglos XIV y XV.* Madrid: Siglo Veintiuno, 1975.

Wachtel, Nathan. "Frontières intérieures: La religiosité marrane en Amérique hispanique (XVII siècle)." In *Passar as Fronteiras,* ed. Rui M. Loureiro and Serge Gruzinski. Lagos, Portugal: Centro de Estudios Gil Eanes, 1999.

———. *La Foi du souvenir: Labyrinthes marranes.* Paris: Éditions du Seuil, 2001.

Wagner, Christine. Introduction to *Le dialogue sur la doctrine chrétienne de Juan de Valdés, 1529,* trans. Christine Wagner. Paris: Presses Universitaires de France, 1995.

Watt, William M. *A History of Islamic Spain.* Edinburgh: University of Edinburgh Press, 1965.

Wilke, Carsten. *Jüdisch-Christlich Doppelleben im Barock*. Frankfurt am Main: Peter Lang, 1994.

Wiznitzer, Arnold. *Jews in Colonial Brazil*. New York: Columbia University Press, 1960.

Yerushalmi, Yosef Hayim. *Assimilation and Racial Anti-Semitism: The Iberian and the German Models*. New York: Leo Baeck Institute, 1982.

———. "Between Amsterdam and New Amsterdam—The Place of Curaçao and the Caribbean in Early Modern Jewish History." *American Jewish History* 72 (1982): 172–192.

———. *From Spanish Court to Italian Ghetto: Isaac Cardoso: A Study of Seventeenth-Century Marranism and Jewish Apologetics*. New York: Columbia University Press, 1971. Reprinted Seattle: University of Washington Press, 1981.

———. *The Lisbon Massacre of 1506 and the Royal Image in the Shebet Yehuda*. Cincinnati: Hebrew Union College, 1976.

———. "Marranos Returning to Judaism in the Seventeenth Century: Their Jewish Learning and Mental Preparation" (Heb.). In *Jewish Studies in a New Europe: Proceedings of the Fifth Congress of Jewish Studies*. Copenhagen: C. A. Reitzel, 1969.

———. "The Re-education of Marranos in the Seventeenth Century." The Third Annual Rabbi Louis Feinberg Memorial Lecture in Judaic Studies. University of Cincinnati, March 26, 1980.

———. *Sefardica: Essais sur l'histoire des juifs, des marranes et des nouveaux-chrétiens d'origine hispano-portugaise*. Paris: Chandeigne, 1998.

———. *Zakhor: Jewish History and Jewish Memory*. Seattle: University of Washington Press, 1982.

Yovel, Yirmiyahu. "Converso Dualities in the First Generation: The *Cancioneros*." *Jewish Social Studies* 4, no. 3 (1998): 1–28.

———. "The Jews in History: The Marranos in Early Modernity." In *Zionism and the Return to History: A Reevaluation* (Heb.), ed. S. N. Eisenstadt and M. Lissak. Jerusalem: Yad Ben-Zvi, 1989.

———. "Kant and the History of the Will." In *Kant's Legacy: Essays in Honor of Lewis White Beck*, ed. Predrag Cicovacki. Rochester, NY: University of Rochester Press, 2001.

———. "Marranos in Struggle" (Heb.). *Sepharim*, Ha'aretz Weekly Book Review, August 14, 1996.

———. "The Mystic and the Wanderer: Conversos in Spain's Golden Age Culture." Unpublished manuscript.

———. *The New Otherness: Marrano Dualities in the First Generation*. The 1999 Swig Lecture, September 13, 1999. San Francisco: Swig Judaic Studies Program, University of San Francisco, 1999. (Also delivered as "La nouvelle alterité: Dualités marranes des premières générations." Centre Alberto Benveniste, Paris, 2002).

———. *Spinoza and Other Heretics*. 2 vols. Princeton, NJ: Princeton University Press, 1989.

Yuval, Israel. *Two Nations in Your Womb* (Heb.). Tel Aviv: Alma, Am Oved, 2001.

Zacuto, Abraham. *The Book of Lineage or Sefer Yohassin*. Trans. Israel Shamir. Tel Aviv: Zacuto Foundation, 2005.

Zeldes, Nadia. *The Former Jews of This Kingdom: Sicilian Converts after the Expulsion, 1492–1516*. Leiden: Brill, 2003.

Zenith, Richard, ed. and trans. *The Selected Prose of Fernando Pessoa*. New York: Grove Press, 2001.

Zeumer, Karolus, ed. *Leges Visigothorum*. Rev. ed. Hannover: Hahn, 1973.

Zürn, Gabriel. "Les séfarades en Allemagne et en Scandinavie." In *Les Juifs d'Espagne*.

Index